Options to Accompany
Business Communication, 7e

xtra!

 ## Xtra!

Xtra! access is an optional bundle with new textbooks. This exciting resource gives students a plethora of reviewing content including eLectures, a Jeopardy-like game called QuizBowl, crossword puzzles to review key terms, chapter quizzes that are graded automatically by the sytem, and a grammar workshop for each chapter.

 ## WebTutor Toolbox on WebCT® or Blackboard®

Enhance your WebCT, BlackBoard, or eCollege course with WebTutor Toolbox! This product is available at no additional cost as an optional bundle when students purchase new texts. WebTutor Toolbox includes such chapter review content as learning objectives, chapter outlines, review questions, practice exercises, and student PowerPoint® slides. Use this content to give your students more ways to study and review through your course managements system!

 ## Creating Dynamic Multimedia Presentations, 3e

©2006
Carol Lehman, Mississippi State University
0-324-31330-6

Creating Dynamic Multimedia Presentations Using Microsoft PowerPoint® goes beyond the traditional step-by-step manual by exploring specific design and delivery techniques that lead to superior PowerPoint presentations. Astonish clients, managers, and peers using the skills acquired right here. Prepared by Dr. Carol Lehman, an expert presenter and leader in the business communication field, this resource will ensure that your students will design and deliver effective presentations. They will learn specific design techniques that allow them to utilize the full functionality of Microsoft PowerPoint to develop creative, dynamic, and highly effective business presentations that will set them apart.

Business Communication

Seventh Edition

Business Communication

Seventh Edition

A. C. "Buddy" Krizan
Murray State University

Patricia Merrier
University of Minnesota Duluth

Joyce Logan
University of Kentucky

Karen Williams
San Diego Mesa College

THOMSON

SOUTH-WESTERN

Australia · Brazil · Canada · Mexico · Singapore · Spain · United Kingdom · United States

THOMSON

SOUTH-WESTERN

Business Communication, Seventh Edition
A. C. "Buddy" Krizan, Patricia Merrier, Joyce Logan, Karen Williams

VP/Editorial Director:
Jack W. Calhoun

Publisher:
Neil Marquardt

Acquisitions Editor:
Erin Joyner

Developmental Editor:
Julie Klooster

Marketing Manager:
Nicole Moore

Content Project Manager:
Tamborah Moore

Manager of Technology, Editorial:
John Barans

Technology Project Manager:
John Rich

Marketing Communications Manager:
Sarah Greber

Manufacturing Coordinator:
Diane Gibbons

Production House:
Lachina Publishing Services

Printer:
Transcontinental Beauceville
Quebec, Canada

Art Director:
Stacy Jenkins Shirley

Internal Designer:
Craig Ramsdell, Ramsdell Design

Cover Designer:
Craig Ramsdell, Ramsdell Design

Cover Images:
© Veer

Photography Manager:
John Hill

Photo Researcher:
Darren Wright

Library of Congress Control
Number:
2006936556

For more information about
our products, contact us at:
Thomson Learning Academic
Resource Center
1-800-423-0563

Thomson Higher Education
5191 Natorp Boulevard
Mason, OH 45040
USA

brief contents

contents

preface

Dear Friends and Colleagues:

Thank you for your interest in *Business Communication*, seventh edition. As authors, we appreciate receiving your ideas for improvement. Revisions and changes in this edition are based on suggestions made by reviewers and users of previous editions.

The text continues to stress a balanced approach to communication by including coverage of correspondence, proposals and special reports, visual aids, teamwork and collaboration, interpersonal communication, listening and nonverbal messages, presentation skills, and employment communication. Communication technology, multicultural and global communication, business ethics, and teamwork are covered in specific chapters and also integrated in content and applications throughout the text.

You will find that the seventh edition maintains a solid focus on basic fundamentals of business communication in areas such as grammar, punctuation, capitalization, reference citations, frequently misused words, and principles of writing and speaking. The Writer's Workshop at the end of each chapter reviews these basic principles in a building-block structure that reinforces basic skills and increases in difficulty as students progress through parts of the book.

As in previous editions, in-depth review and discussion questions and application exercises are included for all chapters. Each correspondence chapter also has 20 or more case problems, and the report application chapter provides data for seven reports. These end-of-chapter activities have been revised and updated to include approximately 50 percent new items!

Research supports teaching by example as a sound instructional approach, and this feature is expanded in the seventh edition. Chapters include not only *needs work* and *looks good* examples but also illustrate actual business e-mails and letters from China, France, Germany, and the Czech Republic. E-mail receives additional attention as business correspondence, and material about writing for instant messaging, blogs, and websites has been added.

New to this edition is a Virtual Assistant simulation, which is included after each part of the book. Students complete tasks related to the content they have studied and interact with prospective and current clients through technology.

By studying and applying the content in this book, students will gain a broad range of knowledge and skills to help them become effective communicators. Faculty who adopt the textbook will find a variety of helpful instructional resources to accompany the text. As always, we welcome and value your feedback.

Sincerely,

Buddy Krizan
Patricia Merrier
Joyce Logan
Karen Schneiter Williams

New and Hallmark Features

The book cover illustrates the key role of technology in communicating messages around the world. Technology could be considered "the mouse that roared." This edition increases coverage of both technology and multicultural and global communication. New topics for global communication include differences in language patterns by persons who speak English as a second language, countries placed on a continuum of high- and low-context cultures and their general preferences for communication, and examples of business e-mails and letters from four different countries. Business use of instant messaging, blogs, websites, and podcasts is covered in different parts of the book.

Hallmark features of the book continue to be that it (a) teaches communication principles by example; (b) uses practical, easy-to-understand language; (c) covers current communication technology, diversity in a global environment, legal and ethical behaviors that build trust and goodwill, and (d) provides extensive guidance for career planning and obtaining employment.

The example-based approach, readability, comprehensive coverage of up-to-date communication practices and behaviors, inclusion of seminars and basic Writer's Workshop, along with the new Virtual Assistant case simulation, make this book appropriate for students who need to improve skills for basic writing, preparation of business documents, speaking and presentation, interpersonal communication, career-decision planning, and obtaining employment. Instructors will find the example and model document approach for teaching concepts helpful for both classroom and online instruction. At the end of chapters, numerous application exercises, case studies, and content summaries for learning objectives reinforce learning and stimulate critical thinking.

Technological, Legal, and Ethical Considerations

The book covers communication for the e-generation and technological advances that allow individuals to self-select what, when, and where messages are received and sent. Legal and ethical issues include those connected to technology use, as well as legal and ethical issues that arise in other business transactions. Ethical behavior is basic to building trust and goodwill and is not only covered in the chapter but also addressed in application exercises and cases throughout the text. New topics include discussions of wi-fi, podcasts, HotDesking/virtual offices, outsourcing, offshoring, hoteling, and business codes of conduct.

Virtual Assistant Simulation

This new feature, which appears at the end of each part of the text, gives students tasks that apply chapter concepts in their job as a Virtual Assistant. These tasks relate to business start-up, job samples for a prospective client, plans for a website, an ethical dilemma, product research, preparation for a speaking engagement, a mail merge, writing a job description and interview questions to hire an assistant, plans for advertising, graphic development for an annual report, and conference planning.

Message Formats

The availability and widespread use of word processing software means that today's entry-level professionals will be creating their own correspondence. Knowing how to format letters, memos, and e-mail is a necessary skill, so the seventh edition begins the correspondence section with a chapter on message formats. Chapter 6 describes and illustrates parts of a letter, punctuation styles, letter formats, and envelope formatting. In addition to illustrating letter formats used in the United States, letter formats from China and Germany are shown in the native language and their English translations.

Comprehensive End-of-Chapter Activities—Approximately 50 Percent New!

End-of-chapter review/discussion questions, application exercises, and case problems give students opportunities to apply their knowledge and develop critical thinking skills. Experiences are provided to work in teams and collaborate in solving problems. In addition to applying concepts from each chapter, cases and application exercises in all chapters incorporate using technology, communicating ethically, and responding to global issues and cultural differences. Collaboration, technology, global, and ethics icons identify these integrated concepts. Students are introduced to situations in the business world and are challenged to react or respond to these issues.

Multicultural and Global Communication

Multicultural and global communication are covered in the second chapter of the book, and integrated into other chapters. Application exercises related to this content can be found at the end of chapters throughout the book. New features include illustration of countries on a high- and low-context continuum for communication preferences, examples from actual business e-mails from France, the Czech Republic, and Germany, the effects of language patterns on English as a second language, and a discussion of corporate culture.

Let's Talk Business

All chapters begin with a message from businesspeople who relate how the content in the particular chapter applies in business settings. This feature brings realism to text content and motivates student interest.

Margin Notes

Brief comments that summarize major content from text material greatly aid student comprehension, enhance their exam preparation time, and provide a review and reinforcement of chapter concepts.

Tips and Hints and Communication Notes

Tips and Hints offer advice that business professionals can use in their daily communication situations. Communication notes relay relevant information related to chapter content and business work experiences.

Needs Work/Looks Good Illustrations

This extremely useful feature offers a direct comparison of good examples and those that "Need Work." The correspondence chapters include ethical and unethical messages and good and poor letters that make requests, approve or disapprove requests, express appreciation, respond to job interview candidates, refuse credit, agree or disagree to adjustments, apply for a job, and compose social business correspondence. These illustrations that show "do's and don'ts" of correspondence aid students in composing successful business messages.

Easy to Read and Understand

An important hallmark feature of *Business Communication* is the well-written, concise but comprehensive and easy-to-understand material. Students at a variety of academic levels use and appreciate the book.

Message Analysis and Writer's Workshop

End-of-chapter activities include a message relevant to chapter content that students are asked to rewrite and improve. Writer's Workshop is a new feature that presents errors for correction in a building-block structure that reviews basic grammar and writing principles and adds new challenges as students move through each part of the text.

Seminars, Appendixes, and Reference Material

At the end of the text, seminars include complete coverage of parts of speech, sentence structure, punctuation, style, and word usage. Document formatting for APA and MLA text citations and reference lists, as well as a sample formal report are in the appendixes. Inside the book cover as a handy reference, you will find proofreading marks and state abbreviations.

Comprehensive Learning Package

Instructional Resources

Instructor's Manual The Instructor's Manual provides resources to increase the teaching and learning value of *Business Communication*. This useful manual includes teaching tips, activities, and guidelines for classroom discussion. Also included in the Instructor's Manual are the solutions to end-of-chapter questions for review and discussion, application exercises, case problems, and the Virtual Assistant feature. For your convenience, we've also included a print version of the electronic test bank.

Instructor's Resource CD This helpful instructor resource includes PowerPoint® slides—a great enhancement tool for stimulating classroom discussion with lectures; ExamView testing software for creating appropriate and challenging quizzes and tests; Test Bank files in Microsoft Word format; and the Instructor's Manual files in Microsoft Word format, all on one easy-to-use CD. Use the IRCD to make printed tests or create transparencies from the PowerPoint slides!

Instructor's Support Website http://thomsonedu.com/bcomm/krizan The Instructor Support Website includes text resources such as downloadable files for the Instructor's Manual, PowerPoint® slides, Test Bank files, and other supplementary materials pertinent to selected chapters and application exercises in *Business Communication*. All of these useful supplements are available at your fingertips through the Instructor's Support Website.

WebTutor™ Toolbox for Business Communication, Seventh Edition This online learning aid can be imported as a course cartridge to supplement any online course component being administered in WebCT™, Blackboard®, or eCollege. This course cartridge provides you with machine-graded quizzes and review questions that help you assess how well students are grasping course content. In addition to the quizzes and review questions, PowerPoints and other study aids are available to help your students review chapter concepts. The content in this course cartridge allows your students to practice and apply their knowledge in an online environment, developed with your students in mind and is especially useful for distance education. WebTutor Toolbox access codes can be packaged with your books at no additional cost—ask your sales representative about how to have this product included with your books!

Student Resources

Text Support Site Available to any student who purchases *Business Communication Seventh Edition*, the text support site (**http://thomsonedu.com/bcomm/krizan**) offers a variety of review materials to help students increase their retention of chapter concepts and test themselves on their knowledge. From machine-graded quizzing to a student version of chapter PowerPoints, students have a wealth of resources available to them at this complimentary website!

WebTutor Toolbox Available at no additional cost when you order the package ISBN, WebTutor Toolbox contains learning objectives, chapter outlines, interactive quizzes, PowerPoint slides, and review questions for each chapter that will help students review and reinforce key concepts. Get a better grade—ask your instructor to set you up with WebTutor Toolbox!

XTRA! XTRA! is a completely online-based resource designed to help students review and reinforce concepts they have learned in class and in *Business Communication Seventh Edition*. Included in this new edition of XTRA! is a grammar workshop, chapter quizzes, a crossword puzzle for each set of key terms, Quiz Bowl (a Jeopardy-like game), and eLectures. All of these resources help students assess their own skills in chapter concepts and allows them to review in an interactive environment. XTRA! access codes can be package at no additional cost with a new book—ask your sales representative about how to have this dynamic tool included with your books!

About the Authors

Dr. A. C. "Buddy" Krizan is a professor emeritus in the College of Business and Public Affairs at Murray State University, Murray, Kentucky. Formerly, he served as assistant dean, department chair, and professor in the College of Business and Public Affairs. He began teaching business communication courses, seminars, and workshops in 1977. He has conducted research on a variety of topics including basic business communication, résumé content, visual aids, proposals, and written and oral messages. He has served in leadership positions for national, state, and local professional organizations. Buddy has made presentations at numerous professional conferences and has published in many professional journals.

Dr. Patricia Merrier is a professor in the Finance and Management Information Sciences Department at the University of Minnesota Duluth. She has over 30 years of secondary and post-secondary teaching experience; business communication has been a part of her teaching assignment for 30 years. Pat has served in a variety of leadership roles within campus, community, and professional associations. Assistant Academic Vice Chancellor, Acting Athletic Director, union president, and NCBEA president are among the posts she has held. She enjoys interdisciplinary and collaborative research and has been successful in having the results of her work presented at meetings or published in professional journals. Her current research interests include interpersonal communication and electronic communication.

Dr. Joyce Logan is an associate professor in the College of Education at the University of Kentucky. She has taught business courses at the high school and university levels and has been a member of NBEA for over 25 years. Joyce currently teaches in the principal preparation and doctoral programs for school leaders. Other experiences in education include school principal, regional coordinator of vocational education, school services director for the Kentucky Department of Education, office head for the Kentucky Tech system, and field coordinator for the American Council on Education. She has conducted research and presented in areas such as Tech Prep, adult education, and technology, as well as school leadership.

Karen Schneiter Williams has been teaching computer technology, business communication, and office administration courses for almost 20 years. Since 1999, she has been at San Diego Mesa College, where she currently serves as Computer Business Technology Department Chair. Throughout her career, Karen has been active in her profession. She has presented at state, regional, national, and international conferences as well as at many teacher training workshops. Karen currently serves as the chair of NBEA's curriculum administrative committee, which has the task of revising and publishing the third edition of the *National Standards for Business Education, What America's Students Should Know and Be Able to Do in Business*. In 2005 she was awarded the Outstanding Postsecondary Business Educator of the Year by the National Business Education Association.

Acknowledgments

We appreciate the support of the following individuals who have reviewed and offered creative and useful suggestions for improving *Business Communication:*

Marion Webb, Cleveland State University

Carmen Christopher, Sampson Community College

Jo Ann Garraway, Jones County Junior College

Bonnie Fox Garrity, D'Youville College

Sandie Idziak, University of Texas at Arlington

Marsha Tomlin, Sam Houston State University

Susan Perala-Dewey, University of Minnesota at Duluth

M. Winifred Morgan, Pennsylvania State University at Abington

David Curtis, Governors State University

Sinceree Gunn, University of Alabama in Huntsville

Luchen Li, Kettering University

Susan F. Heywood, University of Phoenix Online, Axia College of Western International University Online, Colorado Technical University Online

Laura Monroe, University of Akron

Shari Jerde, University of North Dakota

Janet Alampi, Central Connecticut State University

Business Communication

Seventh Edition

Part 1
The Communication Environment

© Stockbyte

Chapter 1
Business Communication Foundations

LET'S TALK BUSINESS

Communication permeates all aspects of our personal and professional lives. It is the key to having positive interactions and to building and maintaining favorable relationships. The ability to communicate and to have that message understood is vital in today's world. The core principles apply, no matter how complex or advanced the technology becomes.

In marketing communication at 3M, knowing the objective of the communication and understanding the target audience are core principles, whether the communication is external or internal. Being aware of the organizational climate, industry trends, and customer preferences helps me create and deliver effective messages. The astute and skillful communicator considers all these factors.

Whether you are preparing e-mail, leading a meeting, writing a report, ironing out a misunderstanding with a coworker, or conveying the vision of an organization, your use of good, basic communication skills will give you confidence that your message will be effective.

Diane Kiekhoefer, Marketing Communications Manager, 3M

Photo courtesy of Diane Kiekhoefer

FIGURE 1.1
Key Ways in Which
Communicating Effectively
Is Important to You

The Importance of Communicating Effectively

- **Getting Jobs You Want** Effective communication will make it possible for you to design a powerful résumé, compose a persuasive application letter, interview with poise and confidence, and get the job you want.
- **Gaining Promotions** Moving ahead in your career depends on communicating your technical competence to others and maintaining effective relationships with them.
- **Providing Leadership** Your ability to motivate and help others achieve rests on your understanding of human nature and on mastering communication skills.

- **Being Productive on the Job** Work performance is enhanced by your ability to listen effectively, speak clearly, and write competently.
- **Relating Positively to Others** Successful business and personal relationships depend on mutual trust and respect; communicating ethically, with concern and compassion, is essential.
- **Assuring the Success of Your Organization** Your organization will succeed only if it has the support of its constituencies—support that comes from effectively communicating with customers or clients about the organization's products or services.

As Diane Kiekhoefer notes in this chapter's Let's Talk Business feature, communication is one of the most important skills you can develop. How well you read, listen, speak, and write will affect the quality of your personal relationships and, as shown in Figure 1.1, will help determine the progress you make in your career.

Research with business professionals reveals that effective communication ranks high among the skills necessary to succeed in business. The number and types of work-related communication activities in which a person engages depend on his or her field and level of responsibility. For example, telemarketers spend the majority of their work hours placing calls to prospective customers; entry-level tax accountants focus on entering and manipulating data; public relations specialists gather information and write news releases; and human resource managers negotiate contracts, train employees, and prepare reports.

Businesses must have effective internal and external communication in order to succeed. Internal operations depend on the day-to-day exchange of information among employees. Performance objectives, job instructions, financial data, customer orders, inventory data, production problems and solutions, and employee production reports illustrate the range of *internal communication* exchanged in the course of doing business. Organizations accomplish long-range planning and strategic decision making by relying on research, reports, proposals, conferences, evaluations, and projections.

External communication builds goodwill, brings in orders, and ensures continued existence and growth. Day-to-day external communications include sales calls, product advertisements, news releases, employment notices, bank transactions, and periodic reports to governmental agencies. External communication that has a long-range impact includes new product announcements, plant expansion plans, contributions to community activities, and annual reports.

As you can see from these examples, most business communication is **transactional:** It involves a give-and-take relationship between the sender and the receiver(s) in order to establish a common understanding. This interaction is the primary feature that distinguishes business writing from journalistic or creative writing.

LO 1
Explain why business communication is important to individuals and organizations.

NOTE 1.1
How and when you communicate vary by field.

communication note

The word "communication" comes from the Latin word *communis,* which means common. When individuals communicate, they try to establish a common understanding between or among themselves. *Business communication* is the process of establishing a common understanding between or among people within a business environment.

NOTE 1.2
Effective communication benefits you and the organization.

Effective communication is essential to both you and the organization for which you work. The material in this book is designed to help you improve your ability to communicate. This chapter focuses on the goals, patterns, and process of communication. It also addresses communication barriers and ways to remove them. Later chapters provide more details about meeting the challenges of communicating in a business environment.

Goals of Business Communication

LO 2
List and explain the goals of business communication.

Effective business communication involves both the sender and the receiver, but the sender must take responsibility for achieving the four basic **goals of business communication:**

1. Receiver understanding
2. Receiver response
3. Favorable relationship
4. Organizational goodwill

NOTE 1.3
The sender has primary responsibility for communication success.

Receiver Understanding

NOTE 1.4
First goal: Receiver understands message as sender intended.

The first goal of business communication, **receiver understanding,** is the most important. The message must be so clear that the receiver understands it *as the sender means it to be understood.*

For communication to be successful, the sender and receiver must achieve shared meaning. Suppose a supervisor sends an e-mail to a subordinate saying, "No one plans for a meeting like you do." Should the worker react with pleasure or disappointment? Is the supervisor praising or criticizing the worker's attention to detail? The message is too vague to guarantee receiver understanding. If one worker says to another, "Will you join me for lunch today?" the sender and receiver might have different ideas about who will pay for the receiver's meal.

It is a challenge for the sender to achieve the goal of receiver understanding. To develop a clear message, the sender must consider the following four issues, which are discussed in detail later in this chapter:

- Receiver characteristics
- Message form and content
- Receiver feedback
- Communication barriers

Receiver Response

The second goal of business communication is receiver response. The **receiver response** may be positive, neutral, or negative. It may be conveyed through words, actions, or both. The situation will determine what is appropriate. If the chair of a committee distributes a memo announcing the time and date of a meeting, those who receive the memo may act in any of four ways. They may (a) notify the chair that they will attend, (b) notify the chair that they will be unable to attend, (c) attend without having notified the chair in advance, or (d) miss the meeting without providing advance notice. The first three actions achieve the goal of receiver response; the fourth does not.

Because this goal is achieved when the receiver demonstrates his or her understanding of the message by providing an appropriate response, a sender should assist the receiver to respond. The wording of the message should encourage response. In a face-to-face conversation, the sender (speaker) can ask the receiver (listener) if he or she understands the message. Further, the sender can ask directly for a specific response.

When written messages are used, the sender can encourage a response by asking questions, enclosing a reply envelope, including an e-mail address, asking the receiver to telephone, or using any one of many other possibilities.

NOTE 1.5
Second goal: Receiver provides necessary response.

NOTE 1.6
The sender should make it easy for the receiver to respond.

Favorable Relationship

The third goal of business communication—**favorable relationship**—focuses on the people involved in the communication process. To establish a strong business relationship, the sender and the receiver should relate to each other in three important ways: positively, personally, and professionally. They must create and maintain a favorable relationship.

Both the sender and the receiver will benefit from a favorable relationship. If the sender manufactures goods or provides services, a favorable relationship might mean job satisfaction, increased sales, and more profits. If the sender is a customer, a favorable relationship could lead to a continued source of supply, better prices, and assistance if problems develop.

The sender should assume primary responsibility for creating and maintaining a favorable relationship. Some of the ways the sender can do this include the following:

- Stressing the receiver's interests and benefits
- Using positive wording
- Doing more than is expected

For example, suppose you have to refuse to work overtime on Wednesday. If you simply say "No," you will do little to promote a favorable relationship with your supervisor. By offering to work overtime on Thursday or by finding someone who is willing to work Wednesday, however, you will have helped your supervisor, taken a positive approach, and done more than was expected.

NOTE 1.7
Third goal: Sender and receiver have a favorable relationship.

Organizational Goodwill

The fourth goal of business communication stresses benefit to the organization. The goodwill of customers or clients is essential to any business or organization. If a

NOTE 1.8
Fourth goal: Organizational goodwill.

© Blend Images

Effective communication helps foster positive relationships between people and between organizations.

company has the goodwill of its customers, it has their confidence and often their continued business. The more goodwill a company has, the more successful it can be.

Message senders have a responsibility to try to increase goodwill for their organizations. They do so by ensuring that their communications reflect positively on the quality of the company's products, services, and personnel.

The way in which an employee handles a returned merchandise situation can be used as an example of how to build organizational goodwill. If store policy dictates that employees should accept returned merchandise even when the customer doesn't have a receipt, the employee could say: "Would you prefer a refund or a replacement?" After the customer has chosen, the employee should complete the transaction quickly and courteously. Doing so might lead to repeat business for the company and enhance its reputation. This behavior allows the employee to generate goodwill for the store and achieve the fourth goal of business communication—**organizational goodwill.**

Patterns of Business Communication

LO 3
Describe the patterns of business communication.

As communicators strive to achieve the four goals of business communication, they send and receive messages that are both internal and external to their organizations. Some of these messages are formal; some are informal. Some messages are work related; others are personal.

Internal Communication Patterns

NOTE 1.9
Organizational communication flows in all directions.

As shown in Figure 1.2, organizational communication can flow vertically, horizontally, or through a network. In **vertical** communication, messages flow upward or downward along a path referred to as the "chain of command." Reports and proposals commonly follow an upward path; policy statements, plans, directives, and instructions typically follow a downward path. **Horizontal** message flow occurs between workers or units of comparable status who need to share data or coordinate efforts. In **network** communication, information flows freely among those who have a link that goes beyond the participants' role or unit within the organization. Members' roles or status within the organization will generally have the greatest influence in vertical communication and the least influence in network communication.

NOTE 1.10
Networks may be planned or unplanned.

A network may be a planned part of the business operation or it may arise from informal interactions. An example of a planned network is a project team formed to computerize a process. An informal network could consist of employees who share interests outside the workplace. Organization-based informal networks, such as company-sponsored softball teams, can be powerful. Members can discuss work-related issues outside the traditional communication structure and then combine efforts to influence the direction of the organization. Personal networks such as those consisting of friends and relatives, classmates and faculty, current and former employers, and current and former coworkers are important sources of professional and personal support.

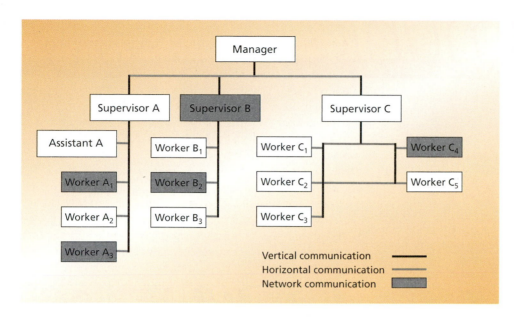

FIGURE 1.2
Business Communication
Patterns

Regardless of the direction in which it flows, communication may have a formal, an informal, or a serial pattern. In this section, *formal* and *informal* refer to the nature of a communication, not the writing or speaking style used to convey a message. You'll learn more about communication style in later chapters.

FORMAL COMMUNICATION

Formal communication is business related. It can be written (memo, report, policy) or oral (speech, meeting). Most organizations keep written records of formal oral communication—copies of speeches, minutes of meetings. Formal communication

- Is planned by the organization.
- Flows in all directions.
- Is essential for the effective operation of the business.

NOTE 1.11
Formal communication is
business related.

INFORMAL COMMUNICATION

Informal communication—sometimes referred to as a *grapevine*—consists of both business-related and personal information. Rumors about company expansion and discussion about a popular TV show are two examples. Most informal communication is oral, but widespread use of e-mail has made informal written communication more popular. Informal communication

- Is not planned by the organization.
- Flows in all directions.
- Develops and maintains positive human relationships.

The following Communication Note provides additional information about the advantages of cultivating an organizational grapevine.

NOTE 1.12
Informal communication
can be business related or
personal.

SERIAL COMMUNICATION

Much of the information flowing vertically and horizontally within an organization involves three or more individuals. For example, job instructions are developed by

NOTE 1.13
Serial communication is
chain transmission of
information.

communication note

A SWEET AND SOUR LOOK AT THE GRAPEVINE

Every organization has a grapevine, but not every organization uses it effectively.

When used to provide comprehensive, honest information to employees in an easy-to-understand manner, the grapevine fills information gaps. Professionals who use the grapevine in this way will find it a useful resource that can help them assess the morale of the organization, understand employees' anxieties, and evaluate formal communication efforts. If an organization's managers ignore or attempt to suppress the grapevine, however, the likely result will be low morale, low productivity, misinformation, and misunderstandings—factors that lead to worker resignations.

In order to take full advantage of the grapevine, managers should

• be as open, honest, and complete as possible when communicating
• monitor the grapevine to learn whether formal messages have been understood or need restating
• identify and work with those who are key purveyors of grapevine information
• ask employees how they use the grapevine

—Lorenzo Sierra, Aon

managers and transmitted to the supervisors who report to them. The supervisors, in turn, transmit the instructions to the workers under their direction. This communication pattern is called **serial communication.**

In serial communication, messages are usually changed—sometimes dramatically—as they are sent from one member of the chain to another. Because each sender may omit, modify, or add details to the message as he or she relays it, special precautions are necessary. Four techniques will assist in maintaining the accuracy of and achieving understanding with serial communication:

Senders should
• Keep the message simple
• Request feedback

Receivers should
• Take notes
• Repeat the message

Although serial communication is typically oral, e-mail has increased its presence in written form. The ability to forward messages without paraphrasing them minimizes or eliminates the distortion customary in oral serial messages. This advantage is lost, however, when those who receive the message add to or comment on it before passing it along. Having to read the additional information can place a burden on the receiver.

NOTE 1.14
Serial communication may be oral or written.

External Communication Patterns

External communication flows between a business organization and the entities with which it interacts. Companies have many external contacts such as customers, suppliers, competitors, the media, governmental agencies, and the general public. These contacts may be domestic or international. The information that flows between a business and its external receivers can be either written or oral. Letters, reports, orders, invoices, and web pages illustrate external written communication; telephone calls and radio or television advertisements are examples of external oral communication.

NOTE 1.15
Organizations communicate with many external publics.

Although external communication is typically formal, it may occur informally as well. Whenever an employee comments about work-related matters to someone not affiliated with the organization, informal external communication occurs. The external audience could be a neighbor, a friend, someone to whom the worker has just been introduced at a party, or someone who accidentally overhears a conversation. Employees represent their organizations both on and off the job; therefore, they should demonstrate good communication skills in their professional and social interactions.

NOTE 1.16
External communication can be formal or informal.

Literally thousands of formal and informal communications take place every day. Effective communication enhances both individual and organizational success.

The Communication Process

Understanding the communication process can help you become a better communicator. The following sections focus on the components of the communication process model and ways to implement the model successfully.

LO 4
Explain the communication process.

A Communication Process Model

The best way to study the communication process is to analyze a model of it. An understanding of the communication process model shown in Figure 1.3 will strengthen your performance as a communicator.

The communication process model operates in an environment that includes the sender, the message, the receiver, feedback, and communication barriers. The **communication environment** includes all things the participants perceive through their senses—sight, smell, sound, taste, and touch.

The communication environment is distracting and complex. Communicators must overcome distractions to achieve the goals of business communication. In addition, they must recognize that each organization has its own culture, a personality that affects the communication environment and the way the communication process is implemented. Leaders (past and present), traditions, attitudes, and

NOTE 1.17
An organization's culture affects its communication environment.

FIGURE 1.3
A Communication
Process Model

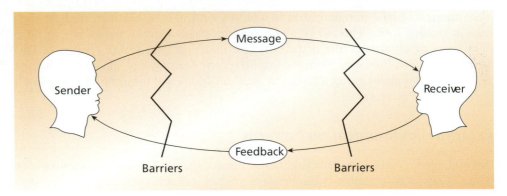

philosophies determine each organization's culture. Some organizations are formal, as indicated by conservative clothing, limited access to leaders, and a preference for written communication. Other organizations are informal—casual dress, open-door policies, and a preference for oral communication. Other factors influencing the culture are the organization's values relating to diversity, seniority, friendliness, teamwork, individuality, and ethics. An organization's culture can be dynamic, changing with its size and leadership. Effective business communicators adapt to and positively influence the development of their organizations' cultures.

NOTE 1.18
The office is a competitive
environment with its
own politics.

Office politics is the name given to the competitive environment that exists within the corporate culture. The competition may be for tangibles such as equipment, pay raises, promotions, or office space; it may also be for intangibles such as status or influence. Any workplace action that represents an informal attempt to protect self-interest, meet personal needs, or advance personal goals could be termed negative office politics. Actions that establish effective relationships, recognize and meet others' needs, build support for constructive ideas, and further the mission of the organization represent constructive office politics. Written rules seldom address competitive strategies and, even when they do, bending and breaking occur. Consider the following example.

Tony and Victor were assigned to work on an important project, one that could have major implications for their careers. They didn't always agree on how to approach the task or on the best solution to the problem, but both were satisfied with the final product.

When Tony and Victor presented their proposal to the five-member management team, it was not received well. Several weaknesses were cited, and the men were asked to remedy them. After the meeting, Tony made appointments with each manager to discuss his or her concerns. He acknowledged the report's weaknesses, asked relevant questions, and gathered useful information. Victor looked for casual opportunities to interact with the two managers he thought were most influential. He tried to distance himself from the proposal by suggesting that he wasn't really happy with it but had been pressured to accept Tony's solution. Both men were trying to maintain or improve their professional status within the organization—one took a positive political approach, the other a negative one.

Because people are human and have emotions, politics exist in every organization. Ronna Lichtenberg, author of *Work Would Be Great If It Weren't for the People*, contends that skill alone is insufficient for survival in today's organizations; people must be good at office politics, too.[1] This view is shared by others, among

---

[1]"Office Politics," *Executive Excellence*, October 1998, p. 14.

them Rebecca Luhn Wolfe, author of *Office Politics: Positive Results from Fair Practices,* who advocates practical, ethical choices based on five rules:[2]

1. Understand your corporate culture. Follow policy unless you are in a position to change it.
2. Know when to hold and when to fold. Each is appropriate depending on the situation; be flexible.
3. Believe in win-win situations. Being able to negotiate a solution can help you survive.
4. Play fair. Respect yourself and others.
5. Think first, act later. Results will be better if based on reason rather than emotion.

You probably won't be able to assess the political environment in an organization until you begin working there. If you find yourself working in an organization where the politics don't match your beliefs or ability to play, you may benefit by changing employers.

NOTE 1.19
Assess the political environment in the organization.

Sender's and Receiver's Roles

The sender and the receiver have important responsibilities in the communication process. If both fulfill their roles, the communication will be successful.

NOTE 1.20
Both sender and receiver have important roles.

SENDER'S ROLE
In the communication process the sender initiates the message. The sender may be a writer, a speaker, or one who simply gestures. The **sender's role** in the communication process includes (a) selecting the type of message, (b) analyzing the receiver, (c) using the you–viewpoint, (d) encouraging feedback, and (e) removing communication barriers.

RECEIVER'S ROLE
The receiver is the listener, reader, or observer in the communication process. The **receiver's role** includes (a) listening or reading carefully, (b) being open to different types of senders and to new ideas, (c) making notes when necessary, (d) providing appropriate feedback to the sender, and (e) asking questions to clarify the message.

Remember, the sender has a greater responsibility for the success of communication than does the receiver. How you can successfully fulfill your role as the initiator of the communication process is discussed in detail in the sections that follow.

Communication Types and Channels

Communication can occur verbally and nonverbally. **Verbal** communication uses words; **nonverbal** communication does not. Although many people associate the term only with spoken words, verbal communication actually includes both written and oral messages.

All communication travels from the sender to the receiver(s) through **channels.** Written message channels include memos, letters, e-mail, web pages, notes, reports, telegrams, newsletters, and news releases. These items may include diagrams, drawings, charts, and tables. Oral message channels take many forms, including face-to-face conversations, telephone conversations, voice mail, in-person conferences, video conferences, and speeches.

NOTE 1.21
Messages may be
- Written
- Oral
- Nonverbal

[2]Rebecca Luhn Wolfe, *Office Politics: Positive Results from Fair Practices,* Menlo Park, Calif.: Crisp Publications, Inc., 1997.

tips and hints

Selecting Message Type and Channel

When selecting the type of message to be used and the channel through which it will pass, ask yourself the following questions:

- **Do I need a permanent record of this communication?** If yes, choose a letter (external audience), a memo (internal audience), an e-mail (either internal or external audience), or a report (either internal or external audience). Written messages can have historic and legal value.
- **Will my receiver(s) readily accept the message?** If yes, a written message is appropriate. If no, oral communication is preferred. The ability to convey emotion and to react to feedback make face-to-face oral communication the best format for persuading receivers or conveying bad news. The size of and distance from the audience must also be considered.
- **Where and how large is the audience for the message?** Face-to-face oral communication can be effective if the sender and receiver(s) are in the same location. A telephone call may work if the number of receivers is small.

Written communication works best when it is impractical to bring receivers together or when the message doesn't warrant the personal touch of face-to-face communication.

- **Is the message long or complex?** If yes, select written communication. The writer can draft and revise the message before it is sent, and the receiver can refer to it as often as necessary to understand the message. Visual aids may supplement the written text.
- **Is timeliness a factor?** Do I need immediate feedback? Use face-to-face or telephone communication for urgent messages or when immediate feedback is important. In some circumstances, e-mail and fax may be viable alternatives. Letters or memos are often used to confirm messages conveyed orally.
- **Is credibility a concern?** Written messages are perceived as being more credible than oral messages. E-mails have less credibility than documents displayed on an organization's letterhead or presented as a report.

NOTE 1.22
Nonverbal communication
is powerful.

Senders must consider several things as they prepare to select the type of message they will send and the channel through which they will send it. Answering the questions listed in the Tips and Hints above will help you make those choices.

Nonverbal messages can be conveyed by both people and objects. The human channels through which these messages pass include gestures and facial expressions. Object-based nonverbal message channels include the appearance and layout of a document and the audio and visual clarity of a videotaped presentation. Nonverbal communication is a compelling complement to verbal communication. When there is a conflict between a speaker's words and actions or between a document's contents and appearance, the receiver will most likely believe the nonverbal message.

The You–Viewpoint

NOTE 1.23
The sender must analyze
the receiver when using
the you–viewpoint.

Using the **you–viewpoint** means that the sender gives primary consideration to the receiver's point of view when composing and sending messages. This is the most powerful concept in business communication, the key to achieving common understanding. To use the you–viewpoint, you must first analyze your receiver.

ANALYZING THE RECEIVER

No two receivers are alike. You must learn as much as possible about how a particular receiver or group of receivers thinks and feels, in general and with respect to the situation about which you will communicate. Specifically, you must analyze the receiver(s) in four areas—knowledge, interests, attitudes, and emotional reaction.

Knowledge. Begin the analysis with a review of each receiver's education and experience. Some of the questions you might ask are these:

NOTE **1.24**
Analyze the receiver's knowledge.

- What is my receiver's highest level of education?
- Does my receiver have education specifically related to the topic of my message?
- How much work experience does my receiver have?
- How much of my receiver's work experience relates to the specific topic of my message?
- Does the receiver have prior experience interacting with me? with my organization?

Answers to these questions will help you decide the vocabulary level of your message, the extent to which you will be able to include technical terms, and the amount of detail the receiver will require.

Interests. Second, analyze the receiver's interests. The sender will want to ask the following questions:

NOTE **1.25**
Analyze the receiver's interests.

- What are the receiver's concerns? needs?
- Does the receiver have a particular motive? seek a particular outcome?

A receiver's position and level of authority may influence the nature of his or her interest in a situation. For example, an employee responsible for production will have a greater interest in the technical details of machine repair than will the manager to whom he or she reports. The manager's primary interests may be the timing and cost of the solution. A careful analysis of your receiver's interest will help you determine what content to include in your message and the approach you take in organizing it.

NOTE **1.26**
Position and level of authority affect interests.

Attitudes. Third, examine the attitudes of the receiver. You'll want to ask the following questions:

NOTE **1.27**
Analyze the receiver's attitudes.

- What values, beliefs, biases, and viewpoints does the receiver have?
- What words or symbols will make a positive impression on the receiver? a negative impression?
- What ideas can be used effectively to communicate with this receiver?

Among the many attributes that can affect receiver attitudes are status, power, personality, expectations, nationality, and culture.

Emotional Reaction. Finally, anticipate the receiver's emotional reaction to your message. Will the message make the receiver happy? make the receiver angry? leave the receiver unaffected? As shown in the Tips and Hints on page 14, your assessment will assist you in determining whether you should use a direct or an indirect approach.

NOTE **1.28**
Anticipate the receiver's reaction to your message.

Analyzing your receiver will assist you in every communication situation. It will enable you to make effective use of one of the most important concepts of business communication—the you–viewpoint.

USING THE YOU–VIEWPOINT

You can use your understanding of the receiver's knowledge to influence the ideas you include and the amount of explanation you give. In addition, you will be able to use words the receiver will understand and accept. You can design the message to address the receiver's concerns, needs, and motivations. Determining your receiver's attitudes will assist you in avoiding or carefully handling negative situations. Finally, anticipating your receiver's emotional reaction will influence whether you use a direct or an indirect approach in your message.

NOTE **1.29**
Use the you–viewpoint to help achieve the goals of business communication.

tips and hints

Predicting Emotional Reactions

- In most cultures, people will accept pleasant or neutral messages when you give the main point in your opening (direct approach).
- A message that could disappoint or anger a receiver might gain greater acceptance if the sender offers an explanation, a reason, or other supporting information before giving the main point (indirect approach).

- If your supervisor, a customer, or other person with whom you communicate indicates that he or she prefers to have the main idea of the message presented before the details, be sure to do so.

NOTE 1.30
Analyze group members individually.

If you are sending the same message to a group of receivers and you want to achieve the business communication goals with every member of that group, each individual in the group must be analyzed as fully as possible. Then, if the receivers are of equal importance to your goals, you must compose the message for the member(s) of the group with the least knowledge about, the least interest in, and the greatest emotional opposition to the subject. For example, web pages can be accessed by literally millions of people around the world, but those who develop materials for the Web will define, analyze, and write for their target audience, not all Internet users.

NOTE 1.31
I–viewpoint messages are rarely effective.

The opposite of the you–viewpoint is the I–viewpoint, which includes the me–, my–, our–, and we–viewpoints. The **I–viewpoint** means the sender composes messages from his or her point of view instead of the receiver's point of view. Poor communicators use the I–viewpoint and choose message content based on their own knowledge, interests, attitudes, and emotional reaction. Only rarely will an I–viewpoint message achieve the goals of business communication.

Examine these contrasting examples of sentences from opposite viewpoints:

I–Viewpoint	You–Viewpoint
I think your report is excellent.	You wrote an excellent report.
You simply do not understand what I am saying.	Perhaps an example will help make the instructions clearer.
We offer three service plans.	Choose the service plan that best meets your needs.

NOTE 1.32
Messages should be receiver centered.

As these examples show, using the you–viewpoint means more than changing a personal pronoun. It requires that the message be receiver-centered, not self-centered. It requires that you emphasize the receiver's interests and benefits rather than your own. When you use the you–viewpoint, the receiver is apt to respond positively to both you and the content of your message. Although using the you–viewpoint may mean you sometimes write passively, the results are worth it.

NOTE 1.33
Be honest and sincere when you communicate.

The recommendation that you use the you–viewpoint in your messages does not suggest that you ignore basic values or compromise ethics. Complimenting someone just so he or she will do what you want is manipulative and inappropriate. Sincerity and honesty are basic to all successful business communication.

FIGURE 1.4
Interoffice Memo Written
from Receiver's Viewpoint

> TO: Members of the Bell Company Community
>
> FROM: Abbott Winthrop, HR Specialist *AW*
>
> DATE: August 23, 200-
>
> SUBJECT: Vacation Fund
>
> What would *you* do if you had to travel 1,000 miles to spend time with a critically ill family member but had no sick leave or vacation time from which to draw?
>
> As a Bell employee, you would probably request additional paid time from the Vacation Fund. Because the need for time off has been great over these past few months, however, the fund has been exhausted. Without additional time donations, current and future needs will go unmet.
>
> Please consider donating some of your unused vacation time to this important fund. A week, a day, or even a few hours can make a dramatic difference for a worker in need. Forms can be obtained from LeAnn Luther (*lluther*, x7008) or online (http://www.bellco.com/~hr). LeAnn is also available to answer questions you have about the program.
>
> Thank you for your past and future donations to the fund.

It will be helpful now to look at an example of a message written in the you–viewpoint. The goal of the message in Figure 1.4 is to persuade readers.

Providing for Feedback

The sender's role in implementing the communication process includes providing for **feedback** from the receiver. Recall that appropriate receiver response is one of the goals of business communication. To achieve this goal, you can

- Ask directly or indirectly for the response.
- Assist the receiver in giving the response.

When a job applicant submits a letter and a résumé to a company, he or she wants the receiver to respond by extending an invitation to interview for a job. To make it easier for the receiver to respond, the sender should be sure the message clearly asks for an interview and includes a telephone number and address where the sender can be reached easily. In a written sales message, the sender should ask for the order and provide a toll-free telephone number, an e-mail address, or an easy-to-use order form. If the communication is oral, the sender can ask tactfully whether the receiver understands the message or has questions. In critical situations, the sender might ask the receiver to repeat the message and explain his or her understanding of it. When speaking to a group, a sender can gain feedback by observing the audience, asking questions, or administering an evaluation. Because the most important goal of business communication is that the receiver understand the message, feedback from the receiver to the sender is essential to confirm that understanding.

NOTE 1.34
Feedback is essential to confirm receiver understanding.

Potential Communication Barriers

LO 5
Identify communication barriers and describe ways to remove them.

Although knowledge of the communication process and skill in implementing it are basic to effective communication, they will not guarantee success. The sender must also minimize or eliminate barriers that could impede the process. A **communication barrier**

NOTE 1.35
Barriers interfere with the communication process.

is any factor that interferes with the success of the communication process (see Figure 1.3 on page 10). These barriers may occur between any two of the communication process steps or may affect all the steps in the process. The most crucial barriers are discussed in the next sections.

Word Choice

NOTE 1.36
Communication Barrier 1:
Poor word choice.

Choosing words that are too difficult, too technical, or too easy for your receiver can be a communication barrier. If words are too difficult or too technical, the receiver may not understand them; if words are too simple, the reader could become bored or be insulted. In either case, the message falls short of meeting its goals. Senders must be careful to choose the correct words for their messages. Misusing a word (e.g., *continuously* rather than *continually*) can impair communication and will reflect poorly on the writer or speaker. Refer to Business English Seminar E for examples of words that are easily confused or frequently misused.

Word choice is also a consideration when communicating with receivers for whom English is not the primary language. These receivers may not be familiar with *colloquial* English—the casual or informal way in which the language may be used.

DENOTATIVE VERSUS CONNOTATIVE MEANING

NOTE 1.37
Communication Barrier 2:
Differing connotation.

A receiver and a sender may attach different meanings to the words used in a message. A **denotation** is the specific dictionary definition for a word. A **connotation** is any other meaning a word suggests to a receiver based on his or her experiences, interests, attitudes, and emotions. Connotative meanings can also be the result of slang or sarcasm. Senders should analyze their receivers as thoroughly as possible to determine what connotations those receivers might attach to specific words.

If you said to one of your subordinates, "Well, that certainly was fast work!" you may have meant the work was completed in less time than you expected. The receiver, however, may attach a different meaning to the statement. Based on what he or she is thinking and feeling at the moment, the receiver may think you meant the work was slow, was done too quickly, or was done improperly. Other specific examples of connotations versus denotations include the following:

Word	Possible Meanings	
assertive	energetic	pushy
compromise	adjust	give in
equitable	fair	equal
frugal	thrifty	cheap
funny	humorous	unusual

IDIOMS

NOTE 1.38
Communication Barrier 3:
Unfamiliar idioms.

An **idiom** is a multiword expression for which meaning cannot be determined from context. The following are examples of common general and business idioms:

General Idioms	Business Idioms
I'm in over my head.	The bottom line is we can't attend.
Drop me a line.	He is a captain of industry.
You're pulling my leg.	It's just a ballpark estimate.
No way!	Will you crunch the numbers?
Keep an eye out for Doug.	Jebco is saddled with debt.

Receivers for whom English is not the primary language may have difficulty understanding frequently used idioms. Therefore, avoid using an idiom unless you are certain your receiver will understand it.

IMPLICATIONS AND INFERENCES

An **implication** is a meaning given through connotation rather than through specific details. An **inference** is a conclusion drawn from connotation rather than from specific details. Although inferences and implications need not occur as a set, a speaker who *implies* something can cause a receiver to *infer* a meaning different from what was intended. For example, a person who says that his work is undervalued may mean to suggest that he doesn't get enough positive feedback from his supervisor. Without specific detail, however, the receiver of the message might infer that the speaker believes his salary isn't high enough. To guard against this communication barrier, senders should always use specific language, and receivers should clarify meaning by asking questions.

Implications may be made and inferences may be drawn from actions as well as from words. For example, suppose that two employees laugh as their supervisor passes. The supervisor may infer that the workers are making fun of him or her. The workers, however, may have wanted to signal that their morale is high or, more likely, to signal nothing at all.

In spite of the problems they can cause, inferences and implications play a role in workplace communication. Intelligent and appropriate inferences are essential to initiative and follow-through on the job; implying rather than directly stating bad news can soften its impact on the receiver. The challenge is to ensure that inferences and implications are appropriate. Carefully analyzing the receiver and situation will help you to meet this challenge.

NOTE 1.39
Communication Barrier 4: Inappropriate implications and inferences.

Grammar, Sentence Structure, Punctuation, and Spelling

Incorrect grammar and poor sentence structure could hinder the receiver's understanding of a spoken or written message. Punctuation and spelling errors may create barriers to understanding a written message. As the number of errors increases, readers often stop reading for content and begin editing. The errors suggest that the person who sent the message either does not know the basics of the language or was too careless to correct the problems. Neither explanation creates a positive impression of the person who sent the message. As a result, the sender could lose credibility.

NOTE 1.40
Communication Barrier 5: Incorrect grammar, sentence structure, punctuation, and spelling.

Type of Message

Selecting a message type appropriate to the situation is essential to communication success. For example, communicating complex job instructions orally will most likely fail because the receiver must rely solely on his or her memory of what was said—or perhaps memory plus sketchy notes. A written message to which the worker can refer as needed will achieve better results. An in-person oral message is desirable when resolving a conflict between employees. Both the sender and the receiver can take full advantage of the nonverbal cues that accompany the spoken words.

If the message is a report on an evaluation of alternative manufacturing processes, the type of message will depend on who will receive it. The report may

NOTE 1.41
Communication Barrier 6: Wrong type of message.

be written or oral, long or short, technical or simple; graphic aids might be used to support verbal content. Often, more than one type of message can be used for the same communication situation.

Generally, the higher the level in an organization to which a message is sent, the more concise the message should be. Top managers view time as a precious commodity; therefore, a brief summary may be more suitable than a long, detailed report. Managers who have greater involvement with operating procedures may derive more benefits from long, technical messages.

Appearance of the Message

NOTE 1.42
Communication Barrier 7:
Poor appearance of
written message.

The appearance of a message affects its readability and influences a receiver's acceptance of its content. Smudges, sloppy corrections, light print, wrinkled paper, and poor handwriting may distract the reader and become barriers to effective communication. Using emoticons and keying all text in uppercase letters can be barriers in e-mail. Senders should examine every document before it is sent to ensure that its appearance does not interfere with its potential for success.

Appearance of the Sender

NOTE 1.43
Communication Barrier 8:
Poor appearance
of speaker.

The credibility of an oral message can be reduced if the appearance of the sender is unattractive or unacceptable to the receiver. In addition, unintended nonverbal signals can distract a receiver and influence the way an oral message is received. For example, if you smile when you sympathetically give bad news, your motives may be suspect.

If the credibility of the message is questioned, the quality of the receiver's understanding, acceptance, and response will be reduced. For success in oral business communication, senders should be sure that their dress, cleanliness, and facial and body movements are appropriate to their professions and to the communication situations they encounter. Wearing a tuxedo to a beach party is as inappropriate as wearing a swimsuit to the office.

Environmental Factors

NOTE 1.44
Communication Barrier 9:
Distracting environmental
factors.

The environment in which communication occurs can interfere with the success of a message. A noisy machine in an area where a supervisor is trying to speak with an employee can become a distracting environmental factor. A supervisor's desk that separates him or her from a worker during a meeting can intimidate the worker and limit his or her ability to respond to the message. Other examples of environmental factors that can be barriers to effective communication include room temperature, odor, light, color, and distance.

The sender has the responsibility to eliminate environmental factors that are communication barriers. If the room in which an oral presentation is to be given is too warm, the sender should try to get the thermostat turned down or to have the windows opened. If the receiver cannot see to read a message because of limited light, the sender should arrange for more light. Environmental barriers can usually be eliminated or reduced, often before communication begins.

Receiver's Capability

NOTE 1.45
Communication Barrier 10:
Receiver's limited
capability.

If the receiver has a disability that causes a communication barrier, the sender can remove or compensate for the barrier by carefully selecting the form of the message

tips and hints

Enhance Your Multicultural Communication Skills

Learn to enhance your multicultural communication skills by following these diversity action steps:

- Expect multicultural misunderstandings to occur sometimes.
- Recognize that our best intentions may be undermined by old assumptions.
- Catch ourselves in these assumptions in order to communicate more clearly and fairly.
- Learn about the cultural styles and values of different groups; understand and appreciate that individual differences exist within groups.
- Don't generalize about individuals because of their particular culture; many individual differences exist within groups.

- Avoid hot buttons or blunders like ethnic jokes, sexual expressions, racially based assumptions, inappropriate touching, and stereotyped job assignments.
- Use "we're all in this together" language to express trust and to foster a spirit of goodwill and partnership.
- Respond to the context and content of a person's words and deeds, rather than assumed motives.
- Don't be diverted by style, accent, grammar, or personal appearance; rather judge the merits of the statement or behavior.
- Consciously seek out new multicultural relationships and challenges.

From David P. Tulin, "Enhance Your Multi-cultural Communication Skills." Reprinted with permission from Tulin DaversiTeam Associates, Wyncote, PA.

and by providing for appropriate feedback mechanisms. Most of the solutions are clear choices. Increased volume, printed text, or a sign language interpreter can help overcome the potential barrier of a hearing impairment. When a visual impairment threatens the success of a written message, print can be enlarged or the message can be given orally. Effective communicators will focus on their receivers' abilities and will work with receivers to ensure communication success.

Ineffective Listening Skills

Failure to listen is a common barrier to successful oral communication. Listening effectively is not easy. One reason listening is challenging is that most people speak 150 to 200 words a minute but are capable of listening at 400 to 500 words a minute. This difference allows listeners' minds to wander to topics other than the message. In addition, listeners may tune out a speaker and begin thinking about how they will respond to the message. Listening is a skill that can and must be learned.

NOTE 1.46
Communication Barrier 11: Poor listening.

Senders can use several methods to overcome the barrier posed by a receiver's poor listening skills. Including phrases such as "Take note of this next point; it is particularly important" alerts receivers to listen carefully. Asking questions periodically will help determine the extent of the listener's comprehension. In some circumstances a poor listener may be encouraged to improve her or his listening skills. One of the most effective ways to remove poor listening as a barrier to communication is to improve the quality of the message and the way in which it is conveyed. Thoroughly analyzing the audience before designing the message will help a sender plan, organize, and deliver an appropriate oral message.

Other Communication Barriers

Several of the most common communication barriers and ways to remove them have been discussed in the preceding sections. In attempting to improve your

NOTE 1.47
Several other barriers can arise.

communication effectiveness, you may also face other barriers that must be eliminated. For example, some receiver-related communication barriers include lack of interest, lack of knowledge, different cultural perceptions, language difficulty, emotional state, and bias. The sender must do everything possible to remove these receiver-related communication barriers. Information in Tips and Hints on page 19 will help overcome barriers associated with cultural differences.

Summary of Learning Objectives

LO 1   *Explain why business communication is important to individuals and organizations.*

Business communication is the process of establishing a common understanding between or among people within a business environment. Good communication skills help individuals enhance self-esteem, become effective employees, and advance in their careers. The quality of an organization's internal and external communications affects its success.

LO 2   *List and explain the goals of business communication.*

Business communication has four goals: (a) receiver understanding—the receiver understands the message as the sender intended it to be understood; (b) receiver response—the receiver demonstrates his or her understanding of a message by providing an appropriate response; (c) favorable relationship—the people involved in the process relate to each other positively, personally, and professionally; and (d) organizational goodwill—the receiver has confidence in the sender's organization and is willing to continue the business relationship.

LO 3   *Describe the patterns of business communication.*

Business communication may be internal or external, formal or informal, work related or personal. Messages may flow vertically upward from workers, vertically downward from managers, or horizontally between or among workers who report to the same supervisor. Serial communication can occur in either horizontal or vertical communication. Messages can also flow between or among workers who, regardless of their unit or status, are part of a network. The grapevine is one type of informal network communication.

LO 4   *Explain the communication process.*

Communication occurs in an environment that includes the sender, the message, the receiver, feedback, and communication barriers. In the workplace, the organization's culture influences the communication environment and determines the nature and extent of office politics. For the communication process to succeed, the sender must analyze the receiver and then design a message that reflects what was learned through that analysis. The message should focus on the receiver's interests, encourage feedback, and eliminate or minimize communication barriers. The receiver must listen or read carefully and be open to senders and to their ideas; making notes, asking questions, and providing feedback are also part of the receiver's role in the process.

Identify communication barriers and describe ways to remove them.

LO 5

The primary barrier to effective communication is failure to use the you–viewpoint. Other potential barriers include word choice; punctuation, spelling, grammar, and sentence structure; appearance of the sender or the message; environmental factors; type of message; receiver capability; and listening. Analyzing the receiver and taking the you–viewpoint will eliminate or minimize these and other communication barriers that might arise.

Questions for Discussion and Review

1. Employers who participate in the annual survey conducted by the National Association of Colleges and Employers (NACE) consistently rank oral and written communication at the top of the list of skills they seek in job candidates—ahead of honesty, integrity, and computer skills. Why are communication skills so important to these and other employers? (Objective 1)

2. Why do organizations value both internal and external communication? (Objectives 1 and 3)

3. Name the four goals of business communication. Identify the most important one, and explain why it has this distinction. (Objective 2)

4. What is *credibility*? Why is it important for a communicator to be credible? (Objective 2)

5. Based on your work or school experience, discuss how roles or status have influenced the way in which people communicated. (Objective 3)

6. B. J. and Shawn worked in different units of a large organization. B. J. had been with the company for about two years and worked in an entry-level position; positive performance reviews resulted in pay raises and increased levels of responsibility but no promotion. Shawn had been with the company for over ten years and managed a growing division. The two, both of whom were interested in physical fitness, had no real interaction until they joined a new health club near their homes. Over the next several months, their common interest outside the office led to conversations at work. People began to notice, and when B. J. applied for and was hired for a supervisory position in Shawn's division, people began to talk. "It's office politics," they said. One person commented, "B. J. didn't earn that promotion. At least six people in Shawn's division are more qualified. B. J. was hired just because of their friendship. Shawn didn't even know who B. J. was until they met at that health club. I heard that B. J. joined that health club because several managers belonged." Was the meeting between B. J. and Shawn coincidence or strategy? Was their friendship genuine or contrived? Did Shawn hire B. J. because of qualifications or friendship? Was the promotion a function of networking? office politics? neither? both? (Objective 3)

7. What techniques can the sender of a message use to ensure that serial communications are accurate? (Objective 3)

8. How can assessing a receiver's knowledge help a message sender overcome word choice as a communication barrier? (Objectives 4 and 5)

9. Which communication barriers do you consider to be more serious, verbal or nonverbal? (Objective 5)

10. Name two communication barriers and explain how each can be overcome. (Objective 5)

Application Exercises

1. List the various channels through which representatives of your school communicate with you. Indicate the method(s) you prefer and why. (Objective 1)

2. Teamwork. Read the following situation and work with another student to list the possible actions the clerk could take to maintain a favorable relationship with the customer. (Objective 2)

Tyrone had worked at Supreme Sub for only three days and was alone at the counter when an angry customer entered the store carrying a partially eaten sandwich. About half an hour earlier, Tyrone had filled the customer's carry-out order for a large turkey and cheese sub. The customer had taken the sandwich to his office and eaten about half before noticing that it was meatless.

3. Teamwork. Obtain a copy of your school's administrative organization chart. As a group, identify the vertical and horizontal communication patterns suggested by the structure. Then, interview one of the administrators to learn whether/how network communication occurs within the structure. As your instructor directs, report your results in a one-page memo or orally to the class. (Objective 3)

4. Ethics. Picture yourself as the author of the "Ask Andy" column in your company newsletter. This month, you receive a letter from Edna, who writes, "I'm tired of all the office politics here. I think that those who participate in office politics are unethical. Do you agree?" Respond to "Edna, the Ethical Engineer." (Objective 3)

5. The company for which you work has offered you two tickets to a sold-out event (e.g., a concert, an NFL game). Two of your friends know you have the tickets; each wants to be the person you invite to accompany you. Write a brief description of how you think each would react if not invited. (Objective 4)

6. Prepare a one- to two-minute oral presentation in which you explain the sender's and receiver's roles in the communication process. As your instructor directs, deliver your presentation to another student, a small group, or the class. (Objective 4)

7. Words and phrases can have connotative meanings not only in business communication but also in classroom communication. For each item in the following list, identify what a teacher might mean when he or she speaks the word or phrase and what a student might interpret it to mean when he or she hears it during class. (Objective 5)
   a. Okay.
   b. Are there any questions?
   c. This is important.
   d. You need to . . . (study, do your homework).

8. Global. Select a culture other than your own. Gather information on that culture's values, attitudes, biases, and viewpoints. As your instructor directs, interview a student or faculty member from another culture, or use Internet or library resources to conduct your research. Share your findings with the class. (Objective 5)

9. Technology. Send a brief e-mail to your instructor explaining why you agree or disagree with the statement *Jargon is technical slang.* (Objective 5)

10. Judy and Paula were finishing their business lunch when the server who was clearing a nearby table dropped a tray of dishes. When she heard the sound, Paula jumped and turned to see what happened; Judy ignored the commotion and kept talking. Write two or three paragraphs in which you indicate whether effective communication occurred and why. (Objective 5)

Web exercises to accompany this chapter are available at **www.thomsonedu.com/bcomm/krizan.**

MESSAGE ANALYSIS
Correct the content, word choice, grammar, and punctuation errors in the following e-mail.

Bill, thanks for recomending that I attend the defective righting seminar at Ross College. It was out standing?

The segment of the seminar I found more useful was the part explaining how to write from the I–Viewpoint. Today's business world is vary competitive, an focusing on the sender can give you the edge you need to maintain favorable relatives.

Youll agree, I'm sure that my massages have improved all ready. I give you partial credit for the change. Lunch at The Derby Deli next weak will be my treat.

Writer's Workshop

The following items may be sentence fragments or contain errors in subject–verb agreement, comma and semicolon placement, spelling, or word choice. Rewrite the sentences to make them correct.

1. Unfortunately the seminar has been canceled.
2. Miller & Sons have opened a retail store in Lima Ohio.
3. Murray Jefferson who joined the firm just 18 months ago has been appointed as manger.
4. The attornies tried to exclaim the terms of the settlement to their client.
5. After the meeting.
6. The meating sight has been changed form the conference room to the auditorium, therefore, more people can attend.
7. The sofa, not the ottoman or the chairs, are on sale.
8. Sally Barb Hank and Hugh have agreed to be candidates.
9. Any staff member who may come into contract with a biohazard while on the job, should have access to protective devices such as gloves masks and goggles.
10. The first group of volunteers are leaving today. The second tomorrow.

Chapter 2
Multicultural and Global Communication

LET'S TALK BUSINESS

I live in London and work as a portfolio manager in the fast-paced world of global finance. Large sums of money trade hands on a daily basis, so communicating vital information effectively in a volatile environment and in a matter of seconds is a required skill. When interacting with brokers and analysts, I must always be cognizant and respectful of different linguistic and cultural backgrounds, but communication within these markets is not as difficult as you might think. In recent years, the way we communicate has changed dramatically due to two factors: monumental leaps in technology (Internet, cell phone, Blackberry) and the globalization of the financial markets. And, not surprisingly, a need for a common language has arisen. English has become

Daniel Knoeppel, Director, UBS-O'Connor Limited, UBS Global Asset Management

Photo courtesy of Daniel Knoeppel

that de facto language regardless of your mother tongue, unless you work exclusively in local markets. Years ago when I entered the financial markets on the floor of the American Stock Exchange, it was a world where interpersonal skills and hard-nosed craft were necessities. Changes in technology have caused a migration away from face-to-face communication toward computer-dependent interaction. Linguistic diversity, however, has not completely disappeared; it is not unusual to overhear a conversation in any number of languages littered with these words: *deal, bid, ask,* and *price ratio*. The reality is that old modes of communication have now given way to two requisite communication skills: English and technological connectivity.

Daniel Knoeppel is a U.S. citizen who lives and works in London, England. His description of financial markets illustrates today's global business environment.

Technological advances and fiber-optic global connections are changing the way companies do business.[1] In addition, companies have turned to **outsourcing** (transferring processes to a service provider) and **offshoring** (moving part or all of a business operation outside the home country) as ways to lower costs and remain competitive. These practices and **e-commerce** (buying and selling via the Internet) have greatly expanded the need for effective communication across a wide range of cultures.

A multicultural business environment requires communicating with colleagues and business clients who represent a variety of cultures. **Culture** has more than one definition. As used in this chapter, it means the customary beliefs, social norms, values, material traits, and behavior patterns transmitted from generation to generation that distinguish groups of people. Cultural background affects how individuals communicate and how they interpret messages received from others.

The first part of this chapter addresses cultural diversity, cultural barriers to communication, and guidelines for overcoming these barriers. The chapter concludes with considerations and strategies for communicating in a global business environment that relies heavily on technology to communicate.

Cultural Diversity in the Workplace

The workplace environment includes employees and customers with a wide range of needs, interests, abilities, and cultural backgrounds. If cultural diversity is not understood and valued, misunderstandings may occur that negatively affect business success. Analyzing the effect of culture on message content and delivery is consistent with the you–viewpoint described in Chapter 1.

Cultural background affects how individuals view the world, what they value, and how they interact with others. Five generally recognized core cultural dimensions are ethnicity, race, gender, age, and physical disability. In addition to these core cultural dimensions for individuals, organizations such as corporations have behavioral expectations, values, and patterns of operation that are referred to as organizational or **corporate culture.** This section of the chapter begins with a discussion of corporate culture and then addresses core dimensions that define differences related to cultural groups and individuals.

Corporate Culture

The culture of organizations defines shared values and behavioral expectations. Sometimes referred to as "the way we do things around here," organizational culture includes values, beliefs, assumptions, behavior patterns, norms, customs, rituals, and symbols that represent the company's vision and its expectations of employees. Learning the culture of the organization and adapting to it includes becoming familiar with formal statements of purpose, philosophy, and standards of conduct. Listening to others in the organization and observing formal and informal business behaviors provide insight about the organizational culture.

NOTE 2.1
Outsourcing moves some operations outside the company; offshoring opens branches outside the country.

NOTE 2.2
Culture means group beliefs, norms, values, traits, and behavior patterns.

LO 1
Explain how cultural differences affect business communication.

NOTE 2.3
Core cultural dimensions include ethnicity, race, gender, age, and disability.

NOTE 2.4
Corporate culture defines shared values and behavioral expectations.

---

[1]Thomas L. Friedman, *The World Is Flat: A Brief History of the Twenty-first Century* (New York: Farrar, Straus and Giroux, 2005), 66–67.

communication note

MICROSOFT CORPORATE VALUES

- Integrity and honesty.
- Passion for customers, partners, and technology.
- Open and respectful with others and dedicated to making them better.
- Willingness to take on big challenges and see them through.
- Self-critical, questioning, and committed to personal excellence and self-improvement.

- Accountable for commitments, results, and quality to customers, shareholders, partners, and employees.

NOTE 2.5
Company websites communicate corporate values and standards.

Leaders of an organization influence what is valued and expected. Frequent display and repetition of phrases or symbols that signify company core values help create shared meanings and understandings that form a corporate identity. Many company websites display a formal statement of corporate values and standards of business conduct (also called a code of ethics). The Microsoft website,[2] for example, uses the phrase "Great People with Great Values." The above Communication Note lists corporate values of Microsoft.

Large corporations such as Microsoft seek personnel diversity that represents the multicultural environment in which the organization operates. The Standards of Conduct for Microsoft states the belief that retaining and fully engaging diverse talents leads to enhanced innovation in products and services.

Cultural Ethnicity and Race

NOTE 2.6
Ethnicity relates to common history; race, to characteristics transmissible by descent.

Definitions of ethnicity and race are difficult to separate. In fact, the *Cambridge Advanced Learner's Dictionary*[3] defines **ethnic** as a national or racial group of people. **Race** is defined as people who share the same language, history, and characteristics or who have particular similar physical characteristics. However, race and ethnicity can be considered largely a cultural and historical construct used to identify groups of people with similar characteristics. Identification choices for race used by the U.S. Census Bureau[4] include American Indian or Alaska Native, Asian, Black or African American, Native Hawaiian or Other Pacific Islander, White, and Other Race. For ethnicity, the Census Bureau uses Hispanic or Latino, and Not Hispanic or Latino. These options will expand as the United States increases in ethnic and racial diversity.

Identifying cultural characteristics, ethnicity, and race is difficult because of overlap between groups and the cultural diffusion resulting from worldwide communication and travel. Increased interaction among varying cultures may decrease cultural

[2]"Microsoft Standards of Business Conduct: Great People with Great Values, Microsoft: About Microsoft," Microsoft, May 4, 2004, http://www.microsoft.com/mscorp/legal/buscond/ (accessed January 7, 2006).
[3]Cambridge University Press, "Cambridge Dictionaries Online: Advanced Learner's Dictionary," n.d., http://dictionary.cambridge.org/define.asp?key=65069&dict+CALD (accessed January 7, 2006).
[4]U.S. Census Bureau, "Racial and Ethnic Classifications Used in Census 2000 and Beyond," n.d., http://www.census.gov/population/www/socdemo/race/race/factcb.html (accessed January 7, 2006).

differences, but change takes place slowly. Languages, dialects, and ethnic symbols are a source of pride in cultural heritage, and some differences will continue to exist.

Because race and ethnicity are not clearly defined, someone may label you in a way that you find inaccurate and offensive. Even if unintentional, such labeling can be a barrier to communication. Cultural variations in backgrounds and experience as well as language or physical characteristics affect communication. Experiences, beliefs, and values influence interactions with one another and serve as a filter through which message understanding and acceptance or rejection take place.

Gender Roles

Gender is another core dimension of diversity. Within cultural groups, societal expectations affect how men and women interact with one another. For example, in the Middle East holding hands in public is considered proper behavior between friends of the same sex but not between individuals of the opposite sex. Cultural attitudes toward the appropriate roles of men and women vary markedly throughout the world.

Although not always true, men and women tend to communicate in different ways. Historically, in the United States and some other countries, society expected men to be decisive and to use language to assert independence and maintain group position; women were to be nurturing and use language to create connections and relationships. These cultural tendencies sometimes continue in everyday business communication. For example, women may be more likely to discuss a problem with others and seek input before making decisions; men may make decisions without consultation because they believe it is their role to do so. Without considering why this behavior occurs, men may misinterpret a woman's need for input as inability to make a decision. Likewise, women may assume that all men who make decisions without consultation are power seekers who do not value the opinion of others, particularly women. In the United States, corporate cultural expectations of teamwork, collaboration, and facilitative leadership as well as societal changes blur these communication differences. However, being aware of the influence that cultural expectations have on behavior patterns and beliefs helps individuals learn to collaborate effectively within diverse work teams.

Age Diversity

Individuals' ages and stages of life affect not only how they perceive the world around them and what they value but also how others perceive them. Cultures tend to associate different ages with special roles in society. Cross[5] defined life stages in the United States as follows:

- 18–22: leaving home; establishing identity and new alliances
- 23–28: regarding self as adult; living and building a future
- 29–34: searching for stability and security; reexamining relationships
- 37–42: becoming one's own person; facing reality and a sense of age
- 45–56: settling down; becoming a mentor and grandparent; gaining self-confidence
- 57–64: mellowing; preparing for retirement; adjusting to aging
- 65+: beginning life review; accepting self; adjusting to different routines

[5]K. P. Cross, as cited in Patricia Cranton, *Working with Adult Learners* (Middleton, Ohio: Wall & Emerson, 1992), 36–37.

NOTE 2.7
Societal expectations of men and women affect how they interact with one another.

NOTE 2.8
Men and women tend to exhibit different communication behaviors.

NOTE 2.9
Age and stage of life affect individuals' values and how others perceive them.

communication note

GENERATIONAL ISSUES

Chuck Underwood, President of the Generational Imperative, counsels companies on managing age differences in their workforce. He says, "For the first time, four generations are active and critical to the American Workforce—the Silent Generation (ages 60–72), baby boomers (ages 40–59), Generation Xers (ages 25–39), and Millennials (24 and under)."

He notes that generational issues are high on the list of employee-relations issues today.

Jordan Robertson and Bob Moos, "As More Gen Xers Supervise Older Workers, Conflict Is Inevitable," *The Dallas Morning News.* Story appeared in *The Standard-Times,* **SouthCoast Today.com,** July 19, 2005, L2. http://www.southcoasttoday .com/daily/07-19-05/102.ca216.htm (accessed January 21, 2006).

Although the age ranges vary for different people and cultures, these life stages not only typify the way roles change as people mature but also indicate differing interests and needs. Thus, an individual's life stage affects his or her interests. Understand that age may affect the message receiver, but avoid emphasizing age or age-related characteristics.

Traditionally, most persons left the workforce at age 62 or 65, but longevity increases and health advances are changing this pattern. One in five persons is 55 or older, compared to one in ten at the beginning of the twentieth century. The Census Bureau projects that by 2010 the number will be one in four. As the number of healthy seniors increases and the pool of younger workers decreases, senior adults are staying in the workforce longer than in previous years and are becoming an increasingly important consumer market.

Physical Disability

NOTE 2.10
The Americans with Disabilities Act removes barriers for persons with disabilities.

Persons with a physical disability comprise another core dimension of cultural diversity. In the workplace, physical disability usually means use of a wheelchair, a cane, crutches, or a walker or difficulty seeing, hearing, speaking, or performing physical activities. U.S. census figures show approximately one in five adults has some type

tips and hints

Communicating with Persons Who Have Disabilities

- Focus on the individual's ability rather than on the disability.
- Use terminology such as "a person who uses a wheelchair" (rather than "a wheelchair-bound person") or "Jane has a speech disability," keeping the focus on the individual.
- When talking more than a few minutes with a person in a wheelchair, sit down so you are on the same eye level.
- If a person with vision disability needs help going down stairs, let him or her take your arm; use verbal cues to direct the person—verbalize the stair, curb, or a chair location ("Be ready to step down"; "The stairs are three steps in front of you").
- Enunciate clearly to permit lip reading and use a combination of gestures, facial expressions, and note passing (if necessary) when conversing with an individual who has a hearing disability.

of disability; among ages 45 to 54, this number rises to 23 percent. Individuals with physical limitations are sometimes patronized or avoided, usually because of the visibility of their difficulty and a lack of awareness of how to interact with them. The Americans with Disabilities Act (ADA) removes unreasonable barriers to employment; its aim is to prevent discrimination against qualified employees with disabilities.

Multicultural Perspectives

Awareness that miscommunication can arise due to ethnicity, race, gender, age, physical disability, and other differences such as religions and lifestyles is the first step toward effective multicultural communication. Greater cultural diversity in the workplace and marketplace increases the need for understanding how cultural background affects communication. The following paragraphs describe potential barriers to effective multicultural communication.

Communication Barriers

A number of communication barriers exist when you are interacting with people from cultures other than your own. Barriers include cultural relativism, ethnocentrism, lack of knowledge and understanding of other cultures, discriminatory behaviors such as harassment, and language differences.

CULTURAL RELATIVISM AND ETHNOCENTRISM

Cultural relativism compares the values and behaviors of different cultures and usually means judging them against standards of right and wrong for your own culture. This approach to other cultures becomes a barrier when you assume that cultural beliefs, values, and behaviors are wrong if they differ from those of your culture. **Ethnocentrism** is the inherent belief that your own cultural traditions and values are

LO 2
Identify cultural barriers to communication.

NOTE 2.11
Cultural relativism means judging cultural values and behaviors, usually against your own standards; ethnocentrism is the belief that your own culture is superior.

Multicultural work teams bring together diverse perspectives, help overcome cultural barriers to communication, and improve products or services for a diverse clientele.

© Digital Vision

correct and superior. People around the world are ethnocentric to a degree. Beliefs, values, and behaviors that differ from those of your culture may seem peculiar, strange, and even wrong. However, as you study different cultures, recognize that there is not just one right or wrong way but that different ways can be equally correct.

LACK OF KNOWLEDGE AND UNDERSTANDING OF CULTURES

Although a particular culture may generally exhibit similar behaviors or characteristics, this does not mean all individuals in that culture are alike. People form **stereotypes** when they assume that behaviors or characteristics typical of a particular culture define all members of that cultural group. Stereotypes result from a limited knowledge of cultural diversity. Numerous resources describe common characteristics of different cultures. Some of these are cited in this chapter. Regard these descriptions as general in nature. Interacting with and learning more about individuals within a culture help dispel stereotypes.

An understanding of cultures means being aware that individuals within each culture have similarities and differences. It means responding to people as individuals while recognizing that cultural backgrounds and experiences influence behavior and communication.

DISCRIMINATION AND HARASSMENT

Discrimination is showing favoritism toward or prejudicial rejection of people because of differences. In the United States, laws prohibit employment discrimination against persons in protected groups, including race, gender, age, religion, national origin, and disability. Discriminatory practices include failing to hire or promote individuals from a protected group, making arbitrary or capricious decisions that adversely affect their employment, or failing to treat them with the same dignity and respect reasonably afforded to any human being.

Business communication between the sexes calls for a clear understanding of remarks and actions that could be construed as sexual harassment. **Sexual harassment** is unwelcome behavior of a sexual nature or with sexual overtones. It may occur for men as well as women. Legally, either of the following conditions constitutes sexual harassment:

- **Quid pro quo** (exchange something for something). Quid pro quo occurs when a positive or negative employment decision depends (or appears to depend) on whether the person submits to or rejects sexual demands.
- **Hostile environment.** This results from unwelcome sexual conduct that creates an offensive environment, interferes with a person's job performance, or causes intimidation.

Quid pro quo is applicable if rejecting advances could affect hiring, firing, promotion, or evaluation. A supervisor who persists with unwelcome advances toward an employee can be guilty of quid pro quo. Also, such harassment could come from an employee who is a friend of the supervisor and who harasses a coworker by threatening to interfere with the coworker's request for promotion if advances are rejected. The employee who is subject to quid pro quo from a supervisor may be reluctant to object to unwanted behavior because of fear of potential reprisals or a negative influence on employment decisions.

A hostile environment can result from frequent interactions that have sexual connotations, such as comments and jokes with sexual innuendoes, as well as touching that may be viewed as inappropriate and of a sexual nature. Examples of behavior that could create a hostile environment include frequent comments on a sexy appearance, a joke with crude language or sexual content, or intentional physical contact when walking past a coworker. Whether an environment is hostile depends on how the recipient of the unwelcome behavior feels about it and the extent to which it creates an intimidating or offensive work situation.

The victim of sexual harassment should make it clear that offensive comments or actions are unwelcome. Rejection may be by verbal or nonverbal behaviors such as evident annoyance or pushing the person away. However, failure to do so does not absolve the offender of guilt as long as the sexual banter or horseplay was not responded to in kind. A victim of continued offensive behavior should report the harassment to the proper person in the organization.

LANGUAGE

Language may be a barrier to communication. An increase in multicultural inter-actions presents language challenges. When organizations communicate with large numbers of people who speak languages other than English—employees, clients, customers, suppliers, and government personnel—misunderstandings can occur. Voices speaking languages other than English can be heard in public places almost anywhere in the United States. In addition, most product directions are printed in more than one language, and universal symbols are commonly used as road signs. Although English has become the language of business, increased global contacts through e-mail, e-commerce, offshoring, and outsourcing, in addition to the num-ber of immigrants coming into the United States, increase language barriers to communication.

NOTE 2.16
Language differences can be a communication barrier.

Some words have different meanings and connotations in different countries and cultures. The Advertising Research Resource Center[6] at the University of Texas gives a number of examples of humorous or lost marketing opportunities because of mixed meanings in different languages. For example, the American Dairy Association's decision to extend the "Got Milk?" advertisements to the Mexico market failed because the Spanish translation was "Are you lactating?" When Kentucky Fried Chicken entered the Chinese market, its slogan "finger lickin' good" came out in translation as "eat your fingers off"! Chinese translation proved diffi-cult for Coca-Cola, which tried twice to get it right. The first translation was "Ke-kou-ke-la" because it sounded roughly like "Coca-Cola." After printing thousands of signs, company representatives discovered the phrase meant "bit the wax tad-pole" or "female horse stuffed with wax," depending on the dialect. After research-ing 40,000 Chinese characters, Coca-Cola came up with "ko-kou-ko-le," which translates roughly to a more appropriate "happiness in the mouth."

NOTE 2.17
Words may have different meanings and connotations in different countries.

Some words and phrases are difficult to translate from one language to another because of mental associations that only native language speakers have for them. For example, sports-related expressions such as "out in left field" would create translation problems in a country that did not have baseball teams.

The first wave of globalization made English the universal language, but current marketing strategies recognize the importance of accommodating geographic or cul-tural target markets. Corporations are shaping their products for local conditions and producing websites in two or more languages. American media giants such as

NOTE 2.18
Corporations respect local languages, and their websites may be in more than one language.

---

[6]"Lost in Translation," Advertising Research Resource Center, Department of Advertising, The University of Texas at Austin, n.d., http://advertising.utexas.edu/research/humor/lost.html (accessed July 15, 2005).

CNN now broadcast in other languages as well as English to compete with regional and other international media. The number of non-English websites is growing, along with newly active Internet newsgroups that use the national language.

English is the common "linguistic denominator" for business.[7] However, globalization is changing the nature of the language. With native speakers a shrinking minority of those who speak English, current thought resists the idea that students of English in other countries should emulate Brighton or Boston English. There is an acceptance that they may embrace their own local versions. Researchers are studying non-native speakers' "mistakes"—such as "She look very sad"—as structured grammar, and an expert in world Englishes at King's College in London asks why Asians, who may have difficulty saying words beginning with "th," should try to say "thing" instead of "sing" or "ting."

Variations of English words exist even in English-speaking countries. For example, the American word for bathroom becomes loo or WC (Water Closet) in British English. In England, the American jello becomes jelly and jelly becomes jam. The British word for a sausage is banger, and a car trunk is a boot. In both Australia and England, an elevator is a lift.

Regional language differences exist within the United States as well. When you need a drink of water, do you look for a water fountain, a drinking fountain, or a bubbler? Do you carry your lunch in a bag or a sack? Do you refer to a carbonated beverage as a pop or soda?

Even the use of parts of speech varies in different languages. In Japanese, the verb is at the end of a sentence. This enables Japanese speakers to begin to express a thought and watch the receiver's reaction. Depending on how the receiver reacts to a message, the verb may be changed, thereby changing the meaning of the sentence. For example, a Japanese language speaker might start to convey a message meaning, "Please go away from me now" but end up with the meaning, "Please stay with me now" by changing the verb, which is said last. Because of the importance of misunderstandings that can occur in language translations, a businessperson with knowledge of language and language subtleties is a business asset.

Nonverbal language influences the receiver's understanding and acceptance of a spoken message. If the message receiver perceives a difference between the sender's verbal and nonverbal messages, he or she is more likely to believe the nonverbal than the verbal communication. In multicultural business communication, nonverbal signals vary as much as spoken languages do. Nonverbal greetings vary from a bow to a handshake, or from a hug to an upward flick of the eyebrows.

Not understanding cultural differences in nonverbal messages causes communication problems. For example, the Japanese consider crossing one's legs by placing one foot or ankle on the knee of the other leg to be impolite or vulgar. The preferred way of sitting is with both feet on the floor with knees together. Thumbs up in America means approval, but in Iran and Ghana it is a vulgar gesture. In addition, the social distance or individual space that persons need for comfort in communication varies in different cultures. If people stand too close when conversing, Germans, Canadians, and Americans may feel uncomfortable; in Middle Eastern cultures, however, conversations may be almost nose to nose.

---

[7]Carla Power, "Not the Queen's English," *Newsweek International Edition*, MSNBC, Newsweek, Inc., 2005, http://www.msnbc.com/id/7038031/site/newsweek/ (accessed July 15, 2005).

communication note

NONVERBAL COMMUNICATION IN GHANA

Anthony Donkor, a native of Ghana, West Africa, and currently a doctoral student at the University of Kentucky, describes nonverbal language used in Ghanaian culture.

"A positive smile sets up the platform for effective communication. It establishes trust. Reaction to a smile brings these thoughts to one's mind: 'I am in the right place; I am in good hands; they care; I have been accepted; I can work with them.' In the Ghanaian culture, the frequent usage of the word 'please' is in both formal and informal discussions. Shaking hands during greetings is better than nodding heads. In addition, waving a left hand at anyone is unacceptable and regarded as an insult. Ghanaian's are not familiar with the act of looking straight into the eyes of other people during a one-to-one discussion. Shying away does not imply a hidden agenda in the Ghanaian perspective. It is a sign of respect. People listen more than look straight into the eyes of their counterparts."

Anthony Donkor, cofounder, Hope International School, Weija-Ghana, West Africa.

Multicultural Communication Guidelines

You can become an effective multicultural communicator if you follow a few simple guidelines. Understanding your own culture, keeping an open mind and respecting differences, adapting to cultural communication patterns, and identifying language differences can improve multicultural interactions.

UNDERSTAND YOUR OWN CULTURE

Improve communication with others by increasing awareness of your own culture and its influences on your beliefs, values, and behavior patterns. Recognize that your cultural background and experiences shape how you think, what you value, and how you communicate. Consider how you might have different beliefs and behaviors if you had been born a member of the opposite sex or a different race or had come to the United States from another country such as India, Russia, or Japan.

KEEP AN OPEN MIND AND RESPECT DIVERSITY

Learn about other cultures, beliefs, and customs without judging them by your own cultural identity and unexamined biases. This is not to suggest that you change your beliefs or disrespect your own culture, but rather that you recognize that cultural values affect beliefs and behaviors and that understanding how others interpret verbal and nonverbal language helps your communication receive the intended response. However, avoid accepting stereotypes that assume that characteristics that may apply to some people in a particular culture are characteristic of all individuals in that culture. Knowledge of an individual's ethnic or other cultural background is only an initial clue to understanding his or her interests, needs, and values.

IDENTIFY AND ADAPT TO LANGUAGE DIFFERENCES

If you are communicating with persons from another culture, learn how that culture's verbal and nonverbal languages differ from your own. Observe and learn the meaning of nonverbal communication signals such as facial expressions, social distance for conversing, and hand gestures. Avoid nonverbal signals that may be offensive.

When speaking or writing, alter language and change traditional word usage to avoid language that offends someone. Be sensitive and considerate of others' beliefs.

LO 3

Explain basic guidelines for effective multicultural communication.

NOTE 2.22
Understanding your own culture helps you understand others.

NOTE 2.23
Be open to learning about other cultures, and respect their differences.

NOTE 2.24
Learn about verbal and nonverbal language differences.

NOTE 2.25
Be sensitive to word meanings by applying good judgment and mutual respect.

When reading or listening, do not be overly sensitive if good intent is evident. Good judgment and mutual respect should prevail.

About 340 million people speak English as their native language, and speakers of English as a second language may soon outnumber native English speakers. About one fourth of the world's population speaks English with some level of competence, and an increasing number of people in other countries are learning English.

NOTE 2.26
The number of speakers of English as a second language equals the number of native English speakers.

English is a common business language. This globalization of the language brings it back in somewhat altered forms. Sentence structure, word usage, and spelling in business correspondence from speakers and writers of English as a second language may vary from the form considered technically correct in countries where English is the native language. These variations should be respected and understood; usage of a second language is not likely to be a perfect match for that of a native speaker or writer. Some sentence structure or word usage may resemble familiar usage in the native language.

NOTE 2.27
Respect English grammar variations used by non-native English speakers.

Multinational and Global Business

LO 4
Discuss communication challenges in a global environment.

"Multinational" and "global" are terms sometimes used synonymously. Both refer to business operations across national boundaries with multiple countries. **Multinational business** implies operations targeted toward and conducted in two or more countries; **global business** is a broader term meaning operations and strategies to serve a world market. Because communication is increasingly global and business practices often blur national boundaries, this concluding section of the chapter refers to both multinational and global business operations as global. The section begins with further discussion of outsourcing and offshoring operations that open new labor sources and markets and then describes adapting to a global environment. The chapter concludes with strategies for effective global communication.

NOTE 2.28
"Global business" refers to business operations across multiple national boundaries.

Outsourcing and Offshoring

When you place a call for technical assistance from your Internet provider, schedule airline reservations, or place an order at a drive-in restaurant, the person answering your call may be in another city, state, or country. Friedman,[8] in his book *The World Is Flat*, gives examples of all those scenarios. India is one of the initial prominent providers of outsourcing operations for large corporations. Call centers for technical assistance and software development for major technology companies have become major sources of employment for India's young, well-educated workers.

NOTE 2.29
Outsourcing for call center operations and software development is a common business practice.

A business supply chain for global business operations could include American designers, Indian software writers, Asian manufacturers, and Singaporean implementation planners or other such configurations. Similar operational networks are producing quality products or services at a lower cost than has been possible with all operations completed in the United States or other industrialized countries.

Outsourcing uses outside workers to perform specialized tasks that can be effectively communicated electronically and completed with a low-cost labor supply. Because of time zone differences and different holiday calendars, strategic location of outsourcing to other parts of the world can allow these functions to take place at

---

[8] Friedman, *The World Is Flat*, 25–42.

night when the home office is closed, thus expanding operations to 24/7. Differences in holidays and work schedules can mean production 24/7/52.

Homesourcing is another form of outsourcing used by American corporations to cut costs and increase efficiency. JetBlue Airways outsourced its reservation system to housewives in Utah who worked from their homes. These home reservationists worked 25 hours a week and came to the JetBlue regional office only four hours a month for updates and new skill training. Some multistate fast-food franchises outsource their drive-through orders to a call center in Colorado Springs. Alltel in Kentucky outsources technical assistance calls to a call center in Kansas. Companies in the United States, Great Britain, Japan, and other industrialized countries currently outsource some or all of their manufacturing or service operations.

NOTE 2.30
Homesourcing is a variation of outsourcing.

Expanding Global Operations

Companies have had offshore operations for over a decade, locating all or part of their business outside the home country. For example, a manufacturing company in Texas may move manufacturing operations across the Mexican border. A software development company in Indiana may expand its service market by opening branches in France, the Czech Republic, and Germany. Another company may relocate all business operations except the administrative home office. New market opportunities in countries such as China are increasing offshore business operations. China's move into world trade opens a vast new market and labor supply.

NOTE 2.31
Offshore and global operations are increasing.

NOTE 2.32
Global executives find communication and language the most challenging cultural differences.

A survey of 101 global executives from 36 countries asked what cultural difference they considered most challenging. The most frequent responses were communication and language.[9] One executive described the challenge as understanding people, what they want, and what motivates them. Another said, "When you tell a person this is what we are going to do, if he doesn't understand, he will not tell you." Understanding the culture is as important as understanding the language. If people don't understand, they may not tell you this because in their culture they avoid telling bad news. Cultural variations affect communication; therefore, a general understanding of the differences in conducting business from one country to another helps avoid misunderstandings. Variations exist among countries. Understanding their history, customs, and perceptions of time, space, and power structures is a starting point for communicating effectively.

Laugh Parade by Bunny Hoest and John Reiner

"WELL, PAT, THE GOOD NEWS IS THAT WE'VE DECIDED NOT TO SHIP YOUR JOB OVERSEAS ... WE'VE DECIDED TO SHIP YOU THERE INSTEAD."

© 2005, reprinted courtesy of Bunny Hoest and Parade

---

[9] Morgan W. McCall Jr. and George P. Hollenbeck, *Developing Global Executives* (Boston: Harvard Business School Press, 2002), 24–28.

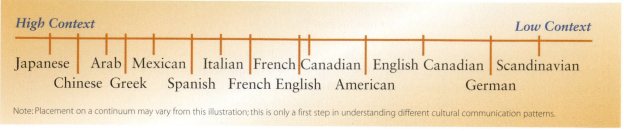

Note: Placement on a continuum may vary from this illustration; this is only a first step in understanding different cultural communication patterns.

FIGURE 2.1
Continuum from
High-Context to
Low-Context Cultures

COMMUNICATING IN HIGH- OR LOW-CONTEXT CULTURES

One way to study global culture and its influence on communication arranges countries on a continuum from high to low context.[10] Traditionally, high-context countries place high value on relationships and favor indirect communication when conducting business. Low-context countries value productivity, prefer direct communication, and give minimal attention to relationship building. High-context cultures assign more meaning to shared history, nonverbal signals, and the context of the message than to what is said. Many contextual stimuli are disregarded by low-context cultures, with intense focus on words, messages, or physical gestures.

NOTE 2.33
Consider high- and low-context cultures when studying global cultures.

Japan, China, and most other Asian countries generally are considered high-context cultures. The United States and Canada as well as northern Europe are low-context cultures. Figure 2.1 shows a general placement of 15 parts of the world on this continuum.

NOTE 2.34
Recognize that differences exist within a culture as well as between cultures.

This classification is an oversimplification because variations exist within low-context or high-context localities. For example, although American culture is classified as low context, communication among family members tends to be high context. Family relationships and members' high level of shared experiences require fewer words because of mutual understandings. Communication between two businesspersons from a low-context culture tends to be direct, specific, and structured linearly and logically. Attention focuses more on what is said than on relationships. In China or Japan, words receive less attention than identifying relationships, establishing mutual understandings, and observing nonverbal body language. Communication is indirect. Figure 2.2 compares general characteristics that affect communication between individuals from high- and low-context cultures.

COMMUNICATING ACROSS NATIONAL BORDERS

NOTE 2.35
E-mail is the most frequent mode of global communication.

Communicating globally by telephone or e-mail minimizes differences in business hours, holidays, and time zones. You can send voice mail or e-mail at any time. Talking directly to persons outside their business hours and workdays is possible by prearrangement or via their cell phone. However, in most cases, such calls outside work time should be made only in emergencies or when requested by the person to be called. E-mail, because of economy and rapid delivery, is the most frequent mode of global communication.

---

[10] This analysis was based on Janet K. Winter and Esther J. Winter, "Contexting: The Relative Directness of Intercultural Communication," *Communication for a Global Society, NBEA Yearbook* (Reston, Va.: NBEA, 2005), 158–171; Charles P. Campbell, "Beyond Language: Cultural Predispositions in Business Correspondence," paper presented at Region 5 STC Conference, Fort Worth, Texas, 1998, http://infohostnmt.edu/~cpc/internationalethos.html (accessed August 9, 2005); Mary O'Hara-Devereaux and Robert Johnson, "Transcending Cultural Barriers: Context, Relationships, and Time," n.d., http://www.csub.edu/tic/options/resources/handouts/fac_dev/culturalbarries.html (accessed November 5, 2005).

communication note

CONVERTING TIME, CURRENCY, AND OTHER MEASURES

World Clock
http://www.timeanddate.com
http://www.timeanddate.com/worldclock/meetingtime.html
http://www.timeanddate.com/worldclock/converter.html

Currency
http://www.oanda.com

Distance, Temperature, Speed, Date/Time, and Others
http://onlineconversion.com

High Context	Low Context
Indirect communication patterns	Direct and specific communication
Fewer words, more nonverbal clues	High value on words rather than shared background
Simple, ambiguous messages	Structured messages with technical details
Highly verbal people perceived as unattractive; smiling associated with nervousness	Informal, smile frequently, and frequent use of hand gestures and facial expressions
Reliance on long-term relationships and underlying meanings	Transitory personal relationships; shared background not assumed for meanings
Long-term view of time	Short-term view of time
Appointments considered flexible; "on time" may be within a half hour, week, or month	Emphasis on appointments, management of schedules, and punctuality
Values family and group authority	Individualism valued
Communication follows spiral logic based on relationships rather than linear progression of ideas	Communication follows linear pattern; emphasizes logic to present ideas and considers the bottom line
Vague, nonconfrontational language preferences	Focus on getting a job done, succeeding, and profitability
Honor and face more important than business; defer to power and position	Transitory personal relationships; ideas and people assumed as equals
Information obtained through private networks	Information readily accessible, shared with others

FIGURE 2.2
Comparison of Communication in High- and Low-Context Cultures

International time zones mean a six- to nine-hour time difference between European or Asian countries and the United States. Time differences allow little or no overlap in normal business hours. Also, many countries in warmer climates tend to close their offices in the middle of the day for the main meal and for rest, although this practice is changing in larger cities such as Milan, Italy.

The days of the week that businesses operate vary around the world. In the United States most business offices operate Monday through Friday. In Korea, the workweek is Monday through Saturday, and possibly Sunday. In contrast, the workweek in Saudi Arabia and other Islamic countries is Saturday through Wednesday, with Thursday and Friday as the days off. Friday is the Islamic day of rest and worship.

NOTE 2.36
Differences in time, workweeks, and holidays affect communication.

Speaking and Writing for a Global Audience

LO 5
Describe key strategies for effective global business communication.

A basic recommendation for communicating with people in other countries is to learn as much as you can of their language. Although you may be unable to speak and write the language fluently, learn at least greetings, courtesy words, and the basic positive and negative signals. Learn a few basic phrases typically used in your communication, and use what you know in your oral and written messages. For example, learn how to say "We want to do business with you," if that is appropriate. Your receivers will appreciate your efforts. They will be understanding and accepting of deficiencies in your use of their language.

NOTE 2.37
Learn and use a few phrases and greetings in the receiver's native language.

The Tips and Hints feature gives suggestions for speaking or writing in English to communicate across cultures. These few simple guidelines can be helpful.

When conducting business in high-context countries such as Japan and China, emphasize relationships, tradition, ceremony, and social rules, and use an indirect communication pattern. This pattern has been described as a spiral pattern of talking about related issues before getting to the business at hand. Initially, time is spent in social conversation and rituals such as handshakes and an exchange of business cards. The business cards should have the information printed in both languages.

Conversely, in low-context cultures such as Germany, Switzerland, and the United States, both spoken and written communication may be depicted as a straight line that gets directly to business. Generally, Germans do not appreciate social small talk.

NOTE 2.38
Adapt your communication style to the indirect or direct style of the receiver.

Express your main message content in much the same way that you normally would, but consider the receiver's preferred style of direct or indirect communication and the importance placed on relationships. For an audience including cultures that traditionally use indirect communication, promote relationship building by expressing interest in the individual or making a connection to a shared interest before moving to the business at hand. Study the letter in Figure 2.3 from a U.S. agricultural supply company to a Chinese businessman who has recently visited the United States to attend an international conference on agricultural production methods. Note the indirect organization of the letter; the writer first shows interest in building relationships before offering to send a brochure of services (the sales message).

NOTE 2.39
E-mail is typically shorter than a letter and more informal.

Frequently, communication across national boundaries is electronic. E-mails are typically shorter than business letters and directed specifically to the purpose of the communication. These messages may have a greater degree of informality than business letters, particularly between individuals who work together in the same company,

tips and hints

Using English to Communicate with People Who Speak English as a Second Language

- Enunciate clearly but speak with a normal tone and pace.
- Avoid long, complex sentences or terms with meanings unfamiliar outside your home area such as "level the playing field" or "daffy idea."
- Learn to say a few words or common phrases or greetings in the message receiver's home language.

- Avoid attempts at humor; misunderstandings may result that offend the message receiver.
- Accept and respect different sentence structures written or spoken to you by someone not a native English speaker.
- Consider the receiver's preferred style of communication.

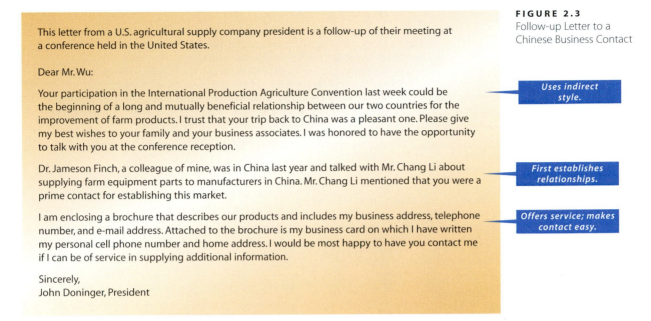

FIGURE 2.3
Follow-up Letter to a
Chinese Business Contact

This letter from a U.S. agricultural supply company president is a follow-up of their meeting at a conference held in the United States.

Dear Mr. Wu:

Your participation in the International Production Agriculture Convention last week could be the beginning of a long and mutually beneficial relationship between our two countries for the improvement of farm products. I trust that your trip back to China was a pleasant one. Please give my best wishes to your family and your business associates. I was honored to have the opportunity to talk with you at the conference reception.

Uses indirect style.

Dr. Jameson Finch, a colleague of mine, was in China last year and talked with Mr. Chang Li about supplying farm equipment parts to manufacturers in China. Mr. Chang Li mentioned that you were a prime contact for establishing this market.

First establishes relationships.

I am enclosing a brochure that describes our products and includes my business address, telephone number, and e-mail address. Attached to the brochure is my business card on which I have written my personal cell phone number and home address. I would be most happy to have you contact me if I can be of service in supplying additional information.

Offers service; makes contact easy.

Sincerely,
John Doninger, President

even when located in different countries. Although some coworkers may be native to the foreign location, the correspondence is likely to be in English.

Regardless of the frequency of correspondence, ideally each person uses good conventions of English, although some messages from another country may use native language patterns or phrases in the content. Messages between frequent business colleagues are usually brief, with less need for detail if the message relates to an issue well known to both sender and receiver. Even though the message is brief, adding words or greetings that convey interest in the message receiver contributes to good working relationships.

Correspondence (e-mail or letter) written in English to someone in a country where English is a second language should follow proper grammatical construction, good writing principles, capitalization, and punctuation as formally taught in the writer's home country. The correspondent using English as a second language may make adaptations of English that fit his or her own country's language structure but that are easily understandable to the recipient. Figure 2.4 shows an actual e-mail chain that was sent between the home office of a U.S. computer software business and a branch office located in France. An **e-mail chain** develops when correspondents use the Reply function of e-mail to keep together in one record all e-mails pertinent to a particular topic. In Figure 2.4, the sequence of messages is numbered in the order sent. The most recent message is at the top. To understand the complete scenario of events, read from the bottom to the top of the e-mail chain.

E-mail, by its brief, direct nature, lends itself to shortcut practices, such as using emoticons, lack of capitalization, and shortcut terms such as CU for "see you" (similar to text messaging). These practices are fine for informal personal messages but are not recommended for business e-mail. They may be misunderstood or may not make a professional impression. Also, as you will learn in the next chapter, employers often use software to monitor messages sent by e-mail and phone calls made from work because of the employer's legal liabilities for employee behavior. Understandably, this monitoring practice is unpopular with employees, but messages sent from work represent the company and can become legal records of that company.

NOTE 2.40
Use good English form but respect language variations by non-native English speakers and writers.

NOTE 2.41
People whose first language is English should follow writing principles, grammar, and punctuation taught in their home country.

NOTE 2.42
Formal and informal e-mail business messages should be professional in tone and appearance.

FIGURE 2.4
E-mail Chain between U.S.
Home Office and Branch
Office in France

This e-mail chain consists of informal internal e-mails in preparation for a European User Conference in Paris, France. Jason Thomas, Analyst Relations/European Marketing Manager in the U.S. office, began this e-mail chain. Responses from the office in France are from Cathy Smythe, Marketing Vice President and expatriate from the United States, and Dominique Chirac, Branch Manager and native of France. Nicolas Sebastian, Sales Representative in France, received copies of the first two messages. Note that the top message is the last one sent; read the sequence of messages from bottom to top. Note, too, that the e-mail headings appear in the language of the receiver's home country. Company and personal names of these real-world e-mails have been changed.

Message 6

*English terms in
message to United
States.*

From: Dominique Chirac
Sent: Thursday, May 12, 2005 11:37 AM
To: Jason Thomas
Subject: RE: Updated EUC Agenda—need pdf file

Salut Jason,

Please find attached the revised French version.

Cheers,
Dominique

Message 5

*French terms in
message to France.*

De: Jason Thomas
Envoyé: Jeudi 12 mai 2005 16:01
À: Dominique Chirac
Objet: RE: Updated EUC Agenda—need pdf file

Salut Dominique,

Here's the finalized PDF of the agenda and the original Excel files for the French and English versions. I created a French version that you'll need to review and finalize. Once complete, I will get it up on the website.

*Receiver's language
for greeting and
closing.*

Merci,
Jason

Message 4

From: Dominique Chirac
Sent: Tuesday May 12, 2005 3:31 AM
To: Jason Thomas
Subject: RE: Updated EUC Agenda—need pdf file

Jason,

*Direct style in all
messages.*

As soon as you have updated the agenda, could you please provide me with a pdf file? I will send it to our customers who did not registered yet. Also, send me the original excel file in order to translate it into French.

Dominique

Message 3

De: Dominique Chirac
Envoyé: Jeudi 12 mai 2005 09:20
À: Jason Thomas
CC: Cathy Smythe
Objet: RE: Updated EUC Agenda

Bonjour,

It is 'compulsory' that we put François Joly's presentation before Bernard is speaking – it is beneficial that tem'post is fully introduced to auditors by La Poste itself. This justified request comes directly from Bernard. I will ask EFSE speakers if they have any feedback on the new agenda. If you have any concerns, please let us know.

Language variation from U.S. English.

Thank you,
Dominique

Courtesy use of English closing.

Message 2

De: Cathy Smythe
Envoyé: mercredi 11 mai 2005 21:47
À: Jason Thomas; Dominique Chirac
CC: Nicolas Sebastian
Objet: RE: Updated EUC Agenda

Jason,

Looks good. Only concern I have is no time between most of the sessions, but I think we can work around that. . . .presenters will have to know they *must* have a hard stop at their presentation end time! Also, Jean-Jacques, it will be important for you to let attendees know they must go straight to the next session (if there is not a planned break).

Cathy

Message 1

From: Jason Thomas
Sent: Wednesday, May 11, 2005 3:21 PM
To: Cathy Smythe; Dominique Chirac
CC: Nicolas Sebastian
Subject: RE: Updated EUC Agenda
Importance: High

All,

Here's the updated EUC agenda with the French and English tracks. A few comments regarding the session tracks.

> I purposely placed the "Dialogue Under the Hood" presentation as the first session track because there's an extra 15 minutes in that session. This is a longer presentation.

> Product and customer presentations were interspersed to make the tracks more interesting. We'll have product demos followed by real-life application examples. This also prevents François and Kent from doing back-to-back presentations.

Please provide your comments to me as soon as possible. I'd like to distribute a finalized version in time for the weekly conference call on Friday.

Courtesy closing in English and French.

Thanks/Merci,
Jason

communication note

ADAPTING WEBSITE DESIGN FOR HIGH-CONTEXT OR LOW-CONTEXT CULTURES

Elizabeth Würth, IT University in Copenhagen, studied McDonald's adaptation of visual images on its websites for high- and low-context cultures. For high-context countries, the websites directed attention to nonverbal communication, relationships, and long-term time perspective. These sites made extensive use of animation, group images, or products placed with an individual. They used subtle navigational clues to encourage patient exploration of the site. For low-context countries, the websites used less-animated body language to convey the message; linear, specific navigational browser windows; and depiction of individuals in relaxed situations such as enjoying a trip to the lake or listening to music.

Elizabeth Würth, "A Cross-Cultural Analysis of Web Sites from High-Context Cultures and Low-Context Cultures," *Journal of Computer-Mediated Communication*, 11(1), 13. Retrieved November 5, 2005, from http://jcmc.indiana.edu/vol11/issue1/wuertz.html.

NOTE 2.43
Corporate web page design and use of animation appeal to the target culture.

Corporate web pages on the Internet are another means of written global communication. Companies often make their web content available in multiple languages. Global marketers study how to appeal to customers in their different target countries. The Communication Note above describes research on website animation adapted for different cultural markets.

Global Communication Strategies

LO 5

Describe key strategies for effective global business communication.

Your goal for effective global communication is to achieve business communication that gets the desired response. This means having the ability to communicate comfortably and naturally with people from a variety of cultural backgrounds. It also means being open to listening and learning, being flexible, and adapting to different cultural settings. Effective global communication requires understanding and respecting differences and recognizing and overcoming possible communication barriers. The same basic communication principles apply. The main difference between business communication within one country and global communication is learning and adapting to the cultural understandings, behaviors, expectations, and languages that are part of the context for communication.

NOTE 2.44
Effective global communication gets the desired response.

Apply these strategies to become an effective global communicator:

- Review business communication principles.
- Analyze the message receiver.
- Be open to and accepting of other cultures.
- Learn about other cultures and apply what you learn.
- Consider language needs.

Review Business Communication Principles

NOTE 2.45
Business communication principles apply to global as well as domestic communication.

A first step in improving communication across country boundaries and across cultures is to review business communication principles. As discussed in Chapter 1, the goals of business communication include achieving a shared meaning between sender and receiver, achieving an appropriate receiver response, establishing a favorable relationship between sender and receiver, and building goodwill for your

communication note

WEBSITES WITH INFORMATION ON COUNTRIES

http://questia.com/PM.qst?a=o&d=9929864
http://en.wikipedia.org/wiki
http://www.infoplease.com/countries.html
http://www.cia/publications/factbook/geos/ja.html

http://dir.yahoo.com/regional/countries
http://www.country.studies.com
http://BBCnews
http://www.Cinadaily.com.cn/english/home/index/html

organization. These goals are important in all types of communication. In addition, the communication process will be the same—analyze your receiver and use the you–viewpoint, select the appropriate form of message, provide for feedback, and remove communication barriers.

Analyze the Message Receiver

Having a general knowledge of the cultural context is a good starting point for analyzing your receiver and using the you–viewpoint. If interaction is face-to-face, you will recognize some things about the individual such as age, gender, race, and physical condition. However, learning more about that person's background, perspectives, and values will require further interaction. Listen, observe, and ask questions as appropriate based on your knowledge of the cultural context.

NOTE 2.46
Analyzing the message receiver requires a general knowledge of cultural context.

Consider how you can learn more about individuals with whom you communicate only by e-mail or letter. You are likely to know little about the person initially. Written messages mask observable characteristics. Use your knowledge of cultural preferences for communication in high- and low-context countries as a beginning. Study the written messages that you receive. Is the style generally direct or indirect? Does the message include words aimed toward relationship building? How and when you ask questions to learn more about a colleague or other contact from another country will be guided initially by your knowledge of that country. Learn more about the country by studying various resources: encyclopedias, websites, travel reference books, and other books and journal articles describe country characteristics. The Communication Note above lists helpful websites for researching customs and characteristics of different countries.

Next, consider how others view your culture. The following analysis describes some perceptions that people from other countries traditionally have held about Americans (a term used worldwide to refer to citizens of the United States).[11] Americans generally speak only their native language and expect to communicate in the English language. They place a value on speaking directly and to the point of the communication. Americans are generally friendly and informal. They are likely to greet others by their first name and shake hands with a firm grip and pumping action. They tend to have a strong sense of humor and laugh and smile frequently.

NOTE 2.47
Understand how other cultures view your culture.

---

[11]This cultural analysis was based on *Culturegram* © (Provo, Utah: BYU, 1999); Lillian H. Chaney and Jeannette S. Martin, *Intercultural Communication*, 4th ed. (Pearson/Prentice Hall, 2007), http://vig.prenhall.com; and Roger E. Axtell, *The Do's and Taboos of International Trade* (New York: Wiley, 1994).

Americans are inclined to be time conscious, frank, and outspoken. Eye contact while conversing is considered a sign of strength and honesty. Americans tend to need personal space. In a business relationship, customary practice is to keep a two- to three-foot minimum distance between themselves and others. An individual's freedom to achieve is valued highly; and work, progress, and success are valued in their own right.

Recognize that these characteristics generally attributed to Americans do not apply to many other cultures nor do they apply to all Americans. Also, be aware that another culture may regard some of these characteristics as offensive. As you communicate with people from different cultures, you will note that there are basic human needs common to most cultures, including needs for food and shelter, safety and security, and social affiliation. However, there may be great differences in values, tastes, beliefs, and behaviors.

Be Open to and Accepting of Other Cultures

NOTE 2.48
Realize that your culture represents one way of believing and behaving—not the only way.

As you think about your own culture, you begin to sense that it represents one way—and not the only way—to believe and to do things. This understanding is essential to communicate successfully with people who believe and do things differently. When conducting business in a diverse global environment, you will want to adopt an open, respectful attitude toward cultural differences of others.

How can you be open and respectful? Be open to learning about other cultures. Be open to different foods, to different ways of doing things, and to different beliefs. For example, unless you are aware of the cultural difference in the value placed on time in a number of countries, you may be offended when working with a person from a high-context culture who is always 10 to 30 minutes late to a meeting. In the United States, people are time conscious and rush to meet deadlines and appointments; in some other countries such as Mexico and Latin America, the pace is slower and the view of time is long term and indefinite.

Be accepting of other people's needs for indirectness in communicating (as in Asia) and for using titles and last names instead of first names (as in Europe). Be open to understanding and be respectful of the different ways people of other cultures think and feel. Learn to tolerate and cope with ambiguity. Understand that information can be interpreted in different ways.

Be patient but not condescending. Do not rush to an early judgment about the way a conversation or business deal is going. You may be misreading a communication situation because of cultural differences. Ask questions. Ask if you are being understood. Obtain feedback.

Learn about Other Cultures and Apply What You Learn

NOTE 2.49
A key global strategy is to learn about other cultures.

Understanding and applying what you learn about different cultures is a key strategy for effective global communication. There is, of course, much to be learned about other cultures. Do not let the volume of information overwhelm you. Seek information about business and social etiquette and lifestyles in the country. Identify social requirements and cultural adaptations that you need to make to strengthen your ability to communicate.

Culture is a complex concept that has interrelated elements. Because much of culture is hidden from view, cultural differences can be intricate, subtle, and difficult to learn. Cultural understanding consists of both factual knowledge and interpretive knowledge. Talking with persons from other countries and visiting other countries help broaden your knowledge of various cultures. Researching and reading reliable resources about particular countries help you learn about their economies, customs, traditions, and social and business practices.

A second aspect of learning about another culture is to learn as much as possible about the people of that culture. This aspect of learning includes a wide range of information from how the people think to the foods they eat. Observe how people relate to each other, their food and apparel preferences, the hours that comprise their workday and the days for their workweek, their negotiation style, their business ethics, acceptable and unacceptable topics of discussion, and acceptable and unacceptable nonverbal gestures. When you have acquired information about another culture, analyze it in the following ways:

- How is it similar to your culture?
- How is it different?
- How can you best bridge these differences?

Consider Language Needs

The extensive use of English as the primary business language is fortunate for English-speaking citizens; however, it is important to recognize that for most people in the world English is a second language. As mentioned earlier, this is also true of many people who live and work in the United States. When English is not your receivers' primary language, your messages must be adjusted to meet their level of understanding of the English language.

If English is your only language and your message receiver does not know English, then you must use an interpreter for oral communication. Expatriates, transnational executives, or others who communicate with persons in countries where a language other than their own is spoken may have occasion to use interpreters for some business interactions. **Expatriates** are persons who live and work in a country other than their home country. **Transnationals** travel frequently across national borders for short periods of time as part of their work. **Interpreters** orally translate messages from one language to another for persons speaking to each other in different languages.

Generally, languages cannot be translated verbatim. Computer translation software can be valuable when translating letters, memos, sales literature, or other messages. Speech recognition and translation software can assist in customizing documents in a particular language. However, a **translator,** competent in the languages involved and qualified in the subject matter, may be required for some situations to ensure that the meaning, not just the words, of the message is conveyed to the receiver. For example, preparing a sales campaign for customers in another country or interpreting a written legal agreement prepared in another language would require a competent translator or review of the computer translation by a person from the targeted country.

Effective global communication requires flexibility, a desire to learn, sensitivity to culture and traditions in a foreign setting, and the ability to apply what you have learned to interactions with others in overseas locations. In addition, combine firmness and business savvy with grace, respect, and kindness. Build appropriate relationships and friendships and network through international societies and trade groups. The Tips and Hints feature on the next page offers suggestions for working effectively with interpreters and translators.

NOTE 2.50

Recognize cultural language differences when communicating in English across national borders.

NOTE 2.51

Expatriates live and work outside their home country; transnationals travel across national borders to work for short periods of time.

NOTE 2.52

When the sender and receiver of a message speak different languages, they may need interpreters or translators.

tips and hints

Working with Interpreters and Translators

WHEN WORKING WITH INTERPRETERS:

- Focus on the message receiver, not the interpreter.
- Avoid long introductory phrases, parenthetical elements, interjections, and complex sentences.
- Talk directly to the message receiver, but keep the interpreter in your range of vision.
- Encourage your interpreter to ask you questions if you are not being understood.

WHEN WORKING WITH TRANSLATORS:

- Select a translator competent in both languages and qualified in the subject matter.
- For important messages, have computer software translations reviewed by a native language speaker to ensure correct interpretation of language nuances.
- Provide for back translation to check for errors by converting the message back into English from the initial translation to another language.

Summary of Learning Objectives

LO 1 Explain how cultural differences affect business communication.

People's background and experiences influence their view of the world and the values, beliefs, and behavior patterns assumed to be good. This cultural lens filters interpretation of messages received and expectations of acceptable behavioral interactions. Unless you realize that cultural differences affect thinking and behavior, misunderstandings are likely to occur. Communication requires mutual understanding.

To apply the you–viewpoint for communication, analysis of the message receiver must include knowledge of cultural influences. Core dimensions of culture include ethnicity, race, gender, age, and disability. Recognize that individuals within each culture have similarities and differences. Learn about general characteristics of different cultures, but recognize that individuals within a culture do not mirror all of these characteristics. Therefore, effective communication across cultures requires a basic understanding of different cultures and knowledge of individual values and interests.

LO 2 Identify cultural barriers to communication.

Cultural barriers to communication include the following:

- Cultural relativism compares cultures, usually against one's own culture. Ethnocentrism assumes that one's own culture is superior.
- A lack of knowledge and understanding of cultures may result in stereotypes that assume general characteristics of a culture apply to all people within that culture.
- Discrimination and harassment are negative actions that sometimes occur between certain cultural groups.
- Language differences create communication misunderstandings.

Explain basic guidelines for effective multicultural communication.

LO 3

As a first step in improving cultural communication, *understand your own culture.* Recognize how your culture affects your beliefs, values, and behaviors as well as your interpretation of messages from others. *Keep an open mind and respect differences.* Be open to learning about other cultures and their beliefs and customs without judging them as right or wrong by your own cultural standards. Respect all people and recognize individual differences within a culture as well as among cultures. *Identify language differences.* Study appropriate resources and observe others to learn both acceptable and offensive verbal and nonverbal language. Respect language variations from individuals who learn English as a second language. *Adapt to communication patterns.* Cultures differ in how their language is structured and the meaning attached to the context of a message. Learning these cultural language variations will help you improve multicultural communication.

Discuss communication challenges in a global environment.

LO 4

A global environment increases business communication with people from other countries, many of whom do not speak English or speak it only as a second language. Business across country boundaries entails variations not only in language and behavior patterns but also in time, holidays, and days in a workweek. Understanding cultural variations is a challenge. First, consider a country's placement on a continuum from a high- to a low-context culture. Traditionally, high-context cultures place high value on building relationships and prefer indirect communication. Low-context cultures value productivity and prefer a direct communication style. Language and cultural variations can cause misunderstandings of verbal or nonverbal messages or the implied meanings of words specific to a particular language.

Describe key strategies for effective global business communication.

LO 5

Review business communication principles. The basic principles of business communication apply to global communication. The goal is to achieve a shared meaning, an appropriate response, a favorable relationship, and goodwill for your organization. *Analyze the message receiver.* Apply the you–viewpoint and analyze the needs, interests, and values of the message receiver. For global communication, this means also analyzing how the culture of different countries affects understanding and acceptability of a message. *Be open to and accepting of other cultures.* Recognize that values, traditions, beliefs, and behavior differ among cultures and that there is not one right way to do things but many different ways can be acceptable. Adopt an open, respectful attitude toward cultural differences. *Learn about other cultures and apply what you learn.* Cultural understanding requires understanding of both factual and interpretive knowledge. Read written resources, talk or correspond with people from other countries, and visit other countries to build an understanding of various cultures. Learn how people relate to one another and become familiar with their food preferences, business practices, and other details of daily living. When you acquire cultural information, decide how you can best bridge the differences between that culture and your culture. *Consider language needs.*

When English is a second language for people with whom you communicate, avoid complex sentences, use synonyms sparingly, and use examples or analogies only if you are sure they will be understood. Attempting humor is risky. When the message receiver speaks another language, you may need to use an interpreter for face-to-face communication or a translator for written messages.

Questions for Discussion and Review

1. Discuss how business practices such as outsourcing and offshoring affect business communication. (Objective 1)
2. What is corporate culture and how does it affect communication? (Objectives 1 and 2)
3. List five core cultural dimensions and give an example of how each influences communication. (Objectives 1 and 2)
4. Define cultural relativism, ethnocentrism, and stereotyping; explain how each one affects communication. (Objective 2)
5. Discuss four guidelines for effective multicultural communication. (Objective 3)
6. Xway Accounting has outsourced preparation of basic income tax forms to technicians working in India. Accountants in the home office will continue to do business tax forms and complex forms for individuals. Customers whose forms are scanned by Xway and sent to India electronically for completion will not be told that their tax forms will be prepared outside of the home office. Discuss one communication challenge that the home office accountants will face and how this challenge may be overcome. Also, what ethical question may be raised about this change in business procedure? (Objectives 4 and 5)
7. Explain three communication challenges that a U.S. expatriate may face when relocated to an office in China. (Clue: Consider high- and low-context cultures.) (Objective 4)
8. What are some of the business communication differences between Canada and Mexico? (Objective 4)
9. If you were communicating with a business contact from Malaysia, how would you change the structure and content of your message? (Objectives 4 and 5)
10. Assume that you are a U.S. marketing consultant who has just opened a branch office in Germany. Your branch manager and marketing representative in the branch office are Germans. They are natives of Germany and have always lived in that country. They speak and write English as a second language. Most communication with the branch office will be by e-mail. How would you expect their messages to differ from those that you receive from stateside contacts, and what guidelines will you follow to communicate effectively with your branch office staff? (Objectives 4 and 5)

Application Exercises

1. What do you consider the most important values passed on to you from your parents and grandparents? (Objective 1)
2. Has anyone used words that were offensive to you because of your ethnicity, race, gender, age, or physical condition? If so, what were they and what was your reaction? Why do you think the person used these words? (Objectives 1 and 2)

COLLABORATIVE

3. **Teamwork.** With a partner read alternate sentences from the following paragraph aloud to each other. (Objective 2)

   ehT qaimtimg also qroved that, sa well sa being a great humter, Cro-Wagmom Nam saw a comsiberadle artist. He dah flourisheb ta a tine whem eno fo eht terrible Ice Ages saw dlotting out much fo Euroqe. He dah estadlisheb hinself amb fought wilb aminals rof livimg sqace. eH surviveb eht ditter colb, amb left beeq bown umber groumb nenorials fo his yaw fo life!

   Discuss with one another the difficulty that you had reading this passage and how you tried to compensate to understand what you were reading. Compare your experience to that of a person who may have dyslexia or a vision problem and to a person reading English as a second language. Make a list of ways trying to read this passage is similar to or different from reading a message written in a language that you are just beginning to learn.

4. **Teamwork.** Form groups of four to seven people. Discuss the importance of diversity initiatives in businesses. Plan an agenda for a seminar that could help people in a business understand the needs and interests of people representing different cultures. (Objectives 1 and 2)

5. **Teamwork. Ethics.** Form groups with four or five students in each. Each member of the group will choose a specific cultural dimension from among the following: ethnicity, race, gender, age, or disability. Each person is to interview three people who represent the chosen cultural dimension; for example, the person choosing age would choose individuals under 16 years of age and over 55. Gender should represent both male and female, and interviewees should include more than one race, ethnicity, and disability. Identify the interviewees not by name but by their cultural dimension characteristic. As a group, prepare a report to submit that summarizes all responses by specific ethnicity, race, gender, age, or disability. (Objectives 1, 2, and 3)

   a. Give an example of a time when you thought you were mistreated because of your ethnicity, race, gender, age, or physical condition.

   b. What do you consider the most important values that you learned from your parents or grandparents?

   c. Has anyone said anything about your ethnicity, race, age, or physical condition that was embarrasing or offensive to you? If so, explain and tell why you think this occurred. If not, explain a word, phrase, or nonverbal gesture that you would find offensive.

6. **Teamwork. Global.** Work with a partner to review the letter to Mr. Wu in Figure 2.3 on page 39 in this chapter. Explain two communication challenges faced by Mr. Doninger in writing the letter. Also, select one strategy for effective global communication and tell how you would improve the letter to Mr. Wu in a way that would be consistent with the selected strategy. (Objectives 4 and 5)

7. **Technology. Global.** India is a well-known location for offshore sites and outsourcing operations for large corporations. Using an encyclopedia, website URLs in this chapter, or other resources, research the culture of India. Write a report about what you learned that may affect communication between a U.S. businessperson and a business colleague native to India who has little knowledge of U.S. culture. E-mail the report as an attachment to your instructor. The following topics suggest possible subheadings for your report. (Objectives 4 and 5)

   a. Business customs

   b. National holidays

   c. Time

   d. Transportation modes

   e. Foods and family customs

   f. Languages

8. **Technology. Global. Ethics.** Interview a student, a businessperson, or a visiting lecturer who is a native of another country or who has spent extensive time in a particular country other than the United States. Prepare and give an oral report using presentation software such as PowerPoint. Ask the following questions. (Objectives 1, 2, and 4)

   a. How do the citizens in this country perceive U.S. citizens?

   b. Describe the style of speaking or writing. Is it direct or indirect?

   c. Give examples of business behavior that are considered appropriate and ethical.

   d. Give an example of a social behavior that is considered unethical in that country.

   e. Describe a typical meal, food that might be served, and table etiquette.

   f. What advice would you give someone going to that country to live and work?

   g. What would be the most difficult adjustment to make when moving to that country?

9. **Global.** Contact an international center at a university (visit, call, or send e-mail). Ask about a study abroad or work abroad program. Develop and present your findings to your class. (Objectives 4 and 5)

10. **Global. Technology. Teamwork.** McBride Industries, an American company, has recently opened a branch office in the Czech Republic. Vladimíra Pokorny, a Marketing Assistant for the Czech office, has received a template of the corporate logo for business cards. The following e-mail chain takes place between him and an associate in the U.S. office, Milton Johnson (U.S.

Marketing Director). Chloe Smith (Vice President, Operations) receives a copy of Milton's letter and replies to Vladimíra. Vladimíra believes the template will print the colors incorrectly for the logo. He copied his first e-mail to three associates in the Czech office. Form work teams of three or four students. As a team, discuss the following questions and develop a written response, using a computer if available. Submit your team report as an e-mail attachment to your instructor. (Objectives 1, 2, and 4)

a. Proofread the first message from Vladimíra to Milton. Identify four variations of English that you believe are due to learning English as a second language.

b. Using the Internet and the world clock, explain how much time elapsed between the time the first message was sent and the time Vladimíra received the first reply.

c. Give examples of friendly, relationship-building words from the four e-mails.

d. Analyze each of the e-mails, and classify it as direct or indirect style. Explain your choices.

Message 4

From: Vladimíra Pokorny
Sent: Wednesday, May 11, 2005 10:54 AM
To: Chloe Smith, Milton Johnson
Subject: RE: vizitky

Milton, Chloe,

Thank you for explanation
Vladi

Vladimíra Pokorny, Marketing Assistant, Czech Republic

Message 3

From: Chloe Smith
Sent: Wednesday, May 11, 2005 4:50 PM
To: Milton Johnson
Cc: Pokorny, Vladimíra
Subject: RE: vizitky

Milton:

I believe Vladimira may be seeing the reversed version of the logo for the first time, and this has brought up some questions. We will be producing a logo standards manual soon that will explain the system.

Here's a brief explanation for what Vladimira is seeing on the business cards. When reversing the corporate logo out of a solid color, the top part of the stylized "M" and the word "software" take on 60% of the background color. The bottom part of the stylized "B" and the word "McBride" take on 15% of the background color. This effect puts visual emphasis on the lighter color similar to how the positive logo places emphasis by using the darker color. So in other words the emphasis is still on the same elements of the logo even though it is handled in opposite manners for positive and negative applications.

Hopefully this explanation helps.

Chloe

Message 2

From: Milton Johnson
Sent: Wednesday, May 11, 2005 3:10 PM
To: Vladimíra Pokorny
Cc: Chloe Smith
Subject: FW: vizitky

Hi Vladimira,

I don't know what to tell you. This template is the corporate design approved by the Board, so changing the colors/design is not an option. In addition, we have already printed cards using this new design without any problems. The only changes in the design (that I can see) is that we replaced the old logo with the new logo on the front of the card and removed the logo on the back of the card. Everything else looks the same to me.

Milton

Message 1

From: Vladimíra Pokorny
Sent: Wednesday, May 11, 2005 5:26 AM
To: Milton Johnson
Cc: Anezka Moravek; Vaclav Prazsky; Manuel Plachky
Subject: FW: vizitky
Importance: High

Milton,

I have received the template for business cards. Thank you.

The template has not changed so far as I can see, the only thing is replacement of the logo. Is that correct? Colors of the logo does not seem to be corporate colors, even the darker and lighter are oposite, (in the logo is darker teal for the lower element, and lighter teal is upper element; and software, where on the business card template it is oposite). Colors also does not correspond to PMS numbers, which I have received from Chloe earlier.

When we print the preview, darker part of the logo is barely visible because of the background which is very similar to darker teal. We would see the solution in replacing darker teal (upper element and software) to complete white. The next possibility is to change the design. Please advice what to do.

Thanks
Vladimíra Pokorny, Marketing Assistant, Czech Republic

Web exercises to accompany this chapter are available at **www.thomsonedu.com/ bcomm/krizan.**

MESSAGE ANALYSIS

Correct the following e-mail. Make necessary changes in punctuation and word usage or other changes necessary to conform to U.S. English grammar and to improve the message clarity.

From: Katherina Schmidt
Sent: Monday, June 27, 2005 10:47 AM
To: Lucas Roth
Subject: RE: German Seminar / Road Show Last week of September

Lucas,

I spoke with Jason again today about the request to help with the seminar, and as this is in conflict with our event, Our help will be limited to helping with having some marketing material ready for the seminar and arranging for some printing services here, that is going to be much easier and cheaper for Jason this way.

It is not my intention to make money by providing marketing support services, and we will be very happy if we can limit this as much as possible, as we have our own sales support objectives to meet. But, should we are required to do that, we are not going to loose money doing it. As we have calculated it before in relation to some of the development projects, own costs per hour are $30 and if we charge that, we do not make any money. $30 will be the hourly rate we will invoice Jason for the services, plus any related travel related expenses. I trust this is fair.

Thank you,
Katherina

Writer's Workshop

The following items may be sentence fragments or contain errors in subject–verb agreement, comma and semicolon placement, spelling, or word choice. Rewrite the sentences to make them correct.

1. In Africka today cellphones are wide used, the cost are low.
2. Twenty persons will attend the Oktoberfest in Cologne depending on interest we'll plan a luncheon or an extend event with dinner.
3. When we visited New York City the twin tower was still standing.
4. Cultural differences effect not only values attitude and management practices but, also impact the process of information gathering.
5. In the last decade public school reform or achievement standards has been the topic of at lease 2,000 newspaper article.
6. Low contest cultures keep business and personal affair separate, whereas, in high contest cultures social life over lap with business.
7. Corporate culture consist of both formal and informal patterns of behavior, new employees have to listen to observe interaction of colleguaes and supervisors to learn the culture.
8. Bronx is the only one of New York Cities five borough on the mainland of the United States.
9. When in a business meeting greeting your hosts and then shaking hands.
10. Effective multicultural communicaters seek to understand the culture background of others and adept to them.

Chapter 3
Technological, Legal, and Ethical Considerations

LET'S TALK BUSINESS

Today's eGeneration is a growing community of consumers demanding higher quality and individualized treatment in a 24/7 world. From their paper correspondence (statements, invoices, and notifications) to cyber media (the Web, cell phones, and interactive kiosks), they expect personalized information on demand and in real time. Companies around the world must be prepared to connect with the eGeneration through high-quality, fully personalized customer communications in print and on the Internet.

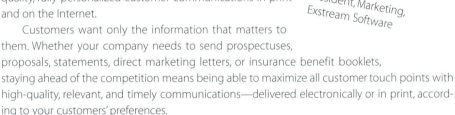

Kelley Sloane, Vice President, Marketing, Exstream Software

Customers want only the information that matters to them. Whether your company needs to send prospectuses, proposals, statements, direct marketing letters, or insurance benefit booklets, staying ahead of the competition means being able to maximize all customer touch points with high-quality, relevant, and timely communications—delivered electronically or in print, according to your customers' preferences.

Kelley Sloane's description of the eGeneration's expectations for personalized information on demand and in real time reflects communication trends resulting from rapidly advancing technology. As you study this chapter, you will learn about the effects of these technology advances on communication. The basic principles of business communication continue to apply; however, current technology, with availability of on-the-go multimedia communication devices, allows individuals to choose how, when, and where they send or receive messages.

This chapter describes technology trends in communication and alerts you to legal and ethical considerations for business communication. A theme throughout the chapter is how technology and legal and ethical issues affect interactions with others. Trust based on legal and ethical behavior is the foundation for productive work environments, customer satisfaction, and goodwill for the company.

Learning Objectives

1

Describe recent technology trends and their effects on business communication.

2

Discuss legal and ethical issues related to electronic communication and e-commerce.

3

Identify legal considerations for different business communication purposes.

4

Describe ethical considerations for communication, and explain how codes of conduct help organizations promote ethical business behavior.

5

Discuss guidelines for ethical business communication.

53

Advances and Trends in Communication Technology

LO 1

Describe recent technology trends and their effects on business communication.

NOTE 3.1
Handheld wireless computers provide communication portability.

NOTE 3.2
Convergence of handheld multimedia increases selectivity of media and specialized content.

Wi-fi, Bluetooth, TiVo®, iPod, podcast, blog, vlog, wiki, GPS, and smart phone—almost every day brings a new technology term related to communication. Are these technology tools changing the way business is conducted? How do they affect communication? Wireless technology and tiny high-capacity computer chips enable on-the-go communication: talking on the phone, using Internet and e-mail connections, viewing videos and movies, and listening to music or recorded audio broadcasts.

Small electronic devices such as handheld computers (also called personal digital assistants or PDAs) provide portability for speaking, writing, listening, or viewing messages via wireless technology and extend the ability to send or receive messages at any time or place. A **global positioning system (GPS)** uses satellite technology and wireless communication to provide directions to specific destinations. See Figure 3.1 for a description of terms used in this section.

Technology advances allow individuals to self-select what, when, and where messages are received and sent. Internet blogs, vlogs, wikis, and other specialized web locations open new possibilities for writing or audio-broadcasting messages to audiences. Audiences for such communication self-select a particular website due to interest in the topic and the ability to choose a convenient time for viewing, responding, or listening. Television programming can be automatically recorded for later viewing on a computer as well as a television screen. E-mail is less time-bound than the telephone because the message sender or receiver selects a convenient time for such messages. In addition, convergence of video, music, camera, telephone, and

FIGURE 3.1
Communication
Technology Terms

Communication Technology Terms

Wi-fi—Wireless fidelity Internet connections at places called "hot spots" that connect to the wireless signal. Laptop or handheld computers with wireless cards can access these signals.

Bluetooth—A wireless technology that allows computers to share files, manage e-mail, and access GPS from a desktop or handheld computer.

TiVo®—A system that finds, digitizes, and records selections from television programs and music for transfer to a laptop or DVD for use at home or on the go.

Podcast—An audio broadcast that posts on the Internet and can be transferred and played on an iPod or other digital music player. Listeners can subscribe to the show for automatic updates and use special software for transfer to a handheld player. Also, podcasts can be purchased and downloaded from the iTunes Music Store.

Blog—A short term for web log. This is an online diary on a web page and can include posted text, photos, or links to other sites. Almost any topic can be blogged.

Vlog—A video web log, or diary of short video clips, regularly updated.

Vodcasting—Videos sold to subscribers via the Internet. Videos of sports events, television programs, or other videos can be purchased and played on an iPod or other video player.

Wiki—A collaborative website similar to a blog but that allows anyone to edit, delete, or modify posted content.

GPS—A global positioning system that uses satellite technology to request or receive directions from your location to your travel destination.

Smart phone—The next generation of cell phones. A wireless, Internet-connected phone capable of most functions a personal computer can do, including easy-to-use software applications.

instant messaging into a single handheld electronic device creates multimedia communication on-the-go, any time and any place. In summary, current technology advances and trends include these characteristics:

- Portability via small, wireless computer devices for on-the-go communication
- Audience selectivity of topic, media, time, and place for receiving and sending messages
- Convergence of audio, video, text, photo, music, Internet, and phone devices

Technology and Business Communication

Major technology trends affecting business communication may be summarized as portability, specialization, and selectivity. These trends increase consumers' control of what, when, how, and where they send and receive messages. In addition, technology brings new ways of working and collaborating as well as new work locations.

NOTE 3.3
Technology advances enable self-selection of messages sent and received.

Wireless and Internet Communication

Cell phones, e-mail, and instant messaging make contacts with employees or customers possible on a 24/7 basis. If the timing of a message is urgent, giving advance notice to the receiver helps ensure that the cell phone or instant messaging device is turned on or the e-mail is read promptly. E-mail transmission sometimes experiences delays and maintenance downtimes, so emergency messages may need to be sent by two communication modes or by scheduling a prearranged telephone call. As with all messages, operate from the you–viewpoint and respect the receiver's time. Be considerate of the receiver's time when sending electronic messages. Avoid making business contacts during off-work hours except in bona fide emergencies. Consideration and courtesy count in maintaining goodwill.

Specialized cell phones provide services for a variety of niche markets such as sports news updates or cheap overseas calls. In Japan, cell phones include a short-range radio chip to beam credit and debit card information to a store register or vending machine. This technology is called a mobile wallet and is entering the market in the United States. Bluetooth technology in selected locations permits customers to use cell phones to download product codes and other information from kiosks. Bluetooth enables wireless connection between computers (handheld, laptop, or desktop) for transferring information or managing e-mail files.

NOTE 3.4
Smart cell phones increase the variety of cell phone capabilities.

Changes in Advertising Media

Technology trends suggest changes in marketing. Electronic devices and services such as TiVo® allow selective recording of television shows, potentially reducing the mass audience for regularly scheduled television commercials. Networks such as ABC and NBC, online magazines such as *BusinessWeek* and *Forbes,* National Public Radio, and some local music outlets offer podcasts to reach new listeners. Podcasting received a boost in users when Apple Computer Inc. made podcasts available for purchase on iTunes, the company's online music store. These programs

Zits by Jerry Scott and Jim Borgman

allow people to download audio programs of interest from the Internet to digital media players for listening at any time—while running, driving, waiting for appointments, or traveling in distant locations. Blogs, vlogs, and instant messaging also provide consumer choice.

NOTE 3.5

Novel, entertaining viral advertising messages encourage spreading the message by personal conversations.

Viral advertising is a recent marketing strategy that uses a novel and entertaining online marketing message. The purpose is to make the message intriguing enough that viewers download it from the Internet to handheld devices to share with others, thus spreading the idea like a virus. Content has to be useful, interesting, and entertaining. This advertising strategy might resemble television commercials such as the talking gecko for Geico insurance or the unique Super Bowl ads.

Videoconferencing

Videoconferencing gives a viable alternative to face-to-face meetings. Unlike in phone conferences, participants can see facial expressions and body language to help interpret spoken messages. Videoconferencing has a number of uses. For example, companies with overseas satellite offices use the technology as do sales representatives or other mobile employees who work away from the home office and physicians who share medical expertise with health-care providers in distant locations.

NOTE 3.6

High-definition video and high-speed broadband connections improve videoconferencing quality.

Broadband Internet connections and high-definition video are improving videoconferencing as well as television quality. Videoconferencing is not new, but higher speed transmission and high-definition video improve sound and picture quality. Video conference rooms can be equipped with large plasma screens, high-quality sound systems, group software, and interactive whiteboards. Whiteboards capture and display media images, notes, or drawings and make them visible to all participants linked through the Internet. The global scope of business operations, along with rising fuel costs and the increasing quality of Internet videoconferencing that resembles in-person meetings, is likely to increase use of videoconferencing to save time and travel costs.

Hoteling

NOTE 3.7

Hoteling reserves office space, phones, and computers for telecommuters or mobile employees.

As discussed in Chapter 2, business outsourcing and offshoring operations keep marketing, production, and delivery on the move. An expanded market outreach and mobile workforce create demand for new workspaces outside the home office. This concept is called *hoteling*. Whatis.com defines **hoteling** (also called **office** hoteling) as the practice of providing employee office space on an as-needed basis. This practice reduces the required square footage for regular office space by providing alternative office space for mobile workers.

Hoteling can support telecommuters as well as mobile employees. **Telecommuting** is working from a location other than the office where business is usually conducted. Although anyone who communicates with his or her office from a car, public telephone, hotel, or client's office might be defined as a telecommuter, the term is more widely applied to those who work from their home. Telecommuters access data and communicate with clients, colleagues, and supervisors electronically. **Mobile employees** could also be called telecommuters, but this term specifically identifies individuals who spend much of their time traveling to a number of work locations.

All videoconference participants can view text or graphics displayed on a whiteboard

© Lance Davies Photography. Courtesy of PolyVision

A hoteling system anticipates mobile employees and other business demands and maintains reserved space to meet that demand. This space, available by reservation, can be located almost anywhere and serves as a remote office with computer ports and communication capabilities. It may be a special room designed for hoteling with tables and chairs or cubicles and can include food service and conference room availability. Hoteling allows mobile employees to maintain their own telephone number extension and voice mailbox.

For some employees, hoteling is an option; for others, it is an assignment. Some businesses are more adaptable than others to office hoteling. Examples of users of hoteling options are real estate agencies, consulting firms, manufacturer representatives, marketing or sales staff, and flex-time workers. The concept of desk sharing through reserved space is sometimes called HotDesking or a virtual office.

NOTE 3.8
Hoteling works well for real estate brokers, consultants, marketing and sales representatives, and flex-time workers.

Intranets and Collaborative Projects

Most businesses use an organization-only computer network called an **intranet** for internal communications. This local business network enables employees to transmit information, exchange ideas, and discuss strategy electronically within the company without going through the Internet. The primary reason for establishing an intranet is the security of having a *firewall* to protect company information from outside intruders, hackers, or others with destructive motives.

NOTE 3.9
An intranet is for internal communication.

As organizations increase their use of cross-functional teams, employees often collaborate to write projects, reports, and proposals. **Collaborative writing software** facilitates group writing. Such software allows several users to work on the same electronic document rather than on a printed copy or an e-mail attachment.

Collaborative writing may be *interactive* **(synchronous)** or independent **(asynchronous).** When collaboration is **interactive,** two or more people work with the same document at the same time and see changes as they are made. Asynchronous collaboration allows individuals to work on the document at different times.

Synchronous collaborative writing software is part of a type of software called *groupware.* Groupware usually is available by subscription or for one-time use at a set price. Software tools with groupware include such options as coordinating

NOTE 3.10
Groupware software allows web team coordination for synchronous collaborative writing or meetings.

communication note

- Spend time getting to know each team member's special interests and expertise.
- Discuss the purpose, style, and format for the finished document.
- Develop clear procedural directions for teamwork.
- Designate a facilitator to coordinate the project and plan group conferences as needed.

- Have individual team members take one subtopic and outline the content.
- Have one person complete a document draft from the content.
- Divide revising, editing, and proofreading tasks among team members.

online web team meetings; sharing files, calendars, schedules, or projects; and working collaboratively on documents in real time to redline and approve changes. Most collaborative writing software packages use the Web as a host site with invited collaborators able to access that site and review, edit, or add to a document residing on the host site. Interactive collaborative writing sessions resemble meetings in that they must be prearranged. In addition, only the host has access to the document between sessions. Examples of group software that permits interactive collaboration are WebEx (www.webex.com), Microsoft Office Live Meeting (www.livemeeting .com), and Conferral (www.conferral.com).

NOTE 3.11

Independent collaborative writing documents usually reside on the web for access by individual team members at their convenience.

For **independent collaborative writing,** the document resides on a computer location that may be accessed at any time by anyone in the writing group. With most groupware, documents would reside on a Web location. This type of collaboration has the advantage of permitting writers to work on the document at their convenience. The disadvantage is that writers must also check periodically to see what changes their coauthors have made. For this reason, writers tend to rely on strikeout and redline techniques or shading to mark the changes. WebOffice (www.weboffice.com), Quickbase (www.quickbase.com), and Projectplace (www.projectplace.com) are examples of groupware for data sharing that allow projects to be set up on the website and made accessible to those who need to view or work on documents.

Some free independent collaborative writing sites can be found on the Web. For example, Writeboard (www.writeboard.com) and Web Collaborator (http:// webcollaborator.com) are available on the Web.

NOTE 3.12

The reviewing tool on Word allows independent document editing and sharing as an e-mail attachment.

NOTE 3.13

Legal issues are binding rules of conduct enforceable by the courts; ethics are accepted group rules for behavior.

Independent collaborative writing may also be completed by using word processing features such as the reviewing tool in Word. This tool allows adding or deleting information and marking all changes. A copy of the changed document can be attached to e-mail and sent to others for review, changes, or comments or be posted to a company intranet site for access by multiple employees. The Communication Note above suggests ways to enrich the collaborative writing experience.

Technology, Legal, and Ethical Issues

LO 2

Discuss legal and ethical issues related to electronic communication and e-commerce.

In this section of the chapter, you will learn about legal and ethical considerations for the use of communication technology. **Legal issues** pertain to laws. **Laws** are binding rules of conduct or actions prescribed and enforced by a governing authority. **Ethical issues** relate to value systems and cultural beliefs about what is acceptable or unacceptable behavior. **Ethics** are principles of conduct governing individual or group behavior. Technology brings with it a number of legal and ethical challenges. These issues pertain to copyright and privacy as well as employee behavior and organizational actions.

Cell Phones and Other Mobile Devices

Ethical and legal issues pertinent to the use of cell phones, handheld computers, and other telecommunication mobile devices evolve as rapidly as the technology itself. Issues center on using these devices in a manner that respects the rights, safety, and privacy of others.

Legislatures have considered laws restricting the use of cell phones in automobiles, citing the danger of driver distraction during phone conversations. To date, federal laws banning cell phone usage have not emerged in the United States, but some states restrict use in automobiles to hands-free phones.

Although talking on a cell phone does not break the law, such an action could result in a legal suit against the company if an employee using the phone while driving contributes to an accident. Employers should take notice of this risk if employees are conducting business by phone while traveling by car. Recently, a brokerage firm paid more than $500,000 to settle a wrongful death lawsuit. A motorcyclist died in an accident when a stockbroker ran a red light while picking up a dropped cell phone.[1] Employers may consider banning cell phones while driving on company time or requiring hands-free cell phones.

NOTE 3.14
Business cell phone usage by employees while driving may lead to company liability for accidents.

Another questionable cell phone practice is the use of its camera to take pictures of people without their knowledge. This becomes even more an invasion of privacy if the pictures are embarrassing to the subject or posted to the Web for others to view. If such pictures are published, to the Web or otherwise, legal action may result.

Ethical use requires courtesy, respect, and concern for others. A common **heuristic** or experiential guide for individual rights says that *your rights end where the other person's begin*. In other words, if your behavior becomes excessively intrusive or dangerous to others, your conduct exceeds your rights. The accompanying Tips and Hints feature suggests etiquette practices to guide use of mobile devices in public places.

NOTE 3.15
Ethical use of handheld communication devices shows respect and concern for others.

[1] W. Mark Gavre, "Cell Phones and Cars: New Liability for Employers," *FindLaw for Corporate Counsel*, 2001, http://library.findlaw.com/2001/Mar/1/132856.htm (February 11, 2006).

tips and hints

Cellular Phone Etiquette

1. **Answer the phone quickly.** A ringing phone irritates those around you almost as much as the conversation that follows. Musical ring tones are even more distracting. Set the phone to vibrate or adjust the ring to the lowest possible volume.

2. **Speak quietly and end the conversation quickly.** Most cell phone users speak louder than normal to compensate for noises in the surrounding area.

3. **Avoid taking or making calls when others are present.** Placing or receiving a call during meetings, while at restaurants, or during group events sends the nonverbal message that the person on the phone is more important than the people around you. If you must use the phone, excuse yourself and leave the room.

4. **Protect the safety of yourself and others.** Talking on the phone while driving can be deadly. Inattention to driving increases the odds of having an accident.

E-Mail and the Internet

Whether employees work on-site or off, organizations are concerned that workers use technology appropriately. Misuse of e-mail and Internet resources not only threatens productivity and creates legal concerns but also may endanger the company's image.

Productivity issues stem from workers' easy access to e-mail and the Internet. Access to these services, which are provided to facilitate business transactions, creates the temptation to waste time. When workers exchange e-mail with family and friends, forward jokes to coworkers and others, play games, engage in day trading, or just surf the Web, they are not engaged in activities that promote the organization or its mission.

Legal concerns about misuse of e-mail and the Internet relate to liability and privacy. Most employers want to trust employees and respect their privacy, but they fear the organization will be liable for the content of e-mail. Computer systems can retain messages long after they have been deleted from the user's mailbox. Gossip, derogatory comments, lewd or obscene messages or graphics, harassing messages, or any number of other items could be retrieved from e-mail files and used as evidence in court cases. In addition, having such messages originate or circulate within the workplace negatively affects the organization's legal responsibility for a harassment-free environment, could ultimately tarnish a company's good image, and decreases productivity.

Even business-related e-mail can haunt an individual or organization, as demonstrated in numerous legal actions. One such example involved state government officials in Kentucky in 2005. Blackberry cell phones used by government employees for phone calls and e-mail were subpoenaed by the attorney general and confiscated from offices in a legal case charging political interference in hiring and promoting employees. Such interference is a violation of state personnel laws. High-ranking government officials had communicated with one another daily by phone and e-mail about these personnel matters. All of those conversations were retrieved and used as evidentiary information for the charges. Another example is the 2002 Enron case. An Enron internal e-mail that referred to shredded documents from an audit became part of legal actions against the company and its accounting firm.

Recognize that e-mail is not private. Your employer can monitor it, computer hackers can intercept it, your adversary in a legal action can review it, law enforcement agents who suspect a crime can obtain it, and your Internet provider can retrieve a copy of it from the e-mail server. U.S. federal law gives a government agency authority under state or federal criminal procedures to secure a warrant requiring communication service providers to disclose the contents of an electronic communication. Illegal use of the Internet, whether from a business or a home computer, is subject to disclosure and may be used as evidence of a crime. Visiting pornographic websites on work time is likely to get you fired; accessing and sending child pornography is a crime, whether from work, home, or a computer in other locations.

The fear of litigation and the concern over wasted time prompt some organizations to monitor workers' use of electronic resources. Special network and e-mail software programs exist for this purpose.

The Fourth Amendment protection against unreasonable governmental searches and seizures pertains to public workplaces. A Supreme Court case, *O'Conner v. Ortega* 480 U.S. 709 (1987), ruled that a *public employee*'s privacy in his or her office must be balanced with the employer's right to conduct a reasonable search based on the circumstances. A **reasonableness test** examines whether the search was *justified at its inception*. This justification requires that there was reason to suspect that evidence of employee misconduct would be found or that access to and retrieval of the file was necessary in the employee's absence. The other part of the test examines the scope of the investigation: its relation to the objectives of the search and its reasonableness as weighed against the nature of the misconduct.

Private employers are *not* subject to the Fourth Amendment restrictions; however, such searches should be based on reasonable suspicion or legitimate business needs, and care should be taken to disclose the contents only in clearly permissible instances. Employers often have a legitimate need to search an employee's e-mail, voice mail, or other electronically stored messages. The Electronic Privacy Act gives an employer the right to access an employee's e-mail and voice mail when they are maintained on a system *provided* by the employer.

NOTE 3.19
Employers may legally monitor computer use by employees.

The final word of advice for employees is to treat e-mail, voice mail, and other electronic messages as if they will be public knowledge. Confine messages to business, and limit the time you spend communicating with family and friends while you are at work. Accessing pornographic websites, sending sexually suggestive messages, or revealing company trade secrets is a recipe for losing your job and may result in legal charges.

NOTE 3.20
Treat electronic messages as if they are public knowledge.

Organizations often choose to develop clear policies on the use of e-mail and other company resources. Such policies become a part of the employee handbook and alert employees that the Internet sites they visit and their e-mail and voice mail are not private. Employers should obtain legal advice on the wording of such policies. The accompanying Tips and Hints feature gives some suggestions for policy content.

Some companies make employment contingent on a prospective employee's willingness to sign a statement saying that he or she has read, understands, and accepts the organization's computer-use policy. Organizations may embed a statement about technology misuse into the system's log-on procedure, requiring users to acknowledge the message and the warning that their computing activities may be monitored.

NOTE 3.21
Companies may require job applicants to accept a computer-use policy as a condition of employment.

tips and hints

Policies on E-mail and Internet Use

1. Be aware that employee e-mail is a part of business records and subject to review in legal actions or when there is reasonable suspicion of misconduct that may damage the reputation of the organization.
2. Don't send animated greeting cards through business e-mail. These messages consume a high volume of processor memory; too many of these greetings (particularly around holidays) could disable the company network.
3. Adhere to professional conduct in the use of e-mail and the Internet. Accessing pornographic sites or sending

obscene or sexually suggestive messages can result in disciplinary penalties or termination of employment and could become the basis for legal action.
4. Treat business e-mail and the use of the Internet as you would the business phone. Keep personal use to a minimum.
5. Avoid viruses by deleting unopened e-mail attachments from unknown sources.
6. Direct questions about proper technology use to management or other appropriate personnel.

Other Technology Privacy Issues

NOTE 3.22
Websites you visit often store a data cookie on your computer.

Internet research is controversial. Technology makes it feasible to gather data about computer users without their knowledge or permission, a practice that many consider unethical and an invasion of individual privacy. As experienced computer users know, many e-commerce sites use tracking software that stores information about you on your computer in a brief text file called a **cookie.** This stored file can be read each time you visit their site; it enables you to be greeted by name when you return to the website and may include your encrypted credit card information to eliminate the need for reentry of data upon subsequent orders. Objections arise because web advertisers may secure information from these files to track your preferences and online shopping habits. To allay concerns about cookies, organizations frequently include a privacy statement on their websites that explains types of data gathered and their use.

NOTE 3.23
Spam is mass mailing of a message to people unlikely to want it.

When the same e-mail goes to multiple persons who, given the option, would not want to receive it, the message is considered **spam.** These mass mailings often promote questionable products, schemes for making money, or services that are only marginally legal. Responding to spam usually leads to more spam and can lead to harassment and identity theft or attempts to steal your credit card number. Organizations use software filters to block some of the spam. It is difficult to block too many terms, or information may be blocked that is not spam. If a persistent spam message comes repeatedly, you can have all messages from that e-mail address automatically sent to Trash.

NOTE 3.24
Phishing uses an illegal copy of a legitimate business logo or information to steal your identity.

Phishing is a common problem with e-mail and sometimes with the phone. The **phisher** uses a logo or other identifying information that appears to be that of a reputable company and asks that you verify your personal information. Sometimes phishers say that they are from a fraud investigation unit or that you have won a prize and must verify your personal information. Legitimate companies don't ask for your personal account information by phone or e-mail, except in sales transactions and on encrypted sites.

If you receive a phishing e-mail that asks for personal information, don't open the link. The phisher is an identity thief. Don't provide your personal information to anyone unless you have verified that person's identity with a trusted source. If you give account numbers, PINs, or passwords to a phisher, immediately notify the companies with which you have accounts. Also, report the phishing e-mail to the company that was falsely represented.

NOTE 3.25
No-call phone lists prohibit unsolicited telemarketing.

Another legal technology issue pertains to telephones. For persons who put their names and phone numbers on a federal no-call list, U.S. law prohibits sending unsolicited advertising through automatic telephone dialing systems or automated telephone equipment with a prerecorded voice message to residential phones, telephone facsimile machines, paging services, or cellular telephones. A number of states have telemarketing laws that establish a *no-call list.* Unsolicited telephone calls to persons on this list can result in a legal penalty.

Computer Fraud

NOTE 3.26
Hackers who access computer data to gain information, extort money, or cause damage commit fraud.

Illegal uses of the Internet include attempting to gain unauthorized access to the computer systems of others or deliberately attempting to disrupt the computer system or destroy data by spreading computer viruses or using other means. The U.S. Code defines **fraud** as intentional unauthorized computer access to a wide variety of computer records (such as government agency computers and computers involved in interstate or foreign communication) to gain information, extort money or other value, or cause damage intentionally.

Computer viruses and worms disrupt businesses and Internet connections. A **virus** program attaches to a file and replicates itself, corrupting the data of the invaded file or attempting to crash the machine. Another type of computer virus encrypts files on the hard drive of computers, locking them to the owner. The owner receives a ransom message demanding online payment for the digital key to unlock the files. **Worms** are a type of computer virus that invades a computer, stealing its resources and using networks to spread itself. Small programs can be attached to an unsuspecting, unprotected third-party computer site. Such a program can send millions of requests for information from that computer to others.

Organizations use firewalls and filters on their computer systems to protect their data, but hackers or terrorists have the capability to breach this security. Antivirus software companies continue to update protective software as new viruses occur. Therefore, you should regularly install antivirus software updates as they become available.

Copyright

Original works of authorship—including written works, art, music, photographs, multimedia, and computer software—qualify for copyright. **Copyright** is a legal right of the owner to control reproduction, distribution, and sale of the work.

Legal use of copyrighted material obtained from the Internet follows the same fair-use guidelines as are applicable to printed, electronic, or other types of work. Copyright law grants a right of *fair use* to the public. Fair use is a privilege, but there is no legally binding answer that defines fair use in a specific instance. Legal interpretations depend on circumstances of the particular use and relate to four factors:

1. **Purpose and character of use.** Nonprofit or educational use is most favorable. Use for commercial purposes should have the owner's permission.
2. **Nature of the copyrighted work.** Information that is general or factual knowledge may be considered fair use even if published. Imaginative, creative work and unpublished work tip the balance toward control of use by the owner.
3. **The amount and portion of the work used in relation to the copyrighted work.** A small amount is most likely to favor fair use, but there is no exact percentage that defines *small amount.*
4. **The effect of the use upon the potential market or the value of the copyrighted work.** If use of the work competes with or takes sales away from the original work or avoids payments for permission in an established permission market, this is a consideration against fair use.

If you are quoting material, be sure to quote it accurately and give credit to the source. Further, you cannot be certain material is free of copyright just because you do not see a copyright notice on the material. In most cases, protected work would have the symbol © or the word *Copyright* followed by the year, but this designation is no longer essential for a person or an organization to prove a copyright violation. When in doubt, request permission to use quoted material.

You do not have to cite a source for information that is general knowledge, such as "Communicators should be sure their messages are ethical and legal." You can say that on your own even though you might have read it in a book or in some other

NOTE 3.27
Copyright is a legal right of the owners to control reproduction, distribution, or sale of their work.

NOTE 3.28
When quoting material or works original to the author, quote accurately and give credit to the source.

publication. Also, copyright laws do not apply to public domain works; works that are not original; U.S. government materials; or ideas, processes, methods, or systems (not original) described in copyrighted works. However, a good practice is to cite the source if in doubt about the copyright.

Plagiarism means stealing and using someone else's ideas or words as your own without giving the other person(s) credit as the source. This theft of ideas or words takes place by using exact quotes or by paraphrasing. **Paraphrasing** is restating ideas (in your own words) but retaining the original meaning. Cite the source when you quote another person's words or ideas and when you reword passages that express someone else's ideas unless those ideas are facts or general knowledge. Paraphrasing or rewording another person's material and making it appear to be your original work is unethical even when it is not illegal. Avoid these problems by (a) understanding and obeying the copyright laws, (b) giving credit to others when using their ideas or words, or (c) not using others' ideas and words.

NOTE 3.29
Illegal copying of software is software piracy and has legal penalties.

Illegal copying of software is **software piracy** and can result in severe legal penalties. You can copy software that is freeware; however, shareware restricts copying. Copyright laws protect commercial software. Laws governing copyright and the fair-use doctrine are complex. Most libraries have the material published by the U.S. Copyright Office on these topics. Business communicators must make themselves aware of the laws and guidelines that apply to their messages.

E-commerce

NOTE 3.30
E-commerce across state lines or with other countries must follow that location's laws.

A legal issue for e-commerce is court jurisdiction that governs which state or national laws apply to the conduct of business transactions. In the United States, interstate commerce is subject to certain federal laws. Conducting business with residents in other countries may mean that such transactions are subject to laws where these customers reside. Laws vary from state to state, and even more from country to country. Consult legal counsel to determine jurisdiction and applicable laws. E-commerce as well as other types of business operations must operate according to such laws.

Electronic signatures facilitate contractual arrangements through e-commerce. A federal electronic signature law endorsed electronic signatures that are logically associated with a record and executed by encryption technology. Furthermore, courts have upheld "click-through" agreements for consumer assent to a contract and contract conditions.

NOTE 3.31
The best practice for a link to another website is to link to the home page.

A common practice on the Internet is linking to other web pages without obtaining permission from the owner. The early culture of website usage accepted this practice. However, because websites have become a critical element of e-commerce, this practice is changing. Use of copyrighted or trademark-protected text or images from a linked page, an artist's artwork, links to internal pages rather than the home page, and links to copyrighted works or defamatory material have become subjects of legal action. If you capture graphics from another website, make sure that you obtain permission to use the copyrighted material.

Links to internal pages in a website can create a problem, not only because the web manager might change internal pages but also because the visitor to the page will not see the web owner's home page. Organizations may use the number of "hits" on the home page to market the site; therefore, skipping the home page could indirectly cause a loss of revenue. The symbol or text that the viewer clicks to go to a linked site is called a **hot zone.** The wording or the symbol used as a hot zone should have accurate text and should not include a copyrighted symbol.

Legal Considerations for Business Messages

You and your organization could be sued or prosecuted if you violate the law in your messages. Thousands or even millions of dollars could be lost. Prison terms might result. To ensure the legality of your written or oral communication, you must be aware of laws, court decisions, and administrative regulations that apply to those messages. Ignorance of the law does not excuse violators.

If you are unsure about the legality of the contents of a message, you should consult an attorney or other authority. Many companies have attorneys available to employees. In addition, company officials—personnel officers, purchasing agents, and others—usually have specialized knowledge of legal requirements in their areas of responsibility.

This section of the chapter gives a brief overview of important legal considerations for contracts, employment communication, and defamation and fraud. This information can alert you to situations with legal implications for communication.

Contracts

Both oral and written communication with your company's customers must meet the requirements of several laws. Among the most important forms of communication is the **contract,** a legally binding agreement between two or more parties. A proposal or offer by one party and acceptance by the other party or parties creates a contract. The contract may involve completing a particular action, providing a particular item or service, or refraining from doing a certain action.

An enforceable contract may result from an exchange of letters—one that makes a clear and definite offer and another that accepts the offer without making conditions on the acceptance—or a series of letters that make clear the parties have reached agreement about material elements of the contract. A contract does not have to be written in a letter or on a particular form if it includes essential elements of the agreement and has the necessary signatures. A valid contract must have the following elements:

1. Offer and acceptance
2. Competency of parties
3. Legality of subject matter
4. Consideration (money, motive, or promise exchanged)

Businesses generally use the services of a lawyer or forms reviewed by a lawyer for all but the simplest contracts. Examples of contracts are agreements for the sale of goods or services, transfer of property or interests in property, and contracts of employment.

"PLAIN ENGLISH" LAWS

Several states have "plain English" laws requiring that contracts be written so consumers can understand them. Certain states specify readability levels, average number of syllables per word, layout, print size, and other content details. These laws require careful analysis of a contract's content. Other states have general guidelines, such as requiring contracts to contain understandable words, short sentences, and

LO 3

Identify legal considerations for different business communication purposes.

NOTE 3.32
Consult an attorney when unsure about the legality of message content.

NOTE 3.33
A contract is a legally binding agreement.

short paragraphs. The principles of business communication given in Chapter 4 will help you meet the requirements of "plain English" laws.

WARRANTIES AND GUARANTEES

NOTE 3.34
Warranties are of two types: express and implied.

Federal law requires the manufacturer or seller to stand behind a purchase of a major product. A warranty must be available for the purchaser to read at the time of purchase. The Uniform Commercial Code, the Consumer Product Warranty Act, the Federal Trade Commission Improvement Act, and similar legislation cover **express warranties** (promises made willingly by the seller) and **implied warranties** (promises created by law). An example of an express warranty is a manufacturer's written promise to replace a product during the first year if it proves defective due to quality of construction or materials. An example of an implied warranty is that the product must be satisfactory for the purpose intended. Promises to consumers and others can be made orally or in writing, so be sure you warrant only to the extent you intend.

Credit and Collection Communication

Many state and federal laws specify the responsibilities of businesses in issuing credit and collecting debts. Here are some of the important federal laws.

EQUAL CREDIT OPPORTUNITY ACT (ECOA)

NOTE 3.35
Credit refusals must be written and must not contain discriminatory language.

This law requires that credit be equally available to all creditworthy customers. This does not mean that all applicants receive credit. Factors such as income, expenses, debt, and credit history determine creditworthiness. The law protects customers dealing with any creditor who regularly extends credit, including banks, small loan and finance companies, retail stores, credit card companies, and credit unions. Anyone involved in granting credit, including real estate brokers who arrange financing, must comply with the ECOA.

When deciding to grant credit, a creditor may not consider your sex, marital status, race, color, national origin, religion, or age (provided the applicant has the capacity to enter contracts). Age can be used in determination of creditworthiness if it has a potential effect on income. A creditor may take into account immigration status and any applicable law or regulation that restricts dealings with citizens or the government of a particular country. Creditors cannot discourage applications by using words that suggest or imply a discriminatory preference. However, they may affirmatively encourage members of traditionally disadvantaged groups to apply. The ECOA requires creditors to notify applicants of action taken on their applications.

FAIR CREDIT BILLING ACT

This law applies to credit cards and open-ended charge accounts such as department store accounts but does not cover installment contracts with repayments on a fixed contract. It protects credit card users against false charges made to their accounts by limiting unauthorized charges to $50. The Act specifies in detail those procedures that consumers and creditors must follow to resolve problems. If your bill contains errors, you must send a letter to the creditor within 60 days giving the amount, describing the problem, and requesting a correction. Enclose information such as sales slips or payment records that support your claim.

FAIR DEBT COLLECTION ACT

This law specifies in detail what debt collectors can and cannot do. The law defines a **debt collector** as a person, other than the creditor, who regularly collects debts from others. Although the law does not forgive any legitimate debt, it requires that debt collectors treat the debtor fairly. A collector may make contacts through mail, telephone, telegram, or fax but cannot make contact at unreasonable times or places, such as before 8 a.m. or after 9 p.m., unless agreed to by the debtor.

FEDERAL TRUTH-IN-LENDING ACT

Full disclosure of credit terms to consumers is a requirement in this law. Lenders and creditors must clearly disclose service charges, finance charges, and the effective annual interest rate. The law covers how the terms and conditions of loans must be specified—such as number of payments and due dates of payments. It also gives the borrower a right to cancel within three business days after signing a contract.

Employment Communication

Managers, supervisors, and employees need to know the legal requirements affecting employment communication. The following laws specify much of what can and cannot be said or written about employees.

Managers must know legal requirements for employment communication.

NOTE 3.36
The terms and conditions of loans must be specified.

THE CIVIL RIGHTS ACT

This law and its amendments prohibit discrimination in employment. Hiring, firing, compensation, and other conditions of employment cannot be based on race, color, religion, gender, or national origin. This Act, first passed in 1964 and since amended, is landmark legislation. Every business communicator should be aware of its requirements. Affirmative action programs have evolved from the Civil Rights Act; the Equal Employment Opportunity Act; and other extensive federal, state, and local employment regulations.

AGE DISCRIMINATION IN EMPLOYMENT ACT (ADEA)

The ADEA deals with a shift in the age demographics of the American workforce. The ADEA prohibits discrimination against workers over 40 years of age. Spoken or written statements that imply age as a factor in an employment decision could have a negative effect if the person contests being rejected for a job or promotion. This Act requires due diligence, record keeping, and documentation on the part of employers in employment actions affecting employees. **Due diligence** is defined as the care that a reasonable person under the same circumstances would use; due diligence entails reasonable but not exhaustive efforts to comply with the law.

NOTE 3.37
The ADEA prohibits discrimination in employment for workers over 40.

LABOR-MANAGEMENT RELATIONS ACT

This law guides communication between managers and workers, particularly as it concerns unions, and prevents employment discrimination based on union activity.

© José Luis Pelaez, Inc./Corbis

The National Labor Relations Board provides details regarding the Act's implementation; the Board's web home page is http://www.nlrb.gov.

NOTE 3.38

Employees can access information about themselves that their employer maintains.

PRIVACY ACT

Employees can access information about themselves as a result of this law. The Act also limits the use of personnel information to the purpose for which it was collected. For example, it is important when serving as a reference that you respond only to specific requests that have been approved by the employee. Further, your comments should relate only to documented job performance. Any reference should be objective, given in good faith, and without malice.

FAMILY EDUCATIONAL RIGHTS AND PRIVACY ACT (FERPA)

This law protects the privacy of information directly connected to a student and includes student records in any medium—digital records, video or audiotape, film, microfilm, microfiche, or written records. FERPA requires written permission from a parent or from the student (if 18 or older) before disclosing any personally identifiable information contained in educational records. Exceptions provided by regulation permit disclosure to a limited set of persons or institutions such as official parties in connection with financial aid, accrediting agencies, or in response to a court order or subpoena.

AMERICANS WITH DISABILITIES ACT (ADA)

This 1990 Act, covering some 43 million Americans with disabilities, is referred to as the most important employment legislation since Title VII of the Civil Rights Act. This Act makes it unlawful to discriminate against people with disabilities in regard to hiring, firing, compensation, training, and advancement. Communicators must be aware of language that the courts might rule discriminatory, such as job descriptions and advertisements calling for applicants with a *high energy level or who are able bodied.* The law covers both physical and mental disabilities. Persons with disabilities are qualified applicants if they meet job requirements and *can* perform the essential functions of the job. Human resource personnel refer to essential job functions as **bona fide occupational qualifications (BFOQ).**

An employer cannot eliminate a qualified applicant from equal consideration for employment if the applicant can perform the essential job functions with reasonable accommodation for the disability. For example, an administrative assistant with a hearing disability could have an amplifier added to the phone to make it possible to handle telephone calls. The amplifier would be a reasonable accommodation; in the employment decision, the disability should not be considered because it could be reasonably accommodated. If this candidate is employed, the ADA requires the employer to provide the accommodation device.

NOTE 3.39

FMLA recognizes the rights of parents and other caregivers to take unpaid work leave to care for family members.

FAMILY AND MEDICAL LEAVE ACT (FMLA)

Passed in 1993, the FMLA recognizes the responsibilities of employees to care for seriously ill family members, to recuperate from their own serious illness, or to care for a new baby or newly adopted child. Certain employers must allow up to 12 weeks per year of unpaid leave for this purpose. The FMLA applies to employers who have 50 or more employees, including part time. The covered individual must have been an employee for a year and worked at least 1,250 hours during the 12 months before the leave. The law describes certain restrictions concerning scheduling, notice requirements, and proof of illness.

Defamation and Fraud

Common law and other legislation cover such important legal considerations as defamation and fraud. These laws restrict what you say about other persons that may damage their reputation or cause financial loss because of misleading or false information.

DEFAMATION

The law does not permit you to make statements that injure the reputation or character of another person. Such statements, called **defamation,** are libelous (written) or slanderous (oral). To be considered defamation, the statements must be false, must have been made for or read by a third person, and must cause some injury. A publication that injures a corporation's credit, property, or business is libelous, also. True statements can be considered defamation if they are made with the intent of harming the other person. In most cases, someone other than the person defamed must read a letter before its contents can be grounds for a court action for libel.

NOTE 3.40
Defamation is written or oral statements that injure another person.

FRAUD

Lying that causes another person monetary damage is called **fraud.** Fraud can be committed by words or conduct or by false advertising and false endorsement of products or services. Fraud exists when these conditions are proven:

NOTE 3.41
Lying that causes monetary damage to another person is fraud.

1. A communicator misrepresents or conceals a material fact.
2. The misrepresentation was made knowingly or with a reckless disregard for the truth.
3. The misrepresentation was made with the intent to deceive.
4. The deceived person relied on the false statement.
5. The deceived person incurred monetary damage.

Ethical Considerations and Codes of Conduct

Ethical communication is essential for individuals and organizations to succeed. Effective interpersonal relationships are built on trust, honesty, and fairness. Promises made are kept. Information is disclosed fairly. Acceptable organizational values should be shared and promoted.

Being ethical is enlightened self-interest. You will pay far more in time, money, and effort to repair the damage caused by false messages than truthful, forthcoming messages would cost in the first place. In addition, it is not always possible to repair the damage caused by an unethical message. Your credibility is likely to be lost, your interpersonal relationships destroyed, and your career impaired.

LO 4
Describe ethical considerations for communication, and explain how codes of conduct help organizations promote ethical business behavior.

NOTE 3.42
Ethical behavior is enlightened self-interest.

An Ethical Communicator

How can you be sure you are an ethical communicator? First, you determine exactly what ethical communication is. Second, you adopt principles or develop systems that work best for you in choosing ethical content for your messages.

needs work

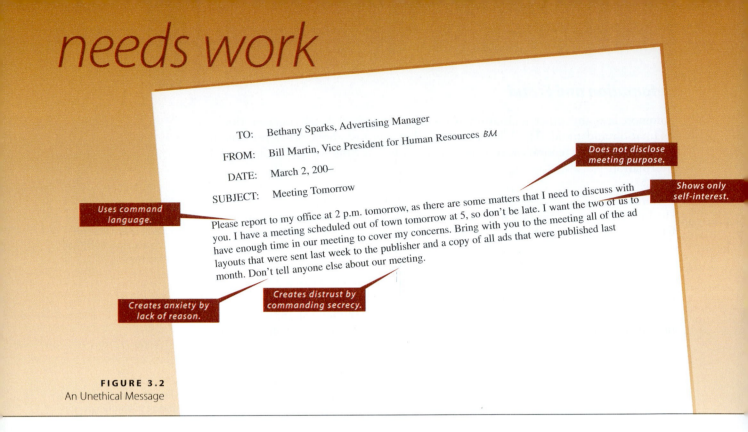

FIGURE 3.2
An Unethical Message

TO: Bethany Sparks, Advertising Manager

FROM: Bill Martin, Vice President for Human Resources *BM*

DATE: March 2, 200–

SUBJECT: Meeting Tomorrow

Please report to my office at 2 p.m. tomorrow, as there are some matters that I need to discuss with you. I have a meeting scheduled out of town tomorrow at 5, so don't be late. I want the two of us to have enough time in our meeting to cover my concerns. Bring with you to the meeting all of the ad layouts that were sent last week to the publisher and a copy of all ads that were published last month. Don't tell anyone else about our meeting.

Does not disclose meeting purpose.

Shows only self-interest.

Uses command language.

Creates anxiety by lack of reason.

Creates distrust by commanding secrecy.

NOTE 3.43
Being ethical means doing the right thing.

DEFINING ETHICAL COMMUNICATION

The word **ethics** is derived from the Greek word *ethos*, meaning character. Being ethical means doing what is right to achieve what is good. In business communication what is right refers to the responsibility to include information in your messages that ought to be there. What is good refers to the result of the communication. The ethical result is to strive for the highest good attainable for all of those involved in the communication. Therefore, **ethical communication** strives for the highest good for all involved and provides information that is fully adequate for the circumstance, truthful in every sense, and not deceptive in any way.

CHOOSING ETHICAL CONTENT FOR MESSAGES

Choosing ethical content for messages requires the same analytical and practical skills as does sound business leadership. Being ethical in your communication requires that you determine—from among all the alternatives—the right and good information appropriate in given situations. Figures 3.2 and 3.3 show contrasting choices for message content.

Ethics in Businesses and Organizations

NOTE 3.44
Only a small percentage of business and professional people are unethical.

Today, we frequently learn about unethical behavior in business and government through the news media. Insider trading, bribery, misleading advertising, misrepresentation of facts, cover-ups, and stonewalling seem to be common practice. In fact, only a small percentage of business and professional people behave in unethical ways. Those who are unethical rarely succeed in the long run, and most of them are not successful even in the short run. Businesses complete millions of transactions daily based on trust and honesty. They advertise merchandise fairly, and they receive orders, ship quality products, and make payments on time. If businesses and their

looks good

TO: Bethany Sparks, Advertising Manager

FROM: Bill Martin, Vice President for Human Resources *BM*

DATE: March 2, 200–

SUBJECT: Meeting Tomorrow

Can you meet with me tomorrow at 2 p.m. in my office to discuss a complaint that has come to my attention about company bias against promoting women into management positions? I believe that it would be helpful for the two of us to review our recent advertising campaigns for content that could support such a claim. One of the allegations of bias mentioned that company ads do not show any pictures of women managers and that the language used shows a strong bias for men in these positions. Please bring with you all ads that were sent to publishers last week and all that were published last month.

Your advertising expertise will be helpful in reviewing with me all recent ads to identify any content that might be considered gender biased or to ensure that such accusations are not supported. My investigation of this claim will be confidential until it is completed.

Please confirm with me your availability for the 2 p.m. meeting. I have another meeting tomorrow at 5 p.m. that is out of town; therefore, I cannot change the time to a later meeting. If you are not available at 2 p.m., let me know if you can meet this Friday at 1 p.m.

FIGURE 3.3
An Ethical Message

customers do not relate in this way, long-term business success and survival are doubtful.

Global Business Ethics

In our global economy, managers face new challenges to ensure ethical operations in foreign lands. To conduct business ethically in another country, managers must be aware of that country's culture, values, and ethics. Organizations must help managers distinguish between practices that are unethical and those that are merely different. Figure 3.4 shows web home pages that relate to business ethics in different countries.

Ethics and Codes of Conduct

Research shows that today about 90 percent of all *Fortune* 500 companies have codes of ethics (also called codes of conduct) to help guide their employees' behavior. Codes of conduct must provide clear direction about ethical behavior when the temptation to behave unethically is strongest. The pronouncement in a code of conduct that *bribery is unacceptable* is useless unless accompanied by guidelines for gift giving and suggested employee responses to unethical situations such as offers of

NOTE 3.45
The most successful businesses have ethical employees.

FIG 3.4
International Ethics Websites

Canadian EthicsWeb	**www.ethicsweb.ca/**
Ethics Resource Center, Washington, D.C.	**www.ethics.org**
Society for Business Ethics (International Organization)	**www.societyforbusinessethics.org**
Institute for Global Ethics	**www.globalethics.org**

bribes. Executives must practice the ethical standards outlined in the code of ethics if the company is to have a successful ethics program.

NOTE 3.46
A company's code of conduct provides direction for ethical behavior.

Texas Instruments (TI) is an example of a company with a long-standing code of ethics. TI published its first written code of ethics in 1961 and has revised it several times to reflect business environment changes. In addition, TI employees receive a copy of the TI Ethics Quick Test on a business-card–size mini-pamphlet to carry with them. This test consists of the following:[2]

- Is the action legal?
- Does it comply with our values?
- If you do it, will you feel bad?
- How will it look in the newspaper?
- If you know its wrong, don't do it!
- If you're not sure, ask.
- Keep asking until you get an answer.

Figure 3.5 shows a portion of the Texas Instruments Code of Ethics. Figure 3.6 lists websites for other corporate and professional organizations' codes of ethics.

NOTE 3.47
Employees' actions should be compatible with the company ethics code.

Companies have training sessions to discuss ethics codes and explain procedures for compliance. Ethics codes are often in employee handbooks and placed on the company's website. In addition, some corporations provide a toll-free hot line for employees to obtain advice on ethical matters. Ethics is not just a U.S. issue. A website for the Institute of Business Ethics (IBE) in England gives guidelines for content of a code of business practice and ethics and how to make codes of conduct effective. Its page may be found at http://www.ibe.org.uk/codesofconduct.html. Most businesses now realize the importance of a strong sense of individual and corporate values.

NOTE 3.48
Ethical standards guide decisions for gray areas of right or wrong.

In many communication situations, you will be faced with gray areas. Most situations are complex, and few are entirely right or entirely wrong. There may be competing interests among your superiors, subordinates, customers, suppliers,

FIGURE 3.5
The Values and Ethics of TI
(Texas Instruments)

- **Integrity**
  "Integrity is the foundation on which TI is built. There is no other characteristic more essential to a Tler's makeup. It has to be present at all levels. Integrity is expected of managers and individuals when they make commitments. They are expected to stand by their commitments to the best of their ability." (From *TI Culture—The I's of TI*)

- **Innovation**
  "Since productivity depends upon the performance of TI as a whole, we stress innovation not only in scientific and technical areas, but also in marketing, in personnel relations, and in short, in all areas of the corporation." (Erik Jonsson, Former Chairman, Texas Instruments)

- **Commitment**
  "Our extraordinary commitment to integrity reflects the value system established by TI's founders early in the company's history . . . integrity that goes far beyond what is ordinarily considered good business to reflect a genuine, deep concern for doing what's right and fair in all business transactions. Keeping our commitments and fulfilling the expectations we create with our promises—both direct and implied—is an uncompromising standard." (Market Communications Strategy Statement)

  **Know what's right. Value what's right.
  Do what's right.**

  Courtesy of Texas Instruments. Excerpts from *The Values and Ethics of TI.*

---

[2] Texas Instruments, "The TI Ethics Quick Test," *Ethics*, n.d., http://www.ti.com/corp/docs/citizen/ethics/quicktest.shtml (March 18, 2006).

National Association of Social Workers	http://www.naswdc.org/pubs/code/default.asp
Society of Professional Journalists	http://www.spj.org/ethics_code.asp
A Blogger's Code of Ethics	http://www.cyberjournalist.net/news/000215.php
National Education Association	http://www.nea.org/aboutnea/code.html
General Motors	http://www.gm.com/company/gmability/
Federated Department Stores, Inc.	http://www.fds.com/company/social_1_2.asp
U.S. Steel	http://www.ussteel.com/corp/corp_gov/ ethics_contacts.htm
Lexmark	http://investor.lexmark.com/phoenix .zhtml?c=irol-govConduct
How to Write a Code of Ethics	http://www.ethicsweb.ca/codes/

FIGURE 3.6
Organization and Corporate Websites for Ethics and Code of Conduct Statements

stockholders, and others. Ethical principles and systems that can help you make decisions on ethical content for your messages are presented in the following sections.

Ethical Messages

Ethical principles that are basic to decisions about message content, found in one form or another in codes of conduct, include the following:

1. Integrity and honesty
2. Personal and professional responsibility
3. Concern and respect for others
4. Fairness to all concerned

These principles can help you be an ethical communicator. Use them on a daily basis to ensure that your messages are ethical.

Developing Ethical Messages

Applying ethical principles exemplifies the you–viewpoint. Expectations are that communication will be honest, fair, and considerate of the receiver's needs. Integrity means being true to ethical principles even when the right thing to do is not the expected response. Considering the message receivers' needs does not mean telling the audience what it wants to hear. It means considering the best content for all concerned; communicating that content honestly, with full disclosure of the reasons involved; and wording it to demonstrate respect and concern.

What effect will the message have on the person directly involved and on all others affected by it? Simply stated, ethical principles provide a fundamental moral imperative that serves as a guide for business communicators. Ethical communicators analyze the communication problems facing them. Then they analyze the message content they could select for their messages. They choose content that will provide the same full disclosure, truth, and straightforwardness that they would want to have if they were the receiver. They consider the needs of persons affected by the message and show respect and concern for those needs through the message tone.

The question the business communicator asks is, "Would I be willing to require all others in the same circumstances to send the same kind of message I am sending?" The answer has to be yes if it is the best message for all concerned.

LO 5
Discuss guidelines for ethical business communication.

NOTE 3.49
Ethical principles require integrity, honesty, responsibility, and respect for others.

NOTE 3.50
Analyze message content based on ethical principles.

NOTE 3.51
An ethical test of your message is whether you believe all persons under the same circumstances should send the same kind of message.

Message senders meet their personal and professional responsibility when they demonstrate by their words, tone, and actions that they are truthful, do not misrepresent or overstate facts, and care about providing the best service or product that meets the customer's needs. Employee actions and communication meet all ethical standards represented by the company and are consistent with the message sender's own ethical values. In addition, business communicators' actions, decisions, and messages reflect caring, concern, and personal and social responsibility.

Being Ethical

NOTE 3.52
Being an ethical communicator requires human judgment based on ethical standards.

Being ethical in your communication is not only essential and the right thing to do, it is also contagious. Others will follow your lead when they observe the success you experience in interpersonal relationships and in your career. You are the message; for the message to be credible, the message receiver has to believe in the honesty, competency, professionalism, and sincere concern for the receiver's needs and the needs of others.

Summary of Learning Objectives

LO 1 Describe recent technology trends and their effects on business communication.

Small portable wireless computer devices provide on-the-go communication with convergence of text, audio, video, documents, photographs and other graphics, television programs, music, and Internet connection. Special interest communication through the Internet offers a forum for communication through sites for blogs, vlogs, podcasts, and wikis. The capability of handheld electronic devices to download media for convenient listening, reading, viewing, and responding allows the message receiver to select content, medium, time, and place.

Portability, selectivity, and on-the-go multimedia formats open opportunities for niche market phone services and new marketing strategies. An increasing number of mobile employees use videoconferencing and hoteling. Intranets, collaborative writing, group software, and Internet host sites enable employees in different locations to work on the same project either synchronously or asynchronously.

LO 2 Discuss legal and ethical issues related to electronic communication and e-commerce.

Legal and ethical issues arise with increasing use of mobile devices and the Internet. Using camera cell phones and conducting business on cell phones while driving raise ethical and legal issues.

Liability of employers for employee use of technology has contributed to privacy issues for e-mail and the Internet. In addition, illegal use of the Internet is recorded not only on the user's device but also on the Internet or intranet provider's server and is recoverable and subject to subpoena in case of legal charges. Organizations need technology-use policies, and employees should treat electronic messages as if they are public knowledge. A variety of technology capabilities creates risks of data gathering, spam, identity theft, extortion messages, and phishing. Copyright laws protect electronic and print works, and users of these works should know and observe legal restrictions. Electronic signatures and click-through agreements facilitate the growth of e-commerce. Websites are becoming commercially important as e-commerce. Therefore, bypassing the owner's home page may affect revenue from advertisements or other benefits that result from the number of "hits" or people accessing that site. Legal actions can result from unauthorized use of copyrighted or trademark-protected text or images from a web page.

Identify legal considerations for different business communication purposes.

LO 3

The contents of messages must be both legal and ethical. When in doubt about legal questions, consult an attorney. Contracts, credit and collection letters, and employment communication are subject to a number of laws, legal codes, and requirements. Further, defamation and fraud can result from false statements that injure another person.

Describe ethical considerations for communication, and explain how codes of conduct help organizations promote ethical business behavior.

LO 4

Ethical communication means determining the right thing to do and demonstrating fairness and respect for the message receiver. Being truthful and honest, fair in advertising, and disclosing all information necessary to avoid harm to others are examples of ethical communication practices. Ethical behavior means not only staying within the law but also being consistent with your own value system and your company's code of conduct. A code of conduct publicly announces the values and beliefs of the organization and makes company expectations a part of the work culture. Making this guide for conduct publicly available increases public respect for the business and its employees.

Discuss guidelines for ethical business communication.

LO 5

Planning, composing, and sending messages requires constant adherence to legal and ethical principles. Is the message content accurate and complete? Have you considered what the receiver needs to know? Have you selected a medium that is appropriate for the message and that will be favorably received? Does the message reflect community and society's standards of behavior and the organization's ethical standards? Does it meet your own personal value system? Trust, honesty, and fairness are basic to interpersonal relationships and apply also to business relationships. Global business transactions raise new legal and ethical issues because accepted practices in one country are not the same in others. Information on international ethics for business helps to guide ethical global practice.

Apply ethical principles and organization codes of conduct to all of your business messages. Consider these principles and your own value system when planning messages. Ethical messages demonstrate integrity and honesty, personal and professional responsibility, concern and respect for others, and fairness to all concerned.

Questions for Discussion and Review

1. Describe three technology trends and how they affect business communication. (Objective 1)
2. How do these technology tools change communication use: Wi-fi, podcasts, and blogs? (Objective 1)
3. Explain the concept of viral advertising, and give an example of an advertisement that might fit this concept. (Objective 1)
4. Describe three legal and three ethical issues brought about by use of e-mail and the Internet. (Objective 2)
5. Identify a portable wireless device, other than a cell phone, and give an example of an ethical issue and a legal issue that could arise with its use. (Objective 2)
6. What are two circumstances that affect interpretation of fair use of copyrighted material? (Objective 2)
7. Describe two types of laws that affect agreements between two or more parties. (Objective 3)
8. Explain why you agree or disagree with this statement: "Only a small percentage of business and professional people behave in unethical ways." (Objective 4)
9. Mitzi Johnson worked for XYZ Company, which had a code of ethics for employees. In the training session, employees received a card that included these tests to determine ethical behavior: *Is it honest? Would you want your action to be printed in the newspaper? Would this behavior have potential to damage the company's reputation?* Mitzi had a friend who lived in another state and worked for a competitor of XYZ Company. Her friend asked her to send a copy of a news article from the local paper that described XYZ's research on a new product soon to be released. Mitzi decided to fax a copy of the article to her friend on her office fax machine. Did Mitzi's action meet all three tests for ethical behavior? Why or why not? (Objective 4)
10. How can a business or organization code of conduct help guide communication by its employees or members? (Objective 5)

Application Exercises

1. **Ethics. Technology.** You received an iPod for your birthday that stores videos and pictures as well as music. Describe how using your iPod would increase your selectivity for content choice, time, and place for viewing or listening. Give an example of an ethical or a legal question that may arise as you use the device. (Objectives 1 and 2)
2. **Ethics. Teamwork.** Form a team of three to five students. Each of you will listen to a television news show for one week or read the daily newspaper to identify situations reported in the news that have legal or ethical implications for communication. At the end of the week, meet and make a list of all of these situations observed by your team. As a team, use group consensus to select five issues for a discussion of the legal and ethical implications. Consider the individual opinions that may arise when discussing what is or is not ethical. Remember that individual ethical standards and opinions about ethics may differ; not everyone agrees about what is ethical. (Objectives 2, 3, and 4)
3. **Ethics. Technology. Teamwork.** For the five issues identified in Application Exercise 2, meet with your team and write three questions about the situation that you need to research further to understand the legal and ethical implications. Use the Internet for this research. As a team, develop a summary of what the team learned about each issue, and present your findings to the class. (Objectives 2, 3, and 4)
4. **Technology. Ethics.** Send an e-mail to your instructor describing an ethical or legal communication that you had to handle at your job or in the classroom. Apply the ethical principles described in this chapter to the situation. (Objectives 4 and 5)
5. **Technology. Ethics.** A friend gives you a copy that he has made of a software program that he purchased. Is this a legal or an ethical issue or both? Explain your answer in an e-mail sent to your instructor. (Objectives 2 and 5)

6. **Global. Ethics. Technology.** Assume that you are a good friend of an executive of a company that markets widgets in the Bahamas. You have stock in this company, and your friend casually mentions that the widget is becoming obsolete. Nothing is mentioned about your stock. Is it legal for you to call your stockbroker and sell your stock? Is it ethical? Research the topic *insider stock trading* on the Internet. Write your answer to these two questions, using your research to explain your answers. (Objective 3)

7. **Ethics. Technology.** Evaluate this statement using the Texas Instruments Ethics Quick Test and the Code of Conduct from Figure 3.5: "It is better to steal from the stockholders of a company than the public because it will receive less media attention." Summarize your evaluation and post it to a class electronic discussion board, if one is available, or send it as an e-mail attachment to your instructor and members of your class. (Objectives 4 and 5)

8. **Ethics.** For each of the following behaviors, explain whether it is illegal and/or unethical and what effect the behavior could have on an employee and employer. (Objectives 2, 3, 4, and 5)
   a. Sending sexually explicit jokes to fellow employees using company e-mail.
   b. Taking personal calls on your own cell phone or pager while at work.
   c. Copying company software for home use.
   d. Blaming a technology glitch for an error that you made.
   e. Using the office copier to make 150 copies of your social club's newsletter.
   f. Taking home pens and paper from the office for other than work tasks for your company.
   g. Overstating an expense item on a travel expense report for reimbursement.
   h. Inflating a selling price and giving the customer a kickback.
   i. Shopping for personal items on the Internet while at work.
   j. Using the cell phone to transact business while traveling in a company car.
   k. Using an employer's stationery when applying for a job with another firm.

9. **Ethics.** Assume that a section of the company policy where you work conflicts with your individual value system. When a situation arises that requires application of this policy for a communication that you are to write, which ethical guide would you follow? What would be the likely consequences? Form a team of three to five students to discuss this question. Summarize your conclusions to share with the class. (Objectives 4 and 5)

10. **Ethics. Technology.** Company officials searching for a way to avoid bankruptcy raised cash with off-the-balance-sheet loans and overstated results by inflating capital expenses and hiding the debt. The company's stock traded on Wall Street. Send an e-mail to your instructor evaluating the actions taken to avoid bankruptcy. Use the guidelines from this chapter for your evaluation. (Objectives 2, 3, 4, and 5)

11. **Ethics. Technology.** Peter Drucker states that "there is no such thing as Business Ethics, there is only ethics." Collaborate with another classmate to write a reaction paragraph to this statement. E-mail the message to your instructor. (Objectives 4 and 5)

12. **Ethics. Technology.** A health spa used the term *micro color* in marketing campaigns to refer to permanent cosmetic makeup. A beauty supply company claimed the right to the term and said it was registered as a trademark for one of its products and that its use by the health spa would cause confusion for its customers. The health spa owner contended that she had fair use because the spa had used this term for the past five years without any question of legality being raised. Review the information in the chapter about fair use. Working with a partner, decide which company you believe will prevail if this case goes to court and why. Send the response to your instructor by e-mail. (Objective 3).

13. An automobile manufacturer planned to sell cars directly to consumers through the Internet. Texas law prohibited auto manufacturers from acting in the capacity of dealers. Based on information in this chapter about court jurisdiction, explain why this manufacturer's e-commerce sales to Texas consumers may come under Texas jurisdiction. (Objective 3)

14. **Ethics. Technology.** A bank charges extra fees to Hispanic customers for opening and maintaining a checking account without meeting the bank's minimum deposit amount. The account has no check-writing privileges although it was advertised to Hispanics as a checking account. Customers must go to the bank to make a withdrawal. Each deposit or withdrawal from the account costs the customer $1.50. Do you believe this action is legal? ethical? Explain your answer, and send it by e-mail to the instructor. (Objectives 3, 4, and 5)

ETHICAL
COLLABORATIVE

15. Ethics. Teamwork. A manager of a department store tries to follow a company policy that prohibits off-the-clock work requirements of employees; however, store managers have to keep payroll costs below a target set by headquarters, and overtime pay is against policy. The store manager decides that the only way to control payroll costs is to require employees to stay at work 30 minutes each day after they clock out to straighten merchandise for the next day. After all, she reasons, the two company policies are in conflict with one another. Write a paragraph explaining whether you believe the action is unethical or illegal and your reasons for this response. Exchange papers with a classmate and critique each other's response. (Objectives 3, 4, and 5)

ETHICAL

16. Ethics. A pharmaceutical company hides indications of a drug's dangerous side effects and delays sending a message to physicians about possible effects until six months after research documented serious illness or death from use of the drug. Describe in writing your beliefs about actions that the manufacturer should have taken to send messages that could have saved lives or prevented serious injury. Explain whether you believe a pharmaceutical company has an obligation to the public greater than, equal to, or less than a manufacturer of automobiles. (Objectives 3, 4, and 5)

ETHICAL

17. Ethics. A friend of a college football coach faxed the coach a description of plays from a rival team's playbook. The coach's team was scheduled to play the rival team the next week. The coach accepted the plays and used them in preparation for the game. In a group of three to five people, discuss this case and decide whether the actions of the friend and the coach were ethical. Explain the reasons for your decisions. (Objectives 4 and 5)

18. Police officers in Cincinnati claimed that under the Fair Labor Standards Act they should be paid time and a half overtime for working more than a 40-hour workweek. The city claimed that overtime pay would create a budget deficit and an undue burden. The statute does not consider payment of overtime an undue burden. Do you believe this is a legal issue and/or an ethical issue? Explain. (Objectives 3, 4, and 5)

ETHICAL
COLLABORATIVE

19. Ethics. Teamwork. Mike took out a loan at the United Bank and Trust and was unable to keep up the payments. The bank sent collection letters to Mike over a six-month period and then turned the action over to a collection agency. The collection agency called Mike at 7:30 every morning for two weeks to demand payment. Calls were also made to Mike's employer and to his neighbor inquiring about Mike's ability to pay. Do you believe this action to be legal? ethical? Explain. Discuss this case with a partner, and send your response by e-mail to your teacher.

20. Locate an example of a contract. Describe the four essential elements applicable to this contract. (Objective 3)
   a. Offer and acceptance
   b. Competency of parties
   c. Legality of subject matter
   d. Consideration

Web exercises to accompany this chapter are available at **www.thomsonedu.com/ bcomm/krizan.**

Message Analysis

Based on what you have learned in this chapter about codes of conduct and from previous chapters for developing messages, revise the following letter that explains the General Standards of Conduct for State Government Employees. Reword for a positive tone as well as clarity and completeness. Edit your letter carefully before submitting it to your instructor. Assume that this letter is to be signed and returned as evidence that the employee has seen the policy.

Dear Employee:

It is my duty to inform you that every employee is required to sign this letter and return it no later than one week after it is received. You should know that your actions will be monitored while you work for this organizations. The Public code of Conduct recognsed that public servant work is for the benefit of the people and is a trust based on concent of its citizens. Citizens are to have trust in the integrety of there government. Therefore, the following general statements of required behavoir are presented:

- *Don't take bribes. Be independent and impartial in decisions.*
- *Don't make decisions and policies outside of established goverment processes.*
- *Don't comit behavioral actions that destroy public confidence.*
- *Do not engage in conflict of interest deals*
- *Don't use public property—technology, copiers, telephones, etc. for private use.*

If you do any of these actions you will be found out and will be fired without an opportunity for explaination.

Have a good day!!!!

Respectfully Yours

Writer's Workshop

The following items may be sentence fragments or contain errors in subject–verb agreement, comma and semicolon placement, spelling, or word choice. Rewrite the sentences to make them correct.

1. A set of morale principals define the term, ethics.
2. The *ABC Journal* publishs articles on business communications.
3. Effective English teachers learn the students how to write speak and listen.
4. Basic communication and enterpersonal skills is fundmental for success in business.
5. Ethic experts argue that you can not teach ethics however you can teach ethical reasoning based on fairness, honesty and responsibility.
6. Jane completed several activities today, at school she left her purse, books, and jacket, paid the bills at the grocery before returning home.
7. Brushing up your technology skills for a good job.
8. Handheld computers, a way to communicate on the go.
9. The professer taught English, mathematics, and foreign language but he had a light teaching load because none of his class had more than six students.
10. Jim and John or the new student who enrolled today are expected to present a demonstration tomorrow.

YOU BE THE
virtual assistant

Here, and at the end of each part of this text, you will assume the role of a virtual assistant—a self-employed professional who provides administrative assistance to clients via the Internet.

Your clients may reside anywhere in the world. You may have met them personally, or you may know them only through e-mail and telephone contacts. They may be entrepreneurs whose businesses may not yet need permanent staff, or they may be established small or large businesses that need temporary help with a special project or during peak work periods. The fees virtual assistants charge vary by region and task; for this activity, use a base rate of $40 per hour.

Just as the size and business focus of your clients vary, so do the tasks you perform for them. For the purpose of this feature, your tasks will relate to running your business and performing communication-related projects for your clients. Each set of tasks will relate to the content of the chapters in that part of the text.

1. Create a name and catchy tag line for your business. A tag line is an easy-to-remember motto or phrase that succinctly describes your service or your approach to business.

2. Design a business card that includes all relevant information about your business.

3. Search the Internet to learn about the International Association of Virtual Assistants. Answer the following questions:

   a. How large is the group's membership?

   b. What are the dues?

   c. What are the benefits of membership?

   d. Does the association sponsor a professional certification? If so, what must you do to earn the certification?

4. You have received an e-mail from Bangladesh, India, from a prospective client. Search the Internet, local library, and local directories from your area to find resources that can provide information on the culture and communication styles in Bangladesh. Make a list that includes information for making future contact with at least four resources that may be helpful for information on the culture, currency, economy, and geography.

5. A client asked you to gather information and draft the text of a ten-minute speech about leadership. You completed the task and e-mailed the text to him for revising and editing. You have just received his reply and are concerned about what you see. All the source references you included (e.g., "As Jack Welch said . . .") were deleted but the quotes and secondary information remained. Decide how to handle this ethical dilemma and prepare the text of the e-mail you will send your client. Remember, if you say nothing, your ethics could be questioned.

Part 2
Effective Communication Development

© Digital Vision

Chapter 4
Principles of Business Communication

LET'S TALK BUSINESS

As a sales representative, I understand the importance of oral and written communication. Success in business depends on building positive relationships with clients. In today's multicultural society, understanding the diversity of backgrounds, interests, and needs is essential to good customer service. Listening to each client's needs, communicating clearly, and taking that extra step to be helpful builds trust that leads to a long-term relationship with the customer. A smile and a helpful attitude are understood and appreciated, regardless of differences in language, age, gender, or ethnic background. Use simple, conversational words that do not stereotype people and that reflect a genuine interest in each person as an individual.

Michelle Jones, Pharmaceutical Sales Representative, Eli Lilly and Company

Photo courtesy of Michelle Jones

Communicating effectively, either orally or in writing, depends on understanding the business client and responding to each situation from the client's point of view. In today's competitive business environment, improving communication with clientele promotes business success.

Michelle Jones reminds us that business success depends on effective communication and that simple, conversational words and the you–viewpoint promote such communication. As you study this chapter, you will see how these principles apply to word choice, sentence construction, and paragraph development. The best way to compose effective business messages, whether oral or written, is to apply these principles of business communication to all types of business messages.

A basic communication principle is to keep your message short and simple. Communicators remember this principle by its initials, KISS, which stands for Keep It Short and Simple. Application of this principle means using short and simple words, sentences, and paragraphs when composing your business messages. As a result, your messages will be concise, easy to understand, and straightforward.

To communicate effectively, adopt a businesslike, friendly, and easy-to-understand style consistent with the KISS principle. Composing short, effective messages takes extra time but is worth it to you and your receiver. Competent communicators build long-term customer relationships and goodwill.

NOTE 4.1
Keep business messages short and simple.

Choosing Words

Words are the smallest units of messages. Give attention to each word used to be sure it is the most effective one. An **effective word** is one that your receiver will understand and that will elicit the response you want. You can improve your ability to choose words by (a) using a dictionary and a thesaurus and (b) following the six principles of business communication described in this section.

LO 1
Identify words that your receiver(s) will understand and that will elicit the intended response.

Use a Dictionary and a Thesaurus

The two most valuable resources for the business communicator are a dictionary and a thesaurus. Use of these tools can increase your power to choose the most appropriate words for each of your messages.

A **dictionary** is a word reference that gives word meanings, acceptable spelling(s), hyphenation, capitalization, pronunciation(s), and synonyms. Dictionaries may be in print or electronic format. Dictionary software can be installed on your computer or read from a CD. In addition, dictionary websites can be found on the Internet by using a search engine. Some of these websites require a subscription fee for full use; others allow use without a cost. An example of a dictionary website can be found at http://www.onelook.com. Also, specialized dictionaries for areas such as technology can be found on the Internet.

A dictionary helps you choose correct words. Similar words are confusing and, therefore, at times are misused. Examples of such words are *effect* and *affect*, *capital* and *capitol*, *principal* and *principle*, *continuous* and *continual*, and *further* and *farther*. See Business English Seminar E for an extensive list of easily confused words.

A **thesaurus** provides synonyms and different shades of meaning. If you have an idea you want to express, use a thesaurus to check for words that represent the idea and find several alternative words that you can use. Each choice usually has a slightly different connotation. A thesaurus can provide the simplest and most precise words for your message. Most word processing programs include a thesaurus.

NOTE 4.2
Use a dictionary to select words.

NOTE 4.3
Use a thesaurus to find synonyms.

Successful managers communicate clearly and concisely.

© José Luis Pelaez, Inc/Corbis

A dictionary and a thesaurus should be readily accessible when composing messages. These two references help you choose words and avoid overuse of the same word by providing **synonyms** (words with similar meanings). In addition to using these references, apply the following six principles to select words for effective messages.

Principle 1: Choose Understandable Words

The first principle of word selection is to choose words that your receiver will understand. Prior to composing your messages, you should analyze your receiver's knowledge, interests, opinions, and emotional reactions. Keep in mind the importance of using the you–viewpoint. When you select words understandable to your reader and consider the reader's opinions and emotional reactions, you are applying the you–viewpoint. Mentally, you are viewing the message from the receiver's perspective and anticipating the receiver's information needs and responses.

An **understandable word** is one that is in your receiver's vocabulary. Consider your receiver's educational level and knowledge of the message topic. The words that will communicate best are those slightly below the receiver's vocabulary level. Examples in the following list of words labeled More Understandable are an appropriate choice for most receivers. These words help you maintain a conversational tone to the message.

NOTE 4.4
Choose words your receiver will understand.

Less Understandable	More Understandable
abdicate	resign
affluence	wealth
ambiguous	uncertain
amicable	friendly
apprehend	arrest
ascend	climb
delineate	clearly describe
diatribe	criticism
emulate	copy
exonerate	clear
expedite	rush
facilitate	help
finality	end
gregarious	sociable
illicit	unlawful
imperious	commanding
incite	provoke
incriminate	blame
initiate	start
palpable	obvious
pompous	self-important
prerogative	right or privilege
trajectory	path
utilize	use
validate	confirm
zealot	fanatic

The words listed under More Understandable in the previous examples are generic for most readers. Notice their brevity and conversational tone.

Appropriate selection of technical words is a special consideration when choosing understandable words. Technical words are terms that have a special meaning in a particular field. They convey precise, meaningful messages among certain receivers and senders. For example, between two accountants the use of the words *accrued liabilities* will be understandable. Using these technical words conveys to accountants a more precise and efficient meaning than using nontechnical language. For most of us, though, *accrued liabilities* is not as understandable as *debts that have not yet been recorded on our books*. Here are some other examples of technical and nontechnical words:

NOTE 4.5
Understandable words are generally simpler and shorter.

Technical Words	Nontechnical Words
acceleration clause	immediate repayment demand for late loan payments
amenities	features of the property
arrears	an overdue debt
bill of sale	written transfer of ownership
bill of lading	shipping document
brief	summary of a legal case
capital-intensive	requiring large sums of money
cerebellum	lower part of the brain
de facto	actual
disbursement	payment of funds
equity	owner's value beyond debt

(continued)

(continued)

Technical Words	Nontechnical Words
font	typeface or print style for characters
freeware	computer software distributed without charge
juried	judged
laissez faire	minimal regulation
mandible	jaw
plumage	feathers
spelunking	cave exploration
symposium	conference
synchronous	at the same time
underwriter	sponsor or insurer

NOTE 4.6
Appropriate technical words are those in your receiver's vocabulary.

You will want to use only those technical words that are in your receiver's vocabulary. To do otherwise reduces the receiver's understanding of your message. If you are not sure if a technical word is in your receiver's vocabulary, do not use it.

In summary, you can best choose understandable words by selecting simple words, short words, and technical words appropriate to the receiver. The following example words shown under More Understandable are for a receiver who is a typical high school graduate and who has no particular knowledge of the topic.

Less Understandable	More Understandable
That investment is a cash cow.	That investment brings a dependable income.
Midori demanded the prerogative to establish her own docket.	Midori demanded the right to set her own schedule.
The garment was made of crepe de chine.	The garment was a soft, silky fabric.
The wind damaged the airplane hull.	The wind damaged the main body of the airplane.
Communication came through Intelsat.	Communication came through the global satellite network.
John worked at the port as a stevedore.	John worked at the port unloading ships' cargo.

Principle 2: Use Specific, Precise Words

NOTE 4.7
Use specific words for clarity.

Specific words are clear and precise in meaning. In your messages use words that are clear and that will leave no question in your receiver's mind about the intended meaning. Words selected for your message should be so precise that they accurately mirror what you want the receiver to understand.

Beetle Bailey by Mort and Greg Walker

Vague or **abstract words** are indefinite words; they do not have a specific meaning that is the same for each receiver of the message. Vague words are not precise; they are the opposite of specific words. **Abstract words** may be nouns that identify an idea, an emotion, a quality, or a belief. Examples are *thought, beauty,* and *miracle.* Because people are not alike in opinions and feelings, abstract nouns have different meanings for different people. Also, some adjectives and adverbs do not have the same meaning for different people. For example, the word *some* in the previous sentence is an adjective. How much is *some*? Is it 5, 10, or 50? The message receiver cannot be sure; therefore, *some* is vague and imprecise in meaning. A speaker or writer who uses the adverb *very* intends to emphasize the word the adjective modifies. However, *very* is imprecise and does little or nothing to help the message receiver interpret the meaning. Additional words add preciseness to meaning only if they provide meaningful, specific details that help interpret the meaning.

Vague or abstract words can create wrong or confusing meanings in your receiver's mind. They state a general idea but leave the precise meaning to the receiver's interpretation. Give preference to specific and precise words in your messages. Specific words add to the meaning of the message. For example, the statement, "Some customers commented that they liked the display" gives a perception that the response to the display was positive. However, the number who liked it is unknown as is the period for receiving comments. With more specific wording, the perception of the display changes to a negative one and indicates justification to change the display: "Three customers commented that they liked the display design; but before noon on Monday, 50 complained about the bold colors in the display." The following examples show vague or abstract words and ways to make them specific and precise:

NOTE 4.8
Vague or abstract words mean different things to different people.

Vague	Specific
many	1,000 *or* 500 to 1,000
early	5 a.m.
hot	100 degrees Fahrenheit
most	89.9 percent
others	business administration students
poor student	has a 1.6 grade point average (4.0 = A)
very rich	a millionaire
soon	7 p.m. Tuesday
furniture	an oak desk

Notice in the preceding examples how adding a few words makes the meaning precise. These additions to the length of your message are worth the clarity gained.

Principle 3: Choose Strong Words

A **strong word** is one that creates a vivid image in the receiver's mind. In the English language, verbs are the strongest words. Nouns are next in strength. (See Business English Seminar A for a review of the parts of speech.)

Give preference to verbs and nouns in your business messages. The strongest verbs are those that express action (*identify, explain, melted, sang*) rather than a state of being (*is, are, was, were*). Use state-of-being verbs sparingly; words of action present a strong, meaningful picture in the receiver's mind. Think of these action verbs and specific nouns as power words. **Power words** have a distinct meaning and create a visual image in the mind of the receiver. For example, the verb *melt* or *melted* creates a mind picture; thus, it is stronger to say, "The ice melted" instead of

NOTE 4.9
Verbs and nouns are strong words.

"The ice disappeared." Adjectives and adverbs that make a noun or verb specific give preciseness and clarity. An example of this is "The water flowed down the bubbling brook" rather than "The water flowed down the brook." However, if you use vague terms (e.g., *very, many, few, some, often*), they distract the receiver from the main points of the message because they are imprecise.

Overuse of adjectives and adverbs, however, reduces their effectiveness. Using too many adjectives or adverbs may lead to overstating a point or position. For example, "I will be the happiest and luckiest person in the world if I win the Frederick Remington print in tomorrow's prize drawing" is an overstatement. "I will be delighted if I win the Frederick Remington print in tomorrow's prize drawing" is a more accurate statement. To have an impact, messages should convey clarity and objectivity without exaggeration.

NOTE 4.10
Eliminate unnecessary words.

Overuse of prepositions and prepositional phrases distracts from the message. Eliminate those that are unnecessary. For example, you might say, "I printed off a copy of the article." A clear, direct statement says, "I printed a copy of the article" or "I printed the article." Another example is "The idea came out of the book," which is less powerful than "The idea came from the book."

A sender who communicates with clarity and forcefulness makes the message easy to read and understand. A concise, powerful message that eliminates unnecessary words and uses power words to create a mental image gets the attention of your receiver. Note how changing words in the following examples creates a stronger message and presents a clearer mental image.

Weak Nouns and Verbs	Strong Nouns and Verbs
The conflict is ongoing.	The war rages on.
The situation was creating contention.	The problem created conflict.
He dived into the water.	He plunged into the waves.

Weak Adjectives and Adverbs	Strong Adjectives and Adverbs
The contract expires in a few years.	The contract expires in five years.
Many people were at the reception.	Fifty people attended the reception.
I very nearly died.	I almost died.

Unnecessary Prepositions or Phrases	Simple, Direct Statement
The action resulted in a disappointed group of members.	The action disappointed the members.
The market sold the item free of a duty charge.	The market sold the item duty free.
Did you pay out rent for the office space?	Did you rent the office space?

NOTE 4.11
Use weak words to soften messages.

Although Principle 3 advocates a preference for strong words, there will be times when you want to soften a message with weaker words. This is particularly true for a bad news message. When you discuss a problem with a coworker, you build better human relations and acceptance of your message if you use the weaker word *situation* instead of the stronger word *problem*, which has negative connotations. In Chapter 8 you will study how word choice affects acceptance of a negative message.

Principle 4: Emphasize Positive Words

NOTE 4.12
Effective communicators have a positive, can-do attitude.

A positive, *can-do* attitude makes a good impression. Communicate a *can-do* message to your receivers by selecting positive words and avoiding negative words.

Positive words convey optimism and confidence. **Negative words** trigger unpleasant emotions in receivers.

Positive words in a message help achieve communication goals: receiving the desired response, maintaining a favorable relationship, and gaining goodwill. Here are examples of negative words you should avoid using:

NOTE 4.13
Positive words help achieve message goals.

Negative Words

accuse	disaster	improper	regret
angry	discouraging	insensitive	sorry
blame	disgust	neglected	terror
complaint	failed	never	trouble
contradict	fault	no	unable
deny	hateful	not	unhappy
disapprove	impossible	obnoxious	wrong

These examples show that unpleasant and negative words are strong words. There will be occasions when you will want to use negative words for emphasis. An example would be a letter to a vendor to replace a lamp broken in shipment. The tone of the letter should be positive, but negative words can emphasize the loss. A sentence might read: "The lamp was broken when it arrived. The glass base was shattered, and the lampshade was torn. The box in which it was shipped was smashed almost flat." Although the words *broken, shattered,* and *smashed* are negative, they emphasize the condition of the lamp and container when they arrived.

As the next examples show, however, you will effectively convey a positive attitude and the you–viewpoint if you emphasize what can be done rather than what cannot be done. Selecting positive words and avoiding negative ones promote goodwill and build relationships.

Employees who are good communicators develop a positive, can-do attitude.

© Myrleen Ferguson Cate/PhotoEdit

Negative Phrasings	Positive Phrasings
Your understanding was wrong.	Let us review the facts.
Your order cannot be shipped until Friday.	Your order will be shipped on Friday.
Your order for the mp3 player will be delayed; the item is not in stock.	Your mp3 player will be shipped direct from the factory and should arrive next week.
It is unfortunate you were unable to attend the meeting.	I look forward to seeing you at the next meeting.
You will not regret your decision.	You will be pleased with your decision.
A code is required to enter the wiki site.	Add your ideas to the wiki by entering this code.
You cannot be enrolled at UCSB until after December 31.	Your enrollment window at UCSB opens January 5.
I regret to advise that we must decline the refund request for your defective mower.	Our professional staff will repair your lawn mower.
The store is not open until 10 a.m. on Monday.	The store opens at 10 a.m. on Monday.

communication note

WORDINESS, OVERUSED WORDS, AND COMPLEX LANGUAGE

Does the following message communicate clearly?
You need to think outside the box and be cautiously optimistic that this process will be cutting edge. Communicate your implementation intentions and prioritize the minimal minutia that you deal with on a daily continuum.

Would this be an improvement?
Be creative in planning and optimistic that implementing this process will be successful. Share the plan with your staff, and find time for effective communication by reducing routine tasks.

Principle 5: Avoid Overused Words

NOTE 4.14
Overused words lose their effectiveness.

An **overused word** is one that loses effectiveness because it has been used too much in normal conversation or in written messages. Because you have heard them over and over, these words have become trite and uninteresting. Keep your message interesting by avoiding overused words such as these.

Overused Words and Phrases

actually	in denial	see ya
awesome	interface	slam dunk
been there; done that	it goes without saying	synergy
below the belt	lean and mean	talk to you later
bottom line	level playing field	user friendly
by leaps and bounds	like	wannabe
change agent	ok *or* okay	what's up
down to the wire	out of the loop	win-win
dude	paradigm	wow
get over it	razor thin	yeah
impact (as a verb)	really	you know

The message in the Communication Note above illustrates how wordiness, overused phrases, and pompous language make a message dull and difficult to understand.

Principle 6: Avoid Obsolete Words

NOTE 4.15
Obsolete words are pompous, dull, or stiff.

An **obsolete word** is one that is out-of-date, pompous, dull, or stiff. Business messages in past years used these formal, unnatural words and expressions, and they continue to appear in today's business messages. Everyday conversation does not use these words, and they should be deleted in business communication.

The use of obsolete words makes a written or oral message formal, stilted, and pompous. The following are examples of obsolete words and phrases that you should avoid:

Obsolete Words and Phrases

enclosed herewith	I hereby send
enclosed please find	in regard to
hereby advise	mind your p's and q's

(continued)

(continued)

Obsolete Words and Phrases

permit me to say	thanking you, I remain
permit us to remind	tower of strength
pleased to inform	trusting you will
regret to advise	we remain
take the liberty of	wish to advise
thanking you in advance	your kind favor

Obsolete expressions are stilted and unnatural. As you read the previous examples, you quickly realized that most people do not use obsolete words in their everyday conversations. However, some people use them in their writing or public speaking because they view a written message or a speech as formal. Such obsolete words should be avoided in all business messages. Conversational language communicates best with receivers.

Developing Sentences

In the first part of this chapter, you learned how to choose effective words. Now you are ready to study the principles that will guide you in combining those words into effective sentences. Businesspeople prefer concise, efficient, effective communication. Use clear, short sentences with active-voice verbs to emphasize your important points. Study the following principles for developing clear sentences.

Principle 1: Compose Clear Sentences

Word choice based on the principles discussed in the preceding sections will help you compose clear sentences. A **clear sentence** uses words that are understandable, precise, strong, and positive. In addition, clear sentences have **unity**; that is, they contain one main idea and have related words placed close to one another. Finally, clear sentences are grammatically correct.

GIVE SENTENCES UNITY

A sentence that has **sentence unity** communicates one main idea—one main thought. At times you may want to include supporting ideas in the same sentence. The general rule, however, is one thought, one sentence. If you have two main thoughts, construct two separate sentences. Examine these contrasting examples of sentences without unity and with unity:

Lacks Unity	Has Unity
International freshman students live on campus, and we have students enrolled from 12 different countries who will graduate this spring.	International freshman students live on campus. We have students enrolled from 12 countries who will graduate this spring.
Cell phone ring tones are popular; iTunes sells music, video, and ring tone downloads.	Cell phone ring tones are popular. iTunes sells music, video, and ring tone downloads.

In the first example, *living on campus* and *enrolled from 12 different countries* are related thoughts but not closely related. In the second example, the first part of the

LO 2

Discuss the elements that create clear, concise, and effective sentences.

NOTE 4.16
Use short, clear sentences; active voice; and appropriate emphasis.

NOTE 4.17
Clear sentences have understandable, precise, strong, and positive words.

NOTE 4.18
Clear sentences have unity.

sentence introduces a thought about the *popularity of ring tones*. The second part conveys the thought that *ring tone downloads are sold by iTunes*. In both examples, the relationship between the two ideas is not clearly stated or understood. Separating these two thoughts into two sentences makes the sentences easier to read and gives each separate sentence unity. However, if paragraphs were constructed for each of the two examples, the related but different thoughts would need additional words, phrases, or sentences that clearly link these thoughts. The last part of this chapter addresses paragraph unity and how to add transitional words to bridge related thoughts.

KEEP RELATED WORDS TOGETHER

NOTE **4.19**
Place related words together in sentences.

Words, phrases, or clauses that describe or limit other words, phrases, or clauses are **modifiers.** Modifiers should be placed in the sentence close to the words they modify. For sentence clarity, the word or words described or limited by the modifier must be obvious. Each of the following Unclear Relationship examples shows in italics both the modifier and word(s) that could be confused. This is followed by the question in the reader's mind.

Unclear Relationship	Clear Relationship
The *restaurant* served excellent *food;* *it* was only two years old. (Was the restaurant or the food two years old?)	The restaurant, which was only two years old, had excellent food.
Sue and Jim laid the *plans* on the table where *they* remained for two weeks. (The plans remained for two weeks or Sue and Jim remained for two weeks?)	The plans remained on the table for two weeks after Sue and Jim laid them there.
Ahenewa and *Mark only* lived in the neighborhood for *two years.* (Ahenewa and Mark were the only ones in the neighborhood for two years? or they only lived there—didn't work there, didn't socialize there, etc.)	Ahenewa and Mark lived in the neighborhood for only two years.

USE CORRECT GRAMMAR

NOTE **4.20**
Clear sentences are grammatically correct.

Clear sentences are grammatically correct. All parts of a sentence should agree. The subject and verb should agree in number—plural or singular. Pronouns should agree with their antecedents in three ways—number, gender, and clear relationship. A clear relationship between the pronoun and its **antecedent** (the word to which it refers) means that there is no question about which word in the sentence is the antecedent. Another important form of agreement is **parallelism**—using the same grammatical construction or word form for parts of sentences that serve the same purpose. Correct grammar is discussed in Business English Seminars A and B.

Grammatically correct sentences have agreement of subject and verb, agreement of pronoun and antecedent, and parallel structure of similar sentence components. The sections that follow illustrate each of these grammatical rules for sentences. Study these examples.

Agreement of Subject and Verb
The Tuesday evening comedy *shows are* my favorites. (plural subject, plural verb)
Josephine's *nephew* or *niece spends* each summer with her. (singular subject, singular verb)

Agreement of Pronoun and Antecedent

Each *student* expected an A grade on *his* or *her* essay. (singular antecedent, singular pronoun)

The alumni *organization* sent *its* members a monthly newsletter. (singular antecedent, singular pronoun)

Students expected *their* grades to be posted promptly. (plural antecedent, plural pronoun)

Catherine described *her* job interview. (feminine antecedent and pronoun)

Alberto and Juliana receive *their* safety training this week. (plural subject, plural antecedent, and plural pronoun; both genders and a generic gender pronoun)

In the Seattle Museum, I saw Asian *art* displayed in the main *lobby that* detailed daily life. (Unclear antecedent. Which one detailed daily life—the art or the lobby?)

In the main lobby of the Seattle Museum, I saw Asian *art that* detailed daily life. (Clear relationship between the pronoun and its antecedent)

Parallel Structure

The Children's Theatre offers a yearly activity agenda: It *has science exhibits, offers plays,* and *provides interactive technology experiences.* (parallel verb phrases—verb plus object)

Each department had a role in planning: *marketing estimated the size of the market, human resources projected personnel needs,* and *marketing prepared recruitment materials.* (parallel clauses)

The company president *asked for an audit, notified employees* to update accounts, and *called an accountant* to schedule the audit. (parallel verb phrases)

Managing costs, planning new products, and *implementing plans* are critical business functions. (verb phrases used as a compound subject)

Principle 2: Use Short Sentences

A short sentence is more effective than a long sentence. Generally, short sentences are easier to understand.

The average length of your sentences depends on your receiver's knowledge of the message content. For an average-level receiver, short sentences should range between 15 and 20 words. The following Communication Note gives a guide for sentence length. Generally, you should use sentences of longer-than-average length only in messages for receivers with a high degree of knowledge. For receivers who have less knowledge of the topic, use short, simple sentences.

Vary the length of your sentences to provide interest and to eliminate the dull, choppy effect of too many short sentences. At times, you need a long sentence to cover the main idea or the relationship of ideas, but be sure that the meaning is clear.

NOTE 4.21
Use short sentences. They are understandable.

NOTE 4.22
Vary sentence length for interest.

communication note

HOW LONG IS A SHORT SENTENCE?

- A sentence fragment may have *1 or more words.*
- Complete sentences usually have at least *2 words* (a subject and a verb).
- Short sentences will average *15 to 20 words.*
- Long sentences are *30 words or longer.*

Any sentence that is 30 words or longer is a long sentence. Examine it for clarity *and* eliminate unnecessary words. Read the sentence aloud to yourself to check it.

A **complete sentence** usually has at least two words—a subject and a verb—and expresses a complete thought. For example, *Paul laughed* is a complete sentence. An exception is a request or command. In request statements such as *Please close the door when you leave*, the subject *You* is not stated but is understood; therefore, this is a complete sentence. *You* is the subject, *close* is the verb, and the thought expressed is complete. *When I started my car* has a subject, *I*, and a verb, *started*, but is a sentence fragment because the thought is incomplete.

What a relief! is a fragment; this expression has no subject or verb, but the thought is complete. Other examples of fragments that express a complete thought are *Welcome!* and *Thank you for your interest in our product*. In informal business writing, sentence fragments that express a complete thought are acceptable. Business letters use a conversational tone, and sentence fragments beginning with *Thank you* or other similar expressions of a complete thought are used as appropriate for the message. Fragments expressing a complete thought can be used for special effect in bulletins or advertisements. **Fragments** look like a sentence followed by a period, a question mark, or an exclamation mark but either do not have a subject and verb or do not express a complete thought. In business messages, confine use of fragments to those expressing a complete thought used in an appropriate context.

Give preference to short sentences because they have several advantages. They are less complex and, therefore, easier to understand than long sentences. Short sentences are efficient. They take less time for the reader or the listener and are businesslike—concise, clear, and to the point. Long sentences can be shortened by omitting unnecessary words and by limiting sentence content to one major idea.

OMIT UNNECESSARY WORDS

NOTE 4.23
Compose short sentences
by omitting unnecessary
words.

An **unnecessary** or **redundant word** is one that is not essential to the meaning of the sentence. Clear and concise sentences are lean. They have only *essential* words. When composing sentences, you should omit unnecessary words. Such words are redundant. Eliminate unnecessary words that repeat the same or similar meaning. *Merge together* and *fair and equitable* are examples of words that duplicate meaning. Read your sentences carefully to eliminate unnecessary prepositions, prepositional phrases, and duplicative and other nonessential words. Compare these examples.

Wordy	Lean
The garden show this spring opens this week; there is a new theme this year called Flower Power.	The spring garden show opens this week with a new theme, Flower Power.
The principles of quality improvement rest on an underlying philosophy of quality that leads an organization to analyze its systems.	Organizations use the quality improvement principles to analyze their systems.
There is a considerable amount of data that lends support to the success of the organization.	Data support the organization's success.
Central Appalachia is broken into four regions that are distinct, serving all of the three states of Kentucky, Tennessee, and Virginia.	Central Appalachia has four distinct regions and serves Kentucky, Tennessee, and Virginia.

(continued)

(continued)

Wordy	Lean
I met the accountant on only one occasion.	I met the accountant once.
We would like to invite you to attend the graduation party.	We invite you to attend the graduation party.
Print out six copies of this report before tomorrow when I have to present the report to the board.	Print six copies of this report before my board presentation tomorrow.
He went up to my home where I live in the east end of the city.	He went to my home in the city's east end.

LIMIT CONTENT

As you will recall, clear sentences convey one main idea. If you have a sentence that is 30 words or longer, you may want to divide it into two or more sentences. Examine the unity of the sentence to see whether dividing it further is appropriate. Remember, you want just one thought unit for most sentences. Avoid beginning sentences with *There are* and *It is*. In most cases, rewording these sentences will limit content and eliminate unnecessary words.

NOTE 4.24
Limit content to achieve short sentences.

Excessive Sentence Content	Simplified Sentence Content
It is a fact that most people do not get enough sleep, probably because of work productivity demands plus handheld computer devices that they watch or listen to for nonstop diversion.	Most people do not get enough sleep. This may be due to stress and constant attention to handheld computer devices.
Airport security closed the Los Angeles airport down when an unidentified man who was wearing baggy clothing was singled out for more screening and fled from the screening area.	Airport security closed the Los Angeles airport when an unidentified man fled the screening area. The man, wearing baggy clothing, ran when selected for more screening.
Rising interest rates are going up; you can buy certificates of deposit with adjustable, changeable rates from your favorite bank or other FDIC insured financial institution.	Interest rates are rising. You can buy adjustable-rate certificates of deposit from any FDIC financial institution.

One technique for changing long sentences to short sentences is to change commas or semicolons to periods when possible. The preceding examples show this technique. Often phrases and dependent clauses can be modified so that they can stand alone as short sentences.

Principle 3: Prefer Active Voice in Sentences

Sentences using the active voice of the verb communicate more clearly, concisely, and forcefully than those in the passive voice. In the **active voice** the subject does the acting; in the **passive voice** the subject is acted upon. For example, *Gloria issued the teaching schedules* (active voice) becomes passive voice when the subject becomes the receiver of the action: *The teaching schedules were issued by Gloria.* The active voice emphasizes Gloria and the action.

NOTE 4.25
Active voice is clear, concise, and forceful.

The active voice is more direct, stronger, and more vigorous than the passive voice. The active voice usually requires fewer words and results in shorter, more understandable sentences. You will want to use active voice for most sentences. Look for the advantages of the active voice over the passive voice in these contrasting examples:

Passive	Active
The home was built in the late 1700s.	The Eli Jones family built the home in the late 1700s.
The $1,000 fine was paid by the guilty party.	The guilty party paid the $1,000 fine.
The flowers were cut for a bouquet by Sonja.	Sonja cut the flowers for a bouquet.
The brick fireplace was painted gray.	The owner painted the brick fireplace gray.

NOTE 4.26
Passive voice can be used to add variety or to de-emphasize ideas.

Although these examples clearly show the power, liveliness, and conciseness of the active voice, passive voice has appropriate uses. Use the passive voice when the subject (*who* or *what*) performing the action of the verb is unimportant or unknown. Also, passive voice can be used to de-emphasize negative or unpleasant ideas. For example, passive voice is appropriate when a customer's order is more important than who shipped it.

Active: The department store delivered the clothing on schedule.
Passive: The clothing was delivered on schedule.

Passive voice emphasizes the customer's order and reflects the you–viewpoint. Further, in the passive voice, the doer of the action—the vendor—is de-emphasized and appropriately left unnamed.

In the next example, you can see how to reduce a negative impression of a doer of the action by using passive voice and not naming the doer.

Active: The department store delivered your clothing late.
Passive: Your clothing was delivered late.

You can use passive voice to provide variety and interest in your messages. However, because of its advantages, active voice should be dominant in your business messages.

Principle 4: Give Sentences Appropriate Emphasis

Giving your sentences **appropriate emphasis** means emphasizing the important ideas and de-emphasizing the unimportant ideas. Every speaker or writer wants a particular message transmitted to the receiver. As you develop sentences in a message, ask yourself, "Should the main idea of this sentence be emphasized or de-emphasized?" Then design each sentence to give the appropriate emphasis.

NOTE 4.27
Use sentence design to emphasize important ideas.

You can emphasize or de-emphasize an idea in several ways: use length of sentence, use location within the sentence, use sentence structure, repeat key words, place emphasis on important points, be specific or general, use format, and use mechanical means. Each of these ways is discussed and illustrated in the following sections.

NOTE 4.28
Length: Short sentences emphasize; long sentences de-emphasize.

USE LENGTH

Short sentences emphasize content; long sentences de-emphasize content. Use short sentences to give your ideas emphasis. Compare these examples:

> The team plans to go to the meeting that will be held on Friday at 7 p.m.
> The team plans to attend the 7 p.m. Friday meeting.

The important content of the message—*the meeting*—receives emphasis in the short sentence. The longer version not only changes the main idea to a dependent clause but also includes unnecessary, distracting words.

USE LOCATION

Beginnings and endings of sentences are the locations of greatest emphasis. What ideas are stressed in these sentences?

> Larry received a raise.
> Larry's salary was raised to $42,000 per year.
> Larry received a raise because of his outstanding performance.

NOTE **4.29**
Location: The beginning and ending emphasize; the middle de-emphasizes.

The first and third sentences begin with Larry's name, emphasizing *Larry*. The first sentence also emphasizes *the raise* by placement at the end. The second sentence gives emphasis to *Larry's new salary*. Use of passive voice at the beginning and placement of the specific amount at the end give more emphasis to the amount. Finally, the third sentence gives the greatest emphasis to *Larry's outstanding performance*.

Sentence beginnings compete for attention with the words that follow them. Endings compete for attention with words that precede them. Words in the middle of sentences, however, have to compete with both the preceding and following words and, therefore, are de-emphasized. For example:

> Transfer to a new position at another facility offers an excellent opportunity for promotion.
> Potential for promotion is a benefit of transfer to another facility; this job change may create opportunities for a management position.

In the first sentence, location in the first and last parts of the sentence emphasizes *the transfer* and *opportunity for promotion*. The second sentence emphasizes *potential for promotion*, de-emphasizes *transfer*, and emphasizes career potential for *a management position*. Location is an excellent way to give appropriate emphasis.

USE SENTENCE STRUCTURE

A short, simple sentence gives the greatest emphasis to an idea. To show a relationship between ideas, emphasize the main ideas by placing them in independent clauses. De-emphasize other ideas by placing them in dependent clauses. The independent clause is similar to the short sentence; it can stand alone as a sentence. Dependent clauses are not complete thoughts; they do not make sense standing alone. See the following example. (Also, Business English Seminar B provides a discussion of sentence structure.)

NOTE **4.30**
Structure: Independent clauses emphasize; dependent clauses de-emphasize.

> The new position offers an excellent opportunity for advancement, although it requires a transfer to another facility. (emphasizes the advancement with the new position and de-emphasizes the transfer)

The two short sentences that follow give approximately the same emphasis to two main ideas.

> Work smarter and faster with technology.
> Health and income problems are the greatest fears of aging.

NOTE 4.31

Ideas share emphasis in a compound sentence.

If you want two ideas to share emphasis—each receiving a reduced amount—you can organize them into a compound sentence:

> Effa Manley was the first woman elected to the Baseball Hall of Fame; she was co-owner of the Newark Eagles.

Organizing these two ideas into one complex sentence, however, emphasizes one idea and de-emphasizes the other. This sentence structure arrangement is called **subordination**. Emphasize one idea by placing it in an independent clause; de-emphasize the other idea by placing it in the dependent clause. Examine the varying emphases in the following examples:

> Effa Manley was the first woman elected to the Baseball Hall of Fame because she was co-owner of the Newark Eagles.
>
> Effa Manley, who was the first woman elected to the Baseball Hall of Fame, was co-owner of the Newark Eagles.

The first example emphasizes *the election to the Baseball Hall of Fame* by placing it in an independent clause. *Co-owner of the Newark Eagles* is de-emphasized by its placement in the dependent clause. In the second sentence, the primary idea of *co-owner* gets the attention as an independent clause in the sentence, and *the first woman elected to the Baseball Hall of Fame* is de-emphasized in a dependent clause.

REPEAT KEY WORDS

NOTE 4.32

Repetition: Emphasize ideas by repeating key words.

Main ideas represented by key words can be emphasized by repeating those words within a sentence. Note the emphasis placed on the key word *connect*:

> *Connect* your business as easy as 1, 2, 3; *connect* your employees with cell phones.

Here is another example of emphasis through repetition of the same root word in different forms:

> An extended-stay hotel makes you feel at *home;* this hotel is your *home* away from *home.*

Repetition of key words also provides coherence and movement in a sentence. Coherence and thought flow are discussed later in this chapter.

TELL THE RECEIVER WHAT IS IMPORTANT

NOTE 4.33

Explicitness: Tell the receiver what is important or unimportant.

You can tell your receiver that an idea is important or unimportant by your word choice. For example:

> High grades and high SAT scores are *essential* for acceptance by a top university.
> The theme of the movie was *less important* than the conclusion.

Of course, there are many words and constructions that indicate the importance of an idea. You can refer to ideas with such words as *significant, of (no) consequence, (not) a concern, high (or low) priority, (not) critical, fundamental,* and *(non)essential.* Your thesaurus will be helpful in choosing words to tell your receiver that an idea is important or unimportant.

BE SPECIFIC OR GENERAL

NOTE 4.34

Specification: Specific words emphasize; general words de-emphasize.

Another way to give appropriate emphasis is to use specific words to emphasize ideas and to use general words to de-emphasize ideas. Here are examples of how this works:

Specific: Tom bought a new *yellow Hummer.*
General: Tom bought a new *car.*
Specific: Roberta has *a 3.9 grade point average.*
General: Roberta has *good grades.*

USE FORMAT

The way you arrange and punctuate a sentence gives emphasis to selected ideas. One way to highlight an idea is to separate it from other information in the sentence. Consider this example:

> Your paper won an award for excellence—congratulations!

"Congratulations" stands out because it is set off with a dash and an exclamation point. Dashes, colons, and exclamation points are strong punctuation marks and can be used to emphasize ideas. Ideas can be de-emphasized by setting them off with commas or parentheses, which are weaker punctuation marks. Ideas set off from the sentence with commas or parentheses are explanations that could be omitted without changing the meaning of the sentence. These ideas add detail to the sentence but are not essential to complete the main thought.

A vertical list attracts more attention than a list of items simply set off by commas in regular sentence format. This example shows how you can emphasize points by putting them in a numbered list. Also, letters or bullets may be used with a list.

> The major conclusions of the study suggested that online delivery of instruction is most effective if these elements are present:
>
> 1. An orientation session
> 2. Interaction among students
> 3. Frequent feedback from the instructor

NOTE 4.35
Format: Emphasize ideas with punctuation and lists.

USE MECHANICAL MEANS

You can emphasize ideas through mechanical means in a variety of ways. You can underline, *italicize,* or use **boldface** type. You can use a different color to highlight selected ideas. The previous sentence, the illustrations, and the margin notes in this book are examples of effective use of color. Other mechanical means include font size, font style, uppercase letters, bullets, arrows, and circles.

Overuse of format or mechanical means to emphasize ideas will distract attention and reduce their effectiveness. Limit their use in letters and memorandums to special situations. The use of mechanical means to emphasize ideas is more common in advertisements, reports, and visual aids.

You can emphasize and de-emphasize ideas as you develop effective sentences. Applying and practicing the principles described in this section will help you strengthen your communication skills.

NOTE 4.36
Mechanics: Emphasize with underlining, type size and font, color, or other means.

Forming Paragraphs

Organizing sentences into meaningful paragraphs is an important part of composing a message. Paragraphs help your receiver understand the message and its intent. You can form effective paragraphs by following five basic principles of business communication. These principles will guide you in determining paragraph length, unity, organization, emphasis, and coherence.

LO 3

Develop clear, concise, logical, coherent, and effective paragraphs.

NOTE 4.37
Paragraphs help organize the receiver's thoughts.

communication note

HOW LONG IS A SHORT PARAGRAPH?

Business Letters and Memos
- A short paragraph can have *1 line.*
- Short paragraphs will average *4 to 5 lines.*
- Long paragraphs are *8 lines or more.*

Business Reports
- A short paragraph can have *2 lines.*
- Short paragraphs will average *6 to 7 lines.*
- Long paragraphs are *12 lines or more.*

Principle 1: Use Short Paragraphs

NOTE 4.38
Use short paragraphs. They are easier to understand.

You will want to use short paragraphs in your business messages. A **short paragraph** helps your receivers organize their thoughts, increases understanding of the message, and appears more inviting to the receiver than a long paragraph. Long paragraphs are more complex, more difficult to read, and harder to comprehend than short paragraphs. Receivers are more likely to read short paragraphs than long paragraphs.

NOTE 4.39
In letters and memos, paragraphs should average four to five lines.

In business letter and memo writing, short paragraphs average *four to five lines.* If any paragraph in a letter or memo is eight lines or more, it is long and should be examined carefully to see whether it can be shortened or divided. Usually, business letters and memos are read quickly, and short paragraphs aid receiver understanding.

NOTE 4.40
In reports, paragraphs should average six to seven lines.

Business reports are likely to be studied carefully, and the paragraphs can be somewhat longer. In business report writing, short paragraphs should average *six to seven lines.* Twelve lines or more in any paragraph of a report is a signal that it is long, and its unity (see Principle 2) should be examined carefully. Criteria for a short paragraph for business letters, memos, and reports are shown in the Communication Note above. These guidelines for the lengths of paragraphs in business messages are recommended averages and should vary, as needed, to accommodate content and to promote reader interest.

NOTE 4.41
First and last paragraphs are usually shorter for greater emphasis.

In most business letters, memos, and reports, the first and last paragraphs are shorter than the middle paragraphs. Often the first and last paragraphs in letters and memos are one to three lines long and consist of only one or two sentences. In reports, the first and last paragraphs may be somewhat longer. Short opening and closing paragraphs are inviting to the reader. They add emphasis to the message's beginning and ending ideas. Parts 3 and 4 of this book include several examples of letters, memos, and reports. Notice the paragraph lengths in these written messages as you study the chapters in those parts.

Principle 2: Give Paragraphs Unity

NOTE 4.42
Clear paragraphs have unity.

Paragraphs should have unity. **Paragraph unity** means that all the sentences in a paragraph relate to one topic. The topic should be covered adequately; however, if the paragraph becomes too long, it should be divided into two or more logical parts. Examine the following paragraphs:

Lacks Unity
USA Today surveyed 1,732 executives to ask if they would choose a completely different field if they could start their career over. The survey population came from a

variety of organizations. Slightly over half, 51 percent, said "Yes." The margin of error is plus or minus 3 percentage points. Thirty-four percent said "Maybe," and 25 percent said "No."

Has Unity

USA Today surveyed 1,732 executives about their career choice. They were asked if they would choose a completely different career if they were starting over. Responses showed that slightly over half, 51%, said "Yes"; 34%, "Maybe"; and 25%, "No." The survey margin of error was + or − 3%.

Giving unity to paragraphs is sometimes more difficult than the preceding examples imply. The following example lacks unity. Can you determine why?

Lacks Unity

The College of Business has proposed that all professors submit their professional development plans online. The new procedure will require all plans to follow the same format. Using the same format will save time for reviewers of professional development plans. All College of Business faculty members must publish one refereed journal article per year and make two presentations at professional conferences.

Did you note that the fourth sentence does not relate directly to the paragraph's main topic? If you did, you are right. The main topic is *submitting professional development plans online*. The fourth sentence shifted the topic to *publishing a refereed article and making presentations*. The fourth sentence is a separate topic that requires its own paragraph or paragraphs.

Principle 3: Organize Paragraphs Logically

Paragraphs can be organized logically using one of two basic plans: the direct plan (deductive approach) or the indirect plan (inductive approach). In the **direct plan** the main idea is presented in the first sentence of the paragraph, and details follow in succeeding sentences. In the **indirect plan** details are presented first, and the main idea comes later in the paragraph.

NOTE 4.43
Organize paragraphs logically using direct or indirect plans.

The content determines which plan—direct or indirect—you will use. Positive news and neutral news can best be presented using the direct plan. Getting directly to the main point and following it with details helps orient the reader to the content.

NOTE 4.44
Present positive or neutral news using the direct plan.

Negative news or persuasive news can be presented best by using the indirect plan. This approach enables message details at the beginning to pave the way for an unpleasant main point, an unfavorable recommendation, or a request for action.

NOTE 4.45
Use the indirect plan to persuade or present negative news.

The sentence that presents the main point of a paragraph is the **topic sentence.** The topic sentence announces the main idea to the reader, or it summarizes the content of the main idea. In the direct plan, the topic sentence is like a headline and will be the first sentence, as it is in this paragraph. With the indirect plan, the topic sentence will be placed later in the paragraph.

NOTE 4.46
The topic sentence states the main point of the paragraph.

As a rule, the first sentence in a paragraph should be either the topic sentence or a transitional sentence. How to provide transition (movement) in a first sentence will be explained later, under Principle 5. Unless there is an important reason to locate it elsewhere in the paragraph, the topic sentence should be placed first in business messages.

NOTE 4.47
The first sentence should be topical or transitional.

The Communication Note on the following page gives examples of the two basic plans. The topic sentences are italicized to show their location in each paragraph.

communication note

Direct Plan (Topic Sentence First)
The NCAA basketball tournament brings March Madness! Excitement builds for fans, coaches, and teams as March approaches.

Indirect Plan (Topic Sentence Within)
Gain the edge! *Call 1.888.555.2387 and enroll in the International Training Certificate program.* The International Training Certificate program offers certification for conducting business with

people from (a) Asian cultures, (b) European cultures, and (c) Hispanic cultures.

Indirect Plan (Topic Sentence Last)
Spring is just around the corner. This means that vacation time is near. When you plan your vacation this year, think of us. Let us send you the "Summer Vacation Planner's Guide." *Call the Newport Coast Travel Agency at 949.555.1234.*

In summary, paragraphs can be organized logically using the direct or the indirect plan. Generally, the direct plan is recommended for good news or neutral news, and the indirect plan is recommended for bad news or persuasion.

Principle 4: Give Paragraphs Appropriate Emphasis

NOTE 4.48
Use paragraph design to give appropriate emphasis.

As you will recall from this chapter's section on sentences, giving *appropriate emphasis* means emphasizing the important ideas and de-emphasizing the unimportant ideas. Many of the same ways for giving appropriate emphasis to sentences apply to giving appropriate emphasis to paragraph content. The Communication Note at the bottom of the page summarizes applicable ways to give emphasis.

Principle 5: Provide Paragraph Coherence

NOTE 4.49
Smooth thought flow provides paragraph coherence.

Providing **coherence** between and within paragraphs means having a smooth thought flow from one sentence or paragraph to the next. You want to encourage your receiver's thoughts to move smoothly and logically through the message. The primary way to ensure coherence is to organize paragraphs logically using the direct or indirect plans discussed in Principle 3.

communication note

Length	Use short paragraphs to emphasize content; use long paragraphs to de-emphasize content.	**Explicitness**	Emphasize an idea by telling your reader that it is important.
Location	Place ideas at the beginning or ending of paragraphs to give the greatest emphasis. The middle of a paragraph is the location of least emphasis.	**Format**	Emphasize ideas by arranging them in lists or using wider margins.
Repetition	Repeat key words throughout the paragraph to emphasize the ideas those words represent.	**Mechanics**	Emphasize ideas by using mechanical means: underlining, boldface, type color or size, type style, uppercase letters, bullets, arrows, or circles.

communication note

TRANSITIONAL WORDS BRIDGE IDEAS

Contrasts:	but, however, by contrast, nevertheless, on the other hand, on the one hand, from another viewpoint	**Emphasis:**	significantly, primarily, most importantly, particularly, especially, in fact, indeed, above all
Examples:	for example, to illustrate, for instance, that is, as follows, like, in illustration	**Conclusions:**	therefore, thus, so, consequently, as a result, accordingly, hence
Sequence:	first, second, third; one, two, three; also, in addition, finally; next, then, finally; to sum up; in conclusion	**Exclusions:**	except, neither . . . nor, except that, all but, except for, all except
		Additions:	in addition, furthermore, also, and, similarly, moreover, as well as, too

Also, you can use transitional words and tie-in sentences to provide coherence between and within paragraphs. Hints for successfully adopting these latter suggestions follow.

USE TRANSITIONAL WORDS

A **transitional word** is a helpful bridge from one idea to the next. Transitional words help receivers see where you are leading them, why you are leading them there, and what to expect when they get there. Transitional words provide coherence by logically linking ideas.

NOTE 4.50
Provide coherence with transitional words.

For example, suppose you present an idea in one sentence, and you want to expand on that idea in the next sentence. By using transitional words such as *in addition, furthermore,* and *also* at the beginning of the second sentence, you help receivers see the relationship between ideas. The following example shows this kind of bridging between two sentences:

> **Adding Information**
> The president announced the new slate of officers. *In addition,* she discussed organizational goals for the year.

Transitional words provide coherence for different situations. The Communication Note above gives examples.

USE TIE-IN SENTENCES

A **tie-in sentence** helps your receiver move from one aspect of the subject to the next. When using the tie-in sentence technique for coherence, repeat the same subject one or more times. To develop tie-in sentences, you can paraphrase the subject, repeat key words that describe the subject, or use pronouns that refer to the subject. Examples of tie-in sentences using these approaches are as follows:

NOTE 4.51
Provide coherence with tie-in sentences.

> **Paraphrasing:** *The student group* asked for a delay in the assignment due date. *These students* explained that the original due date conflicted with final exams.
> **Repeating Key Words:** *Raising funds* for scholarships is a worthy activity. However, *raising funds* requires an extensive time commitment.
> **Using Pronoun Reference:** *Students* submitting applications to MBA programs must register for the GMAT test by April 1. *They* will receive confirmation of *their* registration by May 1.

Using Unbiased Language

The use of unbiased language is a final and important consideration in the composition of messages. Fair and balanced treatment of all individuals regardless of race, gender, culture, age, ability, religion, or socioeconomic status is essential in a democracy. Such treatment is vital to creating and sustaining favorable human relationships.

Avoid words that reflect unfavorably on any group or individual. The use of such language will offend not only those persons referred to in the message but also the message receiver or others who respect people, regardless of differences. To increase your effectiveness as a communicator, analyze your messages to ensure language is unbiased.

Avoid Gender-Biased Language

Using unbiased gender language is a special challenge because of the structure of the English language. The English language implies stereotyping of males and females because of (a) the generic use of masculine singular pronouns—pronouns used to represent both men and women; (b) the generic use of the word *man*; and (c) the use of certain words, phrases, and constructions that tend to stereotype a group or an individual.

Some English-language listeners and readers subconsciously tend to picture a male when words such as *man, he,* or *chairman* are used. This is true even though such word use generically represents both men and women. Avoid stereotyped images in your messages. The examples that follow suggest possible language alternatives to gender stereotyping.

Biased	Unbiased
chairman	chair, moderator, group leader
policeman	police officer
salesman	sales agent, representative, sales associate
businessman	executive, businessperson, manager
executives and their wives	executives and their spouses
mankind	humanity, people, human race
manned	staffed
mailman	mail carrier, letter carrier
Each chairman must submit his program to the membership committee.	Each chair must submit a program to the membership committee.
When a student carries a computer to class, she is able to take notes easily.	When students carry computers to class, they are able to take notes easily. (*Note that the pronoun and antecedent must agree in number.*)
If an employee is late, give him one warning.	An employee who is late should receive one warning.
the ladies and the men	the women and the men, the ladies and the gentlemen
Gentlemen: or Dear Sirs: (letter salutations)	Ladies and Gentlemen: (or avoid salutation by using the Simplified letter style shown in Chapter 6)

Avoid Other Biased Language

To treat people of different races and cultures in a bias-free manner, avoid all negative stereotypes of any group. Chapter 2 gave guidelines for avoiding stereotypical language. A key point in respecting diversity is to think of people as individuals. Avoid categorizing groups of people as having specific common characteristics and do not use terms that set them apart from others. Unless a description of the individual or group is essential to the message meaning, omit references to race, religion, age, or disability. For example, leave out the terms in italics in the following sentences: "The *Jewish* investor from New York City funded the construction of the regional mall." "The *white* teacher spoke to the inner-city youths." "The *old* man exercised in the mall."

NOTE 4.54
Avoid negative stereotypes.

If reference to race or ethnic background is required, use terms that do not have unfavorable associations. Connotations of words sometimes change, so learn the preferred term if reference to race, ethnicity, age, or disability becomes necessary. Individuals from Mexico may prefer the term *Hispanic* as an ethnic description. *Senior* is usually preferable to the terms *elderly* or *old person*. When referring to a person with a disability, use people-first language and focus on the person, not the disability. Use *patient with AIDS* instead of *AIDS patient* and *person with mental illness* instead of *mentally ill person*. In most cases, these categorical designations are not essential to the meaning of the message and should not be used.

NOTE 4.55
Use no language that belittles, offends, or embarrasses other people.

Composing with Style

The most effective communicators use the principles that have been reviewed in this chapter. You, too, should find them effective. One other important dimension of your communication is your personality. Once you have mastered the basic principles for writing described in this chapter, give attention to developing your unique writing style. Your writing and speaking should reflect the interesting person that you are. As you become proficient in writing, your style will emerge.

LO 5
Apply your own composing style to personalize your messages.

NOTE 4.56
Compose messages that reflect *you*.

Be yourself. Use words and combinations of words that not only are understood by your receiver but also reveal who you are—words that give life and distinction to your message. There are many combinations of words that will send the same basic message to your receiver. Use the words that communicate clearly and concisely and that reflect your personality.

One of America's outstanding orators, Patrick Henry (1736–1799), showed what could be accomplished with style. The first sentence shows how he might have made one of his famous statements; the second sentence is what he actually said:

> **Not This:** If I can't have freedom, then I would rather not live.
> **But This:** Give me liberty, or give me death!

One of the leaders in advocating full rights for women, Susan B. Anthony (1820–1906), was extremely effective in awakening the American nation to inequities based on gender. Contrast the way she might have expressed her basic belief in equality for women with the way she actually expressed it:

> **Not This:** There is no reason to give women fewer rights than we give men.
> **But This:** Men, their rights and nothing more; women, their rights and nothing less.

Another powerful communicator who moved Americans, Martin Luther King, Jr. (1929–1968), used the principles of communication coupled with his own unique

communication note

When composing the message, did I . . .
- Choose understandable words?
- Use specific, precise words?
- Choose strong words?
- Emphasize positive words?
- Avoid overused words?
- Avoid obsolete words?
- Compose clear sentences?

- Use short sentences?
- Prefer active voice in sentences?
- Give ideas appropriate emphasis in sentences?
- Use short paragraphs?
- Develop paragraph unity and coherence?
- Organize paragraphs logically?
- Give ideas appropriate emphasis in paragraphs?
- Avoid biased language?

selection of words. What he could have said and what he did say are sharply contrasted in the following illustration:

Not This: It is hard for others to hold you down if you never give them the chance.
But This: A man can't ride your back unless it's bent.

Finally, from another effective writer and speaker, John F. Kennedy (1917–1963), we have this contrast in what could have been said and what was said:

Not This: Do not inquire about what you can get the government to do for you; instead find out what you can do for the government.
But This: Ask not what your country can do for you; ask what you can do for your country.

Effective communicators give thought and time to what they say and write. You, too, with study and effort, can improve your ability to be an effective communicator in your professional career and your personal life. Remember to use the you–viewpoint, apply the principles of business communication, and be yourself—you will then be a powerful business communicator.

The checklist in the Communication Note above will help you use the principles of business communication. When drafting and revising messages, refer to this list to be sure you have used each principle.

Summary of Learning Objectives

LO 1   ***Identify words that your receiver(s) will understand and that will elicit the intended response.***

Words are the smallest units of messages, and you will want to choose effective words for your messages. The six principles of choosing words are (a) choose understandable words; (b) use specific, precise words; (c) choose strong words; (d) emphasize positive words; (e) avoid overused words; and (f) avoid obsolete words. The two most valuable resources for the business communicator are the dictionary and the thesaurus. Remember to have both a hard copy and an electronic copy of each.

Discuss the elements that create clear, concise, and effective sentences.

LO 2

Businesspeople prefer concise, efficient, effective communication. Therefore, you will want to use clear, short sentences that use active voice verbs and that give appropriate emphasis to important ideas. The four principles of developing sentences are (a) compose clear, grammatically correct sentences with unity and clear relationships between words and ideas; (b) use short sentences because they are more understandable than long sentences; (c) use active voice in sentences and clearly identify the subject doing the action; and (d) give your sentences appropriate emphasis using sentence length, location, structure, key word repetition, format, and other sentence design elements.

Develop clear, concise, logical, coherent, and effective paragraphs.

LO 3

Combining sentences into paragraphs is an important part of composing a message. Paragraph organization provides smooth thought flow and helps the receiver understand the message. The five principles for developing effective paragraphs are (a) use short paragraphs because they are easy to understand; (b) give paragraphs unity, which means that all the sentences in a paragraph relate to one topic; (c) organize paragraphs logically using the direct or indirect plan; (d) give paragraphs appropriate emphasis by stressing the important ideas and de-emphasizing less important ideas; and (e) provide for smooth thought flow and paragraph coherence.

Use appropriate alternatives to ensure unbiased language in messages.

LO 4

Message analysis includes ensuring unbiased language for fair and balanced treatment of all individuals regardless of race, gender, culture, age, ability, religion, or socioeconomic status. You will want to avoid all words that have unfavorable denotations or connotations in their reflection on any individuals.

Apply your own composing style to personalize your messages.

LO 5

The most effective business communicators use the principles that have been reviewed in this chapter. There is one other important dimension of your communication—your personality. Use words and combinations of words that not only are understood by your receiver but also reveal who you are—words that give style and distinction to your message.

Questions for Discussion and Review

1. Define the KISS principle of business communication and discuss the advantages of its use. (Objective 1)
2. Explain how a dictionary and a thesaurus can help you be a more effective communicator. (Objective 1)
3. Define "technical words" and explain how you would make decisions about their use in your business messages. (Objective 1)

4. Give three examples of vague or abstract words and how they could be made more specific. (Objective 1)
5. Describe five characteristics of grammatically correct sentences. (Objective 2)
6. Why are short sentences preferred in business communication? How can long sentences be shortened? (Objective 2)
7. Discuss when to use active voice and when to use passive voice in sentences. Write a sentence in passive voice and then change the sentence to active voice. (Objective 2)
8. Explain why a sender should use short paragraphs in business messages. Tell what the average length of short paragraphs should be for (a) letters and memos and (b) reports. (Objective 3)
9. Discuss why and how unbiased language should be used in business messages. (Objective 4)
10. How can you follow the principles of business communication in your composing efforts and still reflect your own personality in your messages? (Objective 5)

Application Exercises

TECHNOLOGY

Technology. For each principle of business communication listed, follow the directions given. Keep the basic message meaning in each of the exercises, and use examples that are different from those in this chapter. Use a dictionary and a thesaurus to assist you in these exercises. Assume that your receiver is a high school graduate with a tenth- or eleventh-grade vocabulary level and no particular technical expertise. E-mail your responses to your instructor.

Principles of Word Usage
Principle 1: Choose Understandable Words (Objective 1)
1. **Select simple words.** Use an online dictionary or word processing thesaurus to select simple, more understandable words to replace these difficult words: (a) mesmerize, (b) exemplary, (c) garner, (d) protocol, (e) decorum, (f) stoic, (g) adversary, (h) jeopardy, (i) segregate, (j) impervious, (k) beguile, (l) impeccable, (m) propriety, (n) pulverize, (o) sequester.
2. **Use short words.** Use a print or electronic thesaurus or dictionary to select short words to replace these long words: (a) whimsical, (b) facsimile, (c) consolidate, (d) reproduction, (e) reasonable, (f) confederate, (g) vacillation, (h) prerogative, (i) clandestine, (j) amalgamate, (k) representation, (l) incorporate, (m) surreptitious, (n) lackadaisical, (o) capacitate.
3. **Use appropriate nontechnical words.** Use an online or print dictionary to select nontechnical words to replace each of these technical words: (a) dividend, (b) prosthesis, (c) equity, (d) hypothesis, (e) asset, (f) invoice, (g) assessment, (h) tabloid, (i) flyleaf, (j) debug, (k) amplify, (l) emporium, (m) generate, (n) chronicle, (o) matriculate.

Principle 2: Use Specific Words (Objective 1)
Select specific words to replace these vague words: (a) book, (b) early, (c) building, (d) equipment, (e) nice, (f) flower, (g) soon, (h) early, (i) transportation, (j) periodically, (k) occasionally, (l) tree, (m) airline, (n) slow, (o) late.

Principle 3: Prefer Strong Words (Objective 1)
COLLABORATIVE

Teamwork. Work with another student to select strong words to replace these weak words: (a) let go, (b) warm, (c) inexpensive, (d) request, (e) suggest, (f) refrain, (g) injure, (h) big, (i) decline, (j) resist.

Principle 4: Emphasize Positive Words (Objective 1)
List five positive words that would be good to use in messages and five negative words a sender should avoid using.

Principle 5: Avoid Overused Words (Objectives 1 and 2)
Write three sentences with each one including an overused word or phrase. Rewrite the sentences substituting different words or phrases that have the same meaning but are not trite from overuse.

Principle 6: Avoid Obsolete Words (Objectives 1, 2, and 3)
TECHNOLOGY

Technology. Rewrite the following e-mail replacing the obsolete words or phrases, using effective sentence construction, and using the direct plan of organization.

Attached please find a copy of notes from the conference on the global economy that I attended last week. I am taking the liberty of sending this to you because I wish to advise you of the changes that are taking place. Permit me to remind you that if we don't watch our p's and q's in this country, the United States will not continue to be a trend setter for the world economy. Labor is cheaper in countries such as China, India, and Russia than in the U.S., and as many as 70 percent of our jobs could be completed in another country because of digital transferability. Trusting you are well, I remain

Joetta Branstetter

Principles of Effective Sentences

Principle 1: Compose Clear Sentences (Objective 2)

1. **Give sentences unity.** Rewrite the following long sentences making them concise and understandable. If needed, divide the content into more than one sentence to express only one main thought in each sentence.
   a. The art show is scheduled to be given on November 14 if all art is submitted in a timely fashion; however, if the artists submit their work late, we may have to reschedule the show for a date at sometime later in the future but only time will tell.
   b. There are 3.6 billion people from China, India, and Russia who potentially will become part of the free enterprise system, and this will make a fewer number of jobs available for high school graduates in the United States.
2. **Keep related words together.** Revise the following sentences to show a clear relationship between the modifiers and the words they modify.
   a. Emilio's CAT scan was read by a radiologist in India because he could send it during evening hours.
   b. The software needs upgrading for our office because it is old.
   c. The fax machine needed repair which was purchased last year.
   d. Postal mail is losing customers to e-mail because it is slower.
   e. The newspapers fell through the bars because they were wet.

Principle 2: Use Short Sentences (Objective 2)

Shorten the following sentences by omitting unnecessary words and limiting content. Divide the content into more than one sentence if necessary.

1. We received your letter of January 15 on company letterhead and responded to it in as quick a fashion as possible.
2. As head of the human resources department, Mr. Srinivas was happy to have been asked and have the opportunity to be a part of an interview team for applicants for the new position.
3. Our services include a logistic audit to evaluate your transportation department and warehouse operation, and the purpose of the audit is to improve your capacity to get your products to market as quickly as possible.
4. Our goal is to affect your bottom line directly in a positive manner.
5. I will call you within the next several days to see when we might schedule an exploratory meeting.
6. The prices that are for the nonfat variety of milk are going up in cost.

Principle 3: Prefer Active Voice in Sentences (Objective 2)

Change the verbs in the following sentences from passive voice to active voice.

1. A lecture must be prepared by the professor.
2. The building was constructed over three years.
3. Proposals are to be prepared in triplicate.
4. The information was faxed to Brunswick Company on Thursday by Cindy Greene.
5. The cross-country race was won by Liz Morse.

Principle 4: Give Sentences Appropriate Emphasis (Objective 2)

Teamwork. Work with another student to create two sentences for each situation.

COLLABORATIVE

1. **Use length.** You want to help students at a local high school understand the importance of performing well on their upcoming ACT test for college admission. Express this idea in a sentence giving emphasis by sentence length.

2. **Use location.** Write a sentence that uses location to emphasize the importance of effective inter-personal relationships to job success.

3. **Use sentence structure.** Write one or more sentences to tell members of a school jazz band that their application to perform in a parade at Disneyland has not been accepted. Use sentence structure to de-emphasize the *no* in your sentence(s). Assume that you are the public relations director at Disneyland.

4. **Global. Repeat key words.** Write a sentence that repeats key words to emphasize that communication technology helps create a global society.

5. **Be specific or general.** Be general instead of specific in writing a sentence that de-emphasizes the grade received on your chemistry final examination.

6. **Use format.** Use format in a sentence to emphasize the number of students in your graduating class who will continue their education.

7. **Use mechanical means.** Use mechanical means in a sentence to emphasize the importance of attending a business seminar on job interviews.

Principles of Paragraph Development

Principle 1: Use Short Paragraphs (Objective 3)

Write a four- to five-line opening paragraph of a business letter or e-mail for each situation below.

    a. Ask for a refund for a book that you are returning because it was damaged in shipment.

    b. Thank a customer for prompt payment of each month's invoice. Assume the customer has been buying from your department store for five years.

    c. Introduce yourself as the new regional sales representative for a book company.

    d. Request a personal leave day to attend the funeral of a close friend.

    e. Ask your supervisor for a transfer to a different work location because of an allergy to potted plants located in your present work area.

Principle 2: Give Paragraphs Unity (Objective 3)

Indicate the sentence that does not belong in each of the following paragraphs:

1. Business communication courses offer students a chance to strengthen a critical skill—effective communication. Managers say that job success depends on strong communication skills. They list these specific skills as critical: developing messages from the you–viewpoint, delegating responsibility, and providing constructive feedback. However, recognition of managerial achievement requires budgeting and planning for the future.

2. Colleges are building more classrooms and hiring more professors to serve an increasing student enrollment. The number of students entering college is so large it is referred to as Tidal Wave 2. Over the next ten years, enrollment projections predict a 25 percent increase in college applicants. College students who participate in clubs and organizations are more likely to graduate than other students.

Principle 3: Organize Paragraphs Logically (Objective 3)

Using the direct plan, indicate the most logical order of these two groups of sentences by listing their letters in that order:

1.   **a.** Economic competitiveness drives school reform.

    b. Schools need to upgrade and integrate strong math and science skills in the curriculum.

    c. All content areas should improve reading skills.

    d. A competitive workforce must have ability to read technical manuals, perform basic math calculations, and apply science skills in a work setting.

2.   **a.** The facts in your request clearly supported your position.

    b. Your request to attend the conference is approved.

    c. Report these expenses to me when you return.

    d. Please keep a careful record of your travel expenses.

Principle 4: Give Paragraphs Appropriate Emphasis (Objective 3)

1. Create a paragraph that emphasizes the importance of getting a college education and de-emphasizes the time commitment that is required.

2. Create a paragraph that emphasizes the importance of having a computer connected to the Internet for your homework and de-emphasizes the cost of purchasing Internet service and computer hardware.

Principle 5: Provide Paragraph Coherence (Objective 3)

Using the indirect plan, indicate the most coherent order for these sentences by listing their letters in that order:

1. **a.** Why should you join the National Business Education Association?
   b. Don't wait. Join NBEA today!
   c. You will receive valuable publications.
   d. In addition, you can exchange ideas with others in your field of study.
2. **a.** The evening meal is a perfect time for families to talk and share events of the day.
   b. Therefore, it will happen only if family members make having one meal together a priority.
   c. Busy lives leave little time for families to eat dinner together.
   d. Family members get support and help from being together.

Comprehensive Exercise 1

Teamwork. Form a group of two or three students, and use your creativity to rewrite the following sentences. While retaining the basic meaning of the original version, draw on your own unique personalities to word the revised versions. Submit your rewritten sentences to your instructor. (Objective 5)

1. Communication skills are essential for success in business.
2. Using the Internet enables communication with the world.
3. Building teamwork doesn't come easy; everyone has to give and take.
4. Cell phones both remove us from people and link us to people.
5. Music on the go is a new way to relax—or is it?
6. Positive relationships take work, attention, and trust.
7. When does higher education become hire education?
8. Financial gains and losses on the stock market come from a willingness to take risks.
9. Learning a foreign language helps you understand your native language.
10. Ability, motivation, expectations, and opportunity come together for successful people.

Comprehensive Exercise 2

Change the language to improve the following sentences to ensure unbiased references to race, gender, culture, age, or disability. (Objective 4)

1. Jack is confined to a wheelchair. (*Hint:* Avoid emphasizing the limitation of the disability.)
2. A company owned by a 65-year-old white woman earned a million dollars last year. (*Hint:* Avoid emphasizing age, race, and gender unless they are essential to the main point of the message.)
3. The exercise program was developed for handicapped people. (*Hint:* Avoid emphasizing the disability.)
4. A young Asian man was arrested for leaving the scene of an accident. (*Hint:* Avoid mentioning nationality when it is not essential to the message.)
5. This is obviously man's work. (*Hint:* Avoid gender-biased language.)
6. The student having difficulty with math should ask his instructor for help. (*Hint:* Avoid language that is gender biased or implies a limitation for one sex.)
7. Dear Sirs: Please accept my application for the position as human resource manager. (*Hint:* Avoid language that is gender biased or limiting.)

Comprehensive Exercise 3

Principles for Choosing Words, Developing Sentences, and Forming Paragraphs

Teamwork. Using unbiased gender language is a special challenge because of the structure of the English language. Form a group of four or five students and develop a list of ten biased words or word phrases and the unbiased alternatives. Develop a sentence using each of the unbiased alternatives for these words or word phrases.

`TECHNOLOGY`

1. **Technology.** Send an e-mail to your instructor explaining why you took this class. Apply the communication principles for word selection, sentence construction, and paragraph development that you studied in this chapter.

`TECHNOLOGY`

2. **Technology.** Use an Internet search engine or a library website to locate and read an article about sentence or paragraph construction. Plan and write a short essay that describes what you learned. Present a two-minute oral report to the class.

`TECHNOLOGY`

3. **Technology.** Use the Internet and a search engine or library website to locate an article about business letter writing. After reading the article, send an e-mail to your teacher giving the title, author, date, source, and a paragraph that rates the article as Excellent, Good, Fair, or Poor and explains your rating. Construct your paragraph using writing principles studied in this chapter for word choice and sentence and paragraph development.

Web exercises to accompany this chapter are available at **www.thomsonedu.com/ bcomm/krizan.**

MESSAGE ANALYSIS

The following message follows the direct plan of organization. Rewrite it using the indirect plan, a positive tone, the you–viewpoint, and simple language.

> *Dear Customer:*
>
> *You should change your home mortgage to direct billing to your bank to make sure that each monthly payment arrives on time and avoids late charges or prevents destroying your credit record. We would like all of our customers to use direct bank payment for monthly mortgage payments because it makes our processing of payments easier and faster.*
>
> *Enclosed is a return envelope with a printed statement that you can sign to authorize us to send your mortgage statement to the bank each month for them to process payment. Also, too, enclose a copy of a canceled check from your bank that shows us the bank name and address for billing.*
>
> *We are doing you a favor by sending you this notice. You should follow our advise and rush it right back to us.*
>
> *Yours truly,*

Writer's Workshop

The following items may be sentence fragments or contain errors in subject–verb agreement, pronoun–antecedent agreement, comma and semicolon placement, number display, capitalization, spelling or word choice. Rewrite the sentences to make them correct.

1. Sandy arrived to class late and set at the back of the room so she could slip out before the end of the class.
2. The whitney-fasig museum was ranked as 5th best in the nation and the local museum have many of the same features.
3. January and febuary this year brought mild weather, however we can expect a few cold days before March thirty one.
4. Have you visited the Career center which is located in Patterson Hall at 1 Wildcat Boulevard?
5. Jose was conversing with a friend that asked Patty and I to join them
6. Marginally effective in the classroom Josh was out standing in Basketball.
7. Each person influences their own destiny, focused effort towards a goal help achieve them.
8. Asking the right questions led to the right answer.
9. The morning star journal printed an article about their staffs' awards by the national press association.
10. Broadway Live present Oklahoma on March 4 at 2 and 6 PM at the austin opera house.

Chapter 5
Print and Electronic Messages

LET'S TALK BUSINESS

We are the managing partners of a company operating five lodging facilities. All facilities are located $1\frac{1}{2}$ to 4 hours from our office. It is important for us to be in frequent contact with our on-site managers, often several times per day, communicating company policies, instituting and monitoring programs, and helping resolve problems. We rely heavily on various communication media: telephone, fax, and increasingly the computer—especially the use of e-mail. With a business that operates 24/7, e-mail allows us to send detailed messages directly to the managers and allows them to respond no matter the time of day or night. The use of e-mail has become increasingly important in our business as partner Ilene Levin has speech problems that make the use of the telephone difficult.

Ilene Levin and Steve Goldfine, Owners, Goldin Properties Midwest LLC

Photo courtesy of Levin and Goldfine

Successful communicators like those featured in this chapter's Let's Talk Business approach writing as a process that includes selecting the appropriate type of message; being aware of the vocabulary level at which they write; and planning, drafting, and finalizing their work. As business owners, Ilene Levin and Steve Goldfine know that output quality is directly related to input quality, and they are willing to do what it takes to achieve the goals of business communication. In this chapter, you will study and apply the techniques associated with developing print and electronic written messages. In later chapters, you will learn how to plan for effective oral communication.

Learning Objectives

1
Identify the advantages and disadvantages of written messages.

2
Use a three-step process to develop effective business messages.

3
Describe how to determine the vocabulary level of business messages.

4
Explain how to develop effective Internet-based messages.

The Advantages and Disadvantages of Written Messages

When faced with a situation that requires communication, your first decision will be whether to convey the message in writing or orally. Each method has advantages and disadvantages. The advantages of written messages are that they

- Provide a permanent record that can be filed and referred to in the future
- Can be reread and studied, which is important if a message is long, is complex, or has been written in anger
- Can be revised and edited to ensure they adhere to the principles of business communication
- Can have legal value

The disadvantages of written messages are that they

- Are generally transmitted slowly; e-mail and fax are notable exceptions
- Are viewed as being more formal, in part because they are permanent
- Do not lend themselves to quick or thorough feedback because there are few nonverbal cues and because the sender and receiver are in different locations
- Require storage, which can be time-consuming and expensive

In contrast, oral messages can be transmitted quickly, are considered to have a more personal tone, and allow for immediate feedback. Because oral messages do not provide a permanent record, however, receivers have limited time to reflect on them. These factors make oral messages unsuitable for complex material.

Developing Written Business Messages

The process for developing written business messages consists of the following three steps:

1. Planning
2. Drafting
3. Finalizing

Carrying out this process may take from a few seconds for routine letters, memos, e-mail, or instant messages to several days for a long written report or a web page. Following the process is essential for developing effective business messages.

Step 1: Plan the Message

The steps taken before putting words on paper or entering them into a computer are called **planning** or **prewriting.** This process incorporates and applies topics covered in Chapter 1, "Business Communication Foundations," Chapter 4, "Principles of Business Communication," and Chapter 10, "Business Research and Report Writing."

ANALYZE THE COMMUNICATION SITUATION

Your first step in planning is to decide what is involved in the specific communication situation. When analyzing the communication situation, you will want to ask yourself the following general questions:

- Who will receive the message?
- Will he or she be the final receiver or an intermediate reader?
- What are the physical and political constraints under which I am operating?
- What does the receiver need to know?
- What action do I want my receiver to take?

Specific questions you might ask when analyzing the communication situation include the following:

NOTE 5.5
Ask general and specific questions.

- Is the receiver internal or external to the organization?
- Has the receiver asked specific questions I must answer?
- Will my receiver view my message as positive? negative? persuasive? mixed?
- What is the relationship between me and my receiver? between our organizations?
- Is my message part of an ongoing dialogue, or does it introduce a new topic?

ESTABLISH PRIMARY AND SECONDARY PURPOSES

After analyzing the communication situation, you will establish the primary and secondary purposes of your message. This will be done within the framework of the four business communication goals:

NOTE 5.6
Relate your primary and secondary purposes to the business communication goals.

1. Receiver understanding
2. Necessary receiver response
3. Favorable relationship
4. Organizational goodwill

The main idea is the primary purpose, and the supporting ideas are the secondary purposes. For example, assume that you can say *yes* to a department head's request to purchase four new computers. This positive message will be sent to a colleague you know well. The memo or e-mail will include the *yes*, plus additional information about items such as purchasing procedure, hardware/software requirements, and budget. Figure 5.1 shows how your purposes might appear for this communication situation.

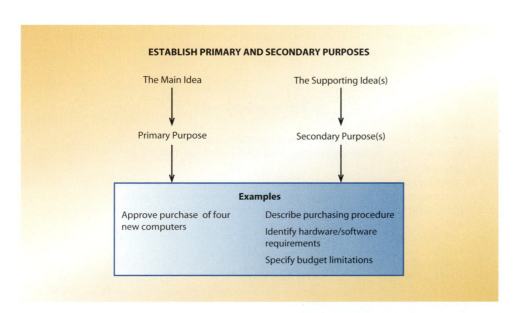

FIGURE 5.1
Simple Message Purposes

NOTE 5.7
Message purposes can be simple or involved.

Another example shows how establishing primary and secondary purposes for a specific message can be more involved. Assume that the message you are developing is a written annual departmental report. The message may include positive, neutral, negative, and persuasive information. The receivers of the report could include employees who report to you, managers at your level in other departments, and upper-level managers. The primary and secondary purposes for your departmental report might be as shown in Figure 5.2.

When you have analyzed the communication situation and have determined the primary and secondary purposes of the message, you are ready to analyze your receivers to enable you to use the you–viewpoint. Because this step is discussed fully in Chapter 1, only a brief summary of it is given here.

ANALYZE THE RECEIVER

NOTE 5.8
Analyze receivers for their knowledge, interests, attitudes, and emotional reactions.

For some communication situations, you will know the receiver of your message so well that little or no analysis will be necessary. In other communication situations, it may be necessary for you to do a careful, detailed analysis of the receiver. Whether your analysis of the receiver requires a limited or an extensive amount of research, the approach is the same. You analyze your receiver in four areas—knowledge, interests, attitudes, and emotional reaction—as shown in Figure 5.3.

NOTE 5.9
A message must be developed so all receivers can understand it.

If you have multiple receivers, you need to analyze each person. For example, if you are writing a memo to five people in your office, analyze the knowledge, interests, attitudes, and potential emotional reaction of each of them. To achieve its goals and purposes, your message must be understandable to the receiver with the least amount of subject knowledge, the lowest vocabulary level, and the most emotional opposition without insulting or being condescending to other receivers.

Your analysis of the receiver will give you important information about the receiver's vocabulary, interests, possible biases, and emotional reaction. From your analysis you can determine the ideas, words, and approaches that communicate your message best in the situation you face.

SELECT THE TYPE OF MESSAGE

NOTE 5.10
Select the most appropriate type of message for the situation.

Written messages can be formatted as e-mail, letters, memos, written reports, or other document types. In addition, they can be handwritten, typed, or keyed into a computer and printed. Format and style will vary with the situation. Memos are used exclusively for internal communication; letters, e-mail, and reports may have either an internal or an external audience.

FIGURE 5.2
Involved Message Purposes

Involved Message Purposes

Primary Purposes
1. To document clearly the department's accomplishments for 200–.
2. To persuade upper management to meet the department's future needs.

Secondary Purposes
1. To instill pride of accomplishment in the department's employees.
2. To inform managers at your own level of the department's activities and needs.
3. To inform upper management of the contributions your department and its employees have made.
4. To convince upper management to finance the department's continuing operation and proposed projects.
5. To maintain favorable relationships with others.
6. To build organizational goodwill for the department.

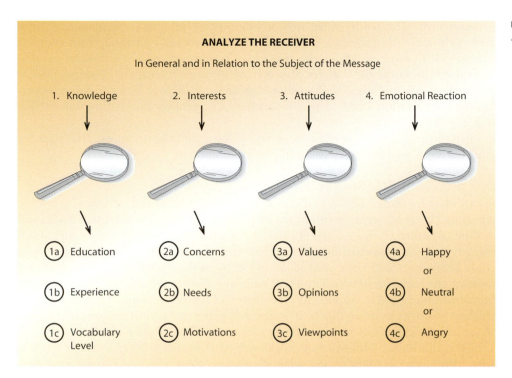

FIGURE 5.3
Analysis of the Receiver

SELECT AN ORGANIZATIONAL PLAN

Business messages may be organized by either the direct (deductive) plan or the indirect (inductive) plan. These two plans have many variations. In Parts 3 and 5 of this text, alternative ways to use the direct and indirect approaches are discussed. The direct and indirect plans for messages are shown in Figure 5.4.

The **direct plan** attempts to achieve the primary purpose of the message by placing the main idea in the opening. The details supporting or explaining the primary purpose follow the opening. The **indirect plan** opens on neutral ground or on a point

NOTE 5.11
Match the organizational
plan to the receiver's
anticipated reaction
to the message.

FIGURE 5.4
Organizational Plans for
Messages

To: Graciela Sanchez
From: Tim Waters
Date: February 23, 200-
Subject: Replacement of Digital Camera

MAIN IDEA

_____
_____
_____

_____
_____
_____

_____
_____

To: Graciela Sanchez
From: Tim Waters
Date: February 23, 200-
Subject: Recall of Digital Camera

_____
_____

MAIN IDEA

_____
_____
_____

_____
_____

of agreement. The sender then provides supporting reasons or explanations that lead to the main idea, which is presented later in the message. Although research has shown that in most situations the direct plan is more effective for positive or neutral information and the indirect plan is more effective for negative information or persuasion, you will want to do a thorough analysis of your receiver before selecting the organizational plan. Variables such as age, gender, and culture will be factors in your decision.

After selecting the type of message you will use and the organizational plan for your message, you are ready to outline message content.

OUTLINE THE MESSAGE CONTENT

NOTE 5.12
Create an outline to
organize your ideas.

In outlining message content, you are organizing your ideas and information for the message. This process can be completed on paper or on the computer using traditional outline structure (I., A., 1., a.), (1., 1.1, 1.1.1), bullet points, or simple indents to identify main and supporting ideas. When you are responding to a message, you could brainstorm and write your ideas on a copy of the document and use numbers to show the sequence in which you will write about them. Figure 5.5 illustrates how brainstorming could be applied to preparation of a claim refusal. Regardless of the method you use, your goal is to arrange and order your information in a logical sequence, which maximizes the receiver's understanding of the message.

The traditional outline method works well when you have a clear idea of what to write. Brainstorming works best when generating ideas and determining how they

FIGURE 5.5
Brainstorming the Message
Content on a Claim Letter

Purpose of Message:
1) Reject request for cash refund
2) Maintain customer's business.
3) Increase goodwill for store by offering economical solution that meets customer's needs

3623 Ocean Valley Drive
Virginia Beach, VA 23450
February 3, 200–

Ideas for Content:
1) Express appreciation for purchase.
2) Pride ourselves on customer service and helping them choose the best camera to meet their needs
3) This camera has all the features needed; larger memory card will solve problem and is economical

Mr. Lars Fenton, Owner
Clear Images Photo Shop
9356 Colony Way
Virginia Beach, VA 23451

Dear Mr. Spear:

I would like my money back on the Nickel 4600 camera I bought at your store during the "December Daze Sale." After using the camera on a ski trip in early January, I found it did not hold as many pictures as I needed. I think your salesperson recommended the wrong camera for me to buy. He should have recommended the more expensive camera so there would be room for all my pictures.

I would like a refund for $181.68, which I paid for the camera. Please send me the refund check and I will send the camera back to your store.

Sincerely,

Susan Mackey

Susan Mackey

Reinforce purchase decision was wise for needs you communicated
All sales final—no cash

relate to one another. In Chapter 10, you will learn more about these and other methods used when preparing lengthy, complex documents such as reports and proposals.

After completing the sequencing of ideas, you are ready to draft the message.

Step 2: Draft the Message

Using your mental or recorded notes from the outlining process, draft the message. Apply the principles of business communication, use the you–viewpoint, and focus on content. At this stage, getting something in writing is more important than generating perfect copy.

NOTE 5.13
You may have one or more drafts.

Even with good planning, experienced writers sometimes encounter **writer's block**—difficulty in putting thoughts into words. The Tips and Hints feature contains suggestions to help overcome this challenging situation.

NOTE 5.14
Tackle writer's block.

Step 3: Finalize the Message

Finalizing a message involves proofreading the document to determine where it needs to be revised and edited. Revising and editing are similar processes with different objectives. Revising focuses on content; editing focuses on mechanics.

REVISE THE MESSAGE

When a writer revises a message, he or she makes changes to its content. To determine what changes to make, read the message—aloud—from your receiver's point of view. Ask whether the primary and secondary purposes have been achieved. Check that you have chosen the correct organizational plan for the message and used it effectively. Determine whether better transitions or bulleted lists would help make your message clearer. Check to see that the principles of business communication have been applied. Verify that all necessary information is included and accurate. Finally, think about the visual image the message creates.

NOTE 5.15
The clearest messages result from revising and editing drafts.

tips and hints

Overcoming Writer's Block

When the words aren't flowing freely or when your mind seems as blank as the computer screen or paper before you, try these techniques for overcoming writer's block:

- Divide the writing project into smaller, more manageable parts. Completing a series of smaller tasks will give you the feeling of accomplishment.
- Start somewhere other than the beginning of the document. Write the middle or end and then fill in the remaining material.
- Change writing methods. Switch between pen and computer, or try a voice recorder. Some people find talking easier than writing.
- Change where you write; go outside, to a coffee shop, or to the library.

- Be sure you have pen and paper or a tape recorder handy at all times. Good ideas often arise when you least expect them, and you'll want to have access to the tools to record them.
- Write during the time of day when you're most productive; be sure to allow a reasonable block of time.
- Take a brief break. A change of scenery, a drink of water, a breath of fresh air, or exercise can help clear the cobwebs.
- Have music playing in the background. If you're anxious or stressed, use soothing music; if you lack motivation, select upbeat tunes.
- Ask a colleague for assistance or "talk the message." The conversation process may help you formulate ideas.

If you detect any weaknesses in the message, make changes to add strength. This is your opportunity to improve your word choice, sentence development, and paragraph formation. In addition, revising gives you another chance to add distinctiveness—a part of your personality—to the message.

NOTE **5.16**
Word processing software helps writers draft, revise, edit, and format text.

The ability to insert, delete, move, and copy text is essential to revising efficiently, and word processing software helps writers accomplish these tasks with ease. However, unless writers cut and paste carefully, they may find that their messages say something other than what they intended.

Word processing software allows writers to move quickly and easily from one part of a document to another while revising a message—for example, from the top of the page to the bottom or from page 43 to page 5. Movement also may be linked to words or phrases. Writers can find the next or every occurrence of a character, word, or phrase. When combined with a replace function, the find feature becomes a powerful revision tool, but one that must be used with care. Unless users precisely define what is to be replaced, they may create a problem in addition to solving one. Imagine directing the software to replace all occurrences of *his* with *his and her* only to find that *This idea has merit* becomes *This and her idea has merit.*

NOTE **5.17**
Choose emphasis techniques wisely.

Word processing software also can assist writers in choosing words and emphasizing text. A **thesaurus** helps writers select appropriate words by suggesting a variety of alternatives. Its use helps avoid word repetition and brings variety to word choice. For emphasis, text may be displayed using **bold**, underscore, *italic,* or other enhancement features. Type fonts (styles) and points (size) can be changed. Margins may be widened or narrowed. Tables can be created. Boxes or other borders can be placed around text. Symbols or images may be inserted to draw a reader's attention to important items. Writers who have access to color printers should determine whether using color will enhance the communication and, if so, how much of which color(s) is appropriate. Some colors (e.g., white, red) have significance within a culture. If your message is designed to reach a person or group within a particular culture, include color as part of your audience analysis.

NOTE **5.18**
Revise to improve content.

With so many options available, writers must choose wisely. Using too many enhancements could impede rather than facilitate successful communication. Decide what you want to accomplish and then choose the best feature to help you reach your goal. In other words, analyze your receiver and the communication situation.

EDIT THE MESSAGE

NOTE **5.19**
Edit to achieve mechanical correctness.

After a message has been revised, it must be edited. During the editing process, the writer proofreads the message to determine whether it is mechanically correct. The writer checks to be sure there are no errors in format, spelling, grammar, punctuation, spelling, or style.

NOTE **5.20**
Spell checkers and grammar checkers assist with proofreading.

A **spell checker** assists with, *but does not replace,* careful proofreading. A spell checker will not detect an error that results in the correct spelling of another word (e.g., *then* for *than*). Recent versions of word processing software automatically correct certain types of errors. If a writer keys *teh* rather than *the,* the software detects and corrects the error. The software also automatically changes the first letter of a sentence from lowercase to uppercase if the writer makes such an oversight. Users may choose to turn off these features when keying material that is intentionally contrary to the rules.

A **grammar checker** analyzes a document and alerts the writer to potential problems with sentence length, vocabulary level, word choice (e.g., *affect* for *effect*), punctuation, and passive voice. The software does not, however, correct the errors. The writer retains responsibility for ensuring that style errors do not create communication barriers. Although they are a good writing aid, grammar checkers are not perfect; they may question things that are correct or fail to question things that are incorrect. Writers always should be sure they have applied the principles of business communication.

The steps in the finalizing process are iterative—one or more of the steps may need to be repeated before the message is ready to sign and send. As they go through these iterations, many writers find that the tasks associated with finalizing a message are best accomplished by printing a copy of the document and using symbols to indicate the location and nature of the changes they will make. Standard symbols for editing and revising are shown at the back of the book. These symbols are especially helpful if the person who writes the message is not the one who prepares the final document. In this circumstance, the symbols themselves become a valuable communication tool. Learn to use these symbols in your revising, editing, and proofreading efforts.

NOTE 5.21
Use editing symbols to aid communication between message preparer and originator.

The results of editing and revising can be seen in Figures 5.6 and 5.7 on pages 122–123. Figure 5.6 shows the draft of a message; Figure 5.7 shows the final version. Note the clarity, power, and you–viewpoint that have been added by applying the principles of business communication while revising the message and the grammar and punctuation errors that were eliminated during editing.

NOTE 5.22
Give the editing and revising tasks high priority.

PROOFREAD THE MESSAGE

Proofreading is done several times during the process of finalizing a document. Proofreading occurs during and after revising and editing. The process involves (a) reading the message for content and (b) reading it again for correct spelling, grammar, and punctuation. Some proofreaders can find more spelling errors by reading the copy backward.

NOTE 5.23
Proofread during and after revising and editing.

Proofreading includes the following steps:

1. If you are using a word processing program, use your spell checker and grammar checker to locate errors. Next, proofread the copy on screen and print a copy of the document in double-spaced format.
2. Proofread the copy by reading the document aloud from beginning to end, focusing on the content. Reread the document looking for spelling errors, grammatical errors, punctuation errors, and style errors. Pay special attention to personal names, numbers, addresses, information in brackets, words displayed in uppercase letters, and unusual words.
3. After you have completed proofreading the document, ask a colleague or an associate to proofread the document. It helps to have another person proofread the document because you might not detect your own errors. If you have columns of numbers, consider reading these numbers aloud with a partner who can check them against the original source.
4. Make the corrections as required and then reprint the document for an additional reading.

You can find proven procedures and techniques for effective proofreading in books at the library. You may also check the Online Writing Lab (OWL) at the Purdue University website at http://owl.english.purdue.edu/, the Writing Center at the University of North Carolina website at http://www.unc.edu/depts/wcweb, or the Writing Center at the University of Wisconsin–Madison at http://www.wisc.edu/writing/ for additional guidelines on proven methods of proofreading.

Proofreading is not a glamorous activity, but it is a critically important one. Errors detract from the clarity of the message and reduce your credibility in the

needs work

Pacific Fields Piano
1800 Mount Diablo Blvd.
Lafayette, CA 94549
(714) 283-5000

May 1, 200–

Mrs. Ronalee Reid
3623 Happy Valley Lane
Lafayette, CA 94549

Dear Mrs. Reid:

We appreciate your recent purchase of a G2F PE Yamaha acoustic piano. You certainly have chosen an extremely high-quality parlor grand piano that will give you many years of joy and satisfaction. A Yamaha piano is the instrument chosen by many of the world's top artists. We want to ensure that enjoyment is possible.

You made a good decision when you bought a G2F PE Yamaha acoustic piano during the Pacific Fields Piano "Winter Sale." The tremendous savings you got on this sale totaling almost $4,000 were made possible in two ways: We (1) buy merchandise in large volumes whenever we can and (2) cut overhead and pass the savings on to our customers.

One of the ways we cut overhead is to make all sales final on items purchased during the "Winter Sale." We make every effort to be sure all our customers are aware of this policy by noting it in all advertisements and posting signs throughout the store.

You will be very glad to learn that you can easily make the piano quieter by purchasing a set of foam baffles. These foam baffles are installed under the piano between the ribs in order to quiet the sound. For $125.95 you can purchase the foam baffles that have complete directions and guides for installation. You can either "do-it yourself" or have one of our technicians take care of it for you at cost. Please call us collect at (714) 555-9011 and tell us your preference.

Once again, thank you for making Yamaha part of your life.

Sincerely yours,

Richard Spear

Richard Spear, Manager
Keyboard Division

FIGURE 5.6
Draft Message

mind of the receiver. Therefore, you or some other competent person should proofread each message carefully. As the one who submits the report or signs the letter or memo, you have the ultimate responsibility for both the content and the accuracy. *No document should be signed or sent—electronically or by more traditional methods—without proofreading it to be sure it is accurate and error-free.*

You may revise and edit some messages many times. Continue revising, editing, and proofreading until you have a clear, concise, businesslike, error-free message that reflects the you–viewpoint.

LO 3
*Describe how
to determine the
vocabulary level of
business messages.*

Determining Vocabulary Level

NOTE 5.25
Message analysis includes
determining vocabulary
level to ensure receiver
understanding.

Message analysis is an aspect of writing related to developing effective business messages. Select the vocabulary level of your messages so that it fits your receivers. As you know, one of your primary concerns in composing effective business messages is using a vocabulary level that your receiver will understand. **Vocabulary level,** as used in this book, refers to the level of difficulty of the words and combinations of words in messages.

looks good

May 1, 200–

Mrs. Ronalee Reid
3623 Happy Valley Lane
Lafayette, CA 94549

Pacific Fields Piano
1800 Mount Diablo Blvd.
Lafayette, CA 94549
(714) 283-5000

Dear Mrs. Reid:

We appreciate your recent purchase of a G2F PE Yamaha acoustic piano. You certainly have chosen an extremely high-quality parlor grand piano that will give you many years of joy and satisfaction. A Yamaha piano is the instrument chosen by many of the world's top artists. We want to ensure that enjoyment is possible for you with your new piano.

You made a good decision when you bought a G2F PE Yamaha acoustic piano during the Pacific Fields Piano "Winter Sale." The tremendous savings you got on this sale totaling almost $4,000 were made possible in two ways: We (1) buy merchandise in large volumes whenever we can and (2) cut overhead and pass the savings on to our customers. One of the ways we cut overhead is to make all sales final on items purchased during the "Winter Sale." We make every effort to be sure all our customers are aware of this policy by noting it in all advertisements and posting signs throughout the store.

You will be very glad to learn that you can easily make the piano quieter by purchasing a set of foam baffles. These foam baffles are installed under the piano between the ribs in order to quiet the sound. For $125.95 you can purchase the foam baffles that have complete directions and guides for installation. You can either "do-it yourself" or have one of our technicians take care of it for you at cost. Please call us collect at (714) 555-9011 and tell us your preference.

Once again, thank you for making Yamaha part of your life.

Sincerely yours,

Richard Spear

Richard Spear, Manager
Keyboard Division

FIGURE 5.7
Finalized Message

Readability Formulas

Readability formulas can be used to calculate vocabulary levels for your messages. These formulas—such as the Gunning-Fog, Flesch-Kincaid, Dale-Chall, and Fry—are described in materials available in most libraries or on the Web. They generally assess the sentence length, the number of syllables or characters in words, and the complexity of sentence structure. Although the counting necessary to use the formulas can be done manually, several of the formulas have been computerized and can be used easily with electronic media. Some word processing programs have readability formulas built into their grammar checkers, and these software programs are able to calculate the vocabulary level of your message.

NOTE 5.26
Readability formulas can be used to check vocabulary levels.

Readability Ratings

The vocabulary-level ratings obtained from readability formulas generally reflect the approximate grade level needed for a person to understand the written material. For example, a rating of 12 would mean that a person would have to be able to read at the twelfth-grade level to comprehend the material fully.

NOTE 5.27
Readability ratings show approximate grade level.

NOTE 5.28
Common sense must be
used with readability
ratings.

Readability analysis does not check the actual words you use or the manner in which you combine those words into sentences. An analysis will not show whether the writing is accurate or inaccurate, interesting or dull, and valuable or not valuable to a receiver. Use readability ratings as guides, and use common sense in applying them.

A message may have a low readability rating because it uses short words and short sentences even though it uses difficult technical words. By contrast, a message may have a high readability rating because it uses long words and long sentences, even though the sentences are easy to understand and the words are familiar. In addition, an appropriate grade level for a message does not necessarily guarantee that the message will communicate effectively. An inappropriate grade-level rating for a message, however, does mean that the message should be examined for word choice and sentence length.

Vocabulary Levels

NOTE 5.29
Business messages are
written at the eighth- to
twelfth-grade level.

As you compose a message for a given communication situation, keep in mind the estimated vocabulary level of your receiver. A message written at too high a vocabulary level will not be understood. A message written at too low a vocabulary level will either insult your receiver or fail to hold his or her attention and interest. Business messages written at the eighth- to twelfth-grade levels will communicate clearly with most receivers.

Readability formulas are important tools for analyzing your messages. Use these tools regularly to analyze the vocabulary levels of form letters or memos, newsletters, speeches, magazines, books, and similar materials that will be read (or heard) by many receivers. Use these tools periodically to check the vocabulary levels of your messages to a single receiver.

Developing Electronic Messages

LO 4
*Explain how to develop
effective Internet-based
messages.*

Technology related to the Internet is constantly evolving and has enabled people to communicate in ways previously not possible. In this section, you will explore concepts and techniques associated with writing for four of these technology-driven media—e-mail, instant messages, blogs, and web pages.

NOTE 5.30
The Internet is a worldwide
network.

When two or more computers are linked to facilitate information transfers, they form a **network.** The **Internet** is the world's largest network, but rather than linking individual computers, it links computer networks.

Created in the 1960s, the Internet was a tool for communication among employees of various government agencies, especially research scientists. Today, the Internet is an international communication medium used by educators, businesses, nonprofit organizations, and private citizens. One of the factors contributing to the popularity of the Internet was the inception of the **World Wide Web.**

NOTE 5.31
The Web makes Internet
access easy.

The Web, which originated at the European Organization for Nuclear Research (CERN) in Geneva, Switzerland, has made the Internet more accessible to those who want to tap its resources. Users navigate the system via a *browser* (a software application used to locate and display web pages) and rely on *hyperlinks* (electronic pointers) to move from one *site* (location) to another.

NOTE 5.32
E-mail is the most-used
Internet application.

E-mail represents the most common Internet application. About 90 percent of all Internet users send or receive e-mail.[1] The Internet can, however, be used for

---

[1] Susannah Fox and Mary Madden, "Generation Online" (PEW Internet & American Life Project, published data memo, December 2005).

many other purposes, including research. Information about how to develop an effective search strategy, how to recognize a credible source, how to cite Internet resources, and how to use the Internet as a research tool can be found in Chapter 10 and Appendix A. Chapter 16 includes information about how to use the Internet to research potential employers and to apply for employment.

Electronic Mail

One of the most common questions business professionals ask today is, "What's your e-mail address?" The reason for the question is simple—e-mail represents an efficient, convenient, and economical method of exchanging messages. Users may select stand-alone or network versions of commercial e-mail software, subscribe to a service, or obtain free e-mail through the Internet.

Once used primarily as an informal method of communicating with friends, family, and colleagues, e-mail has evolved into an acceptable and official communication method. Today, many individuals and organizations have found that they receive more e-mail than they do print mail. Some business organizations now use e-mail rather than paper as an official method of communicating with employees.

Whether content is embedded within the text of a message or created separately and conveyed as an attachment, e-mail is becoming the medium of choice for message transmission. The result is that writing has become an essential part of nearly everyone's job. Because of its role in official business communication, e-mail is developed using the same three-step plan as other written messages—plan, draft, and finalize. These steps were thoroughly described earlier in this chapter, so that discussion will not be repeated here. Rather, this section will focus on the e-mail features and guidelines that will help you complete those steps.

E-MAIL FEATURES

E-mail systems may be internal or external. Internal systems allow users to communicate only *within* an organization. External systems allow users to communicate with others in the same organization or, by using the Internet, to channel messages to users outside the organization.

E-mail resembles a memo. The writer enters the receiver's name and the subject. Salutations, closings, and signatures are not needed, but many users include them to make the message seem more personal. The software automatically enters the sender's name or e-mail address and records the date and time of the message.

A feature used to personalize e-mail is the **signature block,** a segment of text added at the end of a message. Signature blocks are like electronic business cards. They typically include the writer's name and information seen on letterhead stationery—company name, mailing address, phone number, e-mail address, and fax number. Also, they may contain other things, such as a company slogan or motto. The signature block should use no more than five lines. Writers should choose carefully when selecting what to include in a signature block. The text goes with *every* message that is sent and, unless deleted by the receiver, stays with the message if it is forwarded.

E-mail programs vary in the number and sophistication of mail management tools they include. To receive the greatest benefit from the software, writers should be thoroughly familiar with the programs they use. One common management tool is an **address book.** This feature offers writers the opportunity to store the e-mail

NOTE 5.33
Speed and convenience contribute to e-mail's popularity.

NOTE 5.34
Use the plan/draft/finalize method when developing e-mail.

NOTE 5.35
E-mails and memos have a similar format.

NOTE 5.36
Signature blocks provide information about how to contact the writer.

NOTE 5.37
Create a distribution list to save time when sending one message to many receivers.

addresses of those with whom they frequently exchange messages. To access the address, the writer uses an **alias,** a code or short version of the name. The addresses may be inserted directly into the e-mail, which reduces the chance for error. The same concept allows a writer to create a **distribution list,** a group of mailing addresses of several receivers, and enter an identifier to retrieve all of them simultaneously. For example, rather than entering the full address for each sales representative every time a message is to be sent, the sales manager might record all information only once and then retrieve it by selecting "Sales Reps" or a similar assigned alias. Recipients will see their name and the names of others in the group in the To line of the heading.

Another useful e-mail feature is auto response. When you are away from the office and unable to respond, **auto response** alerts those who send e-mail to you that you will not be able to respond immediately.

E-mail programs can have many of the same features found in word processing software. Users can check spelling as well as move and copy passages. Writers can format messages by adjusting margins and can use emphasis features such as bold, italic, and underscore. These emphasis features, however, are useful only when senders and receivers use the same software program.

NOTE 5.38
Emphasis techniques can have special meaning in e-mail.

It is very difficult to express emotions in e-mail because it lacks intonation, gestures, and a shared physical environment. Certain emphasis features, however, have a special connotation in e-mail. Anything displayed entirely in uppercase letters, for example, suggests the sender is shouting at the receiver. Exclamation points, when used often or in a series (!!!), suggest greater volume. To intensify a portion of a message, a sender may *place the text within asterisks.*

NOTE 5.39
Business e-mail deserves the same attention as other business messages.

If you've used e-mail to communicate only with friends or family, or if you've heard that grammar and spelling aren't important in e-mail, the statements in the preceding section might make you wonder why e-mail software has *any* editing features. The reason is simple: In business communication, the only difference between an e-mail message and a paper message is the channel through which it is transmitted. When e-mail is used in a business setting, the extent to which a writer edits a message depends on his or her analysis of the situation and the receiver.

E-MAIL GUIDELINES

NOTE 5.40
Set high standards for e-mail quality.

Those who receive business e-mail from you will judge both you and your organization by the quality of your messages. You will want to create and maintain a professional image. Using the following guidelines will help you apply the same high standards to business-related e-mail that you apply to paper messages:

- **Make the subject line count.** Use a brief and descriptive phrase to convey your real message to your receiver. For example, if you are asking the reader for a favor, your subject line might be "Request with Deadline."
- **Keep the subject line short.** Some systems limit display space, and you won't want your subject line to be truncated (cut). If you forward a message, change the subject line to reflect the message you are sending or it could become a cumbersome mess of commands such as "FW: RE: FW: FW: RE: Budget Update."
- **Cover only one topic in each message.** Limiting yourself to one topic allows you to use the subject line effectively, helps ensure that each item gets the attention it deserves, and permits the receiver to take action on each message and then delete it.

- **Make your message inviting.** Use short line lengths, short paragraphs, conversational language, positive words, and traditional format.

  using all lowercase lettersfailing to correct typographical errrs and omitting punctuation may mean you can create messages faster but it makes the message hard to read readers are accustomed to seeing material in a mixture of characters and use punctuation to guide them through a message varying from what is normal affects comprehension.

  Take the time to correct errors, or your readers may find your message as difficult to read as you found the previous paragraph.

- **Use position wisely and keep messages brief.** Deliver the most important information in the opening sentence or paragraph. If the message is longer than one screen, the receiver might not bother reading it. If you need to transmit lengthy documents via e-mail, use the attachment feature. Be sure your message directs the receiver to critical parts of your attachment.

- **Use attachments carefully.** Not all computer programs are compatible when it comes to attachments. Confirm in advance that your receiver has the software necessary to access what you send. If you're sending a text file, for example, tell the receiver what program you used to create it. Opening a Corel WordPerfect file using Microsoft Word can result in a message that resembles hieroglyphics. When you have multiple attachments, consider sending them separately. Some e-mail programs don't support multiple attachments; others have limited mailbox space. Also, be sure to include the attachment! Completing that task before writing the message will ensure you don't have to send a second message just to convey the attachment.

- **Hold your temper.** Remember, you're communicating with a person, not a machine. Don't send messages when you're angry or upset. If you feel the need to vent, write the text of the message then let it *and you* rest for at least 24 hours before adding the receiver information and sending the message.

- **Eliminate emoticons; use abbreviations and initialisms wisely. Emoticons** are the symbols [e.g., :)—smile] writers use to reflect emotion; use them only in personal e-mail. *The Unofficial Smiley Dictionary* at http://paul .meron.ox.ac.uk/ascii/smileys/html illustrates and explains e-mail emoticons. **Abbreviations** are shortened forms of words (e.g., Jan. for January). **Initialisms** are letter combinations that substitute for words (e.g., FYI for For Your Information or QFR for Quarterly Financial Report). Learn and use the abbreviations and initialisms your organization has adopted, and use only those that your receiver will recognize quickly and interpret correctly.

- **Know when *not* to use e-mail.** Because it lacks the cues supplied by body language, voice tones, and shared environment, e-mail doesn't have the communication richness of a face-to-face or telephone communication and the formality or authority of a letter. Consider other communication channels when messages

NOTE 5.41
Treat e-mail attachments with care.

NOTE 5.42
E-mail is inappropriate in some situations.

communication note

COMMUNICATING VIA E-MAIL REQUIRES CAREFUL PLANNING

Few technological advances have affected the way we communicate as radically as the advent of e-mail. The medium is often used in lieu of a "telephone conversation," with the author inaccurately assuming the same level of privacy. This cavalier attitude toward e-mail is typically inconsequential; however, in cases where the information is privileged or thoughtless, there can be repercussions. It is a good policy to treat e-mail as you would any other business correspondence, taking care to ensure the information being sent is accurate with regard to both context and content. This approach alleviates embarrassment not only to the author but the corporation as well.

Courtesy of Sherri Novitsky, Administrative Director, Metropolitan Rehabilitation Services.

are time sensitive (scheduling or canceling a meeting on short notice), when the message is simple and the receiver is nearby (cubicle-to-cubicle conversation), when the topic merits face-to-face discussion (performance appraisals, negotiations, grievance settlements), or when the message contains content that will have significant emotional impact on the receiver (e.g., job termination). Requests or claims submitted by e-mail, however, may be refused by e-mail; the decision rests on the emotional stake the receiver has in the situation.

- **Choose "reply" or "reply to all" as appropriate to the situation.** Ensure that your message gets to its target audience and no one else.
- **Set the context for your response.** Edit the subject line *(Request Response—Yes!)*, recap the original message, or include some or all of the original message in your reply. Most e-mail programs distinguish between old and new text by placing a > or other symbol before each line of text retained from the original message.
- **Avoid e-mail chains.** Replying to or forwarding e-mail messages without deleting unnecessary text from earlier messages creates an e-mail chain. Long chains increase the chance that confidential or potentially embarrassing material will reach an unintended audience. Long chains also waste reader time and use storage space needlessly.
- **Respect confidentiality.** Never forward confidential information unless you are authorized to do so. If you receive a blind copy (BCC), recognize that the primary receiver doesn't know you also received the message. Do not mention the message to the primary receiver or to anyone else. If you don't want your message forwarded to others, explicitly request that it remain confidential.

NOTE 5.43
Proofread e-mail before sending it.

- **Proofread the message before you send it.** Most systems do not allow messages to be canceled or retrieved after a user gives the *send* command. To make matters worse, it takes just a few keystrokes for the receiver to forward the message to one, a few, or literally thousands of additional receivers.

As mentioned in the above Communication Note, electronic messages require the same attention to planning and development as do letters and memos.

NOTE 5.44
Be a courteous e-mail user.

The speed by which e-mail can be transmitted has led communicators to expect quick responses to their messages. Courteous e-mail users check their messages once or twice every day and strive to respond within 24 hours. They read items once and decide whether to respond immediately, delete the message, or move the message to a project-related folder. E-mail users are also careful about viewing attachments they receive. Computer viruses are often sent as e-mail attachments; when the attachments are opened, the virus is activated. Unless your employer directs you to delete all attachments received from sources outside the company, a good rule is to save the attachment as a file so that virus detection software can be applied.

Although the advantages of e-mail are significant, there are also some disadvantages you should consider before deciding to send an electronic message. First, there is no such thing as a private e-mail. Some organizations monitor employee e-mail, and with some e-mail systems the e-mail administrator has access to all messages in the system. Also, e-mails are hard to destroy because they are backed up and are recoverable. Therefore, do not include any information in an e-mail that would cause embarrassment or that you would not publicly disclose. In some situations the sheer volume of e-mail an individual receives may make it difficult to make a timely response. Finally, avoid sending spam by following the suggestions in the Tips and Hints feature below.

NOTE 5.45
Lack of security and delay in responding may make e-mail less effective.

Instant Messaging

One of the fastest-growing forms of electronic or Internet-based communication is instant messaging, often abbreviated IM. Forty-two percent of Internet users (more than 53 million Americans) use instant messaging.[2] **Instant messaging** is a text-based computer conference involving two or more people.

IM has become popular because, unlike e-mail, it allows spontaneous interaction in real time. If the person you want to reach is available in your instant messaging contact list, your message appears instantly in a window on his or her screen. Flexibility in accessing remotely located users in a timely and economical manner is extremely helpful for organizations. Fifty percent of IM users indicate they regularly save time on tasks, and 40 percent of IM users say instant messaging has improved teamwork and workflow.[3]

NOTE 5.46
Instant messaging is a text-based Internet conference in real time.

NOTE 5.47
Organizations use instant messaging to reach remotely located users quickly and economically.

---

[2] Eulynn Shui and Amanda Lenhart, "How Americans Use Instant Messaging" (PEW Internet & American Life Project, September 1, 2004).

tips and hints

Are You Spamming Unknowingly?

You could be spamming readers of your e-mail and not even know it. Spam filters on personal computers and corporate networks are designed to snare unwanted incoming e-mail based on a variety of characteristics, including the sender's e-mail address, words in the subject line, and even words in the body of the message. If your e-mail is flagged, your readers may never see it.

So what can you do to avoid being caught in the spam trap? Here are three guidelines to follow: (a) don't send attachments with an e-mail unless you know the recipient, (b) be as specific as possible in your subject line, and (c) stay away from message-subject words that spam filters search for initially.

Here are some of the snags that will catch your e-mail in the spam trap:

- The From field appears not to contain a real name or ends in numbers.
- The Subject field includes the term "offer."
- The Subject field has exclamation marks and/or question marks.
- The Subject field starts with a dollar amount or "For Only."
- The Subject field contains "Guaranteed."
- The Subject field contains "Free."
- The Subject field contains "Congratulations."
- The body of the message contains one or more lines of "YELLING" (e.g., all caps).
- The message has at least 70 percent blank lines.
- The message contains too many images without much text.

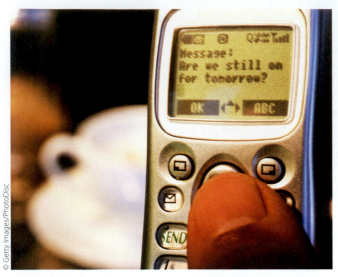

© Getty Images/PhotoDisc

Individuals can instant message anywhere and any time.

Like e-mail, IM lacks the expressive features of face-to-face communication. Also, the slang common in IM may be difficult for new or inexperienced users to master quickly. Instant messaging slang includes initialisms (e.g., TTYL—talk to you later, OTP—on the phone, TMI—too much information), words formed by combining letters and numbers (e.g., b4, 4warned), replacement letters in words (e.g., thankz, billz), and symbols that replace vowels in words (e.g., t%k, b&). Instant messaging is not totally secure because the messages are maintained on servers controlled by the provider of the utility.

Probably the most-used feature of instant messaging is the "away" message alert. Other features allow the IM user to create a chat room, share files and links to websites, use the Internet instead of the phone to talk, view images, and stream content.

NOTE 5.48
Instant messages should be concise; limit a message to one or two thoughts.

Messages that are sent through IM should be brief and concise, including all pertinent details. Most instant messaging programs limit the amount of text you can send in a message. A thought or two is all you should send at one time (think of an instant message as a postcard without the postage). The content is similar to that in an e-mail or a memo. Keep your message casual but professional (no misspellings or typographical errors, wise use of initialisms, and no emoticons). This form of electronic communication should be positive. It is not intended to replace face-to-face conversations dealing with bad news or highly personal information.

Blogs

NOTE 5.49
A blog focuses on a particular topic.

A **blog** is a website to which entries about a particular interest area are posted on a regular basis and displayed in reverse chronological order (most recent posting at the top). The term *blog* is a shortened form of **weblog** or **web log.** The postings often contain hyperlinks to other topics of interest and invite reader comments that may be read by all viewers. Text and hyperlinks dominate, but some blogs emphasize images and videos (such a blog is called a **vlog**).

NOTE 5.50
Blogs are dynamic, are easy to use, and often have a "voice."

A blog has certain attributes that distinguish it from a standard web page. For example, blogs are designed to log "real time" events. The home page is regularly updated with new information, which makes it a **dynamic web page.** Blogs also have a "voice," which means they may contain the writer's opinion and they may invite comments from the readers. **Bloggers,** the participants in a blog, like the ease of posting comments. Usually information is entered into a simple form and then submitted. Blogs can be set up quickly (knowledge of HTML is not required) and updated easily, even when the blog owner is away from his or her own computer.

NOTE 5.51
Businesses use blogs in a variety of ways.

The value of blogs in business is still being debated. Business blogs are used to promote and defame companies, to argue economic concepts, to disseminate information, and more. Many professionals rely on blogs to stay current in their field. Some organizations are using blogs on their intranets to keep employees aware of new projects and initiatives. Other businesses, such as Intuit, Microsoft, and Adobe,

---

[3] Ibid.

use blogs as customer communication tools. According to John Battelle, "Blogs work because people have something to say, and others find what they say valuable."[4]

Effective steps for writing in a blog include the following:

1. **Determine the purpose of and the audience for the blog.** Knowing what you want to accomplish and whom you are writing to will allow you to be more focused. Adopt a tone and vocabulary appropriate for your intended audience.
2. **Write in the proper format.** Blogs use a conversational writing style. Edit and revise your materials before you post. Omit unnecessary words and select colors and elements that support your posting without distracting from the message. Be authentic and honest; infuse postings with your personality, energy, and passion so the blog evolves into a conversation with the audience. Proofread blog postings so they give a positive and professional impression of you or your business.
3. **Establish credibility for the blog.** To have a credible blog, you need to monitor it actively and update the content regularly. Credit any sources you use in your postings, and exchange links and ideas with your audience. Offer feedback mechanisms for readers and listen to their feedback.
4. **Create an archive.** When you add something to a blog and invite others to link to it, you must keep your words online, in their appointed place, indefinitely. Always provide a permanent location, a **permalink,** where each of these items may be found.

Websites and Web Pages

A **website** contains a group of related web pages. The opening screen, or **home page,** of a website acts as a table of contents. From this screen, users link to other pages or sites by clicking on icons or phrases designed for that purpose. The convenience and speed of this process result directly from the way in which the home page is organized.

NOTE 5.52
A website may have one or more pages.

Building an effective website involves five steps:

1. **Determine the purpose and audience.** Websites may have one or more purposes. Sites are designed to inform, persuade, and/or entertain. Each site owner also hopes to generate goodwill. Good websites have an overall strategy for the entire site, plus a goal for every web page. A common error that beginning writers for the Web make is to assume that everyone enters the website at the home page (some enter the website via a link from another website). To determine the purpose of your website ask the following questions:

NOTE 5.53
Every web page should have its own goal.

   - **Why are you writing the document?** Are you trying to generate sales? Are you trying to inform customers? Are you trying to save money on advertising costs?
   - **What is the primary message?** Each page should have a key message you can summarize in one sentence.
   - **Who do you want to visit your website?** Once you have identified your audience, you should adapt the tone and vocabulary to that audience.
   - **How to you want visitors to your site to respond?** Do you want them to write for more information on a product? Do you want them to order something from your website?

If you answer these questions before beginning to write, your web content will be focused, and focused content brings traffic to a website.

NOTE 5.54
Web pages need to be written so they can be scanned easily.

---

[4] John Battelle, "Why Blogs Mean Business," *CNNMoney.com, Business 2.0,* February 2004, www .business2.com/b2/subscribers/articles/print/0,17925,575603,00.html (accessed February 19, 2006).

One characteristic common to all web audiences is that they spend most of their time scanning material. If they don't find what they want quickly—within the first minute—they will probably leave your site and may never return. To help site visitors find what they want and find it fast, you will want to use short, specific headings (4–8 words), short sentences (15–20 words), short paragraphs (4–5 lines), and short summaries (30–40 words). The Tips and Hints on the following page offers more suggestions for those writing for the Web.

NOTE 5.55

Content in a website may include links.

2. **Develop the content.** Site content may consist of original material or material supplemented by links to other sites. Most people who search the Internet are seeking information; a site that contains only links won't meet their primary need and won't be visited frequently. Materials you prepare yourself should adhere to the principles of business communication. They should also be prepared with full respect for copyright, fair use, and intellectual property rights. If you establish links to other sites, be sure those sites meet your high standards. Those who view your site will construct an image of you or your organization based not only on what you prepare but also on where you might direct them.

NOTE 5.56

Organization and navigation are key to a well-designed website.

3. **Design the site.** Organization is the key to site design, and an outline will help you create an easy-to-navigate site. Visiting other sites can help, too. The design theme should be consistent throughout the web pages and not detract from the contents of the website. A consistent design can help establish a site's identity. The design should allow for ease of use. Links should always be in dark blue text because web viewers identify blue text with a hyperlink. The design will also need to balance control and accessibility. If control of the design elements is restricted so everyone sees the same thing, you may be sacrificing the accessibility for some viewers (e.g., a person who is visually impaired may need to enlarge the font to read it). Use graphics wisely. A few well-chosen graphics add interest; too many add to the load time.

4. **Address technical issues.** Every web page is an HTML document. Users may write their own HTML, create it using commercial software, or hire a commercial service to perform the task. To be accessible to readers, each site must have a URL and reside on a computer equipped with server software and connected to the Internet. If your website requires certain software to view portions of the site, direct visitors to websites where the needed software can be downloaded.

NOTE 5.57

A regularly updated website has maximum credibility.

5. **Develop the credibility of the site.** A user-friendly design and effective navigation enhance the credibility of a website. Web users also want to know the site represents a "real" person or organization, so a name and address should be on each page of the site. For maximum credibility, websites need regular maintenance. The site's contents will determine how frequently updates are needed, but quarterly reviews are the outside limit. During an update, verify that all sites to which you link are still active and appropriate; software is available to assist with this task.

Summary of Learning Objectives

LO 1   *Identify the advantages and disadvantages of written messages.*

Written messages provide a permanent record, accommodate lengthy and complex content, can be reread and studied, and can be edited and revised. Unfortunately,

tips and hints

Guidelines for Writing for the Web

Following these guidelines when writing for a website can ensure that your receiver will get your intended message:

- **Write for the skim-reader.** To help your readers find what they want fast, use headings that are short (4–8 words), specific, and a summary of what is to come. Put keywords in your headings. Sentences should be no longer than 20 words. Vary paragraph length, but limit the length to 65–100 words maximum. Bulleted lists can be used to emphasize important items; an effective length is 3–5 bulleted items. Each web page in the website should use the inverted pyramid structure. This structure starts with the main point, a description, or a summary of what is on the page. Traditionally, readers scan documents by reading the first few words of a paragraph; that is why it is important to use the inverted pyramid structure.

- **Use plain English.** By definition, a web page is an international document because it is posted on the World Wide Web. Write in plain English so readers from around the world can read and understand your website. Using plain English simply means using short sentences, simple words, the you–viewpoint, active voice, and positive language. You need to avoid slang, idioms, metaphors, phrasal verbs, short words with multiple meanings, and clusters of "mini" words (e.g., "in terms of," "for the purpose of," "in a position to").

- **Implement standards for web accessibility.** Federal agencies and departments and any organizations receiving federal funding are legally bound to make their websites accessible to everyone, regardless of technological or physical disadvantage. The web writer can provide alternative text for every nontext element on a website (ALT-text). ALT-text simply describes the image element that is on the web page. For more information on web accessibility go to http://www.w3.org/WAI or http://www.access-board.gov/508.htm.

- **Optimize searchability of the website.** One of the goals of a writer is to have the website ranked high in search results. High search ranking equates to heavy traffic in the website. Meta keywords and description tags are two tools the writer uses to improve search results. Search engines use four criteria to evaluate searchability: (a) relevance, (b) prominence, (c) link popularity, and (d) currency (updated content) of web pages. Relevance and prominence are the two factors the writer can affect. To determine relevance, search engines compare the number of times a query word is used in the website text; this factor highlights the importance of word choice. Search engines also enhance the ranking if the query word is positioned by the writer in a place of prominence (title, meta description, or body text).

- **Revise, edit, and proofread.** Proofread, revise, and edit the content for your website several times before you publish it. Most web writers review the site at least three times and find that the finalizing process can take from 30 to 50 percent of the time it took to develop the content. Revise first for content, tone, and style; then, edit for grammar and spelling. The final website will be the first (and sometimes last) impression readers will have of the organization represented by the website.

they are also transmitted slowly, are more formal, produce delayed and reduced feedback, and require storage.

Use a three-step process to develop effective business messages.   LO 2

The three-step process for developing business messages is simple but critical to your success in communicating. The three steps are as follows:

Step 1: Plan the Message. Planning involves asking general and specific questions to assess the communication situation, establishing primary and secondary purposes, analyzing the receiver, selecting the type of message, selecting an organizational plan, and outlining the message.

Step 2: Draft the Message. The second step in developing an effective written business message is to put thoughts into a written draft—an effort that focuses on getting something on paper rather than worrying about format, spelling, grammar, and mechanics. Writer's block may occur during this process, but it is a problem that can be overcome.

Step 3: Finalize the Message. The third step in developing an effective business message involves revising, editing, and proofreading the document. Word processing software can be a valuable tool in this process.

LO 3

Describe how to determine the vocabulary level of business messages.

Using a vocabulary level that your receiver will understand is a primary concern in composing effective business messages. Vocabulary level, as used in this book, refers to the level of difficulty of the words and combinations of words in messages.

Any of several readability formulas can be used to calculate vocabulary levels for your messages. Many grammar-checker programs are able to calculate the vocabulary level of your message. Business messages written at the eighth- to twelfth-grade level will communicate clearly to most receivers.

LO 4

Explain how to develop effective Internet-based messages.

E-mail, instant messages, blogs, and web pages are electronically transmitted written messages. Although they may be created to meet personal goals, they also play a critical role in business. When used for business purposes, electronic Internet-based documents should be developed following the same planning, drafting, and finalizing process used for letters, memos, and reports.

Questions for Discussion and Review

1. Compare written and oral messages on the factors listed below. Which type of message earns the higher rating? Why? (Objective 1)
   a. Ability to be edited
   b. Permanence
   c. Tone
   d. Feedback
2. Explain why spell checkers and style checkers do not replace proofreading. (Objective 2)
3. Discuss the advantages and disadvantages of using word processing software programs when drafting messages. (Objective 2)
4. Discuss the factors to be considered when analyzing the receiver of a message to ensure your intended message is received. (Objective 2)
5. For each of the following situations, indicate whether the direct or the indirect organizational plan would be most appropriate and why. (Objective 2)
   a. One of your sales representatives applied for the district sales manager position and was not chosen; you need to notify her that she did not get the job.
   b. You need to notify a human resources colleague that he is to attend a seminar next week on the new insurance plan that will be instituted in six months.
   c. You have been asked to schedule a time to talk with an employee who has been accused of sexual harrassment.
   d. You need to schedule a meeting with your supervisor to discuss your performance appraisal.
   e. You need to notify someone in your department that his or her requested vacation date will not be approved.
6. Explain how a message made up of short words and short sentences could have a high readability rating. (Objective 3)

7. Discuss how the statement "Luck is what happens when preparation meets opportunity" applies to the topics in this chapter. (Objectives 2 and 4)

8. What advice would you give to someone who consistently deletes the text of incoming e-mail before adding a one- or two-word reply? (Objective 4)

9. How has e-mail changed your expectations about communication turnaround time? For each situation below, indicate how long you would expect to wait for a reply. Take part in a class discussion of your responses and your reasons for them. (Objective 4)

   a. An e-mail request for a quote on auto insurance submitted to the e-mail address given on an insurance company's website.

   b. An e-mail to your business communication instructor, sent at noon on Wednesday, inquiring about an assignment due Thursday.

   c. An e-mail to your best friend, a student at a different school.

   d. An e-mail request for a $5 rebate submitted to an office supply store's website.

   e. A product inquiry submitted to the e-mail address given on a manufacturer's home page.

   f. An e-mail complaint about a product that you purchased over the Internet.

10. Is it ethical to send blind copies of e-mail? Is it unethical to forward them to others? Discuss. (Objective 4)

11. List and explain two guidelines to follow when creating e-mail and one to follow when replying to e-mail. (Objective 4)

12. Why is audience analysis important when designing a web page? (Objective 4)

Application Exercises

1. Briefly describe (a) two specific situations in which you would choose to use oral communication and (b) two specific situations in which you would choose to use written communication. Give your instructor a printed copy of the descriptions and your rationale for the medium you chose for each situation. (Objective 1)

2. You have just received a letter from a customer who purchased new rims for his car from your tire store several months ago. He paid for the rims when he ordered them because they were a special order. The rims arrived after a month and were mounted on the wheels. Three days later the customer returned, complaining that the car vibrated when he drove over 60 mph. The tire store balanced the wheels at no charge to the customer. The same vibration problem happened two more times, and the tire store balanced the tires at no charge each time. After the car experienced the same problem again, the customer became very upset and asked for a cash refund for the rims because they did not fit his wheels and provide a smooth ride even though they were custom made. Your company does not offer cash refunds. Answer the following questions: (Objective 2)

   a. What is the purpose of your letter?

   b. What information would you include in the letter?

   d. What alternatives can you offer to the customer?

   c. Which organizational plan would you use in this situation, direct or indirect?
   Report your findings to the class.

3. **Teamwork. Technology.** Form a four-person group consisting of two subgroups. Each subgroup will find an appropriate substitute for the words in the following list. One subgroup will use a traditional (book) thesaurus, the other the electronic thesaurus feature of a word processing software program. Both subgroups should record the time it takes to accomplish the task. Compile the findings of the two subgroups into a visual that compares the two methods. (Objective 2)

   a. archaic
   b. remuneration
   c. entirety
   d. sundry
   e. assimilate
   f. exemplify
   g. preposterous
   h. irritable
   i. ubiquitous
   j. fortuitous
   k. superfluous
   l. veritable
   m. acquiesce
   n. monumental
   o. symbolize

COLLABORATIVE
TECHNOLOGY

4. Technology. Use the spell-check feature of your word processing program to check for errors in the following paragraph. Compare the results with errors you find as you proofread the text. (Objective 2)

> *Paula were working a loan in the jewelry department. Tree choppers approached the counter while he was rapping an other customers' pack age. Max, the stationary department clerk, offered to provide assistants. Pauline expected. All six customs were served quickly.*

5. In conjunction with the launch of a new program of study, your school will host an open house on the second Tuesday of next month. You have been asked to announce the event to the students in your school and to the community. Analyze the two groups of receivers and then outline the who, what, when, where, and why information you would include in the message to each group. As your instructor directs, submit your work by e-mail or use it as a springboard to class discussion. (Objective 2)

6. Revise and edit the following message so that it communicates more clearly and concisely to an American receiver with an average reading level (Objectives 2 and 3):

> *I recently was petitioned to consummate an assessment of my supervisor. He registered very prominently in several of the domains on the assessment.*
>
> *He competently imparts intent and instructions, gives acknowledgment for a pursuit commendably completed, and exemplifies enterprise in dilemma analysis. He is adaptable and has an immense sense of comicality.*
>
> *The only area I see opportunity for betterment is his aptitude to empower the labor to others on the unit.*

7. Technology. During the past few weeks, you've received many—too many—e-mails that contain chain letters, jokes, recipes, and other nonbusiness material. An occasional message of this nature is a nice diversion and can enhance morale within an organization, but too many clog the system and reduce productivity. Prepare an e-mail that politely but firmly asks the senders of these messages to stop. Send the message to your instructor. (Objective 4)

8. Teamwork. Work with one other student. Exchange the messages you wrote in Exercise 7 and read them silently, then aloud. Discuss whether and how the tone you thought you used in your message paralleled the tone the receiver conveyed when he or she read the message aloud. What, if anything, should be done to improve the message? (Objective 4)

9. Ethics. Teamwork. In a group of three to five students, research on the Internet how blogs and instant messaging are being used in business. As a class, discuss your findings. (Objective 4)

10. Teamwork. Technology. Work with one other student to search the Internet for information on how e-mail, instant messaging, and blogs have affected writing skills, including tone or voice, spelling, grammar, and style. Write an e-mail to your instructor summarizing your findings. (Objective 4)

11. Global. Technology. Access the home page of two companies based in countries other than the United States and two similar companies in the United States (e.g., financial institutions, airlines). In which ways do the home pages for companies based outside the United States differ from those for companies based in the United States? Did any of the companies make their pages available in languages other than English? Present your results in a memo to your instructor. (Objective 4)

12. Teamwork. Form a three-person group. Assign each person in the group one of the Internet-based electronic message systems: e-mail, instant messaging, or blogs. Have him or her informally interview five students and three businesspersons, asking them if they use the technology, and, if so, what they believe are the advantages and disadvantages of each. Summarize your responses in a memo to your instructor. You may also use your responses to start a class discussion. (Objective 4)

13. Technology. J. J. Peak plans to send the following e-mail to his new boss, someone who has been with the company only three weeks. Knowing this is a business message and that J. J. hasn't had much time to develop a casual, working relationship with his new boss, convert the message to one more appropriate to the situation. Send the revised document to your instructor as an attachment to an e-mail, indicating what is attached. If you are unfamiliar with the initialisms and emoticons used in this message, first try to interpret them based on context, then ask your instructor.

> *THX 4 reviewing the proposal I plan 2 submit 2 Mears, Inc. YOU CERTAINLY MADE LOTS OF SUGGESTIONS!!! :'(FYI the dew date is 4.1. Then TPTB at Mears will do a pelim screening & invite 3 bidrs to make F2F presentations. I'll let ya know ASAP after I hear from em. FWIW I think r chances are xlnt :-D If u have any ??? plz call. TAFN T2UL8R*

Web exercises to accompany this chapter are available at **www.thomsonedu.com/bcomm/krizan.**

Message Analysis

Using what you have learned in this chapter and previous chapters, revise and edit the following letter. Be sure to proofread the document before submitting it to your instructor.

> *Dear Mrs. Finch*
>
> *It is with alot of pleasure that I am riting you today to offer you a speshal offer to stay at the Forest Glen Inn in beautiful Carmel, California. This bed and brekfast is recently remodeled and we are now excepting reservations for June and July. If you book a room for any weekday nite which is Monday thru Thursday your room rate will be $125.00 a nite.*
>
> *All of our guest rooms has a private bath ether a tub/shower or a steam shower. Yur room rate includes a free wine and cheese reception in the afternoons from 5-6 on the patio which overlooks the ocean. In the morning you will be delited with our gourmet breakfast, which is served from 7:00 thru 9:00 A.M.*
>
> *Carmel is a beautiful village situated right on the Pacific Ocean about 100 miles south of San Francisco. Just emagine waking up to the sound of waves breaking on the shore and beautiful sunny days. It is know for being a artist's haven. There are about 8 art gallerys on every block. If you are a golfer bring your clubs because we have several world klass golf courses within just a few miles' of Carmel.*
>
> *Book now! Rooms is limited and they are filling up fast! You can reserve yur room by calling 1-888-555-2236.*
>
> *Very Truely Yours*

Writer's Workshop

The following items may be sentence fragments or contain errors in subject-verb agreement, pronoun-antecedent agreement, comma and semicolon placement, number display, capitalization, spelling, or word choice. Rewrite the sentences to make them correct.

1. If the building on Wallace Avenue and 7th Street is condemed we will make a bid on the property then we will raise the building.
2. 52% of the respondents indicated they plan to lease there next car, 38 percent plan to bye.
3. Michelle completted a three-day training workshop on our new Accounting system, and recieved a certificate of complesion.
4. As a result of a nation-wide marketing campane the passed 6 months we experienced a 23% increase in sales.
5. Everybody knowes Maureen have been looking for a different job—if she gets a promotion I think she'l stay.
6. The attornies adviced us too seek an injunction.
7. The repair bill for the scanner and lazer printer were send to Irene for her aproval.
8. You may get your 30-day trial subscription by calling our toll free number or return the postcard that was in the binding of the magasine.
9. Thank you for excepting my invitation to speak at next months' meeting of the Association For Electronic Commerce (ACE).
10. The communication workers' strike lasted sixty-two days than they settled for a 3% raise for both of the next two years.

YOU BE THE virtual assistant

A virtual assistant uses technology not only for communicating with clients and completing work for them but also for promoting his or her business. In this activity, you will be called upon to implement the principles of business communication as you use technology.

1. Design a letterhead for your business. Save the letterhead file for use in later assignment.
2. This morning, you received the following e-mail from a prospective client at Challenger Engineering who had inquired about your willingness to edit technical documents for his firm on a project-by-project basis. You responded that you had strong writing skills and, as other projects permitted, would be interested in contracting with Challenger. Complete the task as requested, and prepare the e-mail and bill you will submit to Greg Hitchcock.

> To: VirtualAssistant@webster.net
> From: greg_hitchcock@challenger.com
> Subject: Work Sample
>
> Thanks for responding positively to my inquiry about your interest in doing contract editing for us. Before we decide whether to proceed, we ask that you edit a brief sample document (attached).
>
> If possible, please return the edited document within the next week. We will, of course, pay you for the time you spend on this task. When you submit your finished document, please also submit a bill.
>
> Greg Hitchcock
> Project Manager
> Challenger Engineering
> 602.555.7465
> - - - - - - - - - - - - -

Attachment Text
Organize, format, and improve the wording of the following text to make it understandable to a member of the general public with at least a 6th grade reading level. This segment of a larger document addresses safety instructions and warnings for one of our consumer hand tools.

Carefully and thoroughly peruse all instructions. These instructions and general safety admonitions apply to all replicas of this apparatus.

Don't be clad in lose clothing or waring trinkets when tool is in commission. These items (clothing and ornaments) can be wedged in moving parts in motion. If you use this equipment while working in the out-of-doors, we advocate that you use rubber souled foot-ware. Long tresses should be sheltered. ALWAYS WEAR EYE FORTIFICATION – When the tool is plugged in, it's operator should ware safety googles at all times. When the tool is plugged in, refrain from traversing with finger on trigger mechanism. Do not utilize this—or any power tool—for any purpose but the one for which it was designed and manufactured. The chord should not be abused by yanking it from the power receptical or by subjecting it to excessively warm temperatures, lubricants, and sharp edges. When not in use or before cleaning, you should unplug the tool. If the tool mechanism should become entangled with a foreign object, cease operation instantaneously. Inspect the tool for damage and, if necessary, have preservation completed prior to endeavoring supplementary operation. This same cautionary approach should be taken if the cord becomes damaged. Be sure you disengage the tool from the electrical socket before examining it to ascertain the extent of the damage. Portable electric hand tools should never be operated in atmospheres that are gaseous or could be the site of an explosion. Any motorized tool could spark, and those sparks could ignight the fumes in the atmosphere. Similarly, electric tools should not be operated in damp or wet locations. Keep tools out of the reach of children. Store them in an arid container out of harm's way, preferably indoors. Also keep pets and any/all spectators at a safe remoteness.

3. Develop a "mock up" of the home page for a website for your virtual assistant business. In addition to your business name and logo, your site will include information about the services you provide, how to contact you, testimonials from people who have used your services, pricing, and other items you think are relevant. Decide whether all information will be on the home page or whether some will be provided on separate pages with links from the home page. Prepare the text of any item appearing on the home page.

Part 3
Correspondence Applications

© Tom Grill/Iconica

Chapter 6
Message Formats

LET'S TALK BUSINESS

Working internationally gives employees and the firm or venture for which they work virtually unlimited opportunities. Operating beyond the borders of your home country creates opportunities for vast financial and interpersonal growth; it also raises the risk of making cultural faux pas and causing communication break-downs.

Early in my career, I was involved in projects and tasks that required extensive written communication with both domestic and international receivers. That experience taught me that format is an important element to consider when preparing written communications.

Erika Ludwig, Senior Internal Auditor, Sauer-Danfoss

Photo courtesy of Erika Ludwig

Today's professional employee is inundated with communications sent via different forms of media. Whether the message is in electronic or hard copy form, making a good first impression remains essential. The aesthetic design of the message will speak to the reader and invite him or her to investigate and discern the content of the message. Use subject matter, corporate culture, and local business customs to help you tailor the design of your message. Doing so will increase the likelihood that your message will be received favorably and reflect positively on you and your company.

You may have heard the expression "You have only one chance to make a positive first impression." That statement is true for written messages as well as for people. In your role as a business professional, you will write messages to internal and external receivers. You will want those documents to create a lasting, positive impression on your receivers. The format you select for each message will contribute to that impression.

In Chapter 5, you learned that letters are used primarily for external messages, that memos are used for internal messages, and that e-mail may be used for either internal or external messages. In this chapter, you will learn the basics of formatting those documents. The information will be applied as you study Chapters 7, 8, 9, and 17. When you encounter format challenges not discussed in this chapter, consult a reference manual such as *HOW 11: A Handbook for Office Professionals* by Clark and Clark.[1]

NOTE 6.1
The format of a document sends a nonverbal message.

Letters

Letters are used for written messages to individuals outside an organization. Letters are also used to communicate formal written messages to employees within an organization.

Standard Parts of a Letter

The number and location of letter parts depend on the format you select. As shown in Figure 6.1, most letters contain seven standard parts: heading, inside address, salutation, body, complimentary close, signature block, and reference initials.

LO 1
Describe the seven standard parts of a letter.

HEADING

The first standard part of a letter is the **heading,** which consists of the letterhead or return address and the date. Business organizations should use letterhead stationery for the first page of a letter. The stationery can be designed and prepared by a professional printer or created using a personal computer. Individuals preparing personal business messages may prefer to use a return address and dateline rather than create their own letterhead.

A **letterhead** contains the name of the organization and its complete mailing address. It may also contain a phone number; a fax number; an e-mail address; a web URL; an organizational slogan, emblem, or logo; and other information that the organization deems appropriate. A letterhead should use no more than two vertical inches of stationery space. Although a letterhead usually is placed at the top of the page, part of the information may be at the bottom. For example, the street address and telephone number of another location may be shown at the bottom of letterhead stationery. The letterhead may be printed in more than one color. Examples of letterheads are shown in Figure 6.2.

The **date** contains the month, day, and year the letter is written. The month should be spelled in full. Figures are not used for the month (e.g., 6/09/08) because there is no universal agreement as to whether the day or month appears first. Dates may be in one of the following two styles:

June 9, 200–
9 June 200–

NOTE 6.2
Letters have seven standard parts.

NOTE 6.3
The date and writer's contact information are the heading.

NOTE 6.4
Limit the letterhead to two inches of vertical space.

NOTE 6.5
Every letter should show the date on which it was written.

---

[1]James L. Clark and Lyn R. Clark, *A Handbook for Office Professionals: HOW 11*, 11th ed. (Mason, OH: Thomson, 2007).

FIGURE 6.1
The Seven Standard Parts
of a Letter

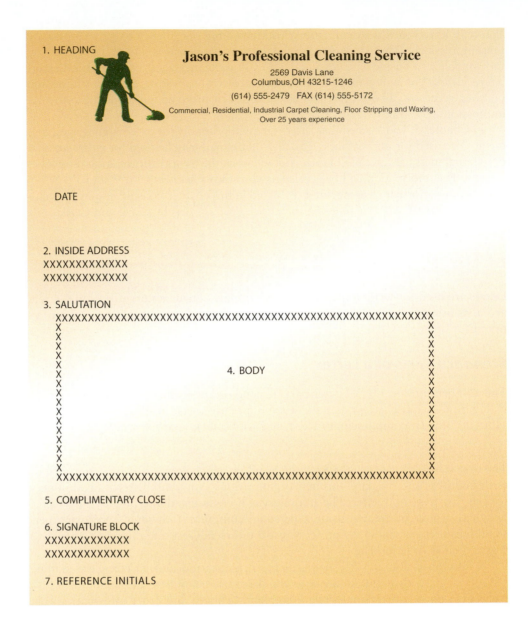

tips and hints

Letterheads with No Address

Occasionally, organizations will print letterhead stationery without including variable information such as an address or a phone/fax number. Perhaps the organization has no permanent mailing address, or the organization may operate from several sites with each needing so little stationery that the cost of printing can't be justified. When using this type of stationery, the writer must key the address and other relevant variables. The sender's address and the dateline are treated as one unit and keyed below the last line of the letterhead; the items should end no lower than two inches from the top edge of the paper.

FIGURE 6.2
Examples of Letterheads

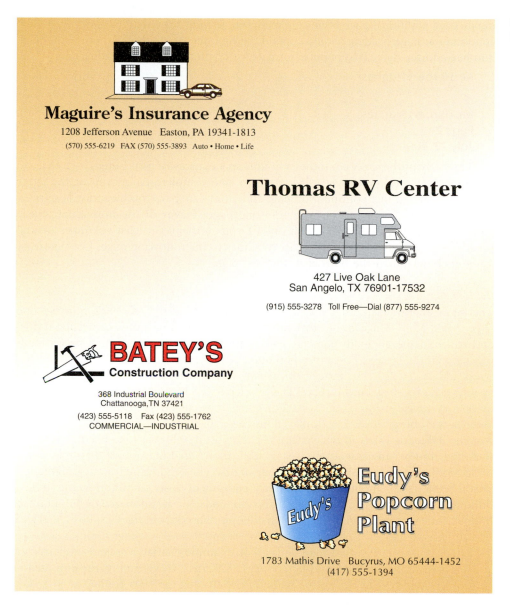

Notice that punctuation is omitted when the day appears before the month in the dateline. Placing the month before the day is the style commonly used in the United States. Placing the day first is the preferred style for international and military use.

The horizontal placement of the dateline (or the keyed return address and dateline) depends on the letter format. The vertical placement of the dateline is determined by the length of the letter. The dateline may be keyed two lines below the printed letterhead or two inches from the top edge of the page.

When a return address is keyed at the top of a personal business letter, the dateline is keyed on the line below it. When the return address appears below the signature block of a personal business letter, the date usually is placed between lines 10 and 15 from the top of the page.

Letterhead stationery is used only for the first page of a letter. Stationery of the same color and quality, but without the letterhead, is used for continuation pages. The head-

NOTE 6.6
Use stationery
without letterhead for
continuation pages.

ing on each additional page begins on line seven, leaving a top margin of one inch. The continuation page heading should contain the first line of the inside address, the page number, and the date. Two popular formats for continuation page headings are

Mr. Herbert Hughes   **2**   **July 22, 200–**

or

Mr. Herbert Hughes
Page 2
July 22, 200–

The body of the letter continues a double space (press Return/Enter twice to leave one blank line) below this heading. At least one complete paragraph of the letter should be carried to a continuation page. If a complete paragraph cannot be carried over, revise the letter so that it is only one page. Never divide individual words between pages. Divide a paragraph only if you can leave at least two lines on the preceding page and carry over at least two lines to the following page. Leave at least a one-inch margin at the bottom of the first page.

INSIDE ADDRESS

NOTE **6.7**
The inside address is the receiver's address.

The **inside address** includes some or all of the following: the receiver's courtesy title (Ms., Miss, Mrs., Mr., Dr., or other title), receiver's name, receiver's professional title, department name, company name, receiver's street address (or some other specific mailing designation, such as post office box number), city, state, and ZIP code. Abbreviate street addresses (e.g., *Ave.* instead of *Avenue*; *Rd.* instead of *Road*) only when necessary to achieve a balanced display. The two-letter U.S. postal abbreviation should be used in complete mailing addresses. For your convenience, U.S. and Canadian two-letter postal abbreviations are displayed inside the back cover of this book.

NOTE **6.8**
Use correct postal abbreviations and ZIP codes.

The ZIP code is keyed one space after the postal abbreviation. The **ZIP code** is a five-digit number that identifies areas within the United States and its possessions. In 1985, the code was expanded by four digits. These additional digits enable the Postal Service to use high-speed automated equipment to sort mail to specific streets, buildings, or floors within buildings. The ZIP code for an address can be obtained online at www.usps.com/zip4 or from media purchased from the U.S. Postal Service or software vendors.

Other countries also use mail codes. For example, Canada uses a six-character code consisting of numbers and letters (e.g., T2K5S3). In Germany, the city identification code is keyed prior to the name of the city (e.g., 53105 Bonn).

NOTE **6.9**
Leave at least two lines between the date and the inside address.

The inside address is always keyed flush with the left margin. Normally, the first line of the inside address is keyed three to five lines below the date. Blank lines can be added if the letter is short, removed if the letter is long.

SALUTATION

NOTE **6.10**
Greet your reader in the salutation.

The **salutation** is the greeting that begins the message. The content of the salutation depends on the first line of the inside address. When a letter is addressed to a company and contains an attention line (discussed on page 146), the salutation is directed to the company and not to the person named in the attention line. If the first line of the inside address is singular, the salutation must be singular; if the first line is plural, the salutation must be plural.

NOTE **6.11**
Select a salutation that reflects your relationship with the receiver.

The formality of the salutation depends on the relationship between the sender and the receiver. A general guide is to use the name that you would use if you met the person or persons face-to-face. Use Ms. for a female receiver unless she specifies another title. If you do not know the gender of the addressee, use the receiver's full

communication note

Notations such as *Personal, Confidential, Certified Mail*, and *Fax Transmittal* are keyed in uppercase letters a double space above the inside address *or* a single or double space below the last notaton on the page (e.g., reference initials, enclosure).

name without a courtesy title (Dear M. L. Benson) or use the simplified letter style (explained later in this chapter). Examples of correct and incorrect salutations include the following:

Correct	Incorrect
Dear Ms. Shelton	Dear Ms. Rita Shelton
Dear Rita	Dear Ms. Rita
Dear Mr. & Mrs. McCoy	Dear McCoys
Dear Jack and Tanya	Dear Adlers
Dear Customers:	Dear Gentlemen:
Ladies and Gentlemen:	Dear Ladies and Gentlemen:

The salutation is keyed flush with the left margin and placed a double space below the last line of the inside address or the attention line, if used. Either mixed or open punctuation may be used. These punctuation styles are discussed on page 148. The salutation is omitted in the simplified format (see pages 150–152).

NOTE 6.12
Leave two lines above and two lines below the salutation.

BODY

The **body** is the message section of the letter. It begins a double space below the salutation. The body is single spaced *within* paragraphs and double spaced *between* paragraphs. The paragraphs may be indented or blocked, depending on the letter format selected.

NOTE 6.13
The message is presented in the body.

COMPLIMENTARY CLOSE

The **complimentary close** ends the message. The word(s) used in the close should match the formality of the message, as shown in the following:

NOTE 6.14
End the letter with a complimentary close.

Formal Business Correspondence	General Business Correspondence	Informal Business Correspondence
Respectfully	Sincerely	Sincerely
Very truly yours	Sincerely yours	Sincerely yours
Sincerely yours		Cordially yours

The complimentary close is keyed a double space below the last line of the body. The first character of the close should begin at the same horizontal point as the first character of the date. Only the first character of the first word in the complimentary close is capitalized. The closing should be punctuated using the same style (mixed or open) as was used with the salutation. The simplified letter omits the complimentary close.

SIGNATURE BLOCK

The **signature block** contains the writer's signed name, keyed name, and title. The name is keyed four spaces (lines) below the complimentary close. A courtesy title is optional in the signature block. It may be included, with or without parentheses, when the gender of the writer is unclear (e.g., Pat, Kim, or Lynn). The name and position title may appear on the same line or on separate lines, whichever creates the more balanced display. If the name and position title are on the same line, a comma separates them. The sender of the message signs the letter in the space between the complimentary close and the keyed name. The signature normally does not include the courtesy title even if it is keyed in the signature block.

REFERENCE INITIALS

Reference initials show who keyed the letter. When the letter is keyed by someone other than the person who wrote it, the keyboarder includes his or her initials in the document. The initials of the writer may also be included, but they are not required. If the writer is someone other than the person who signs the letter, display the writer's initials with those of the keyboarder. The writer's initials should be upper-case letters; the keyboarder's, lowercase. The sets of initials may be separated by either a colon or a diagonal. Place the reference initials flush with the left margin a double space below the sender's title. Examples of reference initials are the following:

> ev (keyboarder's initials)
> NRE:pd (writer's initials:keyboarder's initials)
> JHT/ras (writer's initials/keyboarder's initials)

Supplementary Parts of a Letter

In addition to the seven standard parts, letters may contain one or more supplementary parts. These parts include the attention line, subject line, company name in signature block, enclosure notation, copy notation, and postscript.

ATTENTION LINE

When a company name is used as the first line of the inside address, the **attention line** can be used to direct the letter to a person, position title, or department within the company. Using a person's name in the first line of the inside address is preferred over using an attention line.

The trend is to place the attention line beneath the company name in the inside address; the same format is used on the envelope. Placing the attention line a double space below the last line of the inside address is more traditional. In either case, the attention line may be keyed with all capital letters or a combination of initial capital and lowercase letters. The word *Attention* should not be abbreviated. Placing a colon after the word *Attention* is optional. The salutation agrees with the first line of the address and not the attention line. Attention line placements are illustrated in the following:

College Station Medical Center
ATTENTION: RADIOLOGY
1604 Rock Prairie Road
College Station, TX 77842-1437

Ladies and Gentlemen:

College Station Medical Center
1604 Rock Prairie Road
College Station, TX 77842-1437

Attention: Beth Ek, Nurse Manager

Ladies and Gentlemen:

SUBJECT LINE

The **subject line** identifies the topic of the letter. It is considered part of the body of the letter. The subject line should be short—less than one line—and should not be a complete sentence. The key words contained in a subject line help office personnel sort and route incoming mail and code documents for storage and retrieval.

NOTE **6.18**
The subject line identifies the topic.

Insurance companies, financial institutions, and government agencies often replace the word *Subject* with the abbreviation *RE* or *In re*. Regardless of the term used to introduce it, the subject line is keyed a double space below the salutation. It may be centered, flush with the left margin, or indented the same number of spaces as the paragraphs. It may be keyed in all capitals or keyed with initial capitals and lowercase letters. In letter styles other than simplified, the word *Subject* is followed by a colon; in the simplified letter, the word *Subject* is omitted. If a letter contains both an attention line and a subject line, use the same format for both. A letter that includes a subject line is shown in Figure 6.3 on page 149.

COMPANY NAME IN SIGNATURE BLOCK

The name of the company may be keyed in uppercase letters a double space below the complimentary close. The company name is placed in the signature block when the letter is contractual in nature or when the letter is printed on plain paper rather than on letterhead stationery. The first character of the company name is aligned with the first character of the complimentary close. An example of a company name in the signature block follows:

NOTE **6.19**
Include the company name in the signature block of letters not printed on letterhead.

Sincerely,

FALCON ACCOUNTING

Jamie Falcon
(Ms.) Jamie Falcon, President

This addition is not commonly used with letterhead stationery, nor is it used in the simplified letter format.

ENCLOSURE OR ATTACHMENT NOTATION

Any item sent with the letter, such as a check, invoice, or photograph, is considered an **enclosure.** When something is included with a letter, an enclosure notation should be keyed a single or double space below the reference initials. The writer may list the items enclosed or merely indicate the number as part of the notation. When items are attached to the letter, use *Attachment* or *Att.* in place of the enclosure notation. Examples of enclosure and attachment notations are as follows:

NOTE **6.20**
The enclosure notation signals something is being sent in addition to the letter.

Enclosure *or* Enc.	Attachment *or* Att.
Check enclosed	Attachment: Reimbursement form
Enclosures 3	Attachments (2)
3 Enc.	Att. 3

COPY NOTATION

A **copy notation** is used when a copy of a letter is being sent to someone other than the addressee. The copy notation may appear as *cc* for *courtesy copy* or *c* for *copy*. The copy notation is keyed flush with the left margin and a double space below the reference initials (or enclosure notation, if used). The names of the individuals or

NOTE **6.21**
A copy notation tells the receiver who else received a copy of the message.

tips and hints

Computer File Notations

If you've ever tried to locate a file saved on your computer hard drive but couldn't recall the name under which you filed it, you'll understand why some organizations record a computer file notation on their documents. The notation, which consists of the path and file name of the document, is recorded below the last keyed line/notation of the document; it should appear only on the file copy, not on the document sent to the receiver.

c:\collect\edison\feb08.doc
c:\chicago\memos\vacation.doc

groups to receive the copies should be keyed after the notation. Examples of copy notations include the following:

cc: Tim Miller   c: Ms. Chin Deng
cc: Tim Miller, Sue Manos   112 West Elm Street
c: Accounting   Skokie, IL 60676-2726

NOTE 6.22
Place blind copy (bcc) notations only on copies sent to people other than the addressee.

A **blind copy notation** is used when it is unnecessary or inappropriate for an addressee to know that a copy of the letter is being sent to other individuals. The blind copy notation should appear only on copies, *not* on the original. Place the blind copy notation where the regular copy notation normally appears. Examples of blind copy notations are:

bcc: Burt LaBlanc   bcc: Mrs. Joan Yang, CPA

POSTSCRIPT

NOTE 6.23
Use a postscript to stress an important point or add a personal note.

A **postscript** may be used to add a personal comment or to emphasize an important point discussed in the body of the letter. It should *not* be used to add information omitted from the body of the letter. The postscript, whether keyed or handwritten, should follow the last notation and be formatted in the same style as the paragraphs of the message. The notation "P.S." usually is omitted.

Punctuation Styles

NOTE 6.24
Use open or mixed punctuation in the salutation and complimentary close.

The two styles of punctuation commonly used in business letters are mixed and open. **Mixed punctuation** requires a colon after the salutation and a comma after the complimentary close. **Open punctuation** omits the colon after the salutation and the comma after the complimentary close. No other letter parts are affected by the writer's choice of mixed or open punctuation.

Letter Formats

LO 3
Format business letters using the full block, modified block, and simplified styles.

Some organizations designate the format for their letters; others permit the originator to select the format. The most frequently used formats are full block, modified block, and simplified.

FULL BLOCK

NOTE 6.25
The full block letter format is efficient to prepare.

In **full block format** all parts of the letter begin at the left margin. This feature makes the document quick and easy to key. Figure 6.3 shows a full block format letter.

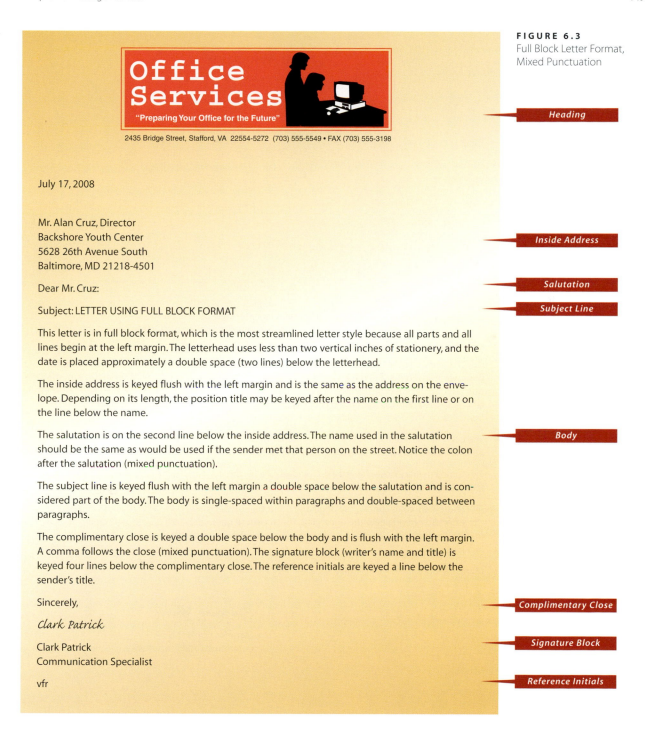

FIGURE 6.3
Full Block Letter Format, Mixed Punctuation

Office Services
"Preparing Your Office for the Future"
2435 Bridge Street, Stafford, VA 22554-5272 (703) 555-5549 • FAX (703) 555-3198

Heading

July 17, 2008

Mr. Alan Cruz, Director
Backshore Youth Center
5628 26th Avenue South
Baltimore, MD 21218-4501

Inside Address

Dear Mr. Cruz:

Salutation

Subject: LETTER USING FULL BLOCK FORMAT

Subject Line

This letter is in full block format, which is the most streamlined letter style because all parts and all lines begin at the left margin. The letterhead uses less than two vertical inches of stationery, and the date is placed approximately a double space (two lines) below the letterhead.

The inside address is keyed flush with the left margin and is the same as the address on the envelope. Depending on its length, the position title may be keyed after the name on the first line or on the line below the name.

The salutation is on the second line below the inside address. The name used in the salutation should be the same as would be used if the sender met that person on the street. Notice the colon after the salutation (mixed punctuation).

Body

The subject line is keyed flush with the left margin a double space below the salutation and is considered part of the body. The body is single-spaced within paragraphs and double-spaced between paragraphs.

The complimentary close is keyed a double space below the body and is flush with the left margin. A comma follows the close (mixed punctuation). The signature block (writer's name and title) is keyed four lines below the complimentary close. The reference initials are keyed a line below the sender's title.

Sincerely,

Complimentary Close

Clark Patrick

Clark Patrick
Communication Specialist

Signature Block

vfr

Reference Initials

MODIFIED BLOCK

NOTE 6.26
The modified block format may have blocked or indented paragraphs.

The date (or the return address and date), complimentary close, and signature block begin at the horizontal center of the page in the **modified block format.** When using the modified block format, writers choose whether to block or indent the first line of each paragraph in the letter body. Letters with blocked paragraphs are more common

FIGURE 6.4
Modified Block Letter
Format, Blocked Paragraphs,
Open Punctuation

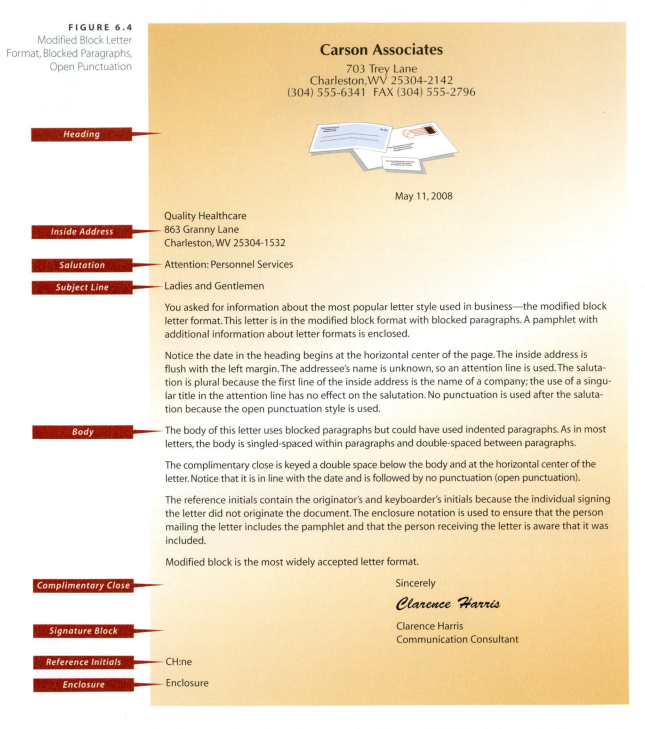

Heading

Carson Associates
703 Trey Lane
Charleston, WV 25304-2142
(304) 555-6341 FAX (304) 555-2796

May 11, 2008

Inside Address

Quality Healthcare
863 Granny Lane
Charleston, WV 25304-1532

Salutation

Attention: Personnel Services

Subject Line

Ladies and Gentlemen

You asked for information about the most popular letter style used in business—the modified block letter format. This letter is in the modified block format with blocked paragraphs. A pamphlet with additional information about letter formats is enclosed.

Notice the date in the heading begins at the horizontal center of the page. The inside address is flush with the left margin. The addressee's name is unknown, so an attention line is used. The salutation is plural because the first line of the inside address is the name of a company; the use of a singular title in the attention line has no effect on the salutation. No punctuation is used after the salutation because the open punctuation style is used.

Body

The body of this letter uses blocked paragraphs but could have used indented paragraphs. As in most letters, the body is singled-spaced within paragraphs and double-spaced between paragraphs.

The complimentary close is keyed a double space below the body and at the horizontal center of the letter. Notice that it is in line with the date and is followed by no punctuation (open punctuation).

The reference initials contain the originator's and keyboarder's initials because the individual signing the letter did not originate the document. The enclosure notation is used to ensure that the person mailing the letter includes the pamphlet and that the person receiving the letter is aware that it was included.

Modified block is the most widely accepted letter format.

Sincerely

Clarence Harris

Complimentary Close

Signature Block

Clarence Harris
Communication Consultant

Reference Initials

CH:ne

Enclosure

Enclosure

than letters with indented paragraphs. The modified block format is illustrated in Figures 6.4 and 6.5.

NOTE 6.27
The simplified format
works well when the
receiver's gender is
unknown.

SIMPLIFIED

The **simplified format** is often used when a letter is addressed to a company rather than an individual, when the gender of the receiver is unknown, or when marital

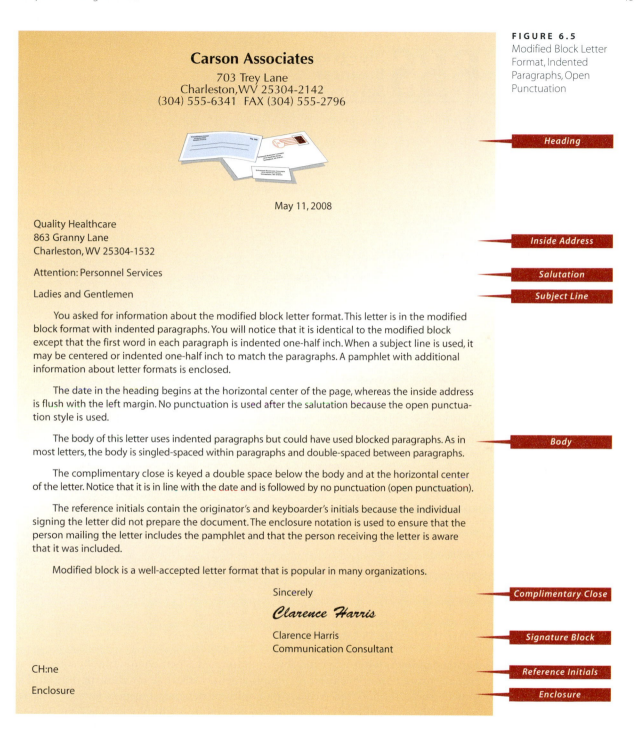

FIGURE 6.5
Modified Block Letter
Format, Indented
Paragraphs, Open
Punctuation

status of a female receiver is unknown. In this style, the salutation and complimentary close are eliminated. A subject line, displayed in uppercase letters without the word *Subject*, replaces the salutation. The writer's keyed signature and title are displayed in one line using uppercase letters. Figure 6.6 shows a letter in the simplified format.

FIGURE 6.6
Simplified Format

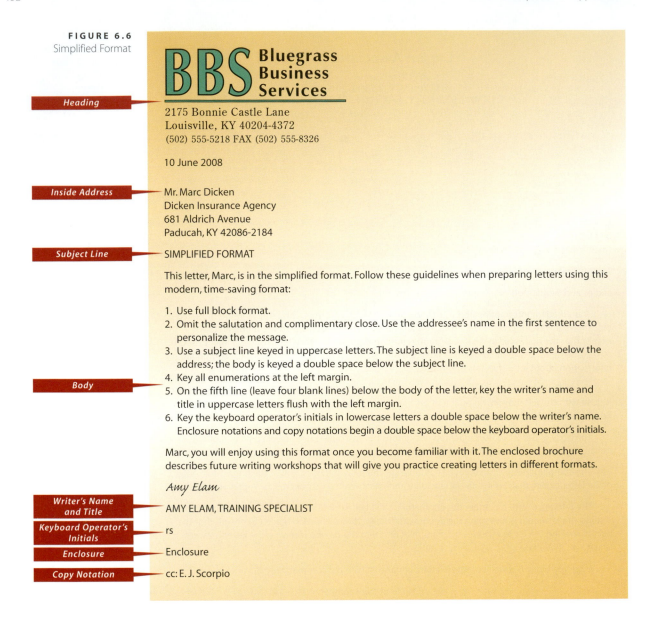

Heading

BBS **Bluegrass**
          Business
          Services

2175 Bonnie Castle Lane
Louisville, KY 40204-4372
(502) 555-5218 FAX (502) 555-8326

10 June 2008

Inside Address

Mr. Marc Dicken
Dicken Insurance Agency
681 Aldrich Avenue
Paducah, KY 42086-2184

Subject Line

SIMPLIFIED FORMAT

This letter, Marc, is in the simplified format. Follow these guidelines when preparing letters using this modern, time-saving format:

1. Use full block format.
2. Omit the salutation and complimentary close. Use the addressee's name in the first sentence to personalize the message.
3. Use a subject line keyed in uppercase letters. The subject line is keyed a double space below the address; the body is keyed a double space below the subject line.
4. Key all enumerations at the left margin.

Body

5. On the fifth line (leave four blank lines) below the body of the letter, key the writer's name and title in uppercase letters flush with the left margin.
6. Key the keyboard operator's initials in lowercase letters a double space below the writer's name. Enclosure notations and copy notations begin a double space below the keyboard operator's initials.

Marc, you will enjoy using this format once you become familiar with it. The enclosed brochure describes future writing workshops that will give you practice creating letters in different formats.

Amy Elam

**Writer's Name
and Title**

AMY ELAM, TRAINING SPECIALIST

**Keyboard Operator's
Initials**

rs

Enclosure

Enclosure

Copy Notation

cc: E. J. Scorpio

Personal Business Letters

NOTE 6.28
Personal business message formats are similar to business message formats.

A **personal business letter** is written by an individual when conducting business of a personal nature. An application for employment, a request for information, and a comment about services received are examples of personal business letters. A good grade of paper should be used for this type of letter. A full block style or modified block style with mixed or open punctuation is suitable. The return address of the sender should be placed two inches from the top edge of the paper. The date should be keyed on the line below the return address; however, the date is not considered a part of the return address. The simplified block format is not recommended for application letters because many individuals interpret the lack of a salutation as being impersonal. Figure 6.7 shows a personal business letter.

tips and hints

Picture-Perfect Letters

- Word processing software programs typically have one-inch default top and bottom margins. Pressing the Return/Enter key six or seven times before keying the date will provide two inches to accommodate the letterhead portion of stationery.
- Keyed material should be placed within the margins created by the letterhead, typically one inch on the left and one inch on the right.
- Word processing software can also allow you to view keyed documents as full pages rather than as simple keyed

text. Use this feature to decide what, if any, adjustments you must make to give your message a "framed" appearance—neither too high nor too low on the page. If adjustments are needed, choose one of the following options:
- Raise or lower the date.
- Add or reduce space between the date and the mailing address.
- Add or remove a line in the written signature area.

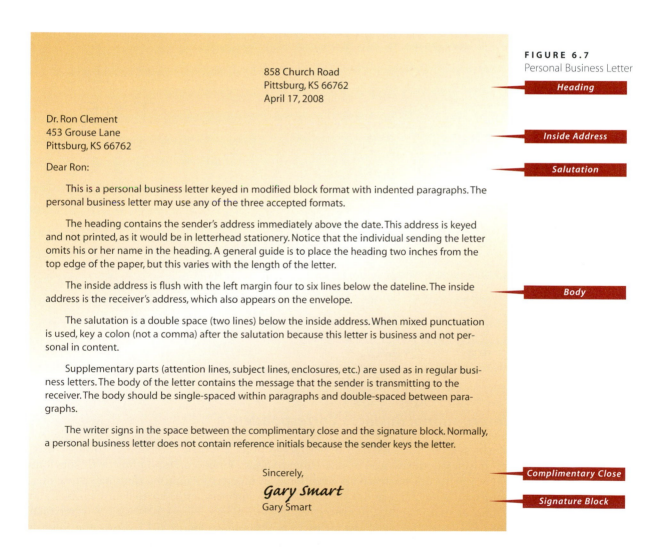

FIGURE 6.7
Personal Business Letter

Heading

Inside Address

Salutation

Body

Complimentary Close

Signature Block

858 Church Road
Pittsburg, KS 66762
April 17, 2008

Dr. Ron Clement
453 Grouse Lane
Pittsburg, KS 66762

Dear Ron:

This is a personal business letter keyed in modified block format with indented paragraphs. The personal business letter may use any of the three accepted formats.

The heading contains the sender's address immediately above the date. This address is keyed and not printed, as it would be in letterhead stationery. Notice that the individual sending the letter omits his or her name in the heading. A general guide is to place the heading two inches from the top edge of the paper, but this varies with the length of the letter.

The inside address is flush with the left margin four to six lines below the dateline. The inside address is the receiver's address, which also appears on the envelope.

The salutation is a double space (two lines) below the inside address. When mixed punctuation is used, key a colon (not a comma) after the salutation because this letter is business and not personal in content.

Supplementary parts (attention lines, subject lines, enclosures, etc.) are used as in regular business letters. The body of the letter contains the message that the sender is transmitting to the receiver. The body should be single-spaced within paragraphs and double-spaced between paragraphs.

The writer signs in the space between the complimentary close and the signature block. Normally, a personal business letter does not contain reference initials because the sender keys the letter.

Sincerely,

Gary Smart
Gary Smart

FIGURE 6.8
Chinese Business Letter

湖南洞庭茶叶有限公司
Hunan Dongding Tea Company Ltd.

报价函

洪城百货公司:
贵方2008年3月16日询价信收悉，谢谢。兹就贵方要求，报价详细如下:
品名: 君山毛尖茶
规格: 一级
容量: 每包100克
单价: 每包100元（含包装费）
包装: 标准纸箱，每箱100包
结算方式: 商业汇票
交货方式: 自提
交货日期: 收到订单10内发货
我方所报价极具竞争力，如果贵方订货量在1000包以上，我方可按95%的折扣收款。
如贵方认为我们的报价符合贵公司的要求，请早日定购。
恭候佳音!

湖南洞庭茶叶有限公司

王海民

总经理: 王海民

2008年3月28日

地址: 湖南省长沙市芙蓉西路45号 电话: 0731-729-8655
传真: 0731-729-8682 邮编: 410006

International Business Correspondence

NOTE 6.29
Letter formats vary internationally.

Business letter formats used by writers in other countries are similar to those used by business letter writers in the United States. When corresponding with someone in a foreign country, learn about differences in letter formatting that may cause misunderstandings. Figure 6.8 shows a sample business letter written in Chinese, and Figure 6.9 shows the same letter written in English. Figure 6.10 shows a personal business letter (job application) written in German; Figure 6.11 shows the English translation. The translation in Figure 6.11 follows the communication pattern of the native language rather than the pattern of American English. Refer to Chapter 2 for more information about language patterns.

湖南洞庭茶叶有限公司
Hunan Dongding Tea Company Ltd.

Pricing Quote

Hongcheng Baihuo Co.:

   Thank you for the pricing inquiry made on March 16, 2008. Based on your requests, detailed pricing information is as follows:

Commodity Name: Junshan Maojian Tea
Quality Rating: First Class
Capacity: 100g/bag
Unit Price: RMB100/bag (including packing charges)
Packing: Standard packing box, 100 bags/box
Settlement: Commercial Draft
Delivery: Pick up
Delivery Date: Deliver goods 10 days after receiving the order form

   The above pricing quote is very competitive. If the quantity of your order is more than 1000 bags, you will receive 5% discount.

   If you think the above pricing quote is consistent with your requirement, please make the order at your earliest convenience.

   We look forward to hearing from you!

                                    Hunan Dongting Tea Company Ltd.

                                    Wang Haimin
                                    Chief Executive Officer: Wang Haimin

                                    March 28, 2008

Address: 45 Furong West Road, Changsha, Hunan   Phone: 0731-729-8655
Fax: 731-729-8682   Zip Code: 410006

FIGURE 6.9
English Translation of Chinese Business Letter

Heading

Subject Line

Salutation

Body

Signature Block

Date

Heading

   Note that standard letter parts are placed differently in these letters than in the formats used in the United States. Note, too, that the Chinese letter places words horizontally rather than vertically, as is customary in other types of Chinese writing.

Envelopes

Envelope paper should be the same color and quality as the letterhead stationery. The envelope must be of adequate size to hold the letter and any enclosures or attachments without unnecessary folding. An envelope should include a return address and a mailing address and may include notations. The envelope feature of word processing software can be helpful when preparing envelopes.

LO 4
Address an envelope properly.

NOTE 6.30
The envelope paper and design should be similar to those of the letter.

FIGURE 6.10
Sample German Personal
Business Letter

Heading

Hans Mustermann
Zickzackweg 90
25602 Hamburg

Inside Address

HSG Bewerbermanagement GmbH
Postfach 442013
20401 Hamburg

Date

10 Januar 2008

Subject Line

Ihre Anzeige in der FAZ vom 07.01.08, Kennziffer 1185FAZ
Führungskräfte im Controlling bei der Beiersdorf AG

Salutation

Sehr geehrte Damen und Herren,

den weltweiten Erfolg Ihres Unternehmens durch Umstrukturierung Ihres Controllings innerhalb der Supply Chain auszubauen ist eine verantwortungsvolle Aufgabe.

In meiner Tätigkeit als IT-Berater konnte ich in den letzten vier Jahren Erfahrung auf internationalen SAP-Projekten in Europa und den USA sammeln. Meine Aufgaben waren die Integration der Produktion und Produktionsplanung in die Supply Chain sowie die Kommunikation mit den Teams Beschaffung, Qualitätsmanagement, Vertrieb und Controlling. Die Aufnahme der Prozesse, deren Implementierung und die Betreuung des Live Systems ermöglichte mir den Einblick in alle Phasen eines IT-Projektes.

Während des Integrationstestes sammelte ich erste Erfahrung bei der Koordinierung eines Teams.

Body

Im Rahmen der Analyse der Materialdisposition im End of Life habe ich mit der Definition des Prozesses und Aufzeigen von Optimierungsmöglichkeiten etwas bewegen können.

Die Möglichkeit, bei der Beiersdorf AG mein bisher erworbenes Wissen aus der Polymer und Technologie Branche einzubringen ist eine Herausforderung, die ich mit Ihrem Controlling Team gerne in die Hand nehmen will.

Für Fragen stehe ich Ihnen gerne zu Verfügung und würde mich über eine Einladung zum Bewerbungsgespräch sehr freuen.

Complimentary Close

Mit freundlichem Gruß

Hans Mustermann

Signature Block

Hans Mustermann

Enclosure

Anlage: Bewerbungsmappe

As William Jaskari notes in the Communication Note on page 158, using correct format when addressing an envelope helps the Postal Service direct your messages efficiently and effectively.

Return Address

NOTE 6.31
The envelope identifies
both the sender and
the receiver.

The **return address** is the sender's address. It should be the same as the one used in the letterhead. Whether preprinted or keyed, the return address is located in the upper left corner of the envelope. The writer's name, initials, and/or location may

FIGURE 6.11
English Translation
of German Personal
Business Letter

be keyed immediately above a preprinted business return address. For personal business letters, return addresses should be printed on labels or keyed on plain envelopes. A keyed return address is single spaced and displayed using a mixture of uppercase and lowercase letters.

Mailing Address

The mailing address on an envelope should be identical to the inside address of the letter, blocked, and single spaced. The first line of the address should be slightly

NOTE 6.32
Use the inside address of the letter for the mailing address on the envelope.

communication note

Once a piece of mail reaches the post office, it may not be touched by human hands until delivery. Our high-tech scanning equipment can read approximately 86 percent of handwritten envelopes and nearly 100 percent of those that are typed/printed. The sender's return address should be placed in the upper-left corner of the envelope so the equipment can distinguish between it and the receiver's address. Always include the five-digit ZIP code, and use the ZIP + 4 if you know it. Properly addressing an envelope is important for timely delivery; it minimizes handling delays within the post office.

Courtesy William Jaskari, Plant Manager, USPS

FIGURE 6.12
Correctly Addressed Envelopes

below and to the left of the center of the envelope. The last line of the inside address must contain only the city, state, and ZIP code. Envelope placement is illustrated in Figure 6.12.

Envelope Notations

Envelopes may have addressee and/or delivery notations. Instructions to individuals handling the addressee's mail are keyed in uppercase letters a double space below the return address. These notations include CONFIDENTIAL, HOLD FOR ARRIVAL, PERSONAL, and PLEASE FORWARD. When an attention line appears below the inside address in a letter, it is treated as an addressee notation.

Delivery instructions should be keyed in all capital letters a double space below the postage stamp or meter mark. This placement facilitates electronic scanning and sorting of mail. Mailing instructions include SPECIAL DELIVERY, SPECIAL HANDLING, REGISTERED, and CERTIFIED.

NOTE 6.33
Envelopes may have addressee and/or delivery notations.

Memos and E-mail

A **memo,** short for *memorandum*, is used for internal business communication. Memos are normally less formal and shorter than letters. E-mail, the electronic version of a memo, is gradually replacing print memos as the primary method for communicating within an organization.

LO 5
Format memos and e-mail properly.

Uses of Memos and E-mail

Memos and e-mail may be used to communicate upward to superiors, downward to subordinates, laterally to peers, and diagonally to other members of a network. Information of all kinds can be conveyed from one department to another through memos and e-mail. In addition, e-mail may be used as a cost-effective alternative to long-distance telephone calls when requesting information and responding to inquiries; it may also be used as a cover document for attached files.

Because e-mail is neither protected nor private, it should not be used to discuss confidential information or significant issues. Also, writers should refrain from using e-mail for long messages or documents requiring a paper copy.

NOTE 6.34
Use memos for internal correspondence.

NOTE 6.35
Memos and e-mail are less formal than letters.

Advantages of Memos and E-mail

Using memos and e-mail has several advantages. One advantage is that the same message can be addressed to several individuals.

NOTE 6.36
Memos and e-mail have similar advantages.

Blondie by Dean Young

If you want to send the same memo to specific employees, you can list all the names and place a check mark after a different name on each copy. Or, you can list all the names and request that the memo be routed from the first-named person through the last-named person. Entire groups can be addressed in a memo and individual copies can be given to each member of the group, or the memo may be placed on a bulletin board. Examples of ways to address memos properly follow:

Specific Individuals	**Groups**
TO: Julie O'Brien	TO: Human Resources Department Employees
Teresa Uland	
Parker Snazza	
TO: See Distribution List	TO: Budget Committee

In the last example, See Distribution List, the names on the distribution list would be listed at the left margin two lines below the text of the memo under a section entitled Distribution List.

When sending e-mail, the writer enters the address of one or more receivers into the *To* section of the message composition template. By using the group address function of the e-mail software, a writer can enter the names and addresses of multiple receivers and assign them to a group file. Entering the group file name in the *To* section of the template directs the message to everyone in the file. The risk of error is minimized because only one address needs to be keyed.

TO: jobrien@catco.com; tuland@catco.com; psnazza@catco.com
TO: budcom@catco.com

A second advantage of using memos and e-mail is that they are less formal than letters and may require less time to compose. Internal messages should be clear and accurate, but they usually do not have to be as polished as letters. Business-related e-mail directed to an external receiver should be informal, not casual. Writers should use correct grammar and punctuation; spelling errors should be corrected. Corporate culture and receiver analysis will dictate whether internal e-mail must meet this standard. Remember, your e-mail message may be forwarded to others. It will reflect on your professionalism as well as on your ability to communicate.

Another advantage of using a memo, or an e-mail, or other written message is that they are visual. Written messages make a more lasting impression than do oral messages.

Memo Format

NOTE 6.37
The receiver, sender, subject, and date are identified at the beginning of a memo.

An organization may use more than one format for its memos, or it may specify one format to be used throughout the organization. Some organizations use printed memo stationery; others ask writers to use customized word processing templates. Both formats typically contain the guide words *To*, *From*, and *Subject* (in that order); they may also include the word *Date*. These guide words replace the date, inside address, and salutation included in a letter. The culture of the organization will determine whether courtesy or professional titles are included with the names in the *To* and *From* sections of the memo.

NOTE 6.38
Memos use full block format for paragraph and notation display.

The body of the memo is keyed flush with the left margin a triple space beneath the *Subject*. As with letters, text is single spaced within and double spaced between paragraphs. A memo has no complimentary close or signature block; the writer simply signs or initials near his or her typed name in the *From* section of the document. Reference initials, notations, and continuation page headings are placed and keyed as they would be in a letter.

A memo prepared using a Microsoft Word memo template is shown in Figure 6.13.

E-mail Format

E-mail software uses **message composition templates,** sets of boxes for variable information (e.g., To, Subject, cc, bcc), and buttons to activate program options (e.g., Send, Attachment, spell check). Most e-mail software programs automatically enter the date the message is sent and the writer's contact information.

Once the appropriate variable information has been keyed, the writer enters the text of the message in the message-composition window. All lines of the message begin at the default left margin. Text is single spaced within paragraphs, double spaced between paragraphs.

To give e-mail a conversational style, writers may open their messages with a friendly greeting and end them with a signature. The formality of each entry depends on the relationship between the sender and the receiver. A message between workers in a department might begin "Hi Bob" and end "Sue." A message between a worker and a superior might begin "Dear Mrs. Burrows" and end with "Ben Chastain, Client Services Representative." Figure 6.14 illustrates an e-mail message.

NOTE 6.39
Enter heading variables into the e-mail template.

NOTE 6.40
Using a greeting and a signature can give e-mail a conversational style.

Stationery

The appearance and weight of the stationery used when preparing business correspondence will influence the impression made by those messages. Businesses usually select stationery that matches the purpose of the message. For example, the stationery used for closing a major business transaction should be of a higher quality than the stationery used for announcing an upcoming sale to credit card customers.

LO 6
Discuss the characteristics of appropriate stationery for letters, memos, and envelopes.

Size

Memos and most business letters are prepared on **standard-size paper,** which measures $8^1/_2$ by 11 inches. Letters from business executives are sometimes placed on $7^1/_4$- by 10-inch high-quality stationery called **executive stationery.**

NOTE 6.41
Match the quality of the stationery to the purpose of the message.

Weight

The stationery most commonly used for business letters is 20-pound bond. This weight measurement approximates the weight of four reams of $8^1/_2$- by 11-inch paper. One ream usually contains 500 sheets.

NOTE 6.42
The standard size for stationery is $8^1/_2$ by 11 inches.

NOTE 6.43
Use 20-pound bond paper for letters.

Color

Selecting the appropriate stationery color is extremely important to the image of the company. White is the most popular color and is acceptable for all correspondence, but another color may be chosen because of its link to a company or industry. For example, a lumber company may choose a light wood-grained stationery.

NOTE 6.44
White stationery is always appropriate.

Company Name

Taylor Enterprises

Memo

To: All Employees

Heading

From: Janet Wilkins, Administrative Specialist *JW*

Date: 03/17/08

Re: Characteristics of Formal Memos

Many questions have arisen concerning proper construction and use of formal memos. The following guidelines should answer these questions.

Formal memos contain several unique characteristics. Some of these characteristics follow:

1. A memo should have a preprinted or keyed heading consisting of **TO:, FROM:, DATE:,** and **SUBJECT:** or **Re.**

2. The individual sending the memo may or may not use a business title. The sender normally does not use a complete signature. An individual's first name or initials are usually written after the keyed name on the **FROM** line in the heading.

Body

3. The memo is not centered vertically as is a letter.

4. Memos, whether formal or simplified, are normally short and contain only one topic; that topic is indicated in the subject line. If more than one topic is needed, separate memos are sent.

5. The body of the memo is in block style beginning a triple space below the heading. The body is single spaced.

6. Informal writing style is appropriate for memos. First person, I, is commonly used as in letters.

Remember that memos should be concise and easy to read; they should not contain any irrelevant information.

Reference Initials

fp

Quality

NOTE 6.45
Use high-quality paper
for all pages of a letter.

The quality of stationery is determined by the amount of rag content in the paper. The **rag content** is the amount and type of fiber (usually cotton) used in the composition of the paper. High-quality stationery usually has 25 percent or more rag content. High-quality stationery also has a watermark showing the name of the company that manufactures the paper or the emblem of the organization that uses the stationery.

Letters should be prepared on high-quality stationery; all pages should be of the same weight, color, quality, and size. The advantages of using high-quality stationery for letters include superior appearance, excellent texture, and long life without chemical breakdown. Memos should be prepared on less-expensive grades of paper.

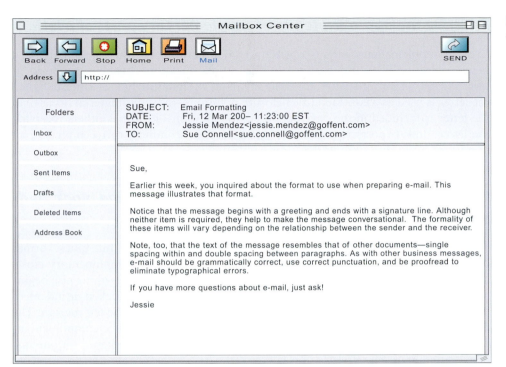

FIGURE 6.14
An E-mail message.

Envelope Paper

Envelope paper should be of the same weight, color, and quality as the letterhead stationery. Also, envelopes should be in proportion to the size of the stationery. For example, standard $8\frac{1}{2}$- by 11- inch stationery requires No. 10 ($9\frac{1}{2}$- by 4-inch) envelopes; executive stationery is $7\frac{1}{4}$ by 10 inches and requires No. 7 ($7\frac{1}{2}$- by 3-inch) envelopes.

Written messages convey a positive or negative image of an organization. Select stationery that reflects the importance of the message.

NOTE 6.46
Select envelopes that minimize the number of letter folds.

Summary of Learning Objectives

Describe the seven standard parts of a letter.

LO 1

The seven standard parts of a letter are (a) heading—a letterhead or return address and the date; (b) inside address—the courtesy title, name, and mailing address of the receiver; (c) salutation—the greeting that begins the message; (d) body—the message section of the letter; (e) complimentary close—a phrase used to end a message; (f) signature block—the writer's signed name, keyed name, and title; and (g) reference initials—the initials of the message originator and/or the keyboard operator. Either open or mixed punctuation may be used with the salutation and complimentary close.

LO 2

Describe the appropriate use of supplementary parts of a letter.

Uses for supplementary parts of a letter are (a) attention line—directs the letter to a person, position title, or department within an organization; (b) subject line—identifies the main topic of a letter; (c) company name in signature block—appears when the letter is used as a contract; (d) enclosure notation—indicates material other than the letter is included in the envelope; (e) copy notation—identifies others receiving the letter; and (f) postscript—used to add a personal comment or to emphasize an important point discussed in the letter.

LO 3

Format business letters using the full block, modified block, and simplified styles.

All standard and supplementary parts of letters written in the full block format begin at the left margin. In modified block letters, the date, complimentary close, and signature block begin at the horizontal center of the page; everything else begins at the left margin. Paragraphs in modified block letters may be blocked or indented. All parts of letters prepared using the simplified format begin at the left margin. The format does not use a salutation; instead, it uses a subject line. The complimentary close is also omitted. In addition, the writer's name and title are keyed on one line using only uppercase letters.

LO 4

Address an envelope properly.

The return address (the sender's address as shown on the letterhead) is keyed in the upper-left corner of the envelope. The mailing address (the receiver's name and address as shown in the inside address) is keyed slightly below and to the left of the center of the envelope. Postal Service delivery instructions are placed a double space below the postage stamp or meter mark. Instructions to individuals handling the addressee's mail are keyed a double space below the return address. Addressee and delivery instructions should be in uppercase letters. The envelope feature of word processing software can be useful when preparing envelopes.

LO 5

Format memos and e-mail properly.

A memo may be prepared on preprinted paper or by using a software template. Both the form and the template will contain the guide words *To*, *From*, and *Subject*; the guide word *Date* may also be included. These items replace the date, inside address, salutation, and complimentary close used in letters. Paragraphs, reference initials, and notations are formatted as they would be for a letter. A writer signs or initials a memo near his or her keyed name in the *From* section. E-mail is an electronic memorandum. Writers use message composition templates to enter variable information and key the message. The paragraph text of an e-mail resembles that of a letter or memo. Writers may use greetings and signature lines to make their messages more conversational.

Discuss the characteristics of appropriate stationery for letters, memos, and envelopes.

The most commonly used stationery is 20-pound bond. Generally, correspondence is prepared on standard-size paper, 8$\frac{1}{2}$ by 11 inches, but some messages may be prepared on executive stationery, 7$\frac{1}{2}$ by 10 inches. White is the most popular color for stationery, but other colors are acceptable. The rag content determines the quality of the stationery. Letters are prepared on higher quality stationery than are memos. Envelopes and stationery should be the same quality and color. The envelope should be an appropriate size for the stationery.

Questions for Discussion and Review

1. List and explain the seven standard parts of a letter. (Objective 1)
2. What formatting guidelines should be followed if a letter is too long to fit onto one page? (Objective 1)
3. What items are included in the signature block of a letter? How and where is the writer identified in a memo? (Objectives 1 and 5)
4. Explain how an attention line and a subject line differ in (a) purpose and (b) placement. (Objective 2)
5. In what way can an enclosure notation help a message reader? a message writer? (Objective 2)
6. Explain where to place addressee and delivery notations on a letter and on an envelope. (Objectives 2 and 4)
7. Name and explain the two punctuation styles that can be used with letters. (Objective 2)
8. Name and identify the placement features of the three business letter formats discussed in this chapter. (Objective 3)
9. Why do organizations choose to use high-quality paper for letters but not for memos? (Objective 6)
10. Name and discuss the four factors to consider when selecting stationery. (Objective 6)

Application Exercises

1. **Technology.** Use word processing or other software to design a letterhead that could be used for your personal business correspondence. (Objective 1)

TECHNOLOGY

2. Respond to the following e-mail from a friend. Follow your instructor's directions about whether to print your message or send it to him or her electronically. (Objective 1)

   I want to apply for a job listed in today's paper, but there's no company name—just a post office box. What should I use for a salutation?

3. Rewrite any of the complimentary closings that are not appropriate for the situation. (Objective 1)

Situation	Complimentary Closing
a. Letter to your state senator	Cordially
b. Letter to a new customer	Respectfully
c. Letter to a long-time customer	Sincerely

4. Correct the following inside addresses and salutations: (Objectives 1 and 2)

   a. AmberQuest, Inc.
   689 City Center Drive, Suite 206
   Aurora, CO 80016-5320

   Dear Ms. Kilichowsky

   b. Ambrose Britton, MD

Plains Clinic
1229 Prairie Road
Emporia, KS 66801-9479

Dear Dr. Britton, MD:

c. G. P. Sellner, Jr.
682 First Avenue
Sacramento, CA 95818-2034

Dear Gary

5. Display the following date, inside address, salutation, and text as (a) a letter using full block format and open punctuation, (b) a letter using modified block format with indented paragraphs and mixed punctuation, and (c) a simplified letter. Assume the letter will be printed on letterhead stationery. (Objective 3)

November 15, 200–, Phillip Begg, Begg & Sons Construction, 97 Baker Road, Arkadelphia, AR, 71923-7205, Dear Mr. Begg, Thank you for responding to RFP #388-A. Your proprosal was submitted on time and is complete.

6. Obtain and examine the letterhead stationery and envelopes used at your school or at another organization your instructor selects, and then answer the following questions: (Objectives 1, 4, and 6)
   a. Are the color and quality of the paper used for the letterhead and envelope the same?
   b. Does the letterhead have a watermark? If so, what is it?
   c. Does the letterhead include a logo, motto, or similar item? If so, is the item also displayed on the envelope?
   d. Does the letterhead include contact information in addition to the name and mailing address of the institution? If so, what?

7. Prepare a memo to your instructor describing the advantages and features of the simplified letter format. (Objectives 3 and 5)

8. Visit the Postal Service website (www.usps.com) or your local post office to learn the difference between certified mail and registered mail. Then, address an envelope (or paper cut to the appropriate size) to be sent by you to the mailing address below using the delivery notation that will provide you (the sender) with proof of delivery or the dates of attempted delivery. (Objective 4)

Mr. Jacob Haroldson
Tessling and Lane, LLP
101 South Fifth Street, Suite C
Yuma, AZ 85364-1319

9. Correct the following memo headings: (Objective 5)
   a. TO: Ebony Cartier
         FROM: Seth Maas
         Subject: Fiscal Year Closing Procedures
         Date: June 1, 200–
   c. 2008 June 09
         SUBJECT: Vacation Requests
         TO: Department Managers
         FROM: John Demgen

Web exercises to accompany this chapter are available at **www.thomsonedu.com/ bcomm/krizan.**

MESSAGE ANALYSIS

Correct the content, word choice, grammar, and punctuation errors in the following message; format it as a memo to Rachel Coker from Paul Martin. Date the memo September 17; create an appropriate subject line. Send a copy to the night shift leader.

> *You're transfer to the knight shift has been approved. I am sure you will injoy working with Jenny Carey; your new shaft leeder.*
>
> *As shown on the attached schedule, you will begin working the night shift (midnight to 8 a.m.) on Monday October 1. Please continue working the day shift (eight to for) thru Friday, September 28th.*
>
> *Rachel, you is an asset to our co, and we are pleased to make this change to assist you in improving your child-care arrangments.*

Writer's Workshop

The following items may be sentence fragments or contain errors in subject-verb agreement, pronoun-antecedent agreement, comma and semicolon placement, number display, capitalization, spelling, word choice, possessives, modifier clarity and placement, or parallelism. Rewrite the sentences to make them correct.

1. Jenkins Enterprises has remodeled there Benson road complex.
2. John will be at the meeting, ask him about the proposal then.
3. Every project has challenges but this one is especially difficult.
4. Sara Redden, the ceo, met with the board of Directers at nine o'clock a.m., dined with her sister at 12 p.m., and golfed with clients at 2 p.m.
5. Each of the candidates must submit an application form with they're letter and résumé.
6. Neither the Benson Brothers nor John have read the twelve-page document.
7. After reading Scotts' report Angie suggested he ad 2 graphs.
8. Connie only offered Ben a 10 percent discount, he had expected more.
9. Bring these forms to accounting and ask Paula Smith the department head to sign them.
10. Why does Amy want to know which of us lead the building tour last week?

Chapter 7

Positive, Neutral, and Social Business Messages

LET'S TALK BUSINESS

In my dual position as manager of the Twin Ports–area Curves business office and manager of a Curves Fitness Center, I use oral and written communication daily. Whether I am composing policy and procedure instructions for managers and staff or teaching a nutrition class, the message must be upbeat yet informative and concise. I use the direct approach for the majority of my messages—I put the main idea up front and then provide relevant details.

Karen Wallis, Manager, Curves

Photo courtesy of Karen Wallis

A positive, helpful attitude is essential for good client relationships. At Curves, we send birthday cards to all members and make a concerted effort to follow up on our members' workout habits and membership status. Things like sending a congratulatory postcard to someone who is making strides toward a goal, greeting clients when they arrive and acknowledging them when they leave, posting member achievements at the club, and giving individual attention to members during their workouts all have a great effect on member retention.

Building strong, positive relationships is the cornerstone of any business. Being able to communicate directly with clarity and a genuine concern for clients and associates will have a tremendous effect on your organization and your career.

A **positive** or **neutral message** conveys pleasant, favorable, or neutral information to the receiver. Such a message may (a) provide routine or unsolicited information, (b) request information or action, or (c) respond favorably to requests for information or action. Routine claim messages, adjustment messages, and social business messages are also discussed in this chapter because they follow a plan similar to that used for conveying positive information. **Claims** are requests for action when a writer has been wronged, **adjustments** are positive responses to claims, and **social business messages** are unsolicited acknowledgments of important events in readers' personal or professional lives.

LO 1
Describe positive and neutral messages.

NOTE 7.1
Positive and neutral messages give favorable or neutral information.

Use the Direct Plan for Positive and Neutral Messages

As Karen Wallis points out in this chapter's Let's Talk Business feature, most of her communications are direct and positive. She's not alone. Most of the communication that occurs within an organization, between organizations, or between an organization and its customers or clients can be described as being favorable or neutral to the receiver. When preparing these messages, writers use the **direct plan.** Placing the main idea early in the message attracts the receiver's interest and encourages him or her to read the entire message. By reading the rest of the message, the receiver learns the supporting details and the benefits he or she will receive. The explanation will have a much better chance of acceptance if the receiver is in a good mood rather than in an apprehensive state.

NOTE 7.2
The direct plan encourages receivers to read and accept the message.

How to Use the Direct Plan

Incorporate into your positive and neutral messages the business communication fundamentals that were presented in Chapters 1, 4, and 5. In particular, analyze your receiver and use the you–viewpoint, as discussed in Chapter 1. The four stages in the direct plan for presenting positive or neutral information are detailed in Figure 7.1.

As noted in Chapter 5, planning is a key step in preparing all business messages. You have analyzed the situation and receiver and determined that he or she will respond favorably or neutrally to the information you must convey. You have decided to use the direct plan and know whether you will transmit your message as a letter, a memo, or an e-mail. The next steps are to determine message content and draft the document. Answering the following questions will help you with those steps:

- What is the most favorable information?
- How will this information benefit the receiver?
- What additional information should be given to the receiver?
- Would a convincing sales appeal be appropriate in this message? If so, what content or theme would work best?
- What friendly message will build goodwill in the close?

LO 2
Describe the four specific guidelines for using the direct plan.

NOTE 7.3
The direct plan has specific steps.

NOTE 7.4
Develop content after analyzing the situation and the receiver and determining the purposes of the message.

FIGURE 7.1
Direct Plan Outline

Direct Plan for Positive and Neutral Messages

I. The **Opening**
   A. Give the positive or neutral information.
   B. Be optimistic.
   C. Provide coherence.
   D. Use emphasis techniques.
   E. Stress receiver interests and benefits.

II. The **Explanation**
   A. Present related information.
   B. Be objective.
   C. Be concise.
   D. Be positive.

III. The **Sales Appeal** (if appropriate)
   A. Personalize the message.
   B. Suggest alternatives if appropriate.
   C. Aim for quick action.

IV. The **Friendly Close**
   A. Build goodwill.
   B. Be concise.
   C. Be positive.
   D. Express appreciation.

Once you have answered these questions, you are ready to implement the direct plan. The parts of the direct plan outline are discussed in the following sections.

Opening

NOTE 7.5
In the direct plan, messages begin with positive or neutral information.

In the direct plan, the message should give the positive or neutral information in the **opening**—the subject line or the first paragraph of the message. The subject line works especially well in a memo or an e-mail because it is a natural part of the heading. A subject line can also be added to a letter, but it's not necessary to do so.

The first sentence of the first paragraph should contain the information that will be most beneficial to the receiver. Use positive words to present the information. Give the main idea emphasis by keeping the opening paragraph to two or three lines. If the message responds to a request or is part of an ongoing communication, use the opening paragraph to set the context for the message you are writing. If you prefer, identify the topic, product, order, or contract in a subject line.

Explanation

NOTE 7.6
The supporting explanation should follow the positive or neutral opening.

The second part of a message using the direct plan should contain the explanation. The **explanation** presents additional information that relates to the positive or neutral information presented in the first paragraph. The explanation is factual and, therefore, needs to be presented objectively. It should be concise but still contain all the details the receiver needs. The explanation should be written optimistically.

Sales Appeal

The **sales appeal** is the portion of a message in which the writer attempts to persuade the reader to take a specific action. It can be effective in many positive and neutral messages, but it is not appropriate in all of them. Situations in which a sales appeal would be used include letters approving charge accounts and messages approving claims. In both cases, the receiver might be informed of an upcoming sale or given a discount coupon to encourage him or her to make a purchase soon. Situations in which a sales appeal would not be appropriate include making a claim and agreeing to speak at a meeting.

The sales appeal, if used, should come after the explanation. Depending on its length and nature, the sales appeal may be placed in a paragraph by itself or combined with the closing paragraph. Adapt the appeal to the situation; if possible and desirable, provide alternatives for the receiver. The sales appeal may tell about an upcoming sale or a new product. Personalize the appeal to convince the receiver that it is in his or her best interest to take immediate action.

NOTE 7.7
Use a sales appeal when appropriate.

NOTE 7.8
The sales appeal should follow the explanation.

Friendly Close

The **friendly close** is the final paragraph of a message. Its primary purpose is to build goodwill. This goal is achieved by being personal and optimistic. The close may unify the message by referring to the good information given in the first paragraph, or it may move to a related subject such as appreciation for an employee's past service or for a customer's business. In an internal message requesting routine information, the closing may be as informal as saying "Thanks!" Regardless of the content, the close in a positive or neutral message should be short and omit clichés.

Skillfully used, the direct plan is appropriate for messages that request information, convey favorable information, convey neutral information, or make or settle claims. With the direct plan, effective messages can increase employee morale, promote customer goodwill, and positively affect those who receive them.

The remainder of this chapter is devoted to discussing the various types of positive and neutral messages used in business communication. It begins with unsolicited messages, moves to requests/responses and claims/adjustments, and ends with social business messages. In each segment, you'll see how the direct plan can be applied to create messages that meet the goals of business communication.

NOTE 7.9
A properly written close builds goodwill.

NOTE 7.10
Businesses send both internal and external unsolicited positive or neutral messages.

Unsolicited Positive and Neutral Messages

An **unsolicited positive** or **neutral message** is a communication initiated by an organization. Examples of unsolicited positive or neutral messages to customers may include an announcement of new products or services, notification of new hours of operation, reductions in prices of merchandise, relocation to a new building, or employment of new customer representatives. Unsolicited positive messages to employees may announce new fringe benefits, an unscheduled pay increase, or a promotion. Unsolicited neutral messages may announce, cancel, or reschedule meetings; they may also give instructions or explain policies or procedures.

NOTE 7.11
Using the direct plan in positive and neutral messages increases their effectiveness.

Pickles by Brian Crane

LO 3

Distinguish between poor and good positive and neutral messages.

Unsolicited positive or neutral messages should employ the direct approach. The direct plan is illustrated in the following case, which shows the development of an unsolicited message from a business to an external receiver. You could use the same plan when developing a positive or neutral message to be delivered in person or by telephone. Here are the details of the communication situation:

The Linc Philips Case

NOTE 7.12
A communication case will help illustrate how to apply the direct plan.

Sandborn Flooring had a display at last weekend's local home show. Those who stopped at the booth were invited to enter a drawing for a 4- by 6-foot area rug. Paula Enroe, the store manager, now faces the task of notifying Linc Philips that he has won and providing details about how he can claim his prize.

The first step in writing is to analyze the situation and determine the purpose and content that will most effectively accomplish the objective of the communication. In the Linc Philips case, the objective is to convey positive information—the receiver has won a prize. For this situation, the ideas should be developed and organized using the direct plan. The following sections illustrate how the content of this positive information letter could be developed. Each section discusses a stage of the direct plan and presents an example of *poor writing* and an example of *good writing*.

OPEN WITH THE POSITIVE INFORMATION

NOTE 7.13
The example of a poor opening lacks the you–viewpoint.

A **poor** opening presenting the positive information follows:

- Thank you for stopping by our booth at the home show.

This poorly written opening is courteous, but vague. It does not mention the positive news that Mr. Philips has won the home show drawing. After reading this opening, the receiver doesn't know the purpose of the message. He might think that he has received a sales letter.

NOTE 7.14
The good opening meets all requirements for presenting positive news.

The following would be a **good** opening for this case problem:

- Congratulations, Mr. Philips! You've won an area rug that will enhance the beauty of your home.

In contrast to the poorly written opening, this one-sentence paragraph meets all the requirements of a direct plan opening. It begins with positive information and emphasizes the you–viewpoint. Because this first paragraph has a positive, personal tone, Mr. Philips will be excited about reading the rest of the message.

PROVIDE AN EXPLANATION

The next step in composing a message using the direct plan is to present an explanation of the conditions under which the positive information—claiming the prize—will be carried out.

A **poor** way to present an explanation to Mr. Philips follows:

- While at our booth, you entered our drawing. We had over 1,000 entries, and when we held the drawing at the close of the show on Sunday evening, the name on the form was yours. Your prize is a rug.

NOTE 7.15
The poor explanation lacks the you–viewpoint, is negative, and minimizes the good news.

The style of this poor explanation is similar to the style of the poor opening; it stresses the writer's interests rather than the receiver's benefits. The I–viewpoint and the tone of the message make the explanation negative or, at the very least, dull. The explanation should contain all relevant facts so that the receiver will not have any questions. In this example, the reader is told very little about the prize and how to claim it.

In contrast, a **good** explanation follows:

- To claim your home show prize, bring the enclosed certificate to our Eastside Mall store within the next 30 days. Your lovely 4- by 6-foot Farleigh Woodland Flowers rug will be waiting for you. If you prefer another pattern, size, or style, you may apply the certificate—valued at $150—toward the purchase of any rug in our store.

NOTE 7.16
The good example meets all requirements for a positive explanation.

This explanation presents the facts in an objective way and answers the receiver's likely questions. The paragraph is written positively. It contains enough information so that the receiver understands what must be done and by when. The positive description of the rug and the mention of its value should convince Mr. Philips that he has won a nice prize.

CONSIDER A SALES APPEAL

A sales appeal should be used whenever a writer attempts to obtain additional business from the receiver. In this case the following is an example of a **poor** appeal for additional business:

- If you don't like the rug you won, you can select a more expensive one and pay the difference. While you're in the store, we'll also show you the pad you should use with an area rug. It costs $59.95, plus tax.

NOTE 7.17
The poor example of a sales appeal is cold and impersonal.

Note the impersonal tone of the message. The writer did not use the you–viewpoint in the sales appeal, and the second and third sentences are apt to reinforce the idea that the letter is designed to generate business for the sender.

This example of a **good** sales appeal is written in a personalized way; it encourages Mr. Philips to think about safety:

- Depending on floor the surface in the room where you plan to use your beautiful new area rug, you may want to consider purchasing a non-skid pad. When used on tile, wood, or laminate surfaces, a pad will hold the rug in place so family members and guests won't fall. We stock a variety of affordable pads;

NOTE 7.18
The good example of a sales appeal is positive and personalized.

Sanborn Flooring
831 Maple Avenue
Syracuse, NY 13212
315.582.2270
FAX: 315.582.6183

April 19, 200–

Mr. Linc Philips
623 Parker Road
Baltimore, MD 21224-7619

Dear Mr. Philips:

Thank you for stopping by our booth at the home show.

While at our booth, you entered our drawing. We had over 1,000 entries, and when we held the drawing at the close of the show on Sunday evening, the name on the form was yours. Your prize is a rug.

If you don't like the rug you won, you can select a more expensive one and pay the difference. While you're in the store, we'll also show you the pad you should use with an area rug. It costs $59.95, plus tax.

If we don't hear from you within 30 days, we will draw another name. So, come in soon.

Sincerely,

Paula Enroe

Paula Enroe
Manager

Weak positive news.

Impersonal, negative explanation.

Harsh tone in sales appeal.

Impersonal close.

FIGURE 7.2
Example of a *Poor* Positive Message

a sales associate can review the features and advantages of each with you during your visit.

END YOUR LETTER WITH A FRIENDLY CLOSE

NOTE 7.19
The example of a poor close is negative and does not build goodwill.

A positive or neutral message should conclude with a friendly close that builds goodwill. A **poor** close, such as the one that follows, would guarantee ill will:

- If we don't hear from you within 30 days, we will draw another name. So, come in soon.

An example of a **good** friendly close that will do much to establish goodwill follows:

NOTE 7.20
The example of a good close is friendly and builds goodwill.

- Stop in soon, Mr. Philips. We're open from 10 a.m. to 9 p.m. weekdays and from noon to 6 p.m. weekends.

This friendly close is written in a positive, personalized, and concise way. It not only encourages Mr. Philips to act but also provides information he needs to do so.

SUMMARY—POOR AND GOOD MESSAGES TO LINC PHILIPS

The Linc Philips case has been used to demonstrate how the direct approach can be used to write effective positive messages. The *poor* paragraphs are combined as a letter in Figure 7.2. This **poor** message fails to use the direct plan for positive information and fails to incorporate the communication fundamentals that are presented in Chapters 1, 4, and 5.

Sanborn Flooring
831 Maple Avenue
Syracuse, NY 13212
315.582.2270
FAX: 315.582.6183

April 19, 200–

Mr. Linc Philips
623 Parker Road
Baltimore, MD 21224-7619

Dear Mr. Philips:

Congratulations, Mr. Philips! You've won an area rug that will enhance the beauty of your home.

To claim your home show prize, bring the enclosed certificate to our Eastside Mall store within the next 30 days. Your lovely 4- by 6-foot Farleigh Woodland Flowers rug will be waiting for you. If you prefer another pattern, size, or style, you may apply the certificate—valued at $150—toward the purchase of any rug in our store.

Depending on the floor surface in the room where you plan to use your beautiful new area rug, you may want to consider purchasing a non-skid pad. When used on tile, wood, or laminate surfaces, a pad will hold the rug in place so family members and guests won't fall. We stock a variety of affordable pads; a sales associate can review the features and advantages of each with you during your visit.

Stop in soon, Mr. Philips. We're open from 10 a.m. to 9 p.m. weekdays and from noon to 6 p.m. weekends.

Sincerely,

Paula Enroe

Paula Enroe
Manager

Enclosure

Positive opening.

Positive presentation of facts.

Polite presentation of sales appeal.

Informative, friendly close.

FIGURE 7.3
Example of a *Good* Positive Message

Goodwill is promoted in the positive letter shown in Figure 7.3. This letter combines the *good* paragraphs. It integrates communication fundamentals into the direct plan outline to produce an effective business communication.

Requests for Information or Action

A **request** is a message expressing the writer's need for information or desire for action; it usually asks for a response. The message may include only one sentence, or it may contain several paragraphs. If several questions are asked, listing and numbering them will aid the receiver in responding.

Use the direct plan outline by presenting your request and stating the reason for it (if necessary) in the opening paragraph. In the second part of your message, give enough information so that the receiver can respond intelligently. Close your message by asking for action. Requests usually do not have a sales appeal section.

After drafting a request, writers often engage in role-reversal. They envision themselves as the message receiver and ask whether the message contains enough specific information to allow them to write a useful response.

Figure 7.4 is an example of a **poor** e-mail asking about a missing delivery. The message lacks the detail the receiver needs to respond quickly and completely.

The e-mail in Figure 7.5 is an example of a **good** request. The message provides all the details and includes a positive close that encourages a prompt reply.

LO 4

Prepare competently a variety of positive and neutral messages using the direct plan.

NOTE 7.21
Requests should be specific.

needs work

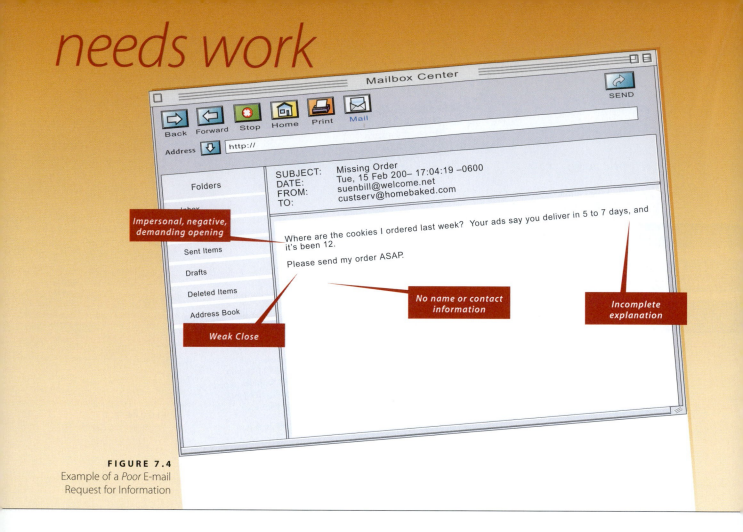

FIGURE 7.4
Example of a *Poor* E-mail
Request for Information

NOTE 7.22
Inquiries about persons
should include only
relevant questions and
should promise
confidentiality.

A request for information about a person must be made carefully to protect the rights of the individual. Begin your message by clearly identifying the person and stating why you need the information. Indicate whether the person about whom you are inquiring authorized your request; enclose a signed release if you have one. The explanation should contain relevant facts—pertinent information that the individual shared with you, requirements that must be met (job, loan, award, etc.), or questions that you need answered. Be sure to ask only those questions that are relevant to the situation. Close by stating that you would appreciate the receiver's sharing the information and by promising to keep it confidential.

Even after crafting a complete, well-written request, you may not get the information you seek. Many companies adhere to the policy of releasing only job titles and dates of employment. If you receive a request for information about someone with whom you work, be sure to check with your firm's human resource department about what information you are authorized to provide.

Request Approvals

Managers of business organizations regularly receive requests from their customers, their employees, and others. These requests may include, for example, a request

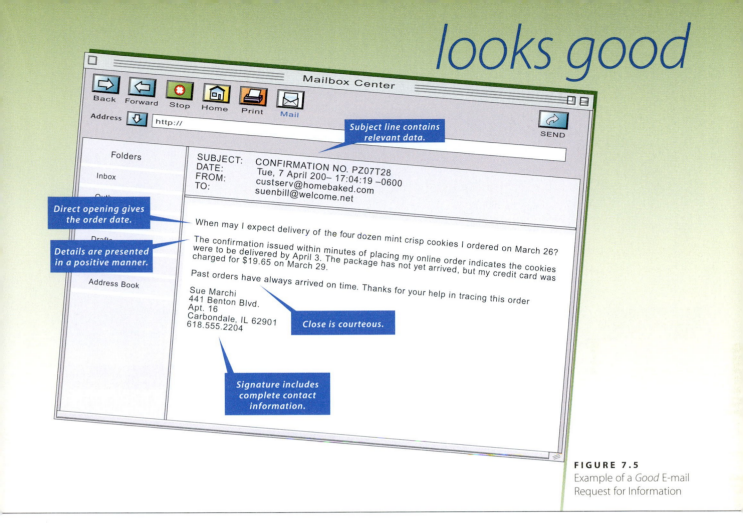

looks good

Mailbox Center

Back Forward Stop Home Print Mail

Address http://

SEND

Folders

Inbox

Drafts

Address Book

Subject line contains relevant data.

SUBJECT: CONFIRMATION NO. PZ07T28
DATE: Tue, 7 April 200– 17:04:19 –0600
FROM: custserv@homebaked.com
TO: suenbill@welcome.net

Direct opening gives the order date.

When may I expect delivery of the four dozen mint crisp cookies I ordered on March 26?

Details are presented in a positive manner.

The confirmation issued within minutes of placing my online order indicates the cookies were to be delivered by April 3. The package has not yet arrived, but my credit card was charged for $19.65 on March 29.

Past orders have always arrived on time. Thanks for your help in tracing this order

Sue Marchi
441 Benton Blvd.
Apt. 16
Carbondale, IL 62901
618.555.2204

Close is courteous.

Signature includes complete contact information.

FIGURE 7.5
Example of a *Good* E-mail
Request for Information

from an employee for a six-month parenting leave or a request from a civic organization for the manager to speak at a conference. Requests should be considered carefully and approved whenever feasible.

The proper handling of a request can build goodwill for an organization. For instance, approving a parenting leave will promote goodwill among employees and reflect positively on the way the public views the organization. Accepting an invitation to speak at a meeting of a civic organization can build goodwill for the company among those attending the meeting. The acceptance letter should convey enthusiasm about the prospect of appearing before the group and emphasize the positive aspects of accepting the invitation to speak.

To illustrate how the direct plan can be used in a positive message communicating approval of a request, assume that you are the president of the Westwood Field and Stream Club. Teresa Livingston, director of the Boys & Girls Club, has requested the use of your Treasure Lake facility so underprivileged children may experience a character-building day. Because you want to build goodwill, you will write a letter to Teresa approving her request and providing details.

A **poor** approval letter for this request is shown in Figure 7.6. It does little to build goodwill for the Westwood Field and Stream Club. Note the absence of the you–viewpoint. Also, notice that the positive information is not given until the second paragraph.

NOTE 7.23
Most business requests are approved.

NOTE 7.24
Goodwill can be improved with proper handling of requests.

needs work

Westwood Field and Stream Club

706 Happy Time Trail
Mountain Home, AR 72653-3185
(501) 555-5219 Fax (501) 555-7729

July 20, 200–

Ms. Teresa Livingston
Boys & Girls Club
1620 Milroy Drive
Mountain Home, AR 72653

Dear Teresa:

Subject: REQUEST TO USE LAKE

I have received your request dated July 14 to use our lake for your annual fishing tournament.

Our members are glad that your organization wants to host a fishing tournament for underprivileged children. We will allow the fishing tournament.

I hope you organize the tournament so that no child is injured while fishing.

Sincerely,

Jack McClendon

Jack McClendon
President

Not written from you–viewpoint.

Unclear explanation.

Approval not given in first paragraph.

Inappropriate close.

FIGURE 7.6
Example of a *Poor* Request Approval Letter

The **good** letter in Figure 7.7 uses the direct plan and should generate goodwill between Teresa and the Westwood Field and Stream Club. The message presents the positive information in the first sentence. The second paragraph presents an explanation that is factual, positive, and concise. A friendly close is given in the final paragraph. A sales appeal—the optional third step in the direct plan—is not appropriate for this situation.

tips and hints

Helping Your Receiver and Yourself

When a business representative makes a traditionally prepared (written) request or claim, basic contact information is included in the stationery's letterhead and signature block. To assist the receiver in replying by mail or phone, individuals should include their name, address, phone number, and perhaps e-mail address as part of the personal business letter format.

Providing the same information when communicating electronically will help your receiver respond. E-mail addresses typically are abbreviated or vague, which makes them impersonal. Unless you have added an identifying signature block that is displayed with every e-mail, include complete contact information with your e-mail requests or claims.

looks good

Westwood Field and Stream Club

706 Happy Time Trail
Mountain Home, AR 72653-3185
(501) 555-5219 Fax (501) 555-7729

July 20, 200–

Ms. Teresa Livingston
Boys & Girls Club
1620 Milroy Drive
Mountain Home, AR 72653

Dear Teresa:

You may hold your fishing tournament for underprivileged children at our Treasure Lake facility on August 25. This event should be an exciting one for the children.

Our resident manager, Owen Cabe, will open the gates at 7 a.m. and close them at 9 p.m. the day of your event. He will also be available throughout the day to answer any questions you may have; his office is in the lodge. The enclosed liability release should be completed, signed, and left with Owen the day of the event.

The docks at the lake will accommodate 25 children and 5 adults. *Everyone must wear a lifejacket while on the docks.* You'll find an assortment of lifejackets and rod and reel sets in the storage shed beside the lodge. The cooler in the shed is for bait; keep whatever perishable foods you bring for meals and snacks in the lodge refrigerator. You will not be charged for use of the facility. We ask only that you treat the buildings and grounds with respect and leave them as clean as you find them. Trash containers are located behind the lodge.

Teresa, you and the children should have an enjoyable day. If you need additional information about our facility, please call Owen Cabe at 555-5219.

Sincerely,

Jack McClendon

Jack McClendon
President

Enclosure

FIGURE 7.7
Example of a *Good* Request Approval Letter

Claims

Claims include requests for merchandise exchange, for refunds on defective or damaged merchandise, and for remedies for unsatisfactory service or work. Your complaint receives greatest emphasis when presented as the first item in the message. Generally, the receiver wants the claim information so that he or she can make necessary corrections as soon as possible. For this reason, and to give strength to your claim, use the direct plan.

The plan for claim messages can be adapted easily from the direct plan used for positive and neutral information shown in Figure 7.1. The *opening* should present the claim and its impact—without placing blame on the receiver. The impact could include the inconveniences suffered and identify specific damages. The *explanation* should provide all necessary additional background that relates to the claim. In this section, provide facts supporting the claim, describe actions that have been taken, and enclose relevant documents such as invoices. In addition, you should specify what you want the receiver to do. Your request must be complete. In a situation involving damaged merchandise, for example, ask or say what will be done with the merchandise. Set a deadline by which corrective action should be taken and, if

NOTE 7.25
Claims are made for many reasons.

NOTE 7.26
Claims are presented using the direct plan.

needs work

1234 Flatrock Drive
Durant, OK 74701
August 2, 200–

Business Publications
29734 Concord Road, Suite B
Boston, MA 02105

SUBSCRIPTION CANCELLATION

Claim not identified in opening.

Six months ago I subscribed to your magazine and paid for the entire period.

Explanation not written in a considerate tone.

I have received only two copies in the six-month period. I want my money back for the subscription.

Send the money quickly.

Close is demanding.

Keith Edwards

KEITH EDWARDS

FIGURE 7.8
Example of a *Poor*
Claim Letter

© Spencer Grant/PhotoEdit

Routine claims are written using the direct approach.

possible, say why meeting the deadline is important. Be courteous; threats are ineffective. There would be no sales appeal in a claim letter. Finally, the *friendly close* should be optimistic.

Figure 7.8 is an example of a **poor** claim letter from an individual who has not received all issues of his magazine subscription. Note that the main objective of the letter—not receiving magazines—does not appear until the second paragraph. Also note that the letter is harsh in its request. In addition, the claim omits the publication name and the subscription period. The receiver needs this information to process the claim. Last, this letter is not written in a considerate tone.

A preferred letter for the same situation is shown in Figure 7.9, an example of the **good** use of the direct plan for a claim. This letter is objective and courteous. The problem is specified in the opening. A concise explanation of the circumstances is given in the second paragraph. A request for cancellation is given politely in the third paragraph. The close is friendly and optimistic.

Claim Adjustments

NOTE 7.27
Legitimate claims should
be approved quickly.

Businesses that receive claim messages should respond to them quickly in order to maintain the goodwill of the customer. A positive response to a claim is known as an **adjustment.** If there is any uncertainty about the legitimacy of a claim, the customer usually receives the benefit of the doubt.

looks good

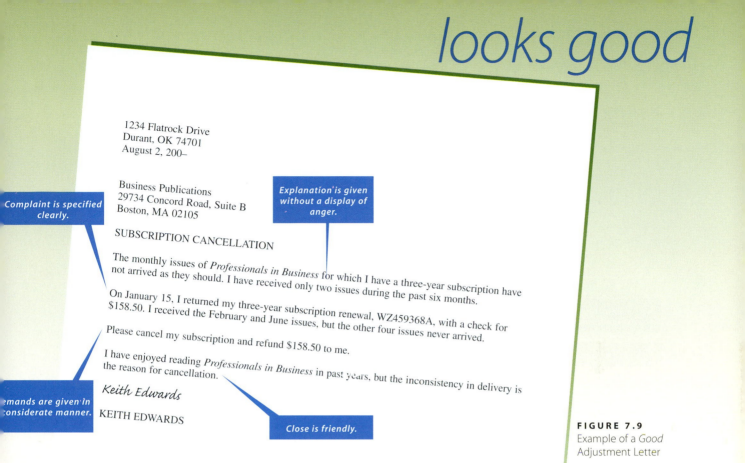

Complaint is specified clearly.

Explanation is given without a display of anger.

1234 Flatrock Drive
Durant, OK 74701
August 2, 200–

Business Publications
29734 Concord Road, Suite B
Boston, MA 02105

SUBSCRIPTION CANCELLATION

The monthly issues of *Professionals in Business* for which I have a three-year subscription have not arrived as they should. I have received only two issues during the past six months.

On January 15, I returned my three-year subscription renewal, WZ459368A, with a check for $158.50. I received the February and June issues, but the other four issues never arrived.

Please cancel my subscription and refund $158.50 to me.

I have enjoyed reading *Professionals in Business* in past years, but the inconsistency in delivery is the reason for cancellation.

Keith Edwards

KEITH EDWARDS

Demands are given in a considerate manner.

Close is friendly.

FIGURE 7.9
Example of a *Good* Adjustment Letter

A letter approving a claim is good news to the receiver; therefore, it should be organized by the direct plan. Beginning with the positive information—the adjustment—will aid in eliminating any negative feelings the customer has toward the company. The explanation should be convincing to regain the customer's confidence. Take responsibility for your or your company's part in the problem, but do so without placing blame on a specific employee or colleague. Instead, focus on what will be done to ensure the problem won't happen again. An apology is unnecessary unless your analysis of the receiver suggests he or she is expecting one. An effective, personalized sales appeal gives the company an opportunity to emphasize to the customer the quality of its products or services. The message should end positively, without any mention of the problem or the inconvenience it may have caused.

NOTE 7.28
Use the direct plan for adjustment letters.

tips and hints

Positive Word Choice

When resolving claims or responding to requests, use the terms *adjust* and *approve* rather than *grant*. The word *grant* is very formal. It suggests that the one acting on the request or claim is the stronger, more powerful player in the transaction.

In reality, both the sender and receiver can gain something important in these situations—goodwill and a reputation for conducting business ethically and professionally.

needs work

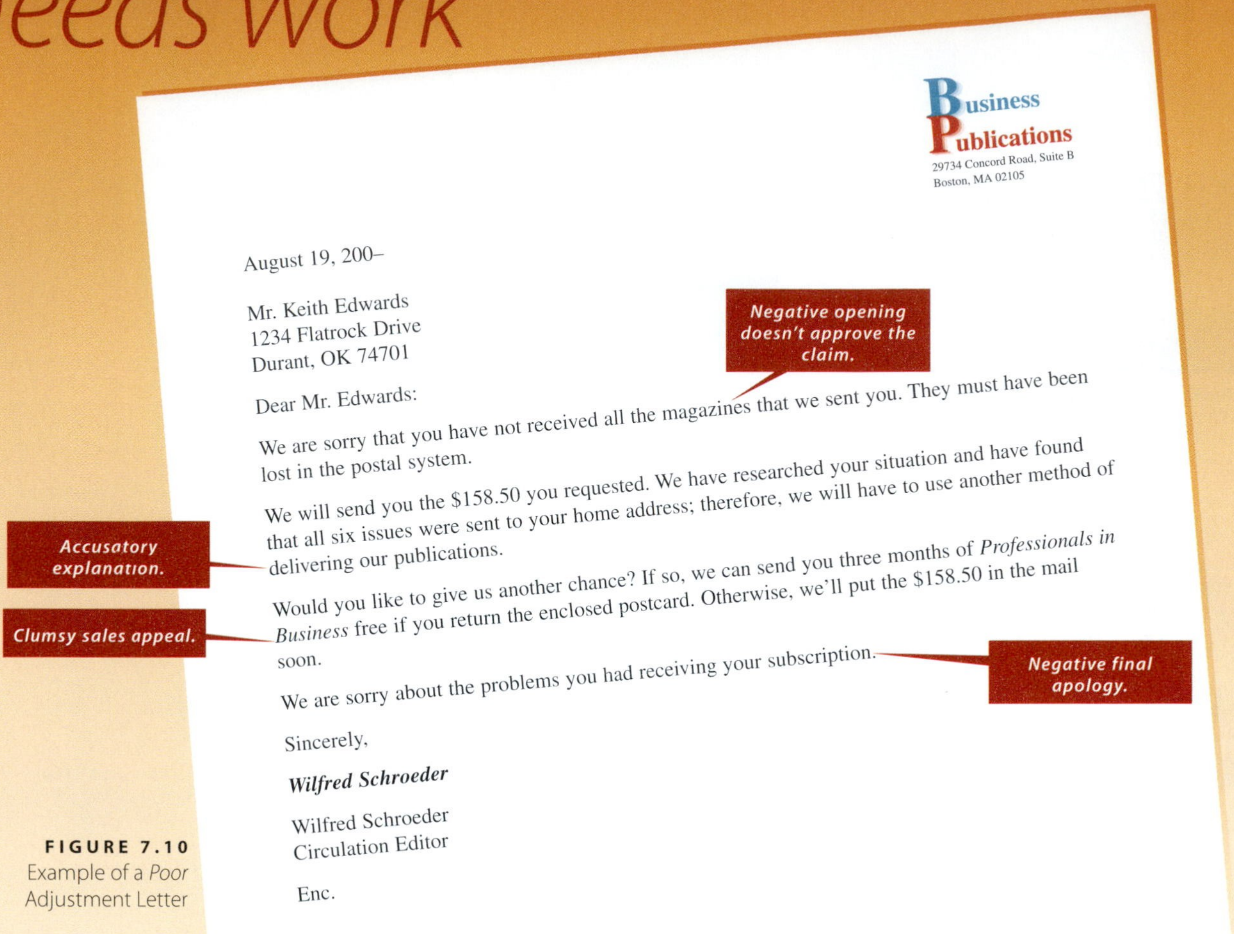

Business
Publications
29734 Concord Road, Suite B
Boston, MA 02105

August 19, 200–

Mr. Keith Edwards
1234 Flatrock Drive
Durant, OK 74701

Dear Mr. Edwards:

We are sorry that you have not received all the magazines that we sent you. They must have been lost in the postal system.

Negative opening doesn't approve the claim.

We will send you the $158.50 you requested. We have researched your situation and have found that all six issues were sent to your home address; therefore, we will have to use another method of delivering our publications.

Accusatory explanation.

Would you like to give us another chance? If so, we can send you three months of *Professionals in Business* free if you return the enclosed postcard. Otherwise, we'll put the $158.50 in the mail soon.

Clumsy sales appeal.

We are sorry about the problems you had receiving your subscription.

Negative final apology.

Sincerely,

Wilfred Schroeder

Wilfred Schroeder
Circulation Editor

Enc.

FIGURE 7.10
Example of a *Poor* Adjustment Letter

An example of a **poor** adjustment response to the claim letter about the magazines that were not received is shown in Figure 7.10. This letter does not get to the positive information until the second paragraph. The explanation places the blame on the postal system and is not convincing. The repeated references to the trouble continually remind the receiver of the negative aspects of the situation. The hollow apology in the close does not build the goodwill of the customer. The you–viewpoint is absent from the letter.

An example of a **good** letter approving an adjustment is shown in Figure 7.11. Note that this letter begins immediately with the positive information. The explanation emphasizes not the wrong itself but what was done to correct the wrong. This explanation should help regain the customer's confidence. In the third paragraph, the writer offers a free subscription that could demonstrate a timely delivery of the magazine. The close ends the letter on a happy, positive note.

Social Business Messages

LO 5

Compose the six common types of social business messages.

Courtesy is never out of style. Therefore, business professionals incorporate social business messages into their communication repertoire. By acknowledging important events in their employees' and customers' personal and professional lives, business writers communicate concern and interest. Showing you care about the receiver generates goodwill. And, as you learned in earlier chapters, goodwill helps build positive, lasting relationships.

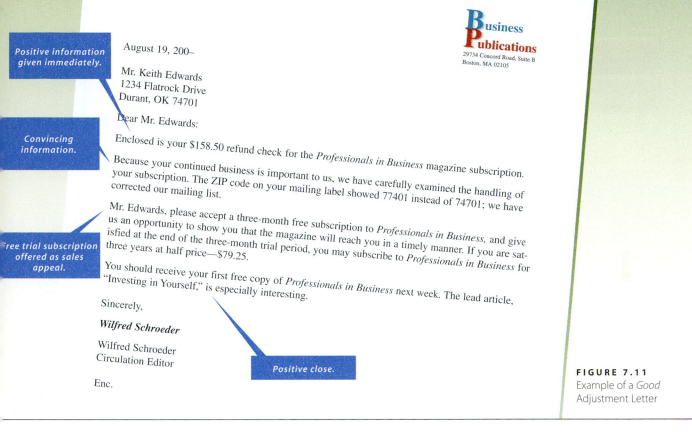

looks good

Business
Publications
29734 Concord Road, Suite B
Boston, MA 02105

August 19, 200–

Mr. Keith Edwards
1234 Flatrock Drive
Durant, OK 74701

Dear Mr. Edwards:

Enclosed is your $158.50 refund check for the _Professionals in Business_ magazine subscription.

Because your continued business is important to us, we have carefully examined the handling of your subscription. The ZIP code on your mailing label showed 77401 instead of 74701; we have corrected our mailing list.

Mr. Edwards, please accept a three-month free subscription to _Professionals in Business,_ and give us an opportunity to show you that the magazine will reach you in a timely manner. If you are satisfied at the end of the three-month trial period, you may subscribe to _Professionals in Business_ for three years at half price—$79.25.

You should receive your first free copy of _Professionals in Business_ next week. The lead article, "Investing in Yourself," is especially interesting.

Sincerely,

Wilfred Schroeder

Wilfred Schroeder
Circulation Editor

Enc.

Positive information given immediately.

Convincing information.

Free trial subscription offered as sales appeal.

Positive close.

FIGURE 7.11
Example of a _Good_
Adjustment Letter

Sincerity is critical to writing effective social business messages. Omit all statements that suggest you are sending the message only to generate additional business. Make the receiver and his or her feelings the focus of your message.

Timeliness is also important. Social business messages should be sent within three days of your learning of the incident or event. Even if you don't learn of the event until weeks or months after it occurs, your message would be considered timely.

The six common types of social business messages are congratulations, condolence, appreciation, invitation, holiday greetings, and welcome.

Congratulations

Everyone enjoys receiving praise. A message that praises the receiver for an accomplishment or an achievement is referred to as a message of **congratulations.** One of the reasons that congratulatory messages are so effective in building goodwill is that organizations and businesspeople do not use them very often.

Congratulatory messages are sent both to individuals and to organizations. Occasions that warrant such messages may be either personal or business in nature. A congratulatory message may be sent to an individual on the occasion of a business-related accomplishment, such as attaining the highest sales for the month, retiring after 30 years of service, or receiving a promotion. You also may send a congratulatory message to an individual for a personal event, such as a birthday, an engagement, a marriage, a birth, or election to office in a social or civic organization. A business

NOTE 7.29
Sincere, timely social business messages build goodwill.

NOTE 7.30
Congratulatory messages are sent for accomplishments or special occasions.

FIGURE 7.12
Message on a
Congratulations Card

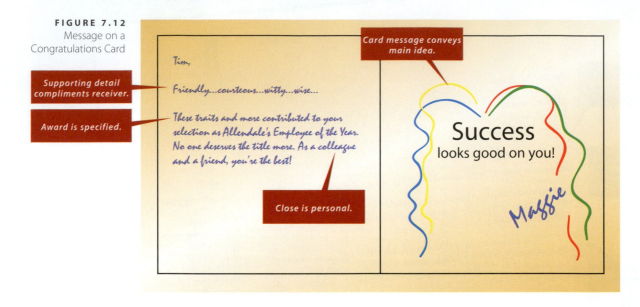

firm could receive a message of congratulations for expansion of its company, relocation to a new building, announcement of a new product, or celebration of an anniversary. The messages may be as formal as a computer-printed letter about a promotion or as informal as a handwritten note attached to a newspaper clipping of a birth announcement.

NOTE 7.31
Use the direct approach in composing a congratulatory message.

Congratulatory business messages should be written in a personal, sincere, direct manner. Immediately mention the honor or accomplishment, and then say why the receiver is deserving. Focus on the receiver from start to finish. End positively without referring to any assistance you or others provided. These references diminish goodwill. A congratulatory message to a colleague is shown in Figure 7.12.

Condolence

NOTE 7.32
Messages of condolence must be sincere.

A message of **condolence** or sympathy may be difficult to write because it deals with misfortune. When written properly, however, the message should leave no doubt about your care and concern. More importantly, it should help ease the pain felt by the receiver.

Messages of sympathy may be sent for an illness, death, natural disaster, or other misfortune. They may be computer-printed letters, handwritten letters, or handwritten notes on blank or printed sympathy cards. Handwritten messages are by far the most personal and most appreciated.

NOTE 7.33
Make a sympathy letter short and positive.

The direct approach should be used for condolence messages. Begin with the purpose of the message—conveying sympathy. Only the necessary details need to be mentioned, and these should be treated positively and sincerely. For example, in a letter of sympathy prompted by the death of a loved one, it is better to assure the survivor that he or she was appreciated and loved by the deceased person than eulogize the deceased person. It is also appropriate to mention a personal detail of the deceased if you know such details: "I remember your mention of the wonderful summer vacations you spent with your grandmother. I know that these memories will be even more precious to you now and in the future."

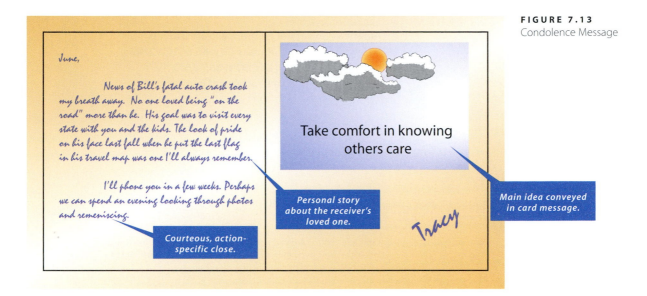

FIGURE 7.13
Condolence Message

If appropriate, a letter of condolence can offer assistance; however, avoid a cliché ending. Make sure your offer is specific and genuine. Your message may be concluded by referring to the future in a positive way. Figure 7.13 shows the message written on a sympathy card sent to the wife of a colleague who died in an auto accident.

Appreciation

Most people do not expect rewards for acts of kindness or thoughtfulness; however, we all enjoy knowing that our efforts are appreciated.

A letter of **appreciation** may be sent for long-time thoughtfulness or for a one-time favor. Some examples of individuals who have shown sustained thoughtfulness include a long-standing, loyal customer; a faithful employee; a friend who has consistently recommended a company and brought it many customers; and a volunteer who has generously contributed time and effort to charitable causes. Letters expressing thanks to such persons are always appropriate. Examples of letters of gratitude for one-time favors include a complimentary letter from a customer to a service department, a letter to a guest speaker who has given an excellent presentation, and a letter to someone who has found a lost article and returned it to the owner.

NOTE 7.34
Messages of appreciation show your gratitude.

Letters of appreciation should follow the direct approach. The good news—the expression of gratitude—should be given in the first paragraph and be followed by supporting evidence in the second or succeeding paragraphs. The letter should conclude with a comment of appreciation in the final paragraph; however, different words should be used in the opening and closing paragraphs. The thought of the letter, not the length of the letter, is the important consideration. Figure 7.14 illustrates a letter sent by the president of a professional organization to thank a member for having served as program chair for a national conference.

NOTE 7.35
Thank the receiver in the first paragraph.

Invitation

A business **invitation** is a request for an individual's presence and is used in various situations. Inviting employees to a small social gathering, asking prominent community

FIGURE 7.14
Letter of Appreciation

Expresses appreciation.

Gives necessary information.

Is personal and sincere.

Uses a friendly close.

---

members to attend a fund-raising event, and inviting civic leaders and selected customers to a company open house are all examples of invitations that are used in the business community. An invitation to a semiannual membership meeting is shown in Figure 7.15.

NOTE 7.36
An invitation may be formal or informal.

An invitation may be handwritten, typed on company stationery, created using computer software, or professionally printed. It may be formatted in a variety of ways, including card, letter, memo, e-mail, flyer, or poster. No matter how the message is formatted, it should include all the necessary details such as the date, time, place, suggested dress, and whether the receiver may bring a guest. For departmental or company-wide events such as picnics, it would be appropriate to indicate whether children are welcome. Be sensitive to diverse living arrangements; use "guest" rather than "spouse."

tips and hints

Doing More Than Expected

When a business professional has represented his or her employer especially well, consider sending a copy of your thank you letter—or a separate one—to the company or organization. The letter can be retained in the individual's personnel file where it can be considered during his or her performance review.

FIGURE 7.15
Invitation

In order to plan efficiently, you should include an *RSVP* notation—that is, a request for a reply to the invitation. The RSVP should specify how and by when to respond:

RSVP 555-7803 **by October 31**	*or*	**Regrets only by May 12** **555-6249**

Holiday Greeting

A **holiday greeting** may be sent before or during any festive season but New Year's Day, Thanksgiving, Hanukkah, Kwanzaa, and Christmas are frequently recognized as social business occasions in the United States. Businesses participating in international trade should be aware of and acknowledge appropriate holidays in the countries where they have employees, customers, or suppliers.

Many companies send year-end greeting cards to employees, customers, and/or suppliers. In recognition of the multicultural nature of the audience for these greetings, writers may choose "Holiday Greetings" or "Season's Greetings" rather than "Merry Christmas" as the message on the card. Typically, the company name is printed in the signature area of the card. Executives and sales representatives may add personalized handwritten greetings to business friends and colleagues.

Although cards are the most common form of holiday greeting, other options are available. As shown in Figure 7.16, a holiday greeting can be printed on stationery that reflects the spirit of the season. The more distinctive the message, the greater the likelihood it will be remembered. Some businesses enclose a calendar, mouse pad, notepad, magnet, or other item that bears the name and/or logo of the sender's company; however, the message itself contains no sales message. The gift and the greeting will be sent in the same package, but there is no enclosure notation because the message is not formatted as a letter.

Welcome

A **welcome** message is used to greet new employees, new customers, and newcomers to a community. Many cities have organizations, such as the Welcome Wagon, that

NOTE 7.37
Holiday greetings may be sent to celebrate festive seasons.

NOTE 7.38
Welcome letters are appropriate for new employees, customers, or community members.

FIGURE 7.16
Holiday Greeting

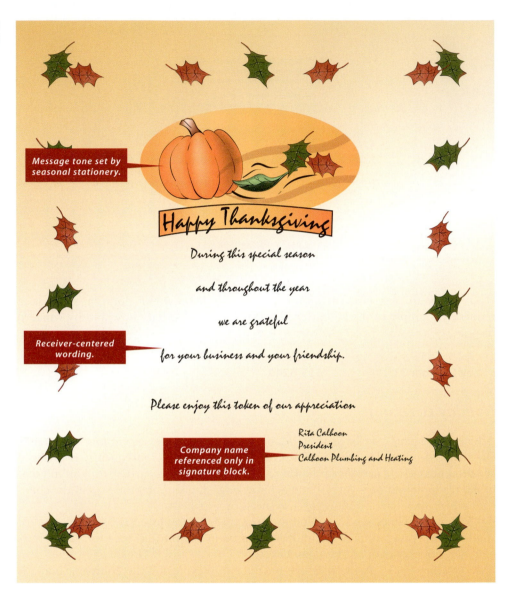

send welcome letters to persons moving into the community. A welcome letter may be used to familiarize new employees with the company or merely to build goodwill. Figure 7.17 is an example of a goodwill-building letter.

Welcome letters are frequently sent to new customers, particularly to those who are establishing credit with the business. These messages are used to congratulate the customer on opening a charge account with the business and to offer an incentive to the new customer to make a purchase soon.

Style in Social Business Messages

LO 6

Describe the criteria for selecting the style for a social business message.

A social business message is an effective way to build a positive relationship with a customer, an employee, or a supplier. Style is important in accomplishing the purpose of the communication.

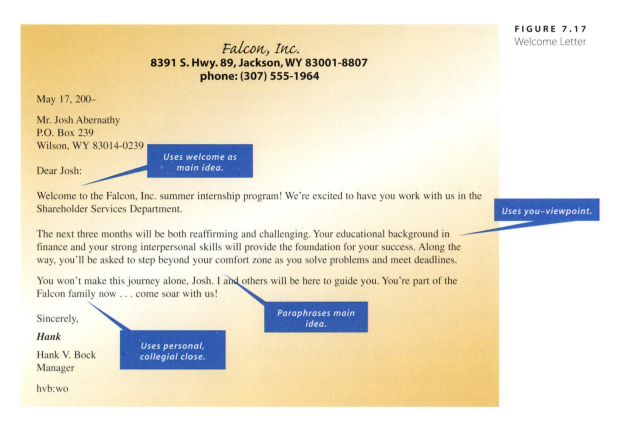

FIGURE 7.17
Welcome Letter

As with all communication, your analysis of the receiver and situation will guide your decision to send a card (print or electronic), a letter, or an e-mail in a social business setting. A handwritten note is appropriate in times of sorrow, but a printed invitation is preferred for a formal social function, whether it is a small wedding or a dinner and dance for several hundred people. A computer-printed message normally is used to welcome a customer or an employee to a business. E-mail and electronic greeting cards are inexpensive and timely; however, neither conveys the personal

NOTE 7.39
Whether to send a card or a letter depends on the occasion.

tips and hints

The Role of Technology

It's your birthday! Which makes *you* feel most special . . . an e-mail, an electronic greeting card, or a mailed birthday card with a handwritten note inside?

E-mail and the Internet offer quick, convenient ways to send personal messages, but they lack the personal touch desired in social *business* writing situations.

- Your e-mail greeting may be overlooked or minimized among the hundreds of messages exchanged in business each day.
- Your receiver's spam detector or virus protection program may block messages from electronic greeting card sites.

- Animation and music may cause your reader to view your card as "cute" rather than professional and sincere.
- Accessing an electronic greeting card site can be time-consuming.
- Neither e-mail nor electronic greeting cards can be placed on display without extra receiver effort.

Sending an e-mail message or an electronic greeting card is preferable to overlooking an event, but taking the time to write and mail a card or letter will make a lasting, positive impression on the reader.

sentiment of traditionally prepared messages. When you want your response to be quick *and* lasting, consider sending an e-mail and then following it with a letter or card.

NOTE 7.40
How well you know the receiver dictates the formality of the message.

The formality of a goodwill message depends on the purpose of the message you are sending and on how well you know the receiver. Put yourself in the place of the receiver and write a message that you would like to receive—whether the message must, of necessity, be phrased in formal language or whether the nature of the message permits you to be relaxed and informal.

Summary of Learning Objectives

LO 1 Describe positive and neutral messages.

A positive or neutral message conveys to the receiver information that is pleasant, favorable, or neutral. The receiver will accept the contents of the message easily; therefore, the message should be constructed using the direct plan.

LO 2 Describe the four specific guidelines for using the direct plan.

Open the letter or memo with the positive or neutral information. Be optimistic, provide coherence, use emphasis techniques, and stress receiver interests or benefits. In the second part of the message, the explanation, present additional information that relates to the positive or neutral information that was presented in the first paragraph. Present the explanation concisely and objectively while including all details that the receiver needs. In the third section, the sales appeal, attempt to persuade the reader to take a specific, desired action. Not all messages need a sales appeal. Complete the message with a friendly close. Build goodwill by being personal and optimistic.

LO 3 Distinguish between poor and good positive and neutral messages.

A good positive and neutral message stresses the reader's interest, the you–viewpoint; a poor message stresses the writer's interest, the I–viewpoint. A good message is written in a positive and friendly style instead of an impersonal manner. The explanation in a good message is concise but gives necessary details; the explanation in a poor message does not contain all relevant facts. A good message uses the you–viewpoint to appeal for additional business; a poor message will be more impersonal. A good message concludes with a friendly close that builds goodwill.

LO 4 Prepare competently a variety of positive and neutral messages using the direct plan.

Incorporate the communication fundamentals in the direct plan when preparing unsolicited positive and neutral messages, requests, request approvals, claims, and claim adjustments. Present the information optimistically using the you–viewpoint.

Use the direct plan: (a) Opening—start with the main idea of the message; (b) Explanation—present additional information concisely but completely; (c) Sales Appeal—persuade reader to take specific action on a related item; (d) Close—build goodwill by being personal and optimistic.

Compose the six common types of social business messages.

LO 5

The types of social business messages are congratulations, condolence, appreciation, invitation, holiday greetings, and welcome. A message of congratulations praises the receiver for an accomplishment or an achievement. Messages of condolence or sympathy may be sent for an illness, death, natural disaster, or other misfortune. Letters of appreciation are sent to acknowledge thoughtfulness. A business invitation is a request for an individual's presence. Holiday greetings may be sent during any festive season. A welcome message is used to greet new employees, new customers, and newcomers to a community. All social business messages are organized using the direct plan.

Describe the criteria for selecting the style for a social business message.

LO 6

Style is important in accomplishing the purpose of the communication. A social business message may be handwritten, computer printed, prepared using computer software, or professionally printed. A handwritten note is appropriate in times of sorrow, but a printed invitation is preferred for a formal social function. A computer-printed message is normally used to welcome a customer or an employee to a business. Commercially produced cards generally are used for brief personal messages; computer-printed letters are used in purely business situations. E-mail and electronic greeting cards are quick and convenient but may lack the personal tone desirable in social business messages. The purpose of the message and your familiarity with the receiver determine the formality of the message.

Questions for Discussion and Review

1. Draw on your experience at work or school. What routine or neutral messages have you sent or received in the past two weeks? Were they presented using the direct plan? (Objective 1)
2. If a writer presents the best news (main idea) in the opening paragraph of a message, why should the receiver read the rest? (Objective 1)
3. Name and explain the four sections of the direct plan. (Objective 2)
4. Which of the following paragraphs would be more appropriate for the sales appeal of a request approval? Explain why. (Objective 3)

   Mr. Williams, I want to invite you to our annual sale. We have many new appliances that would look nice in your home. We are giving our customers a 25 percent discount during this sale.

   Mr. Williams, you may be interested in browsing through our store and selecting from the many washers, dryers, freezers, dishwashers, and other appliances that would complement the refrigerator that you recently purchased. These appliances are now being featured during our annual fall sale. You may be especially interested in the new Model 450 flat-screen television that is being offered at a 35 percent discount during this sale.

5. How can enumerating the questions in a request help both the person who writes the message and the person who responds to it? (Objective 4)
6. What benefits can be gained from an effective sales appeal in an adjustment message? (Objective 4)
7. Why are threats ineffective when making a claim? How do you react when someone makes an angry threat? (Objective 4)
8. Claims and condolences concern negative or unpleasant circumstances. Why are they written using the direct plan? (Objectives 4 and 5)
9. Describe the content that should be included in an invitation. (Objective 5)
10. What determines whether a congratulatory business message is timely? (Objective 6)

Application Exercises

1. Write a message subject line to present the main idea for each of the following situations: (Objective 1)
   a. You're ill and will miss class today. The assignment that's due is attached to your e-mail.
   b. You aren't sure your local agent gave you correct information about the water damage clause in your renter's insurance policy, so you're writing the regional office to inquire and express concern.
   c. The strategic planning committee meets every Tuesday from 1:30 to 3 p.m. The next meeting will start at 2 p.m. The agenda for the meeting is attached.
2. Take a ten-minute walk through the halls of your school. Look for posters or other items that fall into the category of positive/neutral news. Prepare a table that shows each document type, its purpose, and whether its idea is presented using the direct plan. For event announcements (invitations), also report whether all relevant information was included. (Objectives 1, 4, and 5)
3. Determine whether a sales appeal is appropriate for each of the following situations: (Objectives 2, 4, and 5)
   a. You are responding to a complaint about the long lines at the checkouts in your store.
   b. You are thanking an employee for delaying his lunch break because 12:30 p.m. was the only time an important client could be at your office.
   c. You are responding to an inquiry from a prospective customer interested in purchasing an in-home theater system.

COLLABORATIVE

4. **Teamwork.** Form teams of three students and design a brochure that could be used to welcome new students to your college. Be prepared to promote your brochure in a class contest. (Objective 5)
5. A recent trend in the funeral home industry is for mortuaries to have websites from which friends and family members of the deceased can send e-mail or electronic greeting cards. The URL for the site, or simply the e-mail address, is included in the newspaper obituary. The messages are printed and given to the family, either as separate items or as part of the guest register. Write a paragraph in which you (a) list the advantages and disadvantages of using this service and (b) offer advice to someone thinking of sending a message in this manner. (Objectives 5 and 6)

Case Problems

Requests

TECHNOLOGY

1. **Technology.** You have searched the Web and found several vendors who offer business promotional merchandise at unit prices your new business can afford. Each of the websites speaks of quantity discounts, but none gives specific details. Design an e-mail that could be sent to these vendors asking for more information. Based on what you've seen, you anticipate ordering 10 dozen mugs, a similar quantity of personal water jugs, 1,000 pens, and 200 miniflashlights. You would consider adjusting those quantities based on the discount terms. Each item would contain your company name, address, phone number, e-mail address, and logo as a one-color display.

2. **Teamwork.** Brian's Food Service is expanding its catering division. It needs an additional enclosed truck with a refrigeration unit; several propane ovens to keep food warm; and storage shelves and cabinets for supplies, serving trays, linens, and food items. Form committees of three students to develop a message that could be sent to several custom vehicle dealers requesting a design for this vehicle. Be sure to include details to make this a complete inquiry.

COLLABORATIVE

3. Your company recently announced a new benefit. According to the announcement, the company will "pay for expenses associated with taking job-related coursework or pursuing a program of study leading to a degree." Courses must be approved by the employee's manager prior to enrollment. A transcript and expense documentation must be submitted after the course ends. As a sales representative, you believe you would benefit from taking *Comm 344 Persuasive Speaking* at Ramsey College next semester. Prepare a message asking DuWayne Sussex, your manager, for approval to take the course. Classes begin in four weeks, and you would like to register as soon as possible.

4. **Technology.** Refer to Case 3. Because your company's educational benefit is new, you have several questions about what expenses are covered. Ideally, you would like the company to reimburse you for tuition, fees, books, meals, and—considering the cost of gas and your 80-mile round-trip commute—mileage. Prepare an e-mail to Renee Runk, HR Specialist, asking for more information.

TECHNOLOGY

5. Assume the role of the vice president of sales at Rampart Publishing. Early in February, you attended a professional conference in another state. Dr. Daniel Loman, the motivational speaker who delivered the keynote address, was especially impressive. You think he would be perfect as the keynote speaker at your company's annual sales meeting. After the session, you spoke briefly with Dr. Loman about the possibility; he gave you his business card and asked you to send him the details. Neither of you made a commitment—you don't know whether he's available during the meeting (November 1–4), how much he charges, or what expenses your company would be expected to pay. Once you have the information, you can decide whether to enter into a service contract with him. Prepare an appropriate message.

Request Approvals

6. Carl Bott, a systems analyst in your department, has requested approval to take a three-week leave without pay immediately following his two-week paid vacation in February. Carl and his brother want to make their childhood dream a reality by backpacking in Australia and New Zealand, and two weeks just isn't enough time. Approve Carl's request with the understanding that you and he will meet twice during the week before he leaves; you will need information about the status of his projects.

7. As ticket manager for "Help Me, Donnie," a popular new TV talk show, prepare a form letter to be sent to people who have requested and will receive tickets to the show. In addition to basic information about time, date, and number of free tickets you're sending, tell the receivers that 18 is the minimum age for audience members. Unless they want to risk losing their tickets to standby viewers, ticket holders should be in their seats 30 minutes prior to taping. Once the show starts, they can't leave; tapings typically last 90 minutes. Include information about attire and behavior. Consider using a sales appeal in this message.

8. **Technology. Global.** Dahui Lian, a Shanghai official with whom you have met on several past visits to China, is planning to come to the United States. Through your visits and subsequent e-mail exchanges, you have been successful in building a relationship with Dahui. Because of that relationship, he has asked for information about gratuity customs (tipping) in the United States. Use print and Internet resources to gather information about tipping in restaurants, airports, hotels, and other situations he might encounter. Write a message summarizing this information and e-mail it to him.

TECHNOLOGY
GLOBAL

9. Every October, your company has an "open enrollment" period during which employees select their health and dental plans for the next calendar year. Once the open-enrollment period ends, no coverage changes can be made. Last year, for the first time, plan information and enrollment were handled only online. Things seemed to go well, but by March you had received over 100 requests from employees asking to change plans because their family physicians and dentists were covered in a higher-cost plan than the one in which they had enrolled. Each person cited the fact that similar plan names and difficulty in scrolling through page after page of provider lists

were the problem. It took some effort, but you were able to negotiate a one-time exception to the "no change" policy. Each person must complete, sign, and return a change request form by May 15. Premium refund checks will be issued; new premium rates will be prorated and applied as payroll deductions starting June 1. Prepare an appropriate request approval letter to be sent to each employee at his or her home address.

TECHNOLOGY

10. **Technology.** Brenda Durwood, one of your employees and president of the Woodland Ski and Snowboard Club, has requested permission to hold the club's annual Gear Swap fund-raiser in the company parking lot on Saturday, February 3. Club members will handle publicity, security, setup, and cleanup; no one will have access to the building. As the company's facility manager, approve Brenda's request. Waive the $150 facility-use fee Brenda has offered to pay. The company donates the fee to local charities, and the flyer Brenda attached to her e-mail request indicates that 15 percent of the proceeds from the swap will be donated to Carver Nature Center, a local nonprofit outdoor education agency. Ask Brenda to stop at your office next week to review and sign the use-authorization form.

Claims

TECHNOLOGY

11. **Technology.** Six months ago, you entered into a one-year contract with Waldo's Fitness Center. In the past two months, much of the equipment has not been working properly. In addition, many days the facility has been too hot to work out because of faulty air conditioning. You have spoken to the local manager about receiving a refund for the unused portion of the contract, but he is unable to release you from your contract. E-mail a message to your instructor that could be sent to the home office of Waldo's Fitness Center requesting a refund for the remaining six months of the contract.

TECHNOLOGY

12. **Technology.** When you took the first can from the 12-pack of ReFresh Lemon Zest soda you bought yesterday, you knew something was wrong. You couldn't see any damage, but it was obvious the can was not full. According to information on the can, comments or concerns should be reported at the company's website. You log on, provide the necessary information about the product, when and where you purchased it, the price, your name, and so on. Now, it's time to explain the problem. Write the paragraph(s) you would enter into the textbox at the site.

13. On July 1, you relocated your business from one Detroit suburb to another. A month prior to your move, you phoned your security system provider and notified its representative to cancel your service effective June 30, the end of a three-month pre-paid electronic billing. When you received your credit card statement on July 17, you saw that the security company had billed you for another three months' service. You phoned again that day and were told by Al Sapperstein, the manager at SEC-ure, Inc., that he would take care of the matter and reverse the credit card charge. You weren't concerned when your August credit card bill didn't show an adjustment, but now that it doesn't appear on your September statement, you're convinced it's time to create a written record of your requests. Write Mr. Sapperstein.

14. For the past six years, Jet Printing has had a display at the regional business expo. Because booth spaces are assigned on a first-come, first-served basis, you always reserve your space and send payment the day you receive the form. In past years, this practice resulted in your booth being located in a high-traffic area. This year, despite continuing your early registration/payment practice, your booth was assigned a space between the bathrooms and the snack bar. When you arrived at the exhibit hall and learned of your location, you asked the on-site director, Bill Reynolds, to approve moving your booth. He told you that he didn't have the authority to make on-site changes and encouraged you to "see what happens and write to the event chair if you aren't satisfied with the results in this location." You're definitely not satisfied. You saw lots of traffic, but very little of it resulted in conversations with potential customers. Write Jean Stanley, Biz-Ex Chair, expressing your disappointment. What procedural change could you suggest to ensure you aren't surprised in the future?

TECHNOLOGY

15. **Technology.** You manage Sunset Lane, a small card and gift shop. On September 3, you ordered four cases of shower gel and four cases of body lotion, one of each in the following fragrances: White Lilac, Jasmine, Morning Dew, and Ocean Mist. The shipment arrived today, September 29. It contained the correct shower gels, but not the correct body lotions. Instead of Jasmine and

Ocean Mist, you received Country Rose and Citrus Breeze. File an e-mail claim with Soft 'n Glow, your supplier. Because your customers often buy shower gel and body lotion as a set, you want the body lotions you ordered. You're willing to keep the first lotion shipment if the manufacturer offers you a satisfactory discount. Add information necessary to make this a complete claim.

Adjustments

16. Dave Barr, owner of Barr Hardware, has contacted your company about a shipment of 500 bags of lawn fertilizer that he received last week. He stated that 48 bags were torn and not saleable. He would like a refund of $200 for the damaged merchandise. As manager of Rapid Grow Fertilizer, write a complete letter to Dave refunding his $200.

17. As customer service manager for Mama Mia's frozen foods, respond to a letter from Jane Gogh, a student at Seaside College. Jane wrote expressing dissatisfaction with your Veggie Lasagne. She didn't ask for a refund but politely explained that she thought the vegetables were "mushy." Respond to Jane's letter. Provide information to restore her confidence in the high quality of your product. Encourage her to try another of your Italian frozen dinners.

18. Roscoe's Personalized Printing specializes in customized printing of items used for business advertisements. Jennifer Fairbanks designed an unusual calendar to be given to her customers during the holiday season. In October, Ms. Fairbanks phoned in an order for 11,000 calendars. You shipped these calendars to her in early December. On January 9, you receive a letter from Ms. Fairbanks stating that she ordered only 7,000 calendars. She is willing to pay $3,500 for the calendars but not the $5,500 you charged her. You believe that she ordered more calendars than she needed; however, you are willing to adjust her bill to continue getting her business. Write a letter to Ms. Fairbanks explaining your decision to adjust the charge in her account to $3,500, and add details to make the letter complete.

19. Sampson's Audio is a regular advertiser in your newspaper, *The Sunday Star*. The company's 4- by 6-inch ad has been a fixture on page 2 of the "Local" section for five years. Last week, another advertiser asked for a full-page spread on page 2. You, the account manager, e-mailed Sampson's and asked permission to move the ad to page 3 for one edition only. The store manager, Rocky Mildano, quickly replied "OK." Apparently, he hadn't checked with Sam Sampson, the owner, before approving the change. Today, you received a voice mail from Sam. He wasn't angry, just hurt that you would treat a long-term customer so shabbily. He asked that next week's ad be free and back on page 2. You will, of course, comply with his request. (a) Prepare an appropriate claim adjustment. (b) Notify the Billing Department to credit the Sampson account.

20. Dan Daily, purchasing manager for the ValueMax supermarket chain, has requested a 10 percent discount on the cost of the 25,000-unit shipment of paper grocery bags delivered to his warehouse last week. The samples he sent support his claim that the logo color is faint and both it and the store name are noticeably off center. You agree. Prepare a letter that approves his claim and retains him as a customer.

Unsolicited Positive and Neutral Messages

21. Technology. The owner of your company recently purchased two pairs of season tickets for the local symphony orchestra concerts. He will retain one pair of tickets but make the other available to employees through a drawing held one week before each of the six concerts. Send an e-mail to your employee distribution list. Announce the good news and tell workers how to sign up for the first drawing, which will be held in ten days. Employees seeking information about concert dates, times, and guest artists can check the symphony's website, http://www.csomusic.org. Similar announcements will be sent prior to each concert.

22. The Board of Directors of City Library has added activities for the summer. These additional activities include an 8 a.m. story hour and a 6 p.m. children's theater production. The children's theater production will change weekly. As secretary of the board, write a letter that could be sent to all of the area schools announcing these activities. A flyer describing the theater productions is being developed by the Children's Art Guild and will be included in your letter.

23. Thanks to an unseasonably warm spring, you will be able to open the first 9 holes of your 18-hole city golf course April 1, two weeks earlier than in prior years. Prepare an announcement that could be placed in the local newspaper.

TECHNOLOGY

24. You work for a company that owns several office buildings in your town. Your employers have decided to change all locks in their buildings from key to card access. Notify the tenants of each building about the change and tell them when it will occur. If all goes well, the process should take no more than a week at each building. As the locks are changed, keys will be collected and cards will be issued. Prepare a form letter that can be adapted to notify each tenant when the work will be done at his or her office.

25. Inspired by a popular television program, and with an eye toward improving employees' general health, your company has decided to sponsor a "Biggest Loser Contest." Those interested in participating must weigh in each Monday during the ten-week program. In addition, they must attend a two-hour session about diet, nutrition, and exercise. The session will be offered at three different times/days during the week before the contest begins. The individual who loses the greatest percentage of body weight will be named the winner and receive a one-year paid membership at 24/7, a local fitness center.

Social Business Messages

26. **Global.** *Appreciation.* Elizabeth Morton spent a semester with your family as an exchange student from Australia. Six months after Elizabeth returned home, you and your family spent two weeks with her and her family. Write a letter thanking the Mortons for their hospitality. Add details.

27. *Congratulations.* You and Jerry Bydalek were finalists for a management position in your organization. Today, you learned that Jerry was selected. Prepare the message you'll write on a congratulatory card to him.

28. *Condolence.* Two nights ago, fire severely damaged the office of Case Travel, which is located one block south of your bookstore. You and Joy Case, who owns the agency, were high school classmates. In addition, her company has planned several trips for your family. Write a letter of condolence that offers specific assistance.

29. *Holiday Invitation.* It's mid-October, time to invite local schoolchildren to dress in costumes and trick-or-treat at West Lake Mall. As mall manager, write to the presidents of the local Parent-Teacher-Student Associations (PTSAs) and the principals of local elementary schools inviting them and the schoolchildren to the event.

30. *Welcome.* You are the president of the Tri-City Industrial Foundation. You have been successful in getting Little Toy Machines, a toy manufacturer, to relocate to your community. This factory will provide employment for 325 people. Write a letter to the president, Roy Stevens, welcoming him and his company.

Web exercises to accompany this chapter are available at **www.thomsonedu.com/ bcomm/krizan.**

Message Analysis

Correct and strengthen the following message that has been written to invite supporters to a post-election party.

> *Jack Galante is having an election night party, after the polls close, at the Williams Cabin on Berlin Road. He will provide the beverages. Some folks have offered to bring snacks, but he thinks there should be deserts, too. Spread the word because I know I will leave someone out and we cannot have that.*

Writer's Workshop

The following items may be sentence fragments or contain errors in subject-verb agreement, pronoun-antecedent agreement, comma and semicolon placement, number display, capitalization, spelling, word choice, possessives, modifier clarity and placement, or parallelism. Rewrite the sentences to make them correct.

1. Baste on the results of the environmental impact study, our expansion plan was modified.
2. The alteration shop repaired the zipper in Teds' coat in fewer then 1 hour.
3. Becky used her capitol for collateral in purchasing the apartment building after she was ensured that the property would appreciate in value.
4. The St. Louis zoo has numerous exotic monkies, colorful peasants, and tigers that have sleek coats.
5. Wile you were on vacation.
6. While you are in Seattle be sure to phone Max Bozwell at Ranier Industries otherwise we may loose their account.
7. Our flight to paris which was scheduled to depart at 7 p.m. was delayed for 3 hours.
8. After you have annulized the datas give the results to Paige or myself.
9. We only ordered thirty copies of the directory but we can get more if necessary.
10. Me and my brother has a pashion for Amusement Parks expecially one's width roller coasters.

Chapter 8
Negative Messages

LET'S TALK BUSINESS

Photo courtesy of Joshua Morehead

The most important consideration when relaying negative messages is to try to resolve the issue and keep the customer's goodwill. Our store operates as a separate entity from package delivery. We act as a third party in resolving problems related to shipping costs or delays. For example, weather may cause late delivery of a package shipped for overnight service. If the delay is caused by weather conditions, UPS doesn't refund shipping costs. When that happens, customers come to us to claim a refund. We explain that UPS cannot refund the money when weather causes the problem. However, we reinforce that we appreciate their business and hope they will continue to come in to see us. We

Joshua L. Morehead,
Assistant Manager,
The UPS Store

say that we will be glad to help in any way we can. There may be something else we can do for them. We always want to do our best to provide good service because we want to keep our customers. If mistakes happen after we ship a package, we are a third party and act as an agent for our customer. We talk to UPS personnel and try to resolve the problem for the customer.

Shipping packages internationally can present another problem. When gifts are sent out of the country, duty and taxes are added. We get complaints about these costs. We explain that U. S. Customs is a separate entity and that these costs are separate from regular shipping charges. We can help by contacting Customs and explaining the charges to the customer, but we want the customer to understand that these charges are not determined by us. Again, the bottom line is to be of service and keep the customer coming back to our store.

A **negative message** is one that conveys unpleasant, disappointing, or unfavorable information for the receiver. Bad news messages such as the claim refusals described by Joshua Morehead about late delivery or extra costs are disappointing and unpleasant for the customer. Other negative messages may refuse a request from a customer or an employee, provide information about an unfavorable policy change, notify job applicants that they were not hired, or inform customers of a product recall.

An effective negative message presents a challenge to compose so that the receiver will understand and accept the information without a loss of friendship or goodwill for the sender. A well-written negative message can resolve a business problem successfully and win a friend for you or a customer for your organization.

Choosing the Indirect or Direct Plan for Negative Messages

The goals of an effective negative message are to receive a positive response and to maintain the goodwill of the message receiver(s). You may develop negative messages using an indirect or a direct plan of organization and content selection. Understanding the receiver's perspective is the most important factor in deciding how to convey a negative message that reflects the you–viewpoint and achieves your goals. Saying no is more serious in some cultures than in others; therefore, effective communication of negative information requires greater cultural sensitivity than does communication of positive messages. Consider these key questions: What message does the receiver expect? How will the receiver respond emotionally to the negative message? Will the message affect the individual's ego or self-esteem?

Use the indirect plan if one or more of the following characteristics apply:

1. The receiver expects a positive response.
2. The negative message affects the receiver personally and will be upsetting.
3. The negative message is of importance, and the receiver will react negatively.
4. The receiver prefers indirect communication due to culture or other reasons.

Research shows that how individuals view and anticipate events affects how they process information.[1] If a customer has made a request for service, adjustment, or credit and expects to receive a positive response, a negative reply will be unexpected and disappointing. The reply may be perceived as unfair or a personal rejection. In the case of refused credit or a poor employee performance review, a negative response is likely to be intensely personal and a blow to the receiver's ego.

The cultural background or personal preferences of individuals affect communication. Chapter 2 noted the general preference for indirect communication by high-context cultures. For example, in Asian countries such as China and Japan, indirect language patterns are a means of saving face for communicators and their audience.

Many situations for negative messages fit one or more of the characteristics that suggest using the indirect plan. However, as a general guide, the direct plan is appropriate if these conditions exist:

---

[1]George A. Kelly, A Theory of Personality: The Psychology of Personal Constructs (New York: Norton, 1963), 46.

LO 1

Describe the nature of negative messages.

NOTE 8.1
A negative message conveys unpleasant, disappointing, or unfavorable information.

LO 2

Explain the reasons to choose the indirect plan or the direct plan for negative messages.

NOTE 8.2
Goals of an effective negative message: A positive response and goodwill.

NOTE 8.3
Use the indirect plan if the negative message will upset the receiver or is unexpected.

NOTE 8.4
Cultural background affects communication preference.

NOTE 8.5
Use the direct plan if the negative message may be expected, will not upset the receiver, or should be emphasized.

1. The negative message may be expected, is routine, or will not be upsetting to the receiver.
2. The negative information needs to be emphasized.
3. Your receiver's preference, cultural or otherwise, is directness.
4. The message responds to a death or tragedy.

An example of a routine message could be a schedule change for monthly staff meetings. Changing or canceling routine meetings will not upset the receiver in most situations. Another type of routine message might be organizational policy changes that have a neutral or minimal negative effect, or a notification that you cannot attend a routine function. A second or third notice of an overdue account may follow a direct plan to emphasize the need for prompt payment.

NOTE 8.6

Follow a receiver's preferred communication style.

If you know the receiver's preferred communication style, use that as a guide. In general, use the direct plan for communicating with people in low-context countries such as Germany or Switzerland. One clue to communication preference is the type of spoken or written messages that the receiver has sent to you. As illustrated in Chapter 7, the direct plan is appropriate for a message of sympathy or regret for a tragedy that has occurred. At such a time, the bad news is already known and is central to the receiver's thoughts.

NOTE 8.7

Generally, follow the indirect plan for an important negative message.

Most negative messages of high importance to you or the receiver will follow the indirect plan if the receiver will respond negatively. When the negative message will evoke a strong emotional reaction such as anger or injury to the receiver's ego, this is likely to affect the business relationship negatively. You may lose the client's future goodwill and business. Examples of such messages are credit refusals and refusal of a request by a long-term customer to fill a sales representative vacancy in your business by hiring his son, who recently earned a business degree in marketing. Both of these examples would require indirect communication to prepare the message receiver for the bad news. Reaffirming the positive relationship and providing a logical explanation before stating the negative message have the advantage of helping the receiver accept the message.

Regardless of whether negative messages follow the indirect plan or direct plan for a particular situation, effective communicators do these three key things:

- Adapt the message to the receiver's viewpoint.
- Emphasize positive, bias-free words.
- Show respect for the receiver's needs and interests.

The remainder of this chapter describes the indirect plan and the direct plan for negative messages and gives example messages for both types.

Writing Negative Messages with the Indirect Plan

NOTE 8.8

Explaining the reason prepares the reader for the negative information.

The indirect plan for organizing the content of a bad news message prepares your receivers for the negative information by first explaining the reason and providing information that is likely to gain a positive reaction and maintain goodwill. With the indirect plan, the sentence or section of the message that conveys the disappointing information follows an explanation of why you must refuse a request or why you must provide unfavorable information. Receivers are more accepting of negative information when they have been prepared to receive it.

Two important advantages of the indirect plan are that it enables receivers (a) to accept the negative information that you must give them and (b) to maintain a satisfactory relationship with you and your organization. The indirect plan has these advantages because it maintains calm through a gradual approach. If the negative information is given first, the receiver may become anxious or angry and ignore the rest of the message even if a fair, reasonable explanation follows the bad news. When the explanation precedes the bad news, the receiver has an opportunity for reason to prevail, anxiety to subside, and understanding to develop before receiving the bad news.

If your message is written or spoken thoughtfully and carefully using the you–viewpoint, the receiver may understand that the negative information is appropriate and may be better able to accept it. An effective presentation of the message may show that the negative message is, in fact, in the best interest of the receiver. The decision may benefit the receiver, which is likely to produce a positive reaction.

NOTE 8.9
The indirect plan prepares the receiver to accept the negative news and maintains a satisfactory relationship.

Using the Indirect Plan

This section gives specific guides for using the indirect plan to write negative messages. In addition, you will want to use the fundamentals of effective communication that are presented in Chapters 1, 2, and 4. Figure 8.1 outlines the steps and specific guides for using the indirect plan to present negative information. The indirect plan can be used effectively for a variety of written and oral negative messages—refused claims, refused requests, unfavorable decisions, or unsolicited unpleasant information.

LO 3
Describe the five specific guidelines for appropriate use of the indirect plan.

Determination of Content

Each communication situation must first be analyzed to determine (a) primary and secondary purposes and (b) the basic content of the message. As you plan and draft an unpleasant message, you will want to answer the following questions: What ideas can I use in the opening to establish coherence and build goodwill in this particular situation? Is there a possibility that the request refusal or unfavorable information could benefit the receiver? Is there an alternative course of action that I can recommend to this receiver? What friendly message can I convey in the off-the-subject close?

Once you have determined the purposes and content of the negative message, you are ready to implement the indirect plan. The following sections discuss the indirect plan outline and review the most important considerations.

NOTE 8.10
Analyze each situation to determine primary and secondary purposes and basic message content.

Opening Buffer

In the indirect plan, the opening buffer should provide coherence, build goodwill, be positive, maintain neutrality, and introduce the explanation. The opening buffer usually consists of one to three sentences. It serves as the first sentence or paragraph in a memo or a letter.

NOTE 8.11
The opening buffer provides coherence, builds goodwill, is positive and neutral, and introduces the explanation.

FIGURE 8.1
Indirect Plan Outline for
Negative Messages

I. The **Opening Buffer**
   A. Provides coherence.
   B. Builds goodwill.
   C. Is positive.
   D. Maintains neutrality; introduces the explanation.

II. The **Logical Explanation**
   A. Relates to the opening buffer.
   B. Presents convincing reasoning.
   C. Stresses receiver interests and benefits.
   D. Uses de-emphasis techniques.
   E. Is positive.

III. The **Negative Information**
   A. Relates to the logical explanation.
   B. Gives negative information implicitly or explicitly.
   C. Uses de-emphasis techniques.
   D. Gives negative information quickly.
   E. Is positive.
   F. Says what can be done (not what cannot).
   G. Avoids an apology.

IV. The **Constructive Follow-up**
   A. Provides an alternative solution.
   B. Gives additional reasoning.

V. The **Friendly Close**
   A. Builds goodwill.
   B. Personalizes the close.
   C. Stays off the negative subject.
   D. Is warm and optimistic.

To provide coherence, the opening buffer puts you and your receiver on the same wavelength. The negative message is tied to a previous conversation, a point of agreement, a memo or letter received earlier, a prior transaction, or some other common ground.

You will want to build goodwill by using courteous, polite words such as *thank you*, *please*, and *I appreciate* and by keeping the receiver's interests central to your message. Use positive words; avoid negative words. Using positive words helps set a favorable tone and helps make your message acceptable. Composing negative messages without using a single negative word is possible and desirable.

Two of the requirements for a good opening buffer—maintaining neutrality and introducing the explanation—are closely related. You will want your receiver to read all the opening buffer and continue into the logical explanation that follows. You do not want to suggest the negative information in the opening. Therefore, the opening buffer should not imply either a yes or a no. It should not lead the receiver in either direction; it should be neutral.

NOTE 8.12
The opening buffer sets the
stage for the explanation.

The final purpose of the opening buffer is to set the stage for the explanation. In the last sentence of the buffer, introduce the explanation by giving your receiver an indication of the central thought of the explanation. In effect, give the receiver the "headline" for the explanation that follows in the next paragraph(s). This sets up the strategy for the logical explanation, which is the next part of your message, and it assists in providing coherence. The following Communication Note gives examples of opening buffers.

communication note

- Thank you for contacting *Executive News* about the book that you received from us. You are a valued subscriber, and we have addressed your concern. [*For a letter refusing a refund but offering an alternative arrangement.*]

- We appreciate your business as a *Gizmo* customer. Customer satisfaction is our priority. [*For a letter refusing a customer request to return a product but offering an adjustment.*]

- You are a valued employee, and your dedication and productivity have been recognized. In return, the company stands ready to support you when concerns arise that require personal leave time. [*In a letter refusing a week of sick leave for a minor family crisis.*]

- The letterhead that you ordered was shipped yesterday. We shipped it UPS, as you requested. [*In an unsolicited letter about an incomplete shipment and a request for additional information before shipping the other items.*]

Logical Explanation

The second part of the indirect plan is the logical explanation. In a memo or letter, the logical explanation usually begins after the opening buffer and often can be handled in one paragraph. If the explanation is short, the negative information may be included in the same paragraph. In some situations, the constructive follow-up can immediately follow the negative information in the same paragraph. This technique buries the negative news in the middle of a paragraph. In other written message situations, the logical explanation may be so long that it requires two or more paragraphs.

One of the most important aspects of the indirect plan is that the reasoning that justifies the negative information is presented *before* the actual negative information. After the opening buffer, you present the reasons explaining why you must convey the negative information. If possible, these reasons should show how the negative information will be in the best interest of your receiver. To be effective, this reasoning must be presented in a calm, convincing, and pleasant manner using the you–viewpoint.

One strong reason should be enough. If necessary, list more than one reason. The specific requirements for the logical explanation are that it relates coherently to the opening buffer, presents convincing reasoning, stresses receiver interests and benefits, uses de-emphasis techniques, and is positive.

The opening buffer will have introduced the explanation. Use coherence techniques to relate the beginning of the logical explanation to the opening and to improve thought flow. You may use repetition of key words, transition words, a tie-in sentence, or other coherence techniques to ensure that the explanation logically links to the opening buffer.

The convincing reasoning that supports the unfavorable information should be composed with the receiver's interests or benefits as the focal points. The receiver's favorable reaction to the words you choose is your goal. If, at the end of the reasoning, the receiver agrees that the negative information represents the best alternative in this situation, you will have composed the ideal negative message.

NOTE 8.13
The logical explanation follows the opening buffer.

NOTE 8.14
One strong reason from the receiver's viewpoint should be enough.

Using policy as a logical explanation is not effective. If policy is the only reason, also explain the reason for the policy.

© Bill Varie/Corbis

Although the ideal logical explanation presents the reasoning in terms of receiver benefit, circumstances will not always permit you to compose the ideal message. You may have to base your reasoning on what is fair for all concerned. Also, occasionally, confidentiality precludes giving any specific reasons. In these situations, you will want to communicate convincingly and persuasively that the matter was carefully considered in the interest of the receiver before reaching the decision.

You will want to use rules of emphasis in the logical explanation. Start with the points that are most favorable to your receiver, and, as you move further into the paragraph, address the least favorable aspect of the reasoning.

NOTE 8.15
The logical explanation uses positive words and tone.

Finally, the logical explanation should be positive. Avoid negative words. For example, use *situation* instead of *problem* and *needed change* instead of *correction* or *error*. In referring to the negative information, avoid negative words such as *failure, cannot, trouble, inadequate,* and *defective.*

Negative Information

After the opening buffer and the logical explanation, you are ready to present the negative information. This step in the indirect plan consists of a request refusal, unfavorable decision, or other disappointing information. If the opening buffer and the logical explanation have been effective, receivers will be expecting the negative information. In fact, in most circumstances, it is possible for you to prepare your receivers so well that they easily will accept the information, refusal, or decision.

The primary goal in presenting negative information is to be sure that the receiver clearly understands this part of your message. In communicating with Americans, Europeans, Australians, and others from low-context countries, you will want to imply the decision clearly or state it explicitly. Wording such as "Therefore, following the company policy seems to be the best alternative for you" leaves a question in the receiver's mind about the nature of the decision such as, "Is it still open for discussion?" or "May I decide what to do?" However, in high-context such cultures as Asian and Latin American, indirect communication is preferred to avoid unpleasantness and "save face."

Even with cultures that prefer directness and clarity, implying rather than directly stating the negative information is usually desirable. It softens the bad news and permits you to present negative information in a positive manner. For example, "Smoking is permitted in the hallways only" is much more acceptable to most people than "Smoking is prohibited in the classrooms and offices." These statements both say basically the same thing; the first just says it positively. For effective communication of negative information, it is better to say what can be done rather than what cannot be done.

NOTE 8.16
Even with the direct plan, in most cases, imply rather than explicitly state negative information.

In some situations, the negative information should be given in explicit terms. These are the times when you believe that an implied refusal would not be strong enough or might be misunderstood by your receiver. In the case of rejecting admission to a college, for example, it may not be possible to imply the refusal. In this type of situation, it is better to present the logical explanation and then explicitly state the refusal in clear terms, such as "Therefore, the committee has not approved your application for admission." This wording can leave no doubt in the receiver's mind. In most cases, though, you will want to imply the negative information to reduce its emphasis.

The recommended placement of the negative information section of the message is immediately after the logical explanation. In a written message, you do not want to place the negative information in a separate paragraph. To de-emphasize the negative, place it in the middle of a paragraph. The negative news may be followed by an additional reason or suggested alternative(s). This placement tucks the negative information inside the paragraph and de-emphasizes it.

NOTE 8.17
The negative information comes immediately after the logical explanation.

The negative information should be given in as few words as possible. Ideally, you can further de-emphasize the unfavorable news by placing it in a dependent clause. As in all sections of a negative message, you will want to use positive words and avoid negative words—say what can be done and not what cannot be done. Also, in most cases for both the direct and indirect plans, you will want to avoid apologies throughout the message because apologies only call further attention to the negative nature of a situation. Do not use apologies such as "I am sorry I must refuse your request" or "I apologize for being slow to respond to your request."

In summary, the indirect plan clearly implies or explicitly states the negative information directly after the logical explanation, uses techniques to de-emphasize the negative message, gives the negative message quickly, is positive, says what can be done, and avoids apologies. After giving the negative information, your next step in the indirect plan is to provide constructive follow-up.

NOTE 8.18
The indirect plan avoids apologies and de-emphasizes the negative message.

Hagar the Horrible by Chris Browne

Constructive Follow-up

In the constructive follow-up section of a negative message, you provide other solutions to the problem or, if that is not possible, you give an additional reason justifying the unfavorable news.

One good way to strengthen your communication and improve relations is to do more than is expected by offering an alternative solution to the receiver. For example, if you were asked to return to your high school on October 24 to speak to seniors about attending college and your schedule would not permit you to do so, you could suggest an alternative speaker or an alternative date. Although you must refuse the request, your suggested alternative may solve the problem and help you to maintain a favorable relationship. In the case of adjustment refusals, you can make a special offer or resell the customer on the product or service.

If you cannot suggest an alternative or offer a solution to the problem, save part of the logical explanation and place it after the negative information. This helps the receiver accept the bad news by de-emphasizing its importance and giving him or her additional justification for it.

Friendly Close

The friendly close moves the receiver's mind away from the problem—the negative information—and provides an opportunity to build goodwill. If you must refuse a customer credit, you will want him or her to continue to buy with cash. If you have to refuse an employee's request, you will want to maintain goodwill and not reduce the employee's productivity.

You can build goodwill in the friendly close by ensuring that it is personalized, off the subject, warm, and optimistic. The wording of the friendly close should fit the receiver and the particular situation. The close should relate to the topic while avoiding the bad news. It could make further reference to the constructive follow-up, or it could express appreciation to a customer for his or her business.

The friendly close should not include anything that reminds the receiver of the negative information. The friendly close should not include an apology such as "Again, let me say how sorry I am that we cannot honor your claim." This only reminds the receiver of the problem. The close can include any friendly remark appropriate to your receiver. The prime requirement is to regain the goodwill that may have been lost due to the negative information.

Implementing the Indirect Plan

This section describes considerations for choosing the delivery mode of negative messages and then gives the step-by-step development of a negative message following the indirect plan. These steps illustrate content for each of the five parts of the indirect plan in response to a case scenario.

Message Delivery Mode

Negative messages of high importance usually are presented best in person. Preferably, this would be face-to-face, but it may be by telephone. Oral communication is particularly desirable if the message will have a strong negative effect on the receiver(s). For example, an employee notice of a policy violation, an unfavorable performance rating, or a suspension would be documented in writing, but the bad news should be presented first face-to-face. The impersonal nature of a written message without having first met with the supervisor could cause a loss of goodwill and productivity. When negative company news personally affects a group of employees, this information should be presented in employee meetings before workers receive a written memo or learn about it from the news media.

Negative messages to customers that cannot be handled orally may be written in a letter or e-mail. In most cases, written messages that require the indirect plan should be written on company or organization stationery as a letter for postal mail. This delivery mode indicates the importance you place on addressing the situation and overcoming any negative impact on the receiver(s). Although e-mail currently is used more than postal mail for written messages, its frequent casual, direct nature may make it poorly suited for negative messages. However, if the negative message is in response to an e-mail request, it may be preferable to respond by e-mail. If e-mail is the most logical means of delivery for the negative message, make a special effort to use a positive, friendly tone and follow the indirect plan to avoid the message being perceived as blunt and impersonal. Follow letter style by using a greeting and complimentary close as well as grammatical conventions.

NOTE 8.23
You may follow an oral negative message with the written message.

The Easi Pickens Case

Customized Auto Accessories, Inc., sells body kits; interior and exterior accent accessories; visors; and wheel, tire, and grill guards through its website. The company operates globally out of a distribution center in Portland, Oregon. It has a supply chain of manufacturers for accessories adaptable to ten different automobile makes and models. Electronic inventory systems ensure an available inventory of high-demand items. However, orders for low-demand specialty items result in an e-mail request by the company direct to the manufacturers for shipment to the distribution center, which sends orders to customers. Order delivery time depends on the type of item requested and the customer's location. In-stock items have same-day shipping and arrive within one to two days. Specialty, low-demand items have a three- to six-week delivery time. On March 20, the Sales and Shipping Department for Customized Auto Accessories, Inc., moved its offices to a different office suite.

NOTE 8.24
A communication case will help illustrate how to apply the indirect plan.

On March 15, Easi Pickens completed an online order totaling $359.64 for his grandson Tom's sixteenth birthday (April 25) to accessorize the pre-owned Sorento Tom's parents are giving him. The online order form would not accept the credit card information, so Easi made a copy of the Internet order and mailed it from the local post office on March 17 with a money order. He had selected chrome sport gauges, a shift plate, gauge plate rings, a chrome rear bumper molding, an auto wood shifter, and an interior chrome molding kit.

On March 26 the order had not arrived. Another e-mail to the company brought an e-mail response that payment had not been received. Easi copied the money order receipt and sent it to the company, along with a copy of the original order and a letter urgently requesting delivery by Tom's birthday on April 25. When the company received Easi's proof of order and payment on March 30, the Distribution Manager, Janet McKee, returned to the previous office location and found Mr. Pickens' original order and the money order, which had dropped behind a table where incoming mail had been placed. The shift plate, gauge plate rings, and auto wood shifter were available and ready for immediate shipment, but the other items required a special order to the supplier. The expected delivery for these items was April 30.

Ms. McKee decides to write a letter to Mr. Pickens, sending an e-mail copy followed by the original letter on company stationery, signed, and sent by postal mail. The printed letter will include a birthday greeting to Tom for Mr. Pickens to insert in the birthday package. Her task is to convey the negative information that only part of the order will arrive by Tom's birthday. At the same time, she wants to make that information acceptable, and maybe even desirable, to Mr. Pickens and Tom.

STEP-BY-STEP MESSAGE DEVELOPMENT

A written message will be developed for this case to illustrate the content. Ms. McKee chose to ship the requested items that were in stock immediately and to send an e-mail copy of the formal letter, which would follow by postal mail. The e-mail would arrive prior to delivery of the partial shipment, which will take one to two days. The response to the letter is likely to be an emotional, negative reaction; therefore, the letter should be written using the indirect plan. By sending a follow-up formal letter with an enclosed special birthday greeting for Tom, Ms. McKee shows that the company places a high level of importance on effectively addressing this disappointment to the customer. The following sections discuss development of each part of this negative message.

Determine Appropriate Content. The primary purposes of the letter to Mr. Pickens will be to convey clearly the negative information that only part of the order will arrive on time and to secure a positive response. The secondary purpose is to develop a good relationship. The content of the message must be developed and organized for each step in the indirect plan. Examples show poor and good content that could be used to respond to the case scenario.

Write an Effective Opening Buffer. The five qualities of a good opening buffer can be illustrated best for this communication situation through contrasting examples. An example of a **poor** opening buffer follows:

• I apologize for the inconvenience. Sometimes mistakes happen, and delivery cannot be made on time; but we will do all we can to make corrections and keep your business.

In analyzing this poor opening buffer, note the negative words used throughout: *apologize, inconvenience, mistakes,* and *cannot.* Although, the buffer does lead to the explanation and possible corrections, it does not maintain neutrality because it reveals the negative information about delivery. The statement about keeping the receiver's business may suggest a greater interest in benefits to the company than to the customer and does not clearly convey the you–viewpoint to build goodwill.

An example of a **good** opening buffer for this situation follows:

- Thank you for your order. We appreciate your choosing to purchase items for your grandson's birthday from our company. We understand the importance to you of prompt delivery.

NOTE 8.28
The good opening meets the customer's needs, builds goodwill, and introduces the explanation.

In contrast to the poor opening buffer, this paragraph effectively meets all requirements of a good buffer for a negative message. Recognizing the customer's needs and expressing appreciation for the order build goodwill. Introducing the topic (order delivery) for the explanation provides coherence.

Provide a Convincing Logical Explanation. The next step in the indirect plan is to build on the opening buffer with a logical explanation justifying the negative information. A **poor** logical explanation might read as follows:

- Your original order and your money order were misplaced, and company policy did not allow us to fill the order until the money was received. This is the reason for the shipment delay. We regret that, due to this delay, part of your order will not arrive in time for Tom's birthday. We will, however, ship the shift plate, gauge plate rings, and auto wood shifter tomorrow because we found your original order and the money order.

NOTE 8.29
The poor logical explanation lacks positive wording and the you–viewpoint.

This logical explanation shows—as did the poor opening buffer—a lack of positive wording and you–viewpoint. This poorly worded explanation is negative and ignores the receiver's interests. Blame is placed on company policy, which the customer probably views as a poor excuse. The positive statement of items that will arrive on time is buried within the paragraph with no justification of why the order and payment were misplaced and have now been found.

Conversely, a **good** logical explanation for this communication situation could read as follows:

- On March 20, we moved our office suite into a larger warehouse. As soon as I received your message today, I searched our previous location and found your original order and payment that had dropped behind the table where incoming mail had been kept. Today, we shipped the shift plate, gauge plate rings, and auto wood shifter by UPS next day air at no additional delivery charge to you. The tracking number for this shipment is 1ZE1428E137. You should receive this shipment tomorrow, March 31.

NOTE 8.30
The good logical explanation uses emphasis techniques for the most positive information.

This logical explanation coherently follows the good opening buffer and extends the thought of prompt delivery by giving immediate attention to locating and shipping the order. The explanation of why it was lost is convincing and remains positive. The explanation doesn't place blame on anyone or on company policy. Instead, the focus is on actions the company is taking to help address the customer's needs. The most positive information is emphasized by placing it at the end of the paragraph. The delivery information could also have been placed at the beginning for emphasis because the beginning and the ending of the paragraph are the most prominent locations. In this case, the letter has better coherence by giving the explanation for delay first. Mentioning partial shipment first would immediately raise questions about the reason for the delay in shipping the other items. After reading the logical explanation for the delay, the receiver is ready to appreciate this delivery and is prepared for the bad news about late arrival of the remaining items.

Give Negative Information Positively.
A **poor** way to tell that part of the shipment will not arrive in time for Tom's birthday follows:

NOTE 8.31
The poorly stated negative message emphasizes negative information and de-emphasizes the explanation.

- The other items have to be special ordered from the manufacturer and *will not arrive* until April 30. The remaining items will be five days late because we do not keep these items in stock. A special order usually takes from three to six weeks.

The paragraph emphasizes lateness of the additional items by mentioning the date and the number of days late and using the negative term *will not arrive*. The last sentence may raise a question about the exact date for arrival of the other items. These items are not specified; thus, the customer cannot verify that their arrival will complete the order. The reason shipment requires additional time is de-emphasized by sandwiching it in the middle of the paragraph.

A **good** way to inform Mr. Pickens of the bad news follows:

NOTE 8.32
The negative information is placed within the explanation to de-emphasize it.

- The remainder of the order consists of special order items, and delivery from the manufacturer for these items requires additional time. These items— the chrome sport gauges, chrome rear bumper molding, and interior chrome molding kit—will arrive on April 30. We wanted you to have the first part of the order as quickly as possible. By the time these shipped items are installed, the second part of the order will arrive and be ready for installation.

This negative information is presented at the end of the logical explanation paragraph. The late date is de-emphasized by being placed within the explanation. Instead of an apology, which would emphasize the negative situation, the explanation paragraph ends with a statement suggesting that spacing delivery timing may be a benefit to the receiver.

Because the message prepares Mr. Pickens to receive the negative information, this delay may be acceptable. In fact, as suggested earlier, he may prefer the alternative solution that you will give him in the next paragraph—the constructive follow-up. He will know also that Ms. McKee respects his needs because she took the time to explain the negative information and immediately ship available items.

Assist the Receiver with Constructive Follow-up.
Is there an alternative solution to late arrival of part of the order? The following is an example of a **poor** constructive follow-up section of the letter to Mr. Pickens:

NOTE 8.33
A poor constructive follow-up includes an apology; this is a reminder of the problem.

- Again, I apologize for the delay. If your credit card had worked for the online order, this late shipment could have been avoided. Using postal mail to transmit a money order slowed down receipt of the original order. Perhaps you should check with your credit card company to see what problem may have developed.

This follow-up message is destructive to a good relationship rather than constructive. The apology continues to remind the receiver of the problem. Even worse, it places blame on the customer for the delay and raises another problem related to the customer's credit card rather than assuming that the company's own website could be at fault.

A **good** constructive follow-up section would be the following:

- With this letter, I am enclosing a birthday greeting for your grandson from our company. The greeting includes an itemized list of the additional accessory items that he will be receiving April 30. If you insert this message in the birthday package with items from the first shipment, Tom will be happy to see that additional accessories are on their way, and he can look forward to their installation.

NOTE 8.34
The good constructive follow-up suggests an alternative solution or additional explanation.

This constructive follow-up suggests a possible solution for not having the full order on time. Although it is not the solution wanted, it is a thoughtful alternative. In effective business communication, additional effort to meet the receiver's needs helps achieve a positive response.

Build Goodwill in a Friendly Close. The last part of the indirect plan is the friendly close. A **poor** friendly close might read this way:

- If you have concerns about the action taken to solve this problem, don't hesitate to contact me. We know how important a sixteenth birthday is.

NOTE 8.35
A poor friendly close reminds the receiver of the negative information.

Obviously, this close continues to remind Mr. Pickens of the negative information. The last sentence is warm and does personalize the close, but it still mentions the negative subject.

A **good** friendly close for the letter to Mr. Pickens is as follows:

- When you have future needs for car accessories, you will find high-quality merchandise at reasonable prices on our website at *http://www.10caa.com.* We appreciate your business; customer service is our priority.

NOTE 8.36
The friendly close builds goodwill by being neutral, warm, and optimistic.

This friendly close builds goodwill by a friendly offer for future service. It mentions the topic of car accessories but does not refer to the negative information of this message.

Summary—Poor and Good Messages to Easi Pickens

In reviewing how to write effective negative messages, two example letters—one poor and one good—have been presented. Both of these letters carry the negative information, but only the good example presents it effectively. The **poor** letter (see Figure 8.2) does not use proven communication guides that enhance understanding and acceptance of negative messages. The poor letter uses the five parts of the indirect plan outline but does not follow the guidelines for effective development of these parts.

needs work

Customized Auto Accessories, Inc.
5515 Marathon Boulevard
Portland, Oregon 97885-8533
(503) 555-1435 Fax (503) 555-3831
http://www.10caa.com

March 30, 200–

Mr. Easi Pickens
1224 Southline Road
Bannockburn, IL 60015

Dear Mr. Pickens:

I apologize for the inconvenience. Sometimes mistakes happen, and delivery cannot be made on time; but we will do all we can to make corrections and keep your business.

Your original order and your money order were misplaced, and company policy did not allow us to fill the order until the money was received. This is the reason for the shipment delay. We regret that, due to this delay, part of your order will not arrive in time for Tom's birthday. We will, however, ship the shift plate, gauge plate rings, and auto wood shifter tomorrow because we found your original order and the money order. The other items have to be special ordered from the manufacturer and will not arrive until April 30. The remaining items will be five days late because we do not keep these items in stock. A special order usually takes from three to six weeks.

Again, I apologize for the delay. If your credit card had worked for the online order, this late shipment could have been avoided. Using postal mail to transmit a money order slowed down receipt of the original order. Perhaps you should check with your credit card company to see what problem may have developed.

If you have concerns about the action taken to solve this problem, don't hesitate to contact me. We know how important a sixteenth birthday is.

Cordially,

Janet McKee

Janet McKee
Distribution Manager

Apologizes.

Has negative wording.

Gives a third apology

Blames the customer.

Reminds of the bad news.

Gives bad news; not neutral.

De-emphasizes the positive action.

Emphasizes the negative news.

FIGURE 8.2
Example of a *Poor* Negative Message

The **good** letter is shown in Figure 8.3. It incorporates the recommended guidelines for effective business communication. The good letter shows how the indirect plan, properly implemented, builds goodwill and improves human relations.

To illustrate further how the indirect plan applies to actual business situations, the following pages give other examples of poor and good negative messages. The last part of the chapter shows appropriate use of the direct plan for certain types of negative messages.

looks good

Customized Auto Accessories, Inc.
5515 Marathon Boulevard
Portland, Oregon 97885
(503) 555-1435 Fax (503) 555-3831
http://www.10caa.com

March 30, 200–

Mr. Easi Pickens
1224 Southline Road
Bannockburn, IL 60015

Dear Mr. Pickens:

Thank you for your order. We appreciate your choosing to purchase items for your grandson's birthday from our company. We understand the importance to you of prompt delivery.

On March 20, we moved our office suite into a larger warehouse. As soon as I received your message today, I searched our previous location and found your original order and payment that had dropped behind the table where incoming mail had been kept. Today, we shipped the shift plate, gauge plate rings, and auto wood shifter by UPS next day air at no additional delivery charge to you. The tracking number for this shipment is 1ZE1428E137. You should receive this shipment tomorrow, March 31.

The remainder of the order consists of special order items, and delivery from the manufacturer for these items requires additional time. These items—the chrome sport gauges, chrome rear bumper molding, and interior chrome molding kit—will arrive on April 30. We wanted you to have the first part of the order as quickly as possible. By the time these shipped items are installed, the second part of the order will arrive and be ready for installation.

With this letter, I am enclosing a birthday greeting for your grandson from our company. The greeting includes an itemized list of the additional accessory items that he will be receiving April 30. If you insert this message in the birthday package with items from the first shipment, Tom will be happy to see that additional accessories are on their way, and he can look forward to their installation.

When you have future needs for car accessories, you will find high-quality merchandise at reasonable prices on our website at http://www.10caa.com. We appreciate your business; customer service is our priority.

Cordially,

Janet McKee

Janet McKee
Distribution Manager

Enclosure

Callouts (left): Is neutral and positive. · Gives a convincing explanation. · [Em]phasizes what can be done. · [Stat]es explicit negative information. · [Pro]vides a reasonable alternative.

Callouts (right): Introduces explanation. · Relates to buffer topic. · Is optimistic; builds goodwill.

FIGURE 8.3
Example of a *Good* Negative Message

Using the Indirect Plan for a Variety of Purposes

With the development of the letter described in the previous section, you compared a poor and a good example of a negative message that followed the indirect plan. With this plan, the message receiver is prepared for the bad news by preceding it with a logical explanation. The negative information is given only once and de-emphasized. In addition, the message presents an alternative means of meeting the receiver's needs.

Critics of the indirect plan suggest that it is unethical and manipulative because it de-emphasizes the bad news to get a positive response. However, in those

LO 4
Prepare effective negative messages for a variety of purposes using the indirect plan.

NOTE 8.37
The indirect plan is ethical when it considers the receiver's needs, helps neutralize a negative reaction, and presents alternative ways to help.

needs work

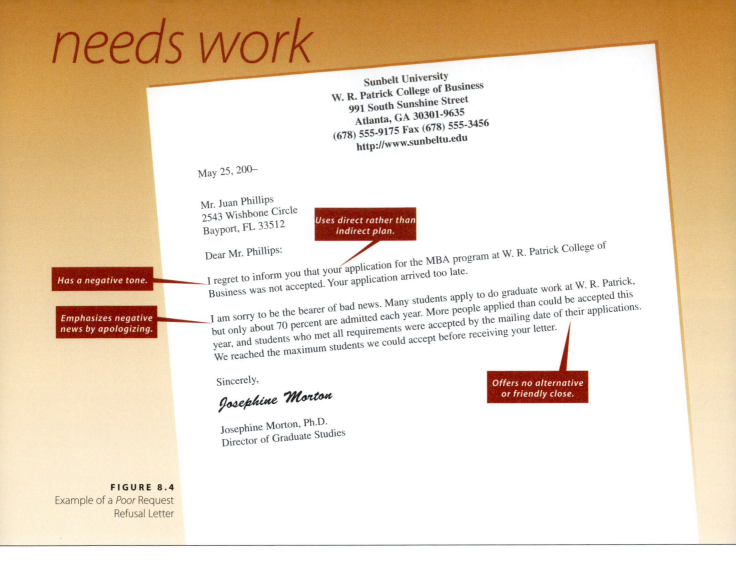

Sunbelt University
W. R. Patrick College of Business
991 South Sunshine Street
Atlanta, GA 30301-9635
(678) 555-9175 Fax (678) 555-3456
http://www.sunbeltu.edu

May 25, 200–

Mr. Juan Phillips
2543 Wishbone Circle
Bayport, FL 33512

Dear Mr. Phillips:

Uses direct rather than indirect plan.

I regret to inform you that your application for the MBA program at W. R. Patrick College of Business was not accepted. Your application arrived too late.

Has a negative tone.

I am sorry to be the bearer of bad news. Many students apply to do graduate work at W. R. Patrick, but only about 70 percent are admitted each year. More people applied than could be accepted this year, and students who met all requirements were accepted by the mailing date of their applications. We reached the maximum students we could accept before receiving your letter.

Emphasizes negative news by apologizing.

Offers no alternative or friendly close.

Sincerely,

Josephine Morton

Josephine Morton, Ph.D.
Director of Graduate Studies

FIGURE 8.4
Example of a *Poor* Request Refusal Letter

instances when a receiver is likely to respond negatively to a situation of high importance to you or the receiver, it makes good sense to convey the message in a manner that helps neutralize a negative reaction and that suggests other ways to help. A sincere message developed with consideration for the feelings of others not only is ethical but also is the central focus of effective communication. An unethical message would conceal information based on the sender's self-interest and with disregard for the message receiver.

This section of the chapter gives examples of a variety of bad news situations that generally require use of the indirect plan. Included are request refusals, adjustment refusals, credit refusals, and unsolicited negative messages.

Request Refusals

Business firms frequently receive requests. These could range from a request from the local high school soliciting paid advertisements for the yearbook to a request from a company employee asking for a two-week leave of absence with pay for job-related professional development. Many of these requests are reasonable, and the company will be able to send a positive response as described in Chapter 7.

looks good

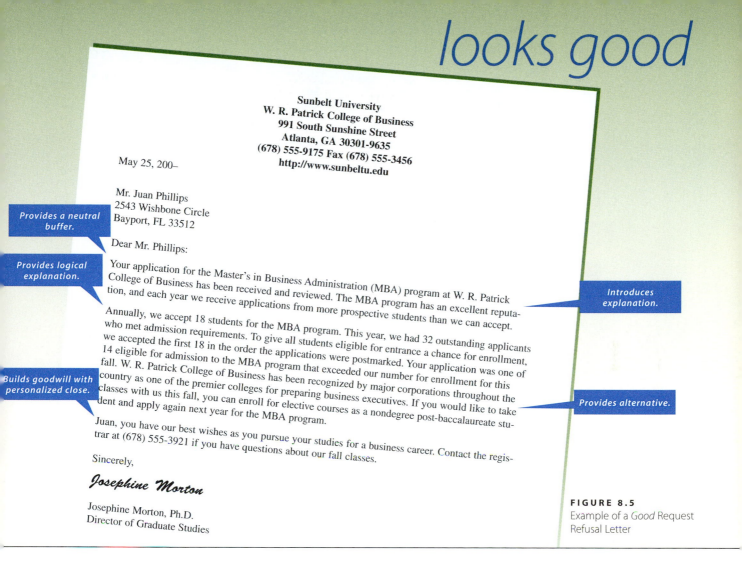

Provides a neutral buffer.

Provides logical explanation.

Builds goodwill with personalized close.

Introduces explanation.

Provides alternative.

Sunbelt University
W. R. Patrick College of Business
991 South Sunshine Street
Atlanta, GA 30301-9635
(678) 555-9175 Fax (678) 555-3456
http://www.sunbeltu.edu

May 25, 200–

Mr. Juan Phillips
2543 Wishbone Circle
Bayport, FL 33512

Dear Mr. Phillips:

Your application for the Master's in Business Administration (MBA) program at W. R. Patrick College of Business has been received and reviewed. The MBA program has an excellent reputation, and each year we receive applications from more prospective students than we can accept.

Annually, we accept 18 students for the MBA program. This year, we had 32 outstanding applicants who met admission requirements. To give all students eligible for entrance a chance for enrollment, we accepted the first 18 in the order the applications were postmarked. Your application was one of 14 eligible for admission to the MBA program that exceeded our number for enrollment for this fall. W. R. Patrick College of Business has been recognized by major corporations throughout the country as one of the premier colleges for preparing business executives. If you would like to take classes with us this fall, you can enroll for elective courses as a nondegree post-baccalaureate student and apply again next year for the MBA program.

Juan, you have our best wishes as you pursue your studies for a business career. Contact the registrar at (678) 555-3921 if you have questions about our fall classes.

Sincerely,

Josephine Morton

Josephine Morton, Ph.D.
Director of Graduate Studies

FIGURE 8.5
Example of a _Good_ Request Refusal Letter

Sometimes, however, a **request refusal**—a denial of something asked for—must be sent. For example, the company receiving the school's request for yearbook support through advertising may budget all advertisements once a year and be unable at this time to allocate additional funds. The company must then refuse this request. The constructive follow-up in this negative message might offer to consider the request for next year's budget. In the case of the employee's request for leave, the dates requested may come at a time of the year when the company will have an occupational safety and health inspection that is critical for continued operation. The leave time must be denied at this time but may be possible at a later date.

Here is another situation that illustrates the use of the indirect plan for a request refusal. Assume that you are the Director of Graduate Studies of the W. R. Patrick College of Business at Sunbelt University. Juan Phillips' application for the MBA program was not accepted because more people applied than could be accepted. Students meeting all requirements were accepted in the order their applications were postmarked. The Director of Graduate Studies must send a letter to Juan denying admission because of the mailing date of his application. Figure 8.4 on the previous page shows a **poor** example of a letter for this situation. Figure 8.5 illustrates a **good** message for this application refusal. This letter builds goodwill by explaining the situation and suggesting an alternative for Juan.

NOTE 8.38
A request refusal denies something asked for.

needs work

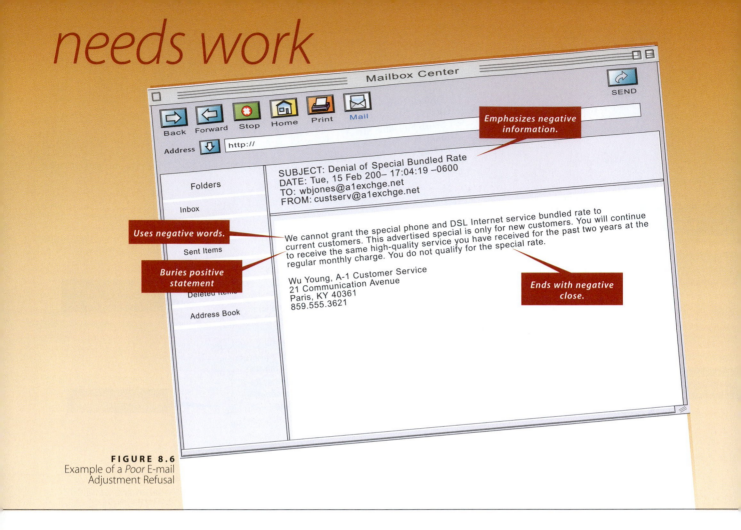

FIGURE 8.6
Example of a *Poor* E-mail Adjustment Refusal

The figure shows a "Mailbox Center" e-mail window with the following annotations and content:

- *Emphasizes negative information.*
- *Uses negative words.*
- *Buries positive statement*
- *Ends with negative close.*

SUBJECT: Denial of Special Bundled Rate
DATE: Tue, 15 Feb 200– 17:04:19 –0600
TO: wbjones@a1exchge.net
FROM: custserv@a1exchge.net

We cannot grant the special phone and DSL Internet service bundled rate to current customers. This advertised special is only for new customers. You will continue to receive the same high-quality service you have received for the past two years at the regular monthly charge. You do not qualify for the special rate.

Wu Young, A-1 Customer Service
21 Communication Avenue
Paris, KY 40361
859.555.3621

Adjustment Refusals

Handling customer claims is a common task for most business firms. These claims include requests to exchange merchandise, requests for refunds, and requests that faulty work be corrected. Most of these claims can be approved because they are legitimate. However, some requests for adjustment must be denied. Although the customer expects a positive response, the company must send an adjustment refusal message. Adjustment refusals are negative messages for the customer. They are necessary when the customer is at fault or when the vendor has already done what can reasonably or legally be expected.

NOTE 8.39
An adjustment refusal requires the indirect plan to retain goodwill.

An adjustment refusal message requires the indirect plan and your best communication skills because it is bad news for the receiver. Your goal is to refuse the claim and, at the same time, retain the goodwill of the customer. You may refuse the adjustment request and even try to sell more merchandise or service. All of this is happening when the customer is probably angry, disappointed, or inconvenienced.

Consider a request from a customer for adjustment to charges for a bundled package of phone and Internet DSL services. The customer has been with this provider for two years. To entice new customers, the provider recently advertised a telephone and DSL bundled package for a total charge that is 25 percent less than the regular cost. This new price does not apply to current customers. Figure 8.6

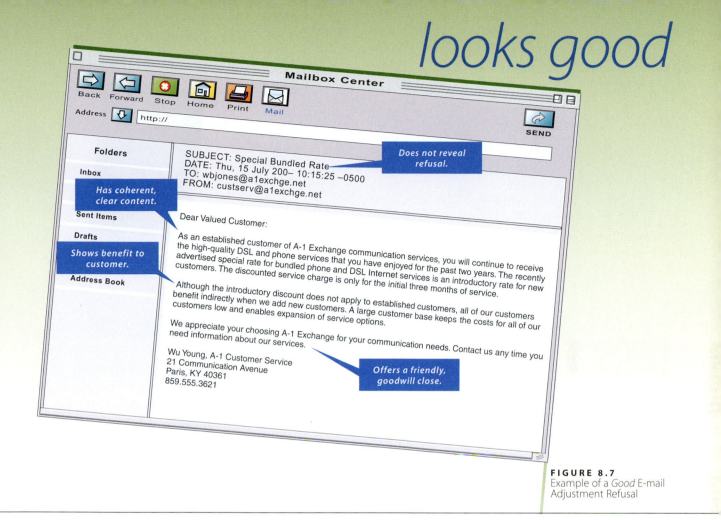

FIGURE 8.7
Example of a *Good* E-mail Adjustment Refusal

shows a **poor** e-mail in which the company does not use the indirect plan and probably loses a customer. On the other hand, the same basic message can be written using the indirect plan and result in keeping a good customer. Figure 8.7 is a **good** example of how this e-mail could be written.

Credit Refusals

Most businesses permit and even encourage qualified customers to buy on credit. It is a strategy that increases sales. The discussion in this section is relevant to in-store credit cards.

Credit applications from customers who have good credit ratings or who have sufficient assets for collateral will be approved. Customers who have problems paying their bills or who own nothing of sufficient value to use as collateral may be refused credit. A message rejecting a credit request is called a **credit refusal.**

Business firms attempt to communicate credit refusals in a manner that makes the answer acceptable to the customer. Businesses want to do this out of common decency and also because they want to continue to serve the customer on a cash basis if possible.

Credit refusals are communicated in the following four basic ways: (a) personalized letters, (b) form letters, (c) telephone calls, or (d) face-to-face conversations. In all cases, the indirect plan is preferable for communicating the credit refusal.

NOTE 8.40
Credit refusals may be personalized letters, form letters, telephone calls, or face-to-face communications.

needs work

March 10, 200–

Clowers Plumbing
2154 Industrial Road
Shreveport, LA 71109

Dear Mr. Clowers:

Negative buffer; not neutral.

I am sorry to inform you that your application for a line of credit with Shreveport Supply cannot be approved at this time. We would like to extend you a line of credit; however, a credit check shows that you owe too much money.

I–viewpoint rather than you–viewpoint.

The competition among plumbers in our area makes it difficult for small plumbing firms to survive. We cannot take a chance on extending credit to a company that is heavily in debt. We hope that your company does not fail, but we can't take a chance.

Again, let me say that I am sorry that we cannot extend a line of credit to your company. If you need any plumbing supplies, please use Shreveport Supply.

Apology; reminder of bad news.

Sincerely,

George Campbell

George Campbell
Credit Manager

jpt

FIGURE 8.8
Example of a *Poor* Credit
Refusal Letter

Figure 8.8 is a **poor** example of a personalized letter in which a supply house denies a customer's application for a line of credit. The indirect plan is not used in this letter. Figure 8.9 uses the indirect plan and illustrates an improved letter for this circumstance. A mutually satisfactory business relationship could develop from this credit refusal.

Unsolicited Negative Messages

NOTE 8.41
Unsolicited negative messages are not a response to a request or an inquiry.

Not all negative messages are in response to a request or an inquiry. An **unsolicited negative message** is a bad news message initiated by the sender. Examples of such messages include communication about price increases for products or services, budget reductions, and staff reductions (layoffs). These messages are especially difficult to compose because they initiate the bad news.

Following the indirect plan but omitting the buffer may be appropriate for some negative messages. This modification of the indirect plan is appropriate for some internal unsolicited communication for situations not related to personnel matters.

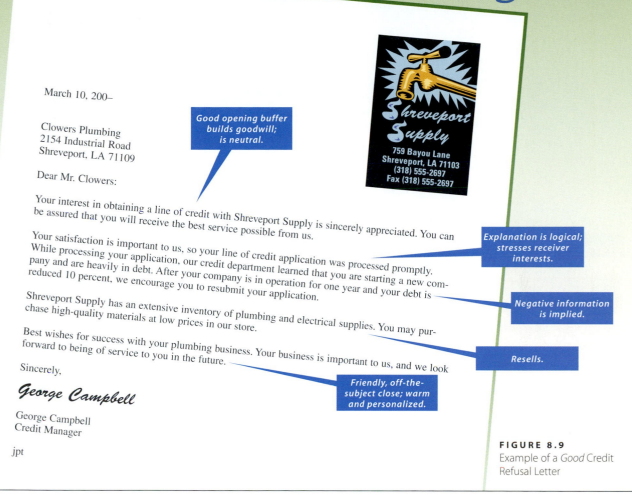

March 10, 200–

Clowers Plumbing
2154 Industrial Road
Shreveport, LA 71109

Dear Mr. Clowers:

Your interest in obtaining a line of credit with Shreveport Supply is sincerely appreciated. You can be assured that you will receive the best service possible from us.

Your satisfaction is important to us, so your line of credit application was processed promptly. While processing your application, our credit department learned that you are starting a new company and are heavily in debt. After your company is in operation for one year and your debt is reduced 10 percent, we encourage you to resubmit your application.

Shreveport Supply has an extensive inventory of plumbing and electrical supplies. You may purchase high-quality materials at low prices in our store.

Best wishes for success with your plumbing business. Your business is important to us, and we look forward to being of service to you in the future.

Sincerely,

George Campbell

George Campbell
Credit Manager

jpt

Good opening buffer builds goodwill; is neutral.

Explanation is logical; stresses receiver interests.

Negative information is implied.

Resells.

Friendly, off-the-subject close; warm and personalized.

Shreveport Supply
759 Bayou Lane
Shreveport, LA 71103
(318) 555-2697
Fax (318) 555-2697

FIGURE 8.9
Example of a *Good* Credit Refusal Letter

This modified indirect plan is similar to the direct plan in tone because it moves quickly to the negative message but differs in that the direct approach gives the negative message before the reason or explanation. The sequence of message steps for the modified indirect plan follows the same pattern as the indirect plan with the exception that there is no opening buffer. An example of using the modified indirect plan is a memo to employees explaining a change in product design. This memo could begin with an explanation of the reason that a particular design feature of the product is no longer effective and move to a description of the product change and its implications for the current marketing plan. For particularly sensitive personnel messages such as a suspension, termination, or change in status that may have legal considerations, rely on legal advice for the message content.

In Figure 8.10, you can feel the impact of the **poor** bad news letter for late payment of shipping charges that were not added to the total payment for the last order. Because this was probably an oversight, the message is unexpected. Its harsh tone and lack of you–viewpoint may lose a regular customer.

needs work

needs work

A Gardener's Dream
Order Reservation Service
P.O. Box 253
Blue Springs, MO 64015
(660) 555-9783 Fax (660) 555-9784
http://www.dreamgarden.com

April 28, 200–

Ms. Betty Martin
151 Grand Tour Drive
Lincoln, NE 68501-3123

Dear Ms. Martin:

This is a notice of late payment for a shortage in the amount of the check sent for your last order. A late payment fee of $10 will be applied if not paid within 15 days. You should have received your order, but you failed to add the shipping costs of $7.95 to the total of your check.

Your full payment is important to us. We hope to receive payment of your balance soon so we can clear our records.

Thank you,

Josh Whitaker

Josh Whitaker, Credit Assistant

No buffer.

Negative words and tone.

No you–viewpoint.

FIGURE 8.10
Example of a *Poor*
Unsolicited Negative Letter

Figure 8.11, a **good** example of an unsolicited negative message, shows how the same information can be conveyed in a more acceptable manner. This letter is positive and has a helpful tone. The opening buffer is neutral but leads to the explanation. The negative message is de-emphasized by its placement in the middle of the second paragraph. The friendly close ends on a neutral, positive note. Which of the two letters would be offensive to you? Which one would be acceptable and likely to keep your goodwill?

There is no need for a communicator to anger, disturb, or hurt receivers—intentionally or inadvertently—through poorly conveyed messages. If this had been a second or third notice for late payment, a direct plan message would be appropriate; but a harsh message negatively worded that is sure to disturb and anger the receiver will not be effective.

LO 5
Describe the guidelines for appropriate use of the direct plan.

Using the Direct Plan for Negative Messages

You are already familiar with the direct plan for message preparation. Chapter 7 describes how to write positive or neutral messages using the **direct plan.** This direct

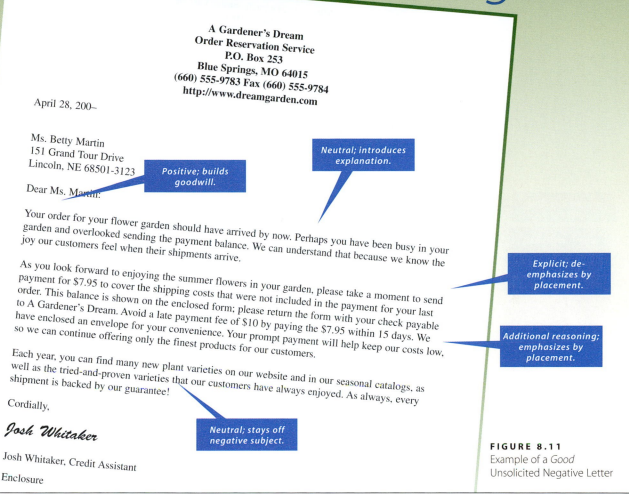

A Gardener's Dream
Order Reservation Service
P.O. Box 253
Blue Springs, MO 64015
(660) 555-9783 Fax (660) 555-9784
http://www.dreamgarden.com

April 28, 200–

Ms. Betty Martin
151 Grand Tour Drive
Lincoln, NE 68501-3123

> *Positive; builds goodwill.*

> *Neutral; introduces explanation.*

Dear Ms. Martin:

Your order for your flower garden should have arrived by now. Perhaps you have been busy in your garden and overlooked sending the payment balance. We can understand that because we know the joy our customers feel when their shipments arrive.

As you look forward to enjoying the summer flowers in your garden, please take a moment to send payment for $7.95 to cover the shipping costs that were not included in the payment for your last order. This balance is shown on the enclosed form; please return the form with your check payable to A Gardener's Dream. Avoid a late payment fee of $10 by paying the $7.95 within 15 days. We have enclosed an envelope for your convenience. Your prompt payment will help keep our costs low, so we can continue offering only the finest products for our customers.

> *Explicit; de-emphasizes by placement.*

> *Additional reasoning; emphasizes by placement.*

Each year, you can find many new plant varieties on our website and in our seasonal catalogs, as well as the tried-and-proven varieties that our customers have always enjoyed. As always, every shipment is backed by our guarantee!

Cordially,

Josh Whitaker

Josh Whitaker, Credit Assistant

Enclosure

> *Neutral; stays off negative subject.*

FIGURE 8.11
Example of a *Good* Unsolicited Negative Letter

plan for negative messages places the main idea in the first sentence or paragraph, followed by the logical explanation, constructive follow-up, and friendly close. The purpose remains the same—to achieve a positive result and maintain or build goodwill. The direct plan is most often used for negative messages that are routine and will not be upsetting to your receiver. It may also be used because of the receiver's communication preference, when the negative information needs emphasis, or when the negative information is already known or may be expected.

These examples of negative messages are appropriate for the direct plan: cancellation of a routine meeting, a request for information that you refer elsewhere, a notification letter to job applicants that they were not selected for the position, or a notice of company policy changes that have a minimal effect on the receiver(s). You may use the direct plan when you know the receiver prefers to learn bad news first and the reasons or rationale later. Your analysis of the situation and the receiver will help you to determine when you should use the direct plan.

Figures 8.12 and 8.13 are examples of **poor** and **good** uses of the direct plan for a negative message to unsuccessful applicants for a job opening. Applicants who do not get the job will be disappointed, but they usually apply to more than one company and do not expect each response to be positive. Also, the main message they want to see first is the news—bad or good—did they get the job? The poor message

NOTE 8.42
The direct plan places the main idea first and is used for negative messages that will not upset the receiver.

LO 6
Prepare effective negative messages for a variety of purposes using the direct plan.

NOTE 8.43
These negative messages might follow a direct plan: canceling a routine meeting, notifying unsuccessful job applicants, or conveying organization news with little receiver effect.

needs work

Mississippi Delta Technical College
2015 Corporate Drive
Jackson, MS 39201-5555
(601) 555-3754 Fax (601) 555-3755
http://www.mdtech.edu

November 18, 200–

Dr. Mark Appleton
P.O. Box 1515
Scottsdale, AZ 85251-7715

Dear Dr. Appleton:

It was a pleasure to get to know you when you came to our campus for an interview. Obviously, you have many contributions to make as an educator.

We have now made our selection for the position of Academic Dean. We selected the candidate who most closely fit the position requirements. Although you were not selected for the position, you have many fine attributes. We apologize for being the bearer of bad news.

Sincerely,

Maurice Helgeson

Maurice Helgeson, Chair
Search Committee

Delays negative message.

Buries the news.

Gives negative, inappropriate apology.

Omits the goodwill close.

FIGURE 8.12
Example of a *Poor* Direct Plan Negative Message

may confuse or irritate the receiver, while the good message tactfully states what the applicant wants to know and includes positive language to create goodwill.

Summary of Learning Objectives

LO 1 **Describe the nature of negative messages.**

A negative message is one that is likely to be viewed as unpleasant, disappointing, or unfavorable by the receiver. A negative message is a challenge to compose. At the same time, it is an opportunity for you as a writer or speaker to resolve a common business problem successfully.

LO 2 **Explain the reasons to choose the indirect plan or the direct plan for negative messages.**

Use the indirect plan when the receiver expects a positive response; when the bad news will be upsetting or a personal disappointment to the receiver; or when the

looks good

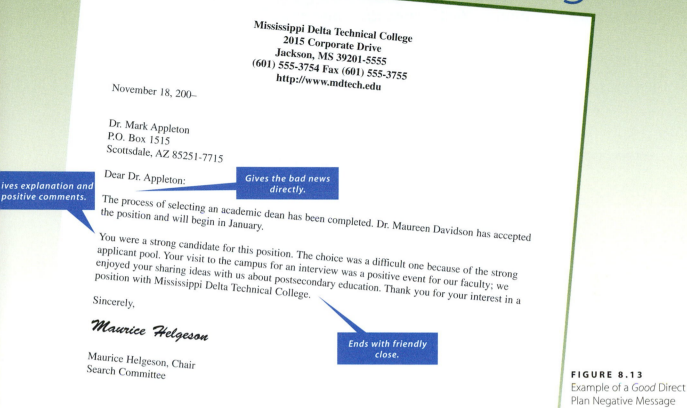

FIGURE 8.13
Example of a *Good* Direct Plan Negative Message

receiver, because of culture or personality, prefers indirect communication. Use the direct plan when the negative message is routine and will not be upsetting to the receiver, the negative information needs to be emphasized, the receiver prefers a direct communication style, or the the receiver has been told of or expects negative news.

Describe the five specific guidelines for appropriate use of the indirect plan.

LO 3

Messages using the indirect plan consist of an opening buffer, logical explanation, negative information, constructive follow-up, and friendly close. The opening buffer should meet the following requirements: provide coherence, build goodwill, be positive, maintain neutrality, and introduce the explanation. The logical explanation usually begins after the opening buffer and often can be handled in one paragraph. The negative information follows the logical explanation and is short—normally one sentence. It may be implied or given in explicit terms and should be de-emphasized. Solutions are provided or additional justification of the unfavorable information is given in the constructive follow-up section. The friendly close should be personalized, off the subject, warm, and optimistic. The friendly close should move the receiver's mind away from the negative news.

LO 4

Prepare effective negative messages for a variety of purposes using the indirect plan.

Incorporate the communication fundamentals in the indirect plan when preparing request refusals, adjustment refusals, credit refusals, and unsolicited negative messages. You should present the information positively using the you–viewpoint. Organize the message in the following order: opening buffer, logical explanation, negative information, constructive follow-up, and friendly close.

LO 5

Describe the guidelines for appropriate use of the direct plan.

For negative messages using the direct plan, present the main topic in the first sentence or first paragraph. This is followed by the explanation, constructive follow-up, and friendly close. The direct plan may be appropriate for negative messages that are routine, will not be upsetting to the receiver, confirm known or expected bad news, or need to emphasize the negative message. Also use the direct plan when you know your receiver prefers to learn the bad news before the reason(s) for it.

LO 6

Prepare effective negative messages for a variety of purposes using the direct plan.

Analyze the situation and the receiver to determine when the direct plan should be used with a negative message. Examples of negative messages that may be appropriate for the direct plan include cancellation of a routine meeting, a request for information that you refer elsewhere, a notification letter to applicants that they were not selected for the position, or a notice of company policy changes that have a minimal effect on the receiver(s).

Questions for Discussion and Review

1. What are negative messages? (Objective 1)
2. Explain how you would decide to use an indirect or a direct plan for development of content for a negative message. (Objective 2)
3. Why does the message receiver's culture affect the choice of direct or indirect plan for communicating negative messages? (Objective 2)
4. Discuss the importance of using the you–viewpoint for effective communication of negative messages. (Objectives 1 and 2)
5. What are two important advantages of using the indirect plan for bad news messages? (Objectives 2 and 3)
6. List and discuss the five major parts of the indirect plan outline and guidelines for developing each part. (Objective 3)
7. Describe three situations that would require a businessperson to use the indirect plan for a negative message. (Objective 4)
8. Explain the placement of the logical explanation and the negative news if a message follows the direct plan. (Objective 5)
9. Describe three situations that would require a businessperson to use the direct plan for a negative message. (Objective 6)

10. Describe a circumstance that would require a businessperson to transmit an unsolicited negative message. For this circumstance, explain the plan of organization that you would use and justify your choice. (Objectives 4 and 6)

Application Exercises

1. Over a 24-hour period, observe and record oral and written communication that you would classify as negative messages because they are unpleasant, disappointing, or upsetting to the receiver. Record the delivery mode of each message, the wording of the message, and whether it followed the direct or indirect plan. Report your list in class for discussion and analysis, rating the effectiveness of each message and justifying the reason for the rating. (Objectives 1, 2, 3, 5, and 6)

2. Select the most effective plan for developing negative messages (direct or indirect) for the following situations and justify your choice: (Objective 2)
   a. A routine meeting is canceled.
   b. A customer's application for a credit card has been denied.
   c. Your planned visit to see a 50-year-old friend who is a resident and native of China has been delayed.

3. Teamwork. Pair with a classmate and discuss why the indirect plan of communicating bad news usually has an advantage over the direct plan, even in low-context countries like the United States. Be prepared to share with your class your opinion about whether most bad news should be communicated indirectly as well as any advantage or disadvantage that the indirect plan might have over the direct plan. (Objective 2)   `COLLABORATIVE`

4. Write an effective opening buffer for the following situations: (Objectives 3 and 4)
   a. Your teacher must indicate to a student that a question was answered incorrectly during a class discussion.
   b. You work part time while attending school. During final exam week, your employer asks you to work overtime the night before you have two exams. You must study for these exams and cannot accommodate your employer's request.

5. Reword the following logical explanations for a negative message so that each has positive rather than negative words and tone. Consider what can be done rather than what cannot. Add necessary details. (Objectives 3 and 4)
   a. Time off cannot be taken without permission of your direct supervisor.
   b. I regret that I will not be able to approve your request for a two-week vacation because company policy does not allow approval for vacation time over one week twice a year.

6. Explain why each of these statements is not an effective way to convey the negative message: (Objective 4)
   a. I am sorry I must refuse your request.
   b. Therefore, following company policy seems to be the best alternative for you.

7. Technology. Your instructor has asked you to speak to the faculty club at your school. Your speech is to be about the benefits of membership in student organizations. You are unable to make the presentation. Send an e-mail to your instructor declining the invitation. Add any necessary details. (Objective 4)   `TECHNOLOGY`

8. Why is the direct plan acceptable for notifying job applicants that they were not selected for a position? (Objectives 5 and 6)

9. Global. Interview a person who is a native of another country to learn how negative messages would be conveyed in his or her homeland. (Objectives 3, 4, 5, and 6)   `GLOBAL`

10. Teamwork. Ethics. Working with three classmates with two on each side of the issue, debate the ethics of using the indirect or the direct plan for negative messages. (Objectives 3, 4, 5, and 6)

Case Problems

Request Refusals

1. You are the franchised dealer for Starlight satellite TV. Last week you ran a four-room installation special in the local newspaper that offered free installation, one-month free service, and a free DVR or HD receiver. Martha Simon, a customer of yours who had the Starlight satellite system installed two years ago, sent an e-mail to you yesterday asking for a free upgrade on her DVR and one free month of service. She had read the special advertisement and thought it was unfair that new customers would get a better bargain than she did when her installation took place. She paid extra for her DVR with installation and did not receive any free service time. The company cannot afford the cost of opening the special offer to current customers. Write a response to Ms. Simon's e-mail. Use effective content consistent with the indirect plan. Keep the language positive. Explain that the special applies to new customers only and that expanding the customer base may help reduce future service cost for all customers. Also, tell her that as a current customer she can receive a 20 percent discount on the cost of a DVR upgrade.

2. Dr. Josephine Markline, a neurologist, is part of a research team with the local university conducting experimental trials of a new drug intended to alleviate tremors for people with Parkinson's disease. In addition to her work with the research, Dr. Markline maintains a regular practice and sees several patients who are in various stages of Parkinson's. George Michelor, a patient whose symptoms have become disabling, sent a request to be given the experimental drug. Dr. Markline must refuse this request because the drug can be prescribed only as part of the approved research trials, and selection of patients for the experiment was completed last month. Approval of this university's trials specified a quota of 15 patients. If the number of participants falls below 15, new participants can be accepted if they meet all requirements when they complete a qualifying physical examination. Write a letter that Dr. Markline can send to Mr. Michelor refusing the request. Include with the letter a brochure that explains requirements for the experimental drug trials. Follow the steps for the indirect plan as you develop the letter.

3. You are the customer service representative for Fly High Airline. The airline awards frequent flyer miles but charges a $50 fee per ticket unless the free flight is booked more than 14 days in advance. The only exception is for a late booking to attend a funeral for a member of the passenger's immediate family. Missy Morganstern, Tempe, Arizona, used her frequent flyer miles to visit her mother, who was ill in California. She had to pay the $50 fee when she booked the flight 10 days in advance. She has requested Fly High Airline to refund the $50 because her mother was seriously ill, and Missy did not know if she would still be alive when she arrived. However, her mother did recover. Develop a message that refuses the request but clearly shows concern for Missy's needs and her emotional state when her mother was ill. The purposes of your message are to overcome a negative reaction to the refusal and to build goodwill for the company.

4. You own a 300-acre farm outside the city. Jack Ripsaw runs a local sawmill and has requested that you let him cut pulpwood from your farm and split the profit 50-50. Mr. Ripsaw's reputation for honesty is not good, and complaints have been voiced from other farm owners that he leaves the fields in disarray with large broken branches scattered where he has cut the pulpwood. Write a letter refusing his request. Use the direct plan to ensure that the answer doesn't encourage further requests. Keep the tone positive to avoid creating ill will.

5. You have been invited to speak at a campaign kick-off reception for Bob Baffle, a candidate for mayor in your city. Bob is a friend of yours, and you plan to support his candidacy. However, the date and time of the event conflict with a work obligation. Write a letter to Bob letting him know that you will not be able to attend. You may suggest a colleague from work, Janice Sivell, who is an outstanding speaker and a strong supporter of Bob's mayoral campaign, and/or you may send a campaign contribution of $250 to show your support.

Adjustment Refusals

6. You own Clean Mist Carpets, a company that uses a chemical process for cleaning carpets and removing stains. You do not guarantee success but have a good reputation for stain removal. Mr.

and Mrs. Carson Jones are placing their house on the real estate market and making repairs to have it ready for their first open house. The family room has a red stain on the carpet that came from the finish on a chair leg. You cleaned the carpet. When you left, the carpet stain appeared to be completely removed. However, you received a message from Mr. and Mrs. Jones asking that their money be refunded and that Clean Mist Carpets pay one-half the cost of a new carpet because the stain reappeared, having wicked from the carpet backing. Their open house is only a week from now; if the stain remains on the carpet, it will be a negative feature that could discourage buyers. Write a letter refusing their request.

7. Seafood Specialties Restaurant offers a shrimp and lobster tail special each Friday evening. You are manager of the restaurant. On Tuesday, you received a request from a customer, Shipley Masters, who ate last Friday's special. According to Mr. Masters, shortly thereafter, he had to go to the hospital emergency room and have his stomach pumped because of food poisoning. He believes his problem came from the Friday special at your restaurant and asks that you pay his hospital emergency room bill. He did not send a copy of the bill or any evidence of his illness. His letter stated the charges were $200. This is the only complaint that you have received; therefore, you have doubts that the illness came from your restaurant. Write a letter refusing the request unless documentation is provided, but make the letter positive to maintain Mr. Masters' goodwill as a regular customer.

8. William Jenson bought a pre-owned Audi with a one-year warranty from Best Motors. After driving the car for a week, he noticed a squeaking sound that appeared to be from the motor. He returned to the service department of Best Motors. The car was serviced and was not making the sound when Mr. Jenson drove it home. The squeak returned the next week. When he brought it back, Mr. Jenson asked that Best Motors find him a similar car and exchange it for the one that squeaks. As owner of Best Motors, you are not ready to take the car back until every effort has been made to determine and correct the source of the problem. Write a letter to Mr. Jenson refusing the request but providing him with another car to drive while his car undergoes diagnostic tests and repairs at no cost to the customer.

9. Nine months ago, Sandra Tucker purchased a computerized sewing machine by mail order from Kunkel Enterprises. The sewing machine was sold with a six-month limited warranty. Sandra has returned the sewing machine to Kunkel because the stitching was poor and the tension could not be adjusted to correct the problem. Although she raised no concerns about the machine during the warranty period, she has requested a new replacement machine. Write a letter to Sandra denying her request but offering to repair the machine at a cost of $90 to Sandra.

10. Wan Yu Tang purchased a cell phone plan from Endless Journey Wireless. His first monthly invoice for service totaled $65, which included a $15 roaming charge. Without understanding the meaning of a roaming charge, Mr. Tang deducted that charge and sent a check for $50, his basic service plan cost. He explained that his basic service charge should be only $50 and asked that you reduce the charges to that amount. Write a letter from Endless Journey Wireless explaining the additional charge and requesting the $15 payment. Write the letter following the direct or indirect plan. Be prepared to justify your choice. Make up additional details as necessary.

Credit Refusals

11. You are the owner of Dale's Clothiers for Men, a business designed to serve white-collar professionals. The policy of your store is to provide credit cards for individuals who have good jobs and excellent credit. One day you receive an application from Jason Williams, a full-time graduate student at your local university. Jason went from high school to college, then to graduate school without ever working full time. He has few assets but not many liabilities because his parents paid for all of his expenses until he started graduate school. He is scheduled to graduate with an MBA in a year. You have decided to refuse his application but do not want to alienate him because he may become a good customer after graduation. Write a refusal letter adding necessary details.

12. Billy Davis has applied for a $9,000 loan to buy a pre-owned automobile. As credit manager of A-1 Finance Corporation, you learn during a credit check that Billy is behind on payments for debts on several credit cards, a home mortgage, and child support. He does not meet the qualifications of a good credit risk with your corporation. Write Billy telling him that you must refuse his credit request on the $9,000 automobile. Add necessary details.

13. Wallenda Jorgenson is in the real estate market to buy a home. She has been attending open houses on her own and has found a house that she wants to buy. She has asked Daniel Thompson, a real estate agent in her town, to be her agent for the purchase. She applied for a loan with a local bank, but her loan was refused because her credit score is too low. She has phoned Mr. Thompson to ask him to help her purchase the house. Word an oral message for Mr. Thompson's phone response that tells her that she will need to be preapproved for a loan before making a formal offer to buy the house. He will help her purchase a home as soon as she can be preapproved for a loan. Also, offer to contact her if a similar property comes on the market with an owner who is willing to carry the loan. In addition to wording the telephone response, write a brief paragraph explaining how your message follows a direct or an indirect plan and justify your selection.

14. You are Finance Officer for Commercial Credit, Inc. Juan Martinez is the owner of a Mexican restaurant. He needs a loan of $200,000 to replace coolers, mixing machines, fry cookers, and commercial ovens. The restaurant is not producing a steady income, and Juan has no other assets as loan collateral. Although Juan is convinced new equipment will solve his income problems, you decide to reject his loan application. Write a letter refusing the loan but with the goal of maintaining goodwill for future transactions.

15. You are the Financial Aid Officer for Liston Community College. Mary Alverez applied for a Pell Grant but did not qualify. Develop the negative message about the loan application. Suggest that you will try to help Mary obtain support from a local organization. Add details as needed. This message will be given face-to-face. Write the Financial Aid Officer's oral message. Partner with another student to role play, taking turns for each to play the part of the Financial Aid Officer and of Mary Alverez. Discuss your positive or negative feelings when you listened to the message in your role as Mary.

Unsolicited Negative Messages

16. You are the owner of Jimmy's Electric, a small electrical construction company. Because of reduction of building in the area, it is necessary that you terminate Milton Young's employment. He is an excellent worker who has been with your company for nine months. You would like to see him come back to work for you when building conditions improve. Develop an outline that you could use when talking with Milton about his termination.

17. For the past year, the local city bus company stopped twice daily at the main entry of Super Mega Shopping Mart for passengers to exit or enter the bus. With the heavy traffic near this entrance, the store manager, Jason Simpson, has decided that a liability factor would exist if one of the passengers were injured near the entrance. Write a letter from Mr. Simpson to Julia Marshall, route manager of the Trans-city Bus Company, telling her that the bus is to load and unload passengers only at the bus stop on the street across the parking lot from the Super Mega Shopping Mart entrance. Supply additional details.

18. Jonathon Green has been a good employee until the past six months. During this time, he has accumulated at least one absence a week and has clocked in tardy 30 times. His productivity has fallen, and you have met with him to discuss these issues and look for solutions to the problems. Yesterday, you met with him to discuss his recent six-month formal evaluation. His overall evaluation for this period has fallen to poor. Previously, all of his ratings were good or excellent. Write the letter that documents and explains the six-month rating. Provide an offer of support and ask that he meet with you to work out an improvement plan. Confirm his previous contributions to the company as a valuable employee, and express your desire to have him once again as a productive, effective employee. Use the indirect plan.

19. Write a letter canceling an appointment that you had scheduled this Thursday at 2 p.m. to meet with your production manager to discuss product goals for the next six weeks. Reschedule the meeting for next week on Thursday at the same time. Use the direct plan.

20. Write a form letter from the local city government director of solid waste to city residents notifying them that as of January 1, garbage service will change from twice a week to once a week. Explain that there is low participation on the second garbage collection day and that making fewer trips with the trucks will save tax money.

*Web exercises to accompany this chapter are available at **www.thomsonedu.com/bcomm/krizan.***

Message Analysis

Nature Unlimited had a spring sale on bird feeders and birdhouses during May. On May 5, Jimme Gomez bought a bluebird house and pole at 20 percent off as a Mother's Day gift. While his mother was out of town the week before Mother's Day, Jimme erected the pole and fastened the birdhouse to it as a surprise for her return. When she returned, his mother told him that bluebirds wouldn't come to her small backyard in the city and asked him to leave the pole but to exchange the birdhouse for a purple martin house. Rewrite and improve the following message to Mr. Gomez from Nature Unlimited. Use the indirect plan to create a positive response and maintain goodwill.

> *I am sorry but I cannot exchange the bluebird house for another birdhouse once it has been installed because I cannot resell it. Your mother will find that the bluebird house is not just for bluebirds, but other birds will use it for nesting. The 20 percent discount on birdhouses is still in effect, so you might want to buy the purple martin house, also. I am sure this would make your mother happy. Purple Martins catch mosquitoes, so this purchase would also protect your mother's health. Again, let me offer my apology for not being able to honor your request. Come by the store to check out the bargains that are still in effect.*

Writer's Workshop

The following items may be sentence fragments or contain errors in subject-verb agreement, pronoun-antecedent agreement, comma and semicolon placement, number display, capitalization, spelling, word choice, possessives, modifier clarity and placement, or parallelism. Rewrite the sentences to make them correct.

1. Businessperson communicate credit refusal in a way that their customers' find acceptable, and helpful.
2. The 1st grade class visited a museum on March 5th.
3. You should do more for your customers then he or she expect.
4. Global Sales in New York city had their most international clients last year.
5. Because of their high overhead costs, most of the customers for Overseas United have switched to another supplier.
6. Representatives of Cummins high school headed by the varsity cheer leaders is encouraging support for their Wildcats in the state basketball tournament.
7. Assignments for the class was to give an oral report; write a two page summary; and a final exam.
8. A good pair of binoculars are essential to bird watching.
9. Soy candles burn cleaner, longer, and are highly scented, they support the American soybean farmer.
10. Stacking papertowels and a heavy pot on top of it, will help prevent a carpetstain from coming back to the damp spot.

Chapter 9
Persuasive Messages

LET'S TALK BUSINESS

The ability to communicate clearly, concisely, and effectively is valued highly at Microsoft. In the technology industry, persuasive messages and presentations are a core part of our daily lives and are used to "sell" ideas both internally and externally. Everyone, from product teams who need to convince development teams that certain features are needed in our software to marketing teams who need to show customers the value in our solutions, needs to have a command of persuasive communication.

Janie Schwark, Sr. Business Manager, US D&PE, Microsoft Corporation.

Photo courtesy of Janie Schwark

To craft a persuasive message effectively, you must understand the audience for your message and understand that audience's goals. You need to present the message from the receiver's viewpoint to gain his or her attention and consideration, yet make sure you can reach your goals as well. To obtain this balance, I often create a grid with my audience's goals on one side and my goals on the other and then look for common points. A framework like this makes it much easier to develop a message that will resonate with your audience members and convince them to do what you need them to do.

Because today's businesses move at such a rapid pace, time is a precious commodity. The more concise you can be, the more likely it is that your message will be looked at in its entirety. You need to provide enough information for the receiver to make an informed decision, but not so much that your audience can't find the key points and tires of reading. One technique that I have found works well is to summarize the key points in bullet format at the end and include a call to action. You are much more likely to get the results you desire if it is easy for your audience to understand what you are asking for.

A **persuasive message** is (a) a request for action when you believe the receiver may be unaware, disinterested, or unwilling; or (b) a communication to try to change the opinion of a receiver. These messages will be viewed as neither positive nor negative by the receiver.

Both internal and external communication use persuasive messages. Examples of persuasive messages in internal communication include a speech asking employees to volunteer to work on upcoming weekends, an employee's memo to a manager requesting that the organization create a scholarship fund for employees' dependents planning to attend college, an employee's recommendation or proposal to establish a day care center, and a letter to employees requesting donations for a charity the company endorses.

A **sales message** is a communication that describes a product or service, its benefits, the available options or models, the price, and related services. It is the most common persuasive message in external communication. Other examples of persuasive messages used in external communication include a telephone call to ask the manager of another company to be the keynote speaker at an annual banquet or a letter to persuade readers to complete a questionnaire. Letters of application or recommendations for employment are also persuasive messages.

In the Let's Talk Business section, Janie Schwark supports the idea that persuasive messages must convince receivers that taking the requested action is in their best interest. The supporting facts in the message must provide enough information for the receiver to make an informed decision. Persuasive messages should usually be presented using an indirect approach.

Use of the Indirect Plan for Persuasive Messages

Use the *indirect plan* to convince the receiver to take an action. The advantage of using the indirect plan for persuasive messages is that it enables the sender to gain the receiver's attention first and then present the benefits that the receiver may gain from fulfilling the request. This approach puts the receiver in the proper frame of mind to consider the request. If the request were given prior to the explanation, the receiver might form objections that would be difficult to overcome. The receiver also might not read the part of the letter that contains the benefits. The indirect plan does require the use of more words than the direct plan, but the result is worth the additional words.

If the message is constructed positively in the you–viewpoint, the receiver is likely to consider the value of the entire message and agree with its contents. An effective presentation will associate the message with the motivating factors in the receiver's mind.

How to Use the Indirect Plan

Analyzing your receiver is especially important when planning a persuasive message. You will have to anticipate what motivates the receiver—his or her goals, values, and needs. You must then build your persuasive message around these factors using the you–viewpoint. Do this by stressing the receiver's interests and benefits.

LO 1
Describe a persuasive message.

NOTE 9.1
Persuasive messages are used to convince receivers to act or to change an opinion.

NOTE 9.2
Persuasive messages are used in internal and external communication.

NOTE 9.3
Convince receivers that it is in their best interest to take action.

NOTE 9.4
Use the indirect plan to convince the receiver to take action.

NOTE 9.5
Use the you–viewpoint.

LO 2
List the goals of a persuasive message.

NOTE 9.6
Carefully analyze the receiver to determine motivational factors.

FIGURE 9.1
Indirect Plan Outline
for Persuasion

INDIRECT PLAN FOR PERSUASION

I. Attention
   A. Capture the receiver's attention in the opening sentence.
   B. Compel the receiver to read or to listen to the entire message.
   C. Be positive and brief.

II. Interest
   A. Build on attention gained in the opening.
   B. Present the benefits to the receiver.
   C. Convince the receiver to continue reading.

III. Desire
   A. Build on the receiver's attention and interest by providing proof of benefits.
   B. Stress benefits to the receiver.
   C. Downplay any negative points or obstacles.

IV. Action
   A. Motivate the receiver to take immediate action.
   B. Be positive.
   C. Make action easy.

NOTE 9.7
The purposes of a persuasive message are to have the receiver consider the entire message and then to take the requested action.

NOTE 9.8
Persuasive messages include requests, recommendations, special claims, sales, collection, and employment.

The two primary purposes of a persuasive message are (a) to get the receiver to read or listen to the entire message, and (b) to have the receiver take the requested action. These purposes are more easily achieved when the indirect plan is used in constructing the message. The basic elements and specific guides for using the indirect plan to construct persuasive messages are shown in Figure 9.1.

The indirect plan can be used for a variety of persuasive messages—requests, recommendations, special claims, sales, collection, and employment. The organization and development of the first five types of persuasive messages are discussed in this chapter; employment messages are covered in Chapter 17. An analysis of the indirect plan for persuasion will be helpful prior to discussing the construction of five sample persuasive messages.

Attention

LO 3

Describe the four elements that are encompassed in the indirect plan for persuasive messages.

NOTE 9.9
Attract the receiver's attention immediately.

NOTE 9.10
Different techniques can be used to get the receiver's attention.

The opening of any persuasive message must attract the receiver's attention. A persuasive message is successful only when the receiver takes the desired action. The desired action is not likely to be taken unless the receiver is motivated to read or listen to the entire message. An attention-getting opening increases the chances that the receiver will read or listen to the entire message and then take the desired action.

The receiver's attention must be captured in the opening sentence. It is important that the opening be concise and positive. In a well-planned persuasive message, the receiver's curiosity is stimulated when a message opens with an interesting point. When a positive emotion is aroused, the receiver will be engaged and continue reading.

Many different methods have been used successfully by communicators to capture the receiver's attention. These methods include using mechanical devices (such as color, drawings, or a picture), the receiver's name in the sentence, rhetorical questions (for example, "How would you like to spend your next vacation relaxing on the beach in Hawaii?"), and interjections. The you–viewpoint must be considered when organizing the content of the message. Any method that gets the receiver's

Sheldon by Dave Kellett

attention may be used if it is relevant to the topic of the message and is not trite or high pressure. Gimmicks may be used but should not give the receiver the impression that an attempt is being made to mislead him or her. For example, beginning a letter with "Would you like to earn an additional $5,000 a month at absolutely no cost to you?" will probably cause the receiver to read no further because the opening statement is unrealistic.

Interest

You must hold the receiver's interest after gaining his or her attention. The receiver will maintain interest when seeing the benefits for himself or herself. When taking the requested action will result in more than one benefit to the receiver, the benefits may be emphasized by listing them. The receiver may hesitate to take the desired action unless he or she clearly sees the value of doing so.

NOTE 9.11
To maintain interest, make the receiver aware of the benefits of taking the action.

Desire

Once you have the receiver's attention and interest, offer proof of the benefits he or she can gain. Remember, the purpose of the persuasive message is to move the receiver to take the requested action. Showing how that action will benefit the receiver will motivate him or her to take the requested action.

Details of the message should intensify the receiver's interest and create desire for action. Anticipate that the receiver's negative reaction will be to avoid the desired action; attempt to overcome these feelings by showing proof of the benefits. Facts and figures can be valuable but should not be overused. Too many numbers

NOTE 9.12
Providing proof of the benefits and values enhances a receiver's desire to take action.

communication note

BELIEVABILITY AND PERSUASION

To hold a receiver's interest and encourage him or her to take action, a persuasive message must be believable. Edward R. Murrow, a famous U.S. broadcast journalist and newscaster who was the subject of the movie *Good Night and Good Luck,* once said, "To be persuasive, we must be believable; to be believable, we must be credible; to be credible, we must be truthful."

or testimonials will confuse, annoy, or bore the receiver. Enclosing a brochure or referring the reader to a website where he or she can learn more may be helpful.

The *interest* and the *desire* sections of a persuasive message may be combined by listing a benefit and then immediately providing proof of that benefit. This arrangement would be used until all the pertinent benefits have been discussed.

Action

NOTE **9.13**
The receiver should feel that taking the action is a logical conclusion.

You are ready to ask the receiver to take immediate action once you have built his or her interest and desire. The action you request of the receiver should be a logical next step. This action should be requested in a direct and positive manner.

NOTE **9.14**
Make it easy to act.

Ensure that taking the necessary action requires minimal effort by the receiver. Ask for a simple action such as checking a choice and returning an enclosed card rather than a time-consuming action such as writing an entire letter.

NOTE **9.15**
If a deadline is necessary, give it.

When the desired action is required by a certain date, clearly state the date. If no time limit is involved, encourage the receiver to act quickly.

A variety of techniques can influence the receiver to take the desired action immediately. A sales letter can offer coupons to be redeemed, specify a date that the offer ends, or suggest that supplies are limited. Collection letters can offer assurance that the receiver's credit will not be damaged if payment is received by a certain date. Including the receiver's name in a drawing for a prize if he or she returns a questionnaire can be used with requests. All these techniques are effective if the receiver feels no undue pressure and sees value in what is offered.

Implementation of the Indirect Plan

NOTE **9.16**
A communication case will help illustrate a way to compose persuasive messages.

The use of the indirect plan for persuasion will be illustrated through the development of a vice president's request to an employee asking her to take on new responsibilities with extensive travel. Here are details of the case:

The Anne Tremmel Case

Anne Tremmel has been a valued employee in the Human Resources Department at Horizon Pharmaceuticals in Somerville, New Jersey, for six years. During that time, Anne has taken on many of the day-to-day operational responsibilities, including the staffing of a new research facility in Newark. Anne has also earned the SPHR certification (Senior Professional in Human Resources). Horizon Pharmaceuticals will be expanding its operations significantly due to the development and FDA approval of several new drugs and the anticipated opening of a new research facility in San Diego, California. Horizon will be hiring approximately 150 new employees in the areas of sales, marketing, and research and development. To accomplish the hiring goal that has been set by the management of Horizon Pharmaceuticals, Michael Cabrillo, the vice president of human resources, will ask Anne to take on the responsibility of interviewing and hiring the people to fill the new positions that will be generated by the opening of this new facility and the expansion of the product line. This new responsibility would require Anne to spend the next six months traveling to college campuses to interview graduating students as well as interviewing candidates at job fairs in the major metropolitan areas of the United States. Horizon will reimburse Anne for all expenses, but these recruiting trips will require her to be away from home and her two small children for four weeks at a time.

The first step in developing business messages is to analyze the situation to determine the content that will best accomplish the purpose of the communication. The following sections show how the content of the Anne Tremmel memo may be developed. Each section discusses a stage of the indirect plan for persuasive messages and presents an example of poor writing and then an example of good writing.

CAPTURE THE RECEIVER'S ATTENTION

The first step in writing a persuasive message is to capture the receiver's attention. A **poor** way of gaining Anne's attention is shown here:

- Because we recently received FDA approval of several new drugs and acquired a research facility in San Diego, California, we need to staff approximately 150 new positions in the next eight months. You have been working in human resources for some time, so you should take this temporary reassignment.

NOTE 9.17
The poor opening is negative and impersonal.

This poorly written opening paragraph begins by telling Anne that she should take a reassignment. It may get her attention but not in a positive way. The paragraph is impersonal and shows a lack of appreciation for Anne's service with the company. She may be reluctant to continue reading the memo if she immediately senses that the company may be taking advantage of her.

In contrast, a **good** opening to gain Anne's attention follows:

- Your work in our human resources department during the past six years has been outstanding; Horizon has benefited greatly from your knowledge and dedication to the field of human resources. Specifically, your recruiting and staffing work at the Newark research facility last year was exceptional.

NOTE 9.18
The good opening is positive and personal.

This good opening gains Anne's attention by recognizing her longtime dedication to the organization. This paragraph uses both a positive approach and the you–viewpoint. It should interest her because it praises her for her previous service. Everyone likes to receive recognition, and this acknowledgment of her efforts should motivate Anne to read the remaining portion of the memo with an open mind.

BUILD THE RECEIVER'S INTEREST

After you have captured the receiver's attention, concentrate on building his or her interest in accepting the request. A **poor** way of building Anne's interest follows:

- I envision this recruiting process will take approximately six months. During these six months, you would be traveling to college campuses and interviewing graduating students. In addition, you would be working job fairs in the major metropolitan areas of the United States. You would be traveling and interviewing for four weeks and then have a break before you start on your next four-week recruiting trip. You have six years with Horizon, so you know the type of employee we are looking for and the process we go through to recruit, hire, and process new employees. This reassignment would not be a promotion, but you would have all your expenses paid.

This poor attempt to build the receiver's interest is similar to that of the poor opening in that it focuses on the negative and trivializes her reassignment. The paragraph is cold and lacks a you–viewpoint; it is of no help in building Anne's interest in accepting the temporary assignment.

A **good** paragraph, which should build Anne's interest, follows:

- As I mentioned to you in our discussion last week, Horizon Pharmaceuticals is rapidly expanding its operations. A new research facility will be opening in San Diego within the next eight months, and within the next six months we will be expanding our sales force due to FDA approval of several new drugs. We urgently need a human resources professional like you who has extensive experience in all phases of human resources to recruit, process, and hire approximately 150 new employees due to the opening of the new facility and the approval of the new drugs. You would be involved in recruiting prospective employees from colleges around the country as well as at job fairs in the major metropolitan areas. The opportunities for promotion to a human resources position at our new facility will be great once it is operational, even though this temporary reassignment would not mean an immediate promotion.

This good paragraph describes in a positive manner the opening of the new facility and the opportunity for a promotion in the future. Anne's interest, now stimulated, will peak in the next paragraph.

PROMOTE DESIRE IN THE RECEIVER

This section should emphasize the benefits that Anne would receive by taking the requested action and attempt to overcome any negative thoughts that she may have. A **poor** attempt to create desire is illustrated here:

- I know it will be difficult being away from home for long periods of time and not working with your colleagues in the human resources department on a daily basis, but I think it would be an excellent opportunity to grow professionally and personally.

This approach will do little to motivate the reader to accept the temporary reassignment. The paragraph is written from the sender's point of view, not from the receiver's. Anne will look at the temporary assignment as nothing more than spending a lot of time away from family, friends, and colleagues.

A **good** attempt to stimulate Anne's desire to accept the transfer follows:

- This reassignment will involve extensive travel, which will be fully reimbursed by Horizon. After every four weeks on the road recruiting, you would have one week off (with pay) before you start the next recruiting trip. And, arrangements will be made to have a virtual assistant work with you to process the paperwork generated by these recruiting trips.

NOTE 9.22
This good example points out the benefits to the receiver.

The benefits that Anne can gain from the reassignment are clearly explained in the good example. The negative aspects of the traveling—time away from family and colleagues and increased paperwork to complete—are handled in a positive way. Anne should now be looking forward to accepting the temporary reassignment.

REQUEST ACTION FROM THE RECEIVER

Once Anne has been motivated to accept the temporary reassignment, request that she do so immediately. Accepting the reassignment should be made as easy as possible for Anne.

A **poor** example of requesting action is shown here:

- Anne, please send me a letter of acceptance if you would like to do this job. If you can't do it, please let me know as soon as possible so I can contact someone else about the job.

NOTE 9.23
This poor request for action is presented in a negative manner.

This paragraph does little to motivate Anne to accept the reassignment. The you–viewpoint is absent. The paragraph is negative; it emphasizes the alternative that she does not have to accept the temporary reassignment.

A **good** example of requesting action may be written as follows:

- Anne, please accept this recruiting position for our newly expanded operations. Your acceptance will provide an exciting opportunity for you to participate in the staffing of a new site and the expansion of our sales, marketing, and research and development teams. Your expertise will make a major contribution to the future success of Horizon. Please e-mail your response to me no later than January 23 at michael.cabrillo@horizonpharmaceuticals.com.

NOTE 9.24
This good example makes it easy for the receiver to take action.

Notice the direct, positive approach used in this paragraph. Accepting the temporary assignment is made easy for Anne; she can simply e-mail her acceptance.

SUMMARY—POOR AND GOOD MESSAGES TO ANNE TREMMEL

Good and poor persuasive messages have been illustrated. The poor paragraphs are combined as a memo in Figure 9.2. This persuasive request does not follow the indirect plan outline as shown in Figure 9.1.

The chances that Anne will accept the temporary assignment are improved in the good message shown in Figure 9.3. This effective persuasive message follows the guidelines described earlier in this chapter.

This case problem shows how the indirect plan can be effective in communicating persuasive messages. To help you better understand the use of the indirect plan in organizing persuasive messages, several examples of both poor and good messages are illustrated on the following pages.

needs work

TO: Anne Tremmel
FROM: Michael Cabrillo *MC*
DATE: January 4, 200–
SUBJECT: Additional Responsibilities

Because we recently received FDA approval of several new drugs and acquired a research facility in San Diego, California, we need to staff approximately 150 new positions in the next eight months. You have been working in human resources for some time, so you should take this temporary reassignment.

I envision this recruiting process will take approximately six months. During these six months, you would be traveling to college campuses and interviewing graduating students. In addition, you would be working job fairs in the major metropolitan areas of the United States. You would be traveling and interviewing for four weeks and then have a break before you start on your next four-week recruiting trip. You have six years with Horizon, so you know the type of employee we are looking for and the process we go through to recruit, hire, and process new employees. This reassignment would not be a promotion, but you would have all your expenses paid.

I know it will be difficult being away from home for long periods of time and not working with your colleagues in the human resources department on a daily basis, but I think it would be an excellent opportunity to grow professionally and personally.

Anne, please send me a letter of acceptance if you would like to do this job. If you can't do it, please let me know as soon as possible so I can contact someone else about the job.

sm

Gains attention negatively.

Emphasizes obstacles.

Fails to show benefits.

Fails to motivate receiver.

FIGURE 9.2
Example of a *Poor*
Persuasive Message

Persuasive Requests

Organizations use both simple requests and complex requests. The simple request was discussed in Chapter 7 and should be constructed using the direct plan. The **complex request** is a persuasive message because in it you will have to convince the receiver to take action. The complex request should use the indirect plan.

In this section, we will be concerned only with complex (persuasive) requests. Examples of persuasive requests are those that seek an increase in staffing for your department, ask for volunteers to walk the precincts for an upcoming election, look for participants for a research project, or request a change in work schedule.

Figure 9.4 shows a **poor** persuasive request to individuals to participate in a heart research study. This example does not create receiver interest. The letter is

looks good

TO: Anne Tremmel
FROM: Michael Cabrillo *mc*
DATE: January 4, 200–

SUBJECT: Recruiting for Horizon Expansion

> **Focuses attention on receiver.**

Your work in our human resources department during the past six years has been outstanding; Horizon has benefited greatly from your knowledge and dedication to the field of human resources. Specifically, your recruiting and staffing work at the Newark research facility last year was exceptional.

> **Continues building interest; keeps attention gained in first paragraph.**

As I mentioned to you in our discussion last week, Horizon Pharmaceuticals is rapidly expanding its operations. A new research facility will be opening in San Diego within the next eight months, and within the next six months we will be expanding our sales force due to FDA approval of several new drugs. We urgently need a human resources professional like you who has extensive experience in all phases of human resources to recruit, process, and hire approximately 150 new employees due to the opening of the new facility and the approval of the new drugs. You would be involved in recruiting prospective employees from colleges around the country as well as at job fairs in the major metropolitan areas. The opportunities for promotion to a human resources position at our new facility will be great once it is operational, even though this temporary reassignment would not mean an immediate promotion.

This reassignment will involve extensive travel, which will be fully reimbursed by Horizon. After every four weeks on the road recruiting, you would have one week off (with pay) before you start the next recruiting trip. And, arrangements will be made to have a virtual assistant work with you to process the paperwork generated by these recruiting trips.

> **Emphasizes proof of benefits to receiver.**

Anne, please accept this recruiting position for our newly expanded operations. Your acceptance will provide an exciting opportunity for you to participate in the staffing of a new site and the expansion of our sales, marketing, and research and development teams. Your expertise will make a major contribution to the future success of Horizon. Please e-mail your response to me no later than January 23 at michael.cabrillo@horizonpharmaceuticals.com.

> **Motivates receiver and makes taking action easy.**

sm

FIGURE 9.3
Example of a *Good* Persuasive Message

written in the I–viewpoint rather than in the you–viewpoint. The receivers will have little motivation to participate in this study.

Figure 9.5 shows a **good** persuasive request written in the you–viewpoint. The message creates receiver motivation to participate in the heart research study. The letter gains attention, builds interest, creates desire, and makes taking action easy.

The following table summarizes the approach used for the two types of requests.

Request	Approach
simple or routine	direct
persuasive or complex	indirect

Recommendations

A **recommendation** is a message that attempts to persuade the receiver to take an action proposed by the sender. Individuals in business, government, and civic organizations

NOTE 9.26
Recommendations are best when organized using the indirect persuasive plan.

needs work

Heart Research Center
474 Park Lane, Suite 210
San Diego, CA 92145-2314
(619) 555-1922 • (619) 555-3781

March 14, 200–

**(INDIVIDUALIZED
INSIDE
ADDRESS)**

Dear (**NAME**):

The Heart Research Center does all kinds of research. We need individuals to serve as guinea pigs for our research.

We want to conduct this research so that we can continue receiving federal grants. Our research may eventually lead to a healthier society.

If you want to participate in our study, read the enclosed brochure that gives all the details.

Sincerely,

Lori McKeever

Lori McKeever
Research Coordinator

sm

Enclosure

Impersonal—does not gain attention.

Selfish—does little to build interest.

Vague—difficult for receiver to take action.

FIGURE 9.4
Example of a *Poor* Persuasive Request

periodically submit recommendations to receivers who are above, below, and at their organizational level. Recommendations are most effective when the indirect persuasive plan is used. Examples of recommendations that should use the indirect plan include a company officer advising the firm to conduct regular training on sexual harassment, a manager creating a new policy, a civic leader using a tract of land for a city park rather than a housing project, and a colleague sending an unsolicited endorsement of an individual seeking employment.

Figure 9.6 shows a **poor** recommendation from Mark Spencer, a vice president, to Jeffrey Burns, the president. Mark is responding to a situation that negatively affects productivity in a department. Mark probably will not be successful in his recommendation if the poor memo is submitted. This memo is not written with the you–viewpoint. It also displays negativity, which hinders communication. In addition, the memo is not written using the indirect plan—the key to successful persuasive messages.

The **good** memo in Figure 9.7 should increase the chances that Jeffrey Burns will proceed with the proposed outsourcing of reprographic services. Note how the indirect persuasive plan presents the benefits—improved production and increased customer satisfaction—*before* the recommendation. This memo gains the president's attention in the opening, uses the you–viewpoint in presenting the reasons

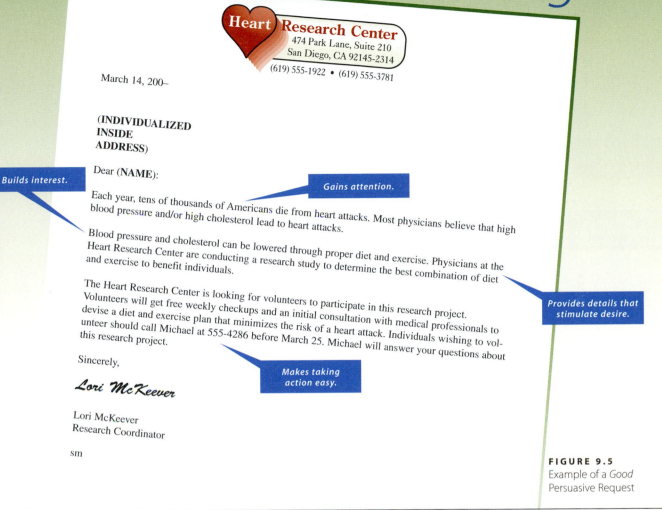

FIGURE 9.5
Example of a *Good* Persuasive Request

supporting the recommendation, and presents the recommendation in a positive, professional manner.

Special Claims

Special claims are unique and should use the indirect persuasive plan. Routine claims use the direct plan and are discussed in Chapter 7. **Special** or **nonroutine claims** are those in which the fault is disputable. The sender may need to convince the receiver that the adjustment or refund is appropriate.

Examples of special claims that should be organized as persuasive messages include the following: You want a concrete contractor, who has guaranteed his work, to replace a newly poured patio because it is not level and drains toward the house. A transportation company has purchased a fleet of 25 trucks, 20 of which had their transmissions replaced in the first six months. The company wants the manufacturer to absorb the cost of the new transmissions. A work of art, which was purchased for $24,000, was found to be a forgery; the buyer demands reimbursement from the gallery that sold it.

NOTE 9.27
Special claims should use the indirect plan.

needs work

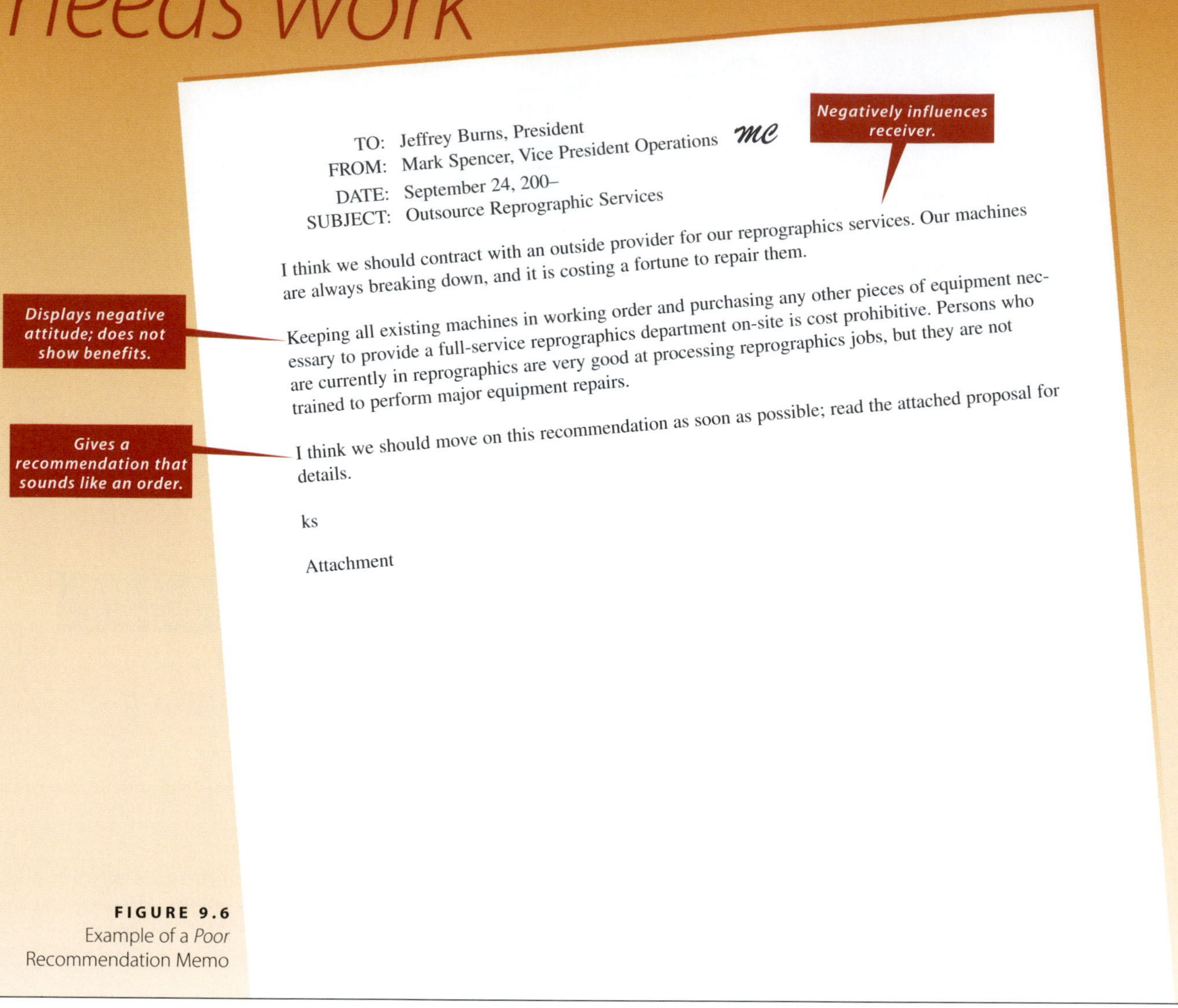

TO: Jeffrey Burns, President
FROM: Mark Spencer, Vice President Operations *mc*
DATE: September 24, 200–
SUBJECT: Outsource Reprographic Services

I think we should contract with an outside provider for our reprographics services. Our machines are always breaking down, and it is costing a fortune to repair them.

Keeping all existing machines in working order and purchasing any other pieces of equipment necessary to provide a full-service reprographics department on-site is cost prohibitive. Persons who are currently in reprographics are very good at processing reprographics jobs, but they are not trained to perform major equipment repairs.

I think we should move on this recommendation as soon as possible; read the attached proposal for details.

ks

Attachment

FIGURE 9.6
Example of a *Poor*
Recommendation Memo

Figure 9.8 is a **poor** special claim letter from Janine Thomas, owner of The Great Event Wedding Planners. Janine contracted with Class Act Video Productions to produce a DVD of the St. Clare/Meadows wedding. After viewing the finished product, Janine found the quality to be substandard. The wedding vows and messages from well-wishers could not be heard because of background noise, and outdoor pictures of the bride and groom had so much light that their faces could not be seen clearly. Janine is upset, and it shows in her letter. The receiver's attention may be gained in the opening paragraph but not in a way that will get the desired reaction. Janine clearly does not give the necessary details. The entire letter is negative, which will irritate the receiver and impede getting the desired action—an editing of the DVD or a partial refund if the DVD cannot be edited.

TO: Jeffrey Burns, President
FROM: Mark Spencer, Vice President Operations *MS*
DATE: September 24, 200–
SUBJECT: Outsource Reprographic Services

MXX Services has developed a first-rate reputation for providing business travelers with the hoteling services that are critical to their success when working away from their offices. Over the past three years, our sales have increased approximately 23 percent. I expect that this level of success will continue into the future.

The increased volume of business and the complexity of that business in the reprographics area are both a positive and a negative for us. It is positive for us because the higher volume of reprographic work we complete generates more income. The negative is that the complexity of the reprographics jobs our customers need requires equipment that has many more options than our current equipment has, and this equipment is expensive. Also, the heavy volume of copying has taken a toll on our existing equipment; breakdowns are occurring, and delays could negatively affect customer satisfaction. Our current reprographics staff are extremely capable in handling the processing of customers' work; however, they are not trained repair technicians.

There is a solution that helps our customers and our business. I would suggest that we contract with an outside provider to supply our facility with the reprographics equipment we need for our operations. We could lease this equipment on a monthly or yearly basis. This contract could also include hiring a person from the outside provider to work on-site at MXX Services to train our current reprographics personnel on the new equipment, serve as a repair technician, and do daily reprographics work. This would allow our current workers to become more productive during their time on the job.

I recommend that we investigate hiring an outside provider for reprographics services as soon as possible; this proposal will benefit everyone. Please contact me if you have questions about the proposal, which I have attached to this document.

ks

Attachment

FIGURE 9.7
Example of a *Good*
Recommendation Memo

The letter in Figure 9.9 covers the same situation but is a **good** message. Notice how Janine shows the receiver the benefits to be gained by editing to improve the quality of the finished DVD. The writer maintains a calm tone and explains the necessary details for the receiver. The positive approach will encourage cooperation from the receiver. Janine is courteous throughout the complaint but emphasizes that the current DVD is not acceptable. Janine also states she still desires to provide her clients with a DVD of their wedding, preferably a quality DVD from Class Act Video Production. Notice that the receiver may fax a response.

The following table summarizes the approach used for the two types of claims.

Claim	Approach
simple or routine	direct
special or nonroutine	indirect

needs work

The Great Event Wedding Planners
3827 Twilight Way Portland, OR 97214   503.555.4732

March 6, 200–

Mr. Randall Stallings, Owner
Class Act Video Productions
3703 SE Brooklyn Street
Portland, OR 97202

Dear Mr. Stallings:

I want the $1,100 back that I contracted with you for the videography of the St. Clare/Meadows wedding. The quality of the DVD was far less than you promised. **[Is negative.]**

You promised a DVD of the highest quality that included opening titles; closing credits; video of the pre-ceremony activities, the ceremony, and the reception including guests' messages; still images; and music. I am very disappointed with the quality of the finished DVD. The sound is not clear; it is very difficult to hear the vows being exchanged or the guests' messages to the couple because of background noises. Also, the pictures that were taken outdoors have so much light in the background that it is difficult to see the bride and groom's faces. The recording of the events of a wedding day is important for my clients. I often receive comments about the joy they experience as they view the DVD and "relive" their first day as a married couple. I am very disappointed with the quality of the video and know my clients, the Meadowses, will be disappointed as well. **[Shows anger.]**

I want you to either send me back my $1,100 and I will return the DVD, or I will keep the DVD and you can refund me $550, half of the cost of this wedding day DVD. Clients should not have to pay for a DVD of such poor quality. Please let me know as soon as possible what you will do so I can let the Meadowses know. **[Demands action rather than makes a request.]**

Sincerely,

Janine Thomas

Janine Thomas
Owner

FIGURE 9.8
Example of a *Poor*
Persuasive Claim Letter

Sales Messages

NOTE 9.28
Some sales messages are
prepared by advertising
professionals.

Sales messages come in many different forms, such as letters, brochures, leaflets, catalogs, radio and television commercials, and billboards. Some of these messages may be prepared by advertising professionals; however, any size business may have a need for a sales message, so you may one day be asked to compose one.

The Great Event Wedding Planners
3827 Twilight Way Portland, OR 97214
503.555.4732

March 6, 200–

Mr. Randall Stallings, Owner
Class Act Video Productions
3703 SE Brooklyn Street
Portland, OR 97202

Dear Mr. Stallings:

Your firm has provided me with beautiful and professionally produced videography for many weddings I have coordinated over the past six years. On November 12, I contracted with Class Act Video Productions to produce the video of the St. Clare/Meadows wedding. I paid half of the fee, $550, in advance. At the wedding reception, I gave your videographer a check for $550, the balance on the contract.

As you know, many married couples go through their wedding day without really being able to take in everything that is happening. That is why a service such as videography is so important; it provides those lasting memories of one of the most important days in a couple's life together—their wedding day. Upon receiving the DVD from you, I viewed it to be sure it included the pre-ceremony activities; the ceremony and reception, including guests' messages; still images; and music—all the events of the day that had been identified in our agreement. Everything was there, but the quality of the DVD was not what we have come to expect from your company. The sound was not crisp and clear; it was difficult to hear the bride and groom exchanging their vows, and the guests' messages to the newly married couple were overpowered by background noise. Also, the pictures of the bride and groom taken outdoors have so much light in the background that it is difficult to see their faces clearly.

I am sure that our goals are the same—to provide the highest quality product to our customer. Therefore, I am requesting that you edit the DVD to clarify the sound recordings and adjust the background lighting of the outdoor pictures. Doing this would provide the professional-quality videography we have come to expect from Class Act Video Productions. If you cannot do this, please issue a refund for $550 to compensate my clients for a DVD that is not of an acceptable quality. Please call or fax your decision to me by March 12 so that I can notify my clients of the resolution of this situation.

Sincerely,

Janine Thomas

Janine Thomas
Owner

Gets attention with praise.

Gains interest by giving details.

Needs more detail.

Makes polite request.

FIGURE 9.9
Example of a *Good* Persuasive Claim Letter

Before you compose a sales message, know the product or service you are going to sell. Know its strengths, its weaknesses, its competitors, and its market. As you compose the message, emphasize the strengths and omit any mention of weaknesses. Your market should be researched carefully to determine how to appeal to your customers and to get their business.

NOTE 9.29
Complete a careful analysis of the product or service before composing the sales material.

needs work

Big Buddies of the Greater Hartford Area
127 Second Avenue Hartford, CT 06106
(860) 555-9371

September 12, 200–

Opening does not grab receiver's attention.

BUY A COUPON BOOK TO HELP THE DISADVANTAGED

The Big Buddies of the Greater Hartford Area are once again selling the $uper $aver coupon book for $40.

Receiver benefits are not pointed out.

This year's $uper $aver coupon book offers an abundance of coupons for discounts on dining, movies, and sporting and cultural events. There are also a wide variety of travel discounts available in the coupon book.

Receiver benefits are pointed out but not emphasized.

The proceeds from the sales of the $uper $aver coupon book go to the Big Buddies of the Greater Hartford Area.

Details of this benefit are not outlined.

Let us know if you want to buy this year's $uper $aver coupon book.

Justin Clark
JUSTIN CLARK, EXECUTIVE DIRECTOR

Request for action is not positive.

FIGURE 9.10
Example of a *Poor* Sales Message

NOTE 9.30
The receiver's attention may be gained through several techniques.

NOTE 9.31
Sales messages may be written for multiple receivers.

Various techniques are used in sales messages to gain the receiver's attention: color, sentence fragments, catchy slogans, famous quotations, testimonials, and descriptions of benefits. A salutation is frequently omitted from the message.

Once you gain the receiver's attention, you must maintain his or her interest to ensure that the entire message is read or heard. A careful analysis of the receiver is critical in preparing the message from the receiver's point of view. Extra care must be taken in the analysis of the receiver because sales messages are usually prepared for multiple receivers.

A **poor** sales message is shown in Figure 9.10. This message is not written from the you–viewpoint. The letter fails to point out and emphasize the benefits of the

246

Big Buddies of the Greater Hartford Area
127 Second Avenue Hartford, CT 06106
(860) 555-9371

September 12, 200–

AN OPPORTUNITY TO GIVE BACK TO YOUR COMMUNITY

**Would you like to $ave $$$ every day on routine expenses?
Would you like to give back to your community at the same time?
If so, the $uper $aver coupon book is for you!**

This year's $uper $aver book offers you many ways to save money. There are 50 percent and 2-for-1 discounts for dining, movies, sporting events, and cultural events. There are coupons that enable you to save money on basic household needs such as groceries, car servicing, and dry cleaning.

And, if that isn't enough, this year there are even more travel discounts than ever before. With the discounts for hotels, airfare, cruises, and car rentals, you can now afford to take your family on that long-awaited dream vacation without going into debt.

How often do you get the opportunity to buy something that pays for itself on the same day you purchase it? Here is how that works: The $40 cost of the $uper $aver coupon book can be saved in just one day by using a $5 grocery coupon, purchasing two movie tickets for $10 with coupons, and using a 2-for-1 coupon valued at $25 at your favorite restaurant. You have just saved the cost of the $uper $aver coupon book. It's that easy!

One of the great benefits of purchasing this coupon book is that you are helping to mentor the economically disadvantaged youth in our city. All proceeds from the sales of the $uper $aver coupon book are being put toward a new recreation center in downtown Hartford and the Big Buddies' after-school tutoring programs.

Order your book today by returning the enclosed postcard. It is never too soon to $tart $aving $$$$. The books also make great gifts!

Justin Clark

JUSTIN CLARK, EXECUTIVE DIRECTOR

Enclosure

Nontraditional technique used to capture receiver's attention.

Interest stimulated by giving details.

Interest maintained by identifying benefits to receiver.

Details tell how receiver is helping community.

Request for action makes response easy.

FIGURE 9.11
Example of a *Good* Sales Message

$uper $aver coupon book to the purchaser. Some general statements are made about the contents of the book, but not enough detail is given to develop a strong interest in it. The request for action is weak. How should the customer "let us know"?

A **good** sales letter is shown in Figure 9.11. Note how this letter stresses the benefits that a purchaser will receive from the $uper $aver coupon book. The subject line is an emotional appeal that stresses the benefits the community will receive from the sales proceeds of the book. Mentioning more specifics of the savings gained by using this book and showing how the book can pay for itself will stimulate interest.

needs work

WILLIAMS APPLIANCE
1712 Pecan Avenue
(662) 555-2376
Batesville. Mississippi 38606-1426
(662) 555-1729

October 14, 200–

Mr. Johnny McCarty
1228 Morgan Road
Canton, MS 39046

Dear Mr. McCarty:

We are so disappointed that you have NOT made a payment on the appliances that you bought from us. We must have our money to remain in operation.

If we don't receive a payment quickly, we will have to take additional action. Since your credit rating was marginal, you should be happy that we gave you credit.

We want my money now, so mail your payment quickly. We don't want to get nasty.

Sincerely,

Charlie Williams

Charlie Williams
Owner

tp

> Attacks the receiver too severely.

> Uses I–viewpoint.

> Makes a demand.

FIGURE 9.12
Example of a *Poor* Collection Message— Appeal Stage

Collection Messages

LO 5

Write messages that are used for the various stages of collection.

A collection message is used by businesses to collect overdue accounts. The two purposes of collection messages are (a) to collect the money due and (b) to retain goodwill with the customer.

Collection messages, generally, are written in three stages—reminder, appeal, and warning. Each stage is progressively more persuasive, and each stage has several steps. The number of steps in each stage will vary according to the type of business involved and the credit rating of the customer.

Reminder Stage

The reminder stage is for customers who intend to pay but just need a reminder. The **reminder** is a simple and sometimes comical message intended to get a receiver to pay a bill. Collection messages in this category are direct and friendly; they must never offend the receiver. These messages are normally only short notes or a sticker on a bill.

Examples of collection messages in the reminder stage include the following:

Past Due
Reminder
Please Remit

NOTE 9.32
Collection messages are designed to collect money and retain goodwill.

NOTE 9.33
Collection messages are written in three stages.

NOTE 9.34
The reminder stage is for customers who forgot to pay.

248

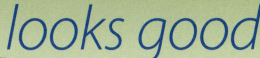

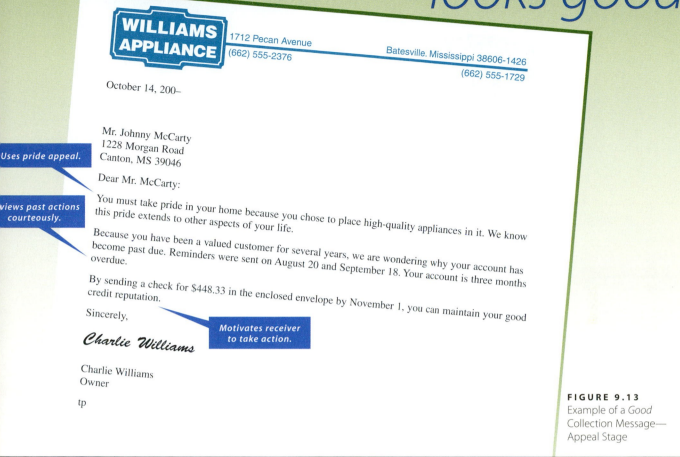

Uses pride appeal.

Reviews past actions courteously.

Motivates receiver to take action.

WILLIAMS APPLIANCE
1712 Pecan Avenue
(662) 555-2376
Batesville. Mississippi 38606-1426
(662) 555-1729

October 14, 200–

Mr. Johnny McCarty
1228 Morgan Road
Canton, MS 39046

Dear Mr. McCarty:

You must take pride in your home because you chose to place high-quality appliances in it. We know this pride extends to other aspects of your life.

Because you have been a valued customer for several years, we are wondering why your account has become past due. Reminders were sent on August 20 and September 18. Your account is three months overdue.

By sending a check for $448.33 in the enclosed envelope by November 1, you can maintain your good credit reputation.

Sincerely,

Charlie Williams

Charlie Williams
Owner

tp

FIGURE 9.13
Example of a *Good* Collection Message— Appeal Stage

Messages in the reminder stage are very courteous because failure to make a payment is often only an oversight. A harsh reminder may well alienate a customer who had intended to pay on time. If the reminder fails, the collection process will proceed to the appeal stage.

Appeal Stage

An **appeal** is stronger than a first-stage message because the customer has failed to heed the reminder notice. You need to analyze the customer carefully before writing a letter of appeal. You will have to select the type of appeal that will persuade the customer to pay. You may appeal to the customer's pride, credit rating, morality, or reputation. Once you have selected the type of appeal to use, construct the message using the indirect persuasive outline.

A **poor** collection letter in the appeal stage is shown in Figure 9.12. This letter is too harsh. It is written from the writer's point of view and will cause anger, which will reduce rather than increase the chances of collection. Necessary details such as the amount due are not furnished.

The **good** collection letter in Figure 9.13 is recommended for the appeal stage. It is written in a positive, courteous tone. The opening paragraph will get the customer's attention by appealing to his pride. The customer should believe that the store is trying to help him maintain his excellent credit reputation. The store's chances of collecting are greatly increased with this letter.

NOTE 9.35
A comical sticker can be used as a reminder.

Please don't make me beg.

NOTE 9.36
The appeal stage must effectively persuade the receiver.

needs work

WILLIAMS APPLIANCE 1712 Pecan Avenue
(662) 555-2376

Batesville, Mississippi 38606-1426
(662) 555-1729

January 20, 200–

Mr. Johnny McCarty
1228 Morgan Road
Canton, MS 39046

Dear Mr. McCarty:

Neglects the you–viewpoint.

All of our customers pay promptly, so we cannot allow you to be delinquent. We have sent collection bills for the past six months with no results.

Threatens receiver.

If you don't get the money to us by February 12, we are going to turn your account over to our attorney. We are giving our attorney authority to do whatever is necessary to collect the money. You will be sorry.

Sincerely,

Charlie Williams

Charlie Williams
Owner

tp

FIGURE 9.14
Example of a *Poor*
Collection Message—
Warning Stage

Warning Stage

NOTE 9.37
Use the warning stage only when the other stages have failed.

Reminders and appeals may not succeed in collecting all past-due bills. When these efforts fail, you must move into the final stage—warning. Until now, you were interested in maintaining the customer's goodwill while trying to collect. When the warning stage is reached, you are interested only in collecting the past-due amount.

A **warning** is the last opportunity for a customer to pay an account before it is transferred to a collection agency, a credit bureau, or an attorney. Use the direct plan to develop your message for this stage. Sending the warning letter by registered mail—so a signature is required—stresses the importance of the message and creates a sense of urgency.

A **poor** warning stage collection message is shown in Figure 9.14. In this poor example, the customer will be inclined to resist because Mr. Williams does not get directly to the warning in a firm manner without displaying anger. Notice that the amount due is never given. The use of threats is illegal and will not increase the writer's chances of collection.

Figure 9.15 shows how a **good** collection letter in the warning stage should be written. This letter gets directly to the main idea—the customer's account is past due, and no attempt is being made to correct the problem. Facts are presented in a positive tone with no sign of anger. In the last paragraph, the customer is told exactly what must be done to avoid legal action.

250

looks good

WILLIAMS APPLIANCE 1712 Pecan Avenue (662) 555-2376

Batesville. Mississippi 38606-1426 (662) 555-1729

January 20, 200–

Mr. Johnny McCarty
1228 Morgan Road
Canton, MS 39046

Dear Mr. McCarty:

> **Gains reader's attention.**

Your failure to make a payment for the past six months has resulted in a past-due account with a balance of $896.66. This situation leaves us with no choice but to refer the account to our attorney.

You are legally obligated for this bill, and legal action is not pleasant for either of us. A lawsuit will be expensive and embarrassing for you.

> **Reminds reader of possible consequences.**

You can maintain your credit reputation by paying the account balance by February 12. Our attorney assures us that no legal action will be taken if you send the payment now. Please send the check in the enclosed envelope prior to February 12 to avoid the legal action.

> **Motivates receiver to take immediate action.**

Sincerely,

Charlie Williams

Charlie Williams
Owner

tp

Enclosure

FIGURE 9.15
Example of a *Good* Collection Message—Warning Stage

Finally, let us summarize the approach that is used in each stage of collection messages:

Stage	Approach
reminder	direct
appeal	indirect
warning	direct

Your use of the indirect plan outline will enable you to compose effective persuasive messages. The ability to do so will serve you well throughout your career.

Summary of Learning Objectives

Describe a persuasive message.

A persuasive message is (a) a request for action when you believe the receiver may be unaware, disinterested, or unwilling or (b) a communication to try to change the opinion of a receiver. These messages will be viewed as neither positive nor negative by the receiver and may be used in both internal and external communication. The supporting facts of persuasive messages must convince receivers that taking the requested action is in their best interest. Persuasive messages should almost always be presented using an indirect approach.

LO 2

List the goals of a persuasive message.

The two primary purposes of a persuasive message are (a) to get the receiver to read or listen to the entire message and (b) to have the receiver take the requested action.

LO 3

Describe the four elements that are encompassed in the indirect plan for persuasive messages.

The four elements of an indirect plan for a persuasive message are the following: (a) Attention—the receiver's attention must be gained in the opening to ensure the message is read or heard; (b) Interest—benefits must be shown to hold the receiver's interest; (c) Desire—providing proof of the benefits will motivate the receiver to take action; (d) Action—make it easy for the receiver to take action and motivate him or her to take the action quickly.

LO 4

Write different kinds of persuasive messages using the indirect plan.

Use the indirect plan when preparing complex (persuasive) requests, recommendations, special claims, sales messages, and some collection messages. The indirect plan for persuasion includes attention, interest, desire, and action.

LO 5

Write messages that are used for the various stages of collection.

The three stages normally used in collection messages are reminder, appeal, and warning. The reminder stage is a short, direct, polite message to a customer who simply forgot to pay. In the appeal stage, use the indirect plan for persuasion. When the other stages fail to collect, move to the warning stage. Messages in the warning stage are constructed using the direct plan and are not concerned about maintaining the receiver's goodwill.

Questions for Discussion and Review

1. When is a persuasive message used? How does anticipated receiver reaction influence the organizational plan used to write a persuasive message? (Objective 1)
2. Why is analyzing your receiver important when planning a persuasive message? (Objective 2)
3. What factors may influence how a receiver will react to a message? (Objective 2)
4. Describe different techniques that a sender may use to gain a receiver's attention in a persuasive message. Give an example of a situation in which each of these techniques can be used effectively. (Objective 3)
5. What organizational plan is most effective for persuasive messages? What are the four basic elements of this plan? (Objective 3)

6. You have been advised by one of your better employees that another company may be calling you for a recommendation about him or her. Develop an outline you could use during the conversation with the prospective employer. (Objective 4)

7. Explain why the following paragraph would be ineffective as the opening paragraph of a letter to Dawn trying to persuade her to take on the reponsibility of membership committee chair for the Students in Free Enterprise (SIFE) chapter on the Belmont College campus. Rewrite the paragraph to be more effective. (Objective 4)

   The local SIFE chapter at Belmont College needs someone to serve as membership committee chair for this school year. You know a lot of the business students on campus, so you should take this position.

8. Explain why the following paragraph would be ineffective in closing a persuasive request message. Rewrite the paragraph to be more effective. (Objective 4)

   If you are willing to participate in the marketing survey of consumer products, read the brochure that is enclosed and let us know of your interest so we can mail the surveys to you.

9. What are the purposes of collection messages? (Objective 5)

10. Are the objectives the same for all three stages of collection messages? Explain your answer. (Objective 5)

Application Exercises

1. Visit a business in your community and ask how the business uses recommendation letters when hiring new employees. Are there specific qualities, positive or negative, that the business uses to select the new employee? Be prepared to discuss your findings in class. (Objective 3)

2. Discuss three situations or messages in which someone tried to persuade you to do something. Analyze the strengths and weaknesses of these oral or written messages. (Objective 3)

3. Collect sales messages in different formats (e.g., letter, flyer, brochure, postcard). Which are effective and which are ineffective? Explain why. (Objective 4)

4. **Technology.** In your marketing class, you have been reading extensively that more and more work in this field is done in a collaborative environment. Your course syllabus indicates that you will have three graded oral presentations. Send a persuasive e-mail to your instructor asking that your final presentation be a group presentation. Use facts and logic to support your request. (Objective 4)

   `TECHNOLOGY`

5. Rewrite the following opening sentences of persuasive messages to attract the receiver's attention. You may use any appropriate attention-getting technique identified in the chapter to make these openings effective. (Objective 4)
   a. *This is your last reminder to renew the service plan on your computer.*
   b. *Many franchisees have indicated their sales are better than ever after using our ad agency.*
   c. *We have been in the financial investment field for 15 years and would like to add your name to our list of clients.*

6. Write a persuasive article for your school newspaper convincing students to participate in the upcoming election of officers for the Associated Student Government. Provide appropriate details in the article. (Objective 4)

Case Problems

Persuasive Requests

1. Your instructor recently talked about the work she has been doing with a not-for-profit organization, Dress for Success. This group works with economically disadvantaged women and encourages self-sufficiency through career development and employment retention. As part of its program, Dress for Success provides each client with a suit when she is ready to interview for a job and a week's worth of clothing once she has the job. You have decided that you would like to collect donations of business suits and professional clothing to give to Dress for Success for its clients. Write a letter that can be sent to friends, family, acquaintances, and classmates asking for donations to this worthwhile program.

TECHNOLOGY

2. **Technology.** You are currently employed by the City of Silver Springs in the accounting department. One of your colleagues, Paul Armstrong, was recently diagnosed with a brain tumor and underwent surgery to remove the tumor. He will require weeks of chemotherapy and radiation and faces several months of rehabilitation after his treatments. You just learned that because of this debilitating illness, Paul has used all his sick leave and will not be paid during this recuperation period. After talking with the human resources department, you have learned that employees can donate their excess sick days, in one-week increments, to Paul so he will receive a paycheck during his time away from work. You have decided to write an e-mail to send to all company employees encouraging them to donate a week of their sick leave to help a fellow employee.

3. Star Electric has provided electricity to the area for many years. Recently, Star upgraded all of its wiring to fiber optics and is expanding into digital cable services. As marketing manager for Star Electric, write a letter that could be sent to residents in the area persuading them to take advantage of these services. These letters may be sent to current as well as potential electrical customers. Add details to make the letter complete.

GLOBAL

4. **Global.** You are program director for the student economics organization on your campus. You have done such an outstanding job that you have been asked to obtain the keynote speaker for this year's state conference. You would like to get an economist from Germany. Write a letter to the head of the economics department at the University of Heidelberg in Germany requesting that he or she furnish a speaker at no cost, except travel-related expenses, for the state conference. Add details needed to make this a complete request.

5. You live on the corner of 15th and Vine Streets. A number of minor accidents have occurred at this corner in the past six months. You are concerned because several children in the neighborhood ride their bikes through the intersection. Write a letter to the city manager, Ray Cantu, requesting that the intersection be made into a four-way stop.

Recommendations

6. Brett Geiger of the human resources department has received complaints from several managers during the past few months about employees surfing the Internet, answering personal e-mail, shopping online, and playing games during the workday. Two managers actually fired employees they felt were using the company's computers inappropriately. However, with no written policy in effect, the managers are uncomfortable and have questioned whether their decisions are binding and/or legal. At a recent meeting, the HR manager agreed to draft a policy on personal use of company computers. You offered to draft the message that will accompany the policy when it is sent to the president. Your goal is to persuade the president to approve the policy and to activate it as soon as possible. Prepare a message to be reviewed at the next managers' meeting

TECHNOLOGY

7. **Technology.** You are a customer service representative for the Trax Computer Corporation. The company's office is located in San Mateo, California, but your customers represent all areas of the United States. Because there is a three-hour time difference between the East Coast and the West Coast, you would like to recommend to your supervisor that some customer service representatives be given the opportunity to have flextime schedules to accommodate your customers.

Prepare an e-mail for your supervisor, Paula Chapman, recommending flextime schedules. Add details that are appropriate and will help persuade her to adopt your recommendation.

8. Samantha Clark was employed by your firm during the summer. She is attending college in your city and is applying for the William Bennett Scholarship. She has asked you to write a letter of recommendation for her. Add details to make the letter convincing and realistic.

9. The city in which you go to school needs a new administration building. One location being considered for the building site is a public park in the downtown area. If this park area is used, many beautiful old trees would be destroyed. An alternative location would be property owned by the city at the edge of town. Write a recommendation letter to the city officials persuading them to select the alternative site. Add details.

10. Tom Wilson, president of the local chapter of Business Leaders of the Future, is interested in becoming the national president of the organization. He has asked you to write a letter recommending him to the nominating committee. Prepare an appropriate message. Add details needed to make your message complete.

Special Claims

11. You recently moved to Phoenix, Arizona, to accept a job with Multimedia Masters. Until you moved to Phoenix, you had no idea how brutal the sun could be. One of your colleagues at Multimedia Masters suggested that you get your car windows tinted to keep the sun's hot rays out, reduce ultraviolet rays, reflect the sun, and cut the glare. Three months ago, you had Mr. Tint, Inc. tint your car windows. You were given a 60-day guarantee on the work, but already the tinted film on the windows has turned purple and bubbled. Write Stephen Aguillera, the manager, and ask for an adjustment because the job is not of the quality it should have been. Add details as appropriate.

12. You hired Kane Lawn Service to install lawn sprinklers and landscape the area surrounding your office building. For this work, Kane estimated the cost would be $12,000; you agreed to pay this amount. However, you did give oral approval to go a little bit above the agreed amount of $12,000 if necessary to complete the job and meet the specifications upon which you mutually agreed. Kane installed the sprinklers but did little to improve the appearance of the area around your building. When the job was completed, Kane Lawn Service billed you $18,500 for the work. You selected Kane because it was a new company trying to get established in lawn service. Write a persuasive claim letter to Kane requesting a $5,000 adjustment.

13. Your elderly grandparents live in Illinois and often tell you how much they like fresh fruit but how difficult it is for them to get it throughout the year. For your grandparents' 50th anniversary gift, you purchased a subscription to a Fruit of the Month Club for them. The first two months, they received their selections of apples and pears and raved about the quality of the fruit and how it arrived as scheduled. The third month, they were scheduled to receive fresh blueberries from Maine and huckleberries from Montana. However, both fruits arrived after the promised date and contained mold. The fruit was inedible. Write Fresh Fruits For You and describe the situation that occurred with last month's fruit selection. Ask for a one-month extension to make up for the inedible fruit that your grandparents received.

14. Mayes' Leadership analyzes a company and then provides personnel training seminars to improve the client organization's operating efficiency. As human resources director, you hired Mayes' Leadership to offer workshops to improve morale and reduce absenteeism at your company. Mayes' conducted many seminars for all levels of employees and managers over a three-month period. Nine months later you have noticed no significant improvement. In fact, absenteeism has increased and morale is at an all-time low. Write a letter to Mayes' Leadership requesting a refund of $95,000 for its consultant work. Add details.

15. You and your siblings planned a party for your parents' 25th wedding anniversary on October 12. As part of this celebration, you made a oral agreement with The Emotions to play live music for four hours. The band charged $3,000 and required $1,500 as a down payment. On October 12, The Emotions did not show, and repeated attempts to reach them by phone that day led only to unanswered voice mail. When you finally reached them on October 15, you found that they thought they were booked for October 19. Write a letter asking them to refund your $1,500 down payment.

Sales Messages

16. The service organization We Care is having a Demolition Derby for a fund-raiser. You have been asked to develop a sales message that could be placed in the local newspaper. Add details and be creative so that the ad will attract spectators to the event.

17. Teamwork. Global. Technology. You are a member of your school's Humanities Student Association, which has decided to organize a retired-persons' tour to the Black Forest of Germany for its service project. Several tasks must be accomplished for this project. Your tasks include the following:

   a. Contact a travel agency or an airline to obtain airfare information.

   b. E-mail a tourist information office in one of the towns in the Black Forest area to obtain necessary information for developing a sales letter about the tour.

   c. Find the exchange rate for euros to U.S. dollars.

   d. Write a form letter that could be sent to the retired people in the area advertising this tour. The letter should include the cost of the tour (airline tickets, lodging, food, and ground transportation). Have interested individuals send a deposit for the tour.

18. Spotlight Résumés is a complete résumé-writing service that assists in preparing résumés, applications to graduate schools, and cover letters. Scott Regis, the owner of Spotlight Résumés, has hired you to write a sales letter to send to all seniors graduating from colleges and universities within a 100-mile radius of Raleigh, North Carolina. Testimonials and quotes from previous clients are available for you to use in your sales message. Also, when clients sign up for this service, they will receive a copy of the book *Spotlight on Effective Resumes.* Add details as necessary.

19. Your student business organization has been contacted by Claudia's, a clothing boutique, for help in promoting a Valentine's Day sale. Claudia's would like your organization to sell coupons for $5 each. The boutique would be closed to the public one evening; the only way a person could enter the store would be with this coupon. In addition to admitting the person, the coupon would entitle the customer to free refreshments and a 25 percent discount on all purchases. Claudia's would donate all of the coupon monies to your organization. Design an advertisement that could be placed in the local or school paper to help your organization with this fund-raiser.

20. Joseph Dunlap is starting PC Dr., a small business that will make "house calls" to service computers. Joseph's company repairs computers, installs networks, designs special software programs, and removes viruses from hard drives. Joseph's fees are hourly for repair work and programming; he charges set fees for other services. Write a sales message to small businesses in your hometown. Add details as appropriate.

Collection Messages

21. Cynthia Robertson graduated from the University of Pittsburgh 14 months ago. She received a scholarship to offset some of her tuition while attending Pitt as an undergraduate, but she took out a loan for the balance of the tuition. Cynthia was to start paying back the loan with regular monthly payments nine months after her graduation. To this date, she has not made any payments on the outstanding loan balance of $46,780. As an employee of College Loan Corporation, your job responsibility it is to follow up on late loan payments. You have sent Cynthia two previous letters without any response. This letter needs to indicate that if her first monthly payment is not received within 30 days, her account will be referred to a collection agency.

22. Kent Fulsom has been a credit customer of Thurman Furniture Store for eight years. He is a good customer but periodically fails to make payments on his account. He is currently four months past due ($235.81); several reminders have produced no response. As credit manager of Thurman's, write an appeal collection letter to Kent requesting payment.

23. Mary Lou's Family Cooking has been operating for 25 years. Several chain restaurants have moved into the area resulting in a highly competitive market. Mary Lou's currently owes an $18,750 balance for grocery products to Hillman's Wholesale. Payment is eight months past due. Because the bill has not been paid, you are now requiring this restaurant to pay for all groceries on delivery. This policy has worked well, but Mary Lou's has made no payment toward the $18,750 past-due balance. Write a letter that will encourage the restaurant to begin paying on the past-due amount. You realize that it may take a year to reduce the balance to zero.

24. Jason Ochi purchased an in-home gym during the Anniversary Sale at Workout City. During the Anniversary Sale, a special promotion was running that allowed Jason to qualify for 0 percent interest for six months because his purchase was over $799. At the end of the six months, Workout City sent Jason a statement notifying him that he needed to pay off the purchase or make payments that included 17.89 percent interest. Jason's six-month 0 percent interest payment has expired, and his first payment was due last week. Write Jason a collection letter that reminds him it is now time either to make the payments as specified in his last statement or to pay for the purchase in its entirety.

25. You are a new employee for Chapel Hill Gas Company. Your supervisor has asked you to use your creative talents in developing a simple message that could be used to remind customers to pay their bill that was overlooked. You want your message to be courteous and not alienate the customer.

Web exercises to accompany this chapter are available at **www.thomsonedu.com/ bcomm/krizan.**

Message Analysis

Correct the errors in the following letter that was written by Kimberly Loften, a wedding planner with Precious Memories, to Matthew and Darla Kingman. Kimberly planned and coordinated Matthew and Darla's wedding seven months ago; Matthew and Darla still owe $2,300 to Kimberly for her services.

> *It has been seven months since I coordinated your wedding and I am still waiting to receive payment for the outstanding balance of $2,300. I am very disappointed that you haven't honored the contract you signed and paid for the services I provided.*
>
> *When we started working together on the wedding plans, I paid the bills as they were incurred and sent you an itemized statement of the vendors' charges. You paid those bills promptly. However, some of the bills were submitted by the vendors after the wedding when you were on your honeymoon. I sent statements to you with the details of the bills and a request for payment. Since your wedding I have not even received an acknowledgment that these statements reached you.*
>
> *If I don't receive at least a partial payment of your outstanding balance by April 20, I will have to take additional steps to correct this situation.*

Writer's Workshop

The following items may be sentence fragments or contain errors in subject-verb agreement, pronoun-antecedent agreement, comma and semicolon placement, number display, capitalization, spelling, word choice, possessives, modifier clarity and placement, or parallelism. Rewrite the sentences to make them correct.

1. The first day back from my business trip was spend returning phone calls, attending meetings, and to answer e-mails.

2. Different cultures interpret gestures in different ways therefore care should be taken in using gestures.

3. At our manager's retreat we reviewed our companies Code of Ethics to see if it was up-to-date.

4. Last month Ricardo speak at Universities in Oxford, Mississippi, Dallas, Texas, Grand Forks, North Dakota, and Duluth, Minnesota.

5. Our company give all it's employees martin luther king junior day as a holiday with pay.

6. Voters have been turning out in steady numbers to cast early ballots in the Ennis School Districts $thirty-five million bond election.

7. The number of retirees with out insurance coverage have increased every year since 2000.

8. Lets keep the merger of our department's among the too of us.

9. Troy ran the marathon and 100-meter dash threw the javelin and discus and participated in the mile relay during the Spring Meet.

10. Robert and Lisa Wilson are happy and proud of the arrival of their first, great, grandchild Zoe Frances that was born March 9.

YOU BE THE virtual assistant

Virtual assistants must communicate with and for their clients. In this feature, you will be asked to prepare electronic and print messages that meet the goals of business communication in good news, bad news, and persuasive situations.

1. Greg Hitchcock, the client with whom you corresponded in the Part 2 feature, was referred to you by Erik Ronding, another client. The work sample you provided for Greg led to your being hired to edit instruction manuals for Challenger Engineering. Prepare a thank you message that could be sent to Erik (AstroTech Corporation, Suite 224 Newsell Building, Denver, Colorado 80127-2281, eronding@AstroTech.com).

2. To celebrate your three-year business anniversary, you and your spouse (or a friend) have decided to take a ten-day Caribbean cruise in late December. Although your experience is limited, you have heard from other VAs that business is typically slow at this time. You want this to be a real vacation and have decided to leave your work cell phone and your computer at home. With travel time, you will be unavailable by phone or e-mail for two weeks. Prepare an e-mail to be sent to those in your client database, and write the text of the voice mail message you will record prior to your departure.

3. Write a one-paragraph persuasive sales message that you can use in various publications to advertise your business. Consider the strong points of using a virtual assistant and the experience or other strengths that make you a desirable choice.

4. Hanna Washington hired you to prepare a brochure for her store, The Book Worm. Once the content was finalized, she paid you for your work then asked you to select a printer and work with her to produce 1500 copies of the brochure. You entered into a new contract with Hanna, completed the work, and sent her a bill. That was nine weeks ago, and you're still waiting to be paid for the 38 hours you spent on this project. The two e-mail reminders you sent were not answered. Now, it's time to send Hanna a second stage collection message (Hanna Washington, The Book Worm, 357 Main Street, Austin, TX 78717-2385).

5. Robert Hughes, a nationally known motivational speaker, has hired you to handle reservations for his half-day seminars. To streamline the process, you asked Mr. Hughes to give you a copy of the acknowledgment letter he has used for this purpose in the past, and he has done so (see the next column). Convert it to a form letter that can be used in a word processing mail merge. Then, test the mail merge using the variable

information provided. Programs operate on the same start/end/food service pattern shown in the sample letter. Not all hotels have adjacent parking ramps, but they will all have some type of parking available; adjust the text to make a generic statement about parking.

September 3, 2007

Ms. Milly Owens
Account Executive
WYCU Radio
680 Railroad Street
Montgomery, AL 36110-4713

Dear Ms. Owens:

Your reservation for the October 6 seminar, "You've Got the Spirit," has been received. You are confirmed to attend this half-day event, which will be held in the Great Plains Ballroom of the Edgewood Plaza Hotel in Montgomery. Your receipt for the $175 fee is enclosed.

Check-in begins at 7:30 a.m., and the program will begin promptly at 8:15. You may park in the ramp adjacent to the hotel. Light refreshments will be available throughout the morning; lunch will be served following the session, which ends at 11:30.

I am confident that you will find this seminar interesting and that you will leave feeling positive and self-confident.

Yours truly,
Robert Hughes
Enclosure

Variable Information:

Contact Information	Seminar Title	Date	Location
Jim K. Falls 206 West Martin Dr. Apt. 212 Bismarck, ND 58503	The Power to Lead	12/1	Main Floor Conference Room Capitol Inn Bismarck, ND
Ebony Carver Nursing Director Regina Hospital 682 East Third St. Casper, WY 82638	One Step Forward	11/16	Meeting Room B Big Sky Hotel Casper, WY
T. J. Ulgin Owner Ulgin Electric 4501 Industrial Way Reno, NV 89509	The Miracle Mind	11/20	Mountain View Room Convention Center Reno, NV
Barbara Thatcher Sill Accounting 733 Goldwater Blvd. Kingman, AZ 86413	Aim High and Fly	11/28	River Room The Bridge Inn Lake Havasu City, AZ

Part 4
Written Report Applications

© Stockdisc

Chapter 10
Business Research and Report Writing

LET'S TALK BUSINESS

One of my most critical roles as a consultant in a national accounting and consulting firm is to communicate highly technical issues and concepts to clients in a manner they can understand and use to improve their business processes. Our "deliverable," or means of communicating this information, is normally a written report. This report serves as a reference source for the client long after our oral presentation of the findings has passed.

One risk we are careful to avoid is losing our audience's attention by burying our major points amid several pages of technical references. Therefore, our firm has adopted standards for language, format, and writing style that succinctly and accurately convey our message. High-level executives are usually very interested in getting to the "bottom line" without wading through voluminous details. Most clients prefer an executive summary at the beginning of the report. In it, we highlight our understanding of the situation, the problem we are solving, our planned engagement activities, our findings, and our recommendations. The remainder of the report contains the detailed analysis enabling the reader to gain more insight into any of the summary points presented early in the report. Flowcharts, tables, charts, and other graphical means are essential in meeting our reporting standards.

Written communication skills are a very important selection criterion for new consultants hired into our firm and are a key component of our employee performance appraisal process.

Timothy Peterson, Director, Consulting Services, RSM McGladrey

Photo courtesy of Grandmaison Studios

Research and report writing are common activities in business. They can be used to develop procedures, to test products, to explore markets, or to gather opinions. The results of research may be reported orally or in writing, informally or formally, to internal or external audiences.

Regardless of their purpose or destination, reports must be based on thorough, accurate, ethical research. As Timothy Peterson notes in this chapter's Let's Talk Business feature, knowing your audience, applying the principles of business communication, and selecting an appropriate format are also important to preparing understandable, usable reports. This chapter, which builds on the communication basics introduced in earlier chapters, is devoted to discussing research techniques and report writing, including formatting. Techniques for making effective oral presentations are discussed in Chapter 15. Because visual aids may be used in both oral and written communication, that topic is covered separately, in Chapter 12.

Report Types and Characteristics

Written reports vary from short, informal reports to long, formal reports. The language can vary from conversational, first-person language to highly structured, third-person language. This section provides a brief introduction to informal and formal reports; each type is then discussed individually.

Informal reports are generally brief. They can consist of a body and a title page or a body only; informal reports often are formatted as memos or letters. **Memo reports** communicate information to individuals within an organization. This style is used primarily for reporting routine information concerning day-to-day operations or to provide a written record. **Letter reports** use a letter format to present information and make recommendations to individuals outside an organization; a subject line may be used to identify the topic of the report. When formatted as correspondence, informal reports may contain side headings to guide the reader from topic to topic. This type of report rarely contains graphic aids and seldom draws on material from secondary sources. Informal reports are usually written in the first person (I recommend that . . .).

A **formal report** may consist of all or some of the following parts: title page, authorization message, transmittal message, table of contents, list of illustrations, abstract, body, glossary, appendix, and bibliography or reference list. The body of the report will span several pages and include multiple levels of headings. Content could be drawn from primary and/or secondary sources. Visual aids help readers interpret information presented as text. Formal reports are usually written in the third person (It is recommended that . . .). Recent trends, however, suggest that informality is becoming more acceptable in formal reports. The degree of formality is based on the culture of the organization and is determined after the report originator has analyzed the receiver(s).

Informal Written Reports

In business, the informal report is used much more frequently than the formal report. There are many different types of informal reports; three of the most common—progress, periodic, and technical—are discussed in the following sections.

Some informal reports may fall into more than one of these categories. For example, a report could be classified as technical and periodic.

PROGRESS REPORTS

A **progress report** (also called a *status report*) is used to inform readers about the status of a particular project. A progress report that flows upward within the organization assists managers in monitoring and making decisions about a project; one that flows downward or horizontally keeps participants or other interested persons informed. The report should inform the reader about the work that has been accomplished, the work that is being done currently, and the work that is scheduled to be done in the next reporting period. Any significant progress or problem(s) should be discussed in the report. The frequency of the reports will depend on the type or nature of the project being discussed. An example of a progress report in memo form is shown in Figure 10.1.

PERIODIC REPORTS

A **periodic report** provides managers with updated information at regularly scheduled intervals. These intervals may be daily, weekly, monthly, quarterly, or annually. Periodic reports follow no set format; many organizations use preprinted forms. A form used to indicate the security status of facilities is shown in Figure 10.2.

FIGURE 10.1
Progress Report

SANBORG MANUFACTURING

835 West Lake Road   Telephone (478) 555-3340
Sparks, GA 31647-0137   Fax (478) 555-3350

DATE: May 16, 200–
TO: All Employees
FROM: Matt Prima, Community Campaign Coordinator   *MP*
SUBJECT: Campaign Update

Thanks to the generosity of Sanborg's employees, nearly $20,000 has been contributed during the first month of this year's Community Campaign. As shown in the following table, we are ahead of last year's totals and well on our way to achieving our $35,000 goal.

Department	Last Year			This Year		
	Donor #	Donor %	$	Donor #	Donor %	$
Accounting	10	56	1,175	11	65	1,230
Administration	31	65	3,565	30	64	3,685
IS	7	78	700	9	73	1,040
Maintenance	21	58	525	24	53	860
Marketing	19	46	3,180	33	57	4,020
Production	115	83	8,625	106	83	8,125
R&D	17	93	1,020	14	78	935

The campaign ends June 15, so please return your pledge form soon. If you've misplaced your form, phone Joan Ruprecht at 3367.

FIGURE 10.2
Periodic Report

DAILY SECURITY CHECK OF FACILITIES		
FAIRCHILD, INC.		
FACILITY	**TIME**	**RESULTS**
Conference Room		
Dining Area		
Human Resources		
Accounting		
Purchasing		
Advertising		
Laboratory		
Assembly Room		
Warehouse #1		
Warehouse #2		
Warehouse #3		
Parking Lot		
OFFICER'S NAME		
OFFICER'S ID NO.		
DATE		
OTHER INFO.		

TECHNICAL REPORTS

A **technical report** conveys specialized information. There are no standard formats or organizational plans for technical reports. However, organizations will often specify particular formats and plans to be used for internal technical reports. Standardized formats make it easy for readers to scan reports for information of particular interest to them. An example of a technical report in letter format is shown in Figure 10.3.

Technical terms need not be defined when a technical report is prepared for someone familiar with the terminology. If the reader does not have the appropriate expertise, however, technical words used in the report must be clarified. A good rule to follow is to remember the principles of business communication discussed in Chapter 4.

NOTE 10.4
Technical terms must be defined if they are likely to be misunderstood by the reader.

FIGURE 10.3
Technical Report

KIRKPATRICK TESTING SERVICE

3477 Ridgeway Road, Chicago, IL 60602-3109
Telephone (224) 555-4490 Fax (224) 555-7861

November 17, 200–

Bridgewater Advertising Company
316A Willow Building
567 Main Street
Carbondale, IL 62901

TESTING RESULTS

On November 10, technicians collected carpet dust samples from various locations in your office complex. Samples were sealed and delivered to our laboratory where they were examined.

Results

Sample No.	Location	CFU*/Gram	Primary Organisms	
1A	Reception Area	590,000 CFU/gm	Cladosporium	90%
			Alternaris	<10%
			Other	<10%
2A	Weber's Office	700,000 CFU/gm	Cladosporium	90%
			Alternaris	<10%
			Other	<5%
3A	Jenkins' Office	800,000 CFU/gm	Cladosporium	86%
			Alternaris	<10%
			Other	<10%

*CFU=Colony Forming Units

Recommendations

Based on these results, we recommend that the carpet be removed and tile or wood flooring be installed. New flooring should reduce the allergy-like reactions you and your employees have been experiencing. If you have questions about the data or this recommendation, please phone.

K. P. Yuli

K. P. YULI
INDUSTRIAL HYGENIST

LO 3

Identify and use the five steps for conducting research.

NOTE 10.5
There is a common, overall approach for conducting business research.

Research Techniques

The systematic procedures used to conduct a business study are called **research methods.** Those who expect to pursue careers in any business field should know how to plan and conduct a research project.

The Steps in Conducting Research

The five steps in conducting research are

1. Plan the research.
2. Gather information.
3. Analyze the information.
4. Determine solution(s).
5. Write the report.

Plan the Research

Planning the research includes stating the problem, setting the boundaries, determining and analyzing the audience, and deciding on the research procedures to be followed.

STATING THE PROBLEM

The **statement of the problem** is a clear, accurate description of what is to be studied. Prior to finalizing the problem statement, managers or other key people might discuss what the research should accomplish or they might agree to conduct a preliminary investigation. Examining files, talking with employees, reading similar reports, speaking with vendors, or making inquiries are activities that could help the researcher(s) clarify what needs to be done. Here are examples of problem statements for studies:

- Determine the best advertising medium for our product.
- Design a new procedure for processing online orders.
- How can we improve employee morale?
- Should we purchase hybrid vehicles for our delivery fleet?

Notice that the first two examples are statements, and the last two examples are questions. Either form is appropriate.

SETTING THE BOUNDARIES

Research needs to have boundaries. The scope, time schedule, and budget affect the boundaries for the project.

Scope. Once the problem has been defined, you will identify the factors to be examined. These factors are known as the **scope** of your research. Brainstorming and cluster diagramming can help you generate possible factors, evaluate them, and decide which are most important.

   Brainstorming means listing or jotting ideas without evaluating or sequencing them. It is a stream-of-consciousness process that can be done alone or with a group and can be completed in various ways. If you are working alone, you could randomly list ideas you think you will include in your report. When working in a group, the person designated as recorder could write ideas on a flipchart and post the lists where all can see and react to them. After listing the ideas, review them to determine whether some should be added, deleted, or modified. The result is a list of factors about which you will gather information.

NOTE **10.6**
Problem statements can use either the statement or the question form.

NOTE **10.7**
What factors will you research?

NOTE **10.8**
Brainstorm alone or as part of a group.

NOTE 10.9
Cluster diagramming
groups ideas as they are
presented.

With **cluster diagramming,** ideas are grouped as they are introduced. The main idea is placed in the center, and the key concepts are placed in various locations around it. As ideas are generated, they are written near the key concept to which they relate. After all ideas have been recorded, they are reviewed. Duplicate ideas are deleted; new ideas are added. Finally, lines are drawn to connect related ideas. Each cluster of ideas becomes a section of the report. A partial cluster diagram showing factors for one of the problem statements given previously is presented in Figure 10.4. Each factor and subfactor could be divided further until all related ideas are included.

You could research many other factors relative to improving employee morale, and you might want to consider some of them later. However, a clear and reasonable scope must be defined for every research project.

NOTE 10.10
What time schedule will
you follow?

Time Schedule.   The person who assigns the project and the person who conducts the research should agree on a completion date. The schedule is set by working back from the report deadline. The **time schedule** should show the major steps in the research and report writing process and the anticipated completion date.

Figure 10.5 illustrates a time schedule known as a **Gantt chart.** As you view the chart, notice that several tasks can be worked on at the same time. For example, you can prepare mailing labels while a survey document is being printed. Time schedules should include enough detail for everyone associated with the project to understand exactly what is to be done and when.

NOTE 10.11
How much will the
research cost?

Budget.   All studies cost money. Even studies that are conducted within an organization will have some costs above normal operating expenses.

A large organization may use a charge-back system to bill one department for having work done by another. For example, if you are conducting a survey for the

FIGURE 10.4
Cluster Diagram

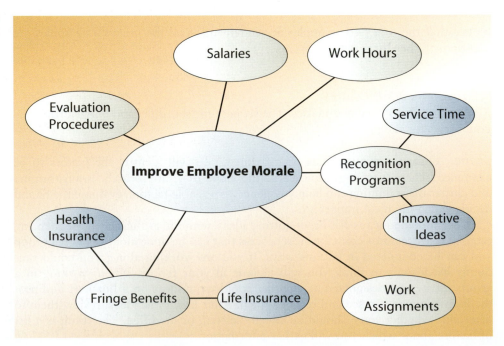

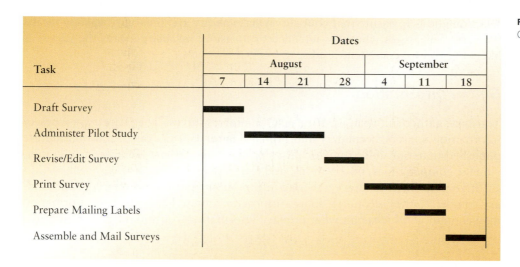

FIGURE 10.5
Gantt Chart

human resources department, the graphic arts department might charge your unit for printing a questionnaire and the final report. In addition, the information systems department might charge for processing survey results. Other research costs could be incurred for items such as personnel time, supplies, and postage. Estimate all costs and have the budget approved before work begins.

DETERMINING AND ANALYZING THE AUDIENCE

Effective communication depends on using the you–viewpoint in all written and oral messages. When a report will have primary and secondary readers, both should be analyzed. If, for example, you are a financial manager writing a report for which colleagues in the field are primary readers, you can use the technical language of finance because it will be understood by other financial managers. If members of the general management staff, members of the production management staff, general employees, or stockholders are secondary readers, you may want to define your terms the first time you use them or include a glossary.

NOTE 10.12
Analyze the primary and secondary receivers.

DECIDING ON THE RESEARCH PROCEDURES

Comprehensive research requires the project to be completed in a step-by-step sequence. The steps to be followed in completing the project are known as **research procedures.**

Deciding on procedures means determining exactly how to carry out each step. Although the procedures you select will vary from project to project, answering the following questions can guide your choices:

NOTE 10.13
Outline the steps in the project.

- What amounts of money and time are available to gather current data?
- Is useful information about the topic available in print or electronic form?
- Is sufficient information available within the company?
- Will surveying employees produce useful data?
- Are the computing resources necessary to collect and analyze data available?
- Will the report be prepared internally or externally?

When conducting research, you may want to seek the advice of one or more specialists. If, for example, you are going to use statistical procedures to analyze survey data, you could seek the assistance of a statistician. He or she can assist with sample

NOTE 10.14
Surveys must have validity and reliability.

selection and help ensure that your survey has validity and reliability. **Validity** means the survey measures what it is intended to measure; **reliability** means the survey is likely to produce consistent results.

Gather Information

NOTE 10.15
Information sources can be primary or secondary.

You may gather information from one or more sources. There are two types of information sources: secondary and primary. **Secondary sources** of information are published materials (electronic or print) on the topic. **Primary sources** include individuals, company files, observations, and experiments.

If your research requires gathering information from both primary and secondary sources, gather secondary source information first. The published information may contain good ideas on what primary information you should gather and how to gather it.

SECONDARY SOURCES OF INFORMATION

Published materials on most topics are readily available in company, public, and college libraries. Experienced reference librarians can provide valuable assistance in finding published information that will be helpful in your research. They can direct you to print or electronic indexes, catalogs, reference books, government documents, computer databases, and other helpful secondary sources of information.

NOTE 10.16
Carefully evaluate all sources.

When gathering secondary information, be sure to evaluate the sources carefully. Not all information found in print or available through the Internet is accurate. When examining a print source or an electronic version of it, consider the following items:

- *Timeliness.* Is the information the most current available?
- *Relevance.* Is the information related to the specific topic I am researching?

Secondary research encompasses both traditional and electronic sources.

© Michael Newman/PhotoEdit

- *Approach.* Is the work an opinion piece or a research report? Are opinions supported by facts or research? Is the research complete and thorough? Was appropriate methodology used to conduct the study? Is the research unbiased?
- *Outlet.* Is the publication reputable? What, if any, review process was used to screen the work for publication?
- *Author.* Is the author an authority on the topic being researched? What are his or her credentials and reputation in the field?

Because no one controls who posts what to the Internet, you will want to consider the following if your secondary information source is a website:

- *Type/Purpose.* Is the site a personal page or one geared toward advocacy, marketing, information, or news? If the URL contains an individual's name or is hosted by a commercial service provider, investigate further to determine credibility.
- *Sponsor.* Is the page owner a group, organization, institution, corporation, or government agency? The domain (.edu, .gov, .com) will help you evaluate the source. Going to the page at the root of the URL (the portion before the first single /) may help you determine whether a person, company, agency, or other entity accepts responsibility for the content.
- *Perspective.* Does either the author or the sponsor bring a bias to what is posted at the site? If so, consider it as you evaluate the content. Look for sites offering alternative viewpoints. Be sure to acknowledge all potential for bias when you use the information.
- *Author/Contact Information.* Who wrote or gathered the materials? What credentials does the person or group possess? "Googling" the author may help verify his or her credentials. Remember, a webmaster is different from an author.
- *Completeness.* Does the site include up-to-date links to other relevant sites? Are links purely internal (same site), exclusively external (outside site), or mixed?
- *Attribution.* Is the information contained at the site original? If not, have the authors appropriately cited their sources? Check to be sure cited information has been abstracted correctly. If the material is copyrighted, you will need to secure permission to use it if the part cited is more than a small part of the publication or is a unique logo, survey, or other author-designed original work.
- *Timeliness.* How current is the information? When was the site last updated? Look for more than a "Last Updated" entry. Read the content, check citations, and look for active links.

Many university libraries offer advice to students about how to evaluate websites. Check the library section of your school's website or speak with a librarian to learn more.

Traditional Searches. An assortment of reference materials can be used in conducting library research: handbooks, almanacs, yearbooks, encyclopedias, dictionaries, books, periodicals, reports, directories, government publications, and audiovisual materials.

Computerized Searches. Computerized searches of published information on a given topic can be a valuable resource. Most reference librarians can assist you in searches that quickly give you an up-to-date bibliography of materials on your

NOTE 10.17
Reference librarians can assist you in locating print and electronic sources.

topic. In addition, they can guide you to databases accessible through the library that have periodicals available in full text.

NOTE **10.18**
Some computerized sources are free; others have access fees.

Computerized sources can be categorized as either commercial or open access. As the name implies, **commercial sources** require users to pay for materials, which may be provided online or as a CD. Many business periodicals, newspapers, and journals offer subscriptions to online versions of their publications. In addition, professional associations may make databases or other resources available to members either free or for a modest fee. Professional organizations may also sponsor newsgroups, discussion lists, chat rooms, or blogs where members can pose questions. Although these online forums can provide leads to reputable sources, they are seldom viewed as credible in and of themselves.

Open-access sources are available free to anyone who has access to the Web. Because anyone can publish anything and post it to the Web, finding good material related to your topic can be challenging unless you have a search strategy. Clearly defining the research topic will help you select the keywords to use during a search. Most computer searches follow the principles of Boolean logic, which relies on three operators: *OR, AND,* and *NOT.* Search engine sites typically offer suggestions on how to use these operators effectively. Search engines can produce different results, so don't restrict yourself to only one. When you find a good source, either record the URL or save it as a bookmark on your browser.

NOTE **10.19**
Accurately cite all sources.

Be sure that you get complete bibliographic information on published materials while you work with them so that it will be available for footnotes or text citations and the bibliography or reference list. Most published materials are copyrighted. You may have to obtain permission to use such information, and you will be required to give credit to the originator as the source. **Plagiarism** is using someone else's ideas or words without giving him or her credit. To avoid plagiarism you must correctly document information found in all data sources, including the Web. Information on documenting sources is given in Appendix A. Plagiarism and paraphrasing are also discussed in the copyright section of Chapter 3.

PRIMARY SOURCES OF INFORMATION

NOTE **10.20**
Primary sources provide unpublished information about the topic.

Your research may require gathering original information—information about your topic that has not been published previously. This primary information may come from an examination of original company records, a survey of knowledgeable individuals, a focus group, an observation of an activity, an experiment, or an interview.

Original records and files are obvious sources of historical information that may be helpful to you. Other sources of primary information—surveys, focus groups, observations, experiments, and personal interviews—may not be as obvious.

NOTE **10.21**
Surveying people is a way to get primary information.

Surveys. To gather opinions and facts from individuals, you can survey them. Surveys can be conducted face-to-face, by telephone, by mail, or electronically.

Each survey method has advantages and disadvantages. Compared with other survey methods, face-to-face surveys are expensive. Personnel must be trained, scheduling and conducting the interviews is time-consuming, and transportation can be costly. The process does, however, produce the most in-depth responses.

Telephone surveys can be conducted fairly quickly and can be relatively inexpensive if done within a local calling range. Those who conduct the interviews generally read from a script and are cautioned not to deviate from it, so training costs are minimized. Response rates for telephone surveys will generally be higher than for

communication note

One of the most common methods of getting feedback about the quality of customer service is the comment card.

- In restaurants, cards are placed in containers on tables or presented to diners with their bill. Cards may be left at the restaurant immediately after the dining experience or completed and returned at a later date.
- Lodgers may find comment cards on the desk or night table in their guest room or have the card presented with their bill at checkout. The procedure for returning the card parallels that used at restaurants—cards may be left

at the checkout desk or completed and returned after departure.

- Retail store associates may present comment cards to shoppers immediately after completing a purchase transaction or include a card with the merchandise receipt.

Comment cards work well in situations where transactions are quick and uncomplicated. Mail or telephone surveys are the preferred methods for getting customer service feedback in situations where transactions are lengthy or complex.

those conducted by mail, but establishing credibility can be challenging in an era when negative reactions to telemarketing have led to widespread use of "no call" lists.

Because they require fewer people to conduct them, mail surveys are generally less expensive than telephone or face-to-face surveys. The process is quite slow; it can take months to get an acceptable number of responses, even with follow-up mailings to those who don't respond to the initial mailing.

Electronic surveys may be conducted online through a website or via e-mail. In a web-based survey, respondents are invited to complete the survey located at a particular URL. This method enables the researcher to incorporate color, graphics, and audio features into the survey. Online surveys can also be programmed to specify required data fields and to prevent respondents from marking more than one response for a question. In addition, the software used to create the survey can be programmed to collect data automatically and to generate ongoing data summaries.

The simplest way to conduct an e-mail survey is to embed the questions into a message that is sent to potential respondents. Receivers are told to use the reply function and answer the questions as they scroll through the message. The simplicity of

Blondie by Dean Young

this method is offset by the limits placed on the researcher's ability to incorporate emphasis techniques such as type font and size variations, color, and graphics into the document. Pretesting the survey is essential to ensure alignment is maintained through transmission and to verify that entering a response will not adversely affect the format of subsequent items.

One way to overcome concerns about format is to send the survey as an e-mail attachment. The respondent can open the attachment and use a word processing program to respond. The completed survey can then be sent as an e-mail attachment to a "reply" message. The number and complexity of steps in this process may deter people from responding. Software incompatibility is also a concern. A third deterrent is the respondent's fear of infecting his or her computer with a virus passed through an e-mail attachment.

Regardless of whether e-mail surveys are embedded or attached, their response rate could be negatively affected by the lack of anonymity associated with e-mail transmissions. In addition, e-mail is very easy to ignore or delete, especially if it spans multiple screens.

When designing a questionnaire, be sure to follow the principles of business communication. The following guidelines may also be useful:

- *Develop the survey questions from the factors being studied.* In a survey to assess employee morale, you might develop questions to seek opinions or facts about employee salaries, fringe benefits, work hours, and other related factors.
- *Sequence questions appropriately.* Start your questionnaire with easy questions that will encourage respondents to continue. Group similar topics. For example, put all questions about salaries in the same section. Arrange questions in logical order, the way people commonly think of the topics.
- *Use clear questions.* Phrase each item so that it will be interpreted uniformly by all respondents. A question such as "What kind of car do you own?" is vague. Based on the respondents' interpretations, the answers could be *convertible, Chevrolet, sports, foreign,* and so on. An example of a clearer way to obtain specific information is, "Please indicate the name of the manufacturer of the car you drive most often."
- *Ask only for relevant demographic data.* If factors such as age, gender, marital status, income, and so on won't be used in your analysis, don't ask respondents to provide the data.

- *Avoid leading questions.* Leading questions influence respondents to give a biased answer. Questions such as "Would it be a good idea to improve the arrangement of our work hours?" will likely be biased toward a yes answer. A better method would be to ask the respondent to rate his or her satisfaction with current work hours. The rating could be along a numeric (e.g., 5 high, 1 low) or verbal (e.g., very satisfied, satisfied, dissatisfied, or very dissatisfied) indicator known as a **Likert scale.**
- *Provide for all expected responses in the answer options.* When it is not possible to be inclusive, use an "other" option and encourage respondents to write an explanation.
- *Avoid skip-and-jump directions.* Complicated directions can frustrate respondents. For example, "If your answer to Question 9 is no, skip Questions 10, 11, and 12 and go directly to Question 13. If your answer is yes, also answer Question 10, but skip 11 and 12 if you do not have children."

- *Choose the appropriate type of question.* Forced-answer questions will outnumber open-ended questions in mail, telephone, and electronic surveys; the opposite is true in face-to-face interviews. **Open-ended questions** let respondents answer in their own words. These kinds of questions must be worded carefully in order to obtain the desired information. Data obtained through open-ended questions can be difficult to interpret and analyze, which is why forced-answer questions are used wherever possible. In the **forced-answer question** style, the researcher provides possible answers to the questions, and the respondents choose among the alternatives. The possible answers should be discrete; that is, use 25–29, 30–34, 35–39 instead of 25–30, 30–35, 35–40. Provide lines or boxes for easy check-mark answers. The lines or boxes for the responses should precede the possible answers.

Once the survey has been drafted, field test or "pilot" it. The feedback you get from this process will assist you in revising the document prior to distribution.

Brief, attractively designed documents accompanied by a message that explains the purpose of the survey help to convey a professional image and encourage receivers to respond. One sheet of paper ($8\frac{1}{2}$ by 11, 11 by 14, or 11 by 17 inches) printed on both sides and folded to resemble four "book" pages is more inviting than four single-sided, stapled pages. Including a confidentiality statement similar to that shown in Figure 10.6 also encourages receivers to reply and enables the researcher to code the questionnaires so that reminders or follow-up requests can be sent to those who do not respond.

NOTE 10.25
Questionnaires should encourage response.

To save time and money, researchers usually send surveys to a selected number of people who are representative of a larger group. This type of survey is called a **sample survey.** A statistician can help determine how to select the sample, how many surveys to distribute, and the minimum number of responses necessary to draw conclusions about the entire group from responses provided by the sample.

NOTE 10.26
Surveys are usually conducted using samples.

Focus Groups. When you are seeking ideas or feedback in qualitative (verbal) rather than quantitative (numeric) format, focus groups are an appropriate research method. These groups, frequently used in market research, involve 6 to 12 participants and a moderator. Clearly defined research objectives; thoughtful, well-prepared questions; unbiased, randomly selected participants representative of the target audience; and a trained moderator are critical success factors. A comfortable site that creates a relaxed atmosphere also contributes to success.

NOTE 10.27
Focus groups solicit qualitative data.

Under the guidance of the moderator, the group discusses a series of ideas or issues—the focus. The moderator must ensure that everyone's thoughts are heard and that no one is influenced by others in the group. The task of keeping records also falls to the moderator. Notetaking is kept to a minimum during the session so that the moderator can concentrate on what is being said and keep the discussion flowing in an appropriate direction. Immediately after the session, he or she will summarize the positive and negative points that arose during the discussion.

No. 56

Your individual responses will be kept confidential; data will be reported only in the aggregate. The number on this form will be used only to follow up with nonrespondents. Once an acceptable number of responses has been received, all documents linking surveys to respondents will be destroyed.

FIGURE 10.6
Confidentiality Statement

Reviewing a video- or audiotape of the session—recorded with full knowledge of the participants—makes this task easier. Information from the notes and tape(s) will be used when the moderator prepares his or her report.

Most focus groups are in-person events, but online focus groups are gaining popularity because they are cost-effective. In addition, online focus groups are especially well suited for research involving sensitive topics, when respondents are geographically dispersed, or when on-site participants are difficult to recruit. The primary disadvantage of online focus groups is the inability to read and react to participants' nonverbal and vocal cues.

NOTE 10.28
Carefully controlled observations may be used to gather primary data.

Observations. Observation is another way to gather primary information for a research project. This technique involves one or more observers watching and recording facts about an activity. Although the observation technique can incur high personnel costs, it is a way to obtain precise information.

A common use of the observation technique is to gather information on how a worker operates a machine in a factory. The worker's repetitive movements might be timed, production records maintained, and conclusions drawn about the efficiency of the procedures. Similarly, observers might be posted in selected areas of cities to count out-of-state cars in order to get a measure of tourist traffic. Many managers and employers use informal observation to obtain information that is helpful to them in performing their jobs.

The observation technique requires careful control. All observers must look for the same thing and record their observations in the same way for the information to be of comparative value. Proper control requires that observers and subjects do not interact.

NOTE 10.29
Experiments may be conducted to gather primary information.

Experiments. Businesses often use experiments to compare two ways of doing something so that the better way can be identified. For example, employees in one plant might be placed on a four-day workweek, while employees in another plant would be kept on a five-day workweek. The employees in the two plants would then be observed and surveyed periodically to determine their productivity and their satisfaction with work hours.

Another approach would be to conduct a presurvey and a postsurvey of a group of employees that you plan to change from a five-day workweek to a four-day workweek. In this approach, employees who are on a five-day workweek could be asked a series of questions about the effect their work schedule has on their productivity and job satisfaction. Then their five-day workweek would be changed to a four-day workweek. After three months, the employees would be asked the same set of questions they were asked before their work schedule was changed. Then the two sets of answers would be compared.

NOTE 10.30
Experiments are a good way to make comparisons.

Experiments are less common in business than in science, but experiments do have their uses. Usually, **experiments** are used to compare two ways of doing something in similar settings. In an experiment, you can easily compare the old way with the new way, compare Method A with Method B, or test-market a new product. Experiments can be expensive. Carefully designed and controlled experiments, however, have provided businesspeople with much valuable information.

NOTE 10.31
Personal interviews encourage in-depth responses.

Personal Interviews. The last way to gather primary information for a research project is the personal interview, a widely used qualitative research technique. **Personal interviews** enable researchers to pose prepared, unbiased, open-ended questions and, based on the respondent's words and nonverbal cues, to ask follow-up questions to expand or clarify what was said. Personal interviews should always be arranged in advance and conducted in an area that is quiet (no interruptions) and comfortable. Interviewers must make the respondent feel at ease and show interest in what he or she says. Questions are sequenced from simple to complex and often begin with demographic items. The interviewer speaks only when necessary, relying on good eye contact and other aspects of nonverbal communication to engage and encourage the respondent. The interviewer may record the meeting, but only if the respondent agrees. Otherwise, the interviewer should take notes and transcribe them immediately after the meeting.

When researchers consider using this technique, they must balance the advantage of in-depth responses against the time and cost involved in gathering, interpreting, and analyzing those responses.

As explained in the previous sections, business research often involves gathering information from or about people. As the Communication Note at the bottom of the page points out, the research should be designed to protect its subjects.

Analyze the Information

Once you have planned your research and gathered information, you are ready to begin your analysis. The information you gathered may speak for itself. It may clearly say yes to adopting a new procedure or product or that employees overwhelmingly prefer the four-day to the five-day workweek. Under these circumstances, the analysis may take only a few minutes. On the other hand, you may have gathered a great amount of complex information. Completing the analysis may take you days, weeks, or months.

NOTE 10.32
Analysis may be a short and clear or a long and complex process.

The word **analysis** means to look at the parts of things separately or in relationship to the whole. The various parts of your information are compared and contrasted in an effort to develop new or better ideas. Facts and figures are interpreted by explaining what they mean—what significance they have. You will not want personal bias of any kind to enter the analysis. Use your brain power—objectively and unemotionally.

NOTE 10.33
Analysis should be objective.

For example, if you were doing research to determine which computer to buy for your office, you would collect information on the type of work you currently are

communication note

RESEARCH OVERSIGHT

Business research is not the only type of research that must be designed with care. Faculty at colleges and universities also engage in research. Schools that have faculty engaged in research involving human or animal subjects will have policies governing such research. Those policies, which are designed to protect the subjects, are typically monitored by a committee or board that reviews the research procedures.

If your school is among those where faculty engage in research, you will want to learn more about its research policies and review procedures. Specifically, you will want to ask about whether and how the policies affect research projects conducted by students as part of their coursework.

doing and the kinds of work you want to do. Next you would gather information about computers, including cost, software compatibility, speed of operation, machine capacity, machine dependability, maintenance availability, potential for upgrading, cost of retraining staff, and other factors. Then you would compare the machines to determine how well they can do what you want done, what their potential is, how dependable they are, and so on. Once you have completed the analysis, you would be ready to determine solutions.

Determine Solution(s)

NOTE **10.34**
Solutions may consist of conclusions and recommendations.

Based on your analysis, you will be ready to offer a solution or solutions to the problem you have been researching. Your solution(s) will be framed as conclusions and recommendations.

A **conclusion** is an inference drawn from the facts; it is a reasoned judgment that you make from your analysis. If you were to select the most important ideas suggested by your analysis, these ideas would be your conclusions. Based on your conclusions, you could state the research answer or **recommendation**—the research solution. In formal studies and reports, you can draw conclusions from your analysis and state them separately from the recommendation(s).

The conclusions and recommendations must be based on the findings and your objective analysis, not your personal opinion of what a good solution would be. Your conclusions and recommendations for a report might look like this:

Conclusions
- Procedure B appears significantly more cost-effective than Procedure A in the two installations studied.
- Dependable equipment for implementing Procedure B on a wide-scale basis is not currently available.
- The XYZ Manufacturing Company currently has in stock 20 Model 3CA machines that can be used to implement Procedure B.
- The XYZ Manufacturing Company projects that it will have 500 Model 3CAs available within six months.

Recommendations
- Immediately lease the 20 Model 3CAs from XYZ and continue to compare Procedure A with Procedure B for three more months.
- Enter an option to purchase 500 Model 3CAs from the XYZ Manufacturing Company.
- If the additional research continues to show that Procedure B is significantly more cost-effective than Procedure A, exercise the option with XYZ to purchase the 500 Model 3CAs.

Write the Report

NOTE **10.35**
Written reports must be readable and understandable.

The final step in a research project is to write the report. This is an important step because you will want to present your results effectively. The writing process for reports parallels that for other messages. You will plan, draft, and finalize your report before submitting it. As part of that process, you will prepare an outline (see Chapter 5) to guide you in organizing the document and in selecting and using appropriate heading levels. The outline will also be helpful as you prepare the table of contents.

The time and effort spent in researching and writing a report are wasted unless the report is read and understood. The probability that a report will be read and understood increases when certain principles of formatting are followed. The remainder of this chapter discusses the various report types and the formatting principles to follow for effective report preparation.

Formal Written Reports

A formal report is prepared for and read by top-level managers inside or outside the writer's organization. Conducting the research and writing the report may take from several weeks to several months. These activities can be completed by one person or by a team.

A formal report generally contains three major divisions: the preliminary section, the body, and the supplementary section. A formal report may contain all or some of the following parts:

PARTS OF FORMAL REPORTS

1. **Preliminary Section**
   a. Title Page
   b. Letter or Memo of Transmittal
   c. Table of Contents
   d. List of Illustrations
   e. Executive Summary

2. **Body**
   a. Introduction
   b. Procedures
   c. Findings
   d. Analysis
   e. Conclusions
   f. Recommendations

3. **Supplementary Section**
   a. Glossary
   b. Appendix
   c. Bibliography or Reference List

Figure 10.8 (see pages 285–295) contains a portion of an actual business report that features many of the parts described in the following sections. The complete report and an additional report are posted at http://thomsonedu.com/bcomm/krizan. Appendix B contains a report that illustrates the content and format guidelines described in this chapter.

Preliminary Section

The **preliminary section** contains all the parts of a report that precede the body. The specific preliminary pages included in the report will vary with the formality of the report. A discussion of the individual parts follows.

TITLE PAGE

A **title page** typically contains the title of the report; the writer's name, title, and department; and the date of submission. The name of the person or company

LO 4
Describe the components of a formal report.

NOTE 10.36
Formal reports may be written for internal or external audiences.

NOTE 10.37
All formal reports should contain a title page.

receiving the report is used when reports are prepared for clients or others outside the organization. The title should indicate the purpose and content of the report.

Some organizations have specific guidelines for the preparation of title pages; others permit artistic freedom. If specific guidelines do not exist, the traditional format may be the best choice. In traditional format, each line on the title page is centered horizontally with equal vertical spacing between items. Titles containing more than one line are single spaced. The title should be all capitals; other lines may be either all capitals or initial capitals.

LETTER OR MEMO OF TRANSMITTAL

NOTE 10.38
A letter or memo of transmittal conveys and introduces the report.

The **letter** or **memo of transmittal,** if used, introduces the report to the reader. A report to readers outside the organization would contain a letter, whereas reports for internal use would contain a memo. In more formal reports, a preface or foreword may be used.

The letter or memo of transmittal should be concise and may be subjective—the writer may include personal comments and/or offer a suggestion or opinion not supported by data. The letter or memo may also refer readers to parts of the report of special interest or suggest special uses of the information. In general, any item worthy of discussion may be included in the letter or memo of transmittal. The message typically ends with a statement expressing appreciation for the opportunity to participate in the project.

TABLE OF CONTENTS

NOTE 10.39
Use a table of contents only when a report exceeds four pages.

A **table of contents** lists all major sections that follow it and the page on which each begins. Its purpose is to aid the reader in quickly locating specific information in the report. A table of contents normally is not used in reports of fewer than five pages. Section heads should be listed exactly as they appear in the body and should be connected to the page number by leaders (horizontally spaced periods). Page numbers are optional for subheadings. The table of contents normally is prepared after the report is keyed or printed in its final form.

LIST OF ILLUSTRATIONS

NOTE 10.40
A list of illustrations summarizes the visual aids used in the report.

Visual aids are identified in a **list of illustrations.** The list may be on the same page as the table of contents, or it may begin on the following page if the report contains more than four illustrations. The list of illustrations uses the same format as the table of contents, with illustration captions instead of section heads. A report may group all visual aids into one list of illustrations, keep tables as a separate category and group all other visuals as figures, or group each type (table, chart, graph, etc.) separately. This section is normally prepared after the report is keyed or printed in its final form.

EXECUTIVE SUMMARY

NOTE 10.41
An executive summary is a capsule form of the report.

An **executive summary** is a brief version of the report; it restates each section of the report in abbreviated form with an emphasis on findings, conclusions, and recommendations. Other common names for an executive summary are *summary, abstract, overview,* and *synopsis.*

The summary, which is approximately 10 percent of the length of the report up to a limit of two single-spaced pages, saves readers time by providing an overview of the report's contents. Reports that include a synopsis in the letter of transmittal generally do not contain an executive summary.

Body

Most formal reports will contain all the information presented in the sections discussed in this part of the chapter; however, some of the sections may be combined. The material in the body may be presented using the direct or the indirect approach. The conclusions, recommendations, or both come at the beginning of the body when the direct approach is used; they come at the end of the body in the indirect approach.

NOTE 10.42
The body of a report may use the direct or the indirect approach.

INTRODUCTION

The **introduction** provides adequate background concerning the study so that the reader can understand the scope and sequence of the report. In addition to general information about the problem and the main issues involved in it, the introduction may include a specific problem statement, outline the purpose of the study, specify the scope of the research, summarize available literature on the topic, or define unfamiliar terms.

Statement of the Problem. The **statement of the problem** clearly identifies the specific problem that was investigated. The statement should be brief but informative.

Purpose of the Study. The **purpose of the study** indicates why the study was conducted. The purpose should help convince the reader that the problem is important and needs to be studied. The purpose may be stated as a question ("Which insurance company will best serve our needs?") or as a statement ("The purpose of this study is to provide information for the selection of the insurance company with the most effective plan.").

NOTE 10.43
The purpose provides the reason for the study.

Scope. The **scope** of the research is defined by the main factors that were studied and generally appears next in the introductory section. It lets the reader know the extent of the research. Boundaries set by the researcher as well as factors over which the researcher had no control are listed in this section of the introduction. These limitations can include resources, time, or geographic boundaries.

Related Literature. **Related literature** is material collected while doing research on a topic being studied. A review of related literature may be included in the introduction if only a limited amount of literature is available about the topic. A separate section should be used when extensive amounts of related literature are reviewed.

Unfamiliar Terms. Definitions of terms unfamiliar to the reader can be included in the introductory section. When many terms need to be defined, however, a glossary should be included in the supplementary section.

PROCEDURES

The **procedures,** or methodology, section describes the steps taken in conducting the study. One purpose of this section is to allow readers to determine whether all aspects of the problem were investigated adequately. This section can also be used by another researcher to conduct a similar study that could validate or disprove the results of the original study.

NOTE 10.44
The procedures section describes steps used in conducting the study.

FINDINGS

Findings are results discovered during the research. This section should be presented in a factual and objective manner without personal opinions or interpretations. Present all findings—positive and negative. Visual aids such as those presented in Chapter 12 can be used to assist the writer in communicating the findings of the study.

ANALYSIS

NOTE 10.45
Significant outcomes and relationships are discussed in the analysis section.

The **analysis** section contains the writer's interpretation of the qualitative or quantitative assessment of the findings. If prior research on the topic exists, the writer compares its results with the findings of the current study. Information in the analysis section assists the reader in determining which relationships are important. In a brief report, writers may describe and discuss their findings in one section.

CONCLUSIONS

NOTE 10.46
Conclusions are drawn from the findings of the study.

A **conclusion** is a statement of reasoning made by a researcher after a thorough investigation. The findings and analysis should support or substantiate the conclusions. In many studies, conclusions are summary statements of the content of the analysis section. No new data should be presented in this section. A study may have one or several conclusions. Because these statements become the basis for the writer's recommendations, the two sections may be combined.

RECOMMENDATIONS

NOTE 10.47
Recommendations are based on conclusions.

A **recommendation** is the writer's suggestion to the reader as to the action(s) that should be taken to solve the problem that was studied. Recommendations should develop logically from the findings, analysis, and conclusions of the study. A study can result in one or more recommendations. If three or more recommendations are presented, they can be listed and numbered. This section may contain only the recommendations, or it may contain both the recommendations and the supportive reasoning for their development.

Supplementary Section

The final section of a written report contains material that relates indirectly to the main topic of the study. This section may consist of one or more subsections, such as a glossary, an appendix, and a bibliography or reference list.

GLOSSARY

NOTE 10.48
Unfamiliar terms are defined in the glossary.

A **glossary** is an alphabetic list of terms used in the report with a brief definition of each. It is used only when numerous unfamiliar terms are included in the text. When the report contains only a few specialized terms, the writer should define them in the introduction or when they first occur in the text.

APPENDIX

NOTE 10.49
Indirectly related material is placed in an appendix.

An **appendix** contains related information excluded from the body to improve its readability. When appending two or more items, label each separately and identify it with a capital letter:

Appendix A: Computer Printout of Daily Sales
Appendix B: Sample Follow-up Letter

All appendixes should be referred to in the body of the report. If the material is not referred to in the body, it is not relevant enough to be included as an appendix.

Some items commonly included as appendixes include questionnaires, computer printouts, follow-up letters, reports of similar studies, working papers, intricate tables, and supporting material.

BIBLIOGRAPHY OR REFERENCE LIST

A **bibliography** is an alphabetic list of all references used as sources of information in the study, including those that do not appear in footnotes or text citations. A **reference list** includes only those sources cited in the text of the report. Consult Appendix A or a style manual for information on how to display entries for various sources.

NOTE 10.50
References are listed in a bibliography or reference list.

Mechanics of Formal Reports

The mechanics of a written report—format, spacing, and headings—are as important as the mechanics of a letter or memo in that they make the first impression on the reader. The reader's first impression of the report will be based on its appearance. A negative first impression may increase the time it takes for a reader to gain confidence in the report writer's credibility.

When preparing the document, the writer must consider general guidelines of report mechanics as well as the guidelines and policies of the organization. The primary consideration in the physical presentation of a written report is that the mechanics improve the readability of the report. Paragraphs averaging six to seven lines make it easy for the reader to concentrate on the written material. Proper spacing between paragraphs and correct margins make it easy for the reader to follow the material. Headings lead the reader from one section to the next by announcing the next topic.

LO 5
List the advantages of correct report formatting.

LO 6
Write formal and informal reports.

NOTE 10.51
The appearance of a report influences the reader's impression of it.

Cover

The **cover** protects the contents of the report; therefore, it is often constructed of lightweight card stock. Information can be printed on the cover or displayed through a cutout section (window). The cover should be attractive and may contain an appropriate picture or drawing that will add to the impact of the report. Many organizations use preprinted covers on which the author can place the variable information. The items generally displayed on a report cover are the title, the name of the author, and the date the report was submitted. Normally, the title is in uppercase letters, and the author's name has initial capital letters. Covers usually are used only on long, formal reports.

NOTE 10.52
The cover provides information and protects the report.

Margins

Proper **margins** are important because they create the white space that makes the report visually appealing to the reader. As a rule, report margins should be one inch on all sides. However, reports that are bound at the left should have a one-and-one-half-inch left margin, and reports that are bound at the top should have a two-inch top margin. Preliminary parts, supplementary parts, and the opening page of major sections typically have larger (two-inch) top margins.

NOTE 10.53
Margins add to the attractiveness of the report.

Spacing

Reports may be **single spaced** or **double spaced.** The trend in business organizations is toward single spacing to reduce the number of sheets of paper that have to be handled.

NOTE 10.54
Most reports are single spaced, but double spacing is acceptable.

In double-spaced reports, use paragraph indentions that are one-half inch from the left margin; no space is added between paragraphs. Single-spaced reports should be double spaced between paragraphs; indenting the first line of the paragraph is optional.

Headings

Appropriate headings help the reader follow the report organization and enable him or her to refer quickly to specific sections within the report. Sections that are of little interest can be skipped or scanned quickly.

NOTE 10.55
Structural or informative headings may be used.

Headings may be either informative or structural. An **informative heading** indicates the content of a section and orients readers so that they can more easily understand the material. A **structural heading** emphasizes the functional sections within the report. Once the type of heading is selected, it should be used consistently throughout the report. An example of each follows:

Informative Heading
CUSTOMERS' ATTITUDES TOWARD WEB POP-UP ADS

Structural Heading
FINDINGS

The ways headings are presented vary according to the style manual used by the organization. Regardless of the method selected, consistency of presentation is vital. An explanation of one widely accepted method follows.

First-level headings (main headings) are centered on the page; the first letter of each main word is capitalized. Main headings may be printed in boldface; the font size may also be larger than the one used for text. **Second-level headings** (side headings) begin at the left margin, and the first letter of each main word is capitalized. The heading is boldfaced and may be displayed in a font size larger than manuscript text but smaller than the first-level heading. The **third-level heading** (paragraph heading) begins at the paragraph point (at the left margin or one-half inch from the left margin if paragraphs are indented), has the first letter and proper nouns capitalized, is boldfaced, and ends with a period. An example of this method is shown in Figure 10.7.

NOTE 10.56
Headings within a level must be parallel.

The headings at each level must be constructed so that they are grammatically parallel. For example, all first-level headings must be parallel; however, first-level headings do not have to be parallel with second-level headings. In the following example, the second-level headings are parallel, but the first-level headings are not:

INCOME FOR FIRST QUARTER
Rent
Dividends
WAYS THAT FIRST QUARTER INCOME IS SPENT
Wages
Insurance
Travel

This example could be corrected by changing "WAYS THAT FIRST QUARTER INCOME IS SPENT" to "EXPENSES FOR FIRST QUARTER."

The rules of outlining should be followed when preparing headings in a written report. When second- or third-level headings are used, each level must have at least two entries.

Ideally, all first- and second-level headings within a report should be set off from preceding text by a triple space (two blank lines) and from following text by a double

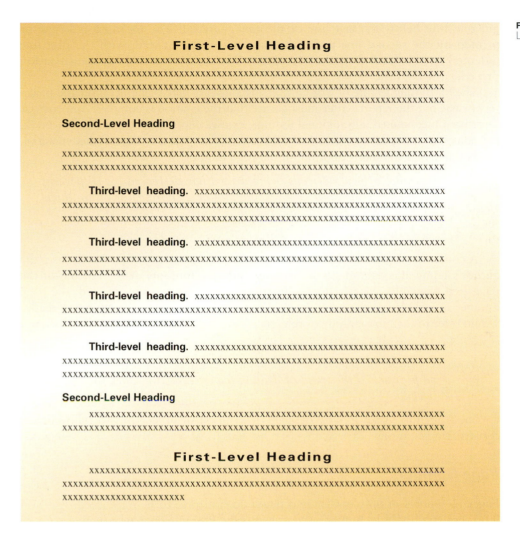

FIGURE 10.7
Level of Headings

space (one blank line). When using word processing software, it is acceptable to use only a double space before and after first- and second-level headings. Text for sections with third-level headings begins on the same line as the heading two spaces after the period.

Footnotes or Citations

Footnotes or **citations** must be used to give credit to the source of quoted or paraphrased material. Because they rely heavily on data gathered through primary research, business reports typically do not contain as many footnotes or text citations as reports in other fields. When sources are cited, however, they are formatted using either of two methods.

The traditional method of footnoting is convenient for the reader when a report contains information gathered from a number of sources. Material to be footnoted is marked by an Arabic numeral that is placed at the end of the quoted or paraphrased material and raised a half line (superscript). The footnote numbers begin with 1 and are consecutive throughout the report. The footnote is separated from the text by a one-inch or two-inch horizontal rule beginning at the left mar-

NOTE 10.57
Information obtained from secondary sources must be footnoted.

gin one line below the last line of the text material. The footnote is keyed or printed on the second line under the rule; it is single spaced, with the first line indented one-half inch from the left margin. The superscript number identification precedes the citation.

NOTE 10.58
Commonly used footnoting or text citation methods are
• Traditional
• Contemporary

The footnoting feature of word processing software makes enumeration and placement easy, but the report writer must ensure that the citation is complete and correct. Information contained in traditional footnotes varies depending on the source—book, periodical, encyclopedia, government publication, newspaper, or unpublished material. An example of a traditional, bottom-of-the-page footnote follows:

The number of new oil wells being drilled has decreased by 10 percent from the number drilled last year.[1] There will be a shortage of oil products if the trend of drilling fewer wells continues for the rest of this decade.

[1]A. W. Hodde, "Oil Production in 2007," Petroleum Quarterly 9 (2008), p. 8.

A contemporary method of citing sources of information within the text uses the author's name and date in parentheses instead of a footnote at the bottom of the page (see Appendix A). If a direct quotation of text or statistics is used, the page number is included in the parentheses. For information about the source, a reader would refer to the bibliography or reference list. An example of this method follows:

The number of new oil wells being drilled has decreased by 10 percent from the number drilled last year (Hodde, 2008, p. 8). There will be a shortage of oil products if the trend of drilling fewer wells continues for the rest of this decade.

See Appendix A for a more detailed description of procedures to follow when constructing citations.

Page Numbers

NOTE 10.59
Reports containing more than two pages should be numbered.

Pages in reports of only one or two pages do not have to be numbered. Pages in long reports should be numbered consecutively. Preliminary pages (pages prior to the body of a report) should be numbered by placing small Roman numerals (ii, iii, iv, etc.) at the center of the page, one inch from the bottom, beginning with the second page. The title page is considered page i, even though no page number is displayed.

The body of the report should begin as page 1, identified with Arabic numerals (1, 2, 3, 4, etc.). For each section or chapter that is started on a separate page, the page number should be centered one inch from the bottom. On the remaining pages of unbound or left-bound reports, the number should be placed on the fourth line from the top of the page in the right margin; on top-bound reports the page number should be centered and one inch from the bottom edge of the page. The page numbering feature of word processing software simplifies the placement process.

Figure 10.8, displayed on pages 285–295, contains a portion of an actual report formatted to meet the company's standards. The complete report and an additional report are posted at http://thomsonedu.com/bcomm/krizan. Appendix B contains a report formatted to meet the guidelines described in this chapter. Although different in style, all three reports are visually appealing, are formatted for readability, and are written to meet the needs of their audience.

McGladrey & Pullen
Certified Public Accountants

Flavorful Foods Company

Treasury and Risk Management Department Review

November 30, 2006

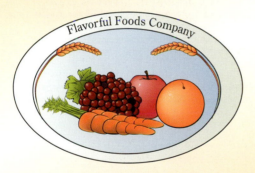

This document is an adaptation of an actual business report. All references to the client (company name, personnel, and other identifying elements) have been removed and replaced with fictitious names. Any resemblance to actual companies or personnel is purely coincidental.

FIGURE 10.8
Formal Business Report

RSM McGladrey

November 30, 2006

Mr. Thomas Bradley
Flavorful Foods Company
10 West Main Street
Ramsey, WA 44789

RSM McGladrey, Inc.
Tim Peterson
227 West First Street, Suite 700
Duluth, Minnesota 55802-1919
O 218.727.8253 **F** 218.727.1438
tim_Peterson@rsmi.com

Dear Thomas:

As discussed, the following is a summary of our evaluation of the Flavorful Foods Company's Treasury and Risk Management departments, including the review of the control procedures of the major revenue and expense cycles. Most of my observations are based on the personal interviews conducted with you, your managers, and the staff at Flavorful Foods Company.

During my meeting with you and Julie, we reviewed some of my initial findings. This report contains those initial findings, along with a few other issues discovered upon further analysis. The objectives of this project were to:

1. Review the systems, procedures, and policies in place at Flavorful Foods Company for the cash management/treasury function at the company's corporate headquarters.
2. Report to company management the results of our review (our findings) and to outline our assessment of the effectiveness of the various controls and procedures in place. This part of the project will also indicate if any gaps exist and will include the specific identification of those gaps.
3. Present to management any recommendations or ideas for improving the control procedures and offer suggestions for additional review processes that may enhance the control environment at Flavorful Foods Company.

Overall, this project is intended to provide you, other management team members, and the company owners with an independent, objective viewpoint on the effectiveness and adequacy of the controls and procedures of the cash management/treasury function.

This report is organized into the following sections:

- Summary and Recommendations
- Process Narratives of areas reviewed
- Flowcharts of areas reviewed
- Test Scripts for certain areas reviewed

It was a pleasure to visit your company and be a part of this review process. We thank your staff and managers for their assistance during our visit to your corporate office. They were prompt and professional in their responses and aided directly in our ability to complete this assignment.

Sincerely,

Tim J. Peterson

Tim J. Peterson, Director, Consulting Services

RSM McGladrey, Inc. is a member of RSM International -
an affiliation of separate and independent legal entities.

FIGURE 10.8
Formal Business Report,
continued

Table of Contents

FIGURE 10.8
Formal Business Report,
continued

SUMMARY AND RECOMMENDATIONS

The systems we reviewed are part of the overall financial systems of Flavorful Foods Company. Most operational areas fell directly under the responsibility of Thomas Bradley, Supervisor of Risk Management, and Robert Petcoff, Supervisor of Corporate Accounting. The company's systems would be classified as mature systems with all procedures and software systems in place for a period exceeding two years. We did note a few of the areas we reviewed were going to be replaced by new software systems or were in the process of a personnel change. When possible, we reviewed the proposed change versus the old system. When the new system was not yet developed, we documented the existing system.

The personnel assigned to the various functions appeared to be well versed on the processes and comfortable with their roles in carrying out their responsibilities.

Overall comments

We did not note any significant control issues in the areas we reviewed. Flavorful Foods Company is a mature company, and the systems in place are not under any major or significant revision or development. Additionally, the company has been subjected to annual audits by independent auditors for several years. We would expect any significant control lapses would be discovered and corrected if they were to exist.

However, mature systems run the risk of complacency as personnel performing the functions may not question the process even if changes in business transactions occur. We are pleased to report we did not see any evidence of personnel becoming complacent about their responsibilities and the control processes at Flavorful Foods Company.

We did observe some areas where we think improvements could be made to the processes and have noted them in the following section of this report. We also have suggested test scripts for areas we felt would benefit from a more frequent in-house or supervisory review.

The following is a recap of the issues we felt were significant and warranted attention by Flavorful Foods Management:

Bank account review

- The company has had a long relationship with Bank Star. Thomas, Julie, and Sandi mentioned the bank relationship is very good, and the bank is proactive in bringing cost-saving ideas and new services to the company for consideration. The company's bank fees with Bank Star are approximately $48,000 annually. According to the personnel interviewed, the company has not conducted a comprehensive review of the transaction fees paid for bank services on the four (4) primary accounts nor has it solicited a request for proposal for bank services from another bank. It should be noted that Julie and Sandi did review the bank analysis statement this summer to determine whether any service fees were being paid that were no longer relevant or whether the services were not being used.

    o Recommendation: A long relationship with a financial institution is normally a desired attribute. However, familiarity sometimes removes some of the competitive elements in a financial relationship allowing fees and other service areas to become less market priced. We would suggest a comprehensive review of the fees and related services provided by Bank Star. A discussion with the Bank Star relationship manager asking for such a review may be all that is necessary. A more direct approach would be to ask Bank Star to respond to a request for proposal for bank services currently provided by Bank Star. It may not yield lower fees, but it will at least establish whether you are paying service fees on a market-based fee structure. We would also suggest the same process be followed with the accounts at New State Bank.

- The company has two (2) checking accounts with Bank Star and four (4) checking accounts with New State Bank. The company maintains approximately $2.2 million in compensatory balances in those accounts to offset bank service fees.

RSM McGladrey, Inc. Page 1

FIGURE 10.8
Formal Business Report,
continued

Flavorful Foods Company   Evaluation of Treasury and Risk Management Departments

- o Recommendation: Two of the accounts are idle with no recent activity. One is established to service a related company in Vermont to avoid any public disclosure of financial data for the company. The other is used to fund other accounts. Having multiple bank accounts typically increase the fees and the administrative efforts necessary to maintain the accounts. It also increases the opportunities for breaches in security and control. We would suggest the company review the inactive accounts to ensure they fulfill their original purpose and, more importantly, to establish whether the original purpose is still intact.

Void check process
- The company is in a transition phase regarding check printing, going from a preprinted check to a printed check that includes micro coding. All checks are printed with a LaserJet printer. Preprinted check stock is secured, and any voided checks are recorded in an Excel spreadsheet. One substantial form of control is the electronic match between the cleared checks and the outstanding checks (electronic files prepared by the bank on cleared checks are matched against the checks produced by the software generating the payment). The procedures for handling voided checks are slightly different for each of the three checks printed by the company.

  - o Recommendation: The procedures for handling voided checks should be consistent, regardless of the check source (CSI, Bordwell, or EasyRecords). The controls, as expressed to us, appear to secure the voided checks through documentation and physical retention of the checks.

Account sweep
- The company has used a single consolidating account for all cash. This account is "swept" if the amount at the end of the day is higher than the "peg balance." Excess cash is invested overnight by the bank and made available the next morning in the checking account. This process has ceased until a new peg balance can be established to support the bank fees. Once this new peg balance has been established, the sweep and overnight investment will resume.

  - o Recommendation/Comment: The sweep process is automatically performed by the bank and monitored daily by the Treasury/Risk Analyst (Julie Thomas). The company periodically uses its Line of Credit (LOC) to fund cash cycles. It was not clear how the presence of an outstanding LOC balance would affect the automatic sweep. The company should ensure that any ability to pay down any outstanding LOC balance should be enacted before an automatic sweep takes place. The company has a core of very talented people working with the cash accounts, and this comment is by no means critical of current procedures.

Lock box
- The company uses two lock boxes, one for each of the two companies (FFC and FSC). All checks, money orders, or other forms of payment received through the mail or common carrier (nonelectronic forms of payment) are presented to the lock box. The funds are deposited daily, and any accompanying paperwork is sent to the corporate office in Ramsey for processing. The bank is working on digitizing the paperwork and will soon provide the company with scanned images that will be available online.

  - o Recommendation/Comment: We have no recommendations for this function. It appears the cash is well monitored, and the company is using technology to ensure access to funds received. One common criticism of lock boxes is the delay in receiving the paperwork used to post to the receivable balances. This was not indicated as a problem for personnel at Ramsey. Company personnel are also very diligent in recording and reconciling, on a daily basis, cash presentations via the Cash Control spreadsheet.

- The bank sends an electronic file to the company with the daily transactions. This file is converted to an

RSM McGladrey, Inc. Page 2

FIGURE 10.8
Formal Business Report,
continued

Flavorful Foods Company   Evaluation of Treasury and Risk Management Departments

Access database file, which is edited by Mary prior to uploading into Bordwell for application to customer accounts. There is no review of this transaction by persons other than Mary. The primary control point is the daily cash control sheet. We are not aware of any comparison between the source document and the transaction loaded into Bordwell.

- o Recommendation: We would suggest the supervisor of this function occasionally check the detailed batch upload into Bordwell against the source documents. We are not suggesting this review be conducted daily; rather, once every other month would be adequate.

EFT, ACH
- The EFT (electronic funds transfer) and ACH (automated clearing house) transactions are approved by the Supervisor of Risk Management. This process allows for control on the funds transferred, and the cash control sheet supports the transactions. Templates are established allowing for consistent processing of the EFT request on repetitive EFT requests. The actual transfer is valid only if the Supervisor of Risk Management enters a password into the bank software for all nonrepetitive EFT transfers. One-time entries are allowed by the Risk Analyst but still require the Supervisor's authorization.

  - o Comment: This process is very well controlled with little evidence of any control issues associated with the process.

- The authorization process for ACH withdrawal requires a form to be initiated and signed by a supervisor. According to our interview, there is no formal review of the authorization forms to remove or delete approved ACH vendors or employees (initiated by the company to pay a few vendor and employee expense checks).

  - o Recommendation: The company should review all ACH authorized transactions periodically to ensure inactive vendors and terminated employees are no longer approved for ACH transactions.

Fixed assets
- The company utilizes a formal procedure for the authorization and acquisition of fixed (capital) assets. The basic policy requires expenditures for fixed assets above $5,000 to be capitalized and approved via the CapEx document. Expenditures above $25,000 would require the President/CEO of the company to approve the request.

  - o Comment: The company's policy is designed to provide pre-acquisition and post-acquisition controls to ensure expenditures for fixed assets are properly approved and accurately recorded in the company's financial records (Asset accounts, Depreciation accounts, Gain or Loss on Sale revenue accounts). We have no recommendations to improve or increase the controls on this function.

- There is no audit process conducted on a CapEx request when the project (expenditure) is completed. The company does check expenditures that are coded to the project when they are paid to ensure they are legitimate for the project.

  - o Recommendation: The company should consider auditing the expenditures authorized against a project upon its completion. We would recommend that expenditures for projects in excess of an arbitrary amount (for example, $50,000) should be reviewed when the project is complete. The invoices and internal costs charged to the project should be compared with the original CapEx request amount. This recommendation is especially appropriate when the CapEx request is justified on some form of economic payback period.

Payroll
- The company has three payroll processes: hourly, salary, and executive. The company prepares the source documents including hour checking, deductions, and miscellaneous pay items. The company outsources the payroll to EasyRecords Corporation. The Supervisor of Corporate Accounting administers the executive payroll on a confidential basis. Human Resources (HR) is responsible for the pay rates, deduction detail, and

RSM McGladrey, Inc. Page 3

FIGURE 10.8
Formal Business Report,
continued

masterfile changes and updates. Accounting is responsible for coordinating the payroll and processing of checks with EasyRecords. The payroll administrator (Susan Johnson) has the ability to update the masterfile.

- Recommendations/Comments: The payroll systems are well controlled with division of key duties in place between Human Resources and the Payroll Department. We feel the controls in place are reasonable and provide consistent processing of each payroll. The personnel assigned to the task are well informed on the upstream and downstream processing of payroll documents. However, there are a few areas where we feel procedural changes can be made to enhance the control environment.

  - Susan has the ability to make masterfile changes even though the Human Resources Department is formally empowered with that task. Password protection or other security means should be in place to prevent Susan's ability to enact changes.

  - There doesn't appear to be a policy in place in the HR Department to approve any masterfile changes. The change request is entered on a spreadsheet and presented to the HR Department for entry. We would recommend a supervisor review all masterfile changes and sign off on the source document (spreadsheet) prior to the update transaction.

  - We recommend the company explore the ability to have all masterfile updates performed during a payroll to be reported to a supervisor for review. EasyRecords may have this report already developed, and it may be possible to request it from them.

- Comment: The executive payroll is deemed extremely confidential requiring the Supervisor of Corporate Accounting to prepare and administer this function. However, it is apparent Susan Johnson is familiar with all aspects of this payroll, including the salaries of the personnel in this category.

Soy payroll
- The soy payroll represents the most significant expenditures of the company. This system is comprised of the acquisition, delivery, and payment for soy delivered to the operating cheese plants. The company has over 100 soy producers (farms) shipping product on a daily basis. The company has contract haulers picking up the soy at the farm and delivering it to the regional plants. The payroll starts with the soy ticket (delivery document specifying quantity, date, and a reference number for a soy shipment) and includes several verifications of the quantity, quality, and price paid for the product. The process is automated through a software system called CSI, a proprietary program developed specifically for this industry. The producers are independent businesses selling product to the company, but essentially they are extensions of the company in several ways. Most producers sell all their output to the company, and the company withholds from the payments to the producers amounts to cover life insurance and other miscellaneous producer obligations.

  - Recommendations/Comments: The system as a whole is well controlled with several check-and-balance procedures incorporated into the system. The CSI software is industry specific and is able to provide several cross-checks of product received and the payment to the producer. There appears to be reliance by the staff administering the soy payroll on the output and electronic batch files created by CSI to validate the transaction. We did not see where the source document (soy ticket) is periodically checked to the system output to ensure the proper recording of the transaction. We recommend periodically checking a sample of source documents to the output to ensure proper recording of the transaction.

Accounts receivable
- The company's accounts receivable function is performed through the Bordwell software system. It is well controlled through the normal system controls within the Bordwell software. The personnel responsible for administering the function (Mary, Sandi, and Marge) were knowledgeable regarding the system and the processes before and after the receivable process. Payments from customers are posted to their accounts electronically through the transaction batch supplied through the lock box system. ACH transactions are

FIGURE 10.8
Formal Business Report,
continued

Flavorful Foods Company   Evaluation of Treasury and Risk Management Departments

monitored through the daily cash control sheet. Aging of the receivables is monitored frequently with calls made to customers three days over their terms.

- o Recommendations: Write-offs of accounts receivable balances appear to be uncommon. The company CFO must approve any accounts written off or adjusted. However, there doesn't appear to be an independent audit of the adjustments or write-offs, and the CFO would be aware only of the transactions presented to her. We recommend a periodic review of sampled customer accounts to determine if any adjustments or write-offs are supported by an authorization by the CFO.

- o Comments: Product returns are monitored through the FUND program. We did not review this function but would recommend the company perform a quick review of this process to determine if the returned products are properly recorded and credits to customers are supported by authorized returns.

Accounts payable
- The Bordwell software supports this function. The function appears to use the controls offered through the software and incorporates traditional accounts payable controls such as purchase orders, three-way matching, and source document signatures for approval. There are three categories of payables: regular accounts payable invoices, purchase order invoices, and WRX invoices. Price and quantity variance are presented to the buyers or authorizing party for approval prior to payment.

  - o Recommendation: There doesn't appear to be a consistent procedure for clearing price variances between purchase orders and invoices. We recommend the company develop a policy directing the Accounts Payable personnel to present invoice variances to the authorizing party (buyers in most cases) for approval prior to entering them into the system.

  - o Recommendation: The Accounts Payable personnel do not have a system to ensure the company takes discounts offered on invoices. We recommend someone check to ensure all discount opportunities are taken.

  - o Recommendation: Vendor masterfile changes are allowed by the Accounts Payable personnel. We would recommend developing a report of all vendor masterfile updates to the Bordwell system. The Department Supervisor should review this report on a regular basis.

Overall system reviews
- The company depends on the use of spreadsheets to communicate several documents and expenditure authorizations within the systems.

  - o Recommendations: We would suggest the company conduct an inventory of all spreadsheets used to generate, authorize, or calculate payments or receipts. These spreadsheets should be audited and the cells, links, and other critical processing be tested to ensure there are no errors or misrepresentations of the data.

- The company has people in backup roles to replace personnel on an extended vacation or sick leave.

  - o Recommendations: The company should consider rotating the backup personnel through the job on a more frequent basis. Job rotation is a very effective control.

PROCESS NARRATIVES
The following section contains the detailed process narrative for each area reviewed during our site visit.

FIGURE 10.8
Formal Business Report,
continued

Flavorful Foods Company   Evaluation of Treasury and Risk Management Departments

Process narrative—bank account maintenance

Person(s) responsible/accountable for function:
Julie Thomas
Sandi Marks

Department responsible for function:
Treasury/Risk Management

Forms or documents used in function:
Not applicable. No standard forms or documents have been identified.

Computer programs used in function:
Not applicable. Computer systems are primarily Excel and online systems offered by the financial institution.

Please list the active bank accounts for the company:

Bank Account Number	Bank	Primary reason for account (e.g., payroll)
141860	Bank Star	Main Checking Account
5300016012	Bank Star	GIF Checking
4114671	Bank Star	Flavorful of Vermont
5330255783	Bank Star	Flavorful Foods Marketing
108937	New State Bank	Producer Payroll
108935	New State Bank	Associate Payroll
136995	New State Bank	Associate Payroll—FFC
113523	New State Bank	Executive Payroll

Process narrative
Flavorful Foods Company utilizes two banks to accommodate Flavorful Foods Company, Flavorful Foods—Vermont, and Flavorful Foods Marketing. The two banks are Bank Star and New State Bank. The Risk Management Department is responsible for the oversight of all bank relationships and transactions.

Bank analysis statements
The bank analysis statement is an important document sent to the company by the bank highlighting all transactional data and the fees associated with bank services. The document will specify whether the company has set a peg balance adequate to cover the majority of normal bank fees. Julie Thomas, Treasury/Risk Analyst, receives the analyses directly from Bank Star and New State Bank. She reviews the statement to ascertain the fees are reasonable and the peg balance is adequate to cover the fees. Julie will occasionally check company records on some transactions to determine the accuracy and appropriateness of the fees on the analysis statement.

Bank signature cards
Signature cards are maintained by the Risk Management Department authorizing personnel to sign checks. Company resolution authorizes the personnel allowed to sign checks. The signature plate stamp that physically imprints the checks is maintained by the Treasury/Risk Analyst. This function oversees all check signing for all companies and bank accounts. There are no limits set on the amount for which the signers are authorized to sign.

Bank reconciliation
Mary, a Financial Accounting Associate in the Corporate Accounting Department, receives most bank statements via the U.S. mail. The only exception is the executive payroll bank statement, which is received by the Supervisor of

RSM McGladrey, Inc. Page 6

FIGURE 10.8
Formal Business Report,
continued

Flavorful Foods Company   Evaluation of Treasury and Risk Management Departments

Corporate Accounting. On a daily basis, the main checking accounts are reconciled via the bank's online system. Deposits and presentations are compared to the company's detailed transactions (deposits and checks written), and any variances are resolved that day. Mary downloads the cleared checks, which are electronically matched with those written through the company's financial system (Bordwell, for example). Payroll accounts are reconciled monthly. Other no-activity accounts are reconciled each month. Sandi Marks reviews and signs off on each bank account reconciliation.

Mary will make monthly journal entries reflecting any adjustments necessary as a result of the reconciliation process.

Check security
Canceled Checks: The company receives the canceled checks from the New State Bank accounts. These checks are filed in a box and retained. The company does not perform a physical comparison of the canceled check to the bank statement (see electronic match mentioned earlier). Canceled checks written on the Bank Star accounts are not received by the company; rather, a CD with the canceled check images is sent to the company.

Blank Checks: The company has safeguards in place for blank check stock. A combination of printed check stock and computer-generated checks is used. Checks are locked in a secure place until they are to be issued (printed). Julie Thomas has access to the checks and will be present with the check signature plate when the checks are signed.

RSM McGladrey, Inc. Page 7

FIGURE 10.8
Formal Business Report,
continued

Flavorful Foods Company	Evaluation of Treasury and Risk Management Departments

Process narrative—accounts payable

Person(s) responsible/accountable for function:
Wilma Rosecran
Jan Wells
Karen Tondry

Department responsible for function:
Corporate Accounting

Please list the forms (if any) used in your function, to whom they are routed, and where they are filed:

Form title or number	Person(s)/function(s) form is routed to (name or function)	Filing location (where form is filed upon completion)
New vendor form	Buyer	Karen updates masterfile
Check request form	Buyer for charity donation	Marge, Judy, and Dianne
W-9 forms	Vendor	Send to Marge to update Bordwell A/P module

Please list any computer programs used in your function:

Name of computer program	Network computer or individual workstation	Function
Bordwell	Network	Enter/maintain invoices
AS400	Network	Run reports
Dbase	Network	Scan/look up invoices

Process narrative
Invoices are received in the Accounting Department either through intercompany mail or U.S. mail. Three types of invoices are received: regular AP invoices, PO invoices, and RSX invoices.

The AP invoices are invoices sent to the buyer for proper approval and account coding. The Department receives these back via intercompany mail.
PO invoices are invoices authorized through the use of a purchase order system. This system assigns a purchase order (PO) number on the invoice. These are matched to the PO through the AS400 and Dbase systems. The line item the invoice is billing is determined and coded to the proper account(s).
The RSX invoices are also purchase order invoices; however, they use a separate system that Karen Tedesco administers. She determines the lines billed and properly codes these invoices, checking for discounts and taxes. She returns them to Jody, Danielle, or Kary for entering into the system.

All three of these invoices are evaluated for any discounts that can be taken and for tax purposes. The invoices are coded for accounts, discounts, and tax and prepared for entry into the Bordwell system. The Associates prepare a control total on the payment totals, the vendor number totals, and the discount totals. These control totals ensure the invoices have been entered correctly. After confirmation, the numbers entered correlate to the numbers in the system, and the batch is released and ready for payment.

RSM McGladrey, Inc. Page 8

FIGURE 10.8
Formal Business Report, *concludes.* The entire report is available at http://thomsonedu.com/bcomm/krizan.

Summary of Learning Objectives

LO 1   ## Distinguish between formal and informal reports.

A formal report may consist of all or some of the following parts: title page, transmittal message, table of contents, list of illustrations, abstract, body, glossary, appendix, and bibliography or reference list. An informal report may consist of only a title page and body or only the body; it also may be formatted as correspondence. Formal reports are usually written in the third person, but informality is becoming more acceptable; informal reports are usually written in the first person. Both formal and informal reports use headings to guide the reader through the document.

LO 2   ## Identify the types of informal reports.

The three most common informal reports are progress, periodic, and technical. A progress report informs readers about the status of a particular project. A periodic report provides managers with updated information at regularly scheduled intervals. A technical report conveys specialized information.

LO 3   ## Identify and use the five steps for conducting research.

The five steps in conducting research are: (a) *Plan the research*. Planning the research includes stating the problem, setting the boundaries, determining the readership, and deciding on the procedures to be followed. Brainstorming and cluster diagramming can help when planning the research. (b) *Gather information*. You may gather information for your research from secondary and/or primary sources. (c) *Analyze the information*. The purpose of the analysis is to make sense, objectively, of the information you have gathered. You will not want personal bias of any kind to enter the analysis. (d) *Determine the solution(s)*. Based on your analysis, you will be ready to offer a solution or solutions to the problem you have been researching. For formal studies and reports, you may draw conclusions from your analysis and state them separately from the recommendation(s). (e) *Write the report*. The final step in a research project is to write the report. It is an important step; you will want to present your results effectively.

LO 4   ## Describe the components of a formal report.

The report cover, which contains the report title and author's name, protects the contents of the report. Report margins are generally one inch on all sides. Reports bound on the left have a one-and-one-half-inch left margin, or top-bound reports have a two-inch top margin. Reports may be single spaced or double spaced. Single-spaced reports should be double spaced between paragraphs. Headings may be informative or structural. Informative headings indicate the content of a forthcoming section; structural headings emphasize the functional sections within the report. Footnotes or text citations give credit to the source of quoted or paraphrased material. Pages of short reports (two pages or fewer) need not be numbered; pages of long reports should be numbered. Preliminary pages normally are numbered with Roman numerals; pages containing the body and supplementary parts of the report are numbered with Arabic numerals.

List the advantages of correct report formatting.

LO 5

Correct report formatting creates a good first impression of the report. It decreases the time necessary for a reader to gain confidence in the report writer's credibility. Formatting a written report properly will improve its readability. Appropriate headings help the reader follow the organization of the material by using appropriate headings.

Write formal and informal reports.

LO 6

Informal reports are normally written in the first person; formal reports most often use the third person. Unlike formal reports, informal reports generally do not contain visual aids or material from secondary sources. The detailed structure of formal reports helps guide the reader through the material. Informal reports are less structured and may be formatted as letters or memos.

Questions for Discussion and Review

1. "If a report has a title page, it's a formal report." Do you agree or disagree with this statement? Why? (Objective 1)
2. How can a writer determine whether to use a formal, third-person style or an informal, first-person style when writing a formal report? (Objective 1)
3. Name and describe the nature of the three common informal report types described in this chapter. (Objective 2)
4. How do preprinted forms or standardized formats help (a) report writers and (b) report readers? (Objective 2)
5. What five steps are followed when conducting business research? (Objective 3)
6. Distinguish between primary and secondary information sources. Give an example of each. (Objective 3)
7. While working as part of a research team, one of your coworkers tells you that failing to cite sources doesn't constitute plagiarism if you're writing an internal report. Do you agree or disagree? Why? (Objective 3)
8. How can a report writer meet the needs of both primary and secondary readers? Give a specific example. (Objective 3)
9. Give an example of a "skip-and-jump" survey question. Why should this type of question be avoided? (Objective 3)
10. What can a researcher do to create a comfortable, supportive environment for a personal interview? (Objective 3)
11. Explain the relationship among findings, conclusions, and recommendations. (Objective 3)
12. What is included in the introduction to a formal written report? (Objective 4)
13. How does the purpose of an executive summary differ from that of a letter of transmittal? (Objective 4)
14. Why is the choice of format important with a formal report? (Objective 5)
15. What factors should be considered when formatting a written report? (Objective 5)

Application Exercises

1. **Teamwork.** Form teams of no more than five people. Each team will select an important current issue or problem on the campus. As directed by your instructor, do one or more of the following (Objectives 1 through 6):
   a. Design a research study that either surveys student attitudes about the issue or investigates the problem by using other research methods and proposes a solution.
   b. Submit a memo to your instructor in which you identify your topic, outline your research plan, and ask for authorization to complete the study.
   c. Submit a progress report to your instructor at the midpoint of your research.
   d. Prepare and submit a formal report to your instructor.

2. **Teamwork.** As directed by your instructor, complete one or more of the following activities:
   a. Form teams to develop a questionnaire that could be used to survey student opinions on the availability of parking at your school. (Objective 3)
   b. Pilot-test, revise, and then administer the questionnaire developed in Application Exercise 2a to the students in three business classes. Tabulate the students' responses and analyze the data. As your instructor directs, report your findings in a memo or an oral report. (Objectives 2, 3, and 6)
   c. Repeat Exercise 2a using the focus group technique. As your instructor directs, report your findings in a memo or an oral report. (Objectives 2, 3, and 6)

3. You're interested in learning what type of backpack is most popular among students on your campus. (Objectives 2, 3, and 6)
   a. Outline your data-gathering plan and share it with the class.
   b. Using the feedback you received from your classmates, conduct your research.
   c. As your instructor directs, report your findings in a memo or an oral report.

4. **Teamwork.** Work with two or three of your classmates to design an experiment to determine how people react to receiving compliments. After getting feedback on your design from members of another team, conduct your experiment. Submit an informal report to your instructor. (Objectives 2, 3, and 6)

5. **Technology. Teamwork.** As a class, identify three keywords that could be used when conducting research about a current business topic (e.g., leadership, ethics). Form small groups and have each group use the keywords with a different search engine (e.g., Google, Yahoo!, MSN). Compare the results to determine how many, if any, sites are listed among the top ten in all searches. (Objective 3)

6. **Teamwork.** Your instructor will place you in a group and ask your group to design an online questionnaire to gather data about college students' preferences about the following:
   a. energy drinks   f. pizza toppings
   b. music   g. candy
   c. magazines   h. TV shows
   d. DVD/movies   i. cellphone ringtones
   e. vehicles   j. spring break destinations

   Present your survey to the class. Modify the survey based on class feedback, and present a copy to your instructor. (Objective 3)

7. Indicate what would be (a) an appropriate statement of the problem and (b) an appropriate list of factors for a study to compare the cost-effectiveness of using paper towels, cloth toweling, and forced-air hand dryers in employee restrooms. (Objective 3)

8. The small company for which you work manufactures and sells camping equipment. Recently, the company's management team decided to expand its sales efforts to include e-commerce. Barbara Kramer, the owner of the company, has read various articles indicating that consumers are dissatisfied with the merchandise return policies used by companies that sell online. She has asked you to prepare a report that provides information about merchandise return policies. State the problem, list the research factors, and indicate the way you would gather data. (Objective 3)

9. **Technology.** Your company uses laptop computers extensively. Because employees take these computers home and on business trips, the equipment is vulnerable to theft. In the wrong hands,

data on these computers could put employees and clients at risk of identity theft. Your supervisor, Tad Peese, has asked you to research the topic of laptop security; specifically, he is interested in information on fingerprint readers and similar biometric devices. Use traditional and/or computerized search techniques to gather your information and then prepare an informal report. (Objectives 2, 3, and 6)

10. Review the online or print copy of a corporation's annual report. Prepare an outline of the report using its major headings and subheadings as your guide. Submit your outline to your instructor. (Objectives 4 and 5)

Case Problems

1. At the request of your dentist, Jennifer Ryan, you surveyed the patients who had checkups at her office during May to determine their dental floss preference. Data gathered from 73 patients are available at http://thomsonedu.com/bcomm/krizan; the data coding legend follows. Prepare a letter report summarizing your findings and recommending what type(s) of dental floss Dr. Ryan should give her patients after their exams.
   - Gender (1 = Male, 2 = Female)
   - Age (1 = 10 or under; 2 = 11–20; 3 = 21–40; 4 = 41–60; 5 = over 60)
   - Style (1 = unwaxed; 2 = waxed; 3 = no preference)
   - Flavor (1 = none; 2 = mint; 3 = cinnamon; 4 = no preference)

2. Your firm will soon be replacing the desktop telephones used by its 47 employees. The unit that's being considered accommodates three features in addition to voice mail and call forwarding. The plan is to install the three most-needed features on all phones. At the request of Ralph Mayberry, the firm's owner, you surveyed the staff and gathered the following data. Prepare a memo report.

Feature	Essential	Useful	Nice	No Need
Speaker	4	1	13	27
Caller ID	11	33	3	0
Call Waiting	5	6	21	15
Conferencing	3	14	1	29
Distribution List	7	2	1	37
Message Waiting Notification	35	4	5	3
Multi-line	7	6	3	31
Transfer	7	6	2	32

3. You are an intern for the Eagleton Eagles, a minor league baseball team. Your supervisor, Matt Marks, has asked you to analyze the following data about the entertainment offered before games, between innings, and after games. Surveys were sent to 738 season ticket holders; 319 surveys were returned, but not everyone answered all questions. Prepare a report that includes conclusions and recommendations. Select an appropriate format.

Feature	Excellent 7	6	5	4	3	2	Poor 1
"First-500" Giveaways (mini bats, hats, T-shirts, seat cushions)	101	93	30	25	15	32	33
Ethan Eagle (Mascot)	14	22	70	96	33	46	32
Pizza Eating Contest	31	14	58	46	43	67	55
Frozen T-shirt Contest	39	47	62	93	21	23	17
Dizzy Bat Race	28	77	19	94	53	18	24
Water Balloon Toss	22	18	113	89	9	16	45
"Fan in the Stand" Trivia	12	56	77	39	56	47	28

(continued)

(continued) Feature	Excellent 7	6	5	4	3	2	Poor 1
Theme Nights (Back to the 50s, Crazy Shirts, etc.)	18	46	79	61	63	18	11
Beverage Batter (half-price sodas if batter strikes out)	68	123	32	19	3	0	0
Post-game Giveaways (coupons, ice cream bars)	24	31	66	119	51	7	4
Post-game Fireworks	144	86	74	60	21	3	12

4. You serve on the professional development committee of a national association in your field. Your group recently sponsored a regional seminar on a pertinent topic in that field. The all-day seminar, held at a large hotel, featured a keynote speaker, a panel, and four small-group sessions scheduled so that each participant could attend two. Refreshments were provided during registration as well as during morning and afternoon breaks, but participants were responsible for their own lunch. Over 300 people attended; 214 of them took time to complete and return the seminar evaluation form included in their registration packet. You have been asked to analyze the results of the evaluation and report to the committee. Prepare an informal report. Create information appropriate to your field (e.g., seminar title, speakers, topics, location). The survey results follow.

	(Very High) 5	4	3	2	(Very Low) 1
Facility	3	17	37	136	21
Keynote Speaker	99	66	41	8	0
Panel (overall)	28	152	31	0	0
Panelist 1	47	113	51	0	0
Panelist 2	0	1	22	143	45
Panelist 3	53	117	39	2	0
Session 1a	94	16	3	0	0
Session 1b	26	41	18	0	0
Session 2a	16	37	10	2	0
Session 2b	23	59	1	0	0
Registration	24	43	119	18	0
Breaks	29	54	71	0	0

Comments (number of similar responses):

Registration table was understaffed during the 30 minutes just before the meeting began. (33)

Serve something other than sweets. (12)

Serve sodas at the morning break. (17)

Need a larger area for registration or a separate area for refreshments. (3)

Session 1a was overcrowded. Those standing in the back couldn't hear. (47)

Moderator lost control of the panel. (5)

Panelist 2 dominated the discussion; he insulted the other panelists and the audience. (71)

AV in Session 2b was inadequate. (4)

Keynote speaker was excellent; she set a positive tone for the day. (18)

Afternoon break needs to be longer; couldn't get refreshments and move to next session. (23)

The panel topic was controversial. Both sides of the issue needed to be presented . . . calmly and logically. (3)

5. In anticipation of upgrading its web presence, the American Woodcrafters' Association asked those who visited its public site during September, October, and November (207 hits; 112 responses) to complete the online survey linked to the home page. You've been asked to analyze the data and identify the strengths and weaknesses of the current site. Report your findings in a memo to Joy McDonald, Communication Committee Chair.

Factor	Very Good	Good	Neutral	Poor	Very Poor
Appearance	23	33	44	8	4
Ease of navigation within site	6	55	41	3	2
Information organization	17	24	42	16	8
Information clarity	11	23	31	35	7

How did you first hear of our site?	Media Broadcast 2	Print Media 33	Word-of-Mouth 19	Search Engine 34	Link from Another Site 19
How often do you visit the site?	First Visit 13	Daily 2	Weekly 24	Monthly 31	Occasionally 37

Did you find the specific information you were looking for?	Yes 27	No 21	Just Browsing 56
Would you recommend this site to others?	Yes 31	No 13	Unsure 53

6. Jubilee Products hired your firm, HR Partners, to conduct a brief employee satisfaction survey. Data received from 336 of Jubilee's 407 employees are available at http://thomsonedu.com/bcomm/krizan. The survey questions and data coding scheme follow. Analyze the data and present your results in a formal report that includes a letter of transmittal and an executive summary.
   - Job Class (1 = Supervisory, Managerial; 2 = Technical/Professional; 3 = Labor; 4 = Administrative Support; 5 = Maintenance)
   - Length of Service (1 = less than 1 year; 2 = 1– 5 years; 3 = 6–10 years; 4 = over 10 years)
   - Questions (rating scale is 1 = strongly disagree, 5 = strongly agree)
     1. I receive useful feedback about my performance.
     2. I am paid fairly for the work I do.
     3. I have the equipment and related resources I need to do my job well.
     4. I receive the training I need to do my job well.
     5. The company encourages a balance between work and personal life.
     6. The amount of work I am asked to do is reasonable.
     7. The company has fair promotion/advancement policies.
     8. I am encouraged to offer opinions/suggestions.
     9. My opinions/suggestions are valued.
     10. The company openly shares plans and information with employees.

7. As part of its long-range expansion and remodeling plan, Simpson Foods gathered input about the features/services its customers consider important in a grocery store. Data from 693 respondents follow. You, the operations manager, have been asked to analyze the data and recommend the features/services that should be included in the remodeled store. Prepare an informal report for Sal Simpson, the owner.

Feature	Essential	Nice	Not Important
Gourmet food section	98	287	308
ATM	186	02	305
Prescription pharmacy	23	66	604
Full-service bank	102	87	504
Deli	317	211	165

(continued)

(continued)

Feature	Essential	Nice	Not Important
Deli eating area	84	195	414
Wide selection of ethnic foods	245	188	257
Fresh seafood	221	183	289
In-store bakery	303	107	283
Potted plants and fresh flowers	71	403	219
Self-service checkouts	123	360	210
Catering department	36	157	500
Grocery bagging/carryout service	29	334	330
On-line shopping (with delivery)	183	299	311
On-line shopping (with customer pickup)	134	267	292
Bio-scan debit card / credit card payment	183	293	217

Web exercises to accompany this chapter are available at **www.thomsonedu.com/ bcomm/krizan.**

Message Analysis

Correct the grammar, punctuation, and style errors in the following text and format it as an executive summary. Consider using numbers, bullets, or other emphasis techniques to highlight important items.

The construction and operation of the first unit of the Hillside Energy Project ("Hillside One") by Ziegler Energy, Inc. ("Ziegler") will provide a substantial boost to both Richland County and the State as a hole.

This report calculates that Ziegler's construction of Hillside One will impact the State's economy in the following ways: $1.04 billion in direct spending on construction to build Hillside One. $300 million in direct spending on operations during a typical plant-year, recurring for the life of the plant. An additional non-recurring $533 million dollars in increased business and house hold spending across Richland County, which will ultimately result in a non-recurring $762 million in increased spending throughout the State, driven by spending on construction. An additional recurring $66 million in increased spending across the County, which will ultimately result in a recurring $91 million in increased spending throughout the State, generated by spending on operations.

This report estimates that Hillside One will also provide an impact in the region and the State by creating thousands of jobs.* Over the course of the 42 month construction period full-time, part-time and temporary construction jobs pique at almost 3,000. A total of over 100 full-time, part-time, and temporary jobs in operations. An additional 1,682 new full-time, part-time, and temporary jobs during the peak year in other sector's across the County, as a result of the creation of construction jobs. An additional 290 new full and part-time jobs in other sectors across the County, caused by the creation of jobs in the typical year of operations.

Significantly, this report assesses the economy impact on the State by Hillside One only. However, it is important to note that Ziegler currently has plans to develop and construct similar full-scale power generation facilities in two additional cites. Thus, if Ziegler is is ultimately successful in developing Hillside 2 and Hillside 3, Richland County could receive potential impacts in addition to those shown here.

*The software used in this projection analysis is driven by data sources that do not distinguish between full-time and part-time employment.

Writer's Workshop

The following items may be sentence fragments or contain errors in punctuation, subject-verb agreement, pronoun-antecedent agreement, infinitive use, abbreviations, number display, capitalization, spelling, word choice, possessives, modifier clarity and placement, or parallelism. Rewrite the sentences to make them correct.

1. Miss Beth Hustad and here husband Mark have volunteered at the summer olympics for the passed twelve years.
2. Jerry only spent $25.00 for tickets to the consert.
3. While locking the door to the store the fire alarm sounded.
4. What is the name of that cozy bussling café on St Charles street in Seattle?
5. What do Lincoln Nebraska Springfield Missouri and Des Moines have in common.
6. Although ice cream comes in many, exhotic flavors Celeste choses vanilla.
7. Every member will receive their ballot by the fist of June and must return it by june 31.
8. Cliff successfully resigned Doctor Tim Bates and Paula Schroeder, m.d. to three-year contracts.
9. Seth promised to quickly compleat the tasks assigned to him.
10. Please e-mail Jeff or myself, when last quarters' sails figures are available.

Chapter 11
Proposals, Business Plans, and Special Reports

LET'S TALK BUSINESS

Proposals are key to our business success. We wrote about 200 the first year we were in business; now, eight years later, we write over 3,000 proposals a year. Each of those proposals must be designed for the prospective client for whom it is prepared. Audience analysis is essential to determining what will best meet the customer's needs. Clear, complete proposals help to establish us and our business as professional, organized, and reliable.

Typically, the proposals we prepare fall into three categories.

Project proposals. These lengthy documents describe the scope of the work we will do and the timeline we will follow.

Complete system proposals. By providing thorough descriptions and itemizing costs, we allow potential customers to compare the quality and price of our equipment against that of other vendors.

Individual component proposals. These brief proposals focus on replacement devices or on accessories the customer may want to use with an existing system.

Service has and will continue to be our competitive advantage. Service begins with submitting a high-quality proposal.

Sean M. Dean and Steven M. Dastoor, Co-owners, Citon Computer Corp.

Photo courtesy of Sean Dean and Steven Dastoor

Formal reports are not the only structured documents used within organizations. Proposals and business plans fall into this category, as do a variety of special reports. Each of these document types is discussed in this chapter.

Proposals

Businesspeople look for initiative. They welcome suggestions about how to change things for the better, to improve productivity, or to enhance profitability. Those suggestions often come in the form of a **proposal**—a persuasive message in which a writer analyzes a problem and recommends a solution. The problem may be a need for equipment, services, research, a plan of action, or other things. The recommended solution may be products, personnel, a business study, a description of work to be performed, or other outcomes. As Sean Dean and Steven Dastoor show in Let's Talk Business, proposals are common in business, and it is important that they be clear, be concise, and meet reader expectations.

Proposals are gambles. They take time to develop and often are rejected. Some proposal developers believe that they are doing well if they win acceptance of one of every ten proposals. Effective proposal writers are risk takers; they assess the probability of success and then decide whether to proceed.

LO 1

Identify the different types of proposals.

NOTE 11.1
Proposals describe problems and offer solutions to them.

Types of Proposals

Proposals can be informal or formal, internal or external, unsolicited or solicited.

Informal proposals generally take the form of letters (external) or memos (internal). **Formal proposals** are highly structured documents that have many of the features found in formal reports. The appearance complements the content and adds to the overall impression the document is intended to create.

Proposals sent to others within an organization are **internal proposals.** These can be proposals to solve problems or to meet needs by improving procedures, changing products, adding personnel, reorganizing departments, expanding facilities, reducing budgets, or making other changes. Ideas for internal improvement, creatively developed and effectively presented, are the lifeblood of organizations.

External proposals go outside an organization to current or prospective customers, to government agencies, or to private agencies and foundations. These messages include proposals to supply products at given prices, to build roads, or to perform audits. This category also encompasses requests for grants of money or goods

NOTE 11.2
Proposals may be
• **Informal or formal**
• **Internal or external**
• **Unsolicited or solicited**

Dilbert by Scott Adams

to support the work of not-for-profit agencies or other groups hoping to meet some societal or humanitarian need. Such requests are submitted to foundations established solely for the purpose of funding projects in areas such as the arts, education, the environment, or human services. They are submitted also to corporations, whose missions often include returning a portion of their profits to the communities or regions in which they do business.

Proposals prepared at the writer's initiative are called **unsolicited proposals.** These proposals represent an independent analysis of another's problems or needs and the creation of possible solutions. Unsolicited proposals may be internal or external. When submitting proposals to foundations or government agencies, the writer must match the goals of his or her organization to those of the foundation or agency.

A **solicited proposal** is prepared in response to a request. The solicitation may be made face-to-face, by telephone, or in writing. Solicited proposals may be internal or external, formal or informal; the same is true of the response. Consider these examples:

- During a meeting, a manager describes a staffing problem and asks department heads to consider the problem and e-mail their proposed solutions to the manager by the end of the week. (informal request; informal response)
- A sales representative phones a client to promote a new or upgraded product. In response, the client says, "Sounds interesting. Put the proposal in writing, and we'll talk about it." (informal request; formal response)
- A package delivery company that plans to replace ten of its vans prepares a Request for Proposal and invites area truck dealerships to reply. (formal request; formal response)

Contents of an Effective Proposal Request

LO 2
Write formal proposal requests.

NOTE 11.3
RFPs help both the writer's and the receiver's organization.

A **Request for Proposal** (RFP) is a formal document that describes a project, product, or service need (problem) and invites potential suppliers to propose solutions. Requests for Information (RFIs), Requests for Bid (RFBs), and Requests for Quotation (RFQs) are similar documents that include similar sections.

A comprehensive, well-written RFP helps both the writer and the responder. The person who issues the RFP benefits because the proposals he or she receives will contain comparable material presented in a comparable format. These features reduce the time needed to review and evaluate the proposals. Those who respond to the RFP benefit because they know what is required and can show how they or their organization can solve the problem efficiently and effectively at a fair cost.

Although the content of a proposal request may vary by organization and purpose, the following items are generally included:

- *Introduction.* The introduction provides background information that profiles your company (e.g., location, goals, size, etc.). It describes the purpose of the proposal request.

- *Project/product/service description.* This section states as specifically as possible what you hope to accomplish or what you need. It describes how the products will be used; includes examples as appropriate; uses clear, accurate descriptions; and avoids using jargon.

- *Vendor requirements* (if any). This section states specific requirements for vendors. For example, you might seek proposals only from vendors in a particular geographic area or only from vendors who have particular levels of experience.
- *Restrictions* (if any). This section lists and explains the time, budget, or other constraints under which you are operating with respect to the topic of the proposal. Including a schedule or stating deadlines will help readers determine whether they can meet your requirements.
- *Proposal guidelines*. The guidelines state what you expect the proposal to include and in what order/format it should be presented.
- *Evaluation criteria*. This section indicates the general qualities of a winning proposal. Although you won't reveal the specific weighting you allocate to each criterion, vendors will appreciate knowing the general parameters for selecting the successful proposal. For example, is time more important than cost? Is safety more important than time? Will the low bidder be offered a contract?
- *Confidentiality statement*. The confidentiality statement indicates whether any, some, or all of the vendor's proposal will be kept confidential and for how long. This section states any expectations you have about whether the receiver should treat information in your proposal as confidential.
- *Submission/contact information*. This section states the deadline for submitting proposals and the date on which the decision will be made or announced. It identifies and provides contact information for the individual to whom questions should be addressed. It also specifies how and to whom the proposal should be submitted.

Accepting a proposal in response to an RFP does not constitute a contract. The information in the documents can, however, become the basis for negotiating the terms of a contract.

Figure 11.1 shows part of a Request for Information. Its purpose is to narrow the field of companies interested in bidding for a consulting contract. The full RFI is available at www.thomsonedu.com/bcomm/krizan. As you review the document, notice the elements it includes and the way each is addressed.

Qualities of a Successful Proposal

Successful proposals have qualities that separate them from unsuccessful proposals. Although success sometimes depends on factors such as luck, politics, timing, and reputation, most proposals must have excellent content and be presented clearly to be accepted. The following qualities usually are required for a successful proposal:

- The purpose of the proposal is stated clearly.
- The problem or need is understood and defined clearly.
- The solution is innovative and presented convincingly.
- The benefits outweigh the costs.
- The personnel implementing the solution are qualified.
- The solution can be achieved on a timely basis.
- The proposal is honest, factual, realistic, and objective.
- The presentation is professional and attractive.

LO 3
Write formal and informal proposals.

NOTE 11.4
Successful proposals have excellent content that is presented clearly.

FIGURE 11.1
Request for Information

DAHL GLASS

DAHL GLASS

Request for Information

Consulting

May 9, 2007

FIGURE 11.1
Request for Information, *continued*

DAHL Glass

i

FIGURE 11.1
Request for Information,
continued

DAHL GLASS

A. *Overview*

Dahl Glass is currently evaluating consulting organizations to assess their ability to assist the company in developing and implementing its global operations vision. Dahl's operations include the following departments: manufacturing, logistics, production planning, customer service, purchasing, engineering, and quality assurance.

Dahl is a multimillion-dollar manufacturer and distributor of industrial glassware headquartered in Utah. The company's U.S. manufacturing facilities are located in Utah, New Jersey, Ohio, North Carolina, and California. Sales representatives are located throughout the country. International plant operations are located in Canada, Mexico, England, France, Germany, and China; distribution centers are located in Brazil and Colombia. Dahl Glass has approximately 1,700 employees worldwide.

The purpose of this Request for Information (RFI) is to gather data that will narrow the field of choices of consulting organizations. All information contained in this RFI is confidential and may not be used for any reason other than responding to this questionnaire.

Table 1
Global Locations and Enterprise Resource Planning (ERP) Implementation Dates*

Location	ERP Implementation Date	Widgets Produced Annually
United States	5/2004	1,200,000
Canada	2/2004	80,000
Mexico	12/2004	40,000
United Kingdom	10/2005	130,000
France & Germany	7/2005	70,000
China	NA	60,000
South America (Brazil & Colombia)	NA	50,000

*Full Suite of ERP modules implemented on the above dates.

1

FIGURE 11.1
Request for Information, *concluded.* The entire RFI is available at http://thomsonedu.com/bcomm/krizan.

DAHL GLASS

B.   *Format and Guidelines*

Responses should be as brief as possible, supplying only the requested information and eliminating any standard response material that does not directly address the issues contained in the RFI.

Your information must be submitted using the supplied Microsoft Word document. Responses should be returned via electronic mail.

Assume all potential contracts will be effective **August 1, 2007**.

Your response will be assumed to comply fully with all terms and conditions of this RFI. Any exceptions must be described clearly in a separate section at the front of your response, even if they are identified elsewhere in the document.

Your request for information must be received no later than *5 p.m. on Tuesday, May 31.*

Submit your response to:

Office of Operations
gnewton@dahlglass.com

A special conference call will be conducted at 2 p.m. on Tuesday, May 24, to answer any questions you may have about the Request for Information. The conference call number is 800.555.7150. The password is *newton.*

Dahl Glass will treat all information that you mark confidential as such, but the company does not assume liability for the disposition of the information contained within your response.

Please note that any costs associated with responding to this RFI are the sole responsibility of the responding organization. This RFI in no way obligates Dahl Glass to enter into a business arrangement with you until the execution of a contract. You also agree that Dahl Glass will neither incur any obligation nor make any commitment to you in connection with this RFI.

2

To convey these qualities in the proposal, the writer must carefully analyze the situation and the receivers, use the you–viewpoint, and apply the principles of business communication.

NOTE 11.5
Proposals should be powerful, persuasive messages.

The proposal should be a powerful, persuasive message. The receivers will look for the benefits to them, their department, the company, the community, society, or some other group to which they belong. The proposal should get the receivers' attention, show clearly the benefits of accepting the proposal, give proof of those benefits, and motivate favorable action.

The Elements of a Formal Proposal

NOTE 11.6
Successful proposals contain specific elements.

Items contained in a proposal vary with the situation and the reader. In solicited proposals, the elements are specified in the RFP. Careful and complete responses should be made to all the elements requested in the RFP. If you think elements necessary to the acceptance of your proposal are missing from the RFP, then you should try to work those parts into the specified format. In unsolicited proposals, you must decide which elements to include. What follows is a list of possible proposal elements:

- Cover letter or memo
- Title page or cover
- Reference to authorization
- Table of contents
- List of illustrations
- Proposal summary
- Purpose
- Problem or need
- Background
- Benefits of the proposal
- Description of the solution
- Evaluation plan
- Qualifications of personnel
- Time schedule
- Cost
- Glossary
- Appendixes
- Reference list

Although all these elements are important for many large proposals, the key elements are the purpose, problem or need, benefits of implementing the solution, description of the solution, qualifications of personnel, time schedule, and cost. All the proposal elements are described in the following sections.

COVER LETTER OR MEMO

NOTE 11.7
The cover letter or memo highlights the contents and encourages action.

The **cover letter** or **memo,** also referred to as a *transmittal message*, introduces the proposal to the reader. A letter is used for an external proposal and a memo for an internal proposal. The cover letter or memo should include content that provides coherence for the reader, reviews the highlights of the proposal, and encourages action.

TITLE PAGE OR COVER

The information contained on the **title page** or **cover** of a proposal can include some or all of the following items: title of the proposal, name and location of the receiver, name and location of the submitter, date of submission, principal investigator, proposed cost, and proposed duration of the project. Consider the image and culture of the receiving organization, and design the cover with those factors in mind. Design features such as color and graphics may be appropriate for some receivers but not others.

The title should be concise, preferably under ten words. Consider which of the six "W and H" questions—what? when? where? who? why? how?—must be answered by the title. The title of the proposal should attract the reader's attention and, because it will be used to identify the proposal, easy to remember. Eliminate meaningless words such as "A Study of" or "An Examination of"; use descriptive adjective–noun combinations.

REFERENCE TO AUTHORIZATION

If the proposal is solicited, the request should be noted in a **reference to authorization**—the permission or request for the proposal. The information contained in the reference to authorization depends on the RFP. For an informal or short RFP, the reference could be as simple as listing the RFP number on the cover or including a line in the cover letter or memo stating "This proposal is in response to your telephone call of May 5, 200–." For a formal RFP, the reference to authorization could be one or more pages following the title page or cover. A lengthy RFP may require an abstract as a reference to authorization.

NOTE 11.8
If the proposal is solicited, its authorization should be noted.

TABLE OF CONTENTS

The **table of contents** lists the titles and page numbers of all the major sections of the proposal. It will assist in orienting readers and will help them locate specific information. The names and page numbers of the appendixes are also included in the table of contents.

LIST OF ILLUSTRATIONS

The titles and page numbers of any tables, figures, graphs, or other illustrations are placed in a **list of illustrations** immediately following the table of contents.

PROPOSAL SUMMARY

The **proposal summary** is the proposal in capsule form. This section, which contains the most vital information from each of the major sections of the proposal, is prepared after the proposal has been written. It should be short. The summary is designed to give busy people a quick but complete overview of the proposal. For short proposals, the summary may be just a paragraph. For a long proposal of 100 to 500 pages, the summary might be one to ten pages. If the RFP specifies a length, be sure to make the summary that length and no longer.

NOTE 11.9
The summary provides an overview of the proposal.

PURPOSE

Following the summary, the actual proposal begins. The purpose should be stated first. The **purpose statement** helps the reader understand clearly (a) the reason you are making the proposal and (b) the nature of the proposal—how it will accomplish the purpose. Example purpose statements follow:

NOTE 11.10
The purpose statement clearly describes the reason for and nature of the proposal.

This is a proposal to reduce manufacturing costs 10 percent by replacing the Assembly Line A conveyor system.

The purpose of this proposal is to increase sales by adding commission sales personnel.

The purpose of this proposal is to improve the environment of the Madison Animal Shelter by securing funding to replace the unreliable, 20-year-old air-conditioning system.

These purpose statements may stand alone or they may be followed by brief explanations. The amount of explanation given depends on the reader's knowledge and his or her need for information.

PROBLEM OR NEED

NOTE 11.11
State the problem being
solved or the need
being met.

The next section should describe the problem being solved or the need being met. This section should use coherence techniques to link it to the section in which the purpose was stated. For example, the first purpose statement given in the previous section might be followed by a problem statement such as the following:

Manufacturing costs for the second quarter are up 5 percent over the first quarter. Most of this cost increase can be attributed to the new labor agreement that became effective March 1. To meet competition, we must find new ways to reduce manufacturing costs.

BACKGROUND

NOTE 11.12
Limit background
information to what the
reader needs.

If necessary for your reader's complete understanding, you should provide background data on the problem. The background section may be combined with the problem/need section or, if both sections are long, it can be presented separately. In the **background** section, you may explain the problem—how it developed, its magnitude, and the consequences if nothing is done.

BENEFITS OF THE PROPOSAL

NOTE 11.13
Benefits of implementing
the solution must outweigh
the costs.

The **benefits of the proposal** represent the outcomes of implementing the proposed solution. The benefits must be stated in the you–viewpoint; they must clearly serve the interests of the reader and/or the reader's organization. The benefits must outweigh their cost. (The cost data will be given later in the proposal.) If your proposal is competing with other proposals, the benefits you cite must be more cost-effective than your competitors' benefits for your proposal to be the winning one.

When presenting the benefits of the proposal, use the emphasis techniques discussed in Chapter 4, but be careful not to overstate the benefits. Make them concrete, realistic, and honest.

DESCRIPTION OF THE SOLUTION

The **description of the solution** should specify what you are proposing be done, who will do it, when it will be done, where it is to be done, how it will be done, and why it should be done. As mentioned earlier, proposals submitted in response to an RFP must provide all the information called for in the request.

Because the solution to the problem is the most important section in the proposal, it will likely be the largest section. This part of the proposal must tie coherently to the information given previously in the proposal. The writer must refer to the purpose, the problem or need, and the benefits of the proposal. The solution must be presented so clearly that readers will understand it and be convinced that it achieves the purpose, solves the problem, and provides the benefits cited earlier.

You will want to stress the innovative aspects of your proposal, the special nature of the resources you are recommending, and the strength of your solution's rationale. Show how these features of your proposal fit your reader's needs or mission. A good way to do this is to relate your solutions directly to each of the benefits given earlier. Those benefits might be listed individually, with each followed by an appropriate part of the description of the solution. The intent is to show clearly that (a) you have carefully thought through all aspects of the proposed solution; (b) it represents a realistic, feasible, and desirable way of solving the problem or meeting the need; and (c) you, your department, or your organization is capable of implementing the solution.

NOTE 11.14
Be sure the description is realistic and persuasive.

EVALUATION PLAN

If appropriate for your proposal, you will want to include an evaluation plan. The **evaluation plan** is a way to measure the degree of success achieved if your proposal is implemented. The evaluation plan could consist of a recordkeeping system; a review by a panel of experts; statistical analysis procedures; a reporting system; or any number of control, analysis, measurement, or judgment techniques.

An evaluation plan is a major element in proposals for research studies. In other proposals, such as increased staffing proposals, the evaluation system might be an employee performance review procedure already in place. In this case, only a brief reference to the existing plan would be needed.

NOTE 11.15
An evaluation plan provides a way to judge the success of proposal implementation.

QUALIFICATIONS OF PERSONNEL

In the **qualifications of personnel** section, you provide biographical information about each key participant involved in implementing the proposal. You show his or her qualifications to provide the services proposed. The information should include the education, experience, accomplishments, successes, and evidence of achievement that directly relate to each participant's involvement in the proposed solution. You are justifying to the reader that these persons are fully qualified to serve in their assigned roles. The appropriate types of data are discussed in detail in the résumé preparation section of Chapter 16.

Depending on the nature of the proposal, the amount of data presented for each individual will vary from a few lines to several pages. In some proposals, brief summaries are presented in the qualifications of personnel section and full résumés are provided in an appendix. If you are responding to an RFP, provide exactly the amount and type of personnel information specified.

TIME SCHEDULE

The **time schedule** is a realistic indication of when activity is to start and when it is to be completed. For simple proposals, the time schedule may consist of a listing of activities and their beginning and ending dates. For elaborate proposals, it may be necessary to use more complex task-time analysis charts such as Gantt, PERT (Program Evaluation Review Technique), or Milestone. If you need assistance in selecting a time-schedule format, most libraries have good reference materials you can use.

COST

The **cost** is the price of the proposed solution. This section may be labeled *Cost, Prices,* or *Budget,* or it may be given another appropriate title. The cost may be presented in logical parts, such as personnel, supplies, equipment, and facilities, or it may be organized by benefits, parts of the description of the solution, time phases, or other appropriate categories.

The cost of the proposed solution must cover your expenses and, if appropriate, a profit. It also must be reasonable in relation to the benefits and the products or services to be provided. If you are following the guidelines in an RFP, the format for the cost section will likely be specified and should be used.

GLOSSARY

Based on a careful analysis of your readers, you may decide to include a glossary in your proposal. A **glossary** lists alphabetically and defines the unfamiliar terms used in the proposal. Include a glossary only when many unfamiliar, specialized, or technical terms have to be used. If there are only a few such terms, define them the first time they are used.

APPENDIXES

NOTE 11.16
Complex supporting information is shown in the appendixes.

To keep the body of the proposal as short and readable as possible, it is sometimes appropriate to place complex supporting information in an appendix. An **appendix** contains items that are indirectly related to the proposal but are excluded from the body to improve readability.

It was suggested earlier that résumés of key personnel might appropriately be placed in an appendix. Other information that might be placed in appendixes includes your organization's history, product specifications, records of past successes with similar projects, letters of support, details that support information in the description section, a questionnaire to be used for the proposed research, or other supporting and reference materials.

NOTE 11.17
Limit appendixes to information that is essential to the reader's needs.

An RFP may specify what appendixes are to be included. Be sure to include only those appendixes essential to the reader's understanding and decision making. If the proposal becomes too bulky, it will be less acceptable to a potential approver, funder, or purchaser.

REFERENCE LIST

If you think it strengthens your case, include a reference list in the proposal. A **reference list** is an alphabetical listing of all sources of information in the proposal, including those items presented as text citations or footnotes.

Writing a Proposal

The task of writing a long, complex proposal may be assigned to a team. When proposal writing is a collaborative effort, it is important to have one chief writer—someone who will be responsible for ensuring consistency and coherence within the document. As suggested in the Tips and Hints feature at the top of page 317, a solo author may ask others to read the proposal before it is finalized and submitted.

Whether written by one person or a team, proposals—like correspondence and reports—require planning. The principles of business communication must be applied as the document is planned, drafted, and finalized.

tips and hints

Get a Cold Reader Review

Writers can become so involved with proposals that they are unable to judge them objectively. To avoid the problem created by close association with the work, a proposal writer should seek the help of a "cold" reader—someone who hasn't worked on the project. The reader should review the RFP or selection criteria and then read the proposal to determine whether all points have been addressed clearly and completely. Asking the reader to summarize the major sections will help determine which, if any, parts of the proposal need to be revised.

Format, too, plays a part in readability and can help to generate interest in the proposal. Headings, margin notes, bullet points, outlines, charts, and diagrams can serve as signs to guide the reader. White space can help to highlight important items.

NOTE 11.18
Use format to enhance readability.

Figure 11.2 is an example of a **poor** internal proposal. This chapter's suggestions for writing successful proposals are not implemented in this memo. An improved proposal for the same situation is shown in Figure 11.3. This example of a **good** informal proposal follows the guidelines for developing and writing successful proposals.

When Henry Wolcot was assigned the task of locating and negotiating a contract for accommodations for an annual meeting for his company, he sent an informal but detailed e-mail request to 14 hotels in six major cities on the East Coast. Figure 11.4 is an example of one of the responses he received—it is an example of a **good** external proposal.

The situation surrounding the message in Figure 11.4 involved representatives of two for-profit businesses. Not-for-profit organizations also engage in proposal writing. An example of a proposal from Goodwill Industries to a private foundation is posted at the website for this text: www.thomsonedu.com/bcomm/krizan.

Proposals are the way that new ideas are conveyed to decision makers. Most of the recommendations in this section on proposals apply to both written and oral proposals. Successful businesspeople develop and submit many proposals during their careers. They are not deterred by rejections. Instead, they follow the suggestion in the Tips and Hints below and try to improve their skills. They keep developing and submitting proposals and realize professional and personal gains when their proposals are accepted.

NOTE 11.19
Well-written proposals can help you advance your career.

tips and hints

When the Answer Is No

If your grant proposal is turned down, learn from the experience:

- Contact a representative of the funding agency and ask to see the reviewers' comments. The comments will help you identify things you will want to change in future submissions.
- Read the summaries of projects that were funded. What did those proposal writers do that you didn't?
- Revise the proposal and submit it to another agency.

needs work

VALLEY
PUBLISHING
COMPANY

Tel: (435) 555-0366   Fax: (435) 555-6630

1222 Century Drive   Logan, Utah 84341

DATE: August 2, 200–

TO: VPC Board of Directors

FROM: Milly Vincent, Public Relations Director *MV*

Subject line is not specific.

SUBJECT: MEETING ROOMS

Based on the number of phone calls and letters I've received during the past few months, I think it would be a good idea if we let folks from the community use our meeting rooms. Now that the Mountain Community Club is gone and the library is being remodeled, someone has to step up to fill the gap, and I think it should be us. What would we gain by letting groups meet here? Good PR . . . something no organization ever has too much of.

Purpose statement is weak; problem is vague.

Let me know soon whether you like this idea, and I'll gather the data needed to determine how much we should charge for our rooms.

FIGURE 11.2
Example of a *Poor* Internal Proposal

Business Plans

LO 4
Draft a business plan.

NOTE 11.20
Business plans are special-purpose proposals.

A **business plan** is a special type of proposal, one designed to persuade a financial institution or a private party to invest money to support a particular venture. The investment may be in a start-up company or in a business that wishes to expand. The plan provides all the information necessary for the project to be evaluated by the funding source.

This section contains a brief description of what a business plan contains and offers several presentation suggestions. When faced with the task of developing a busi-

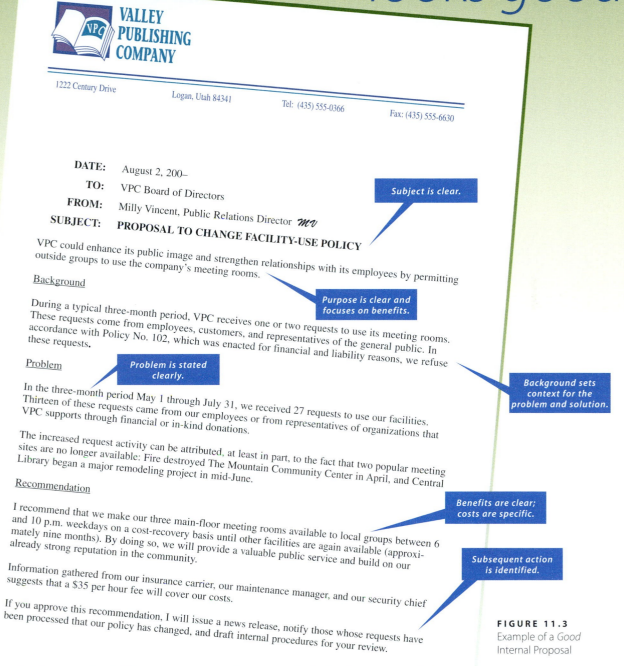

looks good

VALLEY PUBLISHING COMPANY

1222 Century Drive   Logan, Utah 84341   Tel: (435) 555-0366   Fax: (435) 555-6630

DATE: August 2, 200–
TO: VPC Board of Directors
FROM: Milly Vincent, Public Relations Director *mv*
SUBJECT: **PROPOSAL TO CHANGE FACILITY-USE POLICY**

VPC could enhance its public image and strengthen relationships with its employees by permitting outside groups to use the company's meeting rooms.

Background

During a typical three-month period, VPC receives one or two requests to use its meeting rooms. These requests come from employees, customers, and representatives of the general public. In accordance with Policy No. 102, which was enacted for financial and liability reasons, we refuse these requests.

Problem

In the three-month period May 1 through July 31, we received 27 requests to use our facilities. Thirteen of these requests came from our employees or from representatives of organizations that VPC supports through financial or in-kind donations.

The increased request activity can be attributed, at least in part, to the fact that two popular meeting sites are no longer available: Fire destroyed The Mountain Community Center in April, and Central Library began a major remodeling project in mid-June.

Recommendation

I recommend that we make our three main-floor meeting rooms available to local groups between 6 and 10 p.m. weekdays on a cost-recovery basis until other facilities are again available (approximately nine months). By doing so, we will provide a valuable public service and build on our already strong reputation in the community.

Information gathered from our insurance carrier, our maintenance manager, and our security chief suggests that a $35 per hour fee will cover our costs.

If you approve this recommendation, I will issue a news release, notify those whose requests have been processed that our policy has changed, and draft internal procedures for your review.

Subject is clear.
Purpose is clear and focuses on benefits.
Background sets context for the problem and solution.
Problem is stated clearly.
Benefits are clear; costs are specific.
Subsequent action is identified.

FIGURE 11.3
Example of a *Good* Internal Proposal

ness plan, most people consult an accountant or a business development specialist. Numerous print and electronic resources are also available to provide background information beyond what is available here. In addition, agencies such as the Small Business Administration (SBA) provide free or low-cost services. The SBA's website at http://www.sba.gov is one of many online that provide sample business plans.

Although the actual format and organization may vary, a business plan will contain the following elements:

NOTE 11.21
Financial institutions expect business plans to contain certain information.

319

FIGURE 11.4
Example of *Good*
External Proposal

546 West Cork Street Baltimore, MD 21214

March 14, 2006

Mr. Henry Wolcot
Travel Director
Columbia Engineering
672 Elm Drive
Springfield, MO 66806

Dear Mr. Wolcot:

CONFERENCE ACCOMMODATION PROPOSAL
September 26 – October 4, 2006 (arrival/checkout)

Thank you for your interest in holding your 2006 meeting at The Harbor Hotel. We are excited
about the possibility of hosting your group.

The net, non-commissionable rates quoted in this proposal (including attachments) are valid
only for the dates specified in your RFI; should the dates of your meeting change, we request
the opportunity to submit a new proposal.

Guest Rooms
60 Single/Double Deluxe Rooms (25-room minimum) $155 + 12.5% tax (each)

Your attendees will appreciate the comfort and convenience The Harbor offers. Each room has
two double beds; a sofa; a desk area; two multi-line telephones with speaker, data ports, and
voice mail; and an in-room safe. Coffee and the daily newspaper are complimentary. Guests
may purchase day passes ($10 each) to Harbor Gym, located within a block of the hotel.

The Harbor is conveniently located near tourist attractions, downtown shopping, and numerous
five-star restaurants.

Meeting Space
The following meeting spaces have been tentatively reserved for your group. Because we appreciate your room and catering business, *meeting rooms are complimentary.*

Date	Time	Number of Participants	Room Setup
Wednesday, September 27; Thursday, September 28; Friday, September 29; and Monday, October 2	8 a.m. to 5 p.m.	60	Classroom (tables and chairs)
Wednesday, September 27; Thursday, September 28; Friday, September 29; and Monday, October 2	8 a.m. to 5 p.m.	20	Classroom (tables and chairs)

FIGURE 11.4
Example of *Good*
External Proposal
continued

Mr. Henry Wolcot   -2-   March 14, 2006

Catering (See enclosed menus for choices and pricing.)

Date	Event	Time	Number of Participants
Wednesday, September 27; Thursday, September 28; Friday, September 29; Monday, October 2; and Tuesday, October 3	Lunch Buffet	Noon to 1:30 p.m.	60
Wednesday, September 27; Thursday, September 28	Dinner Buffet	7 p.m. to 11 p.m.	80
Weekdays September 27 through Tuesday, October 3	Breaks	10 to 10:30 a.m. 3 to 3:30 p.m.	80

Contract

The rates in this proposal are available through 4:30 p.m. (EDT) April 15, 2006. After receiving confirmation that you accept our proposal and after learning your catering preferences, we will submit a contract for your signature. A 50 percent deposit will be due when the signed contract is submitted.

We are very interested in having Columbia Engineering hold its event at The Harbor Hotel. To learn more about our property and to view photos of our guest and meeting rooms, visit our website at www.TheHarborHotel.com. Should you need additional information, we will provide it.

Sincerely,

Natalee G. Former

Natalee G. Former
Sales Manager

Enclosures: Menus

- *Executive summary.* The executive summary describes the highlights of the plan and helps capture the interest of the reader. It provides a brief, crisp introduction that discusses the nature of the business and its proposed location, how much funding you need and why, and the period for which money is needed.
- *Ownership/management/staffing description.* This section describes the proposed ownership and legal structure; it gives information about the experience, skills, training, and qualifications of key personnel.
- *Product/service/market identification.* This section identifies the size, location, demographics, and other relevant information about your market. It explains your pricing strategy and how you plan to advertise and market your product or service.
- *Administration/production factors.* This section provides information about equipment and facilities, production techniques, quality control mechanisms, management structure, accounting systems and controls, and any other factors specific to your product or service.
- *Growth and development potential and plans.* This part of the business plan presents a one- or two-year projection linked to improving or expanding products, services, or markets. It describes changes in required staffing and identifies additional investment that might be required.
- *Financial information.* The financial section provides detailed, realistic information about how much the project will cost, money that will be provided through other sources, and what financial security you can offer lenders. This section contains a one-year monthly operating budget and cash flow projection. It also forecasts a first-year return on investment, identifies the breakeven point, and supplies projected income statements and balance sheets for two years.
- *Appendixes.* Documents that relate to or further explain or support the plan are included in an appendix or appendixes. Résumés of key personnel, letters of intent, and copies of contracts or leases are among the items that may be included.

As you can tell from the item descriptions, the business plan is a complex document—one that poses a writing challenge. Like other forms of business writing, the business plan should reflect the principles of business communication and show evidence of thorough planning. Because a business plan is a persuasive message, it should contain the attention, interest, desire, and action elements described in Chapter 9. It also should be designed to reflect a professional image. The Tips and Hints offers suggestions related to these topics. A business plan related to the establishment of a

tips and hints

Business Plan Do's

- Keep your plan concise—20 to 40 single-spaced pages plus appendixes.
- Make sure the plan is easy to read and to understand—use headings and tabbed dividers.
- Eliminate typographical and grammatical errors.
- Accurately describe the market opportunities for the business.
- Acknowledge and address the risks involved.
- Convey the strength and depth of your management team.

- Explain your assumptions; make certain they are realistic.
- Limit your use of jargon and technical details. Define any terms you must use.
- Refrain from providing highly confidential or proprietary information.
- Use professional packaging (cover sheet, binding) that reflects the type of business you are proposing; gimmicks detract from content.

permanent structure for a farmers' market is begun in Figure 11.5 and shown in full on the Web at www.thomsonedu.com/bcomm/krizan.

Special Reports

Some business reports require special content or format considerations. Three common special reports are policies, news releases, and performance appraisals. A fourth common special report, minutes, is included with the discussion of meetings in Chapter 13.

LO 5
Develop clear policy statements.

Policies

A **policy statement** serves as a guideline for employees, customers, or others to follow.

Policy statements affecting employees normally will be assembled into a manual or posted to the Web. This manual can be used to orient new employees and can serve as a reference for long-time employees. Policies affecting customers may be posted in a highly visible location or printed on transaction documents. A retail store's return policy, for example, could be printed on a cash register receipt or on a card that is attached to the receipt at the time of sale. An emergency closing policy such as the one shown in Figure 11.6 might be contained in a manual, posted at a prominent place in the building, and/or posted to the organization's website.

Policy statements should be written in the third person and should be clear, concise, and complete. Policies written for managerial personnel are broad guides that allow flexibility; policies for nonmanagerial personnel are narrower and more restrictive.

NOTE 11.22
Policies should be broad for managerial personnel and specific for nonmanagerial personnel.

News Releases

A **news release** is a special business report containing information that will be of interest to the public. News releases need to be newsworthy, accurate, timely, concise, and positive. Common subjects for news releases include employee hires, promotions, or achievements; business expansion; employee layoffs; product recalls; and introduction of new products.

LO 6
Write an effective news release.

A customer returns merchandise to a retail store.

FIGURE 11.5
Business Plan

Elkhart Farmers' Market Business Plan

March 2006

Northern Indiana Sustainable Development Partnership

FIGURE 11.5
Business Plan,
continued

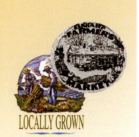

**Elkhart Market Gardeners' Association
Business Plan**
March 2006

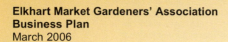

1. **Executive Summary**
2. **Business Description and Operations**
    2.1. Description of Business
        2.1.1. Mission and Objectives, Including Proposed Building Project
    2.2. Market Analysis and Strategy
        2.2.1. Competition
        2.2.2. Interpreting Survey Results
        2.2.3. Keys to Success
3. **Financial Plan**
    3.1. **Historical**
        3.1.1. Tax Returns
    3.2. **Vendor Income**
    3.3. **Financial Projections**
        3.3.1. Key Assumptions
        3.3.2. Source and Use of Funds Statement
        3.3.3. Income Statement, Balance Sheet, Cash Flow
            3.3.3.1. 2005–2006
            3.3.3.2. 2006–2007
            3.3.3.3. 2007–2008
            3.3.3.4. Further 2-Year Projections
        3.3.4. Depreciation
4. **Non-Market Issues**
    4.1. WIC
    4.2. EMGA and Benefits to the Local Community

EMGA Business Plan
i

FIGURE 11.5
Business Plan, *continued*.
The full business
plan is available at
http://thomsonedu.com/
bcomm/krizan.

:ommunity will benefit in many ways from supporting the Elkhart Farmers'
at and its affiliated organization, the Elkhart Market Gardeners' Association
;A). As noted in the marketing strategy section of this plan, the presence of
ing farmers' market is perceived to provide the surrounding community with
isiasm for information about nutrition and sustainable agriculture; social
ction in a vibrant community space; economic development for local
ice growers; tourism-related retail opportunities for local crafters and
ns; new business opportunities for startup businesses; employment and
ation for youth; and federal program support such as the USDA's Women,
s, and Children's Program and the Senior Farmers' Market Nutrition
am.

irsue these opportunities, the EMGA has filed for status as a 501(c)(3)
ofit organization, collected survey data on the Elkhart Farmers' Market
ties, and developed a market business plan that includes fund-raising for a
ng project.

EMGA Business Plan
1

	Winter County Library	Policy: 37
		Passed: 01/08/1996
		Modified: 11/12/2004

EMERGENCY CLOSINGS

This policy shall apply in the event of an emergency such as severe weather, utility failure, fire, or terrorism.
- **The safety of library personnel and patrons will be the primary consideration in the decision to close.**
- **The Director or Assistant Director, working in collaboration with public safety departments and emergency service providers, shall have the authority to close the facility.**
- **In the event of a closure, the Director or Assistant Director shall notify local news media.**
- **In the event of a closure, the Director or Assistant Director shall prepare and submit a closure report to the Library Board of Trustees.**

FIGURE 11.6
Policy Statement

The **inverted pyramid format** should be used for news releases. The inverted pyramid format begins with a summary lead that tells who, what, where, when, and sometimes why or how. Develop the body of the release by giving the details in descending order of importance. This organizational pattern respects both news agency personnel, who will cut material from the bottom to meet space constraints, and the general public, who may not read or listen to the entire story because of time constraints. If your release is to encourage people to attend an event, present information about location, day, date, time, and cost early in the message. Including a quote from someone associated with the announcement or event creates interest and gives the news item a personal touch.

NOTE 11.23
News releases should be written in the inverted pyramid format.

The news release should be double spaced with the company's name and address keyed or printed at the top. The contact person's name and telephone number also should be on the news release. Special instructions ("FOR IMMEDIATE RELEASE" or "FOR RELEASE ON MAY 2") should be keyed in all capital letters at the top. Notations such as "Photo attached" should be placed after the text.

Give each release a title appropriate to the content. A lively, funny title such as "Chatham Chili Cookoff is HOT, HOT, HOT!" may work well for an event, but a merger, a promotion, or a product recall needs a more professional, serious, businesslike title.

The city, state, and date should precede the text on the first line of the body. Placing the notation "-30-" or "###" beneath the last line of the text informs the news agency that the release is complete; for releases longer than one page, "more" should be printed on the bottom of each page that is to be continued. Figure 11.7 shows a sample news release.

Performance Appraisals

LO 7
Prepare a constructive performance appraisal.

A **performance appraisal** reports a supervisor's evaluation of an employee's job performance. The appraisal is a tool for providing feedback that reinforces positive behavior and identifies areas needing improvement. A written appraisal is prepared and discussed with the worker before it becomes part of his or her employment

NOTE 11.24
Performance appraisals help the employee and the organization.

FIGURE 11.7
News Release

Sanford and Bailey
Suite 212, 1314 Pine Ridge Drive Pocatello, ID 83204 208.555.7452 Fax: 206.555.2839

NEWS RELEASE

FOR IMMEDIATE RELEASE

Sanford & Bailey Expands

Pocatello, ID (February 12, 2008) Joan Armstrong and Philip Yeavil have joined Sanford & Bailey as staff accountants.

Ms. Armstrong, CPA, will specialize in trust accounting. An MBA graduate of Clark College, she has five years of experience working with estates and trusts. Mr. Yeavil will specialize in audits. He is a recent graduate of Lewis University.

Sanford and Bailey has operated in the Pocatello area since 1943. The firm provides reliable, accurate accounting service to residents and businesses throughout southern Idaho. These hires bring the number of accounting professionals employed at the firm to 31.

(Photos Attached)

CONTACT:
Pamela Boddle
208.555.6342
pboddle@SanfordBailey.net

###

---

record. Often the employee is asked to sign the appraisal to acknowledge that the supervisor has discussed it with him or her. Employees who disagree with the supervisor's appraisal may have an opportunity to write a response and have it included in the file, too. Information contained in Chapter 13 will be useful in preparing for and conducting the performance appraisal meeting.

No employee should be surprised by information contained in a written performance appraisal. Good management practice dictates that duties and expectations be conveyed to employees in advance and that informal feedback—praise, criticism, and suggestions for improvement—becomes a routine part of supervision. Nevertheless, supervisors must approach the writing of a performance appraisal as they would any other business document. They must identify the purpose, analyze the receiver, and select the appropriate approach.

An evaluation that will be received positively or neutrally should follow the direct pattern; evaluations that contain negative news should be presented indirectly. Because the appraisal will become the basis for human resource decisions such as pay raises, promotions, discipline, and terminations, assessments must be supported by factual evidence. Saying "Paul has submitted four of his last six monthly reports three to ten days after they were due" is more descriptive than "Paul does not submit reports in a timely manner."

Brevity is also a factor in preparing performance appraisals. Many organizations have developed forms that supervisors must use, and space may be limited. If

FIGURE 11.8
Performance Appraisal

Performance Appraisal

Employee: Darren Corel **Department:** Maintenance

Duty: Vacuum, sweep, or mop/scrub floors and stairs once per day as appropriate for their surface.

Standard: No visible dirt or streaks; wet surfaces are clearly marked with caution cones.

Evaluation: Darren performs his duties efficiently. Employees and guests have remarked positively on the condition of our lobby as well as the offices and hallways he maintains. During inclement weather, it can be difficult to complete regularly assigned tasks and keep the lobby safe for employees and guests. Three weeks ago, an employee slipped and nearly fell because the floor near the main door was wet.

Action/Follow-up: Darren and I will develop a strategy for handling unexpected weather-related cleaning demands and review its effectiveness within three days after the next event.

Employee's Signature: *Darren Corel* Supervisor's Signature: *Allen Blaizer*
Date Reviewed: June 16, 2007

necessary, the writer should continue his or her comments on another sheet and attach it to the form. The organization may ask the worker to sign both the form and the supplement. An honest appraisal, devoid of humor and sarcasm, is most effective. Omit comments such as "He sets low standards and consistently fails to achieve them." Figure 11.8 represents one section of a performance appraisal.

Summary of Learning Objectives

Identify the different types of proposals.

LO 1

A proposal is an analysis of a problem and a recommendation for a solution. The recommended solution may be products or personnel, a business study, work to be performed, or any of several other ways of solving a problem. Proposals may be informal or formal, internal or external, unsolicited or solicited. External proposals can be directed to prospective clients, government agencies, or private agencies/foundations.

Write formal proposal requests.

LO 2

A Request for Proposal (RFP) is issued to solicit proposals for specific projects, products, or services. A thorough, well-written RFP helps readers decide whether to apply. Proposals submitted in accordance with the requirements of an RFP should contain comparable elements presented in a comparable fashion, which makes evaluation easier.

LO 3 Write formal and informal proposals.

Proposals are common in business and must be written as persuasive messages designed to win the reader's approval of the writer's recommendation. Successful proposals must have excellent content and be clearly presented.

LO 4 Draft a business plan.

A business plan is a proposal for funding to start or expand a business. The proposal will provide information about the people, products, potential, and financing of the business. A realistic, thoughtful, well-written business plan has the greatest opportunity for success.

LO 5 Develop clear policy statements.

Policy statements serve as guidelines for the operation of a business. They should be clear, concise, and complete.

LO 6 Write an effective news release.

News releases should be written in the inverted pyramid format. The body should contain the most important facts first and least important facts last. It should not contain a conclusion.

LO 7 Prepare a constructive performance appraisal.

Performance appraisals provide feedback to workers and help them improve their performance. Appraisals typically become the basis for human resource decisions such as pay raises, promotions, discipline, and termination. Statements should be concise, clear, and concrete. Comments should be organized directly for positive or neutral evaluations and indirectly for negative evaluations. A written evaluation should be discussed with and signed by the worker to show he or she has reviewed it.

Questions for Discussion and Review

1. Refer to the Let's Talk Business feature that opens this chapter. Decide whether each of the proposals discussed there would be internal or external, unsolicited or solicited, and formal or informal. (Objective 1)
2. In what way(s) does a well-written RFP benefit the organization that issues it? How does it benefit the organization that responds? (Objective 2)
3. How does the Attention/Interest/Desire/Action plan (described in Chapter 9) for writing a persuasive message apply to writing an unsolicited internal proposal? (Objectives 1 and 3)
4. How does the purpose of a proposal's cover letter or memo differ from the purpose of the proposal's summary? (Objective 3)
5. To whom might an entrepreneur present his or her business plan? Why? (Objective 4)

6. Assume you want to start a business in the community in which your school is located. What resources are available to you—locally or through the Internet—as you approach the task of drafting a business plan? (Objective 4)

7. What purposes do policy manuals serve in organizations? (Objective 5)

8. Work with your instructor to select and locate a copy of a policy that applies to students at your school (i.e., adding/dropping a class; using the Internet to download music; posting flyers to bulletin boards) and answer the following questions about it: (Objective 5)
   a. When was the policy created and/or last modified?
   b. How are students made aware of the policy?
   c. Who enforces the policy?
   d. What, if any, penalty is applied if the policy is violated?

9. What is the inverted pyramid format? Why is it used when composing news releases? (Objective 6)

10. How can a performance appraisal help a worker? the worker's organization? (Objective 7)

Application Exercises

1. **Technology. Teamwork.** Individually or as a group, develop a proposal on one of the following topics. The proposal is to be sent to the appropriate administrator at your college. (Objectives 1 and 3)

   `TECHNOLOGY`
   `COLLABORATIVE`

   a. Installing vending machines in every campus building.
   b. Creating a separate parking lot for those who carpool.
   c. Installing more/better lighting in campus parking lots.
   d. Using pesticide-free lawn treatments.
   e. Eliminating final exams.
   f. Establishing a dress code for business students.
   g. Changing the name of the school's mascot.

2. **Teamwork.** George Urban and Helen Felix graduated from your school and later started their own business. Because they believed their education contributed to their success, they recently pledged $50,000 to the business division, payable at $5,000 a year. The only stipulations George and Helen placed on their donation are that the funds be awarded to student groups through a competitive grant process, that students set the criteria for the awards, and that students decide who receives the awards. The head of the business program has asked you to form a five-person committee charged with the task of setting the criteria for and announcing the grant opportunity. Work with four students in your class and prepare a clear, complete informal (memo, e-mail) RFP that announces the grant opportunity. Submit the message to your instructor. (Objectives 1 and 2)

   `COLLABORATIVE`

3. **Teamwork.** Refer to Application Exercise 2. As directed by your instructor, work with your group to prepare a proposal that responds to an RFP created by another group in your class. (Objectives 1 and 3)

   `COLLABORATIVE`

4. Write a proposal using all 18 proposal elements discussed in this chapter. The subject of your proposal can be (a) permitting employees to bring pets to work, (b) instituting job sharing in administrative support positions, (c) purchasing a Segway® (two-wheeled, self-balancing transportation device) for use by security staff in a shopping mall, or (d) any work-related topic approved by your instructor. (Objective 3)

5. **Technology.** You volunteer at a Boys and Girls Club in your community. The playground equipment at the club is old and potentially unsafe. You've decided to explore the possibility of applying for foundation funding to buy and install new playground equipment. Use the Internet to locate three foundations that fund proposals of this nature. (Objectives 1 and 3)

   `TECHNOLOGY`

   a. Prepare a memo to the club's director, Myron Tulley. Report your findings and volunteer to prepare the grant proposal.
   b. Prepare a grant proposal that meets the guidelines of one of the foundations.

6. **Teamwork.** As your instructor directs, work independently or as a member of a team to prepare all or selected parts of a business plan designed to obtain the funding necessary to start one of the following businesses: (Objective 4)
   a. An Internet-based business related to your major.
   b. A consignment clothing store for students on your campus.
   c. A specialty coffee shop.

7. **Technology.** Write (or e-mail) three businesses and request copies of their policy on accruing and awarding vacation leave time. Summarize your findings in a memo to your instructor. Describe the format of the policies, including whether they are numbered, dated, and so on. (Objective 5)

8. A student organization to which you belong recently returned from its national conference. One of the highlights of the conference was announcement of "Chapter of the Year"—and your group won! Prepare an appropriate news release; add details to make the release interesting. (Objective 6)

9. Interview a representative of a local newspaper or area radio or television station to learn how the organization uses news releases. If possible, obtain copies of one or two news releases received within the past month. Report your findings to the class and discuss the format/content of the releases class members obtain. (Objective 6)

10. **Teamwork.** Work with three or four of your classmates to develop a job description for the role of business communication student. Then, prepare a performance appraisal that discusses whether you meet the standards. If appropriate, include recommendations for self-improvement. (Objective 7)

Web exercises to accompany this chapter are available at **www.thomsonedu.com/ bcomm/krizan.**

MESSAGE ANALYSIS

Revise, edit, and reformat the following pet policy statement for The Shady Lake Inn.

Pet Policy

The Shady Lake Inn is a family-friendly lodging facility. Some of our guests consider their pets to be members of their family and enjoy sharing vacations with them; others have no pets or prefer to vacation without their animals. This policy has been adopted to meet the needs of both groups. Date: February 12, 200–

--only small (under 30 #; easily held or carried] healthy wellmannered dogs and cats are permitted. – When reserving a room, the guest must state that a pet will accompany them.*–Guests with pets will pay a daily $25 fee to cover the cost of additional time:effort involved in cleaning the room. *Pets may be prohibited during some holidays or during special events.—Pets are not permitted in the lobby restaurant or other common areas;--Pets must be under owner control at all times and kept in carriers or crates at knight or while their owners is out of the room. –7 outdoor excess main floor rooms will be designated "pet friendly" rooms; all other rooms will be "pet-Free.—Guests with pets will sign a Responsibility/Release agreement at check-inn.

Writer's Workshop

The following items may be sentence fragments or contain errors in punctuation, subject-verb agreement, pronoun-antecedent agreement, infinitive use, abbreviations, number display, capitalization, spelling, word choice, possessives, modifier clarity and placement, or parallelism. Rewrite the sentences to make them correct.

1. When ordering refreshments for next weeks' meeting, be sure to request fruit and bagels, as well as donuts and roles.
2. Yesterdays' **"Montgomery Monitor"** contained an article about hybrid vehicals and how there becoming popularer becuz of the energy crises.

3. Read and draft a proposal to respond too the r.f.p. from Baker Bank/ the dead-line is Thu., june 31st.

4. Each of the travelers must have their Passport ready for examination when we enter France.

5. Did Sal say it was him whom forgot to turn the copier off before leaving the office last night.

6. Jody planes to ask for a four % raise, but will be happy if she receives 3.

7. After you pass the class we will reimburse your tuition and fees; the from you must complete fill out is availabe at the HR websight.

8. Allen Gardner—the founder of Gardner granite, describes himself as "having a stone face when she tells a joke.

9. Cicily chose new carpet for her office which will be installed the 1st week of Septem.

10. Marvin budgeted allocated $2,000.00 for his trip to montreal but his expenses actuarially came too 2 thousand two hundred and 30 dollars.

Chapter 12
Visual Aids

LET'S TALK BUSINESS

As manager for one of the nation's leading engineered wood products companies, I use visual aids to help organize and simplify the information I present. Visuals provide order and sequence to information documents, as well as maintain subject continuity. Whether I am discussing market data, financial information, sales figures, or any other aspect of our company's goals, visual aids are used to underscore the highlights of key ideas. Visual aids keep me focused and prevent the omission of key points of information.

James Thomas, Vice President/General Manager, Eastern Division, Trussway Ltd.

Graphs, statistical information, and financial data presented visually to our management group reduce misinterpretation and give our operations team a clear message. Visual aids play a vital role in giving confidence to our sales and management staff when they make presentations to important clients. Visual aids add realism by giving our company the ability to import graphics.

Visual aids add the sight component to our company's business needs. Engineering and technical information can be explained, understood, and retained far easier when visual aids are used as a component of communication. Our financial team uses visual aids to communicate and compare budget information from profit-and-loss statements to actual performance. Our procurement department uses visual aids to track historical data so that market cycles can be monitored and purchases made at opportune times. Our human resources staff provides management with graphs and charts to track employee data that can visually help solve issues that might take days to interpret through timely statistical computations. Organization charts and flowcharts are used to provide an understanding of our company's management structure, process and procedure information, and job-flow information.

A **visual aid** is an illustration used to improve comprehension of a written report or oral presentation. The American Management Association found that comprehension from an oral presentation increases from about 10 percent to as high as 50 percent with the use of visual aids. This increase assumes that the visuals are well planned to help clarify major points or confusing ideas. Poorly designed, unreadable, or overly complex visuals may actually decrease the quality of the report or presentation. Visual aids may be in the form of tables, graphs, charts, drawings, photographs, diagrams, or maps. As James Thomas indicates in Let's Talk Business, visual aids can complement and increase understanding of written or oral communication. Visual aids may reduce the volume of text in written reports by displaying details or a logical sequence that clarifies and enhances the written explanation of the topic. For oral or written presentations, effective visual aids should achieve these purposes:

- Improve clarity of complex ideas.
- Improve retention of information.
- Provide interest and variety.

In this chapter, you will learn about selecting and developing effective visual aids for both written and oral communication. Visuals become an integral part of either written or oral messages and should be designed to emphasize and clarify major points.

Using Visual Aids in Reports

When used properly, visual aids help communicate ideas. Each visual added to a report should have a specific purpose: a drawing, a logo, or a photograph identifies your company; a graph shows relationships between expenses and income or indicates trends; a map shows location; a diagram displays detailed parts of a product or process; and a table provides data details too cumbersome for written text. Appropriate use and placement of visuals enhance the effectiveness of your communication.

Placement of Visual Aids

Visual aids (also referred to as *illustrations*) should be placed within the written text that relates to the topic. If space permits, place the visual on the same page with the text that refers to it. If the illustration will not fit on this page, place it on the following page. Avoid dividing a visual aid between two pages. Place the illustration on one page even if this placement separates it from the related text.

Illustrations that relate only indirectly to the copy and interest only a few readers should be placed in an appendix rather than in the body of the report. Usually, such information provides additional detail that is not essential to understanding the basic report content and could be distracting if inserted within the text of the report.

The report text refers to a visual aid prior to its appearance. This text reference is a powerful tool that guides the reader to the items you want to stress. The reference may be stated in various ways: "as shown in Figure 2," "(see Table 12)," or "Illustration 3 shows . . . ." Reference to a visual should be subtle and not distract from the text thought flow.

LO 1
Describe the purposes of visual aids in written and oral communication.

NOTE 12.1
Visual aids improve clarity, retention, interest, and variety.

NOTE 12.2
Visuals should have a purpose.

LO 2
Prepare and properly label figures and tables for written reports.

NOTE 12.3
Visuals may be illustrations, figures, or tables; place them on the page that refers to them or on the following page.

NOTE 12.4
Visuals with extra detail may go in an appendix.

NOTE 12.5
Report text refers to each visual by number.

Identification of Visual Aids

NOTE 12.6
Formatting and numbering
of visuals should be
consistent.

If a written report has more than one visual aid, all visual aids within the report should be numbered. Methods of numbering visuals vary. One method is to call all visual aids *illustrations* and number them consecutively throughout the report—Illustration 1, Illustration 2, and Illustration 3. A second method (recommended for most papers for publication and for formal reports) follows the *Publication Manual of the American Psychological Association* (referred to as the APA style manual).[1] The APA style manual divides visual aids into two categories, figures and tables, and numbers each category consecutively using Arabic numbers. Figures include all visuals other than tables. If the report contains more than one section or chapter, the illustrations may be numbered consecutively throughout the report (Figure 1, Figure 2, Figure 3; Table 1, Table 2, Table 3); or they may be numbered by sections or chapters (Figure 1.1, Figure 1.2, Figure 2.1; Table 1.1, Table 2.1, Table 2.2). The traditional style uses either separate numbering for tables and figures or numbers both as figures. In your textbook, you will see that all illustrations (including tables) are called figures and are numbered by chapter. The most important consideration in numbering illustrations and in formatting other visual components is consistency throughout the report or formal paper.

NOTE 12.7
Visual titles may begin at
the left or be centered at
the top or bottom.

Titles follow the figure or table number and may be printed in uppercase letters, uppercase and lowercase letters, or sentence format. Titles may be placed in the center or begin at the left margin. The title is a brief descriptive phrase that explains what the table or figure shows.

NOTE 12.8
The title briefly says what
the table shows—who,
what, when, where,
and why.

The title and content of the table or figure should make the meaning clear. The reader should not have to refer to the text to understand the illustration. Consider the five Ws for headline writing—who, what, when, where, and why—as a guide for wording the title to make the meaning clear.

The APA style manual is used widely by social science (including business) writers for academic papers, formal reports, or manuscripts for publication. The Modern Language Association (MLA) style of notation generally is used for literary writings.[2] Business reports may vary from APA format and use a more traditional style. Again, consistency in numbering, placement, and formatting of the title is of most importance. Figures in this chapter illustrate visuals in two different formats: APA and traditional. Use these figures as a guide for proper placement and capitalization of titles, headings, and source notes when you use APA or traditional style. Note the differences between the two styles.

Identification of Sources

NOTE 12.9
Avoid plagiarism by adding
a source note that gives
credit to those who
prepared the visual.

Follow the same consideration for acknowledging sources of visual aids as is used for text sources. When content comes from another source, add a **source note** that gives credit to that source. For publication, authors must obtain permission to reproduce or adapt all or part of the table or figure from a copyrighted source. The source note is placed below the table or figure. If the APA format is used, the title of a figure is at the bottom; therefore, add the source note for the figure below the title. With tables, place the title above the table and a source note or special explanation below

---

[1]*Publication Manual of the American Psychological Association,* 5th ed. (Washington, D.C.: American Psychological Association, 2001).
[2]*MLA Handbook for Writers of Research Papers,* 5th ed. (New York: The Modern Language Association of America, 1999).

the table. If you originated the content of an illustration, a source note is not needed. Two examples of a source note are these:

TRADITIONAL STYLE (OFTEN USED BY BUSINESS WRITERS)
Source: Marjorie Kelley, *History of Modern Dance* (Fairmont, NJ: Worksworth Publishing, 2006), p. 223. Copyright 1999 by Art Works. Adapted with permission.

NOTE 12.10
Traditional style for source notes uses the word Source; APA uses Note.

APA STYLE (USED MAINLY BY WRITERS IN SOCIAL SCIENCES FOR ACADEMIC WRITING OF MANUSCRIPTS FOR PUBLICATION AND FORMAL REPORTS)
Note. From *History of Modern Dance* (p. 223), by M. Kelley, 2006, Fairmont, NJ: Worksworth Publishing. Copyright 1999 by Art Works. Adapted with permission.

Developing Visual Aids

You must be knowledgeable about the various types of illustrations before you can select those that will most effectively accomplish your purposes. The most frequently used visual aids in business reports are tables, charts, and graphs. In a formal written report, the titles and text used should be consistent with font styles and sizes used in the headers and text of the report. For a consistent, professional appearance, spacing, horizontal and vertical lines, and placement of titles should be consistent throughout the report for all similar visual aids (i.e., tables, figures, or illustrations).

NOTE 12.11
The most frequent visuals in business reports are tables, charts, and graphs.

Tables

A **table** displays content arranged in vertical columns and horizontal rows. This makes data comparison easy. Tables usually show exact numerical data. All data in tables should be presented in an orderly arrangement for clear reference. In addition to the table number and title, the first row includes column headings that identify the categories of information in each column. The first column may have headings that identify the types of information across the remaining columns in that row. Column headings and row identifiers clearly describe the data but are short enough not to detract from them.

LO 3
Describe five types of tables and charts and explain an appropriate use for each type.

NOTE 12.12
Column and row headings in tables identify types of data.

Tables are efficient for presenting detailed data in a small amount of space. Using the *table* function of word processing software makes constructing tables easy to do. There are two kinds of tables: word tables and numeric data tables. The format of tables (lines, spacing, and title placement) is determined by a standard format used by a particular business or by guidelines for tables given in style manuals such as MLA and APA or business handbooks such as *A Handbook for Office Professionals: HOW 11*. The style illustrated in *HOW 11* is referred to in this chapter as *traditional* style.

Use portrait orientation (8½ by 11 inches) for most tables inserted in reports. However, if the table requires more columns than will fit within the report margins, you may construct the table using landscape orientation (11 by 8½ inches).

NOTE 12.13
Most tables in reports use portrait orientation (8½ by 11 inches).

WORD TABLES
Word tables may be used for a variety of purposes. If you research information about a topic from three to six major authors, you may compare their definitions of terms or major concepts by listing the authors' names as the category in the first

NOTE 12.14
Word tables summarize content categories in columns and rows.

FIGURE 12.1
Word Table—APA Style
for Formal Report

Table 1
Computer Technology Access by Online Students in a Community College Course

Participant (Fictitious names) *n* = 15	Internet connection at work/home	Computer used for class
Aimee	DSL	Home
Anne	No response	Home/work
Angela	T1	Home
Betty Sue	DSL	Work
Delilah	T1	Home/work
Desiree	Cable modem	Home
Gail	Cable modem	Home
Isabel	T1/dial up	Home/work
Janice	Cable modem	Home
Jolene	Dial up	Home/work
Kerry	T1	Home/work
Maggie	Cable modem	Home/work
Maureen	DSL/dial up	Home/work
Olivia	Dial up	Home/work
Sheila	T1/dial up	Home/work

column, with different terms or concepts for comparison in the second column. A literature review might use a word table in this way. A business report showing equipment needs might list different models of the same item of equipment in a word table showing characteristics of each model for comparison. The word table in Figure 12.1 has three column headings that identify three major categories for interview data from research about online instruction: *Participant, Internet connection,* and *Computer used.* In this table, the participant names in the first column serve as row identifiers. Each name (row identifier) tells who gave the responses displayed in the other columns in that row.

A table describing characteristics of different automobiles might include four major categories: Brand Name, Model, Safety Features, and Fuel Efficiency. These would become column headings, and each brand name would be a row identifier.

NUMERIC DATA TABLES

NOTE 12.15
Numeric data tables present statistical or mathematical data in tabular form.

Place statistical or mathematical data in tables when including these data in the text of the report would become complex and difficult to understand. Use the text of the report rather than a table to describe data if a table has two or fewer columns and rows and if the data could be stated clearly in a few sentences. Figure 12.2 shows statistical data presented in a numeric data table.

NOTE 12.16
Arrange numbers from high to low or low to high.

Just as is true with word tables, numeric data tables have brief, descriptive column and row titles. Arranging numbers in order, high to low or low to high, rather than listing them randomly helps the reader find and interpret displayed data.

Charts

NOTE 12.17
Three types of charts are commonly used in business: organization charts, flowcharts, and pie charts.

The three types of charts commonly used in business reports are organization charts, flowcharts, and pie charts. Using such charts eliminates lengthy text descriptions; little explanation would be needed other than a text reference to each chart. The

Figure 2

**PERCENTAGE OF U.S. SCHOOL-AGE POPULATION
WHO SPEAK A LANGUAGE OTHER THAN ENGLISH AT HOME**

Year	Total Population Ages 5–17 (in millions)	Other Language Number (in millions)	Other Language Percentage of Total Population
1979	44.7	3.8	8.5
1989	42.3	5.2	12.3
1992	47.7	6.3	13.2
1995	47.5	6.7	14.1
1999	52.7	8.8	16.7
2000	52.5	9.5	18.1
2001	53.0	9.8	18.5
2002	53.0	9.8	18.5
2003	53.0	9.9	18.7
2004	52.9	9.9	18.9

Source: U. S. Department of Commerce, Census Bureau.

FIGURE 12.2
Numeric Data Table—Traditional Style for Business Report or Oral Presentation

first two types, organization charts and flowcharts, clearly present relationships and procedures. The pie chart illustrates the proportion of parts to the whole.

ORGANIZATION CHARTS

An **organization chart** illustrates relationships among departments and among personnel within the departments. The chart may depict the entire organization or a selected portion of it.

Most organization charts place the senior position at the top of the chart. Other positions are placed on the chart in descending order of supervisory relationships. Solid connecting lines show supervisory and direct reporting relationships. Broken or dotted lines indicate advisory or collaborative staff relationships. Figure 12.3 illustrates an organization chart.

NOTE 12.18
Organization charts illustrate relationships among departments and personnel.

NOTE 12.19
Solid lines show supervisory relationships and direct reporting; broken lines, advisory and collaborative relationships.

FIGURE 12.3
Organization Chart

Busy Street Electronics

Chief Executive Officer

Business Officer   Sales Manager - - - - - - Marketing Director

Account Clerks (3)   Sales Representatives (5)   Asst. Marketing Director

Figure 3. Organization chart of a small electronics company. Solid lines connecting positions denote a direct reporting relationship; dashed lines indicate collaborative and advisory relationships.

FLOWCHARTS

A **flowchart** illustrates a step-by-step progression through a complex procedure. Such procedures could include the steps to manufacture a product, the route that a form follows for processing, or the steps to follow in carrying out a company policy or an improvement plan.

Complicated written directions are clearer and easier to follow when accompanied by a flowchart rather than a text description only. The chart should be kept simple enough to be understood easily. Boxes of various shapes connected by arrows illustrate the direction that action flows to complete a procedure. Box size is determined by the number of words in the label not by the importance of that particular step in the procedure. Figure 12.4 illustrates steps in developing slides for an oral presentation.

PIE CHARTS

A **pie chart** can be used to show the distribution and relationships of the parts to a whole. To make the chart easy to read, begin slicing the pie at the twelve o'clock position and continue in a clockwise direction. Arrange the pieces in descending order of size. If you combine several smaller pieces into an "Other" category, place this piece last. "Other" should not be the largest segment. Label individual pieces by showing the quantity or percentage of each piece.

Pie charts are easy for most readers to understand, but remember certain considerations. All pie charts within a report should be the same size. A pie chart should contain a minimum of two pieces and a maximum of eight. When you use more than eight pieces, labels on a pie chart become difficult to read. The percentages shown in a pie chart should total 100.

To emphasize a specific segment, use an exploded pie chart. In an **exploded pie chart,** one segment is separated from the rest of the chart for emphasis. Figure 12.5 shows an exploded pie chart to emphasize the percentage of interest on a home loan.

Graphs

A graph is a drawing that represents relationships of quantities or qualities of categories of items to each other. A graph presents a simple format that permits the

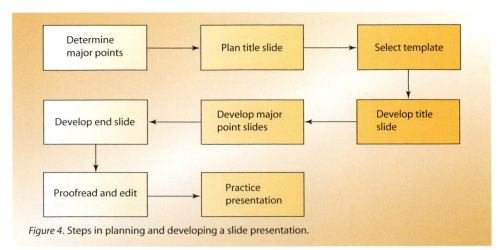

Figure 4. Steps in planning and developing a slide presentation.

FIGURE 12.5
Exploded Pie Chart—
APA Style

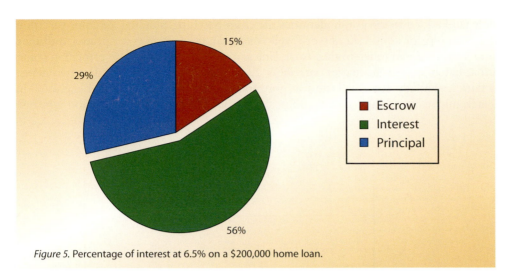

Figure 5. Percentage of interest at 6.5% on a $200,000 home loan.

reader or the viewer to interpret the information and make comparisons quickly. Pie charts visually show relationships and could be classified as a type of graph; however, they are generally considered charts because of their simplicity for a single purpose—showing the relationship of parts to the whole. Computer software programs make constructing graphs easy, and some of these programs refer to all types of graphs as charts. Regardless of their classification, graphs are used frequently as easily interpreted displays that show mathematical or statistical relationships. They usually give less numeric detail than is shown in tables. If a graph becomes complicated, using a table may be the best choice.

NOTE 12.25
A graph shows qualities/quantities and relationships.

Bar and line graphs are the most frequently used graphs in business organizations. Both of these types of graphs have several variations.

BAR GRAPHS

A bar graph is effective for comparison of differences in quantities. Changes in the lengths of the bars graphically show these differences. Bar graphs may be a horizontal or a vertical design. The horizontal bar and vertical column bar graphs are excellent for comparing different data types at one time or comparing the same data type for a sequence of times. For example, sales of different products for the fourth quarter would work well for a horizontal bar graph, and total sales for each quarter of the year could be displayed as a vertical column graph.

NOTE 12.26
A bar graph helps compare differences in quantities.

Frequently used bar graphs are of five types: simple, broken, multiple, stacked, and positive-negative. All bar graphs except a positive-negative one should begin with zero at the bottom or extreme left and use the same increments throughout.

In a **simple bar graph,** the length or height of a bar indicates quantity. Use a bar width that makes a good visual impression. The width of individual bars should be the same throughout a graph. If the bar width becomes too narrow, the graph is too complex, and the data should be logically divided into categories and presented in more than one graph. A simple bar graph is illustrated in Figure 12.6.

NOTE 12.27
A simple bar graph shows quantity by the length or height of a bar.

If you need to depict large amounts in a graph, it may be impractical to include all amounts from zero to the highest amount. In such cases, a **broken-bar graph** may be used, as shown in Figure 12.7.

NOTE 12.28
A broken-bar graph breaks columns for large amounts to begin at zero.

A graph representing several different items may be termed a **multiple-bar graph.** Bars on this type of graph represent different items, and different cross-hatching (patterns), shading, or color variations can be used to distinguish among the items.

NOTE 12.29
A multiple-bar graph shows quantities of different items at one time.

A legend added to the graph identifies the cross-hatching, shading, or color variation for each type of item. Colors work well when you are using a color printer, and they add a professional touch to the visual. Unless a written report will be printed in color, cross-hatching and shading of bars show differences better than color. For two items, a dark and a light color will show as gray and black and be distinguishable printed in black and white. Make sure that the shades on different bars have good contrast

FIGURE 12.6
Simple Bar Graph—
APA Style

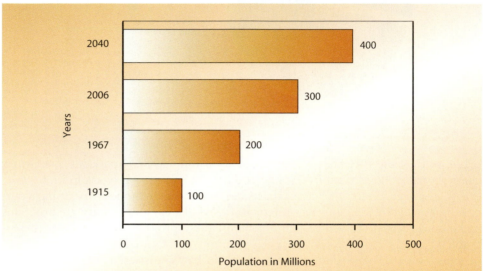

Figure 6. Hundred million population milestone years and the estimated year to reach the next hundred million milestone.
Note: From U. S. Census Bureau and Social Security Administration.

FIGURE 12.7
Broken-Bar Graph—
Traditional Style

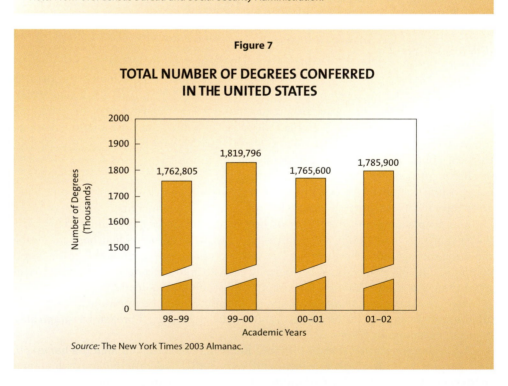

Source: The New York Times 2003 Almanac.

FIGURE 12.8
Multiple-Bar Graph—
APA Style

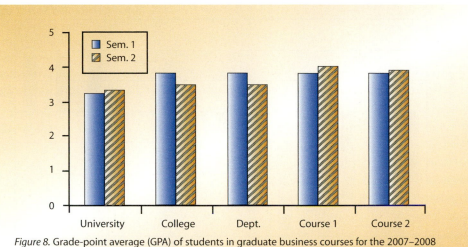

Figure 8. Grade-point average (GPA) of students in graduate business courses for the 2007–2008 academic year at XYZ University.

between them. With bars representing more than two items, cross-hatching used on one or more of the bars helps identify what each bar represents.

A multiple-bar graph becomes cluttered and difficult to read if its bars represent more than four different items. Figure 12.8 shows a multiple-bar graph.

A **stacked-bar graph** (see Figure 12.9) represents elements within a variable. This type of graph is useful in demonstrating differences in values within variables by dividing each bar into its parts. Values should be included for each part, and the parts should be identified on a legend with cross-hatching, shading, or color variations, as in multiple-bar graphs.

A **positive-negative bar graph** shows plus or minus deviations from a fixed reference point. The bars go up or down from this fixed reference point. Relationships between positive and negative values can be illustrated clearly using a positive-negative bar graph as shown in Figure 12.10.

NOTE 12.30
A stacked-bar graph shows elements within a variable.

NOTE 12.31
A positive-negative bar graph shows plus or minus deviations from a fixed reference point.

FIGURE 12.9
Stacked-Bar Graph—
APA Style

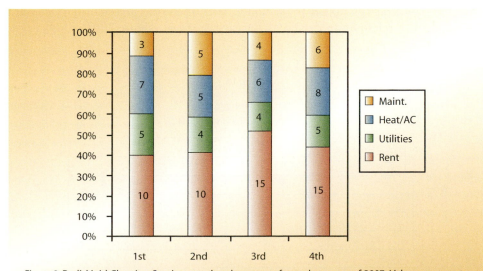

Figure 9. Redi-Maid Cleaning Services overhead expenses for each quarter of 2007. Values represent dollars in thousands.

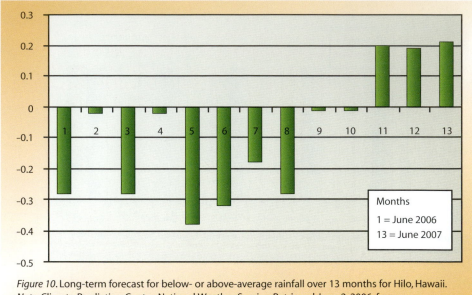

Figure 10. Long-term forecast for below- or above-average rainfall over 13 months for Hilo, Hawaii.
Note. Climate Prediction Center, National Weather Service. Retrieved June 2, 2006, from
http://www.cpc.noaa.gov/products/pacdir/CCAH.shtml.

LINE GRAPHS

NOTE 12.32
A line graph illustrates
changes over time.

NOTE 12.33
A multiple-line graph
shows changes over time in
more than one variable.

A line graph illustrates changes over time. Trends can be portrayed effectively by showing variations within each time period.

A line graph shows a line or lines on an equally divided grid. Include all the data so that the graph conveys an accurate picture. A line graph may use a broken grid if the variation is spread widely. The graph may be a **single-line graph** that illustrates variations of one variable over time or a **multiple-line graph** that shows changes in more than one variable. For multiple-line graphs, differentiate the lines by using dotted, broken, and solid lines or by changing the symbols (triangle, square, circle, and diamond) for each variable. Color variations may be used but require a report printed in color or a computer projection as part of an oral presentation. A legend should identify the lines and symbols for each variable. Figure 12.11 illustrates a multiple-line graph.

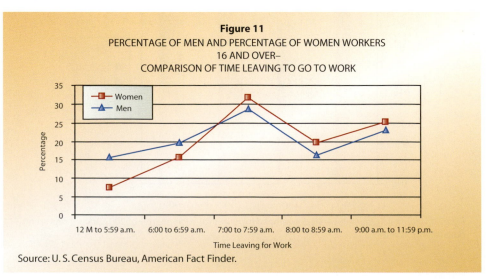

Source: U. S. Census Bureau, American Fact Finder.

Other Visual Aids

Although the most commonly used visual aids are tables, charts, and graphs, these are not the only effective visual aids that can be used for reports. Graphic aids such as maps, photographs, pictographs, and drawings are used infrequently but can be effective in conveying selected information. Any relevant visual aid that clarifies and strengthens the communication could be considered for use in a written report or presentation.

A **map** can be effective in showing location and helping a receiver visualize geographic relationships. The complexity of maps ranges from simple sketches to detailed, multicolored presentations. The content of the map determines the size of the visual aid.

A **pictograph** is similar to a bar graph in that it emphasizes differences in statistical data, but instead of bars, images of items or symbols represent the data. For example, dollar signs ($$$$) might represent money amounts. A legend on the pictograph or a note underneath it should explain the value of each picture or symbol. The pictograph in Figure 12.12 graphically accentuates the increase in new house construction over a period of time by using pictorial representations of houses rather than a plain bar.

A personal touch can be added to a written report or oral presentation by including a **photograph** of a facility, a product, or an employee. For effective communication, the photograph should be clear and well planned. The background should be uncluttered, and the focus should be on the person, object, or facility to be emphasized. A photograph can stimulate interest in a topic by helping the viewer visualize the message.

A **drawing** may be the most effective means of communicating a complicated idea or procedure. The drawing removes clutter that might be distracting in a photograph. A diagram such as the one shown in Figure 12.13 emphasizes details and reflects parts or components not visible when viewing the total object.

LO 5
Describe three other types of visual aids.

NOTE 12.34
Other visual aids include maps, photographs, pictographs, and drawings.

NOTE 12.35
A map shows location and geographic relationships.

NOTE 12.36
A pictograph is similar to a bar graph but uses images or symbols rather than bars.

NOTE 12.37
A photograph that is clear and well planned can stimulate interest.

NOTE 12.38
A drawing removes distracting clutter to communicate a complex idea.

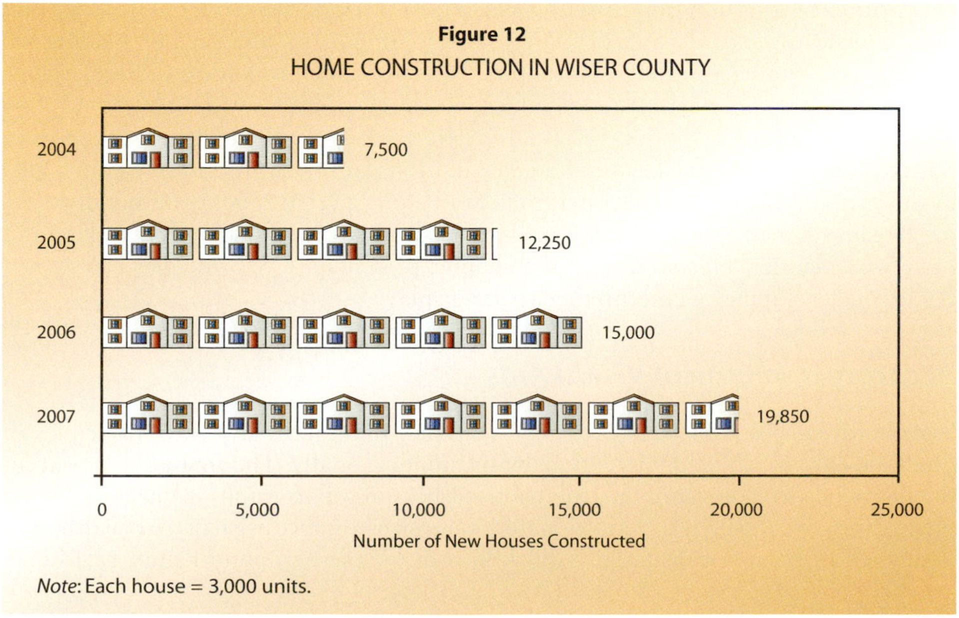

FIGURE 12.12
Pictograph—Traditional Style

Figure 12
HOME CONSTRUCTION IN WISER COUNTY

2004 — 7,500
2005 — 12,250
2006 — 15,000
2007 — 19,850

Number of New Houses Constructed

Note: Each house = 3,000 units.

FIGURE 12.13
Drawing—APA Style

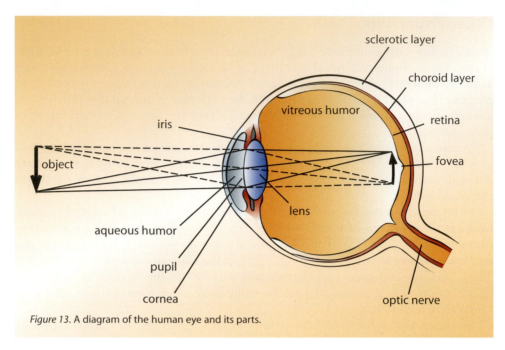

Figure 13. A diagram of the human eye and its parts.

Planning and Interpreting Visual Displays

LO 6

Explain ethical and other considerations for developing visual aids.

Computer hardware and software make an easy task of developing visual aids for either written messages or oral presentations. However, planning visual displays before you create them requires careful thought about content and the best method for display. In addition, as a viewer of visual aids, do you know how to analyze their structure for accurate interpretation?

NOTE 12.39
Planning visuals requires careful thought about content and display media.

A primary consideration for visuals is that they support the overall message and do not mislead the reader or viewer. Visual aids support the message by making the content easily understood. In a written or oral report, they provide a picture, a summary, a comparison, or numeric detail in a format that is easier to understand than a text or an oral description. All visuals are referred to in the text or presentation, but the content of the visuals should give additional information beyond statements in the text and depict it in a format that can be interpreted quickly and easily.

NOTE 12.40
Visuals should support the message and not be misleading.

Be sure that the visual display of data is accurate and presented in a clear and organized manner. This section of the chapter presents a few principles to use as a guide for developing or interpreting visual displays.

Accurate and Ethical Visual Aids

NOTE 12.41
Disproportionate graph image sizes can be misleading.

Visual aids can be misleading. Misrepresentation may occur if certain principles of development are violated—intentionally or unintentionally. The first guide for accurate visuals is to make sure that the width of bars in a bar graph or image sizes in a pictograph are equal. Disproportionate image sizes or inconsistent bar widths can deceive the viewer. For example, a quick look at the pictograph in Figure 12.14 may

FIGURE 12.14
Inaccurate Pictograph
Because of Unequal Size

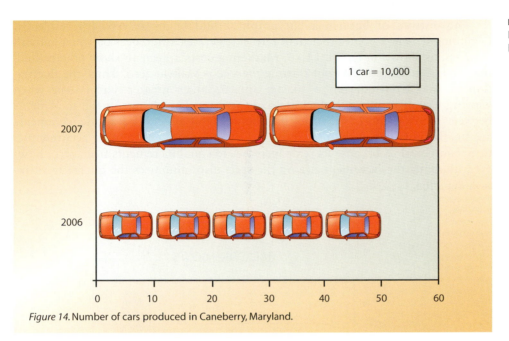

Figure 14. Number of cars produced in Caneberry, Maryland.

give the impression that the number of cars produced was greater in 2007 than in 2006 because that car is larger. In fact, the opposite is true.

In creating and interpreting pictographs and bar graphs, remember the importance of consistent image size and bar width (Principle 1). In a pictograph, the number of images, not their size, determines the value; in a bar graph, the height or length of the bars, not their width, represents the value.

A pie chart that pictures a disproportionate section of the whole and does not represent the actual percentage for each part is not an accurate visual (see Figure 12.15). The construction of this graph could deceive the viewer into thinking the sales tax in Pie Chart A is one third of the tax revenue; it is actually one fifth, as shown correctly in Pie Chart B. Chart A is drawn incorrectly. Proportions of each part displayed must match the values of those parts (Principle 2).

NOTE 12.42
Follow specific principles for creating and interpreting pictographs and bar graphs.

FIGURE 12.15
Pie Charts Showing
Disproportionate and
Correct Divisions

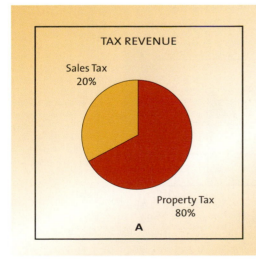
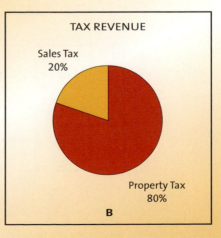

The bottom of bars in a bar graph should begin at zero (Principle 3), Beginning bars at a point other than zero exaggerates differences between individual bars, as shown in Figure 12.16. Marketing costs appear to show greater fluctuation in Bar Graph A by not starting the y-axis scale at zero. Thus, the fluctuation of costs from quarter to quarter appears much greater than is true when viewing Graph B, which begins the scale at zero. The change in the increments between major points of the scale contributes to this effect. These scale increments are smaller in Graph A than in Graph B. Graph B represents a more accurate picture than Graph A because its scale increases in equal increments from zero; however, doubling the increment size on the scale also minimizes the quarterly variation depicted.

FIGURE 12.16
Differences in Costs Appear
Greater in A Than B Because
the Baseline Does Not
Equal Zero

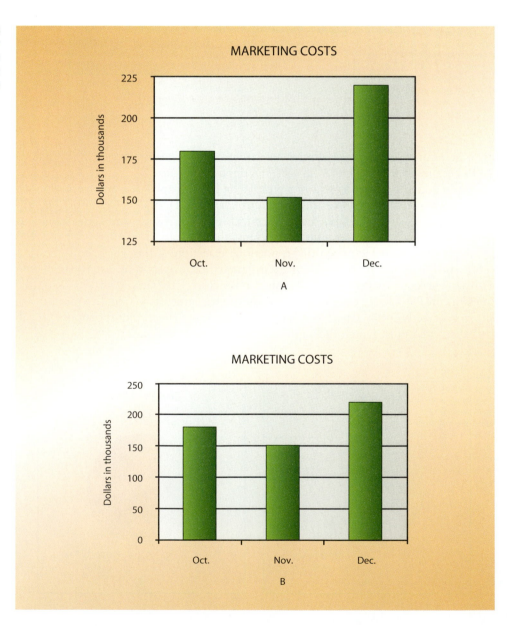

Improperly constructing a line graph deceives the viewer. Inconsistent intervals on the *y*-axis can make changes appear greater or lesser than they actually are. Notice that in Figure 12.17 salaries of women and men appear closer together when the increment between major points is increased. The labels of the *x* and *y* intervals should be evaluated critically. Therefore, the fourth guiding principle is to start the *y* scale at zero. The fifth guiding principle is to recognize that small increments between scale values increase the appearance of variation, while large increments make differences appear smaller. Without attention to the scale on the *y*-axis, variations can be misinterpreted.

Text or oral statements about visuals should be reflected clearly in the visual display. The text or presentation usually makes one or more summary statements or conclusions about what is shown in a table or figure. When developing or interpreting a table or figure, make sure the visual display matches the statements about it. The sixth principle for visual displays is that statements or conclusions about visuals in a written report or oral presentation must be consistent with the visual data depiction.

NOTE 12.44
Inconsistent intervals on the *y*-axis make changes appear too large or too small.

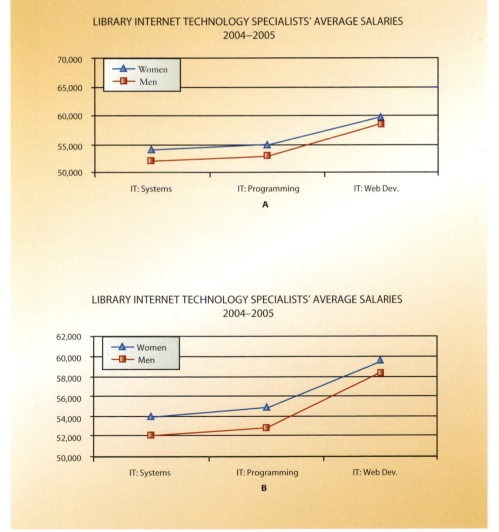

FIGURE 12.17
Increasing the Increments between Value Points on a Line Graph Scale Makes Value Points Appear Closer Together in A Than B

NOTE 12.45
Incomplete data lead to
incorrect conclusions.

As shown in Figure 12.18, incomplete data lead to incorrect conclusions. If you made a statement about a trend in student enrollment as shown in Figure 12.18(B), what would you say? Would this same statement match the data in Figure 12.18(A)? Showing only odd years makes it appear that there has been a steady increase in enrollment. Including the missing even years shows a variable picture of increases and decreases. Therefore, the final guiding principle for developing or interpreting visuals is that trend data, in particular, are not accurate unless all time intervals are shown.

FIGURE 12.18
Omission of Data Shows
Only Odd Years in Graph A
and Misrepresents the
Actual Picture of Enrollment
Shown in B

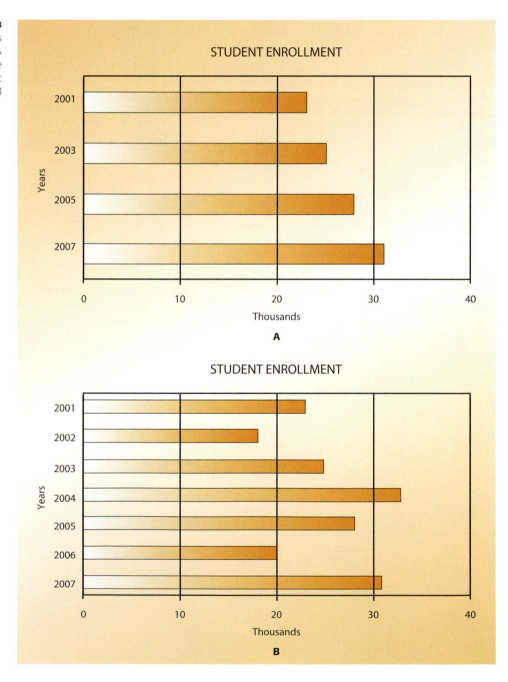

Other Development Considerations

Colors and shadings of colors that can be computer-generated for visuals are almost endless. You can use color differences to enhance visual effects that

1. Attract attention. (Emphasize key information.)
2. Show contrast. (Use different colors or cross-hatch patterns for comparison of different data categories.)
3. Create moods. (Yellow, orange, and red are warm colors that should be used to highlight. Red is associated with *danger* or *stop* and could be used for a negative trend. Green, blue, and violet are cool colors associated with oceans and harmony and are good background colors.)

There should be good contrast on a visual between text and its background. For reading with a lighted environment, dark type on a light background gives the best contrast. For oral presentations given in a darkened room, light type on a dark background is most visible.

About 10 percent of the population is color blind, so do not use green and red next to each other because these two colors present the most problems for people with color blindness. Use different symbols or dashed, dotted, and solid lines for line graphs even if you are color coding. This redundancy will assist viewers who have a problem distinguishing color. Pure blue shouldn't be used for text or fine details, particularly on a black background.

Graphics programs that apply the same color and design pattern throughout give an attractive, uniform appearance to similar visual aids. For both slides and transparencies made with a graphics software program, selecting a predesigned format is usually wise because colors have been selected to complement one another.

Selecting the right type of visual to achieve your purpose is an important consideration in planning visuals for development. The Communication Note compares the purposes for different visual aids for written reports and presentations. To be effective, visuals should meet the needs of the reader or audience rather than be a crutch for the writer or a script for the presenter.

NOTE 12.46
Color in visuals can attract attention, show contrast, and create moods.

NOTE 12.47
Avoid using green and red next to each other; 10 percent of people are color blind.

NOTE 12.48
Using the same colors and patterns throughout a visual program gives a uniform appearance.

communication note

USING VISUAL AIDS: WRITTEN REPORTS AND ORAL PRESENTATIONS

I. **To improve clarity of complex ideas**
   A. Tables and graphs make data comparison easy.
   B. Organization charts and flowcharts present relationships and procedures.
   C. Pie charts show relationships of parts to the whole.
   D. Bar graphs compare differences in quantities, different data types at one time, or the same data type over time. Multiple-bar graphs represent different items at one time.
   E. Stacked-bar graphs represent differences in values within variables.
   F. Drawings remove distracting clutter to emphasize detail.

II. **To improve retention of information**
   A. Tables, graphs, charts, pictographs, maps, photographs, and models improve understanding and, thus, promote retention of information.
   B. Slides and transparencies summarize important points.
   C. Handouts promote note taking and make information available for future review.

III. **To provide interest and variety**
   A. Pictographs attract attention by using symbols or pictures to graph data for comparison.
   B. Maps show geographic locations and relationships.
   C. Photographs and multimedia stimulate interest.

Selecting Appropriate Presentation Aids

LO 7

Select and prepare appropriate visual, audio, or multimedia aids for oral presentations.

Unlike a written report, which draws only on the receiver's sense of sight, an oral presentation can appeal to sound, sight, touch, taste, and smell. Sound (audio) and sight (visual) are generally the most useful. Whether used separately or in combination (multimedia), presentation aids can assist in conveying a message. Used effectively, they can spark interest, add variety, make the message understandable, and hold audience attention. Used ineffectively, they can be a distraction and create boredom. Chapter 15 will give specific attention to planning and delivering oral presentations. In this section, the discussion will focus on effective visual, audio, and multimedia presentations.

NOTE 12.49
Oral presentations can appeal to all senses: sound, sight, touch, taste, and smell.

Visual Presentation Aids

NOTE 12.50
Visual aids used frequently for oral presentations are slides, transparencies, handouts, flip charts, posters, and objects.

The most common visual aids used during a presentation are slides, transparencies, handouts, flip charts, posters, and objects. Thoughtful planning of the purpose, content, design, and appropriate use of visual aids helps ensure that visual and multimedia aids create attention and assist the audience in understanding and remembering the message.

SLIDES AND TRANSPARENCIES

Slides and transparencies are two visual types that can be developed using presentation software. The results can be colorful and professional and work well with groups of various sizes. Although the software requires limited practice for use, the time and talent required to prepare and produce effective slides or transparencies can be substantial.

NOTE 12.51
Keep the number of slides reasonable for a single presentation; keep content brief on each slide.

One general guide for development of slides and transparencies is to keep the total number reasonable for use with a single presentation. The beginning, the ending, and the most important points to be made during the presentation should be your guide for development. Presenters often try to put most of the presentation on slides or transparencies. Too many slides or transparencies and too much content on each one will lose the effect of emphasis and interest. Each visual should be brief enough to be read and interpreted at a glance. Information overload garbles the message and buries the point, as shown in Figure 12.19. For content, use keywords rather than sentences and paragraphs. Use graphs, simple tables, charts, pictures, or other graphics as appropriate to present or illustrate major presentation points.

NOTE 12.52
Presentation visuals use sans serif fonts, lower- and uppercase text, and 36- and 24-point fonts.

Type font size and style promote or detract from readability, as does spacing. General guidelines suggest simple, sans serif fonts such as Arial or Helvetica. **Serifs** are the small endings or curlicues found on letters in type fonts such as Georgia or Times New Roman. These serif fonts are best for long passages of printed text, but are not as easily read as Arial or Helvetica fonts when displayed electronically. UPPERCASE IS MORE DIFFICULT TO READ than lowercase. Lowercase characters and a mix of capitals and lowercase are more distinct than uppercase and easier to read. Electronic displays of italics are not easily read. Recommended presentation font sizes are a 36-point title and 24-point bulleted text. Projecting a printed page with a font too small to read frustrates your audience. Letter spacing should also make words and phrases easy to read—not spaced too close or too far apart.

FIGURE 12.19
Slides with Overloaded Text
and with a Brief, Meaningful
Message

Are you ready to learn how to podcast? It is so-o-o easy!

Study sample podcasts. Get a microphone for your computer and sound-editing software. Find a web hosting provider. Then follow these steps:

- Record your message saving the audio on your computer.
- Refine your message with sound-editing software.
- Convert the file to MP3 format.
- Transfer file to a Web hosting provider.

Congratulations! You are a podcaster!

To get exposure, submit your podcast to iTunes.

Are you ready to podcast?

Plug microphone to computer

- Record your message
- Refine with sound-editing software
- Convert to MP3 format
- Transfer file to a web hosting provider

HANDOUTS

Handouts can present an outline or illustrate major points from the presentation. Some handouts have space for participants to write notes by slides. Handouts can include more information than is on the slides if the developer believes additional information will be helpful to the audience. Handouts that you will refer to in the presentation should be distributed before you begin. Handouts with complex supplementary material should be distributed after your presentation. Listeners can concentrate better on your comments if they do not have to worry about taking notes, but too many handouts or lengthy handouts that are difficult to read can be distracting.

You can use computer presentation software to print one or more slides on a page as an **audience handout.** The more slides printed on a page, the smaller the type font will appear. The maximum number to be easily read would be two or three to a page. Four or more to a page may be difficult to read.

FLIP CHARTS AND POSTERS

Flip charts are economical, easy-to-use aids that work best with small groups. Charts may be prepared in advance or spontaneously, as part of an interaction with the audience. Their advantage in interactive settings is that each sheet may be posted for reference and can serve as a tangible sign of accomplishments. Prepared charts should be designed on paper before being transferred to the flip chart pad. Printing is generally more readable than cursive writing. Penciled notes added when the chart is finished can help remind you of key points to make. Remember that charts require some sort of stand; be sure the pad you select fits the stand.

Posters may include text, charts, graphs, pictures, and pictographs. They work especially well for blueprints and drawings. Be sure to consider how posters will be displayed and whether they will be visible during the entire presentation or revealed as they are used. You may also need a pointer to help highlight important items.

OBJECTS

In many business presentations, you will have something to display either in final form or as a cutaway model that shows parts. If the physical objects or models used as visual aids are not large enough for every member of the audience to see, consider giving each member an object or circulating one or more of the items among audience members. Introducing the sensory dimension of touch into your presentation can reinforce the message but does detract from active listening. Before making objects available to your audience, consider both the benefits and disadvantages to your overall presentation.

Audio Presentation Aids

The use of recorded sound can add variety and impact to supplement your presentation. Cassette tapes, CDs, or podcasts may be used as audio aids. Whatever the medium, the recording quality should be high and the volume sufficient for all members of the audience to hear without strain or discomfort. Because recorded audio sounds are, in a sense, disembodied sounds, use them sparingly. An audience can tire quickly of simply listening to sound without having visual stimuli.

Multimedia Presentations

Computer presentations with projection equipment provide great versatility in visual or audiovisual presentation aids. You may add audio to slides and have fades, dissolves, or similar transition effects incorporated into the presentation. A speaker, for example, may decide to use progressive disclosure and reveal the subtopics of a bulleted list one by one. Sound could signal the addition of an item, or the item could fade into the background as new items emerge. When moving from one topic to another, the old image could slowly dissolve. For a lighter effect, you could have an animated object or character erase the text. Some software programs offer pre-animated templates. In either case, you can choose the speed at which transitions take place.

Computer links can be inserted into podcasts, vodcasts, blogs or other websites, photographs, or video clips for use as appropriate to contribute to major points, introduce a topic, or create attention. Options are many and varied. Use these aids sparingly to ensure that they complement your presentation without being a distraction from the message. The presentation topic can help you decide which to use without detracting from content.

Use of a video or podcast should be brief but might be a recorded quote appropriate to the message. In a similar way, you could use a picture or a short passage from a blog related to the presentation topic, or a brief (half- to one-minute) video clip from a movie. To use one of these audio or visual multimedia clips as part of a presentation, you should link it to the other visuals to be accessed quickly for viewing. Your job as a presenter will be easier if you have another person operate the computer and projection equipment. If you do this, be sure to practice together before the presentation. With presentation software, remember that equipment and software at the presentation site must be compatible with that used to create the presentation. If Internet resources are to be used, for example, a connection to the Internet must be available. Speakers must also prepare for unexpected equipment or network failure.

NOTE 12.59
Computers with projection equipment offer audio, video, and Internet presentation aids.

NOTE 12.60
Presentation software and equipment must be compatible with the presentation site media.

PC and Pixel by Thach Bui

© Artattack Comix 2006

Summary of Learning Objectives

LO 1

Describe the purposes of visual aids in written and oral communication.

Communication can be improved by summarizing complex figures in charts and graphs, by identifying your company through the use of a drawing or photograph for a logo, by showing relationships in a chart, by indicating trends in a graph, or by abstracting cumbersome details into a table. Effective visual aids help improve understanding of complex ideas, increase retention of information, and add interest and variety.

LO 2

Prepare and properly label figures and tables for written reports.

All visual aids should be identified by appropriate titles. Consider the five Ws (who, what, when, where, and why) when developing the title. Visual aids within a report should be numbered, and each should be referred to in the text by its number. All visual aids in a report may be called *illustrations* and be numbered consecutively throughout the report or be separated into categories such as *figures* and *tables* and be numbered consecutively within each category. Figures may include all visuals other than tables. Titles follow the figure or table number. Titles may be in uppercase letters, uppercase and lowercase letters, or sentence format. They may be placed in the center or begin at the left margin and be above or below the table or figure. Exact placement depends on the style manual followed; however, placement and letter case for titles and categories for numbering must be consistent throughout a report.

LO 3

Describe five types of tables and charts and explain an appropriate use for each type.

A word table shows comparison of definitions of terms or major concepts. Numeric data tables make comparison and comprehension of numbers easier than would be possible by showing the number detail as part of text. Both word and numeric data tables have a main title and brief descriptive row and column titles. Organization charts show supervisory and direct reporting relationships for an organization or a selected portion of it such as a department. Solid lines connect positions with supervisory responsibility, and broken lines connect positions with advisory or collaborative staff relationships. Flowcharts illustrate a step-by-step progression for a complex procedure. Arrows connecting the boxes illustrate the direction action flows to complete the procedure. Pie charts show relationships of the parts to a whole and indicate the percentage of each part. A pie chart should have at least two parts and not more than eight; the percentages of all parts equal 100.

LO 4

Describe five types of graphs and construct graphs for various purposes.

A bar graph can be effective for comparing differences in quantities. These differences are shown by different bar lengths. In a simple bar graph, the bar length or height indicates quantity. It is impractical to include all amounts from zero to the highest amount in graphs that depict large amounts. In such cases, a broken-bar graph is used. Multiple-bar graphs represent several different items at one time on a single graph. Because bars represent different items, cross-hatching, shading, or color variation distinguishes among the items represented. A stacked-bar graph represents different values within a variable by dividing each bar into its parts with cross-hatching, shading, or color variations used to identify parts. A positive-negative bar graph shows plus or minus deviations from a fixed reference point and shows relationships between positive and negative values. A line graph illustrates changes over time and effectively displays trends within a period. All the data should be included to produce an accurate picture. A line graph can have either a single line or multiple lines. A multiple-line graph shows changes in more than one variable, with lines differentiated by using dotted, broken, and solid lines or by using different symbols for each value.

Describe three other types of visual aids.

LO 5

A map shows location and geographic relationships. A pictograph is similar to a bar graph and emphasizes differences in statistical data. It differs in that images or symbols of items are used instead of bars. A personal touch can be added to a business report by including a photograph of a facility, a product, or an employee. A drawing can communicate a complicated idea or procedure by omitting clutter and emphasizing details or by showing a diagram of parts.

Explain ethical and other considerations for developing visual aids.

LO 6

To avoid deception, remember that a pictograph shows value by the number of images, not their size. In a bar graph, the height or length of the bar, not the width, determines the value. When looking at a bar graph, be aware that the bars must begin at zero to avoid exaggerating differences between bars. Intervals on the y scale of a line graph should be consistent. Labels of a visual aid should also be critically evaluated. Visual aids should have good contrast between text and its background. Use color to attract attention to key information, contrast data, and create moods by association with connotative meanings.

Select and prepare appropriate visual, audio, or multimedia aids for oral presentations.

LO 7

Visual, audio, or multimedia presentation aids, used effectively, can assist in creating interest and variety, make the message understandable, and hold audience attention. Slides and transparencies can be colorful and professional and work well with various size groups. They should be used for the beginning, the ending, and the most important presentation points. The type font, size, and spacing promote readability. Handouts present an outline or illustrate points in a presentation. Flip charts may be prepared in advance or as part of interaction and be posted to show results of interaction. Posters can be developed for most visual aids and work well for blueprints and drawings. Physical objects or models may be circulated to reinforce the message. Audio and video may be included with computer presentations. Links to multimedia clips can add interest to a presentation.

Questions for Discussion and Review

1. What are three ways that visual aids complement your business reports? (Objective 1)

2. Assume that you are preparing a visual aid that will not fit on the page with the text that relates to it. Where would you place this visual aid in the report? (Objective 2)

3. You are writing a formal report that includes a variety of visual aids: three tables, a pie chart, a bar graph, and a pictograph. (a) If you are using APA style, which would be numbered as tables and which would be numbered as figures? (b) Describe three differences that you observe between APA and traditional style for placement and punctuation of titles, headings, and source notes for tables and graphs. (Objective 2)

4. What is a guide for wording the visual aid title to make the meaning clear? (Objective 2)

5. You have a large amount of numeric data to include in your report. What type of visual aid would be most appropriate? Why? (Objective 3)

6. You have several items to compare differences in quantities. What type of graph would you prepare? Why? (Objective 4)

7. What is the difference between a pictograph and a drawing? (Objective 5)

8. Explain three flaws in development of graphs that could mislead the reader. (Objective 6)

9. What is the main consideration in deciding how many slides to include in an oral presentation? (Objective 7)

10. How can multimedia from the Internet be incorporated in a slide presentation? Give an example. (Objective 7)

Application Exercises

TECHNOLOGY

1. **Technology.** Use the Internet to locate an annual report or other written report from a major corporation that includes visual aids. Write an analysis of the report, including the following information: name of the company, type of report, type and purpose of visual aids, numbering and placement of visual aids, references to them in the report, and your evaluation of how well each aid contributes to the reader's understanding of the report. (Objectives 1, 2, and 3)

2. Construct a chart that shows the percentage of each type of expenditures for operating expenses (in millions) of Amazon.com for the year ended December 31, 2005. Add a figure number, proper title, and source note. Dollar units are in millions. Operating expenses: Fulfillment, $745; Marketing, $198; Technology and content, $451; General and administrative, $166; Other operating expense, $47. Total operating expenses were $1,607 million. Information source: Amazon.com, "2005 Annual Report," Amazon.com Investor Relations: Annual Reports and Proxies. (Objective 2)

3. Create a word table that gives definitions for six types of multimedia presentation aids. Use the APA style to format and place the number and title of the table. Assume that this table is the first visual aid in a written report. Study Figure 12.1 on page 336 as your guide for APA style. (Objectives 2 and 7)

4. Prepare a visual aid that shows the steps in developing an oral presentation. (Objectives 3 and 7)

5. Construct a graph for the following data. Include appropriate content, placement, and format for the number of the visual (assume it is the first visual in a report), title, and source note. Assume that the report will be produced with a color printer. Use APA style. (Objective 4)

> Best Fit Shoe Store keeps a record of the number of each brand of running shoe sold quarterly for the calendar year. For the second quarter of 2007, sales receipts showed 49 pairs of Adidas; 78 pairs of Asics; 64, Brooks; 133, Reebok; 96, New Balance; 53, Nike; 86, Saucony; and 44, Others. This information came from: Best Fit Shoe Store. (2007). Second Quarter Report—Running Shoe Sales. Los Angeles: Author.

6. Construct a graph that shows Student Housing at Be Smart University for 2007. This graph is for an oral presentation and will not need a figure number but will need a title. Follow traditional style for the title as shown in Figure 12.2 on page 337. Assume that the graph will be a computer-projected slide, so be sure the font size is readable for a group and select contrasting colors for each type of housing. Use a white background with black lettering. Number of students in types of housing: Res. Hall, 4,000; Campus Apts., 1,000; Off-campus Apts., 2,500; Off-campus Houses, 1,000. Print a full-page copy of the graph to submit to your teacher. (Objectives 4 and 7)

7. **Technology.** Construct a visual aid showing the grades you have in this course. Send the visual to your teacher as an attachment to an e-mail. (Objective 4)

8. Prepare one of the following visual aids that could be used in a written report: (a) a map that shows how to get from your school or university library to your classroom; (b) a pictograph that shows the number of households in your town for the past three years, estimating the numbers for each year; or (c) a photograph of a local building or park. Give your visual aid a figure number and title following APA style. If needed, add a source note. (Objective 5)

9. **Teamwork. Technology.** Join two of your classmates to research misleading visuals. (a) For one week, each of you will look for visuals that could be misleading. Keep notes of your findings and compile them for a group report (written or oral with visuals) that describes what you found, where you found the visuals, and why you believe them to be misleading. (b) Study Graph A and Graph B in Figure 12.16, page 346. Predict what the appearance of the quarterly variation will be if the graph *y*-axis starts at zero and increases in increments of 25 to a maximum of 225. Then work together to construct a graph with these specifications. Write a paragraph explaining how the graph met or differed from your prediction. Send a copy of the graph and the paragraph in an e-mail attachment to your instructor. (Objective 6)

10. Describe the presentation aid that you would construct to best illustrate the data for each of the following situations. Create your own title for each one. Write an introduction to the aid and write an example comment that could be used to direct your reader to some aspect of the data. (Objective 7)

   a. Your presentation requires that the audience have supplementary material to take home after the conference. Select a topic of interest to you.

   b. You want to have visuals to illustrate the main points of a conference presentation on study habits but will have no computer equipment available; overhead projectors and screens are in all conference meeting rooms.

   c. You will have a computer and projection equipment in the conference meeting room. You are giving a presentation on how to access the university library from an off-campus site.

   d. You are explaining how to construct a small table and would like to have a flowchart visible to use with a pointer during the presentation.

   e. You are giving a presentation on your career choice. You can use a computer and projection equipment to illustrate major points in a colorful and professional presentation.

Web exercises to accompany this chapter are available at **www.thomsonedu.com/bcomm/krizan.**

Message Analysis

The following paragraph is from a formal written report about how U. S. workers travel to work each day. Rewrite it to present the data clearly and free of punctuation, spelling, or grammatical errors. Include a visual to display the data.

> *The increase in oil prices has stimulated a review of the transportation used by US commutors to and from work each day. Many businesses have tried to strongly encourage carpooling or the use of public transportation but with miniscule success. The most recent figures shown by the united states census report shows that 77% drive alone, 5 percent take public transportation, 10 percent carpool with others, two percent walk, and 6 % use other options such as biking, boating, or other means of to regularly commute to work. These figures show that carpooling is the second highest percentage for commutors. Perhaps we are making progress after all.*

Writer's Workshop

The following items may be sentence fragments or contain errors in punctuation, subject–verb agreement, pronoun–antecedent agreement, infinitive use, abbreviations, number display, capitalization, spelling, word choice, possessives, modifier clarity and placement, or parallelism. Rewrite the sentences to make them correct.

1. If it rains tomorrow we will stay home, how ever if it doesn't we will go to the beach.
2. You can excess leading edge cases published by top researchers at our new web sight.
3. The basketball tournament begins next week, every one will want to regularly attend.
4. The *Publication Manual of the American Psychological Association* is a style manual used by authers of manuscripts to accurately meet publication requirements for A.P.A. format.
5. Cricket has a huge fan base in england, other popular sports are socker; lawn tennis; and rugby.
6. I have never been able to fully understand the use of infinitives, this particular phrase alludes my understanding.
7. There appears to really be only 1 reason why Miss Smith asigns so much home work.
8. The C.D.-R.O.M. disk has became the storage media of choice in more offices.
9. Janie williams earned a PH.D. in physics.
10. John Mosby lives at 2548 Genre Avenue, Northeast in Louisville; last year he lead the parade in the Derby Festival.

So far, the messages you've originated have related to your virtual assistant business. Work for clients has been based on materials they provided to you. In this feature, you will expand on those responsibilities and generate draft documents for your clients.

1. Jonas Doney has requested that you send him a proposal for a brochure that explains the cultural and economic climate of your state. The brochure will be sent to representatives of industries interested in relocating there. Prepare an outline of the message content for the brochure.

2. Celia Stryker and Stan Anthony have hired you to help them promote the opening of their business, the Coffee Cup. The specialty coffee shop is located on the corner of Star Street and Borderline Road in Hartford, Connecticut 06112. The shop will open two weeks from today; regular hours are Monday through Saturday, 7 a.m. to 9 p.m. In addition to coffee, the shop will offer pastries, sandwiches, and salads. Patrons may dine in or carry out. Celia was formerly manager of The Haven, a popular family restaurant owned by Stan. Draft a news release and send it to Celia for her approval; she will be the contact person listed on the release (860-555-3872). If you need additional information, ask for it in the e-mail that accompanies your draft (coffeecup@newengland.net).

3. Your last task before proofreading the annual report you've assembled for Ridgedale Bank is to prepare the last four visual aids. Use the following data, and prepare the appropriate graphic aids. The first figure in each set is for the year of the report (e.g. 2007); the second figure is for the prior year (e.g., 2006)

   a. Table Title: Financial Highlights
   Revenue and Net Income presented in $ millions
   Revenue for year ending 12/31: 59,236; 48,103
   Net Income: 12,734; 9,643
   Earnings (per share of common stock): 2.92; 2.81
   Dividends (per share of common stock): 1.21; 1.03
   Average common shares issued and outstanding (in millions): 2951; 2365

   b. Pie Chart Title: 200– Revenue ($ in millions) (fully taxable-equivalent basis)
   Business and Financial Services: 11669.49
   Investment Banking: 12380.32
   Investment Management: 3411.99
   Consumer and Small Business Banking: 31158.14
   Other: 616.05

   c. Pie Chart Title: 200– Net Income ($ in millions)
   Business and Financial Services: 2189.03
   Investment Banking: 1533.17
   Investment Management: 1447.86
   Consumer and Small Business Banking: 6158.16
   Other: 613.78

   d. Bar Chart Title: Total Bank Assets Five-Year Summary ($ in millions)
   (Reminder: First figure is for the year of the report; remaining figures are for prior years.)
   1,001,348
   923,637
   753,419
   622,756
   436,717

4. Ed Pappas, owner of Pappas Furniture City, has asked you to gather information about energy efficient lighting. He's interested in learning whether installing energy saving fluorescent bulbs in the 200 lamps on display in his 50,000 square foot store could result in cost savings. The lamps are lit 12 hours a day. He doesn't want a detailed cost analysis, but he's willing to buy two to three hours of your time to do preliminary research. Use the Internet or other sources and prepare an informal report to be e-mailed to Mr. Pappas (MrEd@pappasfurniture.com).

Part 5
Oral and Nonverbal Communication

© The Image Bank

Chapter 13
Interpersonal Communication and Teamwork

LET'S TALK BUSINESS

We are connected to our partners and associates in a business or profession by our relationships with them. Those who work together to produce a product or provide a service are connected by relationships.

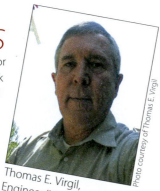

Thomas E. Virgil, Engineer/Manager, Qualcomm, Inc.

Photo courtesy of Thomas E. Virgil

One thing I have learned in ten years of engineering in the wireless communications industry at Qualcomm, Inc., is that we are all customers and providers in our relationships with each other. The focus of a project at Qualcomm may be engineering oriented, but the development of that project is an entrepreneurial venture. A leader provides knowledge about a project and proposes direction and boundaries. The leader promotes ideas about product requirements, plans of action, and engineering methods to the team members. The quality of the relationship between the leader and the team members determines the level of understanding. The leader–team relationship also determines the amount of input from the team members. Thus, the team members have relationship roles as customers and providers. Ultimately, they will produce the product of the project.

To achieve the goals of the project, additional customer and provider relationships must be established with management, the human resources department, the legal department, the information technology network, and the equipment providers. In all cases, these relationships are established by communication between individuals and groups. The quality of the relationships is determined by the quality of the communication.

The ability to create positive business relationships with colleagues, customers, and others is an important skill. In his work at Qualcomm, Inc., Thomas E. Virgil faces the challenge of developing those relationships with people in his physical location and over long distances. To be successful, Thomas needs excellent interpersonal communication skills. Interpersonal communication—what it is and how it is used in business settings—is one of the topics you will explore in this chapter.

The Elements of Interpersonal Communication

Interpersonal communication is the term applied to the verbal and nonverbal interactions that occur in both one-on-one and small-group settings. "People skills" and "soft skills" are terms often used to describe a cluster of personal qualities, habits, attitudes, and social graces that make someone a good employee and a compatible coworker. Each of us possesses soft skills but to varying degrees.

Interpersonal communication is a cornerstone in what social scientists refer to as the **communication climate**—the quality of the personal relationships that exist within an organization. These relationships are directly influenced by the soft skills of the people within the organization. The communication climate reflects the workers' perceptions of whether the organization trusts, respects, and values them—factors related to job satisfaction and commitment. Interpersonal communication is linked to leadership potential and teamwork, qualities employers seek in those they hire. A positive communication climate is a key to success in business.

Interpersonal skills have always played a role in business, but as the United States moved from an industrial to a service-oriented economy, that role grew in importance. Today's service economy puts a premium on people skills and relationship-building among coworkers, departments, organizations, and customers. Developing and maintaining these relationships is a goal of business communication.

Cultural diversity, globalization, organizational restructuring, worker specialization, and technology contribute to the current emphasis on interpersonal skills. Workplace diversity and globalization call on workers to be aware of and sensitive to the ways in which an individual's culture affects his or her attitudes and actions in the work environment. Organizational restructuring often results in downsizing, redistributed workloads, and pressure on those who remain. Worker specialization increases the likelihood that senders and receivers won't speak the same technical language. Technology increases the speed at which work is processed and reduces the number of face-to-face encounters. These changes have resulted in an increased demand for employees who are flexible and adaptable and who can solve problems creatively, manage time efficiently, work well under pressure, and accept and learn from constructive feedback. An employee's failure to practice or possess these soft skills can create communication barriers. As Figure 13.1 illustrates, employers want to hire candidates who have intangible soft skills.

Interpersonal communication skills exhibit themselves in the style with which people write, speak, and behave. Techniques for enhancing your written communication skills are covered in the correspondence section of this book. Here, you will focus on how listening, speaking, and nonverbal communication are used to build positive relationships, to give and receive constructive feedback comfortably, to manage conflict effectively, and to be an effective team member.

LO 1
Identify the components of interpersonal communication and soft skills.

NOTE 13.1
Interpersonal communication skills are used in one-on-one and small-group interactions.

NOTE 13.2
Organizations that show they trust, respect, and value their workers have a good communication climate.

NOTE 13.3
Workers with strong people skills are in demand in today's work environment.

FIGURE 13.1
Employers Seek Applicants
with Strong Soft Skills

Employers Rate the Importance of Candidate Qualities/Skills

Quality/Skill	Rating
Communication skills	4.7
Honesty/integrity	4.7
Teamwork skills	4.6
Strong work ethic	4.5
Analytical skills	4.4
Flexibility/adaptability	4.4
Interpersonal skills	4.4
Motivation/initiative	4.4
Computer skills	4.3
Detail-oriented	4.1
Organizational skills	4.1
Leadership skills	4.0
Self-confidence	4.0

(5-point scale where 1= Not at All Important and 5 = Extremely Important)
Source: Job Outlook 2006, National Association of Colleges and Employers.

Positive Relationships

LO 2

Develop skills for building positive relationships.

Positive relationships don't just happen. They are built over time, and they require ongoing maintenance. Trust and respect are key elements in building and maintaining relationships. Efforts to convey respect can be undermined by the way in which we communicate.

This section focuses on two topics related to building and maintaining positive relationships—conversations in various settings and relationship repair.

NOTE 13.4
Positive relationships don't happen by chance.

Conversations

NOTE 13.5
Relationships begin with cautious conversation.

Relationships generally start with conversations. At first, the interaction will probably be cautious. The participants reveal more of their personalities and share information about their lives as trust and comfort grow. People begin to connect on personal, emotional, and intellectual levels. At the office, this may mean speaking about family or friends, hopes and fears, and problems and solutions. The nature and extent of the topics discussed will vary with each relationship. A worker might share less with a superior or subordinate than with a colleague, and more with one colleague than another. The key elements in any relationship are the levels of trust and comfort.

NOTE 13.6
Workplace relationship patterns parallel personal relationship patterns.

This pattern of trust and sharing in the workplace parallels that used in other parts of life. Consider your best friend. How did you meet? What were your early conversations about? What do you discuss now? Do you share things with one friend that you do not talk about with another? The patterns you observe in your school and social lives will be reflected in your work life as well.

One-to-one oral communication, including conversation, is a valuable business tool. In fact, it is probably the most important form of interaction used in business. It occurs in both structured and social business settings, it is essential to good customer service, and it forms the foundation for workplace interactions among employees. More critical business decisions are made during conversations between two people than in any other forum.

Whether conversations occur in person, via the telephone, or during a web-based videoconference, they are dynamic situations. Sometimes you will be a message sender; sometimes you will be a receiver. Therefore, you must listen carefully (Chapter 14), continually analyze your receiver (Chapter 1), and adjust your delivery based on feedback (Chapter 1). In addition, you must apply the principles of business communication (Chapter 4). The success of a conversation also depends on using care in developing and sending the message and on eliminating communication barriers that threaten the conversation (Chapter 1).

Before we identify factors associated exclusively with successful face-to-face, telephone, and social business conversations, we must understand the conversation process.

THE CONVERSATION PROCESS

Conversations generally take place in five stages:

NOTE 13.7
Conversations occur in stages.

1. Greeting
2. Introduction
3. Exchange
4. Summary
5. Closing

Greeting. The greeting opens the channel for a conversation. "Hello," "Good morning," and "Tamikka, this is Christopher" are verbal greetings; a wave, a nod, and a smile are nonverbal greetings.

NOTE 13.8
Greetings may be verbal or nonverbal.

Through gestures, tone, and words, you provide information about your relationship with the receiver. Smiling warmly, extending your hand, and saying, "Hi, Mike. It's good to see you again" portrays a very different relationship than does a stern face and a curtly uttered, "Hello." Similarly, you might greet a coworker or personal friend by saying, "What's happening, Joe?" but choose "Good afternoon, Mr. Orsinelli" for a prospective client or the president of your firm.

Whatever your relationship with the receiver, be sure that the tone of your greeting matches the tone of your message. A positive, upbeat, carefree greeting would not be a good match for a message conveying bad news. Once the greeting has occurred, the conversation moves to the introduction stage.

Introduction. During this stage, the person initiating the conversation previews what will follow. Introductions should be brief and informative. "Joshua, you have extensive experience leading product design teams with members from different facilities. Do you think videoconferencing is the most effective technology for these meetings?" alerts the receiver to the topic of the conversation and helps frame the context for his or her role in it.

NOTE 13.9
Introductory remarks should be brief yet informative.

An introduction may be direct or indirect. For example, if you believe you deserve an above-average increase in salary and your analysis of your boss tells you he or she prefers the direct approach, introduce your conversation topic by saying, "Considering my performance this past year, I think that I deserve an above-average raise. May we discuss this?" Your introduction makes your position on the topic clear. On the other hand, when a division manager needs to discuss a budget cut with a department supervisor, he or she might say, "We need to discuss your department's budget request." This introduction defines the topic, provides a buffer to the negative news, and serves as a smooth transition between the greeting and the exchange, the third stage of the process.

Exchange. As the word *exchange* implies, the business of a conversation is conducted in a give-and-take format. During this stage of the process, the purpose of the conversation comes to the forefront. For example:

Catherine: Stan, are you free to meet with Lew and me at 10 Thursday morning? We need to go over sales projections for the next six months.

Stan: I already have a meeting scheduled from 9 to 11 on Thursday. Could we meet at 10 on Friday instead?

Catherine: Yes, that works for me. I have an appointment at 11:30, but this should only take an hour.

Stan: OK. I'll put it on my calendar. Will you confirm with Lew to see if it works for him?

Catherine: Sure.

In this example, the exchange is brief and direct. In another situation, the exchange might be longer and use the indirect approach. Specific techniques for a productive exchange are offered later in this section in "Keys for Successful Face-to-Face Conversations."

Summary. The fourth stage in the conversation process, the summary, allows the parties to reflect on the exchange, to recap the items discussed during a long or complex exchange, and to indicate that a conversation is ending. This stage of the process does for the end of a conversation what the introduction does for the beginning—it serves as a bridge.

Either the sender or the receiver may summarize a conversation. By saying, "Please have a tentative agenda for the training workshop on my desk by Wednesday morning" or "Call me if you have questions," a supervisor signals to a worker that their conversation about an upcoming training workshop is about to end. By saying, "I'll make the changes we've agreed to and have the tentative agenda on your desk by Wednesday morning," the employee indicates readiness to end the exchange and move to the final stage, the closing.

Closing. The closing is the cordial conclusion to the conversation. Depending on the situation, the closing may be verbal, nonverbal, or a combination of the two. After finalizing a sale with a new customer, for example, a sales representative might say, "It's been a pleasure doing business with you, Mrs. Phelps. I'll process the order today. About a week after the voice recognition software has been installed, I will phone to be sure you're satisfied with it. Good-bye." The wording makes it clear the conversation has ended; the process has been completed.

Whether spontaneous or planned, successful conversations are honest, objective, sincere, and reasonable. Common courtesy should be a hallmark of all conversations. Effective interpersonal relations and communications depend on these attributes.

COMMUNICATION STYLES

In business situations such as those discussed in this chapter, you may witness different communication styles. The three most common styles are passive (sometimes called nonassertive), aggressive, and assertive.

Passive. When you communicate in the **passive** mode, you give priority to the rights of others. This results in allowing others to make choices for you, rejecting the validity of your own feelings, and withdrawing from the situation. Passive communication is conveyed to others by a hesitant, tentative voice with an apologetic tone. Some examples of what a passive communicator might say include, "I don't care; you decide," "Forget I mentioned that," and "Go ahead with Sean's recommendation. My idea wasn't that good anyway."

Aggressive. The opposite of the passive communication style is the **aggressive** style. The person who communicates aggressively does so at the risk of disregarding everyone else's rights or feelings. Aggressive communicators are often hostile, blaming, demanding, and rude. They tend to use negative "you" statements and speak in a loud voice. You might hear the following from an aggresssive speaker: "You are incompetent. How could you possibly expect to be taken seriously when you submit a report like that?" or "You really blew it this time" or "That is one of the most ridiculous ideas you have ever come up with."

NOTE 13.16
An aggressive communicator disregards others' rights and uses intimidation to make his or her point.

Assertive. Using **assertive** communication is usually very productive because the goal is to meet the needs of all parties to the highest degree possible. Those who communicate assertively respect the rights and feelings of others while standing up for their own rights. They effectively influence, listen, and negotiate so others choose to cooperate or communicate openly and willingly. When addressing others verbally, assertive communicators use factual information, not personal judgments; they avoid exaggeration; they use "I," not "you"; their words reflect ownership; and they speak in a firm voice. Some examples of assertive verbal communication might include, "I would like to offer my suggestion without being interrupted," "The figures in this report are from the second quarter; they should be third-quarter figures," and "I get upset when you don't do what you say you will do." Although at times you may use all three of these communication styles, passive and aggressive communication do not typically achieve your goals or those of your organization; assertive communication is productive and efficient and projects respect for all involved in the communication.

NOTE 13.17
Assertive communication achieves goals, is productive, and respects the rights of all involved in the conversation.

The process, techniques, and communication styles described in this section apply to all conversations; those described in the next three sections relate to special forms of conversation—face-to-face, telephone, and social business.

KEYS FOR SUCCESSFUL FACE-TO-FACE CONVERSATIONS

Face-to-face conversations have an advantage over written and telephone communication because both the sender and receiver can use nonverbal cues to help them convey and interpret a message. The following techniques will help make a face-to-face exchange productive:

NOTE 13.18
Several techniques can be used to make conversations productive.

- Carefully choose the location.
- Minimize interruptions.
- Speak effectively.
- Choose appropriate language.
- Send clear, appropriate nonverbal cues.
- Ask questions.
- Accommodate diversity.
- Listen with your ears and eyes.

Carefully Choose the Location. Conversations may take place in your office, in someone else's office, or at a neutral site. The purpose of the meeting should dictate the site and seating arrangement. Furniture can be a barrier to open communication. In a small office, a chair placed beside the desk creates a more welcoming atmosphere than does a chair placed opposite the desk.

NOTE 13.19
Place furniture to encourage open communication.

Restaurants are neutral sites that provide the opportunity for both social and business interaction. When meeting a business associate at a restaurant, select a table away from major traffic flow and wait there for your guest. Seat yourself across the table from your guest; be sure the guest has the seat with the fewest distractions.

Minimize Interruptions. Interruptions affect your ability to hold a meaningful conversation. Ask staff to answer telephone calls, have your calls transferred directly to voice mail, or simply let your phone ring. Keep your office door partially or fully closed to discourage interruptions. In a work cubicle, turn away from the entry. When off-site, turn off your pager or cell phone or set it to signal messages by vibrating rather than ringing.

Speak Effectively. Strong, effective messages are short and simple. Always think before you speak, carefully choose your words, and structure your sentences so that the receiver will understand them. Most receivers want to hear only those details they need to understand the message. They react favorably to the ideas of a sender who is concise and to the point without being abrupt. People also appreciate having others call them by name. The Tips and Hints feature below provides helpful suggestions on this topic.

Vary your pitch, speed, and volume to hold your listener's interest and to emphasize important points. Use the tone of your voice to reinforce the message you are communicating. Enunciate words clearly and pronounce them correctly. Eliminate vocal distractions such as *um* and *uh*. Avoid vocal expressions that show impatience (humming, speaking abnormally fast) and that do not support your message (sighing).

Choose Appropriate Language. Your purpose, analysis of the situation, and analysis of the receiver will guide you in determining appropriate word choice and how assertive you should be. Remember, though, that assertiveness does not mean

tips and hints

The Importance of a Name

A person's name is his or her most important possession. In the business world, introductions are typically based on a person's rank or position in a company. Individuals of lower rank or status are introduced to those of higher rank or status. If you introduce two people of equal rank to each other, introduce the one you know less well to the one you know better. The only exception to this is when you are dealing with a customer or client. The customer or client should be introduced first even if you are with someone of higher rank in your company. Always mention both the first and last names distinctly, including titles. Until asked to do otherwise, use the courtesy title and surname of customers, clients, or people who hold positions above yours within your organization. Address peers or others in the organization by their given name.

When you forget someone's name, be open and honest; admit your memory lapse. The specific approach you take will depend on the situation. When someone who phones you fails to give his or her name and you are unable to identify the caller by voice or from context, apologize and ask the caller's name. If the individual approaches you and addresses you by name, say, "It's good to see you again. I remember meeting you (indicate event or time) but don't recall your name."

To initiate a conversation, begin by introducing yourself and reminding the person about where and when you met. Use the same strategy if you begin conversing with someone and sense he or she doesn't remember your name. Comfort, not embarrassment, is your goal.

aggressiveness; assertiveness does not alienate others. Be assertive by stating your views in a clear, direct, and honest manner, respecting your own rights and feelings as well as the rights and feelings of the receiver.

Keep your emotions in check because in business relationships people are expected to be calm and controlled. It is possible to disagree without being disagreeable. Successful businesspeople do not argue, they discuss. They do not dominate the discussion. They avoid sarcasm, vulgarity, and inappropriate tears or laughter. They don't embarrass themselves or others.

NOTE 13.22
Control your emotions.

Send Clear, Appropriate Nonverbal Cues. If appropriate to the situation, smile. When you offer someone a genuine smile, you show acceptance and build trust. People speak more freely when they feel safe, and a smile conveys safety.

NOTE 13.23
Use nonverbal cues that match the situation.

Generally, the gestures and other movements used during conversations are smaller and more subtle than those used when speaking before a group. The proximity of the person or group with whom you are conversing makes your facial expressions more noticeable. Be sure any touch is appropriate to the situation, the person, and the culture. Touch can be perceived to signal playfulness, control, support, gratitude, affection, intimidation, harassment, aggression, or other motives. Respect the personal space of those with whom you speak.

Limited eye contact may be thought to signify dishonesty, fear, or lack of interest—all barriers to effective communication; it may also be the accepted norm and show respect in some cultures. Let your receiver and the circumstances govern your behavior.

Ask Questions. Asking questions is a good way to encourage another person to communicate. Carefully structured questions can help you gather facts, determine your receiver's needs, and encourage dialogue. Good communicators understand and use both closed- and open-ended questions.

NOTE 13.24
Use questions to obtain facts and learn about feelings.

A **closed-ended question** is designed to produce a one- or two-word answer; this type of question works best for fact finding. An **open-ended question** requires a longer answer and promotes a dialogue. Use this type of question when you want expanded answers or background information. Open-ended questions also work well when your receiver or the situation is emotional.

NOTE 13.25
Use closed- and open-ended questions.

If, for example, you are trying to help a subordinate improve the quality of his or her work, you will have a more meaningful exchange if you ask, "What can I do to help you do a better job?" than by asking, "Do you need help to do your job?" The open-ended question invites the employee to suggest things that each of you can do to improve the work. In this situation, the closed-ended question invites a one-word response—and resentment or anger. Conversely, if you need to know when an order was shipped, you will get the data you want faster by asking, "What was the shipping date on the Vanguard Security order?" than by asking, "What's happening with the Vanguard Security order?"

Once you've asked a question, give the receiver time to respond. Fast-paced questioning could be perceived as interrogation, which will stifle rather than stimulate discussion.

Accommodate Diversity. Recognize and accommodate cultural or other differences during your conversations. Consider language differences; nonverbal communication differences; and factors such as values, attitudes, religion, political systems, and social orders. Be alert to and considerate of physical or other disabilities that affect communication. Chapter 2 provides information about these and other elements of workplace diversity.

NOTE 13.26

Attentive listening shows
your interest in the
speaker.

Listen with Your Ears and Eyes. People often think about what they are going to say next instead of listening to what the other person has to say. By giving the speaker your full attention, you can participate effectively in the conversation and show the other person you believe that he or she is important and interesting.

Giving the speaker your full attention will allow you to "hear" both verbal and nonverbal cues. Any deviation from the person's normal speech pattern and nonverbal behavior must be considered in the context of the situation. Negative words or an angry tone may signal disagreement or fear; a fast pace may signal nervousness, enthusiasm, or excitement. Darting eye movements, frequent shifts of body weight, and changes in posture must also be interpreted. You may tell an employee that you have decided to give some of his or her job responsibilities to a coworker. If the employee's shoulders slump or if he or she becomes teary-eyed while saying, "Fine. Good." you know that the employee does not view your decision as either fine or good. Before you can move forward with the business discussion, the employee's feelings must be addressed.

NOTE 13.27

Paraphrasing helps you
clarify and retain what
you hear.

To verify or acknowledge what you hear, paraphrase the message or ask relevant questions. Repeating what was said will help you retain what you have heard. When the speaker pauses, count to three before you speak. Interruptions can destroy the comfortable atmosphere you want to create, but a carefully placed "Let me see if I understood you to say . . ." or "So, what you are recommending is . . ." can keep the line of communication open.

NOTE 13.28

Listen with empathy.

Empathy means understanding how a person feels; it does not mean you agree with how the person feels. Listening with empathy is especially important when someone comes to you with a problem. After the problem has been described, ask how you can help. Offer advice only when encouraged to do so. Sometimes just listening is all the help the person needs.

KEYS FOR SUCCESSFUL TELEPHONE CONVERSATIONS

NOTE 13.29

Telephone conversations
are important business
tools.

The telephone is important for sending and receiving business messages and can be valuable in building interpersonal relationships. For some message receivers, the entire image of a company rests solely on the quality of their telephone interactions with representatives of the organization. The following suggestions will help you improve the quality of your telephone conversations.

- Use the telephone equipment and system properly.
- Be businesslike.
- Be considerate.

NOTE 13.30

The telephone amplifies
sounds.

Use the Telephone Equipment and System Properly. Hold the telephone mouthpiece one to two inches from your mouth and talk directly into it. Speech faults, accents, and other sounds are magnified during telephone conversations. Never chew gum, eat, or drink while on the phone. Before placing or receiving a call, remove earrings, bracelets, and similar jewelry that may interfere with proper use of the telephone. Know how to transfer calls, arrange conference calls, use a speaker phone, set up callbacks, and use other special features of your system. Employees who are not able to use the company telephone system properly will be perceived as inefficient, as will the organization.

Be Businesslike. When the telephone rings, be ready to talk when you answer; end all conversations with others in your office. Identify yourself immediately. Some phone systems produce a different ringing sound or have a screen display code to indicate whether a call originated inside or outside the organization. You may wish to include your organization and department name only for calls from outside the organization.

As you speak, create and hold a mental image of the person you call. This technique will help you maintain a businesslike manner. The method will also help keep the conversation receiver-centered and your voice conversational. Because you cannot be seen, your voice has to carry the whole message and convey its tone. Use the caller's name and cordial terms such as *please, thank you,* and *I appreciate.* Remember to smile; the tone of your voice is more pleasant when you smile.

If the caller is angry or has a complaint, stay calm. Realize that the caller is upset with a situation or policy, not with you personally. When you or your company has made an error, acknowledge it without placing blame or making excuses; then, move on. Do what you can to correct the problem; if you promise action, set a reasonable time frame and do what you promise.

After the conversation has ended, let the caller hang up first. This simple gesture reinforces the impression that the caller is important and has your undivided attention. It also minimizes the need for a second call because the caller thought of something else to say but was cut off before he or she could do so.

When you place a call, the telephone may be answered by a support staff member or channeled to a voice mail system. Be prepared to leave a clear, complete message that includes at least your name, your phone number, and the purpose of your call. Be sure to pronounce and spell your name clearly; slow down when giving your phone number. It is also a good idea to leave the date and time you called.

Whether at home or at the office, be sure your outgoing message is current and complete. Resist the temptation to record a generic "I'm unavailable to take your call" message; provide your callers with real information about when you will be available to take or return calls. Invite your caller to leave a message. Be sure, too, that your message is businesslike. Friends or family members may enjoy a humorous greeting, but a client or prospective employer could view the greeting—and you—as unprofessional. Also, international callers may be confused by messages using colloquial English or by messages recorded at a faster than normal speaking rate.

Be Considerate. Place your own calls. Having an assistant place your calls and then keeping the called party waiting while you get on the line makes it appear that you believe your time is more valuable than the receiver's. Such a procedure is inconsiderate and gets the conversation off to a bad start.

When taking calls, answer on the first ring, if possible, but certainly no later than the third. When you must ask a caller to wait while you gather information, return at 15- to 30-second intervals to report your progress and assure him or her that you will be back to the conversation as soon as possible. If it becomes obvious that your off-phone efforts will take longer than a minute or two, offer to return the call at a specified time. Be sure to keep a pencil and notepad close to the telephone. Before using a speaker phone, ask whether the other person objects; honor the person's preference for privacy.

KEYS FOR SUCCESSFUL SOCIAL BUSINESS CONVERSATIONS

In the professional world, the way you interact with others says a lot about your values and how you do business. As an employee, you may be asked to attend social events for or about your profession or organization. You may find these functions

NOTE 13.31
Project courtesy and a businesslike manner.

NOTE 13.32
Create clear and complete voice mails.

NOTE 13.33
Placing and taking your own calls is efficient and courteous.

NOTE 13.34
Interactions in a social business setting reflect how you do business.

present a networking opportunity, or they may simply be an opportunity for you to become acquainted with other individuals from your organization or your professional field. The following guidelines will help you enhance your social business interactions:

- Practice basic social conversation rules.
- Choose appropriate topics.
- Observe social business etiquette.

Practice Basic Social Conversation Rules. Project a polite and professional image at social business functions by making eye contact and smiling when introducing yourself. You will project an image of confidence and approachability. Shake hands firmly when greeting someone. If you are asked to wear a name tag, put it on the upper right shoulder so when you shake hands, people can follow your arm straight to your name. If you are seated, stand when someone is introduced to you. New acquaintances should be addressed by their title and last name until they ask you to use their first name. If you have met someone before and are renewing the acquaintance, indicate when and where you met. Carry business cards to give to people you meet.

Open conversations with "safe" topics when you are meeting someone for the first time. Keep the conversations moving by limiting your responses to a minute or two. Do not monopolize any one person's time. When conversing with someone, show that you are focused on the conversation by keeping eye contact, nodding, smiling, and using other nonverbal gestures. And, at all times, practice common courtesy. Don't interrupt the person talking or finish his or her sentences. Do not criticize others; it is very unprofessional and may have negative consequences. End a conversation by acknowledging the other person and the pleasure of meeting him or her.

At social functions, it is always a good idea to keep your hands as free as possible. Don't carry a huge notebook or bag. If you must eat or drink something, hold it in your left hand so your right hand is free for handshakes.

Choose Appropriate Topics. Stay away from negative conversation and never tell rumors or point out faults in others. These actions build mistrust and are generally unpleasant and unprofessional. There are, however, several topics that are safe for conversations at business social events. Current events are always in style; however, avoid topics involving politics and religion. Instead, concentrate on local events or topics that can be found in a business publication or professional journal. Sports is always a topic that people are eager to talk about. You don't have to be an expert, but at least know what sport season it is and the name of any local teams. If those topics have escaped you for the moment, you can always talk about the function and its goal and/or sponsor. New employees especially can take the opportunity to find out more about the organization sponsoring the event or the professional organization that represents their career field. Personal questions such as "Where did you go to school?" or "Where do you live?" or "Do you have any vacation plans?" can always be used as fallbacks.

Observe Social Business Etiquette. Appearances are important; dress conservatively and in attire appropriate to the event. In most cases, business or business casual attire will be a good choice. Turn off cell phones and pagers or set them to vibrate when attending a social business function. Be on time to social events, but never early. And, don't bring uninvited guests. If someone compliments you, accept it with a simple "Thank you"; don't launch into a long story.

Attend social business events; they are an integral part of your professional life. If you aspire to a higher-level job, this will be just one of the responsibilities you will perform. Employers like to see how their employees act in social settings.

The effectiveness of any conversation depends on several factors—the words and how they are delivered, the appearance of the participants, and the social graces that the participants display. In all situations, project a confident, credible, and professional image.

Relationship Repair

Sometimes, despite the good intentions of those involved, relationships are damaged. Rather than let pride or indifference cause them to walk away from a damaged relationship, effective communicators take steps to rebuild it.

The obvious thing to do, of course, is apologize. Sometimes a simple "I'm sorry" is all that's needed. When this simple statement doesn't accomplish its goal, however, the speaker must make an additional effort. Acknowledging that he or she played a part in the failure is an option, but the speaker must do so sincerely and without expectation that the receiver will also claim responsibility. Relinquishing dual responsibility is a sacrifice that demonstrates the speaker's commitment to rebuilding the relationship.

Depending on what caused the relationship to weaken, positive actions may be the glue that's needed to mend it. This is especially true when the relationship has a history of broken promises. Actions can replace or complement an apology or acknowledgment.

Finally, both parties must let go of the problem that caused the relationship failure. Until they do, the relationship cannot regain its strength or grow stronger.

NOTE 13.39
With effort, damaged relationships can be repaired.

Feedback

Feedback is the communication to a person or a team of people regarding the effect their behavior is having on another person, the organization, the customer, or the team. There are two kinds of effective feedback—positive and constructive. Positive feedback (sometimes referred to as praise) is easy to give and nice to receive. For most people, the opposite is true of constructive feedback.

Whether the feedback is positive or constructive, it is always specific; focuses on a specific behavior, not the person's intentions; is sincere and honest; describes actions or behavior that an individual can do something about; and is well timed. The manner and approach you use to deliver feedback will determine what impact it has. Feedback is necessary for organizations to operate at optimal levels.

LO 3
Give feedback effectively and receive it appropriately.

NOTE 13.40
There are two kinds of effective feedback—positive and constructive.

Positive Feedback

Positive feedback involves telling someone about good performance. Be specific when giving positive feedback. For example, say, "The report you turned in yesterday was well written and understandable; you made your points about the budget very effectively" instead of "Good report." This type of feedback will have a

NOTE 13.41
Positive feedback is a motivator.

greater impact if it is given as closely to the event as possible. Positive feedback is not difficult to give but is sometimes overlooked as the powerful motivator it can be. Most people want to be recognized, so recognition fosters more of the appreciated action.

Constructive Feedback

NOTE 13.42
Constructive feedback is not criticism.

Constructive feedback alerts an individual to an area in which his or her performance could improve. Constructive feedback is not criticism; its main purpose is to help people understand where they stand in relation to the expected job behavior. Constructive feedback is a fact of workplace life. Therefore, it is important that we learn to deliver it effectively without fear of a negative response or reprisal. It is just as important that we accept it with an open mind and learn from it, even if our natural instinct is to defend ourselves and our actions.

GIVING CONSTRUCTIVE FEEDBACK

NOTE 13.43
Receiver understanding and acceptance are the goals.

The following list contains suggestions to help you maximize the chances of having your receiver understand and accept feedback.

- Be sure you have the authority to critique the receiver. If you don't, he or she will most likely reject the feedback and resent you for delivering it.
- Have clear expectations of what should occur when you provide the constructive feedback. If you don't, the outcome will not provide the information necessary for the receiver to understand what should have occurred, how the behavior did not meet the expectation, and how to change the behavior to get the desired result.
- Give feedback on one relevant concern at a time. People become overwhelmed, confused, or dejected when faced with a long list of complaints. Be assertive but consistent. Repeat and clarify the issues, but do not argue about them.
- Check your facts. Avoid using absolute words such as *never* and *always*. If your receiver identifies even one small element of your concern as being false, he or she could focus on it, argue about it, and move the conversation away from the issue at hand. Once a sender's credibility on an issue is compromised, the goal cannot be accomplished.
- Provide feedback privately and calmly, preferably face-to-face. Feedback is difficult enough to receive without being embarrassed in the process. Give the receiver an opportunity to retain his or her dignity and to use every available verbal and nonverbal cue. Be sure no one interrupts your meeting with a phone call or office visit.
- Be specific and helpful. Comments that are clear, specific, and show receiver benefit will be most effective. Rather than saying, "Your proposal is disorganized, contains computational errors, and is a writing disaster," say, "All the elements of a good proposal are here; they just need to be reordered. By placing the strongest element first, we can capture and hold the reader's attention. Double-check your figures and be sure grammar and punctuation are correct." Vague, self-serving suggestions could cause the receiver to feel anxiety or doubt.

NOTE 13.44
Focus on the receiver; use the you–viewpoint.

- Use the you–viewpoint; comment on the action or issue, not the person. "Not giving your full attention to a customer gives the image that we don't think he or she is important" or "You'll make a more positive personal and corporate impression if you give the customer your complete attention" works better than

"You aren't paying attention to the customer when you are having a conversation with someone else at the same time."

- Be sure the receiver knows your feedback in one area won't cloud your overall judgment of him or her. Show respect and appreciation for what the person has done in other areas. By scheduling the meeting for early in the week or early in the day, you will have opportunities to see the individual in positive, reassuring situations shortly after the meeting. Evaluate personal items (e.g., hygiene, dress) only when they relate to work performance.
- If appropriate, accept partial responsibility for the problem. An introduction such as "Perhaps my directions weren't clear" can temper the impact of the constructive feedback that follows.
- Be aware of the verbal and nonverbal cues that accompany your message. Use a conversational pace and tone. Use "blameless" gestures. Pointing with a pen or your finger, for example, creates an aura of accusation.
- Allow the receiver time to process and respond. Even when the receiver knows the purpose of the meeting is to discuss behavior or work performance, hearing the message may have an emotional impact. Accept silence and emotional displays. Listen actively and empathetically. When people believe they have been heard and understood, they are less defensive.

NOTE 13.45
Allow the receiver to absorb and respond.

RECEIVING AND ACCEPTING CONSTRUCTIVE FEEDBACK

Perhaps the only thing more difficult than giving constructive feedback is receiving it. When faced with constructive feedback, people generally respond with "fight or flight" behavior. Fighting manifests itself as defensive, argumentative, or counterattack remarks. Fleeing can be physical (e.g., avoiding face-to-face or telephone contact) or mental (e.g., tuning out). In the long run, neither method solves the problem as effectively as (a) accepting the comments or (b) seeking more information.

NOTE 13.46
Accept constructive feedback without becoming defensive.

Accepting. Feedback can be based on facts, perceptions, or both. If, for example, your supervisor identifies several customer service calls that were handled improperly, he or she may perceive that you were careless or didn't understand what should be done in a particular situation. Arguing about the facts (improper handling of customer service calls) is futile, but you can redirect the perception by pointing out that these identified phone calls are the exception, not the rule, in your work performance. You can also acknowledge that you understand why he or she might feel you did not represent the company as you should have. Acknowledging the other person's feelings doesn't mean you agree with them. Say what you will do to minimize the likelihood that the problem will be repeated.

NOTE 13.47
Accept the facts; redirect the perception they create.

Seeking More Information. Showing interest in what prompts the constructive feedback can help you decide how to fix whatever prompted it. To that end, consider doing the following:

- Ask for specific examples. "Can you play back the phone conversation in which you indicated I raised my voice to the customer and did not give the correct response to the situation?"
- Describe a situation and ask whether it illustrates the problem. "Does the volume of my voice in the conversation with Mrs. Copley and the solution to her concerns with her purchase illustrate the problem?"

NOTE 13.48
Clarify the concern by seeking more information.

- Paraphrase to focus on an outcome. "Are you saying that how I handled Mrs. Copley's concerns was not the best solution to maintain customer goodwill and that it has created problems for our company?"
- Keep your focus on specific ways that you can sharpen your skills. Specific, achievable goals are motivating. Ask how you can improve. "Do you have specific suggestions that might help me?"

After receiving constructive feedback, be sure to take action to remedy the situation. If the critic's suggestions result in improvement, thank him or her; if problems persist, ask for another opportunity to discuss the situation. Keep in mind that a continuously improving organization is made up of continuously improving employees.

Conflict

LO 4

Describe techniques for resolving conflicts.

NOTE 13.49
Conflict can arise from various sources.

NOTE 13.50
Responses to conflict vary by person and situation.

Conflict is inevitable. To deny it is to prove it. Conflict can occur in your personal life or at work. In the workplace, conflict may arise between you and a coworker, between two employees you supervise, between your department and another, or between your organization and a customer or client.

Conflict can arise from differences in personalities (e.g., extrovert and introvert), goals or expectations, values or beliefs, circumstances (e.g., money and time), or facts (e.g., different sources). Conflicts associated with values and beliefs tend to be the most difficult to resolve because they are so deeply rooted. When faced with conflict, you have four options:

- *Accommodate.* This approach should be used when the issue is less important to one person than to the other or when maintaining the relationship is more important than the issue. It is also the logical approach when one person knows he or she can't win or wants to bank a favor.
- *Compromise.* This approach works best when the parties have some areas of agreement on which a mutually acceptable solution can be built or, as in accommodating, when the relationship is more important than the issue.
- *Overpower.* This approach should be used only in an emergency or when the issue is more important than the relationship.
- *Collaborate.* This approach requires people to work together and seek a solution that satisfies both parties. It fits best in situations that may repeat themselves or when the relationship has been long-term. The collaborative approach allows for creativity in developing a resolution and gives participants a sense of accomplishment that together they have resolved the issue without losing anything.

NOTE 13.51
Conflict may be good or bad.

Conflict may be constructive or destructive. At its best, conflict results in solutions to problems, develops cooperative working relationships among participants, fosters creative thinking, and helps individuals develop understanding for one another. Healthy conflict is marked by the ability to disagree on one issue while working collaboratively on others. At its worst, conflict sabotages relationships, destroys morale, polarizes people, lowers productivity, and takes attention away from other important issues and activities. Unhealthy conflict is not issue specific; it transcends both time and situations. Fortunately, destructive conflicts can be resolved. The techniques that follow can be used when you are directly involved in the conflict or when you are an outside party with a vested interest in seeing it resolved.

General Techniques for Handling Conflicts

Several conflict resolution techniques apply to situations in which you are a participant and to those in which you are a facilitator:

- *Act promptly.* The longer a problem goes unattended, the greater the chance it will escalate into a major issue. If the conflict involves emotions, the parties will need 24 to 48 hours to cool off.
- *Schedule a meeting.* Whenever possible, meet face-to-face so that the participants can take advantage of nonverbal cues. Choose a neutral location so neither party has a territorial advantage.
- *Use active listening.* Every conflict has two sides, and each person fervently believes his or hers is the accurate or "right" side. Both people want to be heard and understood. Before a conflict can be resolved, both parties must be able to separate what happened from how they feel about it. Paraphrasing can be valuable in this effort.
- *Communicate honestly.* Keep egos out of the situation and don't play games.
- *Focus on the problem, not the person.* Laying blame delays resolution. The parties must respect themselves and each other.
- *Brainstorm solutions.* Look for win-win opportunities; negotiate if necessary.
- *Formalize the solution.* Putting the solution on paper allows both parties the opportunity to see as well as hear it and minimizes the likelihood that they will later disagree on the solution.
- *Implement the solution and set a date for follow-up.* The follow-up creates an air of accountability.

NOTE 13.52
Conflict resolution requires good interpersonal skills.

Participant's Responsibility for Handling a Conflict

One person in a conflict must initiate resolution. Although some perceive the person who takes the first step as the weaker party, others believe he or she is the stronger. In the workplace, the latter is more likely to be true.

NOTE 13.53
Take the first step.

Critically analyze the situation and your role in it before you approach the other person. If you don't know the basis for your position, you won't be able to explain it. Keep your emotions under control; place organizational goals above personal goals.

When you approach the other person, do so with sincerity. Issue an invitation rather than a directive. Telling the other person that you must meet will create more tension.

During the meeting, let the other person tell his or her story first. Paraphrase to verify that you understand both facts and feelings. Ask for specific examples and facts, but choose your words and tone carefully. Getting angry, arguing, telling the person how he or she should feel, making statements that ridicule or criticize the other person, or telling him or her to be quiet and listen will make the situation worse. As you listen, look for areas of agreement. When you tell your story, begin by citing areas on which you agree. Then move to those on which resolution will be necessary. If the list is short or simple, begin immediately to look for solutions. If

NOTE 13.54
Listen before speaking.

the list is long or complex, schedule a second meeting with the understanding that you'll each come to it with possible solutions.

Facilitator's Responsibility for Handling a Conflict

NOTE 13.55
Left unattended, conflict
will escalate.

As a supervisor or manager, you will have responsibility for building a team, a group that will work with each other and with you to achieve goals. Productivity declines, lowered morale, absenteeism, accidents, and emotional outbursts are all signs that conflict may exist. When conflict emerges within your group, you have an obligation to see that it is resolved before it escalates.

You may learn about a conflict by (a) observing it, (b) being told of it by one or both parties involved in it, or (c) being informed by a third party. Sometimes intensity can be mistaken for conflict; simply hearing raised voices isn't sufficient to presume conflict exists. If you believe you observe conflict or are told of it by a third party, document it.

The situation is more tenuous if one party to a conflict tells you about it. You must acknowledge what you are told without giving the impression that you agree with the person. Taking sides or giving the impression that you are taking sides creates animosity and enemies. Similarly, you must refrain from placing blame or forcing the parties to apologize. Trying to identify who is at fault is unproductive; it causes you to look backward rather than forward. Being forced to apologize humiliates the parties and can increase the animosity between them.

Regardless of how you learn about a conflict, deal with it in private. Invite the parties to meet with you separately and then together. Use the individual meetings to determine the real source of the conflict and its severity. Unless the key issue is identified and resolved, it will resurface. Use the group meeting to encourage teamwork and problem solving. During the joint meeting, the facilitator acts as an emcee; he or she introduces topics, clarifies, refocuses, and summarizes. Remember that your goal is to help the parties resolve their disagreement. You could cause resentment if you approach the situation with the goal of saving or rescuing.

Teamwork

LO 5
*Develop the skills
associated with leading
and participating in
teams.*

NOTE 13.56
Together Everyone
Achieves More.

Teamwork has permeated the corporate and nonprofit sectors of American organizations. Teams are and will remain a basic unit of both performance and change because of their proven capacity to accomplish what other units cannot. In specific situations, they can have a significant impact. Teams are one of the most popular work units in organizations because of their flexibility (they can be quickly assembled, deployed, refocused, and disbanded) and their productivity (they deliver tangible performance results).

The concept is simple—by working together, people can accomplish more than any individual can achieve by working alone—but the execution can be complex. A successful team requires persistence, energy, and focus on the part of the team leader and the team participants. Because teams are so common, you should know about the various types of teams, know how teamwork benefits you and the organization, be aware of the conditions that must exist for effective teamwork, and learn how to be a good team leader and a good team member. In the Communication Note that follows, employers point out that they look for teamwork and leadership skills in their prospective employees.

communication note

WHAT EMPLOYERS ARE LOOKING FOR

On May 2, 2005, CollegeGrad.com released the results of a survey on the criteria employers ranked as most important when hiring new employees. Here are the comments from two of the employers surveyed.

Be congenial, have a "get-it-done" attitude and be a team player— anything less than that will draw down the company's productivity and your career growth.

—Ron Guzinski, Assistant Vice President of Human Resources, GEICO

We screen by major, GPA, demonstrated leadership and experience, so the key differentiators for us are communication skills and maturity—how effectively does the student speak and write and is he or she comfortable in front of a variety of audiences.

—Elizabeth Polak, Talent Acquisition Manager, University Relations, Owens Corning

Source: CollegeGrad.com, "New Survey Results Detail What Top Employers Want Most," May 2, 2005, http://www.collegegrade.com/press/whatemployerswant2005 .shtml (accessed May 28, 2006).

Types of Teams

Teams can be categorized generally as self-managed, process-improvement, cross-functional, or virtual. Any of these types of teams can be made up of people from different cultures and may be referred to as a multicultural team. Multicultural teams are known for their capabilities to produce innovative results and to manage large, complex projects. However, multicultural teams are successful only when the members can bridge their cultural differences.

NOTE 13.57
Teams may be categorized by type.

SELF-MANAGED TEAMS

Teams that have a great deal of autonomy and share the leadership role are considered to be self-directed or self-managed. Self-managed teams are ongoing groups with decision-making authority for nearly every aspect of product production or service delivery from inception to conclusion. Every member of the self-managed team shares equal responsibility for the finished product. Team responsibilities generally include planning daily work as well as hiring, firing, and training. This structure exists in organizations that have adopted teamwork as an operational model.

PROCESS-IMPROVEMENT TEAMS

As the name implies, process-improvement teams are charged with making changes to a process. Their focus may be increasing quality, reducing costs, providing speedier service, or eliminating redundancy. Once changes have been proposed and/or implemented, the team is disbanded.

CROSS-FUNCTIONAL TEAMS

Members of these teams are drawn from various functional areas and charged with accomplishing a particular task, completing a particular process, or providing ongoing input about various issues. This type of team draws its strength from the perspectives and diverse viewpoints its members can present.

VIRTUAL TEAMS

Virtual teams are a current organizational reality due to the globalization of business. One advantage of virtual teams is that groups can transcend the boundaries of time and location. A company with offices in North America and Asia can establish teams with members on the two continents and effectively lengthen the workday by having the project handed from one team to another across time zones.

Virtual teams also level status differences that can occur when people representing various levels within an organization meet in person. As a result, ideas are more likely to be evaluated on merit; team members contribute more often and more freely because they feel a certain level of anonymity when communicating electronically. In addition, the convenience of these meetings often means that more people can contribute; better decisions may result from broader input as well as from ready access to files and other materials.

Teams that cover a wide area can have a deep impact, but a team that is separated by geographical distance presents unique challenges. Those challenges include agreeing on what and how technology will be used to support the team's effort. Some managers perceive that motivation and morale building are more difficult in virtual teams, but computer technology has been so well integrated into our personal and professional lives that concerns about the ability to create team spirit without face-to-face meetings is declining.

The virtual team also needs to determine the use of language to avoid the risk of misunderstanding. More details on how virtual teams function and use technology to achieve organizational goals are in the section of this chapter called "Other Meeting Formats."

Benefits and Drawbacks of Teamwork

NOTE 13.58
Teams have personal and organizational impact.

Teams have both advantages and disadvantages.

On a personal level, participating on a team can help you increase your knowledge of the organization, broaden your perspective of areas within the business, develop a sense of camaraderie with coworkers, be more visible within the organization, learn about the various management styles used by team leaders, and improve your own project management skills.

At the organizational level, teams help organizations gain a competitive advantage. In addition, they can help increase productivity, improve communication, encourage creativity, facilitate problem solving, and increase the quality of decisions. The negatives of working in a group include loss of control; pressure to conform; and uneven distribution of workload, a phenomenon also known as "free riding" or "social loafing." With effective team leadership and participation, these disadvantages can be neutralized or eliminated.

NOTE 13.59
Communication, cohesiveness, and potential for growth foster team success.

For teams to function effectively, the following conditions must exist:

- *Communication must be open and honest.* Members must trust and respect one another. Ideas should be offered freely and listened to with patience and courtesy. Decisions should be based on an idea's merits, not on the popularity or power of the person who offers it. Personal attacks reduce the comfort level within the team and can promote retaliation or reduced participation.
- *The team must be cohesive.* Members must share and be committed to the team's goals and vision. When some members are excluded, the spirit of cooperation is threatened. Members must be free to interact with each other and with the leader.
- *Growth should be fostered.* The needs of the individual, the team, and the organization must be considered. At the individual level, participation should offer the opportunity for personal and professional growth. Keeping the group to a workable size helps make this happen. When teams exceed ten members, communica-

tion and coordination pose challenges. Balanced contributions are more difficult to achieve in a large team; some members may even try to be anonymous.

- *Accomplishments must be recognized.* When teams achieve their goals, they should be recognized for their accomplishment. All members—not just the leader—should receive recognition.

Meeting Leadership and Participation

Meetings are the common vehicle through which teams plan, report, and coordinate efforts toward reaching their goals. Depending on their jobs and the industries in which they work, managers report spending anywhere from 30 to 60 percent of their time in meetings. Unfortunately, many businesspeople view meetings as boring, intrusive time wasters. Knowing how to lead and participate in meetings is, therefore, essential to helping you make them worthwhile, productive experiences.

NOTE 13.60
Meetings are held for sharing information and solving problems.

KEYS FOR EFFECTIVE SMALL-GROUP MEETING LEADERSHIP
Sometimes effective teams arise naturally; more often, they need guidance and leadership. The person primarily responsible for the success of a team is the leader. The keys for successful small-group leadership are presented in the following paragraphs.

Determine the Purpose of the Group. The scope of the group's responsibility and authority must be defined. Will it make recommendations, or does it have the power to act? Is the group an ongoing one, designed to share information and solve problems as they arise, or is it a special team formed to brainstorm solutions to a specific dilemma? The purpose of a group will influence the way in which it accomplishes its work. Therefore, the leader must ensure that the group's purpose is clearly communicated to and understood by all members.

NOTE 13.61
The way a group operates is influenced by its purpose.

Determine the Purpose of Each Meeting. Planning, brainstorming, sharing information, solving problems, and training are among the reasons for which meetings may be held. Groups that meet regularly (e.g., quarterly meeting of sales managers) may have more than one purpose for each meeting. Members might share information about human resources needs and, at the same meeting, brainstorm about ways in which space may be reallocated.

NOTE 13.62
Hold meetings only when necessary.

Before scheduling a face-to-face meeting, be sure it needs to be held. Meetings, even regularly scheduled weekly or monthly meetings, should be canceled if no issues need to be discussed or no decisions need to be made. Consider, too, whether another format might better serve the group. A two- or three-person conversation, an e-mail, or a telephone conference might be more efficient. Although face-to-face meetings have a social dimension, socializing should not be the only reason for meeting.

All too often, people are invited to meetings because the leader doesn't want them to feel left out. Although appropriate in many settings, courtesy is insufficient reason for including someone at a meeting. The larger the group, the less productive the session will be. Limit attendance to those who are instrumental in achieving the group's goals.

NOTE 13.63
Keep groups to a manageable size.

Plan the Meeting Agenda. The group leader must prepare the meeting agenda carefully. The topics to be discussed should be listed in some logical order, in a sequence that serves the purpose of the group. The leader may group similar topics

NOTE 13.64
Prepare and distribute the agenda and related materials in advance.

to avoid repetition. He or she may also allocate a time limit to each point to be discussed on the agenda.

For a formal meeting, copies of the agenda and all related materials should be distributed a few days in advance of the meeting so that the members can prepare. It is critical that everyone knows what to expect before coming to a meeting. When the volume of attachments is small, e-mail is a suitable distribution method. Outlines for two styles of agenda are presented in Figure 13.2. Either could be modified to include the name of the person responsible for each item and to indicate the approximate time to be devoted to each item. For informal meetings with very limited scope, a telephone message describing the date, time, place, and topic may be sufficient.

The time at which a meeting is held can have an effect on its success. Scheduling a meeting for early morning (e.g., 8:15 a.m.) suggests importance; starting at an off-hour time (e.g., 10:45 a.m.) encourages punctuality; selecting an odd starting time (e.g., 1:17 p.m.) captures interest; and scheduling meetings for times just before lunch or at the end of the day encourages timely adjournment. Finally, keep meetings brief. Attention and interest wane after about an hour. If meetings must be longer than an hour, schedule a short break, then reconvene.

The first time a group gathers, list the names of participants on the agenda. Be sure to list the names of guests any time they attend. Knowing who will attend a meeting helps the participants plan for the event.

Select and Prepare the Meeting Facility. Most routine business meetings are held on-site. Off-site meetings encourage efficiency by minimizing interruptions such as telephone calls; facility rental, transportation, and time costs may, however, make them desirable primarily for sessions devoted to strategic planning or similar purposes.

The group leader or a support staff member should arrange for the meeting room and be sure that it is properly prepared. Items to be considered include adequate seating; seating pattern in the room; writing surfaces and supplies; extra copies of the agenda and related materials; room temperature, ventilation, and noise level; audiovisual equipment, cords, and power sources; lighting and location of light switches; and refreshments. Preparations should be completed well in advance of the meeting and checked about an hour before the meeting starts. The leader should arrive a few minutes early to make a final check of the facility.

FIGURE 13.2
Sample Agenda Outlines

Traditional Agenda	Functional Agenda
Group Name Time, Day, and Date of Meeting Location	Group Name Time, Day, and Date of Meeting Location
Participants and Guests Call to Order Minutes of Previous Meeting Reports of Standing Committees Reports of Special (ad hoc) Committees Old Business New Business Announcements Adjournment	Participants and Guests Action Items Discussion Items Information Items

Lead the Group Discussion. During the meeting, the primary role of the leader is to assist the group in achieving its purpose. This means keeping the group focused on its tasks and not allowing the discussion to stray to unrelated topics. It also means moving from one item on the agenda to the next in a timely manner without stifling adequate discussion. The leader must discourage private discussions among members. Asking members to share their comments with the entire group could bring new insights to the topic or discourage future side conversations. Another strategy is to stop the meeting until the side discussions cease.

Good group leaders talk very little during a meeting; they do not believe they have all the answers and they do not insist on providing them. Rather, a good group leader serves as a facilitator—someone who motivates participants to work together effectively and who secures group decisions after adequate discussion. A leader must walk the fine line between providing guidance and giving up control, between making tough decisions and letting others make them, and between doing difficult things alone and letting others learn to do them. Too much control or too little guidance, direction, and discipline can stifle the capability, initiative, and creativity of the team. Unless the leader anticipates having to exercise authority during a meeting, he or she should sit among the members rather than at the head of the conference table.

Encourage Appropriate Participation. The group leader is responsible for eliciting the best contributions possible from each participant. The following Tips and Hints box lists ways to encourage members to participate in discussions. The group leader should create an environment in which ideas are offered freely and responded to constructively. Whenever anyone presents an idea, ask the others to indicate its strengths as well as its weaknesses and to suggest specific ways to eliminate the weaknesses. If the group is a committee formed of employees from different levels in an organization, some higher-level people might intimidate some of the lower-level people. Avoid creating this situation. All employees should be considered equal in order to obtain effective contributions from all participants.

NOTE 13.67
Lead the discussion to achieve the group's purpose.

NOTE 13.68
Encourage meaningful contributions.

tips and hints

Strategies for Appropriate Participation in Meetings

The leader of the meeting should take responsibility for providing all attendees an equal opportunity to participate. Here are some strategies that a group leader may use to achieve full participation of the group.

When members speak too much:

1. Remind the group that everyone has a voice and it is important that everyone be given an equal opportunity to comment on topics during the meeting.

2. Limit discussions on a specific topic to reduce repetitiveness and redundancy.

3. Thank the speaker, summarize the views presented (this shows you listened), and then invite another member to speak.

4. Sit next to the dominant person so it is more difficult for him or her to get the leader's attention to speak.

5. Ask the talkative person to serve as recorder so he or she has less time to participate.

When members speak too little:

1. Ask direct questions; draw on the individual's expertise relative to the topic.

2. Ask for the member's viewpoint on "safe" topics before seeking input on controversial or complex issues.

3. Speak to members individually outside the meeting setting prior to the meeting. Tell them their contributions are valuable to the team, and ask what can be done to make them more active participants.

NOTE 13.69
Be aware of time without
discouraging discussion.

Be Time Conscious. An effective meeting should start and adjourn on time because the time of team members is valued. The leader needs to keep the meeting moving—an hour is enough to cover most agendas, and people lose concentration beyond that length of time. Periodically, the leader may need to remind the group of its time constraints. Comments on time must be made judiciously, however, or they will restrict discussion.

Be sure to stick to the agenda. Allowing a member to introduce topics not on the agenda usually results in hasty, uninformed decision making. The group is disadvantaged because only the person who introduces the new topic has had adequate time to prepare to discuss it. Manipulative group members may try to use this tactic to advance a personal or hidden agenda. Such behavior destroys team unity.

Just before the meeting ends, summarize what has been accomplished and clearly state who is to do what by when. If appropriate, set the date of the next meeting.

NOTE 13.70
Resolve conflicts before
they damage teamwork.

Resolve Group Conflicts. Often participants in group meetings take opposing positions. This is natural and healthy. When disagreements intensify, however, they can lead to animosity or defensiveness, both of which can destroy a group's ability to work as a team. The leader must resolve conflicts before they reach a destructive level. When conflicts arise within your group, follow the suggestions in the Tips and Hints box below.

NOTE 13.71
Appropriate records must
be maintained and shared
in a timely manner.

Maintain Appropriate Records. The leader should ensure that a record of the group's activities is maintained. Some groups conduct highly structured meetings. These groups closely follow the rules of parliamentary procedure and keep detailed records. Most business meetings, however, are less structured. Decisions are reached by consensus rather than by vote. If motions are made, they typically follow discussion rather than precede it.

tips and hints

Strategies for Resolving Group Conflicts

The first task in conflict resolution is to be sure the basic issue in the disagreement is clear. If the conflict continues after clarification of the issues, the leader has several strategies that may be implemented, including the following:

1. Ignore the conflict; in time it may resolve itself.

2. Organize talks between all parties and try to come to an agreement/compromise between conflicting members.

3. Invite an outside advisor to facilitate the discussion and try to come to an agreement.

4. Try reversing the roles. Agree to argue the other side for 15 minutes and then express that viewpoint as persuasively as you can. There may be recognition that the other side has validity.

5. Brainstorm for new ideas. Often conflicts occur because both sides think there is only a limited solution.

6. Call for a deliberate defocusing by temporarily adjourning the meeting for a few hours or a day to give everyone a chance to reflect on the issues.

7. Throw out the bad solutions and things you agree won't work rather than trying to find the right answer. This will narrow the focus and may result in a new idea coming forth.

8. Call in a mediator to work with the individuals and the behavior problems that caused the conflict originally.

9. Institute a trial solution. This may reassure reluctant participants because the decision is not permanent.

10. Remove the conflicting member(s) from the group, but be aware that this could lead to further conflict.

Depending on the formality of the group, photocopying notes made on the agenda may be a sufficient record. If a more formal written record must be maintained, delegate the recording task to someone who isn't part of the group. Having a support staff member or other individual take notes gives members the opportunity for full participation without distraction. If staff support isn't available, the leader should keep the record or ask a member to do so. The member may volunteer, be elected, or agree to serve when asked. In groups that meet regularly, the task of recording and distributing minutes is often rotated among members. Another option is to have major points or actions listed on newsprint or flip charts during the meeting so that all members can see and agree on what is to be recorded. Minutes are then prepared from these notes.

Minutes are an official report of the proceedings of a meeting. They serve as an official record, assist in refreshing memories of participants, provide information to individuals who were not present, and help prepare members for upcoming meetings. Unless law or policy mandate that verbatim records be kept, minutes should be reports in summary form.

NOTE 13.72
Only pertinent information should be included in minutes.

Minutes should concisely and accurately report all pertinent information. All motions and resolutions should be recorded word-for-word as presented. Individuals presenting motions and resolutions should be identified by name in the minutes. It is important to indicate that a motion was seconded, but the name of the individual who seconds a motion need not be recorded. The outcome—approval or defeat—should be included also.

The following parts normally are included in minutes:

- Committee or organization name
- Date, time, and location of meeting
- List of those who attended
- Reference to approval of last meeting's minutes
- Chronological record of the meeting
- Time of adjournment
- Signature of the secretary and/or chairperson

These parts will vary depending on the purpose and formality of the meeting. Style will also vary based on the parliamentary authority used by the group. Figure 13.3 on page 388 shows an example of minutes for a meeting of a committee of a nonprofit organization.

Minutes or notes should be distributed promptly following each meeting. This procedure will enable members to note any corrections while the meeting is still fresh in everyone's mind. Minutes of one meeting also serve as a platform from which the agenda for a subsequent meeting can be developed. E-mail can be an effective tool for distributing and receiving feedback about meeting records.

The fluid nature of business suggests that someone may be the leader of one group and a participant in another. To be effective, the business professional must recognize and accept his or her role in each situation.

KEYS FOR SUCCESSFUL SMALL-GROUP MEETING PARTICIPATION
The following keys for successful small-group participation will increase your effectiveness in team meetings.

Prepare to Participate. Every member of a team should learn as much as possible about the group's purpose. If an agenda is provided in advance, information can be

NOTE 13.73
Participation requires preparation.

FIGURE 13.3
Sample of Meeting Minutes
for a Nonprofit Organization

SOUTHERN CALIFORNIA SECTION

BUSINESS EDUCATORS INC.

EXECUTIVE BOARD MEETING

February 8, 2007

12:30 p.m.–2:30 p.m.

MINUTES

The meeting was held at C & S Restaurant in Temecula.

1. CALL TO ORDER

   President Alberts called the meeting to order at 12:30 p.m. on February 8, 2007.

2. ROLL CALL AND DETERMINATION OF QUORUM

   A quorum was established. The following Board Members were present: Karen Alberts, President; Linda Prescott, President-Elect; Jessica Williams, Secretary; and Stephen Weisblat, Treasurer. Absent: Richard Holman, Past-President. Guests: Christopher Weatherly, Shirley Bergland, and Sarah Covington.

3. MINUTES OF JANUARY 11, 2007, MEETING

   Copies of the minutes of January 11, 2007, Southern California Executive Board meeting were distributed to the Board prior to the February 10 meeting. The minutes were approved with one correction: page 2, ". . . The conference will be held in Tampa, Florida, ..." [Prescott/Weisblat/unanimous]

4. COMMITTEE REPORTS

   4.1.   Legislative

          Christopher Weatherly, Legislative Chair, attended the Legislative Day in Sacramento on January 26, 2007. He met with three legislators and four legislative aides to stress the importance of support for funding and bills for career and technical education on all educational levels.

   4.2.   Scholarship Awards

          Sarah Covington, Scholarship Chair, announced that we will be awarding four $150 scholarships in the spring. Any student who is or will be studying business or computers at the postsecondary level is eligible to apply. Announcements and materials will be mailed to all members. All applications must be submitted by April 9, 2007.

5. OLD BUSINESS

   Newsletter articles are due to Nancy Popeil by February 23.

6. NEW BUSINESS

   The current website does not create a "presence" for our organization. A three-person committee was formed to work on the organization's website design and content. Shirley Bergland agreed to serve as chair of the committee, which includes Linda Prescott and Richard Holman. After developing a design, determining the links to affiliate organizations, and assessing what content should be on the website, she will submit her recommendations to the Executive Board for approval.

7. ADJOURNMENT

   The meeting was adjourned at 2:20 P.M.

Jessica Williams

Minutes Submitted by Jessica Williams, Secretary

Frank & Ernest by Bob Thaves

gathered on each topic to ensure intelligent participation. All available background information should be studied.

Participate Appropriately. Members should arrive on time and be ready to devote their full attention to the meeting. Other work-related problems should be set aside temporarily. Members should participate by making clear, concise comments; asking relevant questions; and voting on issues. Participants must maintain objectivity in their comments and control their emotions. Lively debate is healthy; arguments are destructive. Honesty must permeate all discussions. Withholding information is unethical.

NOTE 13.74
Leave personal and work-related problems behind.

Listen Effectively. Meetings can challenge listening skills. Group members will spend most of their time listening to other participants' comments and must strive to keep their concentration. Members should not have side conversations, gaze into space, or exhibit other behavior that detracts from effective listening. Participants can be surprised when, without warning, a speaker asks them what they think. Listeners must be ready to become speakers at any time.

NOTE 13.75
Concentrate on what speakers say.

Take Thorough Notes. Bring paper and a pen (or an electronic device that allows you to take notes) to every meeting. Use them to record key words, ideas, dates, and activities. Using an outline format or writing notes directly on the agenda for each item as it is discussed will help you take notes while still being an active participant in discussions.

Be Courteous. Participants must respect the rights and opinions of others. Opinions should be expressed tactfully, avoiding any indication of self-righteousness or disrespect. By accepting different viewpoints and by being willing to discuss them, participants can help encourage open discussion. Members should not interrupt, even when the speaker pauses mid-thought. Avoid sarcasm; use humor carefully.

NOTE 13.76
Be courteous and fair to speakers.

Other Meeting Formats

Now and in the future, we can expect more work to be accomplished by **virtual teams**—people who are connected via e-mail, groupware, conferencing software, and Internet technologies.

NOTE 13.77
Alternative formats can be effective.

The following paragraphs describe five common ways in which technology can be used in virtual teams.

E-MAIL AND GROUPWARE

NOTE **13.78**
Technology supports
virtual teams.

E-mail and groupware (calendaring/scheduling, real-time meetings, bulletin boards, group document handling, and project tracking) support the work of virtual teams by allowing team members to exchange messages and share documents.

AUDIO CONFERENCING

NOTE **13.79**
Audio conferences use
modified meeting
procedures.

Audio conferences use telephone technology to link participants. The typical audio conference begins with a roll call to determine whether all participants are online and whether the connection is clear. Next, the leader verifies that all participants have received the agenda and appropriate supplementary materials. If not, accommodations must be made (fax or e-mail the materials; summarize materials as items are presented). Once these tasks have been accomplished, the group works through the agenda.

Because members cannot see one another and may not recognize a speaker's voice, participants should introduce themselves every time they speak. Speaker identification also helps the recorder keep accurate notes. If a member must leave the call for any reason, he or she should announce the departure.

Although audio conferences do not permit use of visual cues, the absence of eye contact sometimes makes people more willing to speak. For some people, meetings are more free and less intimidating in this mode.

VIDEOCONFERENCING

NOTE **13.80**
Videoconferences permit
long-distance, face-to-face
communication.

Videoconferencing is an electronic version of a long-distance, face-to-face meeting; it allows participants to see and talk with other participants in real time. It is preferred over audio conferencing when the meeting involves bargaining, persuasion, images, or complex topics. The effectiveness of videoconferencing lies in the ability to observe and react to participants' facial expressions, body language, and voice intonation, all of which enhance the communication.

Diverse software can communicate easily thanks to an international standard for videoconferencing. There is usually a standard location for a videoconference server that takes all the information and distributes it to other conference locations. In order to take part in a videoconference, each meeting participant must be at a site equipped with a video camera (or web cam), a microphone, speakers, a viewing screen, a PC hard-line connection, and a hub server. Depending on the organization, the site may be an individual's office, a conference room, or a commercial facility. The equipment the individual uses may be a simple, relatively inexpensive PC-based system or a costly, highly sophisticated system requiring special operating equipment and technical support personnel. The quality of the picture and the number of sites that can be displayed simultaneously vary with the nature of the equipment.

NOTE **13.81**
Whether basic or
sophisticated, equipment
should be tested in
advance.

Regardless of the site or the nature of the equipment, the procedures for conducting a videoconference parallel those used to conduct an audio conference. The meeting begins with a roll call to ensure that all group members are connected and that the equipment works properly. If participants are not familiar with one another, each displays a large-print name card at his or her station. The meeting then proceeds according to the agenda and within the framework of the technology used to link the sites.

WEB-ASSISTED TECHNOLOGIES

Web-assisted technologies allow users from all over the world to hold group meetings or live presentations over the Internet. A number of industry experts expect web conferencing to be adopted faster than any technology that has preceded it and anticipate widespread adoption for all manner of collaborative communications by 2010. As a desktop-centered technology, web conferencing represents the same kind of instant access to others as the telephone does.

Web-assisted technologies can be put into three categories—conferencing, casting, and caching. Web conferencing is real-time (synchronous), two-way communication; webcasting is real-time, one-way communication; and web caching is not real-time communication, which means it can be stored and viewed at a later time or date.

Web conferencing is a synchronous conference over the Internet that connects participants in different locations who sit at a computer. The primary feature of a web conference is screen sharing that allows conference participants to see whatever is on the presenter's screen. Usually this is accompanied by voice communication, either through a traditional telephone conference or through **Voice over Internet Protocol (VoIP),** which allows an exchange of voice data over an Internet connection through computers. Sometimes, however, text chat is used in place of voice. The interaction in web conferencing may take the form of keying questions or comments into the computer or voting on issues through the participant's desktop. The Internet without video offers some anonymity so participants may be more comfortable asking questions through the computer keyboard than in person. Another advantage of web conferencing is the savings of time and money on travel. One possible drawback is the attention span of the participants. Unlike a face-to-face meeting where everyone can see what other participants are doing, the privacy of an individual's office may encourage multitasking during the web conferencing (writing e-mails, checking notes for an upcoming meeting, etc.). All participants in a web conference should be provided with the agenda and support materials in electronic form prior to the meeting. A roll call or "check in" is usually conducted to verify that all participants are available and ready to take part.

Webcasts use streaming media technology and send the content from a single source to many receivers simultaneously using only an Internet connection. Webcasts are more about dissemination of information than the socialization of individuals for business purposes. Because they are a one-way communication, webcasts are less personal than videoconference. The ability of participants to observe and react to intonations of voice and nonverbal cues may be minimized if the site of the webcast is set up for a large audience. Also, the sender cannot see the nonverbal cues the audience is making. Although this makes webcasts less personal than videoconferences, it makes them more cost-effective. Roll calls and "check-ins" with webcast sites are omitted. The agenda and any materials that will be referred to during the webcast should either be sent as electronic files to known participants prior to the scheduled conference or be made available at the webcast sites.

Web caching allows people to download the material originally sent over the Internet and store it on a local server; the receiver can then review the material at a convenient time. That means, of course, that there is no interaction between the sender and receiver. This technology eliminates lag time and bandwidth problems, which makes the Internet seem more responsive, and reduces network traffic. As with web conferences and webcasts, any supporting materials should be made available to the audience prior to viewing.

NOTE 13.82
Web-assisted technologies connect people in distant geographic locations.

NOTE 13.83
Web conferencing provides real-time, two-way communication for virtual meetings.

NOTE 13.84
A webcast disseminates information to many receivers simultaneously.

NOTE 13.85
Web caching allows information to be stored on a local server and be reviewed at a later time.

Webcasts are used to reach a large number of people simultaneously. Some companies use webcasts for shareholder meetings so shareholders at a distance can "attend the meeting."

© Cindy Charles/PhotoEdit

ELECTRONIC MEETINGS

Group decision support system (GDSS) software combines the power of networked personal computers with specialized software to enable teams to work together better and faster whether at the same site or at different locations. The number of participants is limited only by the number of stations on the network.

GDSS meetings begin with members signing in and, if the group is meeting for the first time, entering a brief biographical sketch describing the skills and experiences they bring to the meeting. This process parallels the oral introductions common in face-to-face meetings. Unlike oral introductions, which may be forgotten soon after they are made, the biographical sketches are stored and made available to members throughout the meeting. The constant availability of information doesn't end with personal sketches. Participants may also use their computers to retrieve data from any other source normally accessible through the network used to link group members.

NOTE 13.86
Electronic meetings allow anonymous input.

As the meeting progresses and issues arise, participants offer facts, opinions, or questions by keying them at their PCs. When a member is satisfied with the message, he or she submits it. All submissions are anonymous, so members are more willing to participate. Contributions are evaluated and responded to solely on their merit.

NOTE 13.87
Electronic meetings can be fast paced.

A facilitator receives all comments and, unless directed to screen them, makes them available to all group members. The method used to view the shared comments varies with the situation in which the group operates. If members are gathered in a room designed specifically for GDSS meetings, items are projected on a large screen for all to see. If members are working from remote PCs, comments are displayed on their computer screens. Contributions may be made (keyed) simultaneously; therefore, the pace of the meeting is more rapid than in other formats. As the Communication Note on the next page acknowledges, some people who are uncomfortable participating in a face-to-face meeting welcome the anonymity they have in a virtual meeting.

Voting, too, can be accomplished quickly and easily. In fact, the ease with which votes can be taken encourages groups to use methods other than the traditional yes or no vote. Allocation, multiple choice, and ranking votes can be tallied and analyzed almost effortlessly.

communication note

The synchronous nature of virtual meetings and discussions allows participants to make comments at the same time and "piggyback" on ideas or comments made by other participants. Individuals who might be reluctant to participate in a face-to-face discussion appreciate the anonymity offered through a virtual environment that does not use video or web cameras.

Virtual discussions or meetings often reduce an individual's fear of social disapproval and evaluation; the virtual setting may also lower inhibition. Because of anonymity, participation and communication may be improved through more objective and honest evaluation of ideas. The result is increased team productivity and effectiveness.

When the meeting ends, all input is automatically stored on the computer, replacing minutes as the permanent record of the meeting. The record can be printed or saved to disk for future reference.

Whether the meetings you attend are conducted face-to-face or by another method, be sure to follow the techniques associated with good meeting leadership and participation.

Writing Teams

So far, information in this chapter has focused on skills other than writing. Sometimes, though, the product or outcome of teamwork is a written document such as a long report or a complex proposal. Therefore, it seems appropriate to comment on writing teams in this chapter.

LO 6
Describe the features of and process used by a writing team.

The Writing Team

The composition of a writing team varies with the task to be accomplished. For one message, the team might be you and your supervisor; for another message, the team might consist of people from various departments, computer and research specialists, and an editor.

Regardless of its size and membership, a writing team will face the same challenges and use the same communication skills as those of teams formed for other purposes. Members must communicate well verbally and nonverbally. They must be effective listeners. Effective group dynamics have to prevail during team meetings. Team members must respect each other and have complementary skills. In a shared writing effort, team members must be open to constructive feedback and be able to disagree with each other while maintaining a respectful work environment. The team must develop loyalty to the team and its purpose. Team members must understand the writing process and be able to implement it. They have to agree on a schedule and adhere to it.

Productive collaborative writing depends on an effective team effort that competently implements the planning and composing process. In the appropriate communication situation, collaborative writing can result in a message that is comprehensive, accurate, and concrete—a message that is more powerful than one individual could develop.

NOTE 13.88
Teamwork can involve writing.

NOTE 13.89
Writing teams have the same characteristics and challenges as other teams.

The Team Writing Process

NOTE 13.90
Adapt the three-step
writing process to the
team format

In team writing, the planning and composing process described in Chapter 5 is usually carried out in the following manner.

Step 1: Plan. Step 1 is a group effort. Team members analyze the communication situation and agree on the primary and secondary purposes. They also analyze the receiver and agree about the organizational structure to use, identify the reader benefits to include, and brainstorm for content.

Step 2: Draft. When two or more people meet to draft a document, the process becomes inefficient. Different thinking and writing styles prolong the process and actually reduce the quality of the product. Therefore, one team member refines the broad concepts developed during the group planning process, seeks data as necessary, and drafts the document.

Step 3: Finalize. Revising, editing, and proofreading responsibilities are split. The person who drafts the document shares it (electronically or in paper form) with members of the team. Each member suggests changes to content and organization and notes typographical, grammar, punctuation, and style errors. When documents are shared electronically, members see all suggestions offered by other team members; when paper is the medium, changes are generally referred to the draft's author. The document may go through several iterations of revising and editing before the group meets to review the final product.

Summary of Learning Objectives

LO 1 Identify the components of interpersonal communication and soft skills.

Interpersonal communication refers to the verbal and nonverbal interactions in one-to-one or small-group settings. Listening, speaking, and nonverbal communication are the primary elements of a person's "people skills," but writing can also reflect them. Interpersonal communication has a major influence on the communication climate of an organization.

LO 2 Develop skills for building positive relationships.

Conversations, the core of positive relationships, follow a five-step process: greeting, introduction, exchange, summary, and closing. The effectiveness of a conversation can be enhanced when participants pay attention to the location, minimize interruptions, speak skillfully, send appropriate nonverbal cues, ask questions, listen for words and emotions, and accommodate diversity. Efficient and effective equipment operation, consideration and respect for others, and a businesslike manner will help make telephone conversations and voice mail successful. Social business interactions can be enhanced by practicing social conversation rules, choosing appropriate topics, and observing business etiquette. Once damaged, a relationship can be repaired by words and/or actions only if both parties are willing to let go of the problem that caused the damage.

Give feedback effectively and receive it appropriately.

Feedback lets individuals know the effect their behavior is having on another individual, the organization, a customer, or the team. It may be positive or constructive. Positive feedback recognizes good performance and is a motivator. Feedback that is given constructively and received positively without being defensive can help an individual grow. Constructive feedback should be given in private and be limited to documented, relevant, work-related concerns. Focus attention on the behavior, not the person; don't let concerns in one area cloud your judgment in another. Accept partial responsibility if appropriate. Use and read nonverbal cues carefully; allow the receiver time to consider and respond to the message. Agreeing and seeking more information are strategies to use when receiving constructive feedback.

Describe techniques for resolving conflicts.

When faced with conflict, people have four options: accommodate, compromise, overpower, or collaborate. The option chosen will vary with the people and situation; culture is a factor. Techniques that apply both to participants and to facilitators are acting promptly, scheduling the meeting, using active listening, communicating honestly, focusing on the problem, brainstorming solutions, formalizing the solution, and implementing and following up on the solution. When a participant initiates resolution, he or she should first do a self-assessment and then sincerely approach the other person. Active listening combined with paraphrasing should reveal areas of agreement as well as areas to be resolved. Both parties should be involved in developing a solution. Techniques used to facilitate conflict resolution will vary depending on how the facilitator learned of the conflict but generally include arranging a meeting; introducing topics; and clarifying, refocusing, and summarizing discussions and agreements.

Develop the skills associated with leading and participating in teams.

Teams—whether self-managed, process-improvement, cross-functional, or virtual—have personal and organizational advantages and disadvantages. To be effective, team members must engage in open, honest communication; be cohesive; foster growth; and be recognized for their achievements. Meetings are the vehicle through which teams plan, report, and coordinate efforts to achieve goals. Both the leader and the participants have responsibilities in ensuring that meetings are productive. Although most business meetings are face-to-face gatherings, technology is being used increasingly to conduct meetings. The technology provides real-time collaboration, allows participants in remote locations to participate easily, reduces the cost of meetings, and enhances participation.

Describe the features of and process used by a writing team.

Successful collaborative writing depends on the ability of the writing team members, the dynamics of the writing team, group loyalty, and the ability of the members to agree on a schedule and adhere to it. The tasks associated with the three-step writing process are completed either individually or as a group.

Questions for Discussion and Review

1. What factors in the business environment have created a demand for employees with a high level of soft skills? (Objective 1)
2. Identify at least five soft skills that employers are seeking in their prospective employees. (Objective 1)
3. What impression does a passive communicator project to his or her receivers? an assertive communicator? an aggressive communicator? (Objective 2)
4. Explain why it is important to learn and use your receiver's name during a conversation. (Objective 2)
5. Give an example of a situation for which you would use an open-ended question and give the reasons this type of question would be appropriate for the situation. (Objective 2)
6. Why is it important to create a mental image of the person you are speaking with on the phone? (Objective 2)
7. Give an example of a social business situation and what your goal might be in attending the function. (Objective 2)
8. What role does the you–viewpoint play in giving constructive feedback? (Objective 3)
9. Should you ever give unsolicited constructive feedback? Why or why not? (Objective 3)
10. What four options do people have when faced with conflict? Explain. (Objective 4)
11. What are some of the negative consequences a business may suffer as a result of unresolved conflicts between employees? (Objective 4)
12. Is conflict always unhealthy? Why or why not? (Objective 4)
13. Identify two advantages and two disadvantages of teams. (Objective 5)
14. Briefly describe what a meeting leader and participant should do before, during, and after a meeting. (Objective 5)
15. Define team writing and explain how teams approach the three-step writing process. (Objective 6)

Application Exercises

1. Interview four people. Ask each to identify the "Top Five" people skills that make someone a good employee or a good supervisor. During a class discussion, combine your findings with those of other class members. (Objective 1)
2. Convert the list prepared in Exercise 1 into a self-assessment. For each item, rate yourself on a 5-point scale, with 1 = poor and 5 = excellent. Identify two items on which you wish to improve, and make a personal commitment to do so. (Objective 1)

COLLABORATIVE

3. **Teamwork.** As best as possible, create and complete this scenario within your classroom or another room at your school: You are attending the fund-raiser that precedes the business meeting of the local chapter of the Society for the Betterment of Management. Your instructor will give you a card indicating the role you are to take (e.g., officer, membership committee member or chair, speaker, speaker's spouse/guest, prospective member, new member, other member, or founding member). Take on this role as you mingle within the group and engage in conversation with individuals or small groups. Remember to introduce yourself or others as appropriate. Spend 15 to 20 minutes in this activity, and then discuss the exercise as a class. (Objective 2)
4. For each of the following situations, give a verbal and nonverbal example of a passive reponse, an aggressive response, and an assertive response. (Objective 2)
   a. You bought a new gas grill at the local discount home center, and it doesn't work properly.
   b. You are the supervisor in the customer service department, and you have been notified that Janelle came in late the last three days and left work early two days this week.
   c. You are in a meeting in the conference room, and Vance is talking to Kyle in a voice that is loud enough to distract and prevent you from hearing the speaker clearly.
   d. You are at a business lunch and someone at your table starts smoking, which offends you and makes it difficult to breathe because of your asthma.

5. **Teamwork.** Picture yourself as the author of the "Ask Andy" column in your school paper. You receive a letter that says, "My boss is always suggesting ways for me to do my job better. When I mentioned this to my brother, he said that giving constructive feedback is part of my supervisor's job. What do you think?" Prepare the response you'll include in your column. Address your response to "Criticized Chris." (Objective 3)

COLLABORATIVE

6. **Teamwork.** As your instructor directs, role-play one or more of the following situations in which you are required to give constructive feedback. (Objective 3)

COLLABORATIVE

   a. You are the leader of a cross-functional team in your organization. One of the members of the team, Jason, monopolizes the discussions at your meetings, interrupts others when they are speaking, and regularly discounts other members' contributions. He does contribute his marketing expertise in the meetings. However, his behavior disrupts the team meetings and reduces the effectiveness of the team. Convey the necessary message to Jason to rectify this situation.

   b. Eleanor recently submitted a report that you had asked her to prepare that contained the sales figures for each of the sales representatives and calculated the commission to which each was entitled. She turned in the report two days late, so you missed the payroll deadline for issuing the checks this month. In addition, a few of the numbers didn't look right so you double-checked her work. You found several calculation errors. Handle the situation in the manner you think is appropriate.

   c. One of your newest employees at Cassie's Casual Wear seems to have a problem staying focused and listening to determine the customers' needs. She often has to ask them several times what they want. Just yesterday you saw two customers walk out of your store because they felt they were not getting the attention they deserved. Approach your new employee, Julie, and offer to go over your expectations for your sales employees and give constructive feedback so that she can achieve those expectations.

7. **Teamwork.** Recall a recent conflict in which you were involved. How did you behave? Did you allow the other person to treat you as if you had little or no value (passively)? Did you treat the other person as though he or she had little or no value (aggressively)? Did you handle the situation with mutual respect (assertively)? Plan a three- to four-minute oral presentation that (a) describes the situation, (b) explains how you reacted, and (c) suggests how the encounter might have ended had you behaved differently. Working in small groups as assigned by your instructor, give your presentation. (Objective 4)

COLLABORATIVE

8. **Teamwork.** Divide the class into teams with one team on each side of the classroom. One team will take the "pro" side of the issue and the other team will take the "con" side of the issue. Each team will try to "pull" members of the other team to its side using reasoning and persuasion. This "tug-of-war" exercise will be based on one of the following items or a controversial issue at your school. (Objective 5)

COLLABORATIVE

   a. Smoke-free campus (no smoking anywhere on campus)

   b. Dress code for business students at your school

   c. Employer's right to monitor workers' e-mail

9. **Teamwork.** Virtual teams are growing as an organizational phenomenon, and web-assisted technologies are being used to facilitate their work. Research several businesses in your city to see whether they are currently using web conferencing, webcasts, videoconferencing, audio conferencing, GDSS, and other technologies for teamwork. If they are not, research companies on the Internet and find at least one that is currently using the technology. Gather information to present to the class about the following: (Objective 5)

COLLABORATIVE

   a. What technology is being used?

   b. How and by whom is the technology being used?

   c. Why was this particular technology chosen?

   d. Has using this technology lowered the cost of doing business?

10. Hold an in-class debate on one or more of the following statements. (Objective 5)

   a. It is not necessary to be a team player to succeed in the business world.

   b. Teams hide a member's individual accomplishments.

   c. Teams are a management fad.

   d. Participating in work teams takes away from a person's real job.

   e. When you are on a team, a few people end up doing all the work.

TECHNOLOGY

COLLABORATIVE
TECHNOLOGY

11. **Technology.** "Free riders," people who don't contribute to a team's success but share in the credit given for team accomplishments, are often cited as a problem in school-based group projects. What can the leader of a student team do to minimize or eliminate the free-rider problem? What can team members do to minimize or eliminate the free-rider problem? Send your suggestions to your instructor in an e-mail.

12. **Teamwork. Technology.** Work with one other student in your class. Identify and arrange to attend a regularly scheduled meeting of some group (e.g., student organization, faculty/staff committee, professional society) at your school or in your community. (Objectives 5 and 6)

   a. Prepare a written report that describes the extent to which the leader and participants followed the guidelines presented in this chapter.

   b. E-mail to your instructor a message in which you describe how you and your teammate divided the work on this project.

Web exercises to accompany this chapter are available at **www.thomsonedu.com/ bcomm/krizan.**

MESSAGE ANALYSIS

Reorder the following items to reflect the minutes of a meeting. Use a format similar to the one shown in Figure 13.3 on page 388.

September 16, 200–

Malmome Kuj (guest, United Way)

Hank Jeffries made the motion to adjourn the meet at 5:50 p.m.; Jennifer Hennessey seconded the motion; the motion passed.

Minutes of last months' meating were approved with a correction on page 3 . . ..Ellie Nordoff was responsibel for contacting the guest speaker for the December dinner meeting. Padgett made the motion to approved the minutes; Jeffries seconded the motion; the motion carried.

Phil Brigham (Chair, Wachovia Securities)

LRC 435

Sylvia Padget (member, City of Escondido)

PROGRAM ADVISORY BOARD MEETING

Hank Jeffries (member, Lockheed Martin)

4:40–6 p.m.

Guest Speaker report was given by Sharon Walker. Sharon announced that on January 4 the President of Websense will be giving a guest lecture on emerging web technologies. The lecture will be held on the Mesa campus in room B409 at 1 p.m. All business and computer science students are encouraged to attend.

Jennifer Hennessey (member, GEICO)

Articulation Committee report presented by Sylvia Padget. State University will be accepted CIS 165 as an equivalent to CISC 112, Computer Literacy.

Sharon Walker (member, Robert Half Employment)

Carlos Marquez (member, faculty at Mesa Community College)

Chair's report given by Phil Brigham. At the President's Cabinet meeting on Septmber 7 it was announced that the Community College would be hiring a outreach person to set up internships for business students with local businesses. It was also announced that the

The next meeting will be held on November 20 in LRC 435 at 4:30 p.m.

Writer's Workshop

The following items may be sentence fragments or contain errors in punctuation, subject–verb agreement, pronoun–antecedent agreement, infinitive use, abbreviations, number display, capitalization, spelling, word choice, possessives, modifier clarity and placement, or parallelism. Rewrite the sentences to make them correct.

1. Fiscal exercise can releive tension, therefore you can take a walk, stretch in your chair, or take the stares instead of the elevate to relax.
2. Their is good stress, and bad stress.
3. When I get to work at 7:00 am, it is quite and I can organize myself and get ready for the day.
4. When I graduated from High School in 2006 I had a summer job in a mens' clothing store wear I was paid six dollars an hour.
5. Is there anyway we can modify the shipping schedule so the new laptops can be installed by July 1st.
6. For your convience I have inclosed a coupon good for a twenty % discount which means you'll pay only 16.95 for a full-year subsribtion to the magazine **HEALTHY LIVING.**
7. Unless a major new customer can be found our 37000 foot bldg will be vacated indefanitely; and, two hundred people will loose they're jobs.
8. Because of the high cost of living in our county we are loosing population to other countys where prices are more reasonable, it means though that those people have to drive a longer distance to go to work.
9. General Supremes' C.E.O. & major shareholder Gaylor court will announce that the company has filed an Initial Public Offering to rays $25 million dollars.
10. This money saving offfer is only valid thru April 31.

Chapter 14
Listening and Nonverbal Messages

LET'S TALK BUSINESS

Approximately 65 percent of the 6,500 employees in our health-care organization are organized under one of 28 bargaining agreements. Therefore, I am presented with many occasions where listening and nonverbal communication take place at the bargaining table.

During traditional, adversarial bargaining, silence may be used as a strategy. Participants simply do not respond to positions or comments of the other party. Silence is accompanied by lack of body movement. This behavior sends a message that allows for jockeying, which is important in seeming to get what you want without giving up your issue.

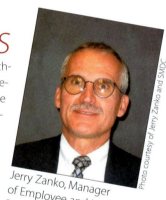

Jerry Zanko, Manager of Employee and Labor Relations, SMDC

Photo courtesy of Jerry Zanko and SMDC

In the more candid interest-based bargaining model, open and honest verbal communication is supported by nonverbal communication. Words, facial expressions, gestures, and body position reflect the participants' desire to solve problems and reach agreement.

In either case, listening—genuine listening—must be worked at. You can understand the *why* behind an issue only if you listen. If you expend your effort in formulating your reply before the other party has fully presented its issue, you lose an opportunity for progress in negotiations, an opportunity that may not present itself again.

The significant roles of written communication have been stressed in the preceding chapters of this book. However, the importance of listening and nonverbal communication should not be overlooked. In studies over the past few decades, employers have consistently rated listening as one of the top five skills they expect employees to have. Why? The average employee spends about three-quarters of each working day communicating. Nearly half of that time is spent listening. Organizations have discovered that one bad listener can undo the work of many good listeners, and good listening skills can improve productivity and increase both employee and client satisfaction. Chapter 13 introduced speaking, listening, and nonverbal communication as components of interpersonal communication and teamwork. In this chapter, you will explore listening and nonverbal communication in greater depth. Chapter 15 discusses how to communicate orally and how to prepare and deliver formal presentations. Figure 14.1 illustrates the amount of time a college student spends in communication activities during the day. Listening and listening-related activities comprise the largest portion.

NOTE 14.1
Employers rank listening as one of the top five skills for employees.

Listening

Listening is challenging because people don't work as hard at it as they should. Because listening seems to occur naturally, we feel that it isn't necessary to put effort into it. However, it is a learned skill; hard work and effort are required if listening is to be effective. Listening is also challenging because people have different reasons for listening. They listen to gain information, to receive instructions, to hear complaints, to enjoy entertainment, and to show respect. The situations in which listening takes place also vary. Listening can occur (a) in one-on-one telephone or face-to-face conversations; (b) in a small group, such as a few employees receiving instructions from their supervisor; and (c) in a large group, such as an audience listening to a webcast of a shareholders' meeting. Jerry Zanko, the HR professional quoted in Let's Talk Business, uses listening in collective bargaining sessions—small-group meetings designed to exchange information and reach agreement about terms

NOTE 14.2
Effective listening is a learned skill.

Activity	Total Hours	Total Percentage
Total Daily Average Hours Dedicated to Communication Activities		
Writing	1.82	8
Reading	1.40	6
Speaking	4.83	20
Listening*	5.80	24
Television*	2.12	9
Radio*	.86	4
CDs/tapes*	1.32	5
Phone*	1.87	8
E-mail	1.33	6
Internet	2.73	11
*Total listening-related activities	11.97	50

N = 206 college students; study conducted by Janusik & Wolvin, 2006.
Source: Laura Janusik, "Listening Facts," *International Listening Association*, n.d.,
http://www.listen.org/Templates/facts.htm (accessed July 3, 2006).

FIGURE 14.1
How Students Use Communication in Their Daily Lives

and conditions of employment. One-to-one conversations are also part of his daily routine, and he is called frequently to speak to student or professional groups.

Hearing versus Listening

LO 1
Distinguish between hearing and listening.

Hearing is a physiological process; listening is a mental one. For example, you may have attended a class session during which the instructor gave directions for assignments and projects to be included in your portfolio for the class. Later, as you began preparing the portfolio, you realized that you could not recall all the items that were to be included. You *heard* the instructions but did not *listen* to them. Listening involves understanding and retaining what is heard.

NOTE 14.3
Hearing is different from listening.

Ineffective listening occurs in the workplace as well as in the classroom. Consider the situation in which Sophie, a new sales representative, had a meeting with Alan, her sales manager, at which time she was given directions on the procedure for submitting travel forms for reimbursement of expenses incurred while on company business. She submitted her first travel form a week later. Much to her surprise, Sophie found she was not reimbursed for all the expenses she submitted. She had not listened carefully, and she had not attached the required receipts. Sophie needs to learn the importance of using the entire listening process.

The Listening Process

LO 2
Describe the five elements of the listening process.

The listening process consists of five elements. Hearing is one of these elements; the other four are filtering, interpreting, responding, and remembering. Figure 14.2 shows the five elements and the sequencing of the listening process.

HEARING

NOTE 14.4
Hearing is a passive activity.

The first element in the listening process, **hearing,** is a physiological process. When we hear, our auditory nerves are stimulated by sound waves. Everyone hears sounds unless he or she has a hearing impairment. Hearing is a passive activity requiring no conscious effort; it is, however, a prerequisite for listening.

FILTERING

NOTE 14.5
Filtering eliminates unwanted stimuli, whether they are external or internal.

The second element in the listening process, **filtering,** is the elimination of unwanted stimuli. The stimuli may be external, such as events occurring around you, spoken words, or physical experiences that affect your senses; these are things over which you have no control. The stimuli may also be internal, such as deadlines you must meet by the end of the workday, information you need in order to make a decision or work on a project, or a headache you have developed because you missed lunch. Whatever the stimuli, you can't focus on all of them at the same time. Filtering allows a listener to focus on stimuli that are of specific interest. Consider an example illustrating both external and internal stimuli: Suppose someone attending a meeting on retirement plan options is seated near an open window through which he or she can see people playing golf, making the listener want to get out and play

FIGURE 14.2
The Listening Process

Hearing ⟶ Filtering ⟶ Interpreting ⟶ Responding ⟶ Remembering a round of golf. The external stimulus is the sight of others golfing, and the internal stimulus is the speaker's information about retirement plans. An individual may have difficulty concentrating on an oral message when his or her filtering process is unable to eliminate or at least minimize distracting stimuli.

INTERPRETING

The third element of the listening process is interpreting. When **interpreting,** the listener's mind assigns meaning to the stimuli. Listeners tend to consider nonverbal cues as well as verbal cues when interpreting oral messages. In addition, a speaker's prior comments and actions are considered when interpreting present messages. As pointed out in Chapter 1, it is important for the receiver to interpret the stimuli in the way the sender intended. However, our minds tend to filter the contents of a message based on our experiences, knowledge, emotions, and beliefs. That means the message received is sometimes different from the message the receiver intended.

NOTE 14.6
The message is interpreted by assigning meaning to the stimuli.

RESPONDING

The fourth element in the listening process is **responding,** a form of feedback that lets the sender know the message was received and understood. There are several types of responses that may be used in the listening process. They include direct verbal responses, such as "That should work well for us"; responses that seek clarification, such as "Tell me more about it"; responses that paraphrase, such as "In other words, what you are saying is . . ."; and a nonverbal response such as a nod or a thumbs-up signal. Feedback will be covered in more detail later in the chapter.

NOTE 14.7
Responding provides feedback to the sender of the message.

REMEMBERING

The fifth element, **remembering,** involves recalling at a later time the information that was interpreted and responded to earlier. The success of this element depends heavily on the association (relationship) placed on the stimuli during the interpretation phase. The normal, untrained listener retains only about half of what he or she hears in a casual conversation or formal oral communication within hours of the event and only about one fourth of it two days later.

NOTE 14.8
Proper association improves recall ability.

The success of the listening process depends on all five elements. If one of the elements is omitted or fails to function properly, the entire listening process is jeopardized. To become a better listener, certain guidelines need to be followed. In the Communication Note that follows, Kenneth R. Johnson stresses that effective listening can solve many communication problems.

communication note

LISTENING: THE DIFFERENCE BETWEEN SUCCESS AND FAILURE

Business and industry leaders agree that listening skills contribute to the success of an organization. According to Kenneth R. Johnson, vice president of R. J. Associates, "the contrast between hearing and really listening can be as different as night and day. And in a business environment, not listening effectively to customers, employees, and peers can mean the difference between success and failure." He goes on to say, "listening effectively to others can be the most fundamental and powerful communication tool of all. When someone is willing to stop talking or thinking and begin truly listening to others, all of their interactions become easier; and communication problems are all but eliminated."

Source: http//www.listen.org/quotations/quotes_effective.html.

Guidelines for Effective Listening

LO 3

List the guidelines for
effective listening.

Most people think they are good listeners, and perhaps they are—at least some of the time. Although listening is more an art than a science, it is a process that can be improved if the receiver takes an active role. The following guidelines can help you improve your listening skills.

CONCENTRATE ON THE MESSAGE

NOTE 14.9

Concentration is key to
effective listening.

People normally speak at 150 to 200 words a minute and listen at 400 to 500 words a minute. This gap between speaking and listening speeds requires the listener to make a conscious effort to focus and concentrate on the message to avoid "mind drift." Focusing your concentration and mental energies on the message is the foundation of effective listening.

NOTE 14.10

Be aware of hidden
meanings.

Mentally summarizing the message is a concentration technique that is effective when the communication is not well organized or when the speaker has a heavy accent. Concentrate on the main points the speaker is trying to convey. Look for hidden messages. Determine whether the speaker is using facts, opinions, or inferences. Do not allow the speaker's physical appearance or vocal qualities to affect your concentration. Focusing on the message will assist you in overcoming barriers that may interfere with your hearing the entire message.

DETERMINE THE PURPOSE OF THE MESSAGE

NOTE 14.11

The three modes of
listening are cautious
listening, skimming, and
scanning.

Oral messages have purposes, as do written messages. As a listener, you need to determine the purpose of the oral message so that you can decide on the mode that you will use when listening. Three modes commonly used to listen to messages are cautious listening, skimming, and scanning.

Cautious Listening. This mode, **cautious listening,** is used when you need to understand and remember both the general concept and all the details of the message. This mode requires more mental energy than the others because of the amount or complexity of material on which you must concentrate. When listening in this mode, your mind has no time to relax.

Skimming. **Skimming** is used when you need to understand only the general concept of the message. When using this mode for listening, your mind has time to relax because you do not need to remember all the details being presented. Listen for main ideas, which are the most important points the speaker wants to make. They may be mentioned at the start or end of the talk; they may also be repeated several times. Pay special attention to statements that begin with phrases such as "My point is . . . ." or "The things to remember are . . . ." Cluttering your mind with insignificant matter causes it to tire, which could cause you to forget the important points.

Scanning. When **scanning,** you concentrate on details of specific interest to you instead of on the general concept. No energy is wasted trying to retain information that is not of specific value. One shortcoming of this mode is that your mind may wander; you may miss material that is important.

NOTE 14.12

Don't allow biases and
prejudices to influence
listening.

KEEP AN OPEN MIND

The speaker presents the message from his or her perspective. Respect the speaker's viewpoint by not allowing your own biases to block what is being said. Don't listen just for statements that back up your opinions and support your beliefs. Your listening ability may be impaired if you are not receptive to the message or if you have a strong emotional reaction to the speaker's use of impact words (also called color words). Another obstacle may be your expectation not to understand a speaker with a dialect different from yours. When you listen with an open mind, both you and the speaker will benefit. The speaker will believe that what he or she is saying is worthwhile, and you may acquire valuable information.

Because a listener can listen at a faster rate than most speakers speak, there is a tendency to evaluate too quickly. Delay evaluating a message until you have heard the entire message. When a listener begins to disagree with a speaker's message, he or she tends to misinterpret the remaining information or distort its intended meaning so that it is consistent with his or her beliefs. Premature evaluations or judgments of a speaker's message benefit no one.

PROVIDE FEEDBACK

Feedback is important. It is your response to the speaker, and it lets the speaker know you are listening. Feedback may be verbal or nonverbal. Use eye contact and body language, such as nodding and maintaining an upright posture. At appropriate times, you may also smile, frown, laugh, or be silent.

The speaker may volunteer more information if he or she receives positive feedback. For instance, an employee describing a problem in the office may expand on his or her comments when you offer feedback such as "Tell me more about . . ." or "Yes, but . . ." or even "Uh-huh." Asking questions such as "What impact will that have on our department?" to clarify the message also provides feedback.

Paraphrasing can be a form of feedback, one that can make the speaker feel as though he or she has not only been heard but also understood. It is important to use your own words in verbalizing your understanding of the message; parroting the words verbatim does not ensure accurate understanding of the message. Engaging in paraphrasing helps listeners concentrate on both the words and the emotions of the speaker. If, for example, a classmate is angry because a team member is doing less than his or her share of work on a project, the classmate might angrily say, "He never does his share of the work, and he always gets away with it." Your feedback should help the speaker regain emotional control. A good paraphrased response might be, "You think he'll be rewarded for the team's performance, and you feel as though you're doing more than your share on the project."

Some listening situations are not conducive to giving any type of feedback to the speaker. These situations include radio, television, and video presentations. Small-group or one-to-one presentations lend themselves best to oral feedback. Each situation should be analyzed as to its appropriateness for feedback. Remember, you listen with your face and body as well as with your ears!

MINIMIZE NOTE TAKING

It may be wise to record complicated presentations for later review. Although your goal should be to have thorough notes, you will not be able to concentrate on listening if you attempt to record everything that is said. Instead, record key words and ideas in an outline. In oral communication situations that are routine or simple, record just the major points. Try to remember what is said without using notes.

NOTE 14.13
Positive feedback will improve the communication process.

NOTE 14.14
Paraphrasing lets the speaker know you understood the message as it was intended.

NOTE 14.15
Taking notes may interfere with the listening process.

Frank & Ernest by Bob Thaves

ANALYZE THE TOTAL MESSAGE

NOTE **14.16**
Use both visual and verbal observation to analyze the message.

Listen "between the lines" to understand the full message. Many cues to meaning come from the speaker's tone of voice, facial expressions, and gestures. People don't always say what they mean, but body language and tone of voice are usually accurate indicators of the intent of the message. Your vocal and visual observations will help you determine the speaker's emotional state and intent, as well as the message content.

DO NOT TALK OR INTERRUPT

NOTE **14.17**
Talking and interrupting interfere with listening.

An individual cannot talk and listen effectively at the same time. Listening should occur more often than speaking. When you are talking, you cannot use all the elements of effective listening. Interrupting a speaker or having side conversations is rude and reduces the effectiveness of the communication. Learn to distinguish between a mid-thought pause and the end of the speaker's comments. When you interrupt, it looks as though you aren't listening, even though you really are.

Barriers to Listening

LO 4
Describe barriers to effective listening.

A **listening barrier** is anything that interferes with the listening process. You should be aware of barriers so that you can avoid letting them interfere with your listening. Some of the more important barriers to listening are discussed here.

PHYSICAL DISTRACTIONS

NOTE **14.18**
Minimize physical distractions to increase listening effectiveness.

The individual responsible for setting up the meeting place in which the listening will occur should minimize physical distractions. Physical distractions may include sensory stimuli such as temperature, smell, and noise. You can limit this barrier by sitting at the front of the room, not sitting near a corridor or an open window, not sitting next to an individual who will talk or whisper during the presentation, and turning off your cell phone.

MENTAL DISTRACTIONS

NOTE **14.19**
Don't let your mind wander when listening.

As a listener, you are responsible for giving your undivided attention to a speaker. Mental distractions may include emotional states of mind (worry, fear, anger, grief, depression), psychological factors (preoccupation, boredom, laziness, daydreaming, shrinking attention span), and biases and prejudices. Because we think approximately four times faster than the speaker can talk, it is easy to let our minds drift to other business or personal interests instead of paying attention to the speaker.

A very common distraction is mentally constructing a comment to make or a question to ask rather than concentrating on what is being said. A related mental distraction is forming an opinion or a rebuttal during a presentation. To listen effectively, keep an open mind—that is, hear *all* of what is said before making judgments.

HEALTH CONCERNS

Good health and well-being play a specific role in effective listening. A hungry, nauseous, or tired listener will find it difficult to focus on the message and listen actively. When these conditions exist, the speaker may wish to repeat the original message later.

NONVERBAL DISTRACTIONS

A listener may give a speaker negative nonverbal feedback. Facial expressions and gestures—frowning, yawning, raising an eyebrow, closing the eyes, or crossing the arms—can convey a message of disinterest or disapproval. Glancing at a watch or a clock may tell the speaker that you are ready for the presentation to end. Avoiding these nonverbal distractions will keep the lines of communication open.

NOTE 14.20
Avoid negative nonverbal actions by giving the speaker positive feedback.

INAPPROPRIATE TIMING

A listener should ensure that a speaker can present his or her message at an appropriate time. A listener often knows whether the time is appropriate. For example, a manager going through a plant may casually ask a worker, "Any problems?" If a supervisor is standing nearby and the manager knows the worker would be reluctant to speak in front of the supervisor, the worker might think the manager really does not want to listen. A more appropriate comment from the manager would be, "If you have any problems, I have an open-door policy and have reserved Wednesday afternoons to listen to employees." This would allow the speaker (the worker) to present his or her message at an appropriate time.

NOTE 14.21
Give a speaker adequate time to present a message.

An individual presenting a message should be given adequate time so that he or she does not have to rush. It is the listener's responsibility to ensure that the speaker will have enough time to present the entire message. For example, if a manager has to leave for a meeting in five minutes and a supervisor enters the office to discuss a complex problem, the manager should make an appointment to meet with the supervisor at a later, more convenient time. The manager should not expect the supervisor to condense the presentation into five minutes.

INEFFECTIVE SPEECH CHARACTERISTICS

A listener must be able to hear and understand a speaker in order to interpret the message. If the words are spoken at low volume or at such a high pitch that the listener has trouble hearing the words, listening will be difficult, if not impossible. Other characteristic speech barriers include articulation, semantics, dialects or a different language, unusual pronunciations, jargon, regional speech patterns (accents), vocalization (tongue clicking, "ums"), and speech impairments. These barriers are difficult to overcome because listeners cannot review a spoken message in the same way they can review a written message. A comfortable atmosphere will cause a speaker to set a more relaxed pace and allow his or her message to be understood more easily. In addition, careful concentration may help a listener deal effectively with characteristic speech barriers. The information in the Communication Note on page 408 suggests that a positive, direct correlation exists between being an effective listener and succeeding in business.

NOTE 14.22
Work to overcome speech barriers.

communication note

EMPHASIS ON LISTENING SKILLS INCREASES AS YOU RISE THROUGH THE RANKS

If you want to move up the career ladder, work on improving your listening skills. Studies have shown that as you rise in the organizational hierarchy, the time spent listening increases. Hourly employees spend about 30 percent of their time listening, managers often spend 60 percent of their time listening, and executives may spend 75 percent or more of their time listening. Does effective listening lead to advancement on the job or do people who are higher on the career ladder learn to listen better because they must? It is probably a combination of the two. But most people in business would agree that in order to be more successful, you must be a better listener.

Advantages of Effective Listening

LO 5
Describe the advantages of effective listening.

One of the best ways to acquire information, hear feedback from others, show respect, and develop better attitudes is through effective listening. Effective listening helps build relationships, solve problems, ensure understanding, resolve conflicts, and improve accuracy. At work, effective listening means fewer errors and less wasted time. Businesses wishing to be perceived as customer-oriented must make the art of listening an integral part of their employee training. Listening builds friendships and careers.

Nonverbal Communication

NOTE 14.23
Nonverbal communication is a message without words.

A **nonverbal message** is one that communicates without words. Nonverbal messages are an important part of the communication process because they provide added information the receiver can use in interpreting what is said. However, the extra information can add to or detract from the meaning of a message. Although listeners may strongly believe what is said, nonverbal behavior may constitute two thirds or more of total communication. People may choose not to speak; however, they can never be uncommunicative nonverbally. Nonverbal signs are a rich source of information. There are many useful business applications for nonverbal communication. It can be used to make stronger connections with clients and colleagues, to determine interest in a product or service, or to convey a certain impression about yourself and your organization.

NOTE 14.24
Establish a baseline to help interpret nonverbal cues.

People constantly communicate through their conscious or unconscious nonverbal messages. As an example, suppose that every day on your way to work you meet the same person at the same place. Each morning as you pass each other you exchange greetings. Suddenly, one morning your greeting is met with indifference; the person does not acknowledge your presence. Later in the day someone asks whether you saw the passerby that morning and you recall your encounter. Would you be so aware of the encounter if the passerby had spoken to you as usual? Probably not. You were aware of the passerby this time because his or her actions differed from what you had determined to be congruent behavior. You used **benchmarking**—a comparison of "what is" against what you have come to expect as typical. You can use this same technique during conversations or business meetings.

When a person's actions vary from what you have observed to be his or her positive nonverbal behavior, it may be time to ask whether the receiver has questions or concerns about what's being discussed or proposed.

Here is another example of how nonverbal messages affect other forms of communication: A prospective customer receives a poorly printed letter announcing a furniture sale. The poor printing is a nonverbal message suggesting carelessness. How quickly will the customer rush to the store for the sale? Which message is more effective—the written words or the nonverbal appearance?

The Importance of Nonverbal Communication

A person should be aware of the impact of nonverbal communication. Nonverbal messages may not always be intended or planned; nevertheless, they clearly communicate to people and influence their interpretation.

Nonverbal messages may aid or hinder communication. The following summarizes the more important characteristics of nonverbal communication:

- *The nonverbal communication can be unintentional.* The sender may be unaware that he or she is sending a nonverbal message and, consequently, may not be aware of the impact that message may have.
- *A nonverbal communication may be more honest than a verbal one.* In a person-to-person communication, the message is sent on two levels—verbal and nonverbal. Nonverbal cues may be transmitted unconsciously and without having been planned. So if the nonverbal cues and the spoken message are not compatible, the receiver of the message tends to base the interpretation and the intent of the message on the nonverbal cues.
- *Nonverbal communication makes, or helps to make, a first impression.* First impressions are powerful. They often result in frozen evaluations, images that can be very difficult to alter.
- *Nonverbal communication is always present.* Neither oral nor written communication exists without nonverbal communication. Examples of nonverbal messages being sent even when the communication may not be face-to-face include tapping the phone receiver, loudly rearranging papers, or silence.

Although nonverbal messages are powerful, a listener should not become so intent on interpreting them that he or she fails to listen to the speaker's words.

Types of Nonverbal Communication

Nonverbal messages come in various forms. Some of the common types of nonverbal communication follow.

PHYSICAL APPEARANCE

Physical appearance is an important type of nonverbal communication. An individual will form a first impression from a letter's envelope, stationery, letterhead, format, and neatness. This first impression will definitely influence the receiver's reaction to the letter.

The physical appearance of a speaker influences an oral message as much as the appearance of a letter influences a written message. Listeners use physical appearance as a clue to the speaker's credibility. That is why an accounting professional

LO 6
Explain the importance of nonverbal messages.

NOTE 14.25
Nonverbal communication has several important characteristics.

LO 7
Identify different types of nonverbal messages and discuss their impact on the communication process.

A speaker's credibility may be judged by his or her physical appearance.

who is dressed in casual, trendy clothes will find it difficult, if not impossible, to be taken seriously when presenting the results of an audit.

Physical appearance also influences a receiver's perceptions of a speaker's socioeconomic status and judgment. For example, an individual who wears designer clothes, custom-made shoes, and expensive jewelry will transmit a nonverbal message. This nonverbal message will be perceived differently by receivers, depending on the occasion for which the individual is dressed. If the individual is going to lunch or dinner at an elegant restaurant, most people would perceive the person to be wealthy and successful. If the individual is washing a car or mowing a lawn, many people would perceive the person to be eccentric or to lack common sense.

BODY LANGUAGE

NOTE 14.26
Physical appearances influence first impressions.

NOTE 14.27
Body language can change the meaning of an oral message.

Whether in conjunction with spoken words or independently, your body sends messages to those with whom you communicate.

An advantage of using body language to respond to a message is that it conveys instant feedback to the sender. A smile is interpreted almost universally as an expression of friendliness and approval. A smile indicates satisfaction, but a frown shows disagreement. The eyes are also a powerful indicator. Failure to look a person in the eye when speaking may indicate shyness, dishonesty, or embarrassment. Eye contact can convey positive emotions such as confidence, agreement, or interest in the subject of a conversation; negative emotions like fear or hatred; or a signal to the sender about when to talk or finish. The frequency of the eye contact may indicate either interest or boredom. Eye contact may be influenced by culture; some cultures identify direct eye contact with disrespect; others value direct eye contact. A raised eyebrow communicates the receiver's uncertainty. And, an individual who glances around while speaking is exhibiting nervousness or lack of interest. Facial expressions continually change during an interaction and are monitored constantly by the recipient.

NOTE 14.28
Posture and body position convey a nonverbal message.

Other forms of body language include body posture, body position, and gestures. The way a person sits or stands communicates a nonverbal message. An individual standing or sitting erectly conveys confidence and pride; a person slumping over may be perceived as being tired or depressed. If an individual leans toward another person during a conversation, body language indicates that the person likes or is interested in the other communicator. If the person leans away from the other person, the posture suggests a dislike of or disinterest in the other individual. A parallel or face-to-face orientation indicates that the interest is focused on the other person. As people become less interested, their bodies tend to angle away from the other person and the focus becomes less. People who are working together on a project are likely to sit side by side while competitors frequently face one another. Leaning slightly forward while standing or sitting communicates that you are approachable, receptive, and interested.

A handshake also communicates a nonverbal message. A person who firmly grips your hand demonstrates confidence; an individual who squeezes your hand so tightly that it causes pain gives the impression of being overly aggressive or inconsiderate. A weak handshake may reflect insecurity or pessimism. Don't rush to judgment, though. A soft handshake could also be related to a person's culture, an occupation, or a health concern. Native Americans, people with arthritis, surgeons, musicians, artists, and others may use a soft handshake by choice. Listen and watch for clues as to why an individual might use a particular type of handshake. Through the Small Business Advocate website, you can access an article that categorizes the types of handshakes and the character of the person delivering the handshake.

People transmit nonverbal messages through their body language.

© Ryanstock/Taxi

It is practically impossible to communicate without some use of gestures. A speaker who doesn't use any gestures when speaking may be perceived as boring, uncomfortable, or nervous. Conversely, people tend to use gestures more when they are enthusiastic or excited. A gesture may be as simple as a thumbs-up to signify approval or a thumbs-down for disapproval. A gesture may be used to emphasize a critical point in an oral presentation. Oral presentations would not be very interesting if the only communicative motion was the opening and closing of the speaker's mouth. Care should be taken in using gestures because, as pointed out in Chapter 2, different cultures interpret gestures in different ways.

NOTE 14.29
Gestures add emphasis and interest to oral communication.

Body language, whether intentional or unintentional, can change the meaning of a verbal message. Unfortunately, many people are unaware of the messages they send through body language.

SPACE

Communication is influenced by space. Space, as used in nonverbal communication, includes the size of a physical area, proximity to another person, and obstacles between you and the person with whom you are speaking.

The amount of space people control influences our attitudes and, therefore, inadvertently is a form of nonverbal communication. The size of a person's office, the number of windows, and the paintings on the wall are all indications of importance within the hierarchy of an organization.

A person in charge wants to keep his or her most trusted aide nearby. Therefore, the proximity of an employee to a supervisor communicates nonverbally the importance of the employee within the organization. The employee's importance also may be indicated nonverbally by parking space location, office size and location, or seating location at meetings.

The design of an office can greatly affect the communication within it. Research has shown that eliminating obstacles such as desks, chairs, and tables will improve oral communication between individuals. Some individuals divide their offices into personal and impersonal areas. This can improve the communication process if the areas are used for the purposes intended. The communication will improve if both communicators are on the same physical level—sitting or standing.

NOTE 14.30
The purpose of the communication will determine the personal space between communicators.

The distance between the communicators will also affect the communication. This distance will vary with individuals from different cultures. Americans tend to require more personal space than do people in other cultures. The purpose of the

communication note

Distance	Purpose of Communication
$\frac{1}{2}$ to $1\frac{1}{2}$ feet	Intimate communication with friends
$1\frac{1}{2}$ to 4 feet	Casual conversation with friends and coworkers
4 to 12 feet	Formal conversation with business associates
More than 12 feet	Speeches and presentations to groups

communication will determine the appropriate personal space between communicators. The table in the following Communication Note shows acceptable distances for personal space in the United States.

TIME

NOTE 14.31
Emphasis on time transmits a message.

Communicators must be aware that the amount of time devoted to a subject transmits a nonverbal message. If the president of a company, for instance, meets with one manager for ten minutes and another manager for two hours, a nonverbal message is being transmitted about the importance of the message or the message receiver.

Punctuality relays a nonverbal message. A person who is always on time is perceived as being well organized. A person who is always late transmits a message that he or she is disorganized or that the appointment is unimportant. For instance, if two people of equal credentials were interviewing for a job and one arrived 15 minutes late for the interview, it is more likely that the punctual applicant would be hired.

The importance of time will vary among cultures. Punctuality is very important with individuals from most European countries; however, a 30-minute delay is customary in most Latin American countries. Asians expect others to be punctual, but they themselves often will be late.

Summary of Learning Objectives

LO 1 Distinguish between hearing and listening.

Hearing is a physical process; listening is a mental one. A person can hear something without listening to it. Listening involves understanding and retaining the message.

LO 2 Describe the five elements of the listening process.

The five elements of the listening process are hearing—the physiological process of the auditory nerves being stimulated by sound waves; filtering—the elimination of unwanted stimuli; interpreting—the listener's mind assigning meaning to the stimuli; responding—giving verbal and nonverbal feedback that the message was received and understood; and remembering—recalling at a later time the information that was interpreted and responded to earlier.

List the guidelines for effective listening.

LO 3

Guidelines that may be followed to improve your listening are (a) concentrate on the message, (b) determine the purpose of the message, (c) keep an open mind, (d) provide feedback, (e) minimize taking notes, (f) analyze the total message, and (g) do not talk or interrupt.

Describe barriers to effective listening.

LO 4

Anything that interferes with the listening process is a barrier to effective listening. A physical distraction is any diversion that interferes with the listener's concentration on what is being said. Mental distractions may include the receiver's emotional state, psychological factors, or biases and prejudices. Health concerns that may affect listening include being hungry, sick, or tired. Nonverbal distractions include the listener looking at his or her watch, yawning, or frowning. Attempting to present a speech or hold a conversation at an inappropriate time can create a barrier to listening. A listener's understanding can be hindered by a speaker's heavy accent or dialect.

Describe the advantages of effective listening.

LO 5

Effective listening helps build relationships, solve problems, ensure understanding, resolve conflicts, and improve accuracy.

Explain the importance of nonverbal messages.

LO 6

The sender of a nonverbal message may be unaware that a message is being sent and, therefore, be unaware of its effect on the receiver. Nonverbal messages may be more reliable than written or oral messages because they are usually unplanned. The receiver of a message may form a frozen evaluation of the sender based on the nonverbal message. Nonverbal communication is always present.

Identify different types of nonverbal messages and discuss their impact on the communication process.

LO 7

The physical appearance of a written message causes the receiver to form a first impression of the message before reading it. The physical appearance of an individual sends a nonverbal message; the way a person is dressed often influences the opinions of others. Body language—facial expressions, gestures, handshakes, posture, and body position—also communicates nonverbal messages. Communication through body language is instantaneous. The size of the physical area, proximity to another person, and obstacles between you and the person to whom you are speaking are all examples of how space can be used to communicate messages. The amount of time spent with an individual and punctuality are examples of how time communicates nonverbal messages.

Questions for Discussion and Review

1. Why do employers rate listening as one of the top skills they expect employees to have? (Objective 1)
2. Distinguish between filtering and interpreting. (Objective 2)
3. What advice could you give to a friend who confides in you that he or she has difficulty concentrating in a class taught by a faculty member for whom English is not a first language? (Objective 3)
4. If you are in a meeting and the speaker is saying something but his or her facial expressions and tone of voice seem to be saying something else, what would you believe, the words or the nonverbal cues? Why? (Objective 3)
5. Identify three internal stimuli and three external stimuli that have prevented you from being an effective listener in the past. (Objective 3)
6. List four examples of feedback you can give to a speaker that would indicate you understand his or her message. (Objective 4)
7. Good listeners can be described as patient and sincere; bad listeners can be described as self-centered and intolerant. What other words describe good listeners? bad listeners? List at least three for each. (Objective 5)
8. List and explain the four characteristics of nonverbal messages. What nonverbal messages might students be sending if (a) they were leaning forward in their seats during the instructor's lecture and (b) if they were looking out the window to watch a touch football game that was taking place on the school lawn? (Objective 6)
9. Explain how physical appearance can affect written and oral messages. What messages might be sent by (a) a coworker wearing jeans and a T-shirt to present an idea for a marketing campaign for a new client, (b) a tattoo, and (c) a scratched-out response on a job application? (Objective 7)
10. Discuss five ways nonverbal messages could be presented in a positive manner when interviewing for a supervisory position in a business organization. (Objective 7)

Application Exercises

COLLABORATIVE

1. **Teamwork.** Conduct the following exercise with teams of five people.
   The instructor will read a factual story (from a newspaper, magazine, or other source) to one member of each team. That person will retell the story to another person on the team; this person will relay the story to another team member, and so on. This will continue until the last member of each team has heard the story. Then the last student to have the story told to him or her will relate the story to the instructor. The instructor will check the story against the original article. The team with the greatest accuracy will win this listening activity. (Objective 1)

COLLABORATIVE

2. **Teamwork.** As directed by your instructor, meet in a small group to discuss the following questions. (Objective 2)
   a. How do you feel when a teacher, manager, colleague, or service representative doesn't seem to be listening to you?
   b. How do you feel when these same people seem to be listening well?
   c. How do you feel when someone with whom you work, a sales associate, or a customer-service worker gives preference to a phone call rather than to you?
   Make a list of the feelings your group identifies and share them with the class. Then, discuss why people might give preference to a phone call rather than an in-person visitor.

TECHNOLOGY

3. **Technology.** During the next conversation you have with a coworker, a family member, or someone not from this class, use paraphrasing at least once. E-mail your instructor to describe the effect paraphrasing had on you and the other person. (Objective 3)

4. **Teamwork.** Bring a newspaper, magazine, or book to class.

   a. Working in a group of four, have one member read aloud for five minutes while the other three members listen—one using cautious listening, one skimming, and one scanning. Compare the results of the three listening efforts and report your results to the class.

   b. Repeat the exercise using different material. Have a fifth person make noise or cause some other distraction. Discuss how the distraction affected each person's ability to listen to the message. (Objectives 3 and 4)

5. **Global. Teamwork.** Conduct an in-class debate on whether ineffective listening is strictly an American problem or whether it exists worldwide. Do the secondary research necessary to support your or your team's position. (Objective 4)

6. Prepare to discuss in class either the pro or the con viewpoint for one of the two following statements. Support your position with examples of situations that have happened or could happen. (Objectives 5 and 6)

   a. Listening builds friendships and careers.

   b. Nonverbal messages hinder communication.

7. **Teamwork.** After the class has been divided into at least two teams, take turns acting out, without speaking, roles presented by the teacher. (Objective 7)

8. **Teamwork.** Form groups of four students. Shake hands with each person in the group and then give either an oral or a written evaluation of the student's handshake. Your instructor may direct each group to develop a form for this purpose or have the class develop one form to be used by all groups. (Objective 7)

9. **Teamwork. Global.** Form groups of four students. Have each group get five to seven pictures (from magazines or pictures they take) of people (from different cultures if possible) illustrating different facial expressions, body positions, and gestures. Identify what emotion or meaning is being conveyed in each picture. Then ask classmates who represent cultures other than those in the pictures if the emotions or meanings conveyed are the same in their culture. (Objective 7)

10. **Teamwork. Global. Technology.** Form teams of three students. Choose a culture you are not totally familiar with but would like to learn more about. Research (through the Internet or interviews) the four types of nonverbal communication in that culture and discuss various nonverbal cues and what they mean or represent in the culture you are exploring. Send an e-mail to your instructor with the results of your findings. (Objective 7)

Web exercises to accompany this chapter are available at **www.thomsonedu.com/bcomm/krizan.**

Message Analysis

You work for Jason P. McDonald, a middle-aged, well-educated man who owns two card/gift shops, a security company, three fast-food restaurants, and a flower shop/garden center. Jason is creative and highly motivated. He credits his success, in part, to his ability to listen effectively. He wants his employees to share his view of how important it is to listen and plans to display attractively designed, framed quotes about listening in the work areas of his various businesses. He's asked you to select three quotes and to use the computer software you have available to create an appropriate design for each. He'll then decide which to have printed and framed. You've searched the Internet and prepared the following list of possible quotes. Now it's time to select the three you want to recommend and to create your design. Be sure you consider the diversity of Jason's businesses as you make your selections.

> *Try to listen carefully that you might not have to speak.—Quaker saying*
>
> *The most basic of all human needs is the need to understand and be understood. The best way to understand people is to listen to them.—Ralph Nichols*
>
> *History repeats itself because no one listens the first time.—Anonymous*

It's my job to talk and yours to listen, but please, let me know if you finish before I do.—Anonymous

The greatest compliment that was ever paid me was when one asked me what I thought, and attended to my answer.—Henry David Thoreau

A good listener truly wants to know the speaker.—John Powell

You cannot truly listen to anyone and do anything else at the same time.—M. Scott Peck

If speaking is silver, then listening is gold.—Turkish proverb

Easy listening exists only on the radio.—David Barkan

Instead of listening to what is being said to them, many managers are already listening to what they are going to say.—Anonymous

It is the province of knowledge to speak, and it is the privilege of wisdom to listen.—Oliver Wendell Holmes

Opportunities are often missed because we are broadcasting when we should be listening.—Author unknown

Listening, not imitation, may be the sincerest form of flattery.—Dr. Joyce Brothers

No one ever listened themselves out of a job.—Calvin Coolidge

Good listeners, like precious gems, are to be treasured.—Walter Anderson

Courage is what it takes to stand up and speak; courage is also what it takes to sit down and listen.—Winston Churchill

Listening is the single skill that makes the difference between a mediocre and a great company.—Lee Iacocca

The beginning of wisdom is silence. The second stage is listening.—A Hebrew sage

Be a good listener. Your ears will never get you in trouble.—Frank Tyger

Know how to listen, and you will profit even from those who talk badly.—Plutarch

Writer's Workshop

The following items may be sentence fragments or contain errors in punctuation, subject–verb agreement, pronoun–antecedent agreement, infinitive use, abbreviations, number display, capitalization, spelling, word choice, possessives, modifier clarity and placement, or parallelism. Rewrite the sentences to make them correct:

1. All questions pretaining to your Pension Benefit should be submitted to James Douglas Human Resources Specialist by 4:00 P.M. on Thursday May 12th.
2. I was surprized alot when I one the raffle at the Company Picnic, I only had one ticket bought.
3. Only five percent of those whom responded to the survey indicated they felt undo pressure to reach the monthly sales quota.
4. Next semester I will take courses in english litrature, international business, spanish and statistics its going to take a lot of studying to do good in these hard courses.
5. Viet ran faster nevertheless he did not win the race.
6. Walter spend the day washing and waxing his car, vacuuming his house, and fed his dog, cat, and bird.

7. Everyone of the swimmers participated in the 50 yard freestile race.
8. After you return from lunch stop by my office to discuss next years' budget, we can not differ the discussion another day.
9. Mr Peters is the best teacher of the two who teach american history.
10. Because Sallys' "to Do list was not on her desk she assumed it had been throne away accidently.

Chapter 15
Oral Communication Essentials

LET'S TALK BUSINESS

Storytelling conjures up images of something told to small children to get them to relax before bedtime. This is just one example of storytelling; in reality, it is much more.

Storytelling is becoming an increasingly important component of business communication. It is a simple tool that everyone from management to maintenance, from service to sales, can use. Storytelling is a technique being used effectively by Ernst & Young, Hewlett-Packard, Walt Disney Imagineering, and many other large and small companies throughout the United States.

Victoria L. Snyder, President, Communication Connection

We live in a fast-paced society, one in which speakers often have only minutes to connect with their listeners. Using stories helps a speaker make a memorable impression quickly and become an unrivaled communicator.

Anyone can learn to become a storyteller. You don't need to have a TV announcer's voice, a scholar's large vocabulary, or a CEO's leadership status. You just need to be natural, open, and willing to communicate honestly.

You can use stories to teach or illustrate just about anything. You can focus stories to inspire people to do their best; to create community; or to make people stop, think, and problem solve. As a professional storyteller and motivational speaker, I weave stories about my sister, whom I call "Princess" Kitty, into talks on a variety of subjects. Audience members relate to, enjoy, and remember stories involving "Princess" Kitty. They also remember the points the stories were designed to stress.

Incorporate storytelling into your life. Practice the skills on people who already spend time with you. In time, you will become a stronger, more memorable speaker and communicator.

Recently, business leaders have come to recognize the story as a powerful and persuasive method of communication. Are you wondering why, in this technologically advanced age, an ancient art like storytelling is emerging as such a viable and effective oral communication skill? As Victoria Snyder notes in Let's Talk Business, storytelling can communicate information, stimulate the imagination, and build community. In addition, corporate stories can communicate the company or organization's values and improve communication among departments. Several of the leading thinkers on knowledge management predict that storytelling will play a key role in the creation and sharing of knowledge in the 21st century because traditional methods of distributing information are not as effective as they once were.

Weaving stories into your oral communication has several benefits. Storytelling is our "native language"; we have been doing it since an early age, so it is a technique with which we are comfortable. Have you ever sat in a presentation or training session where so much information was dumped on you that you couldn't remember much of what was said, but you were still able to remember a story that was told? When you listen to a good storyteller, you listen actively. You experience the story as if it were your own; you become emotionally involved. For a story to come alive and captivate the audience, the content, structure, and performance must be crafted carefully. That means the storyteller must organize the story to achieve a particular goal, choose words and nonverbal cues that will enhance the story, and rehearse until he or she is satisfied that the message will be communicated clearly to the audience.

As much as storytelling can enhance the oral communication process, there are times when it is not appropriate. For example, if an audience is expecting an oral communication that is a numerical analysis of an audit, storytelling would not be appropriate to the situation. Also, if the storytelling could be deceptive and cast suspicion on the credibility or reputation of a person or an organization, it would not be ethical to integrate it into the message. The concept of storytelling introduced in Let's Talk Business is just one technique that can make a point, teach a lesson, and move people to action. Read the Communication Note on page 420 to see how Doug Walker uses storytelling in his company and to read a sample story for business.

Both written communication and oral communication are vital to your personal success and to the success of the business or organization where you work. Other parts of this book have been devoted to general foundations and principles of business communication and their application to written, interpersonal, and teamwork communication situations. In this chapter, you will learn how those foundations and principles relate to oral communication. Specifically, you will learn how to improve your voice and presence and how to prepare and deliver a formal oral presentation.

The amount of time you spend giving presentations will vary widely depending on your position and level of responsibility within an organization. Certain jobs require extensive oral communication. Sales representatives regularly make informative and persuasive presentations to prospective customers. Mediators must present convincing arguments for their proposed solution(s) to all parties involved in a specific situation. Public relations specialists must organize and moderate news conferences. The list could go on, but the jobs identified illustrate the fact that effective oral presentations are a thread common to many careers. Your success will depend not only on *what* you say, but also on *how* you say it—on the quality of your voice and the strength of your presence. You must speak clearly, intelligently, and confidently.

NOTE 15.1
Storytelling is used to inform, to stimulate imagination, and to build community.

NOTE 15.2
Some jobs involve extensive oral communication.

communication note

REAL-WORLD APPLICATION OF STORYTELLING

Doug Walker, the chief executive officer of WRQ, has been telling stories at his software company since he cofounded it more than 20 years ago.

In weekly company meetings, he tells stories that showcase employees who have solved customer problems or improved customer operations. He's found the weekly stories transform dull mission statements into something employees can understand and help keep them motivated.

"We need people to be motivated about coming to work, and storytelling helps us do that," Walker said. "Having a strong team is your competitive advantage. And if we lose that, we lose our business."

Source: Kristina Shevory, "Moral of Story Is That Stories Build Morale," *The Seattle Times*, November 17, 2004, http://seattletimes.nwsource.com/html/eastsidenews/2002092977_eastbiz17e.html (accessed July 19, 2006).

A KNOWLEDGE-BASED STORY WITH A MORAL

Stories are used within business for a variety of reasons. Following the story you will find the moral.

The Talking Shoes

One cold winter weekend when my husband had the flu, he was looking around for something to do that was entertaining but not too taxing. He dug out an old adventure game he'd picked up for the computer a while back. We started the game up, and the computer immediately began to play sounds and music VERY LOUDLY.

After we struggled back into the room (holding our ears), we managed to find the panel in the software that would turn down the sound. However, this was an old game, and with our newer sound system we found that we had exactly two volume settings: deafening and silent.

We were just about to give up and turn off the game when I saw a pair of shoes sitting in front of the desk. I quickly took each one of the small computer speakers and stuffed it deep inside a shoe. Not only did the shoes muffle the sound perfectly, but they made a hilarious narrator for the story!

Sometimes the best solutions to technological dilemmas are not technological at all. Technology does not exist in a vacuum, but in the real world.

Source: Cynthia Kurtz, "The Talking Shoes," http://www.research.ibm.com/knowsoc/stories_talkingshoes.html (accessed July 3, 2006).

Enhancing Your Voice Qualities

LO 1

Enhance the basic quality of your voice.

To improve your oral communication, you must train your speaking voice.

Proper Control of Breathing

High-quality sound with adequate volume depends on the proper use of one raw material—air. You can relax your sound-producing organs and prepare them for speaking by taking a few deep breaths. By controlling the amount of air you inhale and exhale while speaking, you can improve the quality of the sounds you make.

NOTE 15.3
Controlled breathing helps produce rich, full sounds.

To have the necessary air control for efficient speaking, you should breathe from your diaphragm. Controlled inhalation of air from this abdominal area requires less effort than chest breathing, allows you to breathe deeply, and provides ample air for speaking. Good posture controls the balance between your vocal cords and helps enrich your voice. When you inhale deeply, keep your shoulders low and level; expand your abdomen, lower back, and sides. The air should go all the way to the diaphragm—a muscle between the chest and the abdomen. When you are nervous, you may breathe shallowly and not fill your lungs; the result may be a wobbly or shaky voice.

NOTE 15.4
Resonators enrich your voice.

When you speak, the exhaled air should come from your diaphragm, pass your vocal cords, and fill the resonators in your head with enough force to cause the sounds to be rich and full. The **resonators** in your head—mouth, nose, and sinuses—are like echo chambers; they enrich the sound of your voice.

Proper Control of Jaw, Tongue, and Lips

The sound produced through the exhaled air is modified by the resonators and formed into vowels and consonants by the **articulators** (tongue, jaw, teeth, cheeks, lips, and hard and soft palates). The "troublesome t's" of tight jaw, tight tongue, and tight lips cause mumbled, muffled speech sounds that are hard to hear and difficult to understand. Pronunciation, enunciation, and sound clarity depend on your jaw being flexible and your tongue and lips being loose and alive.

NOTE 15.5
Articulators form the vowels and consonants to make words.

Practice freely flexing your jaw by saying *idea, up and down,* and *the sky is blue.* Now say those same expressions with a tightly clenched jaw. Notice how clenching your jaw muffles the sounds. For more jaw-flexing practice, count from 91 to 99, and say *fine, yes, no, pay, buy,* and *like* over and over.

For practice in freeing your tongue and making it come alive, say *either, left,* and *wealth.* Try to say the same words holding your tongue still. Now count from 21 to 29 and let your tongue move freely and loosely. Say *health, thin, think, alive,* and *luck.* Practicing these and similar words will increase the flexibility and mobility of your tongue.

To free your lips—important controllers of voice quality—say *when, where, be,* and *back.* See what happens to your enunciation when you try to say these words without moving your lips. Other words to practice that will help to free your lips are *west, window, puff, lisp,* and *lips.*

Deep breathing and controlled use of your jaw, tongue, and lips will enable you to achieve full, rich tones—the voice quality displayed by announcers and broadcasters in the radio and television industries. Practice until deep breathing and keeping your jaw, tongue, and lips flexible come naturally.

Using Your Voice Effectively

You are ready to improve the use of your voice once you have control of the basic sound-making mechanisms. The important characteristics of voice quality are pitch, volume, speed, tone, emphasis, enunciation, and pronunciation. These aspects of using your voice effectively can each be improved by using a tape or video recorder for self-analysis or by obtaining feedback from a family member, a friend, or others.

LO 2
Use your voice effectively.

Pitch

Pitch refers to the highness or lowness of your voice. A voice that is too high or too low may be distracting to your listener or audience. Pitch has two important aspects:

- Finding your natural pitch and, assuming it is not too shrill or too deep, using it
- Varying your pitch to provide interest and emphasis while speaking

FIND YOUR NATURAL PITCH AND USE IT
To determine your natural pitch, yawn deeply three times. Then say aloud, "My natural pitch is . . . ." Yawn deeply, and say the words again. Your pitch should have become deeper, richer, and fuller. Yawn and repeat the words a third time. Let your voice rest for at least one minute. Now, once again say, "My natural pitch is . . . ." With this exercise you will have found your natural pitch.

NOTE 15.6
Use your natural pitch to avoid damaging your vocal cords.

To avoid damaging your vocal cords, find and use your natural pitch. When you are excited, nervous, or frightened, the muscles tighten around your voice box. The resulting tension in the vocal cords produces a greater frequency of vibration and, consequently, a higher pitch. If this pitch is higher than your natural pitch, you could strain your vocal cords. Speaking in a pitch that is artificially lower than your natural one could also cause you to strain your vocal cords. Strained vocal cords can result in a hoarse, raspy voice or a temporary voice loss.

If you think your pitch is too high or too low, consult a speech correction specialist. Most colleges have or can refer you to a speech correction specialist. With exercises prescribed by a professional, your natural pitch can be brought to a more attractive, pleasant level.

VARY YOUR PITCH WHILE SPEAKING

The second aspect of improving the use of your voice is **inflection,** which is a change in pitch while speaking. We do not speak naturally on one pitch level all the time. The voice slides up and down as we express different thoughts, feelings, and emphases. The interesting, enthusiastic speaker varies the pitch of his or her voice and avoids the dullness of a monotone voice—a voice with a sameness in pitch level. Nothing will lose an audience faster than a monotonous voice, regardless of the quality of the content of the message.

NOTE 15.7
Varying your pitch adds interest and holds audience attention.

You can make your presentation style interesting and hold the attention of your audience by using pitch variations effectively. Indicate comparisons by using the same pitch level; indicate contrasts by using varied pitch levels. "The market is up (moderate pitch), and its gains are solid (moderate pitch)" shows equal emphasis. "The market is up (high pitch), but its gains are not solid (low pitch)" shows contrast. Make a question clear and forceful by raising your pitch at the end. Emphasize the ending of a declarative sentence with a definite drop in pitch. When a speaker's voice rises at the end of a declarative sentence, he or she sounds tentative rather than confident and the audience may think the speaker is expressing an incomplete thought.

Consciously varying your pitch while speaking is one of the most important ways to improve the effectiveness of your voice. Pitch variety holds your listeners' attention and helps them understand your messages.

Volume

A major aspect of using your voice effectively is **volume**—the intensity of sound. Proper volume control enables you to be heard appropriately by your listeners. Volume control also enables you to vary your emphasis to achieve dynamic, forceful oral communication.

USE THE APPROPRIATE VOLUME LEVEL

NOTE 15.8
Shouting can create a communication barrier.

The first goal of volume control is to be heard by every member of the audience. The value of what you have to say will be lost unless the audience can hear you. You want to project your voice, not shout. Shouting can create a communication barrier.

Feedback is an important part of the communication process. You can obtain feedback about your volume level by asking whether you are being heard clearly. Another source of feedback is the nonverbal signals you get from your listeners. Does your audience seem to be getting restless? Are people straining to hear you? Make adjustments as you go based on audience feedback.

VARY YOUR VOLUME FOR EMPHASIS

The second goal of voice volume control is to vary your volume level for emphasis. You can communicate strength, power, forcefulness, and excitement through louder speech. You can create a mood of sorrow, seriousness, respect, and sympathy by lowering the volume of your voice. Both methods can be used to attach importance and emphasis to what you are saying.

You can maintain the attention of an audience, regardless of its size, by varying the volume of your voice. In a one-to-one situation, your voice should be conversational; with a larger group, volume can show a wide range depending on your communication goals.

NOTE 15.9
Give emphasis by varying your volume.

Speed

Changing the speed of your oral communication provides interest and emphasis. The monotone voice we all try to avoid uses not only the same pitch and volume level but also the same speed.

The rate at which you speak should be adapted to the message and the size of the audience. Simple points and illustrations may be made at a quick pace. However, complex or technical material and main points necessitate a slower pace. The slower pace may be achieved by drawing out the words or by using pauses, both of which allow the receiver time to concentrate on and absorb what is being said. Pausing is essential to effective oral communication; it should be thought of as part of the presentation. Speakers use pauses to project confidence and poise, to show they are in control of the presentation, to breathe properly, and to compose themselves at difficult points in a presentation. It is especially effective to pause for emphasis before and/or after major points. A caution—do not overdo the pausing or it will be difficult for the audience to distinguish between what is important and what is supporting or less critical information.

Speed can also be used for emphasis and to convey emotion. Stress selected parts of your message by speaking slowly. Convey excitement with a high rate of speed, seriousness with a slow rate. The important point is to vary your rate as you speak.

Interactive communication will generally have a wider range (75 to 250 words a minute) than will one-way communication (75 to 150 words a minute). Rapid speech may impair enunciation and pronunciation. Try to achieve a balance between speed and clarity. Learning to phrase well will help with pacing and will make the message easy to understand.

NOTE 15.10
Match your speed to your message and audience.

Tone

Tone is possibly your most important voice quality. **Tone** is the way the message sounds to a receiver. Your tone can convey feelings such as concern, irritation, confidence, tentativeness, excitement, calmness, disrespect, courtesy, and detachment. The same sentence, spoken with a different tone, can have a dramatically different meaning. The words, *I know what you mean,* can be said with a concerned tone, conveying understanding; with an irritated tone, conveying frustration; or with a skeptical tone, conveying mistrust.

Most business communication situations call for a friendly, objective, businesslike tone that conveys warmth, strength, and respect. You will not want to sound

NOTE 15.11
Tone conveys meaning through emotions.

negative, overly formal, insincere, condescending, prejudiced, weak, or disrespectful. You should consciously determine the tone you use when you speak.

Emphasis

NOTE 15.12
Different emphases =
different meanings.

You can give emphasis to your oral communication by varying your pitch, volume, speed, and tone. The following exercise will help you vary your emphasis and give different meanings to the same words. Say each of the following sentences aloud, giving emphasis to the highlighted word:

- *You* can improve your voice. (Stresses who)
- You *can* improve your voice. (Stresses ability)
- You can *improve* your voice. (Stresses action)
- You can improve *your* voice. (Stresses ownership)
- You can improve your *voice.* (Stresses what)

Did you vary the emphasis in each sentence by using different pitches? volumes? speeds? Probably you used a combination of these techniques. Now, repeat each sentence in the exercise and emphasize the highlighted word by varying your pitch. Next, say the sentences and vary your volume by saying the highlighted words louder than the others. Then, repeat the sentences and vary your rate by saying the highlighted word slowly and the rest of the words quickly. Finally, say the sentences and vary your tone from a disinterested to a caring quality.

From your use of the different emphasis techniques, you can see how powerful voice variety can be. You can generate interest and communicate different meanings. You can strengthen the force, power, and effectiveness of your oral communication by using variations in your voice.

Enunciation

NOTE 15.13
Sound each word part
clearly and accurately.

Enunciation refers to saying all the sounds in a word clearly. Sound each part of a word clearly and accurately by moving your tongue and lips fully. We sometimes become careless and move our articulators less than we should. One type of enunciation error that results from doing this is the dropping of end letters from words, especially "ing," "ed," "d," "e," or "t." An example of correct enunciation is sounding clearly the g's in words ending in *ing.* Say *talking* instead of *talkin, going to* instead of *gonna,* and *studying* instead of *studyin.* Another source of poor enunciation involves running words together. Instead of saying *"What did you get?"* it may sound like *"Whatdjagit?"* or *"What's that?"* may sound like *"Wazzat?"* Slowing the rate at which you say individual words will help to correct errors in enunciation. Give each word its fair share of time so that each part can be sounded properly and each can be heard distinctly.

Eliminating these enunciation problems from your speech requires practice and diligence. High-quality enunciation reflects favorably on your intelligence and credibility.

Pronunciation

NOTE 15.14
Join sounds correctly for
proper pronunciation.

The way in which you join sounds to say a word is called **pronunciation.** You can make sounds distinctly (enunciate clearly) but still not pronounce a word correctly. The dictionary is your best source of information for correct pronunciation of individual words. The first pronunciation given in a dictionary is usually the preferred one. The second pronunciation is acceptable but less common.

As in the case of high-quality enunciation, the correctness of your pronunciation reflects on your intelligence and credibility. Your listeners expect you to speak correctly. Doing so minimizes the potential for a communication barrier and helps receivers focus on the content of your message. Good oral communicators pronounce words correctly. They say *library* instead of *libary, February* instead of *Febuary, was* instead of *wuz, again* instead of *agin, just* instead of *jist, because* instead of *becuz, to* instead of *ta, the* instead of *da,* and *our* instead of *ar.* Some errors in pronunciation occur because you are using unfamiliar words; other errors occur because you are hearing people you spend time with pronounce the word incorrectly. If you are not sure how to pronounce a word, do not use it until you check a dictionary or learn from another person how to pronounce it correctly.

Analysis

You can improve the effectiveness of your voice by analyzing its qualities and the way in which you use it. You can perform this analysis in several ways. You can record your voice on a tape recorder for self-analysis. You can ask a family member who speaks effectively and correctly to analyze your oral communication. You can ask an instructor at school for feedback, or you can seek the advice of a speech correction professional. Regardless of the method you choose, taking the time to analyze your voice qualities and to improve them where necessary will help make you a better oral communicator.

NOTE 15.15
Analyze your voice to improve its effectiveness.

Strengthening Your Presence

You can further improve your oral communication by strengthening your personal presence. Your **presence** consists of your poise and bearing. It includes your tangible and intangible nonverbal communication. The important aspects of presence are confidence, enthusiasm, sincerity, friendliness, eye contact, body actions, and appearance.

LO 3
Strengthen your personal presence.

Confidence

Whether you are talking to one person or several, your receiver(s) will sense the level of confidence you possess. For a strong presence, business professionals need the right amount of confidence—neither too little nor too much.

TOO LITTLE CONFIDENCE

In one-on-one situations, too little confidence is referred to as *nervousness;* when speaking to larger groups, it is called *stage fright.*

Speaking with too little confidence causes discomfort for both a speaker and an audience. A speaker's discomfort may be reflected in a quivering voice; shaking hands; perspiration; inability to think clearly; inability to respond to questions; or other unpleasant mental, emotional, or physical symptoms. Listeners will exhibit their discomfort through nonverbal cues or through side comments to others in the audience. Speakers who lack self-confidence may not be able to say what they want

NOTE 15.16
Lack of confidence causes nervousness.

to say in the way they want to say it. As a result, they may lose credibility with their audience and reduce the effectiveness of the communication. Neither the speaker nor the audience will find the communication experience pleasant or productive.

For some individuals, too little confidence is caused by negative thinking and unrealistic expectations. Speakers should accept that they do not necessarily have to be admired or respected by everyone in the audience. In addition, they must realize that it is normal to misspeak occasionally; they must not allow such errors to reduce their confidence level.

TOO MUCH CONFIDENCE

NOTE 15.17
Overconfidence produces negative reactions.

Too much confidence can also inhibit oral communication effectiveness. The over-confident speaker projects a know-it-all attitude and a lack of concern for the audience. Your audience will respond negatively to overconfidence by rejecting you and your message.

AN EFFECTIVE LEVEL OF CONFIDENCE

NOTE 15.18
Concentrate on the audience and use the you–viewpoint.

Self-centeredness causes *both* underconfidence *and* overconfidence. Speakers who concentrate exclusively on themselves and do not consider their receivers will be perceived as having either too little confidence or too much. To achieve an effective confidence level, keep the emphasis on your listeners and use the you–viewpoint. You won't be too concerned about yourself if you are thinking about the needs, concerns, and interests of others. As a speaker, you need to sound authoritative as opposed to authoritarian, knowledgeable but not a know-it-all, and definitive rather than hesitant.

Other ways of developing an effective level of confidence include careful preparation, diligent practice, and attention to your personal appearance. Sustain confidence by maintaining eye contact with your audience; talking in a strong, clear voice with sufficient volume; and observing and reacting to audience feedback.

Enthusiasm

NOTE 15.19
An enthusiastic speaker holds the listeners' attention.

Enthusiasm is contagious—if it is genuine. When you are enthusiastic, your audience will become enthusiastic and positive about the ideas you express. Dullness can cause receivers to let their minds wander; it can even put some to sleep. Enthusiasm can excite listeners, spark their interest, and keep them alert.

You can project your enthusiasm by speaking with energy and animation. Variations in pitch, volume, and speed will assist in showing enthusiasm. Facial expressions such as smiles and raised eyebrows indicate enthusiasm. Eyes that are wide open, alive, and sparkling also show enthusiasm. Energetic and definite gestures and body movements help, too. Recognize the importance of building a positive, enthusiastic presence; practice every time you have an opportunity—in conversations, oral reports, discussions, and speeches.

Sincerity

NOTE 15.20
Sincerity strengthens credibility.

Effectiveness is enhanced if the audience perceives the speaker to be sincere. Inappropriate gestures or facial expressions reflect insincerity and an apparent lack of concern for an audience. In addition, an insincere speaker may have difficulty gaining or maintaining credibility. You communicate sincerity when the general tone of your oral presentation conveys that your message is important. Your message should be presented in a warm, friendly, and caring manner.

Friendliness

The speaker who can project a congenial, gracious, caring, and respectful image—a warm friendliness—can relate more effectively to a listener or to an audience. A smiling face, a well-paced approach, and a genuine concern for feedback exhibit friendliness and an honest interest in your receivers. This friendliness conveys believability and genuineness that can engage an audience.

NOTE 15.21
Friendliness builds positive relationships with listeners.

Eye Contact

Appropriate eye contact reflects confidence, interest, honesty, and sincerity. Failure to establish eye contact reflects a lack of confidence and may cause you to project an image of weakness, insincerity, fear, and dishonesty.

Be sure the amount of eye contact you have with your audience is appropriate for the cultural mix in that audience. American audiences expect more eye contact than do Asian audiences but less than French.

When making a presentation, be sure to engage receivers in all areas of the room. Make each person feel that he or she is having a one-on-one conversation with you. Convey the impression that, although you need to talk to others in the audience, you will return to the individual again.

NOTE 15.22
Make every receiver feel important.

Body Actions

Some nonverbal signals that occur during oral communication fall under the heading of body actions. These nonverbal signals include facial expressions, posture, gestures, and body movements. Each of these topics will be reviewed briefly here. They are discussed in more detail in Chapter 14.

FACIAL EXPRESSIONS

Regardless of the words you say, your eyes and your face will convey your true feelings. Show your sincerity and friendliness in your facial expressions. As you practice for a presentation, look in the mirror to see whether you appear to be interested, enthusiastic, and friendly. If not, practice the necessary facial expressions until your nonverbal signals match your verbal message.

NOTE 15.23
Facial expressions will be read as your true feelings.

GESTURES

Your hands, arms, shoulders, and head can convey important supporting nonverbal signals. Sitting stiffly behind a desk or standing immobile behind a lectern results in a dull, uninteresting appearance. Use gestures that support and strengthen your verbal messages.

Gestures should be natural, not contrived. When gestures emphasize a point or give a visual picture of your words, they add energy to your message and engage the audience's attention. Raising the arms with palms facing upward, for example, can accent a verbal message that asks the rhetorical question, *What is the answer?* Pointing to an item on a visual aid helps stress the point being made.

NOTE 15.24
Use natural gestures to strengthen your nonverbal message.

Gestures should be varied, not repetitious. To develop gestures appropriate for you and the situation, practice in front of a mirror until you find movements that are natural and comfortable for you.

POSTURE

An upright, correct posture will improve your appearance and give you a feeling of confidence. You do not want to appear pompous or stiff but rather natural and comfortable. While standing, keep your weight evenly distributed on your feet. Do not lean on a lectern, table, or chair. When seated, keep your back straight. Do not slouch or hang one leg over a chair arm. Correct posture reflects self-confidence and shows respect for your listener.

OTHER BODY MOVEMENTS

Some body movement is important to hold attention and to relax your muscles. These movements should be graceful, unhurried, and natural. You can draw an audience's attention to a visual aid by turning your body toward it or walking to it. As with facial expressions and gestures, you can observe and practice your body movements in front of a mirror until they feel comfortable and convey the correct nonverbal message.

Appearance

The final aspect to consider in strengthening your presence is your appearance. Your personal appearance can be either a barrier or an asset to effective oral communication. Appearance is an important part of the total communication environment, particularly as a first impression.

You have to accept and work with the raw material of your own basic appearance. What you do with what you have is what will influence your audience. Choose tasteful clothing. Be sure both your clothing and your accessories are appropriate for the occasion and the audience. You should be neatly groomed. Good appearance not only sets a favorable stage for oral communication, but it also serves to increase your confidence and improve your credibility.

Preparing and Delivering Presentations

Business professionals often find it necessary to make oral presentations. The purpose of most oral presentations will be either (a) to inform the audience of certain facts or (b) to persuade or motivate the audience to accept a point of view or take a certain action. Occasionally, you may be asked to deliver a presentation designed solely to entertain. Regardless of the purpose of a presentation, your career and your organization will benefit when you prepare and deliver it effectively.

Types of Oral Presentations

Oral presentations in business take many forms. Depending on your position, you may be asked to address a group of employees about a new policy or a recently implemented procedure or be asked to report to company officers on the status of the development of a new product. You might be called on to introduce a speaker, give an interview to the media, facilitate a focus group, or present at a professional meeting. Generally, making such presentations will serve you and your organization well.

Business presentations may be formal or informal, internal or external, short or long, delivered to small groups or to large ones. The situation will help guide you in selecting a delivery style. The four delivery styles from which you may choose are manuscript, memorized, impromptu, and extemporaneous. The features of each are described in the following paragraphs.

NOTE 15.29
Choose a delivery style appropriate for the situation.

MANUSCRIPT

A manuscript oral presentation is written word for word and then read to the audience. Used frequently in broadcast journalism, in high-level politics, or in situations where the audience is extremely large, this style is rare in business. Exceptions occur when precise wording is required, as during a crisis; when a speaker must give several different presentations to various audiences within a short time frame; or when an exact record of the speech must be kept. One of the difficulties associated with this presentation style is maintaining eye contact with the audience without losing your place in the text or being aware of audience feedback. Speakers who read their manuscripts also risk having the pages get out of order. Finally, it is very difficult to prepare a manuscript that sounds conversational; writing usually has more complex than simple sentences. Complex sentences do not translate well into an oral format.

NOTE 15.30
A manuscript presentation is read to the audience.

MEMORIZED

As the name implies, a memorized oral presentation is one in which the speaker has memorized the content verbatim. This style virtually eliminates the need for notes, but the delivery may appear "canned." In addition, a speaker risks forgetting parts of the presentation. Disadvantages include not being able to adapt the presentation to feedback from the audience and having the speaker's concentration broken by a question from the audience. Memorizing a speech typically requires a large investment of time. A better method is to memorize parts (for example, the opening and closing) rather than the entire presentation.

NOTE 15.31
A memorized presentation is learned verbatim.

IMPROMPTU

A presentation given without the benefit of time to prepare is referred to as an impromptu oral presentation. The advantages of an impromptu presentation are the natural feel of the delivery, the large degree of eye contact, and the opportunity to respond to audience feedback. For example, in a meeting of the company's sales force, a sales manager might be asked to say a few words about the sales efforts of his or her staff for a particular period. There are disadvantages to this type of speaking situation, including the lack of organization, increased speaker anxiety, increased use of verbal fillers, and the inability to prepare visual aids to support the presentation. Remaining calm and thinking quickly are keys to doing a good job in an unexpected speaking situation.

NOTE 15.32
An impromptu presentation is one that is given with little or no preparation.

EXTEMPORANEOUS

An extemporaneous oral presentation is prepared and delivered from notes or an outline. The extemporaneous style works well in interactive small-group settings as well as in predominantly one-way, large-group settings. It is a spontaneous, natural way to relate to an audience. It permits good eye contact, allows free movement,

NOTE 15.33
An extemporaneous presentation is prepared in advance and given from notes.

allows advance preparation, and enables the speaker to respond to audience feedback. This presentation method is the basis for the discussion in the rest of this chapter. The following Tips and Hints box provides advice for speakers who work from note cards.

Keys for Successfully Preparing an Effective Oral Presentation

LO 5

Identify the steps to follow in preparing an oral presentation.

The foundation for a successful oral presentation is preparation. Speakers who do not prepare are telling the audience members they are unworthy of the speaker's best effort. Thorough preparation builds a speaker's confidence and assures the audience of an interesting and informative presentation.

NOTE 15.34
Preparation is the key to success.

How much time does it take to prepare for a presentation? Although some speakers say they spend an hour preparing for each minute of oral presentation, no one formula works in every situation. The audience and the speaker's familiarity with the topic will influence preparation time. The steps in planning an oral presentation are described in the following sections.

DETERMINE YOUR PURPOSE

NOTE 15.35
Determine your purpose and state it clearly.

The first step in preparing for an oral presentation is to determine the purpose of the message. Stating the purpose in terms of the expected result will help to narrow your focus. When the primary purpose of an oral presentation is to inform, you want the audience to learn, to understand, or to know more about the topic. That is the expected result. When the primary purpose is to persuade or motivate, you want the audience either to adopt your viewpoint or to take specific action. That is the expected result. Here are some sample purpose statements:

- To inform those attending an annual employee recognition dinner about the awardees' contributions
- To inform the audience about the soon-to-be-released version of XYZ computer software
- To persuade employees to contribute to the United Way through payroll deduction

tips and hints

Preparing Note Cards for a Presentation

1. Use note cards that are 3 by 5 inches or 5 by 7 inches. Note cards do not bring attention to shaking hands.

2. Use black ink and large print; colored print can be difficult to read. Leave two or more blank lines between items.

3. Write each point or subpoint on a separate card. Include key words, phrases, and statistics (keep to a minimum) to explain or reinforce your point. The purpose of a note card is to *guide* the presenter.

4. Use numbers, not bullets, on note cards. Numbers help you stay in order easier than bullets.

5. Use color-coding to signal the transition to a new point or to a visual aid.

6. Number the cards sequentially.

7. Punch a hole in the upper-right corner if you are left-handed or in the upper-left corner if you are right-handed, and insert a 1- or 1½-inch O-ring into the hole. Place the ring on the index finger or thumb of your nondominant hand. You should find it easy to move from one card to another without fear of dropping the set.

- To persuade management to increase the employee discount from 10 to 15 percent
- To motivate employees to be flexible with the changes that will be implemented due to a reorganization of departments

ANALYZE YOUR AUDIENCE

The second step in preparing an oral presentation is to decide exactly who will be in the audience and why. A captive audience is generally less receptive than one who attends voluntarily. Consider how the time of the presentation will affect the audience. People often get lethargic after a meal, can be tardy or slow to tune in for an early morning session, and become preoccupied near the end of the day.

Analyze each member's knowledge, interests, attitudes, and potential emotional reaction regarding your topic. For large audiences, you may need to examine these factors in categories such as receivers' age, gender, and profession. When speaking to an established small group within your organization, consider not only demographics but also politics. Learn the history of the group. Does the group interact formally or informally? Are members generally conservative, or are they open to change? Who are the key decision makers? Who are the informal leaders? What concerns or objections might participants have? Build the oral presentation on your analysis of the audience.

NOTE 15.36
Learn about your audience.

GATHER SUPPORTING INFORMATION

When you have stated your purpose and analyzed the audience, you should determine the points you want to make. A good presentation typically has three to five main points no matter the time made available for the presentation. These points represent the essential information you want to get across to the audience. You are now ready to gather ideas and materials to support the development of your oral presentation. Conduct your research for an oral presentation in the same manner that you would if preparing for a written report. When preparing your speech, use primary sources, print and electronic secondary sources, and/or personal experience for examples, illustrations, explanations, quotations, statistics, testimonials, comparisons, and analogies related to your topic. Use only credible sources and realistic examples. Be sure to record citation information for material drawn from copyrighted sources.

NOTE 15.37
Gather information from a variety of sources.

ORGANIZE YOUR PRESENTATION

As you gather information, you may find that you have far more material than can be conveyed in the time you have available. Resist the temptation to include all the material; an audience can absorb only so much information in one sitting. If an idea can be left out and the purpose of the presentation is still accomplished, that point probably is not necessary. Sort the material you have collected into three sets:

NOTE 15.38
Organize your presentation based on your main points and analysis of the audience.

- Materials you **must** include (those closely related to your main idea)
- Materials you **should** include (those that support your main idea)
- Materials you **could** include (related background materials)

The "must" items will definitely be in your presentation, as will some from the "should" set. The information that supports your main idea should emphasize or clarify the main idea. Information you do not use in your oral presentation will be helpful when responding to questions or during informal discussions that may occur as a result of the presentation.

© Getty Images/PhotoDisc

Oral presentations with visual aids to support the message are common in business.

NOTE 15.39
Choose presentation aids that strengthen your message.

NOTE 15.40
Each part of a presentation must be prepared carefully.

NOTE 15.41
Use the opening to capture interest, preview your topic, and establish rapport with the audience.

Once the material is organized, you can determine which, if any, presentation aids to use.

SELECT APPROPRIATE PRESENTATION AIDS

Unlike a written report, which draws only on the receiver's sense of sight, an oral presentation can draw on sound, sight, touch, taste, and smell. Most speakers will find sound (audio) and sight (visual) most useful. Whether used separately or in combination (multimedia), presentation aids can be an asset in conveying a message. Visuals can spark interest, add variety, increase comprehension and retention of material, and help to hold an audience's attention. They should, however, always be simple, clear, and pertinent. The content and the placement of visual aids within the presentation must be planned carefully. After determining the content to be included in the visual aids, you must determine what type of visual aid will best emphasize, enhance, and clarify the message. Selection and preparation of presentation aids are covered in detail in Chapter 12.

PREPARE YOUR PRESENTATION

You know your purpose. You have analyzed your audience. You have gathered supporting data and prepared your presentation aids. You are now ready to put all this information together in a coherent oral presentation.

Some speakers write a full-text manuscript and then discard it after making notes from it. Other speakers work exclusively from an outline recorded on note cards or sheets of paper. Outlining is discussed in Chapter 5. However you arrive at your fully developed presentation, remember that it will have three parts:

1. Opening
2. Body
3. Closing

The Opening. An effective opening is crucial. The audience evaluates your credibility and capability as a speaker in the first few minutes and, regardless of what you do later, it is almost impossible to change that evaluation. A good first impression will serve you and your audience well throughout a presentation.

Use your opening to get audience attention and interest. Effective ways to open a presentation include a surprising statement, a quotation, an anecdote, a story, a question, a problem statement, a historical reference, an impressive statistic, a visual aid, a reference to the situation, or an illustration. A personal story may help you bond with an audience. Avoid leading with a prepared joke. When a joke fails, you risk losing your audience and undermining your self-confidence. Never use off-color humor or tell a story that embarrasses an audience member. Regardless of the method you choose, be sure the opening relates closely to your topic and is brief.

View the opening as an opportunity to show your audience why the topic is important to them, to give an overview of the talk, and to lead into the body of your presentation. The introduction sets the mood for the presentation and establishes rapport between you and the audience. If the person who introduces you has not done so, tell the audience whether you will take questions during or after the presentation.

The Body. Most of the actual information, details, and evidence you present to the audience will be contained in the middle of the presentation—in the body. Because the purpose of the body of a presentation is to get your key points across, it is important that you identify clearly each main point in the body as you come to it. This "reorientation" can be done with verbal references or visual aids. If you do not clearly identify the main points, your audience will lose interest and the presentation will not be successful. So, plan this portion of your oral presentation carefully. Supplement your knowledge and experience with research and examples. Gather two or three times as much material as you think you will need, and use the best in your presentation.

Storytelling strategically placed within the body of your presentation can help lighten the mood of the audience, maintain listeners' interest, and reinforce an important point.

Decide which organizational pattern(s) work best for your topic and audience. As shown in the following Tips and Hints, you have several organizational patterns from which to choose. The Tips and Hints box on page 434 offers guidelines for developing the body of a presentation.

The Closing. The closing should summarize the main points of your presentation, specify what the audience should do, and leave the audience with a positive feeling about you and your topic or ideas.

NOTE 15.42
The body contains most of the information about your main points.

tips and hints

Selecting an Organizational Pattern

When preparing your presentation, you want to assemble your ideas into a logical sequence that will help you achieve your objective. Speakers have several patterns from which to choose when they organize their presentations. The method you choose depends on the topic and your objective.

1. **Chronological.** Arrange by time. This pattern could be used to review pertinent material from oldest to newest or from newest to oldest or to describe a procedure or process with tasks to be completed in a certain order. This pattern works well for informative and persuasive messages because it allows the speaker to integrate valuable background information.

2. **Topical.** Split the topic into subtopics. Organize the subject according to its logical parts. This pattern is especially useful for presentations designed to inform or entertain.

3. **Spatial.** Follow a direction according to physical space. Describe from top to bottom, bottom to top, left to right, right to left, inside to outside, outside to inside, room to room, or desk to desk, or follow some other spatial flow pattern. Consider this pattern when making informative or entertaining speeches involving space.

4. **Causal.** Show cause/effect relationships between events. Use this technique when attempting to persuade. Sometimes this pattern has a third element—solution.

5. **Comparative.** Show the similarities and differences of the subject matter on a category-by-category basis; this pattern may also be referred to as compare/contrast. It can be used with informative, entertaining, or persuasive presentations.

6. **Problem and solution.** Describe the problem(s), and then present the solution(s). This pattern is appropriate for persuasive messages.

7. **Direct or indirect.** Start or end with the main point, depending on whether your receiver will perceive the message as good or bad news.

tips and hints

Developing the Body of an Oral Presentation

As you develop the body of an oral presentation, consider these guidelines:

1. *Hold the listeners' attention.* Use short sentences (no longer than 25 words) built around the active voice. Vary sentence length and use concrete language. A conversational speaking style using the you–viewpoint is usually very effective. Use examples, illustrations, or stories to create images for your listeners.

2. *Emphasize your main points.* Use repetition, specificity, and mechanical means. Tell your listeners what is important and reinforce it by referring to it again as you transition to the next main point. You can use audiovisual aids to give

emphasis and use statistics and examples to support main points.

3. *Keep your presentation simple.* Audiences cannot comprehend complex, detailed information presented only orally. If you have complex material, put it in a handout. Avoid jargon and acronyms unless your audience will be familiar with them. Provide a smooth transition from one point to the next within the body. Limit uninterrupted talking (talking without any audience activity) to no more than 20 minutes.

4. *Involve your listeners in the presentation.* Have the audience participate in small-group discussions, exercises, demonstrations, and a question-and-answer session.

A conclusion should not catch the audience by surprise. The words and nonverbal signals should point to the end of the message. Say, "In summary," "In closing," "To review," or "In conclusion." A more subtle way to signal closure is to pause and lower the pitch of your voice. Making a significant change in your stance relative to the lectern is another way.

NOTE 15.43
End with a summary and call to action.

The summary should be a simple statement designed to recap the main points of your presentation. It may be followed by advice on how to use the information or by a clear statement of action the audience should take based on your presentation. Use the you–viewpoint so the audience has a connection to you and your topic.

The techniques suggested for opening a presentation also work well for closing it, but choose a different technique than that used in the opening. The closing is an important point of emphasis for your presentation.

As part of the conclusion, the speaker may choose to take questions from the audience. This phase of the conclusion allows the audience to interact with you, to clarify ideas, or to get more information. Responding to questions and answers will be covered in more detail later in the chapter.

How you design the conclusion will depend on your initial purpose for the presentation. Regardless of the design of your conclusion, the presentation should end on a positive, professional note. And, remember that a strong conclusion is nearly as important as a strong introduction because the beginning and the end are the parts most often remembered.

REHEARSE YOUR PRESENTATION

NOTE 15.44
Rehearse your presentation aloud using your notes and audiovisual aids.

Using the notes and presentation aids you have developed, rehearse your oral presentation. Plan your hand gestures and walking patterns. Practice how, when, and where you will move. Rehearsals will help you identify and correct distracting mannerisms such as those listed in the Tips and Hints box on the next page. Anticipate questions that might be asked. Identify three to five questions you hope will be asked and three to five that you hope won't be asked. Prepare to answer both sets.

tips *and hints*

Mannerisms That Distract

Use rehearsals to identify and eliminate these and other mannerisms from your delivery:

- Using fillers (for example, uhm, OK, like, ya know)
- Grasping the podium tightly
- Tugging at or playing with clothing or jewelry
- Having your back facing the audience when presenting visual aids
- Overusing gestures so they no longer seem natural
- Touching your hair, face, or ears
- Clicking a pen
- Clearing your throat

- Looking at your watch
- Adjusting or removing/replacing your glasses
- Tapping the lectern or projector with a pen, pencil, or pointer
- Shaking your finger at the audience
- Picking at your fingernails
- Rocking back and forth on your feet
- Pacing back and forth nervously
- Jingling the change in your pocket
- Looking far above the audience members' heads

If you will be speaking into a microphone, be sure you know how to use it effectively. Follow the suggestions in the Tips and Hints box at the bottom of this page. Microphones come in four styles: platform, handheld, lavaliere (clip and hanging), and remote. Platform microphones are the most restrictive; remote units are the least restrictive.

To get feedback on your presentation, rehearse in front of a mirror or before friends, relatives, or colleagues. You can use an audio or a video recorder for this

NOTE 15.45
Get feedback on your content and delivery.

tips *and hints*

Working with a Microphone

Follow these suggestions when using a microphone during a presentation:

1. If you are using a microphone attached to the podium, adjust it to give 6 to 12 inches of space between it and your mouth. Stay within this range or sounds will be lost or distorted. Speak over rather than into the microphone. Remember that each time you turn your head to the right or left, sounds will be lost. Make sure that the microphone does not block your face or interfere with gestures and movement.

2. Lavaliere microphones should be placed 8 to 10 inches below the chin, ideally in the center. Make sure pins, tie tacks, necklaces, and hair are out of the way of the microphone. If you're using slides in your presentation, fasten the microphone slightly more toward the side where the slides are since you'll be looking at the slides from time to time as you speak. A lavaliere microphone can be wired or wireless. If it is wireless, the transmitter pack will need to be attached

to clothing in the back of your body near your waist, so wear something with a belt or pocket to keep the transmitter in place and out of the way.

3. Sound levels should be checked in advance and set to compensate for sounds absorbed by a room full of people. If you must check the microphone at the start of a presentation, do so by asking audience members to raise their hands if they cannot hear you well. Blowing into the microphone, tapping on it, or asking, "Can you hear me?" are signs of amateurism.

4. Obvious as it may seem, know when a microphone is on or off. You don't want to get your presentation off to a great start only to find the microphone was off. And, remember to step away from, turn off, or remove the microphone after you have finished. You don't want audience members to hear comments that were not intended for them.

purpose. This practice will help you decide which parts of your content and delivery need to be modified or fine-tuned. It also gives you experience in handling your audiovisual aids efficiently. It is the only way you can be sure of the length of your presentation. When a speaker goes beyond the expected time, audience members will leave—physically or mentally.

Rehearsing your oral presentation is essential to its success. Practice will increase your familiarity with the material and your confidence in delivering it. If you go into a presentation underprepared or unprepared, you will be preoccupied with yourself and your message and lose the opportunity to establish rapport with your audience.

Keys for Successfully Delivering an Effective Oral Presentation

LO 6

Demonstrate the techniques to be used when delivering an effective presentation.

All the material you studied earlier in this chapter applies to the delivery of an oral presentation. You will want to use your voice effectively and project a strong presence. You will want to vary your pitch, volume, and speed for emphasis while speaking. Enunciate sounds clearly and pronounce words correctly. Your poise and bearing should convey confidence, enthusiasm, sincerity, and friendliness. Establish appropriate eye contact with your audience, and use natural gestures. Dress appropriately for the audience and the situation.

You have prepared your oral presentation, and now you are ready to deliver it. Here are keys to guide you in successfully delivering your oral presentation.

START POSITIVELY

NOTE 15.46
Become familiar with the site.

When you are scheduled to speak in an unfamiliar facility, visit it at least an hour in advance of your presentation. Acquaint yourself with the room arrangement, and determine whether everything you need is or will be in place before your presentation. Check the lectern and make sure it is the right height for you. Learn how to operate the equipment controls and locate the power supply and room thermostat. Identify who can help if things go wrong.

Arrive five to ten minutes prior to your scheduled speaking time whether speaking in a new setting or in a familiar one. Make a final check to ensure that the lighting, temperature, sound system, audiovisual equipment, lectern, and seating arrangement support and strengthen your presentation. Be sure your notes and visual aids are with you and in correct order. If possible, greet members of the audience as they arrive. Introduce yourself and get the names of as many attendees as you can. Smile, it will give the impression that you are enjoying yourself. This brief activity helps establish your credibility and should increase your comfort and confidence level.

When the program starts and you are awaiting your turn to speak, look pleasantly and confidently at the audience. At the appropriate time, move to the position designated for the speaker. If speaking in an auditorium or classroom-style setting, walk to the lectern with authority. If making a presentation in a conference room, follow the protocol of the group (for example, move to the head of the table; stay seated). Whatever the setting, use your body language to tell the audience there is no place you would rather be than there with them. Take a moment to collect yourself. Arrange your notes and presentation aids before beginning your message if you have not had an opportunity to do it prior to your introduction.

NOTE 15.47
Establish rapport with the audience, and then begin.

Once you have begun building a rapport with your audience by establishing eye contact, begin your presentation. Go right to your opening; omit casual, unplanned remarks and platitudes such as, "It's my distinct pleasure to be here with such a distinguished group of professionals." It is good to memorize the first part, if not all, of the opening. In this way you can concentrate on the audience and your delivery and not have to worry about checking your notes.

Remember that your delivery is part performance and part content. Both must be well prepared for a successful delivery.

REMAIN CALM

Some speakers suffer from a phenomenon known as speaker anxiety or stage fright. Ironically, it's not the speaking that causes nerves, it is the fear of self-embarrassment. One way to handle nerves is to realize that even the most practiced and professional speakers have some apprehension about speaking to an audience. Accept nervousness for what it is—part of the preparation for speaking. Speaker anxiety can be a good thing because it heightens your senses and gets your heart pumping. You will be able to think clearly and speak confidently. Learn to relax. Until you are called to begin your presentation, sit comfortably, but keep your back straight. Remember that you will be more aware of your nervousness than your audience will be.

A second way of dealing with the stage fright that threatens to detract from a successful delivery is to use imagery. Picture yourself rising and moving to the speaking area. Hear yourself speak in a loud, clear, confident voice. See yourself using natural gestures. Picture the audience responding positively to your message. Remind yourself that you have prepared thoroughly.

Calm can be achieved once you have risen and moved to the area from which you will speak. Just before you begin, inconspicuously take a few deep breaths. Inhale slowly, hold your breath for four or five seconds, then exhale. Finally, concentrate on the you–viewpoint. Focus on the audience's needs, interests, and concerns. Remember that you are there to benefit your listeners and that they want you to succeed.

NOTE 15.48
Handle speaker anxiety by thinking positively and concentrating on the you–viewpoint.

USE PRESENTATION AIDS EFFECTIVELY

You have chosen aids that complement your presentation and have designed them so that the audience can read or hear everything in them. You have practiced handling them efficiently. To use them effectively during your delivery, simply take advantage of your careful preparation. The Tips and Hints box on page 438 contains advice for using visual/multimedia aids developed with presentation software.

If you have developed a packet of materials to share with your audience, tell them so they can listen to what you have to say. Distribute handouts at the appropriate time. If all the information you want the audience to have is on the handout, distribute the materials after you finish speaking. If the handout is more of an outline with only key ideas and no details, you may wish to distribute it before you start talking so audience members may take whatever notes they feel are necessary.

NOTE 15.49
Use presentation aids with poise and confidence.

EVALUATE AUDIENCE FEEDBACK

Maintain good eye contact with the members of the audience so that you can receive feedback on how the presentation is progressing. Assess your listeners' changing reactions and make necessary adjustments to keep their attention and interest. Are you sure they can all hear you? If not, speak louder. Can they all see the visual aids? If not, make adjustments. Is their interest waning? If so, change your pace, pick up your enthusiasm, and start involving them in some way. Do they seem not to understand a point? If so, ask them questions, paraphrase, or ask a volunteer to explain his or her

NOTE 15.50
Adjust your presentation based on audience feedback.

tips and hints

Using Presentation Graphics Software

Following these guidelines will help you effectively use presentation software:

1. *Know your equipment and software.* Be sure cords do not present a hazard to you or your audience. Try to rehearse with the equipment you will use when giving your presentation. Audiences get impatient with delays and feel their time is being wasted. Always have a backup plan in case equipment fails; it is all right to have "low-tech" transparencies to back up your high-tech presentation (provided you have arranged to have an overhead projector as a backup).

2. *Position equipment so that you can see the monitor and use the computer while facing the audience.* Better yet, use a remote mouse. Doing so will free you to interact with your audience and minimize the need to move back to the computer every time you want to change a slide. Such movement interrupts the flow of your presentation and distracts your audience.

3. *Don't just read the slides.* Provide more information than what appears on the screen. The screens should contain only key points and phrases, not all the information gathered for the presentation.

4. *Move slowly from slide to slide.* Electronic presentations tend to make you speak more quickly than usual.

5. *Don't let the slide show be a distraction.* Don't feel compelled to use every transition, animation, and sound available on your software. Remember, the audience should concentrate on you and your message.

6. *Use blank (background only) screens where ideas will pause.* Begin with a title screen; end with a slide that recaps your major points, provides information on how to contact you, or shows only your slide show background pattern.

understanding of the point. Do members of the audience show signs of physical discomfort? If so, ask them about it and have the necessary adjustment made. Using the feedback you get from an audience can strengthen the effectiveness of an oral presentation.

END POSITIVELY

Endings, like beginnings, are important points of emphasis. Deliver the closing with a clear, strong voice. Your poise and bearing should be at their best even if the body of your presentation did not meet your highest expectations. At this point, eye contact with the audience should be 100 percent. You should be focusing exclusively on your audience and using the you–viewpoint.

Dilbert by Scott Adams

tips and hints

Handling the Question-and-Answer Session

During a question-and-answer session, you may encounter four types of questions: (a) information-seeking, (b) opinion-seeking, (c) hostile or negative, and (d) off-target. The following tips will help you make the experience a positive one for you and your audience:

1. If time is limited, let your audience know in an inviting manner, such as "We have about 25 minutes before this session ends; this would be a good time to ask questions."

2. If no one asks a question, start the process yourself. You might say, "A question I am often asked is . . . ." Ask the question and then answer it with a brief (less than 30-second) direct response.

3. When a question is asked, listen carefully. Repeat the question so that all may hear it and you have a moment to organize your thoughts before responding.

4. When answering, use a conversational style and look primarily at the person who asked the question.

5. Deflect hostile or negative questions by rephrasing them before answering. If the person is not satisfied with the changing of the question's wording, tell him or her that you will be glad to talk about it following the Q & A session. Never argue with a questioner; it not only tarnishes your image but also causes the audience to sympathize with the questioner. If someone asks a question unrelated to the topic, offer to meet with him or her after the presentation to discuss it.

6. When answering a question, try to refer to topics covered during your presentation, but keep the response concise and to the point.

7. Be conscious of the nonverbal messages your gestures and body language convey as you respond to a question.

8. If an audience member makes a comment instead of asking a question, when he or she takes a breath, interrupt and thank him or her for the comment and ask for the next question.

9. Don't evaluate questions. If you praise one questioner and not another, the person not receiving praise might think his or her question was not worthy. Such value judging might discourage others from asking questions.

10. Be prepared to end the session with a few brief remarks related to your presentation.

RESPOND TO QUESTIONS

Question-and-answer sessions are common in business presentation settings. In a large-group setting, questions are generally posed after the presentation has ended. In a small-group setting, questions may arise during or after the presentation depending on the audience or on the speaker's preference. When speaking to an audience of clients or to people holding positions higher than yours within your organization, it is best to answer questions as they are asked. In other settings, specify as part of your introduction or opening whether you will take questions during the presentation, after the presentation, or both.

Answering questions gives speakers an excellent opportunity to relate positively to the audience, to clarify and reemphasize points, and to alleviate any concerns the audience may have. Some questions may relate to the specifics of your content; others may be about a related topic or condition. Be prepared to answer both types. If possible, prepare answers to anticipated questions before the presentation and practice them. Particularly, be prepared to defend any assumptions you may have made; for example, if you are assuming a certain number of items will be sold, be sure you can justify this assumption with evidence. Following the guidelines in the Tips and Hints box above will help your session go smoothly.

When you have finished, smile and graciously accept the applause or thanks the audience offers you. Later, reflect on the experience. Note what worked well and what you would like to improve.

NOTE 15.52
Use question-and-answer sessions to strengthen your relationship with the audience.

Using the guidelines that have been presented in this section will help you to prepare and deliver effective business presentations in traditional settings. Not all speaking situations you encounter, however, will be traditional. Several special situations are described in the next section.

So far, material in this chapter has focused on how to make an individual presentation. Team presentations are also common in business. The Communication Note below offers suggestions for making successful team presentations. Teamwork is discussed in detail in Chapter 13.

Communicating in Special Presentation Situations

LO 7

Identify tasks and techniques associated with special presentation situations.

Other speaking situations you may encounter in your professional career are discussed in this section—emceeing an event, introducing a speaker, and participating in a media event.

Emceeing an Event

The master of ceremonies, known informally as the **emcee,** plays a significant supporting role in the success of an event. It is his or her responsibility to ensure that the event begins, moves along, and ends in a timely fashion. He or she sets the tone for and maintains the continuity of the event.

NOTE 15.53
Emcees are responsible for setting the tone and maintaining the flow of an event.

The specific duties performed by an emcee will be determined by those who plan the program. At the very least, an emcee will be expected to welcome the audience, introduce a series of speakers in a predetermined sequence, and close the program. Additional responsibilities may include introducing those seated at a head table, acknowledging dignitaries seated in the audience, assisting program participants, and serving as moderator of a question-and-answer session. The procedure for

communication note

TEAM PRESENTATIONS

Effective team presentations can help you gain more business in today's competitive workplace. In many respects, team and individual presentations are similar. They both require preparation, structure, audience analysis, and rehearsals—all essentials of oral communication. There are, however, some differences.

Sometimes a team presentation appears to be a group of loosely connected parts instead of a unified presentation. The first step to achieving a unified message is for the team to agree on the purpose of the presentation and determine how to accomplish the team's purpose. The next step in creating an effective team presentation is to identify who will do what in the presentation. Play to each team member's strengths to determine the role he or she will assume. Typically, you want someone who is dynamic to do the opening and closing, someone who is detail-oriented to cover the technical and support section, and someone who is a quick thinker to handle the questions.

Carefully coordinate the presentation sections with transitions to avoid presenting a series of mini-presentations equal to the number of team members instead of a team presentation. You can achieve a unified presentation by referring to the next section or point or to key points made by other speakers. Use "we" statements instead of "I" to demonstrate an integrated team. Having all team members use only one presentation style (one PowerPoint show, for example) instead of several individual styles creates a unified and seamless presentation.

First impressions are lasting impressions. And, a well-executed team presentation is a reflection of the cohesiveness of the organization itself.

introducing a speaker is described in a separate section; the remaining duties are covered in the following paragraphs.

WELCOMING THE AUDIENCE

The welcome, more than any other factor, will set the tone for the event. Begin by greeting the audience and then pausing briefly to allow conversations and activity to cease. Once you have gained the attention of the audience, give your name and welcome the group to the event. You might say, for example, "Good evening, ladies and gentlemen. (pause) I'm Adam Davenport, your host for this year's Chamber of Commerce Recognition Dinner. Thank you for joining us tonight." Be sure to smile, scan the entire room, and speak in a clear, confident voice. Next, provide a brief overview of the agenda for the event. The entire welcome should take less than two minutes—no longer than five if you are also expected to prime the audience with a few humorous comments.

NOTE 15.54
Introduce yourself, greet the audience, and provide an overview of the event.

INTRODUCING THE HEAD TABLE

Although an emcee does not determine who sits where at a head table, he or she should follow a standard pattern for introducing those seated there. The pattern calls for moving from the emcee's far right to center, where the lectern is typically placed, then from the emcee's far left to center. Before beginning, the emcee should specify what each individual should do (e.g., rise, then be seated; rise, remain standing), and tell the audience to hold applause until all head table guests have been introduced. Correct pronunciation of each name is essential. The emcee should have good eye contact with the audience and occasionally look or gesture toward the people being introduced. The introductions should be simple and brief—name and title, role in the organization, or reason for being seated at the head table. If appropriate, the emcee could also make a lighthearted remark or tell an anecdote about each person. Format consistency is the key.

NOTE 15.55
Pronounce names carefully and correctly.

ACKNOWLEDGING DIGNITARIES

Those who plan the program may wish to have the emcee introduce some attendees not seated at the head table. These individuals may play a prominent role in the community or have some past, special tie to the group. Knowing in advance that each dignitary is actually at the event and where he or she is seated will make the process flow smoothly. Once again, the emcee should specify the actions to be taken by the audience and those being introduced. Names should be pronounced correctly. If several guests are to be introduced, decide how you will achieve smooth transition without being wordy. "Also with us tonight" and "Another special guest" are examples of introductory phrases that can be used as transitions.

NOTE 15.56
Recognize prominent attendees.

ASSISTING PROGRAM PARTICIPANTS

The emcee should introduce himself or herself to each program participant before the event begins. He or she should clarify seating arrangements, explain the sequence of events, verify the time the participant has been allocated, tend to special requests, and confirm the accuracy of personal information such as name pronunciation and title. In addition, the emcee should be sure that the sound system and other equipment are working properly. The emcee should arrange for a pitcher of water and several glasses at or near the lectern. He or she is responsible for assisting or knowing who has been assigned to assist the speaker with tasks such as distributing materials and operating equipment.

NOTE 15.57
Be courteous and efficient.

By keeping on schedule, the emcee assists not only those who participate in the program but also those who attend. If the participant exceeds the allotted time, the emcee must ask him or her to stop. Because the emcee is typically seated next to the lectern at a head table, passing a note saying "Your time has expired; please end now" should be sufficient. If the emcee is seated elsewhere, another method of signaling time must be devised. The emcee should select a method based on room and seating arrangements and then inform each participant of it.

After the speaker finishes his or her presentation, the emcee should rise, extend personal thanks to the speaker, and then thank the speaker for the entire group. The personal remarks are made privately, as the emcee shakes the speaker's hand; formal thanks are given so the entire audience can hear. The formal thanks should identify the speaker by name and relate in some way to the topic. "Thank you, Representative Fuller, for sharing with us how your bill for security measures against identity theft (HB 387) will affect us in our daily lives" completes the task in one sentence. Depending on the speaker and topic, a longer, perhaps humorous, statement would be appropriate.

MODERATING A QUESTION-AND-ANSWER SESSION

The primary tasks of an emcee during a question-and-answer session are to call for questions, repeat the questions after they have been asked, keep time, and thank the speaker.

After the presentation has ended and the speaker has been thanked for giving it, the emcee informs the audience of the time available and asks for questions. Often, this request will be met with silence. Audience members may need time to formulate their questions and summon the confidence to ask them. The emcee should give them this time by asking the first question. Doing so relieves the pressure that silence can place on both the audience and the speaker.

As audience members stand or raise their hands to be recognized, the emcee should acknowledge them, listen carefully to the question, and then repeat the question to ensure that all in the audience know what was asked. If the question is long, the emcee should paraphrase. If the question is complex, the emcee should divide it into logical subquestions and pose each separately.

In some settings, audience members are asked to write their questions on cards. The cards are collected and given to the emcee, who then reads them on behalf of the audience members. When this protocol is followed, the emcee should quickly scan the questions and select a fairly simple one as the first question. While the speaker is responding, the emcee can decide which of the remaining questions will be asked and in what order. Similar questions may be paraphrased. Several questions should be thought-provoking. Of course, all questions should be in good taste.

When the allotted time has expired, the emcee thanks audience members for their questions and the speaker for responding to them.

CONCLUDING THE EVENT

Once all parts of the program have been completed, the emcee issues a general thanks to the entire group and bids them farewell. The remarks may include a brief summary of the events or a reference to the featured speaker's presentation. The emcee allows program participants to leave the stage area first and remains in the room until the majority of guests have left or are clearly engaged in conversation.

The emcee at a formal event serves the same purpose the host or hostess serves at a social event. He or she is responsible for ensuring that those who attend feel welcome and have an enjoyable time. That can occur only if the emcee recognizes that his or her role is important to the success of the event but that he or she is not the focus of the event. In other words, the emcee must maintain the you–viewpoint. This same unselfish approach must be used by the emcee or whoever introduces a speaker. Specific techniques for that task are covered in the following section.

Introducing a Speaker

When you are asked to introduce a speaker, accept the invitation with enthusiasm. The experience will give you a chance to enhance your own speaking ability and to provide a valuable service to the speaker and the audience.

The process you follow in preparing for and delivering a speaker's introduction will parallel that used for a longer presentation. You must identify your purpose, gather information, develop the presentation, rehearse, and deliver the introduction with skill and confidence. Your introduction might be entertaining; however, the primary purpose of an introduction is to inform audience members of who the speaker is, what the topic will be, why the topic is important to them, and what credentials qualify the speaker to make the presentation.

In some cases, the speaker will write his or her own introduction. When this occurs, the person designated to introduce the speaker should practice the introduction and give it with style and enthusiasm. When you are responsible for preparing the introduction, remember that the best source of information about a speaker is the speaker. As soon as you learn you will be making the introduction, obtain a copy of the speaker's résumé. Review it and make a few notes to be used in your introduction. Consider consulting secondary sources for information about the topic. Ask program planners whether a formal question-and-answer session will be conducted and, if so, determine whether you or the emcee will serve as moderator. If program planners are flexible, ask the speaker to indicate whether questions should be asked as they arise or held until the presentation is completed. Include that information as part of your introduction.

Several days prior to the event, phone or meet with the speaker to gather additional information and to verify the accuracy and appropriateness of items you intend to use. Try to include more than facts and figures in your introduction. You will make the speaker seem more real if you include some personal information or an anecdote about him or her. Such information can be obtained from the speaker, from a friend or colleague of the speaker, or from your conversations with him or her.

As you prepare your introduction, remember that you have very little time— generally no more than two minutes—to make the audience eager to hear the speaker. Because your time before the audience will be brief, you could either memorize your presentation or give it extemporaneously. Whichever style you choose, be sure to practice. Do not, however, rehearse so much that you destroy the professional, self-confident, and friendly demeanor you wish to achieve.

On the day of the presentation, introduce yourself to the speaker long before you are to make the introduction. Confirm whether the speaker will remain seated or stand at your side while you make the introduction. When it is your turn to speak, rise, face the audience, smile, and begin to speak. Establish good eye contact with your audience. At some point during your introduction, look or gesture toward the speaker.

When you've finished your introduction, lead the applause (if appropriate), step to the side, greet the speaker with a handshake, and inconspicuously return to your seat. If applause is appropriate at the conclusion of the presentation, be the one to

NOTE 15.61
Draw material for an introduction from a variety of sources.

NOTE 15.62
Rehearse the introduction to be sure it is brief, informative, and inviting.

lead it. Convey your thanks to the speaker either as part of the program or in a more informal setting after the presentation ends.

Participating in Media Events

You may be asked to participate in a media event as part of your daily work activities or as a special assignment. Three media events in which you may be asked to participate are a news conference, a radio interview, or a television interview.

NEWS CONFERENCES

This type of media gathering is used to publicize an event or to make an announcement to the general public. Typically, a news conference is only 20 to 30 minutes (including questions and answers) in length. Representatives of the news outlets attend the conference, and then they communicate the pertinent information to their audience.

NOTE 15.63
Introduce yourself and keep remarks short.

If more than one person will be speaking at a news conference, the order of the speakers should be determined in advance. It is preferable to have each person who will be speaking come to the microphone and introduce himself or herself. Each speaker should keep his or her remarks short. If you have several speakers, each may be able to speak for only a few minutes; not all participants must speak. Speakers should distribute copies of their statements to the media; these can be ready in advance and included in the media kit, a packet of information given to each attendee. If a reporter directs a question to a specific individual, that individual should respond; however, if the question is not for a specific speaker, the host should answer the question.

RADIO OR TELEVISION INTERVIEWS

You may be asked to participate in a radio or television interview to publicize an event, to make an announcement to the public, or to represent your organization's position on a particular topic. When you are interviewed for print media, your words carry your message; but with radio and television interviews, your voice is the primary factor affecting the interpretation of the message. Therefore, it is critical that you speak clearly and at a pace that is easily understandable. Don't read from a text; you may sound highly rehearsed, and the emotion in your voice may be missing. Because there will be microphones used during the interview, avoid making noise when others are talking (this includes the shuffling of papers or note cards). Make a conscious effort to avoid using fillers in your message. Do not interrupt others.

NOTE 15.64
Focus on speaking clearly and with a positive tone.

During a radio interview you will have to rely entirely on your words and voice to convey your message to the audience. Try to vary your voice and maintain a positive tone to hold audience interest. It is appropriate to use notes during the radio interview. Because a microphone is very sensitive, take care to be quiet when moving papers or note cards.

NOTE 15.65
Create a focused 10- to 15-second "sound bite."

Television interviews may be scheduled for a few minutes but only 10 to 15 seconds may actually appear on air. Therefore, it is critical that you focus on what you are saying and create a succinct 10- to 15-second "sound bite" that will get the interviewer's attention and make your point. In a television interview, the audience can "hear" your message through your words, your voice, and your appearance. The television camera magnifies everything you do, including your facial features and gestures. Pay particular attention to the nonverbal cues you are projecting. When participating in a television interview, look directly at the person who is asking the question, not the camera. As with a radio interview, if you have notes on cards or paper, take care not to make noise that the microphone can pick up. Wear clothes that are appropriate and don't distract from your message; avoid spots, stripes, small patterns, and all black or white.

Good preparation and attention to the basics of oral communication will help you deliver effective oral presentations, whether they are traditional presentations or media event situations.

Summary of Learning Objectives

Enhance the basic quality of your voice.

LO 1

Speakers who want to improve the quality of their voice pay attention to the way in which they breathe. Inhaling deeply and exhaling so that air is forced from the diaphragm produces deep, rich sounds. Controlling the articulators relates to speaking clearly. The jaw should be flexible; the tongue and lips should be loose.

Use your voice effectively.

LO 2

Finding, using, and varying the natural pitch of your voice will protect your vocal cords from damage and will help to make your speech patterns interesting. Vary your volume, both to be heard and to emphasize important points. Interest and emphasis are achieved by varying the speed at which a message is delivered. Tone is used to convey meaning; a businesslike tone that conveys warmth, strength, and respect is desirable. Speaking clearly and pronouncing words correctly are also important factors.

Strengthen your personal presence.

LO 3

Speakers who have good personal presence concentrate on their receivers, not on themselves. They are genuinely enthusiastic about the message they convey. An effective speaker conveys friendliness and sincerity through words and nonverbal cues involving posture, eye contact, facial expressions, and gestures. Speakers choose clothing and accessories appropriate to the occasion and the audience.

Classify delivery styles by type.

LO 4

Presentations may be delivered in any of four styles: manuscript, memorized, impromptu, or extemporaneous. Manuscripts are written in full and read to the audience. Memorized presentations are written in full and delivered without notes. Impromptu presentations are spontaneous and arise from a particular situation with little or no time to prepare. Extemporaneous presentations are thoughtfully prepared and then delivered using notes. Extemporaneous is the style preferred for business.

LO 5   *Identify the steps to follow in preparing an oral presentation.*

Determining the purpose of a presentation and analyzing the audience are the first two steps in preparing for an oral presentation. Gathering materials, organizing the presentation, and deciding whether to use presentation aids are additional steps. The presentation consists of an opening, a body, and a closing. Once the speaker has prepared the notes or outline from which the presentation will be given, he or she rehearses to get feedback about how to refine both content and delivery.

LO 6   *Demonstrate the techniques to be used when delivering an effective presentation.*

When the actual presentation occurs, the speaker should remain calm, begin positively, use presentation aids effectively, make adjustments based on audience feedback, end positively, and respond to questions from listeners.

LO 7   *Identify tasks and techniques associated with special presentation situations.*

Emceeing an event, introducing a speaker, and participating in media events are among the special speaking situations a business professional might encounter. Emcees are often called on to welcome participants and guests, introduce those seated at a head table, acknowledge special guests, assist program participants, moderate a question-and-answer session, and close an event. Sometimes an emcee introduces the featured speaker; at other times another participant has this privilege. Introductions must be brief yet informative. When participating in a media event as a speaker, it is crucial that you present the information you have to share in a very succinct and clear manner because media outlets work with "sound bites," not full speeches.

Questions for Discussion and Review

1. What are resonators and articulators, and how do they work together to create a strong, rich voice quality? (Objective 1)
2. Identify three uses of the pause when presenting your message to an audience. (Objective 2)
3. Explain how pitch can be used to show comparisons and contrasts. (Objective 2)
4. How can a speaker determine whether he or she is speaking at an appropriate volume? (Objective 2)
5. Identify someone you think is an excellent public speaker. List at least five qualities that this person possesses that make him or her an effective speaker. (Objectives 1, 2, and 3)
6. Describe how appearance can affect the audience's perception of a speaker and his or her message. (Objective 3)
7. What are the three purposes of an oral communication message? Identify a business scenario that would be appropriate for each purpose. (Objective 4)
8. Discuss the impressions given by a speaker who does each of the following: (Objective 5)
   a. Rocks back and forth on his or her feet
   b. Scans the audience by looking above members' heads
   c. Sits on the meeting table or a desk while speaking
   d. Keeps a hand in the pocket of his or her jacket and jingles the coins or keys kept there

   e.   Ends his or her presentation by saying, "Well, I guess that's it."

   f.   Constantly runs fingers through his or her hair

9. While developing an oral report for a marketing class, Sara, one of your team members, locates an article that fits perfectly with your topic. Sara suggests that the group take several paragraphs from the article and use them in the oral report without mentioning the source. How would you handle the situation? (Objective 5)

10. What advice would you give to a coworker who declines invitations to speak to professional and community groups because he or she is too scared? (Objective 6)

11. How should a speaker handle disruptions such as people arriving late or cell phones ringing? (Objective 6)

12. Discuss the role an emcee plays in the success of an event. (Objective 7)

Application Exercises

1. Teamwork. Divide the class into teams of two. Each team member should select a children's book or an excerpt that can be read to his or her partner in about ten minutes. Each reader should use his or her voice qualities to make the book "come alive." When each person finishes reading, the listener will critique the voice quality and delivery. The comments for the reader should concentrate specifically on the volume, tone, inflection, speed, and pitch of the reading voice. Critiques should be honest and offer constructive feedback. (Objectives 1 and 2)

COLLABORATIVE

2. Practice keeping your jaw, tongue, and lips flexible by saying the following sentences aloud three or more times each: (Objective 1)

   a.   Loose lips sink ships.

   b.   Which wristwatches are Swiss wristwatches?

   c.   Peter Piper picked a peck of pickled peppers.

   d.   Hickory dickory dock, the mouse ran up the clock.

   e.   She sells seashells by the seashore. The shells she sells are surely seashells. So if she sells shells on the seashore, I'm sure she sells seashore shells.

   f.   A skunk sat on a stump and thunk the stump stunk, but the stump thunk the skunk stunk.

3. Technology. Access a videotape or webcast of a recently delivered speech on a business-related subject that is of interest to you. The library at your school is a good resource for videotaped speeches, and the following URLs have current webcasts available: http://webcast.oii.ox.ac.uk/?view=Browse and http://www.microsoft.com/events/executives/webcasts.mspx. Observe the voice qualities and speech techniques that are used as well as the presence that the speaker projects. Write your instructor an e-mail that includes the source information for the speech, the oral communication qualities and techniques you observed, and your critique of the speaker's delivery (keep in mind that some pauses in the transmission of a webcast would not have been seen in person; they are due to the transmission of the webcast). (Objectives 1, 2, and 3)

TECHNOLOGY

4. Give emphasis to the important points in the following paragraph by varying (a) your pitch; (b) your volume; (c) your speed; and (d) your pitch, volume, and speed in appropriate combinations. (Objective 2)

> *Your degree of success in providing leadership to others relates directly to your ability to speak clearly, intelligently, and confidently. Your effectiveness will depend on the quality of your voice and the strength of your presence.*

5. Read the paragraph in Exercise 4 three times. Each time, vary your posture so you are (a) standing, head low, shoulders curved forward; (b) seated, almost reclining, with legs extended and crossed at the ankles; and (c) standing, shoulders squared, back straight. Which posture felt most comfortable? Which made you feel most confident? (Objective 3)

6. Teamwork. Sit back-to-back with another student in the class so that neither of you can use nonverbal cues to complete this exercise. Take turns saying the following sentence aloud three times: "Why were you late for the meeting?" Each time you speak the sentence, change your tone to reflect one of the following sentiments: concern, irritation, detachment. See whether your partner

COLLABORATIVE

is able to determine which emotion you are conveying through your words. (Objective 3)

7. Teamwork. Form groups of four to five students. Have each person in the group speak for one minute on one of the following topics (no two persons in the group should speak on the same topic):

    a. Ways to live a healthy lifestyle

    b. PowerPoint use for classroom instruction: too much or too little

    c. Strategies to reduce stress in your life

    d. Places you would include in a tour of your school or campus for a prospective student and why

    e. The person who has influenced your life most and why

    f. An important lesson learned from previous or current work experience

The speakers should practice trying to show a strong, positive personal presence. Listeners should provide constructive feedback. (Objective 3)

8. Teamwork. Technology. Global. Each member in a group of three should locate an article related to some aspect of global business or business communication. Randomly assign the style (manuscript, memorized, or extemporaneous) by which each member will deliver a two-minute summary of the article. After all presentations have been given, discuss the strengths and weaknesses of each method from the perspective of the speaker and the audience. Summarize your conclusions in an e-mail to your instructor. (Objectives 4, 5, and 6)

9. Teamwork. Global. Technology. Work in groups of three students. Each group will identify a country about whose customs they would like to learn more. Each member of the team will be responsible for researching one of the following customs—commonly used gestures and non-verbal cues, tipping, and gift-giving. After the research is done, the team will prepare and deliver a three- to five-minute team presentation about the customs for the chosen country. Keep in mind a team presentation is not three individual presentations; it is a unified effort. During each presentation, various listeners should give nonverbal cues for the speaker to interpret and respond to. After all group members have spoken, the listeners should provide constructive feedback. (Objectives 5 and 6)

10. Prepare and deliver a five-minute presentation on a topic approved by your instructor. Include at least one quote, one visual aid, and your presentation notes. (Objectives 5 and 6)

11. Technology. Research storytelling in business on the Internet and share with the class in a two-minute presentation an interesting fact you learned about storytelling, who uses it, and how it is being used. As part of your presentation, share with the class a story you found or created. (Objectives 5 and 6)

12. In this Application Exercise, you will be doing the groundwork for an oral presentation to your classmates. First, identify which of the presentation topics listed below you will use. Second, analyze your audience and identify the purpose of your presentation. Third, prepare several attention-getting introductions for your chosen topic. Fourth, determine which organizational pattern would be most appropriate for developing the body of the presentation and why. Fifth, identify three to five main points you would cover in your presentation on the topic (you don't need to do the in-depth research for this presentation). Finally, write a conclusion for the presentation topic. (Objectives 5 and 6)

    a. The importance of time management during your first year at college

    b. The advantages of the college's requirement that all students have a laptop computer

    c. The advantages of making the campus a totally smoke-free environment

    d. The benefits of joining a student organization

    e. How to sell products on eBay

    f. How to avoid identity theft

    g. The advantages of outsourcing jobs overseas

13. Teamwork. Global. Technology. Work with six of your classmates to research the appropriate way to introduce people from a culture other than your own. Demonstrate for the class how you would introduce a head table that included political and business leaders from the United States and the country you selected. One group member should act as emcee; the others should be the head table guests. (Objective 7)

14. **Teamwork.** Divide the class into two-person teams. One person will be the interviewer at the campus radio station; the interviewee is the president of the local SIFE (Students in Free Enterprise) chapter at your school. The interviewer will construct questions to ask during the radio interview about an upcoming fund-raiser that SIFE is sponsoring, but he or she will not be sharing these questions with the interviewee before the interview. The interviewee *must be prepared* to answer any questions asked of him or her about the organization or fund-raiser. Tape the interview and critique the responses, paying particular attention to the voice qualities and delivery or responses. Also critique the quality of the questions asked to determine whether they provided substantive information for anyone listening to the radio interview. (Objectives 1, 2, 3, and 7)

COLLABORATIVE

15. You have been invited to return to your high school and speak with business students about your school and your major. Prepare the opening to your presentation; include an anecdote or a quote. As your instructor directs, deliver the opening to a small group or your entire class. (Objectives 5, 6, and 7)

16. **Technology.** You, as student body president, have been asked to emcee the Fourth Annual Senior Awards Banquet in three months. In this capacity, you will be introducing a local businessperson of your choosing to present the awards. Research background information to use in your introduction for the presenter. Once you have received the information and verified its accuracy, you will need to send an e-mail of the introduction for the presenter to your instructor. (Objective 7)

TECHNOLOGY

Web exercises to accompany this chapter are available at **www.thomsonedu.com/bcomm/krizan.**

MESSAGE ANALYSIS

Revise and edit the following memo to reflect good organization and to ensure that its format and mechanics are accurate.

DATE:	October 18, 200–
TO:	Managers
FROM:	Robert Olivio
SUBJECT:	**Presenting Via Videoconferencing**

In videoconference presentations the quality and clarity of the sound and detailed explanations directly will impact the quality of the experience for the members' of the audience in remote locations. Not hearing the message correctly may result in misunderstandings and misinterpretations. This could be costly therefore you will need to maximize your presentation skills for this technology. Please follow these guidelines and share them with those in your units who make videoconference presentations.

Speak clearly and try to maintain a constant volume

Uses pauses when talking to allow sufishunt time for the audience to digest what you are saying particularly if you are speaking to audience members for who your language is not their first language. These pauses accomodate time delays in transmission created by the remote link

Show the audience you know they are out their by recognising them at the start of the presentation.

When using PowerPoint or transparencies be clear about which slide you are talking about by number preferably, and indicate when you are moving on to the next. If possible prior to the presentation sent electronic copies of the slides the audience can refer to.

More maybe less when doing a remote presentation. (You can't see non-verbal cues the remote audience is sends while you are presenting and they are listening; this can only be observed when they are speaking and the video and microphone are on at their location.) Explain clearly each new section of the presentation and summarize. Pause to suggest questions or topics that the audience may like to pay particular attention to during the session

(continued)

Carefully consider how to present quantitative data. It can be difficult to explane and pointers to indicate specific items is not all ways easy to see in the videoconference.

Keep the sound clean; and avoid creating back ground noise that can be magnified for the remote audience such as paper shuffling and clicking your pen

Remind locations to turn off microphones so the speaker only can be heard during the presentation

We will have scheduled a training session for all managers who lead regularly videoconferences at 2:00 PM on October 29 . However, if you need to conducts a videoconference before than, please use these guidelines.

Writer's Workshop

The following items may be sentence fragments or contain errors in punctuation, subject–verb agreement, pronoun–antecedent agreement, infinitive use, abbreviations, number display, capitalization, spelling, word choice, possessives, modifier clarity and placement, or parallelism. Rewrite the sentences to make them correct.

1. Each of the resorts has an 18 whole golf coarse on sight or near by.
2. After useing Clear away for 6 weeks you will both notice that rinkles disappear and age spots fading
3. The A.M.A. has announced that they will present this years Outstanding Marketer award to Jacob Jackson principle in The Liberty Group.
4. One of the more interesting articals I will have read in the last year was Dealing with Technology and Keeping Your Sanity in the Tech Review magasine.
5. The mayer of Brookings Bend Colorado have announced that the towns' one hundred and twenty fifth anniversary celebration will be held on June 13th starting with a parade at 10AM and will finish with fireworks in the City Park at 10PM.
6. For your convienence I have inclosed a coupon good for a ten % discount which means you'll pay only 13.95 for a full-year of "the Money Manager's Guide.'
7. Sherri abundantly made it clear wha she thinks is the problem and whose fault it is.
8. 63% of Del Mar residence gave there aproval through a telephone survey that they feel the City is doing a good job of providing the necesary services they reqwire.
9. Roger Blake and his oldest daughter Cynthia have openned a public acctg firm in the Providence Bldg. On 2d street.
10. With 20 year's experience as a restaurant owner Cyril Wagner should have little difficulty establishing creditability as a caterer.

In addition to completing assignments for clients, virtual assistants—like other small business owners—look for opportunities to promote their business. Some of the tasks you'll complete in this feature will relate to business promotion.

1. You've accepted an invitation to speak to the Women's Business Network (WBN) meeting in your community. The general topic on which you've agreed to speak is *listening*. Use the material in this text, and materials you locate in print or Internet sources, to assemble five PowerPoint slides you can use during your presentation.

2. Beth Jackson, your contact at WBN, will introduce you at the meeting. She's asked you to write the text of the introduction you want her to give. Do so, and e-mail it to her (bjackso3@jetcom.net).

3. Tasha Brady, Human Resources Manager at Center City Power, has asked for your help in locating someone to conduct a full-day seminar for its employees. The focus of the seminar should be communicating to provide high-quality customer service. Do an Internet search to locate possible speakers. Based on your evaluation of the information presented at the sites generated by your search, select three individuals to recommend to Tasha. Send Tasha an e-mail (Tasha-Brady@ccpower.com) that includes your rationale for recommending each speaker, the URL for each site, and other information you believe to be relevant.

4. One of your regular clients is the Blue Ridge Condominium Association. After each monthly meeting, the president of the Association sends you an audio tape of the meeting. You listen to the tape and prepare meeting minutes based on what you hear. The following text represents your draft of the minutes for the meeting held a week ago today. Revise, edit, and format the document.

   Present (5): Dick Westman, Diane Woodward, Jennifer Brooks, Tim Black, Kym Kennedy. Absent (2) George Miner and Gregg Iverson.

Guests: Wendy Carpenter, Barnett Wagers, Ty Simpson Meeting held in the community room; convened by president (Westman) at 7 p.m. Quorum present.

Minutes of last month's meeting (held on the 10th) were approved as distributed.

Old Business Ms. Carpenter reported on behalf of the Rules and Regulations Committee. Four modifications were presented (see attachment). Kennedy moved and Brooks seconded a motion to adopt the proposed changes; approved 5-0. President Westman commended the committee for its efforts. Kym Kennedy was assigned the task of duplicating and distributing the Rules and Regulations to residents.

New Business: Legal Services: The president cited the need to hire legal counsel. Two firms experienced with residential issues were suggested (Barton and Weir; Grey, Mathers, and Beverly). Following discussion, members agreed to request fee information from Barton and Weir. Brooks was assigned the task and asked to report at the next meeting. Accounting Services—needed to set up and conduct periodic records reviews and to assist with preparing tax forms. The Association's property management firm, Denison and Associates, has recommended that a contract be negotiated with Patrick Conparta, CPA with Michaels, Probst, and Flynn. Annual fee is estimated to be $500. Motion by Black was seconded by Woodward and passed unanimously.

Member Concerns . . . Some residents are placing doormats in the hall, which poses a tripping hazard. (referred to Safety Committee) . . . Several of the shrubs need trimming (concern will be referred to Building and Grounds Committee) . . . the National Night Out gathering in August was a success; can a similar event be held each spring? (question goes to Hospitality Committee) Meeting adjourned at 8:30 p.m.

Part 6
Employment Communication

© Stockbyte

Chapter 16
The Job Search and Résumé

LET'S TALK BUSINESS

The résumé is your primary method of communicating with prospective employers. It announces your desire to fill an existing vacancy and describes the qualifications you possess that allow you to meet the requirements of the role successfully.

It's likely, though, that a busy hiring manager will have only a few moments to review your résumé. That's why it's essential that you grab his or her attention immediately. To do so, your résumé must be targeted to the company and position you seek. Rather than sending a standard, one-size-fits-all version of your résumé, adjust the content to each opening. For example, if you apply for a position with a publishing firm, highlight your experience as editor of your college newspaper.

Diane Domeyer, Executive Director, OfficeTeam

Photo courtesy of Diane Domeyer

Many companies screen candidates by using specialized software that scans résumés for keywords or terms from the job description that relate to the required qualifications and expected duties of the role. Employers often look for phrases that demonstrate knowledge of certain software programs; "Microsoft Office" is a common example. So be sure the objective, work history, and skills sections of your résumé contain plenty of keywords.

Above all, it's critical that your résumé is clean and error-free. In an OfficeTeam survey of executives, respondents cited typos and grammatical errors as the most common résumé mistakes. I've often seen simple goofs—such as the job seeker who applied for a position as an "office manger"—derail even the most talented applicants.

If your résumé effectively communicates to a prospective employer that you are an ideal fit for the open position, you have a strong chance of being called for an interview and could eventually be offered the job you seek.

Your most important business communication will be about your employment. Diane Domeyer in Let's Talk Business emphasizes the importance of a well-written résumé. During your life, you will spend most of your waking hours at work. Your work should be enjoyable, challenging, and rewarding. If you carefully analyze your qualifications and job preferences and research companies and their postings, you will be able to create an effective résumé that will help you realize your employment goal. After completing this chapter and Chapter 17, you should have a plan for successfully obtaining employment—employment that best matches your interests, values, and qualifications. Also, in these chapters you will discover how to use the Internet to assist in finding a job and launching your career.

NOTE 16.1
Employment communication is your most important communication.

You will conduct a job campaign to obtain employment. This campaign will include

- Analyzing your qualifications and job preferences
- Obtaining information about employment opportunities
- Developing résumés
- Writing application letters
- Preparing employment applications
- Interviewing for a job
- Preparing other employment communication

The first three steps in the job campaign are discussed in this chapter; the last four steps are discussed in Chapter 17.

Analyzing Your Qualifications and Job Preferences

Because *you* are the product you are selling in your job campaign, you need to know yourself well. You want to sell yourself honestly and fairly; therefore, you should concentrate on your most positive attributes—your accomplishments, education, experience, and personal traits. All communication with prospective employers should focus on how your skills and abilities can contribute in the position for which you are applying.

LO 1
Identify and evaluate your qualifications and job preferences for employment.

Your first step when you begin a job search is to inventory your qualifications, strengths, and interests. Then, you are ready to identify the types of positions in the job market that are a good match for you. Your campus career center is a good place to start. Ask to take an interest inventory or career decision-making test to assist you in focusing your job campaign. These career decision-making tests or other assessment tools can help identify your strengths and weaknesses; pinpoint your interests and match them with your strengths; clarify your values and what matters to you, such as making money or feeling you make a difference in the world; reveal the overlap among your strengths, interests, and values; and identify appropriate careers.

Analyzing your qualifications is an important part of your job campaign and includes an inventory of the skills, personal attributes, experiences, and accomplishments that you bring with you to the job marketplace. The results will be valuable as you construct your résumé. Your résumé is your calling card; it will be your primary tool in securing interviews. The second part of your analysis examines job

NOTE 16.2
Analyzing your qualifications means inventorying skills, attributes, experiences, and accomplishments.

characteristics that are important to you. Researching the job market informs you of the kinds of jobs available in your field, as well as their requirements, and helps you decide the type of job you want. Your job campaign may be aimed at one particular solicited job—accountant for Kaiser Permanente, for example—or it may involve sending unsolicited applications to a large number of potential employers. In either case, you will need to analyze your qualifications in relation to each job and its requirements.

In most cases, you should begin your personal inventory several months before you begin your employment search. In fact, inventorying your qualifications and career choices should begin well in advance of seeking employment. As a student, you would be wise to begin a prospective job file in your sophomore or junior year. Use it to store information that will be useful in your personal inventory, career choice, and job search. For example, keep documents such as diplomas and awards; recognition letters, memoranda, or certificates of special accomplishments; part-time or full-time employment dates and records of earnings; and military experience records. In addition, note special training or assignments that demonstrate job skills.

NOTE 16.3
Emphasize facts about you and your accomplishments.

In analyzing your qualifications, start by brainstorming (alone or possibly with friends and relatives) a list of facts about yourself and your accomplishments. The most important facts are evidence of your accomplishments—your achievements, honors, and knowledge. In addition, list your special qualities that could benefit a company. To create your inventory, label five pages at the top as follows: "Individual Profile" on the first page, "Education" on the next, "Experience" on the third, "References" on the fourth, and "Job Preferences" on the fifth page. These pages are worksheets to help you analyze your qualifications and strengths for the job market. At a good time of the day for you, find a quiet place and start thinking of facts about yourself. Suggestions for the kinds of facts to list are in the following sections. You will add information to these pages over a period of weeks or months, and they will provide a readily accessible source of information for you throughout your job search, application, and interview process. Figure 16.1 shows the five worksheet headings to use for these pages of your self-analysis.

Individual Profile

NOTE 16.4
Develop your individual profile.

Start with the Individual Profile page because it will be the easiest category. Do not try to organize or evaluate the information at this point. The information on the Individual Profile sheet should include your name, temporary and/or permanent address, telephone number(s), and e-mail address. If you have a temporary address, give the expected end date for this address. You may want to include your fax number; if you have an online résumé, include its Uniform Resource Locator (URL).

FIGURE 16.1
Job Search Worksheets for
Self-Analysis Inventory

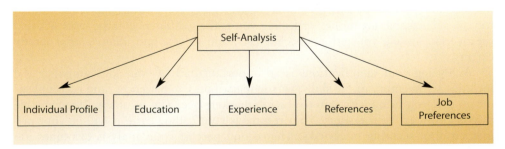

Your Individual Profile should include a list of your interests and hobbies, community service activities, public-speaking experience, work-related church activities, volunteer work, and organization memberships. As appropriate, include your accomplishments, offices held, experience gained, and honors or awards received.

List your special talents or skills, such as an ability to use specific software programs, write computer programs, or speak or write foreign languages. Next, list transferable competencies that can be applied in more than one work environment, such as writing effectively, solving problems, and making decisions. Last, list personal attributes that you would bring to a job, such as enthusiasm, initiative, motivation, sincerity, dependability, a sense of humor, integrity, or adaptability. Include on your Individual Profile any personal information that might be of interest to an employer. For example, list your salary expectations, career objectives, and willingness to travel or relocate.

On this Individual Profile page do not list your height, weight, birthdate, marital status, number of children, or religious affiliation. It is illegal for recruiters to use such information to select employees unless it is a requirement of the job; for example, age is relevant to job requirements if your position is to market or sell liquor because state law prohibits minors from holding such positions. An application for a modeling position may require a photograph. Some of the information from your Individual Profile will be used in preparing your résumé. Other parts of it will assist you in choosing specific jobs, writing application letters, answering questions during interviews, and completing employment forms. Categories of information to include on your Individual Profile inventory page are summarized in the following Communication Note.

Education

On the page labeled Education, list the schools you have attended. For each school, list its name; its location; the dates you attended; your major; your minor; your grade point average (GPA) in your major and overall; and the certificates, diplomas, or degrees you received. Indicate any special groupings of courses such as a series of office technology or accounting courses that qualify you for the position or positions in your job campaign. Enumerate computer software and hardware skills; specify any special projects you completed, such as a web page or a database.

NOTE 16.5
List all your schools, key facts, and achievements.

communication note

TYPES OF INFORMATION ON AN INDIVIDUAL PROFILE INVENTORY

Name	Willingness to travel	Honors and awards
Address	Public speaking activities	Salary expectations
Phone number	Work-related church activities	Interests and hobbies
E-mail address	Special computer skills	Career objectives
Fax number	Volunteer work	Foreign language skills
Website (if online résumé)	Organization memberships	
Community service	Strong personal attributes	

Describe teamwork experiences and group projects. List any education-related honors or awards received (such as outstanding student, membership in honorary organizations, dean's honor lists, certificates of recognition or appreciation, and scholarships). Specify any special research reports you have prepared. Indicate all extracurricular activities (such as professional or service organization memberships, fraternity or sorority activities, intramural or intercollegiate athletics participation, community or special service activities, and study/travel abroad experiences). Identify leadership roles that you held in organizations while a student. List any other information related to your education that might be of interest to an employer. Keep in mind that this is an inventory of your strengths for the job market—a laundry list of relevant items that can help you obtain a position that matches well with your career plans. The Communication Note at the bottom of this page illustrates items from the Education inventory section.

Experience

NOTE 16.6
Emphasize your responsibilities and accomplishments for each job.

On the Experience page of your inventory, list all of your work experience—part-time and full-time. Keep in mind two basic categories as you reflect on each job you have held:

1. Responsibilities
2. Accomplishments, such as achievements, knowledge or skills acquired, and contributions while performing the job

Most people make the mistake of listing only their job responsibilities on their résumé. Although employers are interested in the responsibilities you have had, they are more interested in how successfully you fulfilled those responsibilities. You should list, and quantify when possible, all factual evidence of successful job performances (such as supervised 16 employees, increased sales by 35 percent, conducted a presentation skills workshop, or earned a promotion to assistant manager). Remember to emphasize your accomplishments by using action verbs such as those in the Communication Note at the top of page 459.

communication note

TYPES OF INFORMATION ON AN EDUCATION INVENTORY

School names, locations, and dates
Diplomas, certificates, and degrees
Major(s) and minor(s)
Grade point average (GPA) or class rank
Job-related courses
Special projects and research completed
Group projects (teamwork examples)
Sports participation
Leadership roles
Computer software/hardware skills

Education honors and awards
Membership in honorary organizations
Academic achievement awards
Certificates of recognition or appreciation
Scholarships
Professional organization memberships
Fraternity or sorority activities
Community service or other activities
Leadership activities
Study/travel abroad experiences

communication note

ACTION VERB EXAMPLES

accomplished	designed	maintained	recruited
acquired	developed	managed	redesigned
adapted	directed	marketed	reduced
administered	documented	mastered	reorganized
advised	doubled	mediated	researched
analyzed	earned	modified	resolved
applied	eliminated	monitored	reviewed
approved	established	motivated	revised
arranged	expanded	negotiated	scheduled
assembled	evaluated	obtained	secured
assessed	forecasted	operated	selected
assigned	generated	ordered	set up
assisted	hired	organized	simplified
attended	identified	originated	sold
audited	implemented	participated	solved
budgeted	improved	performed	staffed
collaborated	increased	persuaded	summarized
communicated	initiated	planned	supervised
computed	inspected	prepared	supported
conducted	installed	presented	taught
contracted	instructed	presided	tested
consulted	interpreted	produced	trained
coordinated	interviewed	programmed	updated
created	investigated	promoted	upgraded
decreased	launched	published	validated
delegated	led	recommended	wrote

List each job held, including military service. For each, list your job title, name and location of employer, phone number of employer, and dates of employment. Indicate your responsibilities and give evidence of your accomplishments. Specify what you learned while performing the job, any innovations you developed to improve job performance, sales quotas or other goals met, letters or other commendations received regarding your performance, promotions, or increases in responsibilities. List what you enjoyed most about each job, reasons you left each job, and beginning and ending salaries received.

Add any other work experience information you think might be helpful in your job campaign. You may include jobs held as a volunteer worker and internships, paid or unpaid. These jobs add to your list of work experience. Including them is of special importance if you have little paid work experience. The Communication Note at the top of page 460 gives examples for an Experience inventory of items for both responsibilities and accomplishments.

NOTE 16.7
Include applicable volunteer work.

communication note

Work experience—part-time and full-time	Volunteer positions held
Salary—beginning and ending	Dates of employment
Job title, employer, and supervisor	Letters or other commendations
Internships—paid or unpaid	Responsibilities
Employers' address and phone	Skills/knowledge gained
Evidence of accomplishments	Reasons for leaving positions
What you enjoyed most	Increases in responsibilities
Promotions	Military service

References

NOTE 16.8

List references who know you or your work well and will give you favorable recommendations.

Individuals who know you or your work well and who are willing to write letters or talk to potential employers on your behalf can provide good references. You should have at least three references and may have more if you have been employed many years. Select as references people who know your character or who are former employers, current employers, professors, coworkers, or business contacts in positions similar to your career interest. Potential employers consider former or current employers the best reference types. At this point, simply list those potential references who will give you a favorable recommendation. Depending on the job you are seeking, you may use all or part of this list.

NOTE 16.9

Request permission from references to list them.

Before using anyone as a reference, ask him or her for permission; if necessary, provide a signed request. Once the person has agreed to be a reference for you, give him or her one of your current résumés so that person can be familiar with your recent activities. Although you will need to deal honestly with any unfavorable information in your background, you do not need to list references who will hurt your chances for employment.

For each potential reference, list the person's name; title; position; organization; business (or home) address; business, home, or cell telephone number; fax number; and e-mail address. When you contact potential references for permission, be sure to ask where they would like to be contacted—at their business, home, or other location. Examples of inventory items for your References are shown in the Communication Note below.

communication note

Employers—current and former	Names, titles, and contact information
People who know your character	E-mail addresses
People agreeing to give a recommendation	Business or home address
People who will give positive recommendations	Each person's preference for contact—home, work, or other
Professors	Telephone numbers
Coworkers	Fax numbers
Business contacts in similar positions	

Job Preferences

When you have completed a thorough analysis of your qualifications, you will be ready to seek information about employment opportunities. You will make good choices when setting job and career targets if you understand the personal factors that influence your performance and job satisfaction, as well as your career-related strengths and interests. One of the personal factors you should consider is your values. By working in a job that matches your values, you greatly increase the chance of enjoying and succeeding in your job. Most people spend a lot of time in their work environment, so you should identify the type of work environment that you prefer and that allows you to perform at your optimum level. Also determine characteristics that are important for your long-term career objective (five or ten years from now). Here are sample questions to get you started:

NOTE 16.10
Analyze personal factors and job characteristics that are important to you.

- Do you like working indoors, outside an office environment, or in varied work environments?
- Do you want to work in a large company with a structured work environment, or do you prefer a small or less-structured company?
- Do you like working alone, working with others, or being in charge?
- Do you prefer to work with people or things?
- Are stability and job security important to you?
- Do you enjoy influencing or persuading people?
- Are integrity and truth in the work environment priorities for you?
- Do you like detail work?
- Do you enjoy teaching others?
- Do you value independence? challenge? chance for growth? opportunity for creativity?
- What salary range is acceptable?
- Are you willing to relocate? If so, to what geographic location?
- What are your long-term career goals?
- What types of positions are consistent with your career goals?

List those job characteristics that are important to you. Then, begin to research the market to learn about requirements and benefits for different types of positions that relate to your preferences. Read newspaper job advertisements, study company websites for positions in your career field, and interview people working in positions of interest. These sources will provide you with job characteristics and responsibilities to help you match your preferences with particular types of positions that interest you. The Communication Note below gives examples of information to consider for your Job Preferences inventory.

communication note

TYPES OF INFORMATION ON A JOB PREFERENCES INVENTORY

Short- and long-term career goals	Position responsibilities
Size of company	Acceptable salary range
Types of positions	Position advancement potential
Type of company	Job location preference
Job characteristics important to you	Job structure or independence

Now that you have completed an inventory of your strengths, interests, and preferences, you are ready to begin a search for employment opportunities that match your job preferences. The next section describes sources of information for locating a position.

Obtaining Information about Employment Opportunities

LO 2

Describe seven sources of information about job opportunities and job requirements.

Finding positions for which you can apply generally requires an organized effort. After you have analyzed your personal qualifications and job preferences, you need to determine available jobs and their requirements and identify prospective employers. The amount of energy you put into organizing your job search will directly affect the speed and success of your search. You should include both *solicited* and *unsolicited* position openings in your job search.

NOTE 16.11
Positions are either solicited or unsolicited.

A **solicited position** is a specific job for which employers are seeking applicants. These jobs are often listed on the Internet, posted by campus career centers, advertised in newspapers or journals, posted internally by an organization, or announced through private or government placement agencies.

A job that is available but is unlisted or unadvertised is called an **unsolicited position.** These positions may be an important part of your job campaign. Unsolicited positions can be obtained by direct contact with a company of your choice. You will learn of the availability of many of these positions through your network of friends, relatives, instructors, and acquaintances. Joining a professional association is important for networking with other individuals in your field. Examples of such professional associations include the Society for Human Resource Management (SHRM) for the career field of human resources, Association of Information Technology Professionals (AITP) for information technology, and American Marketing Association (AMA) for marketing. Such a network can help provide you with information on available positions as well as keep you current in your career field.

NOTE 16.12
Use a variety of resources in your job search.

An effective job campaign requires careful, documented research. You will want to use a variety of appropriate sources in your job search. Your career objectives will determine what sources are the most useful to you. Don't limit the resources you use. The more types of resources you use, the greater your job choices will be and the faster you will get optimum results. The following sections discuss possible resources you can use when searching for a job.

Campus Career Centers

NOTE 16.13
Visit your campus career center for career information and services.

Your campus career center is a valuable source of information about jobs. Whether you are an undergraduate student looking for your first career position or a graduate seeking a change in employment, the campus career center can provide many services.

Among the placement services offered by most campus career centers are job-related publications; lists of local, regional, national, and global job openings; information on employers and salaries; arrangements for on-campus interviews with company representatives; maintenance of a credentials file; advice on the preparation of résumés and application letters; guidance about or training for a job interview; and sponsorship of career/job fairs. These services are free or offered at minimal cost.

Materials such as the *Occupational Outlook Handbook,* the *Dictionary of Occupational Titles,* the *Job Choices* series, job-related periodicals, trade association publications, government publications, and individual company publications may be available. The CD-ROM software program *Job Power Source* can assist with your job search. This program or similar ones will help you set career goals, determine your work style, and find jobs.

Begin your job search with a visit to your campus career center.

Two major services of campus career centers are lists of specific job openings and, in larger schools and colleges, on-campus interviews with company representatives. Generally, the lists of job openings are published in print or electronically and updated periodically. Campus career centers will post these listings on campus and may mail them to graduates. If you find an available position that interests you, request that the campus career center assist you with contacting the employer by sending your credentials or by arranging an on-campus interview.

NOTE 16.14
Job-related publications aid the job campaign.

To take advantage of your campus career center's services, register with that office. This registration will involve the careful, accurate, thorough, and neat completion of your credentials file. The credentials file contains information about your education and experience. Your Education and Experience inventory pages will be helpful when preparing credentials for your file. In addition, career center personnel may suggest that you contact references for letters of recommendation to be placed there.

NOTE 16.15
Register with the campus career center and complete your credentials file.

Completing your credentials file will serve you well in your job search. The credentials file will be available and, with your permission or at your request, will enable the career center to provide this information to potential employers in a timely manner.

Many positions are obtained through the services of a campus career center. It should be your first source of information when you initiate a job search.

Networking Contacts

Networking is the top source of job leads today. More than 65 percent of jobs today are identified initially through networking. **Networking** is the process of developing relationships and alliances with people who can identify job leads and assist with the job search. This resource should play a major role in your job search.

NOTE 16.16
Networking is developing relationships with people who can provide valuable information about jobs and job openings.

Begin with a list of people you know. These individuals may be associates in professional associations and other organizations, friends, neighbors, relatives, former teachers and classmates, former military acquaintances, and persons with whom you have worked (in either paid or unpaid positions). Go through your list and place a check by the names of those who are most likely to know about employment opportunities or have contacts in your career field. Develop a telephone call sheet for these people. You will need to have columns for the person's name, telephone number, date called, and information gained. You have three goals to accomplish with your list of contacts: (a) gain information about specific types of positions or companies, (b) identify referrals for job contacts or introductions to people who may be helpful, and (c) create awareness that you are seeking employment opportunities.

The purpose of these contacts is to seek their guidance and advice—not to ask them for a job. Request a short meeting with the individual; this meeting is known as an informational interview. You can gain the information you need more easily person to person than by phone.

These contacts may not know of job opportunities but may know someone in the career field. Getting the name of such a person enables you to make another contact to learn more about jobs related to your career objective. When you call, explain the purpose of your call (that you are interested in employment in this career field and that his or her name was suggested as someone knowledgeable about the field), and mention by name the person who suggested this contact. Having a mutual acquaintance who considered him or her a knowledgeable contact creates a positive opening. Suggest a date and time for a short meeting to discuss careers in this field. At such a meeting, you may not only learn valuable information about this type of position but also learn of a job opening or get another contact name. The Communication Note that follows gives an outline for making calls to your contacts.

NOTE 16.17
Personal contacts take time but can give you an edge.

Networking with acquaintances to learn about careers and employment opportunities may seem time consuming; however, personal contacts and acquaintances often open the door for an interview that leads to a good position in a particular career field. A recent survey found that more than 80 percent of all job openings are never advertised. This further emphasizes why limiting your job search to solicited position openings or traditional strategies is not as productive as networking.

Talking directly with people to whom you are referred by a mutual acquaintance gives you an opportunity to gain information that will give you an edge over other applicants. It offers a higher potential for results than sending résumés as your first contact for employment. However, you should have copies of your résumé with you when you meet with your network contacts. At the appropriate time, leave a résumé with the contact. The Tips and Hints box on page 465 identifies additional strategies that can maximize your networking opportunities.

communication note

CALLS TO NETWORKING CONTACTS

Opening comments: Identify yourself and open with general, friendly comments such as "Hello, Bill. This is Ken Aldrich. I haven't talked with you since you returned from your vacation. How was houseboating on Lake Powell?"

Creating awareness of job search: "Bill, I am currently investigating employment opportunities that will get me started toward my career goals. I know that you have considerable experience as an accountant, and this is the career that I would like to pursue."

Requesting a meeting and suggesting a time: "I would like an opportunity to schedule a half-hour meeting with you to learn about the job responsibilities, benefits, and opportunities for advancement. Would next Wednesday at 8 p.m. be convenient for you?"

Confirming the meeting and closing the call: "Thanks, Bill. Wednesday at 8 p.m. will work for me. I appreciate your taking time to meet with me to share information about your work. I know it will be helpful. I will see you next Wednesday."

tips and hints

Successful Networking Strategies

1. Build your network before you need it.

2. View networking as a communication exchange and relationship builder.

3. Treat every networking contact with professional respect.

4. Develop your list of questions before you meet with your contacts.

5. Discuss your target job with your contacts.

6. Be considerate of your contacts' time.

7. Do not ask for a job! Your goal is to gather information on your target job and the requirements for that job, an industry, or a specific company; possible job leads; and names of others to include in your network.

8. Take a copy of your résumé to the informational interview and leave a copy with your contact if he or she asks for it.

9. Follow up on *all* leads.

10. Send thank you notes to contacts after a telephone conversation or an informational interview.

11. Stay in touch with your contacts throughout the search. Even if they don't know of an opening at the time of your initial contact, they may have one to share with you later.

12. Let your contacts know when you get a job.

The Internet

The Internet provides another means for seeking your career position. You can find a number of websites for accessing information on how to conduct a job search on the Web, what the trends and job market are in your field of study, how to learn about the various companies, what the job requirements are for specific positions, which companies have openings in your field, and how to develop and post an online résumé.

NOTE 16.18
Explore popular career center websites.

A good place to start your job search is on your campus career center's home page, which will have links to other job-related resources. The following Communication Note lists websites that can be helpful in a job search. Even though you may locate positions on the Internet and post your résumé online, don't rely on the Internet as your only job search method. Using a variety of sources to locate employment opportunities increases your chance for success.

communication note

WEBSITES FOR CAREER PLANNING AND JOB SEARCH

http://www.naceweb.org
http://www.careerbuilder.com
http://www.monstertrak.com
http://www.rileyguide.com
http://jobstar.org/tools/resume/index.cfm
http://www.jobfind.com
http://www.careermag.com
http://jobopenings.net
http://www.careers.org
http://www.careers-in-business.com
http://www.quintcareers.com

http://www.careerjournal.com
http://www.jobweb.com
http://usajobs.opm.gov
http://www.ajb.dni.us
http://www.collegegrad.com
http://internships.wetfeet.com
http://www.career.com
http://www.jobbankusa.com
http://www.computerjobs.com/homepage.aspx
http://www.bls.gov/oco
http://www.careeronestop.org

These are only a few of the website addresses for job searching online. You may contact your campus career center staff or browse Internet directory indexes for additional sites. When using the Internet in your job campaign, be aware of the following: (a) sites change frequently, (b) you may appear to be a passive applicant for a position if you use the Internet to post a résumé or apply for a job and do not follow up, and (c) the competition is fierce; tens of thousands of people may be applying for a particular job posting on the Internet.

NOTE 16.19
Check company websites for job openings.

Many companies have a web page and often have information on their website about job openings and their application process; a number of companies now accept online applications. If you have identified specific companies as potential employers, locate their web page. Using the company name or an abbreviated version of the name followed by *.com* may locate the home page. The **.com** ending signifies a commercial enterprise. A search by company name on an Internet directory or search engine such as Google.com is another means of locating a company's website.

Newspaper and Journal Advertisements

NOTE 16.20
Classified ads are sources of job leads.

The classified advertisement sections of newspapers and many trade or professional journals are sources of information about job openings. You can obtain trade or professional journals for your field at your school library or a public library.

NOTE 16.21
Generally, journal ads are national in scope; newspaper ads are local.

Although journal job advertisements generally are national in scope, newspaper job advertisements are a source of information about specific positions in a given geographic area. Classified advertisements of position openings often carry information about job requirements and salary. Classified ads in major newspapers can be accessed easily on the Web. Most newspapers have several editions, and the job opening advertisements may vary from edition to edition. If you wish to relocate to Miami, for example, be aware that the edition of the *Miami Tribune* distributed within Miami will likely contain a more comprehensive listing of job openings than the edition distributed elsewhere. If you plan to relocate to a specific area, you may want to subscribe to one or more of the papers published there or access the online edition of the newspaper.

Private or Government Employment Agencies

NOTE 16.22
Private agencies can be sources of job listings.

Private employment agencies bring together job seekers and employers. Some agencies focus on matching applicants with part-time jobs; others focus on matching applicants with full-time or temporary-to-permanent positions. Private employment agencies work best if you are looking for an entry-level position or a specialized skill position. Private employment agencies are in business both to provide these specialized services and to make a profit. Therefore, either the employee or the employer will have to pay the fee charged. Before using a private employment agency, be sure that you understand clearly what services are provided, how much the fee will be, and who is to pay the fee.

NOTE 16.23
Professional organizations may maintain job listings.

Another category of private employment agency is the nonprofit service of professional organizations. Some professional organizations publish job opening announcements, provide a hotline with recorded job listings, assist in linking job seekers and employers at professional conferences, and maintain a credentials file service. These services are usually offered at low or no cost to members. To determine services available to you from professional organizations, ask a professional in your field.

Public employment agencies can be found at all levels of government: federal, state, regional, and local. There is usually no charge for their services.

At the federal government level, the U.S. Office of Personnel Management administers an extensive employment service. There are hundreds of area federal employment offices throughout the United States that are sources of job opportunities within the U.S. government. You can locate your nearest federal employment office by contacting any federal government agency in your area. The U.S. government's official website for jobs and employment information can be found at http://www.usajobs.opm.gov/. America's Job Bank also lists jobs that can be found in the 50 states and can be viewed at http://www.ajb.dni.us.

State governments provide employment services. These services are more extensive than the employment services provided by the federal government. They maintain data for employment opportunities both in the private sector and in the state government; however, recent studies have shown that state employment agencies are usually aware of only about 10 percent of the job openings in their area. State employment offices provide career counseling, job search techniques, training, and referrals to upgrade education or training. There is no charge for these services. Most states have regional employment offices throughout the state to serve local geographic areas. You can locate these services by looking under the name of your state in the telephone book, by contacting any state government office, or by searching the Web.

NOTE 16.24
All levels of government provide job listings and employment information.

Local and regional government agencies provide employment services to link potential employees with positions within their agencies. Cities, counties, and regional service units are all sources of jobs. Usually, you can locate their employment or personnel offices by looking in the telephone book under the name of the government unit, city, county, or region.

Many cities and chambers of commerce publish directories listing the names, addresses, and phone numbers of businesses in their localities. These directories often contain the names of top executives and department managers and are a good source for contacting individual businesses for possible unpublished job openings. Also, a search engine on the Web can help locate this information.

Web Page Profile

You can learn about prospective employers through company web pages, and you can develop and post your own web page profile for employers to access. Some employers will actively search the Internet for new employees through a university or a professional organization website. What makes a web page profile unique is that employers will come to you with information about a job instead of you seeking them.

NOTE 16.25
A web page profile may attract the attention of employers who actively search the Internet for new employees.

A **web page profile** is usually your résumé posted electronically; however, it typically includes additional details that are not on your résumé as well as links to work that is included in your business portfolio. Some people even make their web profile page interactive so they can showcase their creativity for prospective employers. web page profiles can be linked to web pages for your major department or to a student organization to which you belong. If you create a web page profile, be sure to include the URL for it on your print résumé.

Job/Career Fairs

NOTE 16.26
Job fairs are an opportunity to interview and collect employer information in a short period of time.

Job/career fairs are a good source of job leads and employer information. At these events, you will have the opportunity to contact many prospective employers in one day. Take copies of your résumé or portfolio with you to the job/career fair.

It is critical that you project a professional image, be well prepared, and convey self-confidence. Because you will be meeting prospective employers face-to-face, the first impression employers have of you may determine whether you are invited for an interview during the job/career fair. You should have a "sales pitch" prepared that highlights your qualifications and the benefits you can bring to an employer.

Job/career fairs can be an excellent source for job leads and employer information.

Other Sources

In an aggressive, vigorous job campaign, you will want to seek assistance from all sources. Initially, throw your net wide and then narrow your search. You may even want to advertise your job interests and qualifications in a newspaper or journal to obtain job leads. You should also explore "hidden positions." To uncover a hidden position, research a target employer, identify a useful service or money-saving idea that you can provide, and present your qualifications convincingly. This may motivate an employer to create a job for you as a result of your creativity and ingenuity.

If you are just finishing school, you will be competing with other new graduates for positions. The sooner you start your job search, the greater your advantage will be. Employers may view a significant gap between school or your last job and the application for employment as a lack of initiative or a lack of employability.

NOTE 16.27
A job search takes several weeks or months; stay positive.

Expect to spend several weeks or months in the job search process. Finding the right position is one of the most important activities that you will pursue. Keep a positive attitude and maintain confidence in yourself and the strengths that you can bring to an employer. Throughout the employment process, keep the focus on how your strengths and skills can make a contribution to the prospective employer.

LO 3
Prepare targeted and general résumés in chronological, functional, or combination format.

Preparing a Résumé

NOTE 16.28
A résumé is a self-marketing tool that summarizes your qualifications.

A **résumé** is a self-marketing tool that summarizes your qualifications. Your résumé should clearly and convincingly translate what you have done in the past into what you intend to do in the future. Everything in it should answer the question "Why should the prospective employer hire me?" Résumés should be written concisely and clearly because estimates show that in their first screening employers spend only about 20 to 30 seconds per résumé.

Although most job applicants use a standard written résumé, some use a videotape, a CD, a portfolio, or an electronic résumé. Practically all applicants, however, must use standard written résumés if they are to be successful in securing job interviews. The rest of this chapter describes how to develop an effective written résumé.

NOTE 16.29
Résumés can take many different forms.

The primary purpose of a résumé, along with an application letter, is to obtain a job interview. Fewer than one in ten employment applications result in an interview. Knowing that this statistic applies to all applicants can help you avoid feeling rejected as an individual. If your résumé is better than your competitors' résumés in both appearance and content, you improve your chances of being that one person in ten who gets an interview. If you do not get an interview, you will not be hired.

NOTE 16.30
The primary purpose of your résumé is to obtain a job interview.

Styles of Résumés

There are two basic types of traditional résumés: targeted and general. Either type can have a chronological, functional, or combination arrangement.

TARGETED RÉSUMÉ

A **targeted résumé** is prepared for a specific job application. It is individually keyed and printed, and it contains information to show specifically how you qualify for that one job. Accomplishments and skills on the résumé are written to highlight the skills, qualifications, and experience requirements described for the position. In addition, for college courses completed within the last five years, list those that apply to responsibilities of the specific job.

NOTE 16.31
Use targeted résumés for specific jobs.

A targeted résumé is powerful and should be used for solicited job applications. A word processing program makes it easy to prepare, personalize, and update your résumé.

GENERAL RÉSUMÉ

A **general résumé** is a description of your qualifications that can be used for any job related to your career objective and sent to more than one potential employer. It is appropriate for use when applying for unsolicited jobs that have similar characteristics. For example, if you apply for management trainee positions or a management internship position in several different companies with similar needs, you can send a general résumé to prospective employers.

NOTE 16.32
Use general résumés for unsolicited jobs.

Formats for Résumés

The three basic résumé formats are chronological, functional, and combination. The *chronological résumé* is referred to also as a *traditional* or *traditional reverse chronological* résumé. The *functional résumé* may be called a *skills-oriented, skills-based,* or *nontraditional* résumé. The third format, the *combination résumé*, uses features of both the chronological and the functional résumé.

CHRONOLOGICAL FORMAT

A **chronological résumé** has information in each section organized by date, with the most recent information listed first within each section. For example, in the section containing your experience, your current or most recent position is described first.

NOTE 16.33
Chronological résumés are organized by date, with the most recent listed first.

The résumé then describes each previous position, with the first position you held listed last. The same chronological approach is used in the sections for education, activities, or community service, or in any other section containing information accumulated over time.

Most employers prefer the chronological format because it gives the information they need in a familiar sequence and helps them compare résumés. If employers have to search too hard to find a vital bit of information about you, your application may go into the reject pile. This format enables employers to identify gaps in your work experience, as it emphasizes dates of employment, names and addresses of employers, job titles, and responsibilities. Both Figures 16.2 and 16.3 show a traditional chronological format for a résumé. Figure 16.2 is a targeted résumé sent in response to a position posting for a property manager for multifamily rental units. The job ad says that the preferred applicant should have excellent people skills, pay attention to detail, and have experience with sales and customer service. Figure 16.3 is a general résumé. Both of the résumés represent a recent college graduate with part-time experience gained while attending school. In the first résumé, Experience comes before Education because of work experience skills relevant to requirements of the targeted job. The Education section of the second student is stronger than Experience and, therefore, comes first on the résumé.

FUNCTIONAL FORMAT

NOTE 16.34
The functional format emphasizes qualifications—skills, knowledge, and accomplishments.

A **functional résumé** provides information in a format that emphasizes qualifications categorized by skills and knowledge and related accomplishments—in other words, by functions. Experiences and accomplishments are grouped under function or skill headings pertinent to your career objective. For example, headings used for functions may include *Management, Marketing* (or *Sales*), *Advertising, Communication,* or *Leadership*. This format is creative and is particularly appropriate for positions such as advertising, designing, or copy writing. Also, the functional format is useful to emphasize your strengths when you have already provided all the standard information to the employer in an application form.

The functional format for a résumé works well for an individual who has been out of the job market for a number of years, has little employment experience, or has held several jobs and needs to combine them to make the presentation more concise or more favorable than separate listings. An example of a résumé in functional format is shown in Figure 16.4. This graduate has a strong experience record related to his career goal.

COMBINATION FORMAT

NOTE 16.35
Combination résumés blend chronological and functional formats.

Some applicants use a **combination résumé,** which blends the strengths of the chronological format with the strengths of the functional format. Combination résumés work well for individuals with little work experience who are just entering the job market. Figure 16.5 displays a one-page combination résumé for a recent college graduate with limited experience other than an internship and part-time work while attending college.

Format for a Résumé

NOTE 16.36
Choose your résumé format for the situation.

The format you choose depends on the job you are seeking. Managers who review résumés and make decisions on who will be invited for an interview generally prefer chronological résumés; therefore, they are more appropriate for most job

FIGURE 16.2
Chronological Format of a
One-Page Targeted Résumé

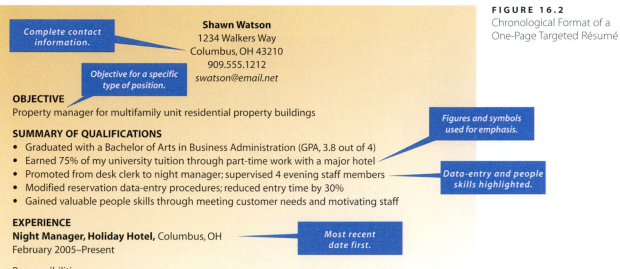

Complete contact information.

Shawn Watson
1234 Walkers Way
Columbus, OH 43210
909.555.1212
swatson@email.net

Objective for a specific type of position.

OBJECTIVE
Property manager for multifamily unit residential property buildings

Figures and symbols used for emphasis.

SUMMARY OF QUALIFICATIONS
- Graduated with a Bachelor of Arts in Business Administration (GPA, 3.8 out of 4)
- Earned 75% of my university tuition through part-time work with a major hotel
- Promoted from desk clerk to night manager; supervised 4 evening staff members
- Modified reservation data-entry procedures; reduced entry time by 30%
- Gained valuable people skills through meeting customer needs and motivating staff

Data-entry and people skills highlighted.

EXPERIENCE
Night Manager, Holiday Hotel, Columbus, OH
February 2005–Present

Most recent date first.

Responsibilities:
- Supervise 4 employees
- Maintain computerized accounting and reservation system
- Greet and register guests
- Balance cash register receipts each night and make bank deposits

Major Accomplishments:
- Developed a batch data-entry system for computerized reservations
- Had no evening staff turnover during 2 years as night manager

Major accomplishments.

Desk Clerk, Holiday Hotel, Columbus, OH
April 2004–January 2005

Responsibilities:
- Greeted and registered guests; assigned rooms
- Entered and verified data in guest registration database
- Completed guest checkouts and recorded cash receipts
- Handled multiple requests to ensure high-quality guest service

Major Accomplishments:
- Promoted to night manager
- Improved registration procedures that reduced guest check-in time by 5 minutes
- Gained communication and problem-solving skills

Appliance Sales Associate and **Building Custodian,** XYZ Appliances, Columbus, OH
June 2003–March 2004

Responsibilities:
- Sold kitchen appliances
- Cleaned and straightened store for the next day

Major Accomplishments:
- Recognized as top salesperson (sales force of 4) for 3 of 10 months of employment
- Promoted from building custodian to salesperson

EDUCATION
BA in Business Administration, The Ohio State University, Columbus (May 2006)
Dean's Honor Roll 5 of 8 semesters
Major courses in business communication, financial management, and organizational planning

SPECIAL SKILLS
Experienced with computer software, including PowerPoint, Word, Excel, Access, and customized computer accounting systems

FIGURE 16.3
Chronological Format of a
One-Page General Résumé
Showing Limited
Experience

GRACIELA M. GUITTEREZ

739 Mountain View Drive
Santa Fe, NM

E-mail: *gmguitterrez@sandia.com*
Phone: (505) 555-1972

General position objective.

OBJECTIVE　　A desktop publishing position

EDUCATION　　Santa Fe Community College, Santa Fe, NM 87508
　　　　　　　　Associate of Arts Degree, June 2006
　　　　　　　　Administrative Assistant Major
　　　　　　　　Certificate of Achievement, June 2004
　　　　　　　　Desktop Publishing Major

Emphasizes education.

Pertinent Classes:
- Administrative Management
- Business Communication
- Records Management
- Accounting for Small Businesses
- Graphic Design
- Microcomputer Applications

Achievements:
- Dean's List every semester; cumulative GPA of 3.93
- Awarded Business Professionals of Today scholarship
- President, Business Professionals of Today, 2005

EXPERIENCE　　Administrative Assistant, Athletics Department, Santa Fe Community College,
　　　　　　　　January 2005–June 2006
- Answered incoming phone calls
- Filed and maintained department and student records
- Assisted with student questions
- Created programs for sports events

Limited experience.

Volunteer, United Way of Central New Mexico, Summers 2003–2005
- Assisted director with presentations to community organizations and fund-raising activities
- Maintained the list of corporate partners
- Created a form letter to send to donors for tax purposes

COMPUTER SKILLS

Word	Dreamweaver	InDesign CS2
PowerPoint	QuickBooks	Outlook
Excel	Access	Publisher
Photoshop	Illustrator	Dragon NaturallySpeaking

Multicultural strengths.

SPECIAL SKILLS AND ACTIVITIES　　Speak and write Spanish fluently
Experience as a high school exchange student in Spain, September 2002–May 2003

campaigns. Chronological résumés make it easy to recognize a continuous job history. Gaps in the job history should be explained on the résumé: 2003–2004, "Completed a mission tour in China," "Studied for the CPA examination," or "Served as a full-time parent after the birth of a child."

If you are applying for a position in a conservative organization or conservative industry, such as banking, public accounting, or manufacturing, you should use the traditional chronological résumé. If you are applying for a position in advertising, sales promotion, or entertainment, your best choice may be the nontraditional functional format. If you are a recent college graduate with little work experience, you may want to use the combination format.

FIGURE 16.4
Functional Format of a One-Page Résumé for a College Graduate with Extensive Work Experience

ANDREW S. CRAWFORD
drew.crawford@bulldog.rr.com

Present Address
9735 Masters Way #36
Athens, GA 30602
Phone: 706.555.1143

Permanent Address (after 5/15/08)
6782 Ocean Breeze Way
Pensacola, FL 32559-7078
Phone: 850.555.6324

Complete addresses given.

CAREER OBJECTIVE—Sales director for a Fortune 500 pharmaceutical company

Specific job objective.

SKILLS DEVELOPED THROUGH EXPERIENCE

Management: Led a team of 114 account executives to sales averaging 12 percent over goal each year; devised strategies for new client prospecting; developed new prospecting forms and reporting procedures that saved account executives an average of 6 hours of paperwork each week; recruited, hired, and evaluated account executives; established and maintained 7 national accounts; and tripled the number of customer accounts in a 2-year period.

Skills by topics instead of job.

Interpersonal: Coordinated and facilitated training sessions for account executives; built rapport with internal and external clients that led to sales increases each year; organized and launched a successful newsletter for clients to keep them informed of changes in the industry and new trends in the field; designed a program to honor the "Top Ten" account executives for their achievements; and provided excellent customer service and follow-up to both internal and external clients.

Skills as past tense verbs.

Training and Development: Conducted sales and leadership training sessions; studied competitors' products to determine selling points for account executives to emphasize about our product in presentations; developed multimedia presentations to be used on tablet PCs when working with a client; and developed workshops that account executives could use for training new customers on the use of our products.

EMPLOYMENT

2005 to present. **National Account Executive**, Merriweather Computer Services, Chicago, IL
2003 to 2005. **Regional Account Executive**, Merriweather Computer Services, Ann Arbor, MI
2001 to 2003. **Account Executive**, Merriweather Computer Services, Cedar Rapids, IA

EDUCATION

University of Georgia, Athens, GA
BA Degree in Business Administration, May 2001
Emphasis in Marketing and Management
Minor in Biology

Job skills, not education, emphasized.

Regardless of the type or format of résumé you use, it should be a carefully prepared, accurate, attractive, high-quality representation of you. It is the primary sales tool you will use to obtain an interview. Through the wording of the content of your résumé, you are conveying to employers information about yourself that will help them determine how you fit their requirements for the position.

Preparing Your Résumé

You are now ready to prepare your résumé with the information you developed when you analyzed your qualifications and the job market. Follow the principles of

NOTE 16.37
There are several sections that are common to all résumés.

FIGURE 16.5

Combination Format of a One-Page General Résumé for a College Graduate with Limited Full-Time Experience

Objective for a job title.

MARY CAROL CHEN
PO Box 515
Coulterville, TN 37373
Home: 510.555.1751
E-mail: *mcchen@net.com*

OBJECTIVE
To obtain a position as a senior accountant

Summary of Qualifications
MBA degree in financial management. One-year accounting internship. Skilled with computerized journal entry and financial reporting. Developed proficiency with commercial and customized accounting software. Set up and implemented an accounting system for a $500,000 net income real estate business.

Accounting and finance highlighted.

Education
Owen School of Business, Vanderbilt University, Nashville, TN
MBA in Financial Management, May 2006
4.0 GPA (4 = A)
Murray State University, Murray, KY
BS in Accounting, May 2005
3.98 GPA (4 = A)
Paducah Community College, Murray, KY
AA in Office Administration, May 2002
3.87 GPA (4 = A)
Student Member of American Accounting Association (2002–2006)

Reverse chronological dates.

Experience
2006–Present, Accountant, Finance Division, MYX Real Estate Properties, Nashville, TN
2005, Accounting Intern (part-time), Promble and Lane Pharmaceuticals, Nashville, TN
2004, Bookkeeper (part-time), Polaris Realties, Inc., Paducah, KY

Skills grouped by categories.

ACCOUNTING
Experienced with maintaining computerized journals and ledgers, making correcting and closing entries, and preparing financial statements. Established and maintained an accounting system for a real estate company with approximately $500,000 net income.

COMPUTING
Gained proficiency with a customized accounting computer system for a pharmaceutical company. Skilled in Peachtree; QuickBooks; Microsoft Excel, Access, and Word; and SQL programming.

COMMUNICATION
Worked with a team of four accountants during accounting internship. Attended weekly Total Quality Management (TQM) team meetings and collaborated to improve accounting practices.

FINANCE
Conducted internal audits of cash receipts and disbursements.

Leadership activities listed last.

Activities
Habitat for Humanity volunteer
Intramural soccer team (Captain, 2005)

business communication, but be creative in presenting the best possible picture of yourself. The following are the major sections commonly used in a résumé:

1. Opening
2. Education
3. Experience
4. Activities, honors, or special skills
5. References

You may not need or want all these sections in your résumé. Also, you may want to arrange them in some other order, or you may choose different or additional section headings such as work history or achievements. For example, if your experience is your strong point, it should be presented immediately following the opening. If you are a recent college graduate and have limited experience, the education section should follow the opening.

More and more companies are scanning paper résumés into an electronic database. **Scanning a résumé** means that the paper document is changed to an electronic format for computer storage and processing. Placing only your name on the first line and using a simple format that begins all or most items at the left margin improves the likelihood your résumé will be database compatible. Scannable résumés are discussed in greater detail later in this chapter. Before formatting a targeted paper résumé, you can contact the human resource department of the prospective company to ask if they scan all résumés and, if so, whether any special formatting is required.

NOTE 16.38
Scanning a résumé transfers it to an electronic format for processing and storage.

Opening

The opening of your résumé should include a heading, your job and/or career objective, and, if appropriate, a summary of your qualifications. The purposes of the opening are to get potential employers to read the remainder of the résumé, to inform them briefly of your interests and qualifications, and to make it easy for them to contact you.

NOTE 16.39
The opening includes a heading and an objective.

HEADING

A résumé heading includes information for contacting you. Your name, address, telephone number, and e-mail address are essential. Be sure that your name is on a line by itself and is in the largest or darkest type. If you include a temporary school address and telephone number, give an ending date for that address and give a permanent address. If you do not currently have a permanent address, you may use your parents' or a friend's address where your mail may be sent; another option is to rent a post office box. If your e-mail address does not project a professional image, get a new one for your job search. Employers may find it difficult to believe that someone at latenightchick@yahoo.com is someone who is dependable and will represent them in a professional manner. In addition, you may want to include your fax number and a web address to showcase a web page profile.

NOTE 16.40
The heading must include your name, address, telephone number, and e-mail address.

Create a voice mail greeting on your telephone that is professional because potential employers will be telephoning your home or cell phone. If you have a web page profile, it should be professional and businesslike. A prospective employer will receive an impression of you not only from the design of your web page profile but also by the content and any links it includes. Features or links that detract from a professional image will hurt rather than help. Remember that the majority of potential employers prefer a conservative, traditional résumé. Here are three examples of résumé headings:

1.

DARCY AMADOR
damador3@cox.net
2791 Jamacha Court
LaSalle, IL 61301
Telephone (815) 555-8114
Fax (815) 555-8327

2.   **DANIEL G. EASTMAN**
                                 dgeastman@mountain.net

Current Address (until 5/30/08):   **Permanent Address:**
P.O. Box 1816   374 Forest Drive
Raleigh, NC 27602-1816   Charlotte, NC 28209
(919) 555-7326   (704) 555-2531

3.   **Lynette MacMillan**
                                 1114 Princeton Street
                                 Claremont, CA 91711
                                    909.555.4339
                                 lmacmillan@gmail.net

CAREER OBJECTIVE

NOTE 16.41
Make sure the career objective matches the position opening.

Prospective employers like to see a Career Objective, sometimes called Objective, in the opening of a résumé so they can tell whether their interests match yours. Your objective can be either specific or general. Use a specific objective for a targeted position and a general objective for a wider variety of positions that match your qualifications and work experience. For solicited positions, read the ad carefully to make sure that the career objective you write fits the position!

Keep the objective brief, clear, and direct. It tells the employer the type of position that you seek. Remember to use words carefully when preparing the objective. Here are examples:

Specific Career Objectives

1. *Objective:* To obtain a summer internship in international marketing with a Fortune 500 company.
2. *Career Objective:* To obtain a position as a webmaster in the health care industry.
3. *Objective:* An administrative assistant position with Third Street Bank.

General Career Objectives

1. *Career Objective:* A position allowing me to utilize my knowledge and skills in the information systems area.
2. *Career Objective:* A career-entry position leading to retail sales management. Long-term goal to become the manager of a major department store.
3. *Objective:* Payroll specialist position with an opportunity for career advancement in an accounting department.

SUMMARY OF QUALIFICATIONS

NOTE 16.42
A qualifications summary gives important achievements related to the objective.

This section provides a brief abstract of your qualifications. Other titles for this section are Qualifications Summary, Key Accomplishments, Major Achievements, Selected Achievements, and Summary of Accomplishments. In this section include *statements* or *phrases* that describe you and your accomplishments. Prepare your Summary of Qualifications section after you have completed the remainder of the résumé so that you can select the most important facts to highlight. Although including this section is optional, some employers like to see a summary statement in the opening of a résumé so they can tell whether your qualifications fit the position requirements.

Items should be specific to your career objective. Use parallel construction. Strong action verbs make a good beginning for each statement (refer to the action verb list in the first part of this chapter). Quantify achievements whenever possible. You may follow the general rules for displaying numbers (see Seminar D) or add emphasis by using figures for all numbers. You may also use % rather than writing *percent*. Select one style and use it consistently throughout the résumé. Here are examples:

1. **Summary of Qualifications**
   Graduated with a Bachelor of Science in Business Administration with emphasis on computer information systems. Worked part-time for four years in a variety of jobs from building custodian to hotel night manager/bookkeeper. Gained experience in working effectively with people and using a computerized reservation system.

2. **General Qualifications**
   - Successful experience in processing insurance claims
   - Youngest adjuster in company history
   - Associate of Arts degree in business: insurance and real estate concentration
   - GPA of 3.5 while working full time

3. **KEY ACCOMPLISHMENTS**
   Supervised 5 employees
   Set up an accounting system for a $500,000 real estate business
   Negotiated a maintenance contract that saved the company $10,000 a year
   Frequently presented at board of directors' meetings

Education

Following your résumé opening, present your strongest qualifications. If you are, or soon will be, a college graduate and have limited experience, your education and related activities will be your strongest qualifications. If you have been employed and your work experiences match well with the job you are seeking, your Experience section should follow the opening.

If you have or soon will be graduated from a postsecondary institution, it is unnecessary to review your high school record in the Education section. However, if while in high school you developed a job-related skill, you may want to include this skill. For example, if you are applying for a position in international business, you may want to state that while in high school you participated in a foreign exchange program and lived abroad for a year. Listing a high school is acceptable also if you wish to return to an area but no longer have a permanent residence address there.

Titles that you might use for this section are Education, Educational Qualifications, Educational Background, Specialized Education, Education and Credentials, Academic Preparation, Professional Education, Educational Data, and Educational Preparation. Remember that all headings at the same level should have parallel construction. If you attended several schools before earning a degree, consider using a statement such as "Degree included courses transferred from . . ." rather than listing each school as a separate entry.

For the chronological résumé, remember that the most recent information is listed first. In the Education section, list the name and location of each school attended and the dates of attendance. Also, for each school show your degrees, major, and other selected information to reflect your achievements and extent of learning. Here are examples:

NOTE 16.43
Education may be the strongest section for a recent graduate.

NOTE 16.44
Place the most recent information first on a chronological résumé.

1. *Education*
   University of South Carolina, Columbia, South Carolina
   Bachelor of Arts Degree, June 2007
   Business Administration Major
   Dean's List last six semesters
   GPA: 3.68 (4.0 = A)

2. *Educational Qualifications*
   Northern Virginia Community College, Annandale, Virginia
   Associate of Applied Science degree in Banking and Finance (2006)
   Courses specific to a position in banking or finance: financial statement analysis, consumer lending, law and banking applications, personal finance, customer service, real estate finance, and international finance
   Linn-Mar High School, Marion, Iowa
   Diploma (2004)
   Ranked 23rd in class of 262
   Leadership Activities: Business Club (President), Student Council (Secretary), Senior Yearbook Editor, Win with Wellness, Soccer, American Field Service (AFS) Student to Italy

3. EDUCATIONAL PREPARATION
   Central Washington University, Ellensburg, Washington
   BS in Business Education, June 2007 (expected graduation)
   Business Education Major and English Minor
   GPA: 3.3 (major)

Experience

NOTE 16.45
Experience is rated highly by employers.

Employers rate work experience as the most important information in a résumé for applicants other than new graduates. More decisions to interview or not to interview an applicant are based on the quality of work experience than on any other factor.

Although all your work experience is important, the work experience that prepared you for the position you are seeking is especially important and should be highlighted. Your experience indicates your record of responsibility and accomplishments, provides the primary sources for references, and reflects your personality and personal preferences. When analyzing your qualifications and preparing an Experience inventory worksheet, you developed the information needed for the Experience section of your résumé. Now you must decide how to present it most effectively.

NOTE 16.46
Focus on your accomplishments.

Your accomplishments should be the focal point of your experience presentation, including what you learned from the experience, your achievements, and your contributions to each position. Your responsibilities for each position may also be listed briefly. Use appropriate action verbs (a partial list of action verbs can be found in the Communication Note on page 459) in your listings of accomplishments and responsibilities. Use present tense verbs for current employment. For each position you should include dates of employment, job title, employer, and employer's location. Remember that for the chronological résumé, you should list the most recent information first.

Depending on the format of your résumé, your experience may be presented using a chronological, functional, or combination format. The examples in Figures 16.6, 16.7, and 16.8 show how the same information might be presented in different formats.

EXPERIENCE

Ranch and Sea Ventures, Santa Barbara, CA
Webmaster/Graphic Designer
(May 2005–present)

Responsibilities
- Design, develop, and publish client websites
- Provide follow-up and maintain client websites
- Perform usability test on websites created
- Lead cross-functional design team
- Create proposals and presentations to secure new clients for business

Achievements
- Grew the client base 50% during a 2-year period
- Successfully completed client projects worth over $500,000 in first 6 months in position
- Provided proposal layout and design for promotional campaign for national retailer under extremely tight deadlines
- Earned Master CIW Website Manager certification

Coastal Images, Santa Barbara, CA
Graphic Designer
(June 2003–April 2005)

Responsibilities
- Designed promotional displays, packaging, and marketing brochures
- Translated subject matter into concrete design for web pages, interactive media, and print projects
- Supervised 4 staff members
- Reviewed mock-up design for printers before final publication
- Developed presentations and proposals to demonstrate fulfillment of client requests

Achievements
- Consistently recognized for innovative ideas and applications
- Received Employee of the Year award in 2004
- Revised art-proofing system so it increased overall quality of production and improved client satisfaction to 97%

FIGURE 16.6
Example of the Experience Section of a Traditional Chronological Résumé

SKILLS DEVELOPED THROUGH EXPERIENCE

MANAGERIAL SKILLS
- Supervised 4 staff members
- Led a cross-functional design team
- Managed all phases of a project (operational, financial, strategic, staffing, and administrative)
- Increased client satisfaction to 97% with a revised art-proofing system
- Grew the client base by 50% during a two-year period

COMMUNICATION AND INTERPERSONAL SKILLS
- Created and conducted persuasive sales and marketing presentations
- Facilitated meetings with team members to create client-driven product of high quality by deadlines
- Participated in team effort to produce streamlined policies and procedures to use with newly hired employees and freelance designers
- Established trusting relationship with designers, vendors, and clients
- Recognized for creative ideas and applications when named the 2004 Employee of the Year

TECHNICAL SKILLS
- Developed proficiency with and applied knowledge of Adobe Creative Suite, Macromedia Studio Suite, and Microsoft Office Suite to print, interactive multimedia, and website projects
- Became proficient at projecting costs for projects that provided value for the client and profit for the employer
- Earned Master CIW Website Manager certification

FIGURE 16.7
Example of the Experience Section of a Functional Résumé

FIGURE 16.8
Example of the Experience
Section of a Combination
Résumé

Ranch and Sea Ventures, Santa Barbara, CA

Webmaster/Graphic Designer
(May 2005 to present)
Design, develop, and publish client websites; provide follow-up and maintain client websites; and perform usability tests on websites created.
Managerial Skills
- Lead cross-functional design team
- Manage all phases of client website creation, development, and implementation
- Increased client base 50% in 2-year period
- Complete complex projects on time

Communication and Interpersonal Skills
- Create proposals for new projects
- Give presentations to prospective clients
- Establish trusting relationships with designers, vendors, and clients
- Facilitate meetings

Technical Skills
- Select most appropriate software to create print, interactive media, or website projects
- Demonstrate proficiency in creating projects with Adobe Creative Suite, Macromedia Suite, and Microsoft Office Suite
- Project cost figures for projects that are a value for client and profitable for employer
- Earned Master CIW Website Manager certification

Coastal Images, Santa Barbara, CA

Graphic Designer
(June 2003 to April 2005)
Translated subject matter into concrete design for print, interactive media, and websites; reviewed mock-up design for printers before final publication; and developed presentations and proposals to demonstrate fulfillment of client requests
Managerial Skills
- Supervised 4 staff members
- Took initiative to revise art-proofing system; client satisfaction rose to 97%

Communication and Interpersonal Skills
- Created and delivered proposals and presentations to prospective clients
- Facilitated meetings among designers, clients, and vendors

Technical Skills
- Demonstrated proficiency in creation of projects with Adobe Creative Suite, Macromedia Suite, and Microsoft Office Suite
- Received 2004 Employee of the Year award for innovative ideas and applications

Activities, Honors, Special Skills, or Other Appropriate Titles

NOTE 16.47
Include special sections
if related to your
qualifications for
the job.

Include additional sections in your résumé if your background justifies them. An example of this might be your work experience. If an internship you had a year ago is more relevant to the position for which you are applying than your current employment, you may choose to have two Experience sections—one for "Related Work Experience" and one for "Other Work Experience." Any additional section that you include should be one that employers would consider positively. For example, if you were involved extensively in extracurricular activities during college, include a separate section on these activities immediately following the education section. Your background may justify a separate section on honors, special skills, computer competence, community service, published works, public presentations, military service, organization memberships, special interests, or any number of other possible categories. If you have a variety of activities, you may combine them into one section simply labeled Activities. The heading of the section should reflect the contents accurately. The important point is that you should not omit any vital information that would enhance your résumé. For the chronological résumé, list the most recent activities first.

Special sections should be placed near related information or at an appropriate point of emphasis. For example, a special section on academic honors should follow the Education section. A special interests section, because it is likely less important, should be placed at the end of the résumé. It is best not to list References in the last section of a résumé; instead list them on a separate sheet. Briefly describe organizations that may be unfamiliar to readers (see Phi Beta Lambda in the second example of the following special sections of résumés).

NOTE 16.48
Place special sections in appropriate locations in your résumé.

1.   HONORS
   Outstanding Employee, Excel Media Solutions, 2005
   Austin Volunteer of the Year Award, 2004
   Outstanding Austin Community College Alumni Award, 2003

2.   EXTRACURRICULAR ACTIVITIES
   President, Phi Beta Lambda (business honorary society), 2007–2008
   Secretary-Treasurer, Phi Beta Lambda, 2006
   Publicity Chair, Phi Beta Lambda, 2005
   Round Rock Representative, Cultural Awareness Program, 2005
   Coach, Round Rock Cross Country Team, 2004
   Business Manager, *Longhorn Roundup*, 2004

3.   ORGANIZATION MEMBERSHIPS
   Professional Development Chair, Information Technology Association, 2007–Present
   Administrative Management Association, 2006–2007 (Chapter Secretary, 2007)
   Habitat for Humanity, 2005–2007
   AFS (American Field Service) Club, 2002–2006 (President, 2005)

4.   SPECIAL SKILLS
   Proficient in Microsoft computer software: PowerPoint, Word, Excel, Access, Publisher, Project, and FrontPage. Speak and write Spanish fluently. Speak and understand limited Japanese. Keyboard at 75 words per minute.

5.   SPECIAL INTERESTS
   Tennis, jogging, basketball, photography, and cooking

6.   INTERESTS
   Gourmet cooking; outdoor activities, including camping, softball, and nature photography

Employment laws prohibit employers from discriminating among applicants on the basis of race, color, religion, age, gender, disability, marital status, or national origin. Employers who have this information prior to selecting an applicant for a position leave themselves open to charges of discrimination. Adding such information on résumés is not recommended. Omit information unrelated to the job you are seeking if you think a given employer would prefer not to have it. For example, do not include a photograph unless it is relevant to job performance (a position as a model may require a photograph).

NOTE 16.49
Omit information not relevant to the job.

If a particular characteristic such as religious affiliation, race, national origin, sexual orientation, marital status, or disability relates to the job responsibilities and would strengthen your job application, you may include it. For example, if you were

NOTE 16.50
Present only the information that will strengthen your application.

applying for an administrative position with the Anti-Defamation League, letting the employer know that you are a member of a Jewish synagogue could be helpful. As a way to provide this type of information in your résumé, you could list the church as one of your organization memberships, citing accomplishments related to your special qualification. Or, you could include the information in a special section devoted to your status. Another way is to mention the unique qualification in your application letter. Application letters are covered in Chapter 17.

References

NOTE **16.51**

List your most important previous employers as references.

Careful development of a list of references is a vital part of your job preparation. Although you want to list only references who will give you positive recommendations, you should list your most important previous employers. In addition, you may want to list college instructors, possibly high school teachers, and—in special circumstances—coworkers or character references. You may list different references for different job applications. Let the nature of the job and its requirements determine the references you think would be the most helpful to the potential employer.

NOTE **16.52**

Provide full information, including a telephone number and an e-mail address.

Instead of taking up valuable space on your résumé, develop a separate reference list to accompany your résumé. Because it is a separate page, place contact information from your résumé at the top of the References page. In certain areas of the country, employers may want you to list the references on the résumé; however, it is better to use this extra space for information about yourself. You do not need to indicate "references available on request" because employers know that you will provide references.

Unless a reference directs you otherwise, provide full contact information—list courtesy title (Mr., Ms., Mrs., or Dr.), name, position, organization, business address, business telephone number, and e-mail address.

NOTE **16.53**

Reference information should make contacting references easy for employers.

Reference information should make it easy for a potential employer who finds your qualifications of interest to pick up the phone, call, and receive a favorable recommendation from one or more of your references. Here is an example of the way a reference list might appear:

REFERENCE LIST
Elizabeth Atwater
1008 Cottage Way
Carlsbad, CA 92009
760.555.8317
libbyatwater@coastal.rr.com

Dr. Alexander Draper, Professor	Mrs. Claudia Weisblat, Manager
Department of Marketing	Hammer and Associates
University of San Diego	3855 Bernardo Center Drive
San Diego, CA 92104	San Diego, CA 92117
619.555.1783 (Work)	858.555.9923 (Work)
adraper480@unisd.edu	claudia.hammerassociates@cox.net
Mr. Robert Owen	Mr. Ben Pyes, Manager
Communications Consultant	Marketing Plus
San Ramon Corporation	13764 Mango Drive
2387 Seboyeta Avenue	Del Mar, CA 92014
San Diego, CA 92130	858.555.7834 (Work)
858.555.1787 (Work)	858.555.7835 (Fax)
rowen1234@sanramon.com	benjamin.pyes@delmarspace.net

Submitting Electronic Résumés

Computer technology provides varied resources for searching and applying for a job. An **electronic résumé** is one that is transmitted in an electronic rather than paper format. Electronic résumés can be classified as either (a) scannable or (b) online.

Scannable Résumés

Many large organizations, such as IBM, Motorola, American Airlines, Citibank, Coca-Cola, Southern California Edison, and UCLA, have developed a streamlined, cost-effective method of dealing with the large number of résumés they receive. They have implemented electronic applicant tracking systems in their human resource departments.

A **scannable** résumé is a paper copy of a résumé that is scanned by electronic technology. The scannable résumé is transferred to a computer database by document imaging technology and then placed in an electronic employment folder. Electronic résumés posted to a job search website, résumés sent by e-mail, or even paper résumés can be scanned into a database. An applicant database tracking system scans résumés from potential employees (for either a solicited or an unsolicited position) by "reading" the résumé and creating a database of the applicant's relevant skills, degrees, and achievements by identifying keywords. After the system compares each résumé with the job openings and job requirements, it identifies the résumés with the most "hits." The scannable résumé that stands out is the one that scores the most hits. The system generates either a letter of invitation for an interview or a letter of rejection, depending on the final recommendation of the human resource personnel. Applicant tracking systems are expensive, so large companies are the primary users. An electronic system such as this virtually ensures that most résumés will never be seen by the human eye. You will need to write your résumé so it is electronically friendly and includes the elements for which the system is designed to search.

You should periodically update your scanned résumé because this database also is used to locate candidates for job advancement. Therefore, if a firm with this type of database system hires you, update your résumé every six months and date your résumé. Even if your employer does not maintain a job advancement database, you should update your résumé at least once yearly. Add your most successful accomplishments for the year to your résumé. Keeping an ongoing job file similar to the one you began with your job search can be helpful for promotion requests or a job change. Keep a record of major accomplishments, awards and recognitions, and assignment changes in this file. Don't let your résumé collect "electronic dust."

What does a scannable résumé mean for you, the prospective employee? You must resist the urge to make a "flashy" résumé that stands out; instead, you need to develop a résumé that scores the most hits.

Keywords

The scannable résumé follows the traditional style and includes *keywords* throughout the document, but particularly in the Summary of Qualifications and Experience

LO 4
Prepare an electronic résumé.

NOTE 16.54
Electronic résumés are scannable or online.

NOTE 16.55
Employees should keep their résumés updated.

NOTE 16.56
Keywords should be nouns specific to the position.

tips and hints

Where Do I Find the Most Effective Keywords for My Résumé?

Keywords play a vital role when you are creating a scannable résumé; you want to score high on the "hits" chart. What can you do to find the most effective keywords for your specific job search and maximize your chances of getting the interview?

1. Search job descriptions and ads on the Internet. Look for words that appear early in an ad or job description; those are probably the most important words.

2. Consult government publications such as the *Occupational Outlook Handbook* (in the library or online).

3. Visit the meetings and websites of professional organizations in your field and listen for current "buzzwords."

4. Scan news stories in trade magazines relevant to your chosen career.

5. Conduct informational interviews with individuals at companies in your field and listen to the terminology used by the interviewer.

6. Visit company websites.

7. Talk to human resource professionals.

8. Read annual reports of organizations for which you would like to work.

NOTE 16.57
Keywords are words commonly used in the career field.

sections. **Keywords** are generally nouns that describe you and are terms recognized and widely used in the targeted position career field. You should use around 20 to 25 keywords in a scannable résumé. The Tips and Hints feature suggests ways to identify keywords appropriate for a job search.

Because the keywords mark an electronic trail, you must learn the keywords that are used in the field for which you are applying so that you have a better chance of being selected for a job interview. Each time one of your keywords matches a keyword for the particular position, you have a hit. The more hits you receive, the better your chance for a job interview. Include only keywords that correctly and honestly describe you and your qualifications. Keywords related to job responsibilities can be included in job titles, department names, companies and organizations, degrees, special skills, and knowledge possessed by the applicant. Keywords pertaining to job requirements might be included in your experience, professional associations, licensure or certification, and interpersonal traits. An example of keywords for an individual working in the human resource area follows.

Equal Employment Opportunity (EEO)	Planning and Organization
Americans with Disabilities Act (ADA)	Job Analysis and Audit
Society for Human Resource Management (SHRM)	Coordination of Team Initiatives
	Organizational Review and Analysis
Merit Pay	Employee Retention
Compensation and Benefits Program	Job Requisition
Certified Facilitator and Instructor	"Time to Fill" Metric
Communicator	Performance Reviews or Appraisals
Master of Business Administration (MBA)	Job Classifications
	Counseling
Malcolm Baldrige Quality Criteria	Supervision
Benchmark Partners	Personnel Database
Business Process Analysis	Applicant Database Tracking System
	Data Analysis
	MS Word

(continued)

(continued)

PowerPoint	Spanish Language Skills
Team Player	Friendly
Self-Starter	Trustworthy
Willing to Train	Reliable
Enthusiastic	Human Resource Manager
People Skills	

Electronic and Scannable Résumé Formats

During your job search, you may be asked to send an electronic résumé. An **electronic résumé** is submitted to an employer by e-mail (either within the body or as an attachment) or entered into an online form or database. Both the electronic résumé and the scannable résumé are relatively plain—some would say unattractive—because they have been stripped of most word processing codes so they can be transmitted and/or processed correctly by electronic software.

The organization and appearance of these résumés are essential to the success of your job search. Your name should be on the first line by itself, followed by your address, telephone number, fax number, and e-mail address. Omit parentheses and brackets, even around telephone numbers; these can blur and leave the numbers unreadable. The type font should be sans serif (such as Arial or Helvetica) and the font size between 10 and 14 points. Use capital letters for your headings; do not use graphics or special formatting such as bold, italics, script, or underlining. Left justify all text, and keep your line length to no more than 65 characters (letters, spaces, and punctuation). Also, avoid special spacing or formatting like double columns, tabs, graphics, and shading because these features may cause the scanner to read the information incorrectly. Some companies do have sophisticated scanning equipment that can read different fonts and styles; however, you cannot be sure of the kind of scanner the company is using unless you telephone first. Your goal is a plain-vanilla résumé.

Preferably, the scannable résumé should be printed by a laser printer with black ink on smooth, white paper. If you have a two-page résumé, do not staple the pages. When sending a paper copy of your résumé, use a 9- by 12-inch mailing envelope to avoid folding the résumé; the fold may cause the scanner to skip words.

To have your résumé selected for human review in this computerized process, you must learn how the computer program works. If you know your résumé will be scanned, find out—from the company or another source—the nature of the computer program so you know what content to include. Figure 16.9 is an example of a scannable résumé with keywords used throughout. This computer-friendly résumé can be read easily and accurately by scanners as well as human eyes.

NOTE 16.58
Scannable and electronic résumés have little if any formatting so they can be transmitted electronically without distortion.

Online Résumés

The Internet provides opportunities for accessing online career centers and company websites for posting your résumé. The online résumé posted on the Web is becoming an important tool in the workplace because many human resource departments are conducting web searches for qualified applicants.

The style of the online résumé differs from the traditional or the scannable résumé in that the contents can be "linked" to more detailed information about your work. It may be referred to as a web page profile if it includes anything more than the résumé; another way to think of the web page profile is as a home page

NOTE 16.59
An online résumé can contain links to more detailed information.

FIGURE 16.9
Chronological
Format of a Targeted
Scannable Résumé

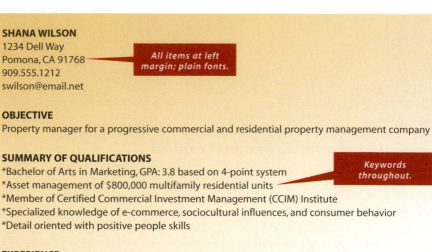

SHANA WILSON
1234 Dell Way
Pomona, CA 91768   *All items at left*
909.555.1212   *margin; plain fonts.*
swilson@email.net

OBJECTIVE
Property manager for a progressive commercial and residential property management company

SUMMARY OF QUALIFICATIONS   *Keywords*
*Bachelor of Arts in Marketing, GPA: 3.8 based on 4-point system   *throughout.*
*Asset management of $800,000 multifamily residential units
*Member of Certified Commercial Investment Management (CCIM) Institute
*Specialized knowledge of e-commerce, sociocultural influences, and consumer behavior
*Detail oriented with positive people skills

EXPERIENCE
Experience first **Executive Manager**, Home Properties, Pomona, CA, 2005 to Present
emphasizes Responsibilities:
work record. *Manage rent rolls, leasing, facility maintenance and improvement, and property promotions
*Analyze vacancy ratios and manage budget
Uses asterisks *Exercise due diligence in notification of late fees and eviction notices
to avoid special Accomplishments:
characters. *Realized a 20 percent return on equity (ROE) over a 2-year period
*Completed a feasibility analysis for 5-year expansion plan
Marketing Assistant, Milwood Industries, Porterville, CA, 2003–2005
Responsibilities:
*Assisted in identification of marketing data needs
*Collected marketing data and proposed plans for promotional actions
*Developed market-product grids and estimated market size
Accomplishments:
*Identified a new global marketing opportunity that resulted in $100,000 in new revenue
*Assisted with development and management of electronic commerce (e-commerce)

EDUCATION
MBA, Marketing, University of California at Santa Barbara, CA, May 2003
BS, Business Administration, California State University, Fresno, CA, May 2002
Outstanding Marketing Student Award, 2002
Pertinent Courses: business communications, financial management, organizational management
and planning, and marketing research

SPECIAL SKILLS
Experienced with computer software, including Microsoft PowerPoint, Word, Excel, and Access, and
customized computerized accounting systems

portfolio targeted to your career field. The web page profile can have links that move to other pages in your portfolio to show detailed examples of projects, proposals, and reports that you have developed. It is important to keep your web page profile professional, as employers will be viewing the information that you have provided. To keep your web presence professional, never link your résumé to any personal information; post your profile in a location separate from your personal website and do not link the two. Contents of a portfolio and its delivery medium are discussed in the Communication Note feature at the top of page 487.

communication note

THE PORTFOLIO—A POWERFUL ASSET IN THE JOB SEARCH

A portfolio is a collection of materials that showcases your skills, achievements, experience, academic excellence, and anything else that is relevant for the interviewer to see. While the résumé summarizes your qualifications, the portfolio proves the existence and strength of your background.

Portfolios can be either print or digital. Digital portfolios are also called online, CD-ROM, electronic, or virtual portfolios.

Be sure your portfolio is well organized, professional, and accurate.

When you post your résumé to the Internet, your résumé may be "shopped" to hundreds of employers at once. This can be both good and bad. Too much exposure could result in your being labeled a "résumé spammer." A good plan of action is to post on one or two large, popular job sites and one or two smaller sites targeted to your preferred industry. Read the privacy policies before you commit to a website; confidentiality and privacy protection vary from site to site. In addition, you will need to make decisions about what personal and contact information you want to appear on the Internet. Posting your résumé may result in several interviews and even job offers. When the job search is over, delete all of your résumés on the Internet, but be aware they may linger in cyberspace for several months or years.

With today's competitive job market, a "one size fits all" résumé no longer works in all job search situations. Job search experts recommend that you create four versions of your résumé. You should have (a) a print résumé with formatting to give to potential contacts or interviewers, (b) a scannable résumé without formatting so it can be scanned easily by the electronic technology, (c) a plain text version of your résumé that you can use to cut and paste into online forms or post in online résumé databases (this is an ASCII file), and (d) an e-mail version of your résumé, which is similar to the plain text version but is formatted for the length-of-line restrictions in e-mail. Using word processing software makes this easy to accomplish.

Refining the Résumé

You will be judged on the appearance of your résumé; it is a potential employer's first impression of you. You should never try to make your information fit another person's résumé format. Apply the following guidelines:

NOTE 16.60
Your résumé may be a potential employer's first impression of you.

Frank & Ernest by Bob Thaves

- Print your résumé—use a laser printer if possible—on white, buff, or some other light-colored paper. Remember, if your résumé is to be scanned, you should use white paper. Use high-quality, clean, 8½- by 11-inch bond paper. Be sure your résumé is neat, unwrinkled, and error free. The quality and clarity of its content will be a potential employer's impression of you.
- Arrange information simply but attractively. Use capitals or a different font size for major divisions of the résumé. As discussed earlier, your goal for résumés that are to be scanned is to prepare a plain-vanilla résumé (without unusual fonts or spacing). Because many companies now scan résumés into a database, using a simple format improves its chances of compatibility with a database file.
- Use action verbs and strong phrases rather than complete sentences. Emphasize relevant achievements, accomplishments, and special skills.
- Draft your résumé carefully to show the employer that there is a clear match between your qualifications and the job requirements. It is important that you learn the jargon of the industry and use those keywords in your résumé.
- Consider giving a draft of your résumé to a classmate whom you don't know well and asking that person to review it. After two or three minutes of this review, ask him or her questions about your résumé. If the reader cannot answer the questions or locate the answers quickly, the résumé is ineffective.
- Proofread carefully; even one error can result in the résumé being eliminated from consideration. Have two other individuals review it to be sure it is accurate.
- Use a Summary of Qualifications to highlight your accomplishments. Many businesspeople prefer a one-page résumé for new college graduates with limited experience. If your résumé is two pages or longer, a Summary of Qualifications section is essential. If you know that an employer specifies the number of pages in applicants' résumés (such as, "Applicant résumés shall not exceed one page"), limit your résumé length accordingly. In most cases, limit the résumé to one or two pages. Be sure that the information is not overcrowded or does not appear so dense as to discourage reading.
- Remember your objective for each job application is to construct the most powerful résumé that you possibly can so you can convince the employer to give you an interview.

Following guidelines given in this chapter should enable you to create your own distinctive résumé, one that will serve you well in your job search. Tailor items to the job requirements, and make your message precise and powerful. And, remember that the most qualified candidate is not always the one to get the interview—the one with the strongest résumé is.

Summary of Learning Objectives

LO 1

Identify and evaluate your qualifications and job preferences for employment.

In analyzing your qualifications, start by brainstorming facts about yourself. The most important facts are evidence of your accomplishments—achievements, honors, and knowledge. In addition, develop an individual profile about yourself, your education, your experiences, people who can serve as your references, and your job preferences.

Describe seven sources of information about job opportunities and job requirements.

LO 2

Career positions can be either solicited or unsolicited. You can find job opportunities and job requirements through (a) job listings with campus career centers, (b) job referrals through a network of personal contacts, (c) positions listed on the Internet, (d) classified ads in newspapers or journals, (e) announcements through private or government placement agencies, (f) a web page profile, and (g) job/career fairs. All of these resources except networking through personal contacts provide information on solicited positions. Unsolicited positions are ones obtained by direct contact with a company of your choice or by advertising your job interests and qualifications through networking or in professional journals and newspapers.

Prepare targeted and general résumés in chronological, functional, or combination format.

LO 3

A résumé is a self-marketing tool that should be written clearly and concisely to summarize your qualifications. The primary purpose of a résumé, along with an application letter, is to obtain a job interview. Résumés can be targeted to a specific position or prepared for a particular type of position in a career field. You may use a chronological, functional, or combination format to prepare either a targeted or a general résumé. A chronological résumé organizes information by date, with the most recent date listed first. A functional résumé categorizes information by skills, knowledge, and related accomplishments and, thus, emphasizes qualifications. A combination format organizes some items by date but incorporates information categorized by skills, knowledge, and accomplishments. The five major sections common in résumés are the opening, education, experience, special activities or skills, and a references page.

Prepare an electronic résumé.

LO 4

Electronic résumés are classified as either scannable or online. The format of a scannable résumé should be simple, with all or most lines beginning at the left margin. Scanning a résumé transfers it to a form compatible with an electronic database. A scannable résumé should include 20 to 25 keywords. Keywords are usually nouns that label your qualifications in terms used in the career field. Because the keywords mark the electronic trail, you must learn the keywords that are used in the field for which you are applying so that you have a better chance of being selected for a job interview. The online résumé can be developed on your computer and then uploaded to your own web page profile. The online computer résumé is becoming an important tool in the workplace. Many human resource departments are conducting web searches for qualified applicants. They also may have their own online application system on their website to receive applicant information keyed directly into electronic forms.

Questions for Discussion and Review

1. Explain why you should complete an inventory of your qualifications and job preferences before beginning your job search. (Objective 1)
2. Give examples of information to list on your Individual Profile inventory. (Objective 1)
3. What information should you list on your Experience inventory that will prepare you to write the Experience section of a résumé? (Objectives 1 and 3)
4. "Networking is a two-way street." Discuss this statement. (Objective 2)
5. Which sources of employment information do you think will yield the best results for your job search? Why? (Objective 2)
6. How can the Internet be helpful in a job search? (Objective 2)
7. How does a targeted résumé differ from a general résumé? Which do you believe would be more effective and why? (Objective 3)
8. Describe the chronological, functional, and combination résumé formats and when each type would be most appropriately used. (Objective 3)
9. What are the potential disadvantages of an online résumé? (Objective 4)
10. What is the difference between a scannable and an online résumé? (Objective 4)

Application Exercises

1. Visit your campus career center and gather information on interest and personality tests they offer or recommend to help individuals determine their career interests. Take one of the tests, have the test evaluated, and write a report to your instructor on the findings. (Objective 1)

TECHNOLOGY

2. **Technology.** List at least ten transferable skills and personal attributes you possess that could be emphasized in the Qualifications Summary section of your résumé. Write an e-mail to your instructor identifying why these skills and traits will make you more marketable in your chosen career. (Objective 1)
3. Analyze the professional organizations in your field of study. List those organizations in which you believe membership would strengthen your job candidacy. Find out whether they offer a student membership and if they post job listings. (Objective 2)

COLLABORATIVE

4. **Teamwork.** Form a group of three or four students and gather employment information and job listings for the following positions. Make an effort to use at least four of the sources identified in the chapter when seeking this information for each position. After the material has been collected, make a presentation to the class and indicate which sources provided the most job listings for a particular position and which sources yielded the best employer information for specific positions. (Objective 2)
    a. Customer service representative
    b. Marketing manager
    c. Payroll clerk
    d. Financial manager
    e. Administrative assistant for a medical office
    f. Web designer
    g. Database administrator
    h. Sales representative
    i. Auditor

TECHNOLOGY

5. **Technology.** Attend a career fair or visit your campus career center and gather information on jobs available in your field. Send an e-mail to your instructor listing five possible positions for which you will be qualified once you graduate. (Objective 2)

TECHNOLOGY
COLLABORATIVE

6. **Technology. Teamwork.** Form a group of two or three students and review the listings in the classified ads of a local or regional newspaper. Assess the employment opportunities in relation to your career interests. Summarize your findings in a presentation to your class and an e-mail or memo to your instructor. (Objective 2)

7. **Technology.** Access job opportunities on the Internet for positions related to your career objective. Assess the job opportunities in terms of your interest in them. Write a letter to your instructor reporting your findings. (Objective 2)

8. List the names of individuals in your personal network of friends, relatives, instructors, and acquaintances who could be valuable to you in a job search. From this list, develop a reference list. (Objectives 1 and 3)

9. **Ethics. Teamwork. Technology.** Read the scenario below; partner with a classmate to discuss the ethical questions following the scenario. Working together, write an e-mail to your instructor explaining your thoughts about the ethics of the situation described in the scenario and what, if anything, Jason should do differently. (Objective 3)

> *Jason had searched for a job as a management trainee for the last three months since his graduation from a business administration program in the local community college. He had been interviewed for three positions but had received no job offers. He was beginning to feel desperate and decided that he had to do something to improve his chances for hiring. He had worked part time as a pizza delivery person while going to school but was fired from that position when he wrecked the delivery vehicle and was charged with reckless driving. He had included this position on his résumé. When asked in the interview about his reason for leaving the position, he just said that he left because the pay was insufficient and that his supervisor was prejudiced against him because of his age—he was only 17 at the time.*

   a. Is there any part of the above scenario that raises an ethical question? If so, what is it and what is the concern?

   b. Explain whether you believe this experience item on his résumé could be a reason for Jason's lack of job offers. If so, should he remove it from his résumé or take a different action?

   c. What advice would you give Jason that might eliminate any ethical concerns and improve his chances for a job offer?

10. Comment on what is incorrect, incomplete, or inappropriate in the following résumé sections. Rewrite each section to make it stronger, adding material where appropriate. Follow the résumé guidelines that were presented in the chapter. (These sections are not parts of the same résumé.) (Objective 3)

   a. **Heading**
   Michelle Harrington
   893 47th Street
   Waukesha, WI 53189
   partygirl@wisc.net

   b. **References**
   Raymond Burns
   Restaurant Manager
   8279 Meadowlark Lane
   Los Angeles, CA 90056
   raymond@mail.net

   Jessica Lee
   1511 Ridge Cliff Lane
   Bloomington, MN 55438
   612.555.0891

   c. **Education**
   Graduated from Lincoln High School in Topeka, Kansas, in 2003
   Finished school at the University of Southern Kansas in 2008; studied multimedia production

   d. **Qualifications**
   I worked cooking on the broiler, the grill, and the fryer
   I also made salads and helped with the prep work before breakfasts
   I think it is important to fill orders quickly and get it right the first time

TECHNOLOGY

ETHICAL
COLLABORATIVE
TECHNOLOGY

My boss says I am a quick learner
I get along well with my boss and my coworkers
Quality is important to me for both the food and the service
I received an Associate of Arts degree in Culinary Arts

11. **Technology.** Assume you worked for your father at his car dealership while attending school. Because you have limited work experience, you want to include this on your résumé. You have written the following duties you performed. Rewrite the tasks you performed using action words and quantify your accomplishments when possible. You may add details as necessary. Present the rewritten Experience section to the class in a PowerPoint presentation. It should be formatted appropriately for a section on your résumé. (Objective 3)

   a. Made appointments for servicing of customers' cars
   b. Checked in customers at the service desk
   c. Wrote work orders for customers; that involved looking up the price of the part and adding 20 percent markup and then looking up in the manual how many hours were allotted to do a particular job and figuring the total cost of labor for the job
   d. Handled money when people paid their bills
   e. Sent out reminders if bills were more than 30 days overdue
   f. Answered phone calls
   g. Received Employee of the Month award in October 2006
   h. Straightened up the parts room to make it easier to find where parts were located
   i. Worked out a system so it was easy to see how many of a certain part were in stock

12. Using the information gathered in Application Exercise 7, prepare a combination general résumé that could be used with at least three of the advertised positions. Partner with a classmate to proofread each other's résumé. Submit your final copy of the résumé with a copy of the applicable ads to your instructor. (Objective 3)

13. Prepare a targeted résumé in chronological format to apply for one of the positions you found on the Internet in Application Exercise 7. Partner with a classmate to proofread each other's résumé. Submit your final copy of the résumé with a copy of the applicable ad to your instructor. (Objective 3)

14. **Technology.** Convert the résumé you developed in Application Exercise 13 to a scannable résumé using keywords throughout. E-mail a copy to your instructor. (Objective 4)

15. You are considering creating an online résumé for your job search. Research publishing to the Web and answer the following questions. (Objective 4)

   a. Where will you publish (or post) your résumé?
   b. Is there a cost attached to publishing your résumé online?
   c. What are some of the questions you will ask before making a decision to publish your résumé online?
   d. Is the security adequate for you to feel comfortable posting your résumé online?
   e. Will you have any links on your résumé? If so, to what?
   f. Are there any particular adjustments you will need to make to your résumé when converting it from a print version to an online version?
   g. Are there any enhancements you will make when converting to an online version of your print résumé?
   h. Will your online résumé incorporate multimedia features? Why or why not?
   i. Is this an appropriate avenue for you to get your résumé to employers in your chosen field?

16. Review Figure 16.9, a scannable résumé illustrated in this chapter, and make a list of words that you believe to be keywords related to property management and marketing. (Objective 4)

Web exercises to accompany this chapter are available at **www.thomsonedu.com/ bcomm/krizan.**

MESSAGE ANALYSIS

From the following Experience inventory, prepare the Experience section of a targeted résumé of an individual applying for a marketing manager position in an international company that does business in North America and Europe. After completing the Experience section, circle ten keywords that you believe to be applicable to this position.

Characteristics important in this company include a background of experience related to marketing with special responsibilities for developing market strategies for solutions, providing sales support, developing and executing a marketing plan, and negotiating deals. This company also values dependability; flexibility; a willingness to assume responsibility; attention to detail; international experience; and strong communication skills, including the ability to speak and write French.

> *MY EXPERIENCE RECORD*
>
> *The French Connection, Rochester, New York. 4/04-present. Marketing Manager. Developed marketing plan that was instrumental in boosting our market share of imported grocery items sold in major U.S. department stores from 15% to 23% in 2005. Developed promotional budgets. Worked with trade show managers to create a show strategy for our products. Created sales tools and trained 50 sales representatives on their use, including representatives in the French-speaking provinces of Canada. Strauss House Publishing Co., Inc., European Division, New York, New York. 8/00-3/04. Acquisitions Editor/Marketing Manager. Conducted market research to determine needs in product line. Acquired new product. Forecasted sales, determined pricing, and calculated profitability margins. Developed promotional budgets and coordinated promotional campaigns. Prepared sales tools for account executives. Strauss House Publishing Co., Inc., European Division, New York, New York. 6/97-8/00. Marketing Associate. Supported sales and marketing team by coordinating sales meetings, trade shows, and executive briefings. Supported Regional Sales Manager by managing sales budget and communicating with sales representatives on marketing issues. Helped sales reps with direct mail pieces, lead generation, and sales analysis.*

Writer's Workshop

The following items may be sentence fragments or contain errors in punctuation, subject–verb agreement, pronoun–antecedent agreement, infinitive use, abbreviations, number display, capitalization, spelling, word choice, possessives, modifier clarity and placement, or parallelism. Rewrite the sentences to make them correct.

1. Analyses, classifying and selection of opportunities for appropriate markets is a important part of global marketing.
2. Women account for only seventeen % of undergraduate computer science majors at universities in the US.
3. She were attending the university of london during the Fall semester.
4. The major advantage for telecommuting are as follows; savings in gasoline; reduction in pollution; and an decrease in traffic congestion.
5. Cohesive work groups has members that work togather towards a common goal.
6. Jeremy was confidently speaking untill the heckler standed up and starting threatening him.
7. Conflict becomes dysfunctional in a organization when it distracks from achieveing organization goals.
8. Reto and Monica flyed on hawaiian airlines to Honolulu wear they boarded a ship for a pieceful seven day cruise of the hawaiian islands.
9. To be a successfull Employee in the Software industry you must work eighty hours per week.
10. Digitel cameras have improved picture taking quality, and cost less than two years ago only.

Chapter 17
Employment Communication and Interviewing

Learning Objectives

1
Write effective application letters for solicited and unsolicited positions.

2
Prepare an employment application.

3
Prepare for a successful job interview.

4
Compose a variety of follow-up letters and other employment-related messages.

LET'S TALK BUSINESS

An essential aspect of securing a new position is the initial communication with the prospective employer. A well-written cover letter and résumé can generate interest; an interview; and, ultimately, a job offer.

Marketing oneself to an employer can be a frustrating and humbling experience; however, a consistent and diligent approach will be rewarded. The major focus in identifying prospective employers should be on the Internet and college placement offices. Nearly all public companies have job posting sites. The college placement office, while often overlooked and underutilized, can offer invaluable assistance to students and companies.

O. Randall Powell,
Vice President, Human
Resources, The Valvoline
Company

Photo courtesy of O. Randall Powell

The initial contact with a company should be made according to its preference. Think of this as the initial screening requirement. A cover letter should state a clear work objective, provide contact and availability information, and indicate travel and relocation preferences. The résumé should be one page and in chronological order. The cover letter and résumé are extremely critical to generating interest for an interview. Without an interview, there will never be a job offer.

494

Chapter 16 covered the first three steps in your job campaign—analyzing your qualifications, obtaining information about employment, and developing a résumé. You are now ready for the next four steps: writing application letters, preparing employment applications, interviewing for positions, and conducting follow-up communications. This chapter covers these steps. In Let's Talk Business, Randall Powell describes the importance of your résumé and cover letter generating interest that will result in your getting a job interview. He also stresses the importance of careful preparation and diligence throughout the job search process.

Writing Application Letters

Once you complete your résumé, you are ready to write a more personal sales message—an application letter. An **application letter** functions as a cover letter in the transmittal of your résumé. It is a marketing tool that highlights your most attractive qualifications as a potential employee and gives you an opportunity to make important points that you cannot cover in a one- or two-page résumé. A strong letter of application lends support to your résumé—but does not repeat the same information. The persuasive message guidelines given in Chapter 9 will help you develop your application letter.

Application letters, like résumés, can be either general or targeted. Again, the choice depends on whether you are seeking a position for which applications are solicited or whether you are submitting an unsolicited application. If you apply for a specific position that has been advertised, use the targeted application letter. If you apply for an unsolicited position or do not know if an opening is available, use a general letter. For some situations, you can combine a general résumé and a targeted application letter into an effective application package. When sending applications to similar types of businesses, for example, you may use the same résumé but personalize each letter with comments specific to the company.

Chapter 16 promotes researching the company before preparing your résumé; this advice applies to the application letter and interview also. The research you gather provides details that help you focus on the potential employer's needs. Organization and position details enable you to explain your qualifications from the you–viewpoint. Highlight specific past accomplishments to show how hiring you will benefit the company. The focal point is not what you *have done*, but what you *can do* for the organization. A targeted application letter will be much more effective if the message includes specific information that pertains to that company. In the section of this chapter titled "Preparing for a Job Interview," you will find a list of specific Internet locations and publications that can help you learn more about specific companies.

For an unsolicited general application or a targeted application for a position advertised with only a post office box for response, learn as much as you can about business operations and work responsibilities applicable to the type of position described. If the information appeals to you, the position described is probably consistent with your background and interests.

In three or four paragraphs, a well-designed application letter achieves the four purposes listed here. These are the same purposes you learned about in Chapter 9 when you read about persuasive messages.

LO 1
Write effective application letters for solicited and unsolicited positions.

NOTE 17.1
An application letter is a marketing tool that highlights your qualifications.

NOTE 17.2
Application letters may be either general or targeted.

NOTE 17.3
Learn about the company before writing a targeted application letter.

1. *Attention:* Gain favorable attention and express your interest in the position.

2. *Interest:* Market your qualifications; identify special strengths and attributes.

3. *Desire:* Describe selected accomplishments that show how you can benefit the company.

4. *Action:* Request an interview or propose a future meeting; make contact easy to schedule.

A successful application letter motivates a potential employer to read your résumé with interest and to arrange an interview. To accomplish this goal, the letter and résumé must create sufficient interest to separate you from the applicant pool and to invite you for a personal interview. It is your responsibility to communicate clearly your value to the employer.

Gaining Attention in the Opening

NOTE 17.4
The opening paragraph gains favorable attention.

In a short opening paragraph (from one to five lines), you want to gain the attention of your reader—to motivate him or her to read the remainder of the application letter. In addition, you want to alert the reader to your interest in a position. This expression of interest is essential to orient the reader to the message and to make a smooth transition to details in the rest of the letter.

The opening can mention who referred you to this position. If the person has a respected and recognized name in the organization or in the same business field, mentioning the name can gain favorable attention. Other openings could indicate your knowledge about the position or the organization, explain why you are interested, or tell how you learned of the position. For example, you could say that you are applying for a position listed with your campus career center, advertised in the newspaper, recommended by a current employee of the organization, or posted on the Internet. For an unsolicited position, you could say that you are highly interested in employment if an opening occurs.

NOTE 17.5
A direct approach works well for a targeted application letter.

The opening of the letter should attract the potential employer's attention; it can be creative or traditional. Creative openings, however, should have a professional tone and appearance and focus on gaining favorable attention. Your choice of opening will be based on applying the you–viewpoint, analyzing your reader, and considering the type of position that you seek. If the opening has been advertised, a direct approach can work well. If you are not sure if an opening is available, use the indirect approach. Here are examples of openings.

- Are you interested in a person with a solid record of accomplishment and a strong work ethic for your management trainee program? (*Gains attention by emphasizing applicant's strengths and identifying the position of interest.*)
- Please compare my qualifications with the job requirements for the staffing specialist position advertised in the job bank of the Society for Human Resource Management website. Consider me an applicant for the position. (*Emphasizes that qualifications match job requirements, identifies the position, and explains how you learned of the position.*)
- Creative! Knowledgeable! Organized! Just what you want in a new copywriter for Lo's Advertising Agency. (*Uses creative opening, emphasizes strengths, and identifies position of interest.*)

- Mr. Chris Schneider, director of information technology for your company, recommended that I apply for the position you have open for a LAN Administrator II. Please note how well my qualifications, as described in the enclosed résumé, match the job requirements listed for your opening. (*Names a company individual, specifies the position, and calls attention to the match between qualifications and job requirements.*)

Convincing an Employer That You Fit the Job

The middle portion of an application letter should convince a potential employer that you fit the job requirements and that your employment will benefit the company. This is the most important part of your letter; it is here that you create interest in your qualifications and a desire to hire you.

In this section of an application letter, you should describe your most outstanding accomplishments that relate to the job requirements. This could be from your work experience, special expertise, or educational accomplishments. Briefly discuss your strengths and how they meet job requirements. When responding to a job advertisement, read the ad carefully; use words in the letter that fit both you and the language in the ad. The order of content may vary in different application letters. The intent, however, is to compose a clear, concise, concrete, and convincing paragraph or two that will motivate the employer to look closely at your résumé. Here are poor and good examples of the second part of an application letter.

Poor:
I will be graduating with a Bachelor of Science degree in Business Administration with a major in marketing this June. This major included sales and marketing courses. I am confident that I have the expertise to be successful in sales. I will work hard to be a good employee. (Repeats information from résumé, includes vague promises rather than accomplishments, and does not link accomplishments to needs of the organization.)

Good:
Mrs. Whitehead, my solid record of experience in sales plus my marketing major match your requirements for a Classic Hardware Marketing Representative. My accomplishments in the sales positions listed on my résumé attest to my marketing skills. Each summer for the years 2004 through 2007, I received recognition as top sales representative in the Western District (a five-state area). Employed full time in hardware sales during the summer and part time during the academic school year, I became familiar with hardware inventory and earned money to pay my education expenses.

I have the personal qualities, as well as the education and experience, that can benefit your organization. I am an energetic, goal-oriented individual who works effectively in team efforts as well as through individual marketing contacts.

Promoting Action in the Close

Now you are ready to motivate the employer to take action—to read your résumé and invite you to an interview. In most application letters, your goal is to get an

NOTE 17.6
The letter creates interest by showing how you can benefit the company.

NOTE 17.7
The letter closes with a positive, pleasant interview request.

interview. The best way to get an interview is to ask directly for it. This request should be made in a positive, pleasant manner.

NOTE 17.8
Make it easy to contact you for an interview.

The closing paragraph is the wrap-up. In the close of your application letter, you should make it easy for an employer to invite you to an interview by providing your telephone number and e-mail address and by offering to be at the employer's office at his or her convenience. Be flexible. Even if you already have your schedule set, you can usually rearrange it to accommodate an interview. An alternate approach is to say that you will call to check the status of your application in one or two weeks. This statement is less passive than waiting to be called. Taking the initiative to follow up the application letter with a call, if expressed courteously, is not likely to offend the prospective employer and may be viewed as a positive factor. Other closing comments should express thanks for consideration or indicate that you look forward to a response. The following examples show appropriate closings for application letters and give their positive aspects in parentheses.

- My experience in financial management, account development, and problem solving will enable me to make significant contributions to the continuing success of Garden Fresh Restaurants. Please call me at (619) 555-1805 or e-mail me at thomas.ryba@gmail.net so that we can arrange an interview. I can meet at your convenience to discuss a future with your company. If hired for this position, I will be a knowledgeable, energetic, and productive employee. (*Includes phone number and e-mail address, maintains a positive tone, asks for an interview at the interviewer's convenience, and reinforces strengths for the job.*)

- May I have an interview to discuss this opportunity with you, Mrs. Wentzell? I believe that my education and experience match your needs and that I could become a valuable part of the team at the Kramer Agency. You can reach me at (919) 555-7812 or e-mail me at sjjohnson@moonriver.edu. At your convenience, I can arrange to meet with you at your office. (*Specifically requests an interview, uses the person's name, emphasizes teamwork, provides contact information, and suggests willingness to accommodate the employer's schedule.*)

- Enclosed is my résumé with contact information and further details about my qualifications and accomplishments. I would appreciate the opportunity to talk with you about how I would fit within your organization. I will call you early next week to arrange an appointment convenient for your schedule. (*Shows initiative and a willingness to meet at the employer's convenience, notes where contact information is found, and maintains a positive tone.*)

- I am excited about the prospect of interviewing for an accounting position with Willis and Flores, a highly respected and long-standing name in public relations. Thank you for your time and consideration in reviewing my résumé. You may reach me by telephone at 319.555.5636 or by e-mail at mhornsby@river.net. Please call me to schedule an interview at your convenience. (*Indicates enthusiasm for the company and knowledge of its history, expresses thanks for consideration, makes contact information accessible, and courteously requests an interview.*)

tips and hints

Tips for Writing an Effective Application Letter

1. Indicate in your letter that you have some knowledge of the organization to which you are applying.

2. Use simple, clear, and direct language; get to the point immediately.

3. Focus on the employer's needs.

4. Use formatting such as bullets, bold, and italics when appropriate. Do not use clipart.

5. Use action verbs and phrases.

6. Maintain a balance between professionalism and friendliness.

7. Demonstrate enthusiasm and confidence, but don't be presumptuous.

8. Check carefully the grammar, punctuation, and spelling, including names and titles. Your letter should be perfect!

Preparing an Application Letter

The application letters you use in your job campaign must meet the same neatness, accuracy, clarity, and conciseness standards as résumés. Application letters should be brief, generally no more than 1 to 1$\frac{1}{2}$ pages.

Use 8$\frac{1}{2}$- by 11-inch bond paper for application letters. The paper should be the same quality and color as was used for your résumé. Never use your current employer's stationery for an application letter. Use a 9- by 12-inch mailing envelope to avoid folding the letter and résumé. Many organizations scan letters as well as résumés, and folds in the paper may cause the scanner to skip the words caught in the fold.

An application letter should be addressed to a specific person. If you need the name, call the organization and ask for the name and address of the person to whom your letter should be addressed. The letter should be prepared individually; even a general application letter for distribution to prospective employers should not be photocopied. If responding to a blind ad, use the simplified letter format with a subject line (see Chapter 6) rather than using "To Whom It May Concern" as the salutation.

A word processing program on your computer helps you prepare several letters and insert variable information in each one. Proofread an application letter carefully for the correct receiver's name, organization, and address. Remember to mention your enclosed résumé within the letter and to include an enclosure notation. Keep copies of the letters and résumés sent to each potential employer. The Tips and Hints feature above gives some guidelines that will make your application letter more effective.

Figures 17.1 and 17.2 show a poor example and a good example of a general letter that could be addressed to human resource managers at several companies. Both of these letters are unsolicited.

NOTE 17.9
An application letter should be brief, no longer than 1 to 1$\frac{1}{2}$ pages.

NOTE 17.10
Application letters and résumés should not be folded for mailing.

NOTE 17.11
Address the letter to an individual or use simplified format.

NOTE 17.12
Proofread your letter carefully; it must be accurate.

needs work

538 Avalanche Way
Laramie, WY 82051
March 21, 200–

Mr. Douglas Josey, President
Rocky Mountain Bank
154 South Second Street
Denver, CO 80208

I am interested in applying for a position with your bank. I was first in my graduating class when I completed a business major at the university in 1999. I left Laramie in 2000 and since then I have held various positions and believe that my education and experience will be valuable to your bank. I would like to come for an interview to discuss my qualifications.

My career accomplishments include 3 years as a software installer, 5 years as a bank teller, and 2 years as a public relations director. Any business could use a person with these experiences. To add to my marketable skills, I periodically take training courses in computer programming and software development.

If you are interested in someone with the high level of skills and knowledge that I have, I would be willing to join your bank for a salary in the range of $65,000 to $80,000 if advancement opportunities are available. Call me at 615.555.2515 and I will arrange a date and time to meet with you.

Yours truly,

Carolyn Henderson

Carolyn Henderson

No position type or major specified.

No salutation with title and name.

Accomplishments unrelated to organization needs.

No text reference to a résumé; no enclosure notation.

No you-viewpoint; premature salary statement.

FIGURE 17.1
Example of a *Poor* General Application Letter

NOTE 17.13
Targeted letters are more powerful than general letters.

Figures 17.3 and 17.4 are poor and good examples of a targeted letter sent in response to a solicited job opening. Targeted letters usually are more powerful than general letters; in a targeted letter you can show specifically how your employment will benefit the employer.

LO 2
Prepare an employment application.

Preparing an Employment Application

NOTE 17.14
An application may be required in addition to a résumé and application letter.

When you apply for a job, you are asked to complete an application for employment. You may be asked to complete an application form even if you have already submitted a résumé and an application letter. With an employment application, a prospective employer has a signed record of your personal and employment history.

looks good

538 Avalanche Way
Laramie, WY 82051
March 21, 200-

Mr. Douglas Josey, President
Rocky Mountain Bank
154 South Second Street
Denver, CO 80208

> **Uses name and title.**

Dear President Josey:

> **Relates skills/experiences to bank needs.**

In May, I will relocate to the Denver area. My research indicates that Rocky Mountain Bank may be the ideal firm to utilize my experience in banking, technology, and public relations. All three of these knowledge areas are important to a new, rapidly expanding bank such as yours.

> **Names specific skills for employment.**

For the past five years, I worked at a branch office of Fourth/Second Bank in Salt Lake City, Utah. I began as a teller, but three years ago, I assumed a half-time responsibility for the bank's computer database and reduced my role as a teller to half-time. A major change that I implemented in the database software saved the bank approximately 100 hours per week of data input time and also improved customer service. Efficient database management can be critical for a bank like yours that has 20,000 customers and continues adding new accounts.

While in Salt Lake City, I served a two-year term as public relations and membership director for the Chamber of Commerce. During this term, our Chamber gained 150 new member businesses. My interest in and development of public relations skills began during my years in Laramie at the university. As a student, I organized a citywide campaign to increase the number of registered voters. As a result, the number of registered voters increased by one third.

> **Refers to résumé that is being sent with letter.**

I appreciate your time and consideration in reviewing the enclosed résumé. I look forward to meeting you and learning more about job opportunities at your bank and how I could apply my skills as part of the Rocky Mountain team. I will be in Denver from April 10 to 15 and will call you on the 12th to arrange an appointment. If you wish to reach me before my April scheduled trip to Denver, you may leave a message on my cell phone at 435.555.5251, or you may e-mail me at chendo@valley.net.

> **Arranges for easy contact.**

Yours truly,

Carolyn Henderson

Carolyn Henderson

Enclosure: Résumé

FIGURE 17.2
Example of a *Good* General Application Letter

Job applicants can apply online for positions at company websites, or they may apply in person at the physical location of the company. It is always a good idea to download a sample application, complete it, and bring it with you when you are applying for employment. If a sample application is not available, use your résumé and reference list for information to record on the form. This way, you will have a reference sheet that lists dates of employment and education, contact information for previous employers, and any other information required on the employment application.

It is important that you read the entire application form before you start filling it out. Follow the directions exactly. Completing the application properly and fully is important. Employers often use the appearance of an application to judge how much importance the applicant puts on the quality of his or her work. The completed application also demonstrates your attention to detail and your ability to follow directions. Be organized; borrowing the prospective employer's pens or telephone book to complete an application does not create a businesslike impression.

needs work

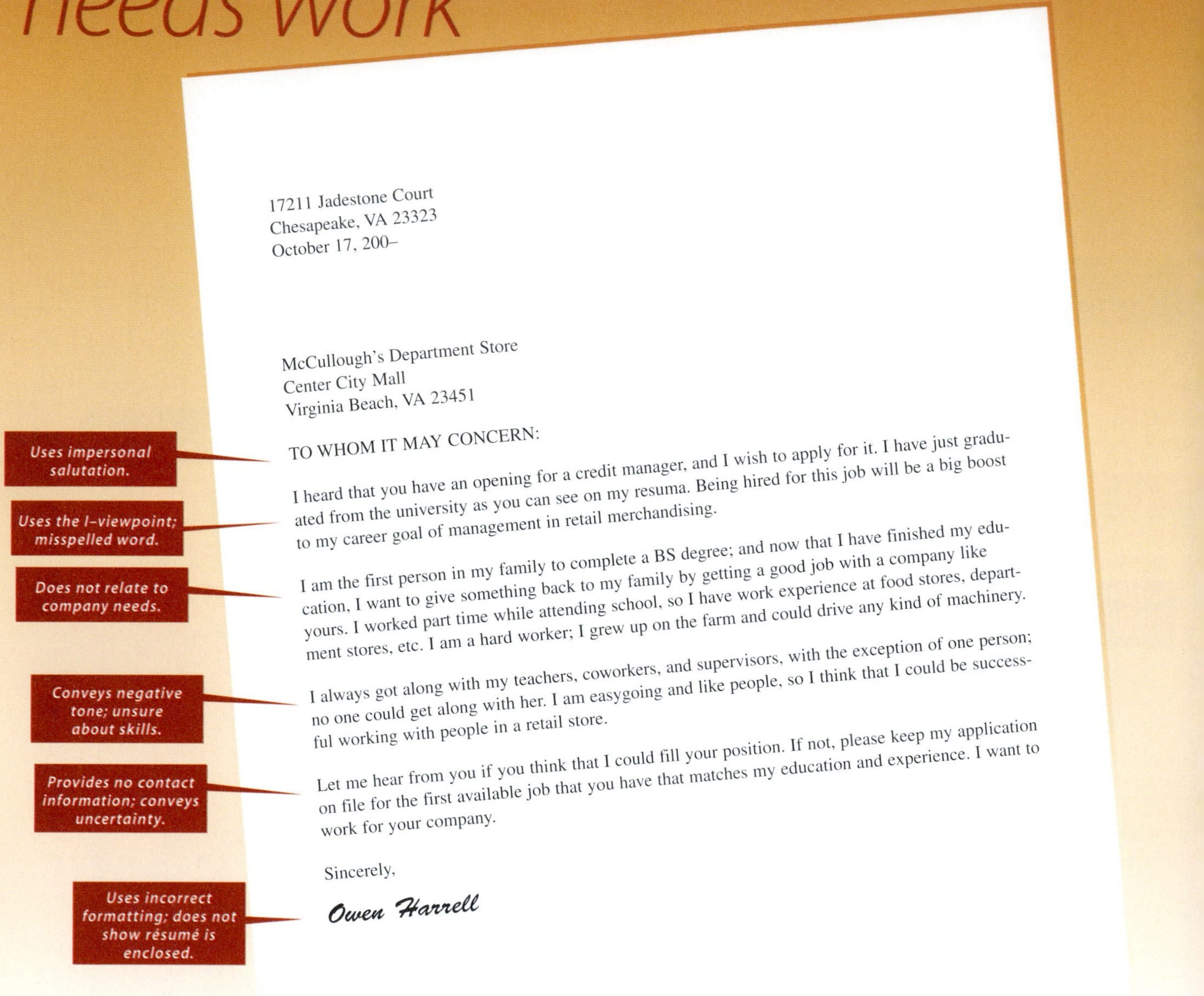

17211 Jadestone Court
Chesapeake, VA 23323
October 17, 200–

McCullough's Department Store
Center City Mall
Virginia Beach, VA 23451

TO WHOM IT MAY CONCERN:

I heard that you have an opening for a credit manager, and I wish to apply for it. I have just graduated from the university as you can see on my resuma. Being hired for this job will be a big boost to my career goal of management in retail merchandising.

I am the first person in my family to complete a BS degree; and now that I have finished my education, I want to give something back to my family by getting a good job with a company like yours. I worked part time while attending school, so I have work experience at food stores, department stores, etc. I am a hard worker; I grew up on the farm and could drive any kind of machinery.

I always got along with my teachers, coworkers, and supervisors, with the exception of one person; no one could get along with her. I am easygoing and like people, so I think that I could be successful working with people in a retail store.

Let me hear from you if you think that I could fill your position. If not, please keep my application on file for the first available job that you have that matches my education and experience. I want to work for your company.

Sincerely,

Owen Harrell

Callouts:
- Uses impersonal salutation.
- Uses the I–viewpoint; misspelled word.
- Does not relate to company needs.
- Conveys negative tone; unsure about skills.
- Provides no contact information; conveys uncertainty.
- Uses incorrect formatting; does not show résumé is enclosed.

FIGURE 17.3
Example of a *Poor* Targeted Application Letter

NOTE 17.15
An employment application should be complete, accurate, and legible.

Employers evaluate three key elements in an application. The first is the information that is entered on the application; it is measured against the skills that are required for a position. The second element is the integrity of the information. With today's increased scrutiny on ethical behavior in business, employers are regularly checking the accuracy of information on applications and résumés. If you can do something, say so; however, do not embellish your skills or education/experience record just to get the job. You can be fired for not telling the truth on an application.

17211 Jadestone Court
Chesapeake, VA 23323
October 17, 200–

Ms. Lisbeth Williamson, Manager
McCullough's Department Store
Center City Mall
Virginia Beach, VA 23451

Dear Ms. Williamson:

Uses positive, direct approach.

Your advertisement in the *Virginia Beach Beacon* for a credit manager appeals to me because the requirements for the position match well with my education and experience. As your credit manager, I believe that I would make an immediate contribution to the continued success of McCullough's Department Store.

Matches skills to job requirements.

Your Requirements

BS degree in Business Finance

Experience in retail credit

Shows enclosure of résumé.

Ability to work with people

Ability to solve problems

My Qualifications

- BS in Business Administration with a Finance specialty; received award as Outstanding Senior in Business Finance.
- Three years' part-time department store experience as Assistant Manager; had responsibility for credit approvals; held three-year bad debts to a maximum of .2 percent.
- Good relationships with colleagues and supervisors; served two years as student council treasurer at the university.
- Managed fund-raising campaign that raised $15,000 for emergency loans for students with a B or above average who needed a short-term loan for tuition.

As requested, I have enclosed my résumé with further details of my qualifications and accomplishments. I look forward to meeting with you to discuss how I would fit into your organization. You may contact me by phone at 757.555.6568 or e-mail at owen.harrell@yahoo.com. I would appreciate the opportunity for an interview at your convenience.

Sincerely,

Owen Harrell

Owen Harrell

Enclosure: Résumé

Makes contact easy; reinforces interest.

FIGURE 17.4
Example of a *Good* Targeted Application Letter

The third element is the legibility of the application. The prospective employer must be able to read the document easily in order to evaluate it. The Tips and Hints feature on page 504 contains suggestions for completing a job application that will present you in the most positive way.

Your completed application is a reflection of you and what you have to offer an organization. Also, it is used as a screening tool. Make a positive impression with your application!

tips and hints

Tips for Completing an Employment Application

1. Practice on a copy of the application if possible. Include as much positive information about yourself as possible; abbreviate to fit information in the allotted space.

2. Leave no blank areas. Write "Does not apply" or "N/A" in the space if the question does not apply; that signifies that you did not forget or overlook the question.

3. Avoid entering a birthdate or a high school graduation date, if possible. This information could be a trigger for an age discrimination issue.

4. Always fill in the space for the Position Desired. Never write "any" or "will do anything." You are sending a signal to the employer that you haven't taken the time to research the company and that you cannot visualize how your skills would fit a position within the company.

5. Write "open" or "negotiable" in the Salary Desired field rather than risk stating a salary that is too low or too high.

6. Write "immediately" in the Availability field if you are available to start the job right away. If you are currently employed, indicate "two weeks" so you can give notice to your current employer and still receive a favorable reference.

7. Fill in job titles; dates of employment; name, address, and phone number of employer; beginning and ending salary; and supervisor's name in the Work Experience section. Make sure dates of employment don't conflict.

8. Use positive phrases like "career change," "returned to school," "reorganization," "moved," or "to take a job with more responsibility" if asked for the reason you left a job. Don't lie; but avoid negative words like "fired," "quit," or "absenteeism."

9. Be truthful in answering all questions. Some applications may ask questions about prior misdemeanor or felony convictions. You may want to fill in the space with "will discuss at interview."

10. Fill out the application form neatly and legibly, using a black or blue pen. Your application, like your résumé and application letter, should be error free. But unlike a résumé and an application letter, which can be word processed, most applications are handwritten.

11. Sign and date your application before submitting it.

Interviewing for a Job

The goal of an application letter and résumé is to obtain a job interview. As soon as you are invited to come for an interview, start preparing for it. The interview can determine the course of your career; it is one of the most important experiences in your life. You want the interview to go as well as possible.

Planning for a Successful Job Interview

You have thought through and carefully prepared for each step of your job search. You have analyzed your qualifications, examined the job market and job requirements, prepared your résumé, and written application letters. Through this process, you have learned about yourself, as well as the job market. In addition, you have organized this information so that you can talk about it effectively and logically.

PREPARING TO ANSWER QUESTIONS

The next step in your preparation is to anticipate questions that might be asked during an interview and to consider the answers you will give. Have a friend or relative ask you the questions to give you practice answering.

Interview questions may be *traditional* or *behavioral style*. **Traditional** questions ask how you *would* handle a hypothetical situation or ask for general information to reveal your job-related attributes or opinions. In contrast, **behavioral** questions focus on specific past situations and how you *did* handle them. You will not know the style of interviewing beforehand; therefore, you must prepare for both traditional and behavioral interviews. In fact, interviews often include a mix of questions—some traditional and some behavioral. Regardless of the style of questioning, the intent is for the potential employer to gather enough information to make a decision about the benefits that you would bring to the company or organization. The underlying question in the mind of the interviewer is, "Would this applicant be the best fit for the position and provide the greatest benefit to the organization?" Keep this in mind as you practice responding to a variety of interview questions.

Traditional Interview Questions. Interviewers ask traditional questions to learn about your education, experience, career goals, and personal history and characteristics. Answers to these questions help the interviewer decide whether you have the education and/or experience, interests, and characteristics that fit the position. Consider possible questions and plan brief but meaningful positive responses that illustrate your past successes and accomplishments. Don't memorize responses or rehearse so extensively that your answers sound "canned." The following list shows examples of traditional interview questions.

Traditional Interview Questions

Personal History and Characteristics
1. Tell me about yourself.
2. What is your greatest strength? your greatest weakness?
3. How is your personality reflected in the kinds of activities you enjoy?
4. Who are your role models? Why?
5. Tell me what you learned from a book you read recently.
6. How do you manage stress?
7. What three words best describe you?
8. What motivates you?
9. Why are you interested in working for us?
10. What skills, ideas, or personal attributes do you bring to the job that other candidates aren't likely to offer?

Education
11. Why did you choose to attend your college or university?
12. Why did you choose your major? minor?
13. Tell me about your education at . . . .
14. How does your college education or work experience relate to this job?
15. Tell me about your course work. What courses did you like best? least?
16. Tell me about your extracurricular activities while you were in school.
17. Tell me about your involvement with your professional organization.
18. Do your grades accurately reflect your ability? Why or why not?
19. Were you financially responsible for any portion of your college education?
20. Do you have plans to get additional education?

Experience
21. Did your customers or clients enjoy working with you?
22. What job-related skills have you developed that are crucial to this job?

NOTE 17.19
Interview questions may be traditional or behavioral.

NOTE 17.20
Responses should cover meaningful accomplishments.

NOTE 17.21
Traditional questions ask how you *would* handle situations.

23. For what kind of supervisor do you like to work?
24. What type of work environment, structured or unstructured, is your most productive or ideal work setting?
25. How would your last employer describe your work habits and your work ethic?
26. What does *teamwork* mean to you?
27. What did you do on your job at ____? What were the most rewarding aspects of that job?
28. Have you ever quit a job? Why?
29. What did you like least in your job at ____?
30. Have you done any volunteer work? What kind?

Career Goals
31. Describe your ideal career (or dream job).
32. Do you like to work alone or with other people? Why?
33. Are you willing to travel?
34. You are younger than most of the people you will supervise. What problems might this pose? How will you resolve them?
35. Where do you want to be in five years? ten years?
36. Because this is your first job, how do you know you'll like the career path?
37. What career paths with this company interest you?
38. What are your aspirations beyond this job?
39. Why did you choose this field of work?
40. What salary do you expect to receive in this job?

NOTE **17.22**

Behavioral questions focus on how you *did* handle past situations.

Behavioral Interview Questions. Increasingly, businesses and other organizations use behavioral questions for all or most of the interview. These questions focus on how the applicant acted and behaved in past situations. Employers support this style of interview because they have found that past behaviors are a good predictor of future behaviors. An added advantage is that answers center on an actual event and are less subjective and less likely to be only an answer the applicant believes the interviewer expects.

NOTE **17.23**

Identify past examples to illustrate your accomplishments.

Prepare for behavioral interview questions by reviewing previous situations at school or at work and how you handled them. Identify specific examples from past events that illustrate positive accomplishments and work attributes. Whenever possible, practice stating these examples with quantifiable outcomes. The following examples illustrate behavioral questions that you may be asked.

Behavioral Interview Questions
1. Describe a major problem you had with another employee at work and how you handled it. Describe why you did or did not confront this employee to resolve the problem.
2. What major problem have you faced in group projects and how have you dealt with it?
3. Describe the most difficult challenge you have faced at work or school. Explain why you believe you met or failed to meet that challenge.
4. Describe a situation in which you were successful (or unsuccessful) in motivating someone.
5. Describe a situation at work or at school where you took the initiative. What was the result? How did you feel?

6. Tell me about a situation at work or at school when you were unsuccessful in accomplishing a task. What could you have done differently?
7. Give me an example of a time management skill you've learned and how you applied it at school or at work.
8. Describe a day at work or at school when everything seemed to go wrong. How did you handle it?
9. Tell me about a leadership role that you carried out at work or at school and how you handled it.
10. Describe the most difficult person with whom you have worked. How did you handle the situation?

Techniques for Answering Questions. When answering questions in an interview situation, there are some basic guidelines to follow. First, be sure you listen to the entire question. Then, you must be clear when stating your response. Feel free to pause before responding. A thoughtful response is better than a poorly phrased quick one. Do not "talk around" the question; answer it honestly, positively, confidently, concisely, and clearly. State your experiences and accomplishments in a specific and positive manner. If you claim to have done something or refer to a specific situation, provide details that support your answer. Don't be modest about taking credit for your achievements; it is important to make these known. Overstatement or embellishment is unlikely, however, to get a positive reaction.

> **NOTE 17.24**
> Answer all questions honestly, positively, confidently, concisely, and clearly.

If you don't understand a question that is asked of you, ask for clarification before attempting to answer the question. Asking for clarification of a question is not viewed negatively unless you ask for clarification on all or nearly all of the questions asked of you. Relate your answers to the job for which you are applying. Take advantage of the opportunity to show your knowledge of the company and the position. Your answers should be brief, but not just yes or no. For example, you may be asked the question, "Do you have plans to get additional education?" You might say, *"Yes, I think it is important to keep up-to-date. I am interested in taking short continuing education courses and, in a few years, working on an MBA degree."* If questions are asked that require you to identify a weakness, turn the weakness into a strength in the answer. In response to, "What do you consider to be your weaknesses?" you might say after reflecting for a moment, *"Well, some people may think I am reserved, but thinking before acting has helped me relate effectively to others."* Another option is to identify a weakness and say what you are doing to correct it. For example, you might say, *"Speaking before large groups is difficult for me, so I've joined a local Toastmaster's club."*

> **NOTE 17.25**
> Think of examples that turn weaknesses into strengths.

Pearls Before Swine by Stephan Pastis

If asked where you want to be in five years, respond with realistic opportunities within the organization. Have two or three positive responses for why the company should hire you. For example, you could say, *"My educational background in finance gives me the basic knowledge to become a credit manager. In my previous position as an assistant manager, I lowered the bad debt ratio from 1 percent to .2 percent. My success in managing credit approvals is an indication of how I can benefit your company by making sound credit decisions. I look forward to becoming part of your organization and expect a long-term mutually beneficial career relationship."*

NOTE 17.26
Give prior thought to a response when asked to "tell us about yourself."

A general request often made early in an interview is "Tell us about yourself." Unless you have given prior thought to this request, the general nature of it can be disconcerting and leave you "clueless" about where to begin and where to end! Keep the response relevant to your education and career development rather than relating a multitude of personal and family details. You could give reasons that led to your career choice, specific ways that your college or university education and any paid or voluntary work experience helped you progress toward your career goals, and reasons why this position is of interest to you. You could say something from your experience similar to this example: *"During my senior year of high school, I began considering a career in public administration when our school implemented a community service project as part of graduation requirements. I worked four hours per week in the mayor's office and was able to help plan and implement an after-school recreation program for inner-city youth. The satisfaction that I gained from this successful effort led to my attending Marshall State University because of its national reputation for offering an outstanding degree in public administration. After graduation, I became excited when you advertised this position as Parks and Recreation Director. It seemed to be perfect timing, a match for my career goals, and a way to help others."*

NOTE 17.27
Think of a positive gained from a negative experience.

When considering how to respond to behavioral interview questions, think of two or three positive and negative experiences that you could use as examples of accomplishments related to the position for which you are applying. If asked to give an example of a negative experience, consider how something positive was gained. For example, you may have worked with someone who was always late arriving at work. He worked the shift following yours at a fast-food restaurant in a part-time job that you held while attending the university. You could not leave your work at the restaurant until he arrived. After waiting for him resulted in your being late to a university class twice, you met with him to resolve the problem in a way that was win-win for both of you. You learned that he did not have an alarm clock and often took a nap and overslept before coming to work. You agreed to give him a telephone call each day at a specific time until payday, at which time he agreed to buy an alarm clock. Before the year was over, you and he became good friends.

With thought, you should be able to come up with a few examples of turning a negative into a positive and strengths that have resulted in successes. Specific examples are more meaningful than general statements such as, *"I have always been able to get along with coworkers."*

NOTE 17.28
Illegal questions could result in discrimination charges.

Techniques for Handling Illegal Questions. Civil rights legislation, Section 504 of the Rehabilitation Act, the Americans with Disabilities Act, the Age Discrimination in Employment Act, the Equal Employment Opportunity Act, and other federal, state, and local laws prohibit discriminatory practices in hiring and affect the content of acceptable preemployment questions. A prospective employer who asks questions unrelated to job requirements and that may have a detrimental effect on groups of people protected from discrimination by legislation is susceptible to charges of discrimination in hiring. An applicant who is not hired may believe interview questions about age, gender, disability, race, ethnic background, or religion resulted in discrimination and may seek a legal remedy.

The following examples illustrate unacceptable questions that could gain information not related to a bona fide occupational qualification for the position. This knowledge leaves the potential employer in a vulnerable legal position if persons not hired suspect the decision was based on discrimination. Furthermore, the person interviewed may resent responding to questions of a personal nature that are unrelated to position requirements. After each of the following questions, the legislation or reason for unacceptability is shown along with the protected group(s).

Unacceptable Questions

How old are you? *(the Age Discrimination in Employment Act—persons over 40)*

You don't look like a native of this country. Where were you born? *(the Civil Rights Act and the Equal Employment Opportunity Act—ethnic background)*

Do you have adequate child care? Who will look after your children while you work? *(the Civil Rights Act—gender)*

Do you have any disabilities? *(the Americans with Disabilities Act and Section 504 of the Rehabilitation Act—persons with disabilities)*

Would you leave a photograph with us? *(the Civil Rights Act, the Equal Employment Opportunity Act, and the Age Discrimination in Employment Act—race, ethnic background, gender, or age)*

Where do you attend church? *(the Civil Rights Act, the Equal Employment Opportunity Act—religion)*

If directly linked to a job requirement, the question is legitimate. For example, if a minor applies for a job that legally requires the worker to be 18, an acceptable question about age would be, "This job requires that a person be 18 years of age. If hired, can you provide proof that you meet that requirement?" Also, a question about disability may be linked to job requirements; for example, "To perform this job requires you to be able to lift up to 50 pounds; do you have any condition that would prevent you from lifting this weight?" The person's appearance in a photograph can give evidence that the applicant is a member of a protected group, and a person's birthplace is a clue to national origin; thus, those questions are unacceptable. Asking for a photograph prior to employment could be acceptable for a position such as a model that requires a certain appearance.

How should you respond if you are asked legally unacceptable questions? Only you can decide. However, you are usually wise to respond calmly. You have nothing to gain by displaying anger or irritation. Such questions are asked for one of two reasons: (a) The interviewer does not realize the question is inappropriate, or (b) he or she wants to observe your reaction (a risky action on the part of the interviewer).

What are ways that you could respond to inappropriate or illegal questions? If asked about your age, you might smile and say, "Age is merely a number. What's more important is that I have the experience and energy necessary to do the job

NOTE 17.29
Unacceptable interview questions do not relate to job requirements.

NOTE 17.30
Displaying anger when asked an illegal question is usually unwise.

NOTE 17.31
Answer an illegal question, evade it, or indicate it is not relevant to the job.

well." Then you can shift the topic back to the position. You can decide to answer the question, pleasantly evade the question, or say calmly that the question is not relevant to the job and shift to another topic.

RESPONDING TO THE SALARY QUESTION

The salary question—the last one on the list of traditional interview questions—is an important one. The employer may have set a salary or a salary range for the position. You should try to get that information before the interview if you can. Also, you should try to learn before the interview what salaries are being paid for similar jobs in the employer's geographic area. Your campus career center may have local, regional, and/or national salary information. Websites with salary information are http://www.salary.com, http://www.salaryexpert.com, and http://www.careerjournal.com. Newspaper employment ads sometimes show salaries, too.

Try to avoid talking about salary until the final stages of the interview, after you have made a good impression and are in a better position to negotiate. If pressed early in the interview for a specific answer, respond in a straightforward, objective manner. You might say, "In researching the job market, the range for this position seems to be between $ and $." Another response could be to ask the interviewer to give you the salary range that this company pays for the position so that you could weigh your answer carefully and give a response related to this specific position.

The most appropriate time to discuss salary is after you have the job offer. In negotiating salary, reinforce the skills that you bring to the company. When considering a salary offer, ask about the total compensation package. Benefits such as health, dental, and life insurance; retirement programs; leave time; and paid relocation expenses can be important considerations. If the company does not agree to the amount you request, you can agree to the figure (if acceptable) and ask that your salary be reviewed for an increase in six months.

PREPARING QUESTIONS ABOUT THE POSITION

Be ready to ask the interviewer key questions of your own. Usually, near the end of the interview you will be asked if you have questions. Do not concentrate just on questions of personal benefit to you, such as ones about fringe benefits, retirement programs, vacation policies, and salary. Your questions might be about such subjects as job duties, the employee evaluation system, management philosophy, company progress and plans, promotion policies, and employee development programs. Here are examples of questions you may want to ask.

1. Please describe the duties of the job.
2. Would you describe the normal routine of this position? Describe a typical day.
3. What kinds of job assignments might I expect the first six months on the job?
4. How is job performance evaluated and how often?
5. How much travel is normally expected? Is a car provided?
6. How much interaction is there among departments? Or, do departments work independently of one another?
7. Do you have plans for expansion?
8. Does your company encourage further education?
9. When do you expect to make a decision?
10. What are some of the strengths you believe the ideal candidate for this position should possess?

An effective exchange of information takes place in a successful job interview.

© Sigrid Olsson/The Image Bank

RESEARCHING THE COMPANY

Learn as much as you can about the company prior to the interview. Secure descriptive materials on the company and its industry directly from the company or its website, your campus career center, the library, the chamber of commerce, the Better Business Bureau, a trade association, trade journals, or the Web.

The Web has many sources of information. A business search engine such as http://www.business.com will provide a number of websites with information about a specific company by entering the company name. Other sites such as http://www.fortune.com, http://www.companiesonline.com, http://www.hoovers.com, and http://money.cnn.com also provide a search option to find company profiles and related data on a large number of companies. Additionally, other websites provide company information such as fact sheets and annual reports for a small fee. Chapter 16 and the first part of this chapter list some of the sources of information on organizations.

NOTE 17.35
Learn about the organization before the interview.

Through your public library, you can access several books and web databases that have information about manufacturers and other businesses and industries. Examples of these databases are Dun and Bradstreet's *Million Dollar Directory* (for large-volume businesses) and *infoUSA*. Your librarian can help you locate these or similar materials. Libraries in some cities also may have copies of company annual reports.

NOTE 17.36
Use the Internet and the library to find information about employers.

Studying materials carefully to gain background knowledge of the organization will help you in the interview in two basic ways: (a) It will aid your communication with the interviewer, and (b) it will set you apart from the other interviewees who learned nothing about the company prior to an interview. Examples of questions you should research about the organization include the following:

1. What is the size ($ and people) of the organization or company?
2. What service or products does the company offer?
3. What is the percentage of annual sales growth in the last five years?
4. When was the company last in the news? Why?

5. What are the strengths of the company?
6. What is the organizational structure?
7. Is the company an international company?
8. What is the corporate culture of the company?
9. What career paths and advancement opportunities does the company offer in your field?
10. What is the salary range for the position?
11. How long has the company been in business?
12. What are the names of top company officers or executives? the human resource manager?

PREPARING YOURSELF PERSONALLY

In the interview, every part of you is being assessed. Your conduct, your skills, and your experience should stand out in an interview; your physical appearance should play a supporting role. Formal business attire is almost always preferred for the job interview. Regardless of whether employees wear formal attire at the prospective workplace, you should dress to impress and show respect for your potential employer. Choose your clothes carefully, give attention to personal grooming, and avoid wearing bulky jewelry or strong colognes. Depending on the industry, men should remove earrings; both men and women should remove tongue studs and facial rings or studs. The interviewer(s) may be dressed in casual clothing; however, employers expect you to dress in a conservative business style for an interview. A suggested general guide follows.

NOTE 17.37
Give attention to grooming and dress for the interview.

Men

- Two-piece conservative suit in a solid color such as blue or gray.
- Long-sleeved white or subdued color shirt with a tie in a plain or simple pattern.
- Polished shoes with socks that match the suit. Remember, your belt should match your shoes.

Women

- Two-piece conservative suit with a knee-length or longer skirt in a solid color such as blue or gray. A business-style, well-fitted pantsuit is also appropriate.
- White or ivory blouse with modest jewelry.
- Polished shoes with plain hosiery.

You can do a practice interview, videotape it, and evaluate your performance as part of your preparation. Some nervousness is natural, but too much nervousness makes a poor impression. Knowing that you are prepared will increase your confidence and help reduce nervousness.

Practice walking, sitting and rising, and shaking hands for the interview. Check in advance to be sure of the date, the place, and the name and title of the interviewer. If the location is unfamiliar, visit the place before the day of your interview. Plan your schedule so that you arrive about 15 minutes early. Allow time for unexpected delays.

Take a portfolio (not a backpack—think "Professional") with the following materials: two copies of your résumé; a copy of your transcript; examples of your course work and work projects; letters of reference; a reference list; and an application form with all the important details such as former employers, addresses, and phone numbers. In addition, take a pen and a small notebook to record notes about the position and the names of the people you meet. Ask for business cards so you will have accurate names, titles, and addresses and can send letters of appreciation immediately after the interview.

Talk (mentally) to yourself and relax before the interview. Build your confidence by telling yourself that you have done all you can to prepare for the interview. You have anticipated questions and have prepared answers, you have learned about the company, and you have prepared yourself personally. You are ready for the interview.

NOTE 17.38
Advance preparation is key to minimizing nervousness and boosting confidence.

Participating in an Interview

View the interview as an opportunity to share your qualifications with an interested person who is knowledgeable in your career field. Greet your interviewer warmly by name and pronounce the name correctly. Let the interviewer take the lead. If an offer is made to shake hands, do so with a firm grip and a smile. Sit when asked to do so. See your role as primarily responding to questions in a businesslike fashion. Keep appropriate eye contact with the interviewer. The amount of appropriate eye contact with interviewers varies depending on the interviewer's cultural background. Other cultural variations that are important in interviews include verbal and nonverbal communication patterns (refer to Chapter 2 for further information on cultural variations in business communication).

NOTE 17.39
Be professional in the interview situation.

The interviewer may intentionally challenge you by asking difficult questions or by appearing disinterested or even irritated to see how you handle different situations. Project a knowledgeable, professional, positive, friendly, and confident image.

Don't smoke, chew gum, eat your lunch, lean back in your chair, lean on the interviewer's desk, act immature, tell jokes, or laugh nervously.

Be alert for signals that the interview is ending. The interviewer may slide his or her chair back, stand, or send you oral signals. When the interview is over, express appreciation for the time and information given you. Indicate that you look forward to hearing from the interviewer. Ask when you will receive notice of the decision or when you may call about the decision. Shake hands, express thanks for the interview, and warmly tell the interviewer goodbye.

NOTE 17.40
At the close, express appreciation for the interview.

After the interview, evaluate your performance. Make written notes of those things that went well and those that you will change the next time you interview. Make a record of the information you learned about the job for comparison with other job opportunities. Record the correct spelling of the names and titles of those who interviewed you, and note what you will want to say in your follow-up communication.

NOTE 17.41
Evaluate your performance and record information for follow-up contacts.

Types of Interviews

Before receiving a job offer from an employer, you will typically have a series of interviews. The interview is the last step in the process to secure a job. You want to be well prepared for the interview because it can "make" or "break" your candidacy for a position. The type of interview or the number of interviews conducted may vary from company to company, from industry to industry, and from position to position. This section of the chapter discusses the various types of interviews: screening, subsequent, telephone, video, online, group, and alternative.

The employee selection process is important to the organization as well as to the potential employee. Both parties in the interview process are looking for a mutually

NOTE 17.42
Interviews may cover one or two stages and use different media.

beneficial relationship in which the qualifications of the applicant meet the needs of the employer.

SCREENING INTERVIEWS

NOTE 17.43
Preliminary screening
verifies your match to
the position.

A **screening interview,** sometimes called a *preliminary interview,* is used to qualify a candidate before he or she meets with a hiring individual for possible selection. In today's job market, this process has become popular and is used frequently to narrow the pool of acceptable candidates. A screening interview is quick, efficient, and low cost. It may take from ten minutes to an hour. It usually starts with a traditional question such as "Why are you interested in this position?" and is followed by behavioral questions. Beware of questions that will eliminate you from consideration. The salary question is the "trick" question that is used most often. When you indicate a figure that is too high or too low, you may inadvertently be telling the prospective employer that you have not done your research on this topic.

NOTE 17.44
Three types of screening
interviews are telephone,
face-to-face, and
computer assisted.

Telephone Interviews. The telephone interview is the most common way to perform an initial screening interview because it saves time and money. Your telephone screening interview may be tape recorded for review by future interviewers. In most cases, someone from human resources does this initial interview; early in the process he or she will ask questions about your technical skills and experience or about personal traits. You may be caught off guard with the initial interview screening call because it may occur in the evening or on the weekend. When you receive a call like this, tell the person you are just finishing something and ask if you may return the call in a few minutes. This will give you time to retrieve your résumé, compose yourself, think about how you are going to "sell" yourself to the interviewer, and mentally rehearse the answers to questions you expect to be asked. Give concise answers (try to keep answers to less than 60 seconds each), and sound enthusiastic and interested. Remember, this is a phone conversation, and you don't have the benefit of nonverbal communication with your interviewer; you must rely on your verbal skills. Have a pen and paper in front of you so you can write down the interviewer's name and take notes as he or she asks questions.

Face-to-Face Interviews. A recruiter or human resource staff person will usually conduct the face-to-face screening interview. He or she is an experienced interviewer who is skilled at judging character, assessing qualifications and skills, and identifying "red flags" or problem areas. Some campus career centers host face-to-face screening interviews.

Computer-Assisted Interviews. Computer-assisted screening interviews are being used increasingly for long-distance candidates. The candidate is provided with a password and a log-in time to access the multiple-choice interview questions that have been posted online. For some candidates, "interviewing" with a computer lessens anxiety; for others, the process is frustrating because they can respond only with their best choice from a group of definitive answers listed. This interviewing method is fast and cost-effective. Once the questions are answered, the computer analyzes the answers and creates a report pinpointing the matches.

If you make a favorable impression on the interviewer(s), you may be asked to a second interview. Not all employers hold screening interviews; the screening of résumés and application letters may suffice as the preliminary step before interviewing. Getting through the screening process is critical for advancing to the next step.

SUBSEQUENT INTERVIEWS

After you have passed the screening interview and/or screening of résumés and application letters, you may be invited to a company's office for one or more additional interviews. The subsequent interviews may include meeting with several individuals in the company separately and/or as a team on a panel. The most common subsequent interview is the one-on-one. Each candidate has his or her own unique interview. This is your chance to market yourself as the best candidate for the job. Talk about your qualifications, what you can contribute to the company, and why you want the job. Weave information you have gathered on the employer into your responses and questions. After the interview, both the candidate and the employer will have a pretty good sense of whether there is a "fit."

NOTE 17.45
After passing screening, you may have one or more additional interviews.

The panel is a group of employees that may include a human resource representative, a potential supervisor, and potential colleagues. This type of interview is usually done to accommodate the panel's time and schedule. When interviewed by a panel, maintain eye contact with the questioner when responding to questions. Be prepared to answer questions from each interviewer. Always bring a paper and pencil with you so that you are prepared to write anything needed during the interview and to record the names of the interviewers. Often the questions asked in a panel interview are the same for all candidates.

TELEPHONE INTERVIEWS

Prepare for a telephone interview as you would for a face-to-face interview; however, you can use notes during the interview. Your reference notes and your résumé should be near the telephone. It is important that you conduct the interview in a quiet area where you won't be bothered or distracted. If possible, use a headset so your hands are free for natural gestures and note taking. Seat yourself in a chair that encourages you to maintain good posture. Speak in a friendly, pleasant voice. A smile can be heard in your voice, so smile while speaking in the same manner that you would if the interviewer could see you. Being unable to see the speaker's nonverbal body language and facial expressions can make it more difficult to interpret the speaker's attitude toward your responses. Keeping a positive mental image of the interviewer will help your confidence.

NOTE 17.46
An interview may be conducted by telephone.

VIDEO INTERVIEWS

A newer form of interviewing uses a videoconferencing system. Video interviews have become popular because they allow companies to interview new recruits at colleges more economically. If you are asked to participate in a video interview, your campus career center will provide you with the information on where the interview will take place. Research indicates that candidates interviewed by videoconferencing rate slightly higher than those interviewed face-to-face. This may result from the interviewer's assumption that the applicant has little or no experience with videoconference interviews and, thus, requires the benefit of the doubt.

NOTE 17.47
Video interviews may take place in a videoconferencing center.

ONLINE INTERVIEWS

Online interviewing uses a combination of video, a camera, a computer, and the Internet. Online interviewing may become more popular because of advancing technology. Either an individual or a team can conduct these interviews. Online interviewing enables employers to screen candidates rapidly and to cut interview costs. With a camera and microphone attached to the computer, online interviews become similar to a video interview.

NOTE 17.48
The computer, microphone, and camera facilitate online interviews.

GROUP INTERVIEWS

NOTE 17.49
Group interviews test a
person's interaction skills.

With group interviews, several people are interviewed at the same time for the same position. Companies use this method to determine how a potential employee will interact in a group situation and to evaluate the employee's potential leadership style. Candidates are asked to solve a problem collectively. This is probably one of the most difficult interview styles because you need to show leadership skills, but at the same time treat other candidates with respect. Group interviews can be overwhelming and stressful for many applicants.

ALTERNATIVE INTERVIEWS

Two alternative styles of interviews are the lunch interview and the interactive interview. Lunch interviews are often used when someone is near the final stages before a job offer is made and the employer wants to see how the applicant performs in a social setting. The key to doing well in this situation is to follow the lead of the interviewer and to remember this is a lunch interview, not a lunch date. That means you need to keep the conversation focused on matching your qualifications to the needs of the employer. The interactive interview is not widely used, but it is gaining ground. Rather than asking candidates the same questions over and over, the interviewer invites the applicant to "show" what he or she can do. This interview style allows you to demonstrate your qualifications and skills with the help of your professional portfolio. The Communication Note feature gives tips on how to use your portfolio to demonstrate your skills and achievements to a prospective employer.

NOTE 17.50
If you are offered a job at
the interview, you may call
back with an answer.

The organization's decision about making an employment offer will result from the interview or series of interviews. You should consider whether you will accept an offer if one is made at the end of the interview. In most cases, any offer of employment would come a few days or weeks after interviewing. If you do receive an offer at the end of the interview, you may want to think about it at least overnight. You could indicate that you are very interested in the position and that, after careful consideration, you will call the next day with your answer. Ask the time of day that would be convenient for you to call, as well as the telephone number. If more time is needed, explain this and give a certain day of the week to call with your answer.

communication note

EMPOWERMENT IN THE INTERVIEW WITH YOUR PORTFOLIO

You have more control of the interview situation with a portfolio. If you show rather than tell the interviewer what you can do, he or she is more likely to remember it. There are typically two ways to use your portfolio in the interview situation: When you greet the interviewer, you can indicate that you have brought a portfolio to demonstrate your qualifications; or when the discussion presents an opportunity to reinforce a qualification, refer to that item in the portfolio.

Portfolios can be either print or digital. The electronic portfolio offers flexibility because a prospective employer can view it before, during, or after an interview; however, it is less secure than a hardcopy version. Therefore, items such as references or letters of recommendation, personal information, and work samples containing confidential information are not appropriate for the electronic portfolio.

The purpose of a portfolio is to prove or demonstrate your skills and accomplishments; therefore, you want it to be professional, organized, and accurate—a reflection of the type of employee you will be.

Preparing Other Employment Messages

Employment communication is not limited to résumés, application letters, and interviews. Other employment messages can include telephone calls, letters, e-mail, and in-person contacts. You may need to follow up on a pending application or communicate your acceptance of an invitation for an interview. You may want to make a follow-up contact after an interview. It will be necessary to communicate your rejection or acceptance of a job offer. If you accept a job, you may need to resign from another job. Finally, you should express appreciation to all those who assisted you in your job campaign. Suggestions for composing these messages are given in the following sections. These examples show the body of the letter only and do not include dates, inside addresses, salutations, and closings. All employment communication requires the appropriate format, as shown in Chapter 6.

LO 4

Compose a variety of follow-up letters and other employment-related messages.

NOTE 17.51
Job-related communication may be in person, in writing, by phone, or by e-mail.

Following Up an Application

If several weeks pass without your hearing about the status of your application with an employer, you may want to initiate a follow-up contact. Remember, many unsolicited applications are not acknowledged. Depending on the circumstances, your follow-up contact can be by letter, in person, or by telephone (be prepared to leave your message on an answering machine or in voice mail). Such a message would be neutral news for the employer; consequently, use the direct plan. Here is an example of such a follow-up message:

NOTE 17.52
Wait two weeks before following up on an application.

Hello Ms. Ames. My name is Sally Welch [spell out name if leaving a message]. About three weeks ago I submitted a letter of application and a résumé for the network administrator position in your information technology department. I have not heard from you, but I am still very interested in this position with Web Solutions.

Since September, I have been volunteering at the San Jose Senior Center where I have designed and installed a network system to link all its facilities. However, my primary goal is still employment at Web Solutions. My skills and experience would be an ideal match for the network administrator position.

If you have questions or need more information, please call me at (515) 555-8261. I look forward to interviewing for the network administrator position.

Accepting an Interview Invitation

Most interview invitations will be by telephone or e-mail. Be prepared to receive this kind of call or e-mail any time during your job campaign and to respond logically, clearly, and maturely. Check the voice mail on your home telephone and the information on your e-mail account to be sure that they are professional. Your communication accepting an interview should use the direct plan (for positive news) and should (a) express appreciation, (b) indicate availability, and (c) convey a positive and optimistic attitude. Here is an example of content for either a written or an oral message:

NOTE 17.53
Telephone and e-mail are commonly used for interview invitations.

Thank you for the opportunity to interview for the position in the human resource department. I am very much interested in meeting with you to discuss the position and my qualifications.

I appreciate your asking me for three alternative dates. Because of my work and class schedules, the best interview dates are April 24, 26, or 27. Any of these three dates will be convenient for me.

I look forward to visiting your offices and learning more about the staffing specialist position.

Following Up an Interview

NOTE 17.54
After an interview, send a letter of appreciation.

A letter of appreciation is appropriate after an interview. If a company has been corresponding with you using e-mail, then it is acceptable that you send an e-mail letter of appreciation. This letter should be sent within one or two days following the interview. If you think you are still interested in the position, you should express that interest in the letter. If you are definitely not interested in the position, a letter of appreciation for the interview is still appropriate. In the latter case, in fairness to the employer, you should withdraw your candidacy. The letter in which you express your continuing interest should use the direct plan, and the letter in which you withdraw your candidacy should use the indirect plan. These letters should be brief, cordial, businesslike, and word processed. An example of a follow-up appreciation letter for a position you wish to obtain is shown in Figure 17.5. It is also appropriate, and good business practice, to send a handwritten note or an e-mail to staff members who assisted in making arrangements for your visit and to those with whom you met informally, perhaps for coffee or lunch.

FIGURE 17.5
An Appreciation Letter as an Interview Follow Up

17211 Jadestone Court
Chesapeake, VA 23323
November 1, 200–

Ms. Lisbeth Williamson, Manager
McCullough's Department Store
Center City Mall
Virginia Beach, VA 23451

Dear Ms. Williamson:

Expresses appreciation for the interview

Thank you for the opportunity yesterday to interview for the position of credit manager for McCullough's Department Store. I appreciated the time that you and other members of your staff spent with me during the morning.

Reinforces match of experience with the position

After meeting with you and your sales team, I am enthusiastic about the position and the growth opportunities that it offers. My experience in retail credit and previous problem-solving accomplishments, both with volunteer work and work experience while earning my Business Administration degree, match well with the responsibilities of the credit manager position.

I look forward to hearing your hiring decision for the position. If you need additional information, please phone me at 757.555.6568 or send an e-mail to owen.harrell@yahoo.com.

Provides information for easy contact.

Sincerely,

Owen Harrell

Owen Harrell

Accepting Employment

The communication offering employment or accepting employment most likely will be by telephone or in person, followed by confirming letters. A letter accepting employment is a positive communication and should use the direct plan: (a) The offer should be accepted, (b) any essential information about assuming the position should come next, and (c) an expression of appreciation should close the letter. An example of a confirming acceptance letter follows:

NOTE 17.55
Use the direct plan for a letter of employment acceptance.

This letter confirms my acceptance of your employment offer of September 25. I am delighted to be joining Midwest Agri-Business in Madison. The work is exactly what I have prepared for and hoped to do. I am confident that I can make a significant contribution to the company.

As agreed, I will report to the human resource office at 8 a.m. on October 23. I will have completed the medical examination, drug testing, and fingerprinting by this date. All employment and insurance forms will be completed for the new employee orientation on October 24.

Thank you for the opportunity to join the Midwest Agri-Business team. I am pleased to be joining your staff.

Rejecting Employment

As is the case with accepting employment, the first communication rejecting employment most likely will be by telephone. An indirect message following up an oral employment rejection may be appropriate. This letter should be brief, cordial, businesslike, and word processed rather than handwritten. The body of a letter rejecting employment might look like this:

NOTE 17.56
An employment rejection should be brief, cordial, and businesslike.

Thank you very much for offering me the position of marketing manager with Fisher Investments. I sincerely appreciate your taking the time to interview me and to share information about this position and your company.

The Fisher Investments position would have offered me a challenging and interesting job. However, I have accepted a marketing position at Money Tree that offers a career path that is more what I had envisioned for myself.

It was a pleasure to meet you and your marketing team. Thanks to all of you for the courtesies that were extended to me.

Expressing Appreciation to References and Others

When you have completed a successful job campaign and accepted an employment offer, share the good news with your references. Also, it will be important to notify any placement service and others who assisted you. These expressions of appreciation for assistance may be by telephone, by e-mail, by letter, or in person. Remember, appreciation messages are organized using the direct plan.

NOTE 17.57
Express appreciation for help given in a successful job campaign.

Resigning from a Job

Once your job campaign is completed, it may be necessary to resign from your present position. It is best that your resignation not be a surprise for your employer. If you can, let your employer know that you have applied for another position while

NOTE 17.58
A job resignation should be oral and in person as well as written.

you are searching. If you think your employer would react negatively to your search for another position, you may want to keep your job search confidential.

Most resignations are given orally and in person and then followed by a written message. Be sure to give your employer the notice required in company policy. If no policy exists, use a standard two-week notice. Resignations are negative messages but are considered routine, and because notice is first given orally, resignations are written following a direct plan. Here is an example of a resignation letter written with a direct plan:

Please accept this letter as official resignation from my position as an administrative assistant, effective Friday, May 29, 2007. I have accepted a position as a human resource staffing specialist with the city of Houston, Texas.

As you know, I have been pursuing my bachelor's degree in business administration while working at Heller Imports. Now that I have my degree, I am ready to start my career in human resources. My time at Heller has been wonderful. The practical skills I obtained here have made me competitive in the job market as a new college graduate. I appreciate the experience and support you provided.

I look forward to continuing our professional relationship.

Summary of Learning Objectives

LO 1

Write effective application letters for solicited and unsolicited positions.

An application letter is a sales letter with *your knowledge and skills* as the products. The major parts of an application letter are the opening to gain attention, the summary of qualifications to convince the employer that you fit the job, and the closing to request an interview and provide information that makes contact easy. Remember that the primary purpose of an application letter is to motivate a potential employer to read your résumé and invite you for an interview. Your sales focal point is to use past accomplishments to illustrate how your employment can benefit the organization.

LO 2

Prepare an employment application.

Many organizations and companies require prospective employees to complete an employment application, even if they have already submitted a résumé and an application letter. It is crucial that the employment application be complete, accurate, and legible. Employers often use this document as a screening tool for applicants.

LO 3

Prepare for a successful job interview.

Preparing for an interview includes reviewing information gathered to this point; learning all you can about the company through research at the library, at the chamber of commerce, or on the Web; preparing to ask and answer questions; dressing appropriately for the interview; and participating in the job interview.

Interview questions can be either traditional or behavioral. Traditional questions ask about your education and experience and how you *would* handle hypothetical situations; behavioral questions focus on specific past situations and how you *did* handle them. Both types of questions are intended to determine how you will perform in the future.

The screening interview eliminates individuals who do not have the required education, work experience, communication skills, and other basic requirements for the position. Subsequent interviews may include one-on-one or panel interviews. Other interview types may include telephone, video, online, group, and alternative. Telephone interviews may be used for screening or for final selection. A video interview uses a videoconferencing system; an online interview uses a combination of video, a camera, a computer, and the Internet. Group interviews involve several people being interviewed at the same time for the same position(s). The lunch interview and the interactive interview are alternative styles that are used less often than other types of interviews.

Compose a variety of follow-up letters and other employment-related messages.

LO 4

Other employment messages that you should be able to prepare are a follow-up to an application letter, an interview acceptance letter, a thank you letter after a job interview, a job acceptance letter, a letter rejecting employment, and a letter of resignation.

Questions for Discussion and Review

1. Discuss the purpose of an application letter. Describe the two kinds of application letters. (Objective 1)
2. How do you address an application letter if you are replying to a classified ad that does not list a contact person? (Objective 1)
3. What content should go in the closing paragraph of an application letter? (Objective 1)
4. If the employment application you submit does not have all the blanks filled in, has smudges on it, and has words crossed out, what impression might the prospective employer have about you? (Objective 2)
5. How would you turn into a positive the answer to the question, "What do you consider your weaknesses?" (Objective 3)
6. What is the difference between a traditional interview question and a behavioral interview question? (Objective 3)
7. Describe how you could gather information about a potential employer. Why is it important to have background information on a future employer? (Objective 3)
8. Why is the direct plan used to write a resignation letter when it contains negative or bad news? (Objective 4)
9. Describe three types of employment-related letters that you may write in addition to an application letter. (Objective 4)
10. Would you follow a direct or an indirect plan in writing a letter accepting employment? Explain your answer. (Objective 4)

Application Exercises

1. Prepare the targeted application letter to accompany the targeted résumé that you prepared for Chapter 16. (Objective 1) (*Hint:* Be sure your letter addresses all four purposes of a persuasive message.)

2. **Global.** Explore business websites or your library resources, and find a company with international opportunities. Write a general application letter expressing your interest in working for that company. (Objective 1)

3. Go to the Student Resources section of the website for Chapter 17. Retrieve and print two copies of the employment application form. Read the directions carefully and then complete the entire form. Transfer the information from your practice employment application to the blank form. You will then have a fact sheet you can use as a reference when filling out other employment applications. (Objective 2)

4. **Technology. Teamwork.** Select ten traditional and ten behavioral interview questions from this chapter or from Internet research. Thoughtfully consider how you would respond to the questions you chose to present yourself in the most positive way to a prospective employer. Write your questions on one sheet of paper and your responses to the questions on another sheet of paper. Practice your responses until you feel comfortable with them (do not memorize because your responses should sound natural, not "canned"). Choose a classmate as an interviewing partner. Ask each other the questions you have chosen and then give constructive feedback on the content and delivery of the responses. (Objective 3)

5. **Technology.** Use a website to locate salary information for a beginning accountant, administrative assistant, computer programmer, and finance manager in the largest city in your state. In an e-mail to your teacher, explain what you learned about the salaries and give the Universal Resource Locator(s) (URLs) for the source(s) that you used to locate this information. (Objective 3)

6. **Teamwork. Ethics.** Form a group of two or three students. Decide what you believe would be the best way to respond to each of the unacceptable questions included in this chapter. Also, discuss ethical considerations for the interviewer and the applicant in regard to asking and responding to legally unacceptable questions. (Objective 3)

7. **Teamwork. Global.** Form groups of three or four students. Each group will choose two countries from the following list: Japan, Mexico, Germany, Australia, Russia, India, or China. If you were interviewing with companies in the two countries you chose for this exercise, describe how each of the following behaviors might differ from interviewing with a company in the United States: (a) greeting the interviewer, (b) responding to questions, (c) closing remarks. Also address how the application letter might differ. (Objective 3)

8. Classify each of the following questions as either traditional or behavioral and prepare a response to each question based on your experience. (Objective 3)
   a. Give me an example of a time when you worked under intense pressure. How did you handle the pressure, what adjustments did you have to make, and what was the outcome?
   b. Are you most productive working alone or with a group?
   c. How do you define job success?
   d. Tell me about a time you didn't perform to your capabilities.
   e. How do you balance your reliance on facts with your reliance on intuition?
   f. How have your career motivations changed over the past few years?
   g. Share an example of your perseverance in a school or work setting. What made the situation difficult, and what motivated you to keep going?

9. **Technology.** Assume your instructor was one of your references. You have just accepted your "dream job." Write an e-mail expressing appreciation to your instructor for serving as a reference. Update your instructor on all the details of your new job. (Objective 4)

10. **Technology.** Assume that you have received an e-mail invitation for an interview from the targeted application letter that you wrote in Application Exercise 1. The message suggested a date and time that would cause you to miss a final examination in one of your university courses.

Prepare an e-mail that indicates your acceptance of the invitation but suggests alternative times and/or dates for the interview. Send your e-mail to your instructor. (Objective 4) (*Hint:* Use the indirect plan.)

11. **Teamwork.** With two classmates, role-play an interview for the position in the application letter that you wrote in Application Exercise 1. Take turns being the interviewer and the applicant. After each of you has played the applicant role, work together to write a follow-up letter expressing appreciation for the interview and confirming your interest in the position. (Objective 4)

    COLLABORATIVE

12. **Ethics. Teamwork.** Assume that you have been employed by a company for five years. Your experiences with the company have been generally positive, but you have not received the promotions and salary increases that you expected. Therefore, for the past three months, you have been applying and interviewing for another position. You have not told your present employer because you believe that you would lose your job. However, your employer called you to his office today to tell you that he has a health problem and will be leaving in three weeks for a one-month overseas cruise based on his doctor's recommendation. He tells you that he has always depended on you and that he wants you to assume leadership of the company while he is gone. You are flattered by his offer, but you believe that it is in your best interest to leave the company and take a new position as soon as you find the right position. You still believe that if your employer knows that you are searching for another job, he will ask you to leave so that he can fill your position with someone else. Partner with a classmate and discuss what you should do and say in response to your employer's request. Decide also what you believe the short-term and long-term effects will be of your response to the situation. (Objective 4)

    ETHICAL
    COLLABORATIVE

13. Assume that you accepted another position the week after the scenario described in Application Exercise 12. Write a letter of resignation from your present job. (Objective 4)

Web exercises to accompany this chapter are available at **www.thomsonedu.com/bcomm/krizan.**

MESSAGE ANALYSIS

List three problems with the following application letter. Rewrite it to strengthen the letter's effectiveness. Add details to your letter as required to improve it.

> *Please consider this letter an application for your company. I believe I could advance my career rapidly as an employee with a company such as yours. I am a quick learner and a hard worker. My business degree is a BS in Finance. I am good in accounting and really enjoy it. If you have an opening for anything, however, I am willing to take the job. What is the salary for a beginning accountant with your company? Please let me hear from you soon as I am eager to get a job and begin my career. I have work experience. I was a counter salesperson with McDonald's for three summers.*

Writer's Workshop

The following items may be sentence fragments or contain errors in punctuation, subject–verb agreement, pronoun–antecedent agreement, infinitive use, abbreviations, number display, capitalization, spelling, word choice, possessives, modifier clarity and placement, or parallelism. Rewrite the sentences to make them correct:

1. A person whom has never interviewed will be most likely to be nervus in a interview.
2. We was purchasing 4 new flash drives to give as birthday gifts at the sale.
3. What affect do you think that the low math grade will have on your chanches for a job as a sales clerk?
4. The job market is tighter now, then it has been for the last several years.
5. As her finanshal planner its' my responsibility to plan out carefully what our investment strategy will be.
6. The english grade on her transcript should of helped her get the newsreporter job.

7. When did you return from your trip to Bangkok, and your trip to Queenland Australia?

8. The Handy shoe Store in Cincinnatti holds a out door shoe sale in October each year, the sale procedes go to the united way.

9. At the department level she was co-advisor of the MBA club; advising students in her office, and she taught job interviewing techniques.

10. Her contributions as a secretary is highly value by the Department.

YOU BE THE
virtual assistant

The number of clients for whom you work and the complexity of the jobs you do has grown, and you now find it necessary to hire someone to assist you in your business. The tasks in this feature relate to expanding your business.

1. Write a job description you can use to hire a word processing clerk to assist you with written projects.

2. You'll advertise your position in the local newspaper(s), with area post-secondary schools, in newsletters circulated to members of the Professional Women's Network (see Part 5 feature) and similar organizations, and on the Internet. Write your ad.

3. Based on the job description you prepared, develop five traditional and five behavioral questions you can use as you conduct telephone interviews with candidates.

4. Respond favorably to the following e-mail from Sarah King, Instructor at Red River Vocational College:

    As I mentioned when you spoke to my Office Technology class last week, Red River is hosting a career fair on March 22

    and 23. The fair would be a good time to meet students and promote your business. Here are the details:

    Location: Gymnasium

    Time: 8 a.m. to 4 p.m. (setup March 21, 5–7 p.m.)

    Cost: $25 (includes table with skirting, 2 chairs, back curtain)

    If you're interested, I'll forward your name and address to those who are organizing the event.

5. The career fair was a very positive experience. Prepare the text of an e-mail thanking Sarah for suggesting you attend (sking09@redriver.edu).

6. Prepare the text of a form message to be sent to each applicant acknowledging his or her application.

7. Prepare the text of a form message to be sent to the applicants you will not interview.

8. Prepare the text of a form message to be sent to the people you interviewed but will not hire.

Business English Seminars

seminar a

Every word in a sentence has a use or function. Knowing word functions will enable you to select the right word, which in turn will help you communicate your ideas effectively. Your understanding of the parts of speech will aid you in selecting the right word at the right time. The eight parts of speech are as follows:

1. **Verb.** A word or phrase that describes the action or state of being (or condition) of the subject
2. **Noun.** A word that names a person, place, or thing
3. **Pronoun.** A word that takes the place of a noun
4. **Adjective.** A word that describes or modifies a noun or pronoun
5. **Adverb.** A word that describes or modifies a verb, an adjective, or another adverb
6. **Preposition.** A word that connects a noun or pronoun to other words in the sentence
7. **Conjunction.** A word that joins words, phrases, or clauses
8. **Interjection.** A word that expresses surprise, emotion, or strong feeling and is not related to other words in the sentence

NOTE SA.1
Knowledge of parts of speech will aid you in communicating.

Verbs

The verb is the most important part of speech in a sentence. It expresses an action or a state of being. Every complete sentence must have a verb. Some sentences—compound, complex, and compound-complex—have more than one verb. A simple sentence may contain a compound verb. (Types of sentences are discussed in Seminar B.) When you are constructing sentences, remember that you should build each sentence around the verb.

NOTE SA.2
A verb is the most important part of speech.

Verb Types

Sentences are constructed using two types of verbs. The two types of verbs are action verbs and state-of-being verbs.

ACTION VERBS

An **action verb** expresses an act. It adds power and precision to your communication. *Create, invest, lose, negotiate, organize, praise,* and *buy* are examples of action verbs. The action verb is italicized in the following examples:

NOTE SA.3
Action verbs are powerful.

> I *check* my e-mail at least twice a day.
> The company *liquidated* its assets.
> Jason *designed* the technology survey last week.

STATE-OF-BEING VERBS

NOTE SA.4

State-of-being verbs are
used to link parts of
sentences.

A **state-of-being verb** expresses the five senses (*hear, smell, see, taste,* and *touch*). Other state-of-being verbs include *is, am, are, was, were, seem, appear, will be,* and *have been*. A state-of-being verb is also called a *linking verb*. These verbs join or link one part of a sentence to another. State-of-being verbs are less powerful and less precise than action verbs. The state-of-being verbs are in italics in the following examples:

> The road repair *will be* completed in January.
> The presidential election *is* history.
> Business *is* returning to normal after Hurricane Katrina.

Verb Tense

NOTE SA.5

Verb tense indicates the
time that action occurs.

Verb tense indicates the time that action occurs. Six verb tense forms are used to indicate time. The six tenses are categorized into two groups—simple tense and perfect tense.

SIMPLE TENSE

NOTE SA.6

The three simple tenses are
present, past, and future.

The simple tenses are present, past, and future. The time of action or state of being of each simple tense is designated by its name.

NOTE SA.7

Present tense expresses
current and continuing
action or general truths.

Present Tense. A **present tense verb** expresses action that is going on at the present time or action that is continuing or habitual. Present tense verbs also may be used to indicate general truths. Verbs showing present tense are in italics in the following examples:

> Athena *is hiring* a virtual assistant. (present time)
> Deanna *tallies* the sales for the department at the end of each day. (continuing)
> Fax machines *facilitate* communication within organizations. (general truths)

NOTE SA.8

Past tense expresses
completed action.

Past Tense. A **past tense verb** indicates action that has been completed. Verbs in the past tense have two forms—regular and irregular. The past tense of regular verbs is formed by adding *-d* or *-ed*. The past tense of irregular verbs is formed by changing the root word. *Regular* and *irregular verbs* in the past tense are shown in italics in these examples:

> Javier *asked* for a raise. (regular—*ask* [root word] + ed)
> Javier *saved* 10 percent of his paycheck each month. (regular—*save* [root word] + *d*)
> Javier *spoke* to a group of high school students about accounting careers. (irregular—root word is *speak*)

NOTE SA.9

Future tense expresses
expected action.

Future Tense. A **future tense verb** is used to indicate actions that are expected to occur in the future. Future tense is formed by using *will* before the present tense form of the verb. The following sentences show verbs in the future tense in italics:

> *Will* the company picnic *be held* on the 4th of July?
> Christine *will send* a copy of her itinerary to Mr. Jepsen.

PERFECT TENSE

A **perfect tense verb** shows action that has been completed at the time the statement is made. The perfect tense requires a form of the verb *have*, along with the past participle of the main verb. (Participles are discussed at the end of this section.) The perfect tenses are present perfect, past perfect, and future perfect.

NOTE SA.10
The three perfect tenses are present perfect, past perfect, and future perfect.

Present Perfect Tense. A **present perfect tense verb** refers to an action begun in the past and completed in the present. Present perfect tense may also refer to habitual or repeated past action. This tense is formed by adding *has* or *have* to the past participle of the main verb. The following examples show verbs in the present perfect tense in italics:

NOTE SA.11
Present perfect tense = *has* or *have* + past participle.

> Mr. Thompson *has served* as the company president for 15 years.
> She *has rented* an apartment near the beach.
> The CEO *has written* many letters to the stockholders.

Past Perfect Tense. A **past perfect tense verb** refers to an action that was completed before another event in the past occurred. This tense is formed by adding *had* to the past participle of the main verb. The verbs in the past perfect tense are in italics in the following examples:

NOTE SA.12
Past perfect tense = *had* + past participle.

> Mr. Thompson *had served* as the company president before his retirement.
> She *had looked* at several apartments before deciding on the one near the beach.
> The CEO *had written* many letters to the stockholders prior to the merger.

Future Perfect Tense. A **future perfect tense verb** is used to express an action that will be completed before a stated time in the future. This tense is formed by adding *shall have* or *will have* to the past participle of the main verb. Examples of verbs in the future perfect tense are in italics in the following sentences:

NOTE SA.13
Future perfect tense = *shall have* or *will have* + past participle.

> Mr. Thompson *will have served* as the company president for 15 years on January 1, 2007.
> She *will have moved* into our apartment before school starts.
> By the end of the quarter, the CEO *will have written* many letters to the stockholders.

Verb Voice

Voice is the term used to indicate whether the subject is doing or receiving the action. Sentence meaning and emphasis are communicated through the proper use of verb voice. The two voices of verbs are active and passive.

NOTE SA.14
The two voices of verbs are active and passive.

ACTIVE VOICE

When the subject of the sentence performs the action, the verb is in the **active voice.** In business communication the active voice usually is preferred because it is more direct and concise. Sentences that use verbs in the active voice identify the one performing the action. The following examples demonstrate how the verbs, shown in italics, are used in the active voice:

NOTE SA.15
The subject performs the action in the active voice.

> Upon returning from a business trip, Illyana *completed* her expense report.
> Elena *is applying* for the sales manager's position.

PASSIVE VOICE

NOTE **SA.16**
The subject receives the
action in the passive voice.

A verb is in the **passive voice** when the subject of the sentence receives the action. The passive voice is used sparingly in business communication. It is used when the subject is unknown or when the writer wants to soften the message to avoid making an accusation. Another use of the passive voice is to emphasize the action rather than the person who performed the action. The passive voice can also be used to eliminate a gender pronoun. It provides variety in sentence construction and keeps reader interest.

Passive voice verbs require a form of *be* (*am, is, are, was, were, been*) as a helping verb, along with a past participle of the verb. Uses of verbs in the passive voice are shown in italics in the following examples:

Donald *was notified* of his eviction by a process server. (Emphasis is on being notified rather than being evicted.)

The list of applicants *was reviewed* by a hiring committee. (The main point is what was reviewed—the list of applicants—not by whom it was reviewed—a hiring committee.)

The books *were audited* before the merger. (A biased statement was avoided by not saying, "He audited the books before the merger.")

Changing the verb voice from active to passive does not change the verb tense from present to past. The tense in the passive voice is expressed by its auxiliary (helping) verb. The following examples show verbs (in italics) in the passive voice in several different tenses:

Training sessions *are offered* each Thursday and Friday. (*passive voice*, present tense)

The company *offers* training sessions each Thursday and Friday. (*active voice*, present tense)

Training sessions *were offered* last summer. (*passive voice*, past tense)

The company *offered* training sessions last summer. (*active voice*, past tense)

Training sessions *will be offered* during the morning in the spring. (*passive voice*, future tense)

The company *will offer* training sessions during the morning in the spring. (*active voice*, future tense)

Verb Mood

NOTE **SA.17**
The three verb moods are
indicative, imperative, and
subjunctive.

Communicators use **verb mood** to express facts, commands, or conditions. The three moods are indicative, imperative, and subjunctive.

INDICATIVE MOOD

NOTE **SA.18**
Use indicative mood to ask
questions or make factual
statements.

The **indicative mood** is used to make statements or to ask questions involving facts. Business writers use verbs in this mood more than in the imperative or subjunctive mood. Examples are in italics in these sentences:

The new version of Microsoft Windows *will be* available in February.
The company *is expanding* into the Northeast.
Are you *going* to the opening session?

IMPERATIVE MOOD

NOTE **SA.19**
Commands, instructions,
and requests are in the
imperative mood.

The **imperative mood** is used to give commands, give instructions, or make requests. Sentences in the imperative mood usually have *you* understood as the subject, and, therefore, it is omitted. Verbs used in the imperative mood are shown in italics in the following sentences:

Write this down before you forget it.
E-mail Katie about the acquisition.

SUBJUNCTIVE MOOD

The **subjunctive mood** can be used to express a wish, a doubt, or an unlikely condition. This mood is rarely used today. Here are some examples; the subjunctive mood verbs are in italics:

If he *were* my father, I would follow his advice. (unlikely condition)
Should the meeting *end* by two, we will be able to see the first pitch thrown out. (doubt)
I wish it *would* quit raining. (wish)

NOTE SA.20
The subjunctive mood is used rarely.

Verbals

A **verbal** is a verb form used as a noun, an adjective, or an adverb. Verbals cannot function as verbs and do not express action or state of being. The three verbals are the infinitive, the gerund, and the participle.

NOTE SA.21
The three verbals are the infinitive, the gerund, and the participle.

INFINITIVE

The **infinitive** is formed by placing the word *to* in front of the present tense of the verb. Several examples are *to rent, to judge,* and *to hire.* An infinitive can function as a noun, an adjective, or an adverb, but it can never be used as a verb. The infinitive is in italics and its use is in parentheses in each of the following sentences. (Some parts of speech are identified in examples in Seminar A and are discussed in depth in Seminar B.)

NOTE SA.22
Infinitive = *to* + present tense of verb.

NOTE SA.23
Infinitives are used as nouns, adjectives, or adverbs.

To remodel her kitchen is Judy's dream. (noun—subject)
Joseph plans *to travel* to Australia this summer. (noun—direct object)
Carmen's dream *to retire* early hinges on her investments. (adjective)
Beth Ann has agreed to replace the lost combination lock. (adverb)

GERUND

A **gerund** is a present tense verb form that can function only as a noun. It is formed by adding *-ing* to a verb. *Typing, creating,* and *manufacturing* are examples of gerunds. Gerunds may be used in phrases consisting of a gerund, an object, and words modifying the object. In the following sentences the phrases are in italics, the gerunds are in bold, and their uses are in parentheses:

NOTE SA.24
Gerunds are used only as nouns.

NOTE SA.25
Gerund = verb + *-ing.*

Designing *brochures* is the responsibility of the graphic arts department. (subject)
Jessie's hobby is **collecting** *Elvis memorabilia.* (predicate nominative)
They enjoy **camping** *in national parks.* (direct object)
Hal was awarded the prize for **selling** *the most fitness club memberships.* (object of preposition)
Mikki, **performing** *in the play,* is the youngest member of the cast. (appositive)

PARTICIPLE

A **participle** is a verb form that can be used as an adjective or as part of a verb phrase. The three types of participles are present, past, and perfect.

NOTE SA.26
Participles are used as adjectives or as parts of verb phrases.

NOTE SA.27
Present participle = present
tense verb + -ing.

Present Participle. The **present participle verb** is always formed by adding -*ing* to the present tense of a verb. The participial phrase is in italics, and the present participle is in bold in each of the following examples:

> All students **planning** *to take an online class* must register by August 10. (adjective)
> Sarah is **renting** *her apartment* to a friend while she travels this summer. (verb)

NOTE SA.28
Past participle
usually = present tense
verb + -d or -ed.

NOTE SA.29
Sometimes the root word
is changed.

Past Participle. A **past participle verb** usually is formed by adding -*d* or -*ed* to the present tense of a regular verb. Irregular verbs form their past participles by changing the spelling of their root words. The past participle is in italics in each of the following examples:

> Last week Nancy *moved* the ribbon display into the quick sale aisle. (verb—regular verb)
> The gardener will be trimming the *overgrown* bushes in the front yard. (adjective—irregular verb)

NOTE SA.30
The perfect participle is
always an adjective.

NOTE SA.31
Perfect participle = *having*
+ past participle.

Perfect Participle. A **perfect participle verb** is always used as an adjective and is formed by combining *having* with the past participle. The perfect participles are in italics in the following sentences:

> Brad, *having displayed* too much anger, quickly left the room.
> Shayla, *having experienced* a tornado before, remained calm.

Nouns

NOTE SA.32
Nouns are words that
identify persons, places,
and things.

A noun names a person, place, or thing. The two main groups of nouns are proper nouns and common nouns.

Proper Nouns

NOTE SA.33
Proper nouns are specific.

A **proper noun** names a particular person, place, or thing. Proper nouns are always capitalized. *Yosemite National Park, Bill Gates, Dallas,* and *USA Today* are examples of proper nouns.

Common Nouns

NOTE SA.34
Common nouns are
general.

A **common noun** identifies a general class of persons, places, things, or ideas. Common nouns are not capitalized. Examples of common nouns are *employee, house, computer, umbrella, college,* and *bridge*. The three classes of common nouns are concrete, abstract, and collective.

CONCRETE NOUNS

NOTE SA.35
Concrete nouns are precise.

A **concrete noun** identifies those things that you can see, touch, hear, taste, or smell. Words such as *director, apple, glass, sand, castle,* and *train* are concrete nouns. Concrete nouns are precise and easily understood, which makes them effective for business communication.

ABSTRACT NOUNS

NOTE SA.36
Abstract nouns are vague.

An **abstract noun** identifies an idea, an emotion, a quality, or a belief. Examples of abstract nouns are *progress, courage, patience, love, surprise, anger,* and *enthusiasm*.

People's opinions and feelings differ in degree; therefore, abstract nouns are less precise than concrete nouns. Abstract nouns should be used infrequently in business communication because they are more difficult to understand than concrete nouns.

COLLECTIVE NOUNS

A **collective noun** is a group of persons or a collection of things. It is normally treated as a singular noun because the group is acting as one body; however, a collective noun would be treated as a plural noun if the group members were acting as individuals. Collective nouns include *family, faculty, department, audience, team,* and *committee.*

NOTE SA.37
Collective nouns identify a group.

Compound Nouns

A **compound noun** is two or more words used to identify one person, place, or thing. A compound noun may be written as one or more words, or it may be hyphenated. When in doubt, consult a dictionary for the correct spelling. Compound nouns can be classified under any of the three classes of common nouns. Examples of compound nouns in each class follow:

NOTE SA.38
Compound nouns are multiple words used to name singular nouns.

Concrete:	bulletin board, board member, mother-in-law
Abstract:	self-esteem, common sense, well-being, life cycle
Collective:	garden club, board of directors, administrative staff

Plural Forms of Nouns

A **plural noun** is used to identify two or more persons, places, or things. The plural of most nouns is formed by adding *-s* or *-es* to the singular form of the noun. Because there are so many ways of forming plurals, consult a dictionary if a question arises. Examples of different ways that nouns are formed as plurals include computer, *computers;* wolf, *wolves;* territory, *territories;* attorney, *attorneys;* brother-in-law, *brothers-in-law;* deer, *deer;* and tomato, *tomatoes.*

NOTE SA.39
A plural noun is normally formed by adding *-s* or *-es* to a singular noun.

Possessive Forms of Nouns

A **possessive noun** is used to show possession or ownership. The possessive form of a noun is indicated by using an apostrophe. The following general guidelines will help you correctly form possessive nouns in written communication:

NOTE SA.40
Possessive nouns show ownership.

1. The possessive of a singular noun not ending with an *s* or a *z* sound is formed by adding *apostrophe s.*
   secretary's desk   lawyer's brief
2. The possessive of a singular noun ending with an *s* or a *z* sound is formed by adding *apostrophe s* to a noun with one syllable and by adding only an *apostrophe* to a noun with more than one syllable.
   Sims's plane   Dickens' book
3. The possessive of a plural noun ending with an *s* or a *z* sound is formed by adding an *apostrophe.*
   girls' lockers   actors' guild
4. The possessive of a compound noun is formed by placing the *apostrophe* or *apostrophe s* after the final word or word element.
   sergeant-at-arms's itinerary   all general managers' budgets

NOTE SA.41
Placement of an apostrophe and addition of *-s* to show possession depends on the noun and the ending sound.

NOTE SA.42
For compound nouns, possession is shown after the last word.

NOTE SA.43
Joint or individual possession of objects influences placement of *apostrophe* or *apostrophe s.*

5. When two or more people share ownership of an object or objects, add an *apostrophe* or *apostrophe s* to the final name.

   Jim and Kristy's horse   Tim and Stewartz' investments

6. When two or more people each own separate objects, possession is indicated by adding an *apostrophe* or *apostrophe s* to each noun.

   Jim's and Kristy's horses   Tim's and Stewartz' investments

---

Pronouns

NOTE SA.44
Pronouns replace nouns.

NOTE SA.45
Pronouns may be classified as personal, relative, interrogative, indefinite, demonstrative, reflexive, or intensive.

Pronouns are used in place of nouns. Pronouns make your writing more interesting because you do not repeat the noun. There are seven types of pronouns: personal, relative, interrogative, indefinite, demonstrative, reflexive, and intensive. Each type of pronoun performs a different function in a sentence.

Personal Pronouns

NOTE SA.46
Personal pronouns refer to specific people or things.

A **personal pronoun** is a substitute for a noun that refers to a specific person or thing. Personal pronouns change their form when they perform different functions and appear in different parts of a sentence. The different forms are called *case forms*. The three case forms for personal pronouns are the nominative, the possessive, and the objective.

NOMINATIVE CASE

NOTE SA.47
Nominative case is used when the pronoun is the subject.

The **nominative case** is used when the pronoun functions as the subject of a sentence or a clause. The nominative case is also called the *subjective case*. Singular personal pronouns in the nominative case are *I, you, he, she,* and *it.* Plural personal pronouns in the nominative case are *we, you,* and *they.* The nominative case is also used when the pronoun follows a linking verb. The italics in the following sentences illustrate the uses of nominative case pronouns:

> *I* will not attend the annual meeting. (subject of sentence)
> When *we* close on the new office building, Neil will announce the purchase to the public in a news conference. (subject of dependent clause)
> It was *they* who surveyed the property. (*it*—subject of sentence; *they*—follows linking verb)

POSSESSIVE CASE

NOTE SA.48
Possessive case shows ownership.

The **possessive case** is used when the pronoun shows possession or ownership. The possessive case does not need an apostrophe. Singular possessive pronouns are *my, mine, your, yours, his, her, hers,* and *its.* Plural possessive pronouns are *our, ours, your, yours, their,* and *theirs.* Several examples of pronouns in the possessive case are shown in italics in the following sentences:

> *His* car was involved in an accident. (shows whose car)
> What are *your* plans for this weekend? (shows whose plans)
> If the report is not yours, it must be *hers.* (shows whose report)
> *Our* vacation was changed because of the weather. (shows whose vacation)
> The company updated *its* logo. (shows whose logo)

OBJECTIVE CASE

The **objective case** is used when the pronoun functions as an object in a sentence, clause, or phrase. Singular pronouns in the objective case are *me, you, him, her,* and *it.* Plural objective pronouns are *us, you,* and *them.* The following sentences show in italics pronouns that are performing these functions:

> Shelia directed *me* to my seat in the stadium. (direct object of a sentence)
> Troy threw the pass to *him.* (object of preposition)
> When we met *him,* Victor was working for our major competitor. (direct object of a clause)

NOTE SA.49
Objective case is used when the pronoun is an object.

Relative Pronouns

A **relative pronoun** connects a group of words containing a subject and verb (a clause) to a noun or pronoun. *Who, whom, whose, which,* and *that* are the relative pronouns. If the word to which the pronoun refers is a person, use *who, whom,* or *whose.* Use *who* when the pronoun referring to a person is in the nominative case and *whom* when the pronoun is in the objective case. Use *which* or *that* if the pronoun refers to a thing. Relative pronouns are in italics in the following sentences:

> The player *who* sacks the most quarterbacks will get the award.
> Patricia doesn't know *whom* her supervisor has chosen to lead the task force.
> In case of a disagreement, *whose* story will you believe?
> The house, *which* was recently painted, is beautiful.
> The bids *that* were submitted were too high.

NOTE SA.50
Relative pronouns link clauses to nouns or pronouns.

Interrogative Pronouns

An **interrogative pronoun** is used within a question. *Who, whose, whom, which,* and *what* are the interrogative pronouns. Pronouns precede verbs in questions. Like other pronouns within sentences, they function as subjects, objects, modifiers, and subject complements. The italics in the following sentences illustrate how interrogative pronouns are used:

> *Who* cut Robert's hair? (subject)
> *Whose* purse was left in the conference room? (modifier)
> *Whom* do you think the Cowboys will hire as a placekicker? (object)
> *Which* bookkeeper handled Anderson's account? (modifier)
> *What* was the reasoning for the reorganization of your department? (subject complement)

NOTE SA.51
Interrogative pronouns ask questions.

Indefinite Pronouns

An **indefinite pronoun** is used to make a general statement about individuals or things. Indefinite pronouns include *each, anyone, one, several, both, many, everyone,* and *nobody.* The indefinite pronouns are in italics in the following sentences:

> *Each* project manager reports to the general manager.
> Did *anyone* see the meteor shower last night?
> *One* of the employees invests 10 percent of his paycheck in the stock market.

NOTE SA.52
Indefinite pronouns do not specify a particular person or thing.

Either Joan or Paul will meet you at the airport tomorrow.
None of the manuscripts was mailed in time to meet the deadline.

Demonstrative Pronouns

NOTE **SA.53**
Demonstrative pronouns substitute for specific nouns.

A **demonstrative pronoun** is used to indicate a specific person, place, or thing. The four demonstrative pronouns are *this, these, that,* and *those.* Demonstrative pronouns are in italics in these sentences:

This budget will need to be revised to maintain a 15 percent reserve.
These tires will last much longer than the old ones.
Is *that* the best solution to the problem?
Are *those* the employees who earned the bonuses?

Compound Personal Pronouns

NOTE **SA.54**
Compound personal pronouns are intensive or reflexive.

A **compound personal pronoun** has the suffix *self* or *selves.* A compound personal pronoun may be an intensive or a reflexive pronoun. *Intensive pronouns* are used for emphasis, whereas *reflexive pronouns* reflect the action of the verb to the subject or to a noun or pronoun in the sentence. Examples of intensive and reflexive pronouns, in italics, follow:

The president *himself* welcomed each person to the celebration. (intensive—emphasizes a noun)
Carolyn will key the report *herself.* (intensive—emphasizes a noun)
The birds saw *themselves* reflected in the stream. (reflexive—refers to the subject, a noun)

Adjectives

NOTE **SA.55**
Adjectives modify nouns and pronouns and make them more precise.

An **adjective** provides additional information about a noun or a pronoun. Adjectives make the meaning of the noun or pronoun more exact by answering such questions as *which one, how many,* and *what kind.* Adjectives also are called *modifiers.*

Adjectives may be regular or irregular. *Regular adjectives* generally are one-syllable words with *-er* or *-est* added when making comparisons. Irregular adjectives usually contain two or more syllables and use *less, least, more,* or *most* when making comparisons.

Degrees of Comparison in Adjectives

NOTE **SA.56**
The three degrees of comparison for adjectives are positive, comparative, and superlative.

Adjectives change form to show degrees of comparison. There are three degrees of comparison: positive, comparative, and superlative. Examples of the degrees of comparison of adjectives are shown in Figure SA.1.

POSITIVE DEGREE

NOTE **SA.57**
Positive degree describes one noun.

The **positive degree** is used to describe one item or one group of items. The positive form is the form used in dictionary definitions. The adjective in the positive form is in italics in the following examples:

His computer has a *large* screen.
The production line at PermaBlend is *efficient*.
The technology budget for this year is *high*.

COMPARATIVE DEGREE

The **comparative degree** is used to show the difference between two items. The comparative degree is formed by adding *-er* to a regular adjective or by adding the words *more* or *less* to an irregular adjective. The adjectives used in the preceding examples in the positive degree are shown in the following examples in the comparative degree:

His computer has a *larger* screen than yours.
The production line at PermaBlend is *more efficient* than the one at Solution One.
The technology budget for this year is *higher* than it was last year.

NOTE SA.58
Comparative degree compares two nouns.

SUPERLATIVE DEGREE

The **superlative degree** is used to compare three or more items. It can also be used for emphasis. The superlative degree is formed by adding *-est* to a regular adjective or by adding *most* or *least* to an irregular adjective. The adjectives used in the previous examples are now shown in the superlative degree:

His computer has the *largest* screen available.
The production line at PermaBlend is the *most efficient* I have seen.
The technology budget for this year is the *highest* it has been in the last five years.

NOTE SA.59
Superlative degree compares three or more nouns.

Absolute Adjectives

An **absolute adjective** is always in the superlative degree. Therefore, it cannot be compared. For example, if the design of a building is *perfect*, another building cannot have a *more perfect* design. Some absolute adjectives are *complete*, *unique*, *right*, *final*, *full*, *square*, *round*, *correct*, *never*, *dead*, and *empty*. Absolute adjectives, however, can be quantified by using the words *more nearly* and *most nearly*.

The portfolio is *complete*.
Jessica's portfolio is more *nearly complete* (not more complete) than mine.
Jessica's portfolio is the *most nearly complete* (not most complete) of any in our class.

NOTE SA.60
Absolute adjectives are always in the superlative degree.

Positive	Comparative	Superlative
strong	stronger	strongest
easy	easier	easiest
good	better	best
effecive	more effective	most effective
favorable	less favorable	least favorable

FIG SA.1
Degrees of Comparison of Adjectives

Compound Adjectives

A **compound adjective** is two or more words used together to describe a single noun or pronoun. Often compound adjectives are hyphenated; sometimes they are not. When compound adjectives are shown hyphenated in the dictionary, they are considered *permanent compounds* and should always be hyphenated. Compound nouns used as adjectives and shown as *open compounds* in the dictionary are not hyphenated. Compound adjectives not shown in the dictionary are referred to as *temporary compounds* and are hyphenated when they appear *before* the noun or pronoun they describe but are not hyphenated when they appear *after* the words they describe. Consult a dictionary for hyphenation of compound adjectives. Compound adjectives appear in italics in the following sentences:

Mike is a *well-respected* attorney. (permanent compound adjective)
Sylvia opened a *money market* account after she was promoted. (open compound adjective)
A *high-speed* fax machine is a necessity for a business today. (temporary compound adjective used before the noun)
Fax machines that operate at a *high speed* are a necessity in business today. (temporary compound adjective used after the noun)

Articles

Although classified as adjectives, *a*, *an*, and *the* are also called **articles.** The article *the* is used to denote specific nouns or pronouns. The articles *a* and *an* are used to denote general nouns or pronouns. The articles are in italics in the following examples:

Zoe attended *the* rock concert.
Zoe attended *a* concert.
Zoe attended *an* uplifting concert.

When the word following the article begins with a consonant sound (*store, beach, car,* etc.), you use *a*; use *an* if the word begins with a vowel sound (*hour, exaggeration, exciting,* etc.). Examples of articles used with words beginning with consonant and vowel sounds are shown in italics:

An administrative assistant will answer your phone when you are away from your desk.
Cassandra is *an* honest individual.
David was *an* excellent athlete and *a* passionate competitor.

Adverbs

Adverbs are modifiers that restrict, limit, or describe verbs, adjectives, or other adverbs. They answer questions such as *how, when, where, why, in what manner,* or *to what degree.* Many end in *-ly.* Examples of adverbs used as modifiers are shown in italics in the following sentences:

The sales dropped *drastically* during the month of November. (dropped *how?*)

A shareholders' meeting is held *annually*. (conducted *when?*)

Training for executives traveling to our Japanese location will be held *here* next week. (held *where?*)

The value of antique automobiles is increasing *extremely* fast. (increasing *how? fast; to what degree?* extremely)

Placement of Adverbs

An adverb may be a single word (speak *clearly*), a phrase (speak *in a clear manner*), or a clause (speak *as clearly as you can*). A single-word adverb can be placed before or after the word it modifies. Prepositional and infinitive phrases and clauses that function as adverbs usually follow the word they modify. An **adverbial clause,** which is a dependent clause that acts as an adverb, precedes the independent clause in a sentence. Seminar B contains a detailed discussion of phrases and clauses.

NOTE SA.64

The placement of an adverb depends on how it is used in the sentence.

Degrees of Adverbs

Some words that are used as adverbs as well as adjectives have positive, comparative, and superlative degrees of comparison. Examples of the degrees of comparison of adverbs are shown in Figure SA.2.

NOTE SA.65

Adverbs also have positive, comparative, and superlative degrees.

Prepositions

A **preposition** connects a noun or pronoun to another word in a sentence. The noun or pronoun that follows the preposition is called the **object of the preposition.** Some of the most frequently used prepositions are *about, after, at, before, by, during, for, from, in, of, on, over, to,* and *with.*

A word group containing a preposition and the object of the preposition is called a **prepositional phrase.** The following sentences illustrate prepositional phrases. The prepositions are in italics, and the object of each preposition is in bold.

NOTE SA.66

A preposition is a connector that needs an object.

NOTE SA.67

A prepositional phrase contains the preposition and its object.

Except *for* **Tuesday,** the office manager will be *in* the **office** all week.

The webmaster *for* our **company** is reviewing the website ensuring it is ADA compliant.

Include a letter *of* **recommendation** *with* your **resume** when you send it *to* **employers.**

Positive	Comparative	Superlative
late	later	latest
early	earlier	earliest
carefully	more carefully	most carefully
effective	less effective	least effective

FIGURE SA.2
Degrees of Comparison of Adverbs

Functions of Prepositional Phrases

NOTE **SA.68**
Prepositional phrases work
as adjectives and adverbs.

Prepositional phrases work as units in a sentence. They perform the functions of adjectives and adverbs and provide variety within the sentence. Examples of prepositional phrases that act as adjectives and adverbs are in italics in these examples:

> Taryn Jones *from the credit union* will speak *in my personal finance class* tomorrow. (The first prepositional phrase acts as an adjective modifying the proper noun *Taryn Jones*, and the second prepositional phrase acts as an adverb modifying the verb *will speak*.)
>
> Will you send the article *to the newspaper*? (The prepositional phrase as an adverb modifies the verb *send*.)
>
> LuAnn is going *to the lake with a friend*. (Both prepositional phrases act as adverbs. They modify the verb *is going*.)

Object of Preposition

NOTE **SA.69**
Objects of prepositions are
nouns or pronouns and can
be modified by adjectives.

As previously mentioned, the object of a preposition is a noun or pronoun that follows the preposition. The object of a preposition can be modified by an adjective, as in the example, "Belinda was proud of *her* grades."

Personal pronouns and *who* have unique objective forms. The objective form of *who* is *whom*. The personal pronouns are *me, us, you, him, her,* and *them*. The objects of the prepositions are in italics in these sentences:

> With *whom* did you work on the Smithers project?
> Did you send an e-mail to *me*?
> I received the most recent sales figures from *him*.
> I saw you at the theater with *him* and *her*.
> Steve designed the work station especially for *you*.
> Harry gave tomatoes to *them*.

Unnecessary Prepositions

NOTE **SA.70**
Omit unnecessary
prepositions within
sentences.

NOTE **SA.71**
Avoid ending a sentence
with a preposition.

Although prepositional phrases can be used effectively to make communication more interesting, effective business communicators avoid inserting extra prepositions within a sentence, choosing incorrect prepositions, or ending a sentence with a preposition. (Ending a sentence with a preposition is acceptable in oral communication if rearranging the sentence is awkward.)

Select prepositions carefully and use only those prepositions that clarify a sentence. The prepositions *to, of, at, for,* and *up* are frequently used unnecessarily. Examples of these uses are shown in italics in the following sentences:

> The team did not say where they were going *to*. (unnecessary preposition)
> The team did not say where they were going.
> The plate fell off *of* the table. (unnecessary preposition)
> The plate fell off the table.
> The mother did not know where her child was *at*. (unnecessary preposition)
> The mother did not know where her child was.
> Who is that phone call *for*? (incorrect)
> For whom is that phone call?
> He walked *up* to the statue and bowed *down* in respect. (unnecessary prepositions)
> He walked to the statue and bowed in respect.

Do you have any idea about what the meeting is? (awkward)

Do you have any idea what the meeting is about? (preferred)

Ellie had a difficult time choosing between chocolate swiss almond, toffee crunch, and tropical sherbert. (incorrect usage of preposition)

Ellie had a difficult time choosing among chocolate swiss almond, toffee crunch, and tropical sherbert. (correct usage of preposition)

NOTE SA.72
Conjunctions are connectors without objects.

Conjunctions

A **conjunction** is used to join words, phrases, and clauses. Conjunctions are also used to introduce clauses. Conjunctions are similar to prepositions in that they serve as connectors but are different in that they do not have objects. Conjunctions are classified as coordinate conjunctions, correlative conjunctions, and subordinate conjunctions. Coordinate and correlative conjunctions join grammatically equal word elements; subordinate conjunctions join grammatically unequal word elements.

Coordinate Conjunctions

A **coordinate conjunction** joins words, phrases, and independent clauses that are of equal importance or rank. Of equal importance or rank means that similar elements are connected; for example, adjectives are connected to adjectives and nouns are connected to nouns. Coordinate conjunctions include *and, but, or, nor, for, as,* and *yet*. The following examples show coordinate conjunctions (in italics) joining words, phrases, and independent clauses:

NOTE SA.73
The three classifications of conjunctions are coordinate, correlative, and subordinate.

NOTE SA.74
Coordinate conjunctions connect elements of equal rank.

Both supervisors *and* cashiers attended the seminar. (joins nouns)

The assistant worked quietly *and* efficiently. (joins adverbs)

The young man ran to the park *and* jumped over the fence to rescue his friend. (joins verbs)

They walked up one side *and* down the other. (joins prepositional phrases)

You have been preapproved for a $350,000 loan, *but* this preapproval will expire on July 15. (joins independent clauses)

Correlative Conjunctions

A **correlative conjunction** is paired with another correlative conjunction to connect two parallel words, phrases, or clauses. The most common correlative conjunction pairs are *both . . . and, either . . . or, neither . . . nor, not . . . but, not only . . . but also,* and *whether . . . or.* Examples, shown in italics, follow:

NOTE SA.75
A correlative conjunction is a pair of connectors that link sentence elements.

Earl *not only* earned a letter in baseball *but also* graduated with honors. (connects verb phrases)

You may have *either* a salad *or* a cup of soup with your main course. (connects nouns)

Christie informed her mother that she would *either* wash the car *or* mow the yard. (connects clauses)

A common difficulty with using correlative conjunctions involves *parallelism*. Be sure that connected elements are equal in rank or parallel in grammatical form. A detailed discussion of parallelism is in Seminar B. The following sentences demonstrate a few parallelism errors. The correlative conjunctions are in italics.

NOTE SA.76
Be sure that connected elements are parallel.

At 11 o'clock Joe will *either* go to class *or* he will eat lunch. (Incorrect—*either* precedes the verb *go*, but *or* precedes the pronoun *he*.)

At 11 o'clock Joe will *either* go to class *or* eat lunch. (Correct—both conjunctions precede verbs.)

Cyndi *not only* cleaned the house *but also* the garage. (Incorrect—*not only* precedes the verb *cleaned* and *but also* precedes the noun garage.)

Cyndi cleaned *not only* the house *but also* the garage. (Correct—both conjunctions precede nouns.)

Subordinate Conjunctions

NOTE SA.77
Subordinate conjunctions connect clauses of unequal rank.

A **subordinate conjunction** joins a subordinate (dependent) clause to the main clause—that is, a dependent clause to an independent clause. Some subordinate conjunctions are *after, although, because, before, since, when, while, where, if, whether, though,* and *until.* The subordinate conjunctions are in italics and the main clauses are bold in the following examples:

Before you submit your report, **check to see that all documentation is included.**
Julia was promoted to vice president *because she was the most qualified.*
The sales projections were adjusted *after the sales territories were redrawn.*

Interjections

NOTE SA.78
Interjections express strong emotions.

An **interjection** expresses strong emotion or feeling. It is not related grammatically to any other word in a sentence. Most interjections do not have any meaning if they are taken out of the message context. An interjection is normally punctuated with an exclamation point. Interjections are seldom used in business writing, but they may be used in oral communication and in written advertising material. The interjections are in italics in the following examples:

No! That is not right.
Wow! Those flowers are beautiful.
Stop! You can't do that.

Application Exercises

1. Identify each verb and indicate whether it is an action or a state-of-being verb. Also indicate whether the verb is in active or passive voice.
   a. The inspection team did an outstanding job.
   b. Because of the expected high temperatures for this weekend, the local power company has asked customers to conserve energy.
   c. The legal papers were delivered to the courthouse five minutes before the deadline.
   d. Antique collectors cherish things from the past.
   e. Did the computer operator detect the virus?
   f. Sam planned a weekend of skiing to celebrate his new promotion.
   g. The proposed regulation establishes limits on how long an airplane can be exposed to snow or freezing rain before being deiced again.
   h. Garden herbs grow best in rich, moist, and well-drained soil.

     i.   The telecommunication office will be closed for the holiday on Monday.

     j.   After the computers were purchased, they were shipped to Dallas.

2. Identify each verb or verb phrase and indicate whether it is in the indicative, imperative, or subjunctive mood.

     a.   If I should win the lottery, I would quit my job.

     b.   Take off your shoes before entering the house.

     c.   Stop the truck immediately.

     d.   Will the new research facility in Durham be operational by August 15?

     e.   Mr. Lee has been late for work four days this week.

     f.   If the stock rises to $90, it will split.

     g.   Market Day is held at the fairgrounds the first Saturday of each month from March through December.

3. Identify each verbal and indicate its form (infinitive, gerund, or participle).

     a.   Asking if you may join people already seated at a table is common courtesy.

     b.   Tim asked his boss for an increase in salary.

     c.   Having won the local contest, Henry will advance to the state level.

     d.   The television network decided to take the lead in limiting pornography in its programs.

     e.   Terry's part-time job in college is to deliver singing telegrams.

     f.   Checking figures for accuracy and preparing reports based on those figures are just two of the daily tasks of an accountant.

     g.   Instead of asking for help in unjamming the printer, Mindy broke it.

     h.   Attending class is an important part of college life.

4. Determine the correct verb form and tense of the verbs that are italicized in the following sentences. Example: The announcement of the resignation *shake* the building. *Shook—past tense*

     a.   Taylor *requests* an update of her retirement benefits last week.

     b.   At the shareholders' meeting yesterday it *is* announced that PPL Corporation has been purchased by New York Tents.

     c.   Next month Taryn *began* working at Pyramid Whole Grains.

     d.   Last week the team *goes* to Boston.

     e.   The city *surveys* the amount of traffic on our street over the next two months to determine if stop signs or speed bumps are needed.

     f.   By the end of the decade, all of Bill and Cindy's children *will have went* to college.

     g.   Morgan *teaches* self-defense classes last semester.

     h.   Geri and I *went* on vacation next month.

     i.   Ty *studies* for his statistics final this coming weekend.

     j.   George fell and *breaks* his leg while he and Maggie *were* climbing in Yosemite National Park.

5. Identify each adjective and adverb in the following sentences, and indicate how the word is used (adjective or adverb). Indicate the word that each adjective or adverb modifies.

     a.   You can easily purchase airline tickets online and directly charge the cost to a credit card.

     b.   Bill was a trustworthy employee who performed his duties admirably.

     c.   Profits were rapidly sliding, and stockholders were becoming increasingly alarmed.

     d.   Their English garden was beautifully designed and perfectly manicured.

     e.   Networks buy new shows from Hollywood studios and later resell them to local television stations.

     f.   The first storm of the season brought much snow.

     g.   The time-lapse photo very clearly showed the third ring around the planet.

     h.   It's a good time to consider buying a new car.

     i.   One good sign is that revenues have picked up dramatically.

     j.   Why did Anne not graduate with her classmates?

6. Common errors occur in the following sentences. Find and correct the errors. Explain each correction.

     a.   Do you know where the children are going to?

     b.   The Habitat for Humanity volunteers painted not only the exterior of the house but also they painted the house's interior.

    c. If I was nominated for the office, I will run a fair campaign.

    d. Larry Page and Sergey Brin are well known entrepreneurs in the technology field.

    e. The workers will either accept the contract or they will strike.

    f. Between Chase and Anita, Chase is the best student.

    g. Where are you sending the truck to?

    h. The employees of Swift Truck Line hired an auditor to investigate the companies pension plan.

    i. John shaped and molded the image of African Americans worldwide.

    j. The laser pointer fell off of the podium during my presentation.

7. Identify the part of speech for each word in the following sentences.

    a. Wow! My stock tripled in value.

    b. My law instructor graded the midterm exam and posted the scores on his office door.

    c. Worldwide, stocks rose in dollar terms.

    d. I had an alarm system installed in my car.

    e. Where did Robin go to school?

    f. Today's hike was longer and required some tricky footwork crossing a beaver dam.

    g. Grant was not well prepared for the interview questions I asked him.

    h. Prior to investing in stocks, an individual should have a thorough understanding of economics.

    i. Did the storm move through the area before midnight?

    j. My short-term career goal is to graduate from college.

MESSAGE ANALYSIS

Correct the following message to reflect (a) correct verb form and tense of the verb in parentheses, (b) proper comparative adjectives, (c) correct placement of adverbs, (d) correct use of prepositions, and (e) correct spelling of words. After correcting all the errors listed above, key a copy of the grammatically correct message and submit it to your instructor.

Cell phones (is) a way of life two day. They (contribute) to (keep) us connected and safe. As cell phone users, we (must recognize) that technology and manners (is) compatable with each other

Cell phone etiquette (follow) the same rules as all good manners. When using the cell phone, softly (speek), (respect) the personal space of others, and (do) not interupt a face to face conversation for a cell call.

(Ask) yourself this question: (Do) you really want to be available 24/7/365? (Do) (be) available all the time make you more truly productive. May be it just (spread) the productivity out over a longer time period. Re-member, the most you (makes) yourself available, the more available everyone will (expect) you to be.

seminar b

A **sentence** is a group of related words that have a subject and a predicate and express a complete thought. A sentence is the basic unit for organizing messages.

You can improve your ability to communicate by becoming familiar with sentence construction and learning how to organize sentence components. Construction of grammatically correct sentences improves your message clarity, expresses your meaning precisely, and increases your message credibility.

NOTE SB.1
A sentence expresses a complete thought.

NOTE SB.2
Correct grammar provides clarity, precision, and credibility.

Parts of Sentences

A sentence expresses a statement, a command, a question, a wish, or an exclamation. The starting point in understanding how to structure sentences is to know their two essential parts: the subject and the predicate.

NOTE SB.3
The main parts of a sentence are the subject and the predicate.

The Subject

The **subject** is the part of a sentence that tells who or what is being discussed. There are three types of subjects: complete, simple, and compound.

NOTE SB.4
The subject tells who or what is being discussed.

THE COMPLETE SUBJECT

The **complete subject** includes all words related directly to the subject. The complete subject is in bold in the following examples:

> **Willie** sleeps.
> **Willie, an eight-year-old dog,** sleeps most of the day.
> **The Technical Support Department** completed the inventory of computers.
> **The 1998 graduates** renewed old memories and made new ones when **they** attended alumni reunion weekend.

NOTE SB.5
The complete subject includes all words related directly to the subject.

THE SIMPLE SUBJECT

The **simple subject** of a sentence is the main noun or pronoun in the complete subject. The simple subject names *who* or *what* is performing the action, receiving the action, or existing in the state of being described in the sentence. The following examples show the simple subject in bold print and the complete subject in italics:

> *The beautiful **pitcher*** fell from the table. (The pitcher names *what* fell.)
> *The rose **garden*** was planted by the local garden club. (The garden names *what* received the action of planting.)
> The ***arboretum*** is a quiet, peaceful place. (The arboretum names *what* exists in the described state of being.)
> *The two **students*** completed a document in Writely software and posted it to a blog. (Students name *who* performed the actions of completing and posting.)

NOTE SB.6
The simple subject is the main noun or pronoun in the complete subject.

*The new school **building*** appeared to be drastically different from the old one. (Building names *what* appeared different.)

THE COMPOUND SUBJECT

NOTE SB.7

Two or more simple subjects connected by a coordinating conjunction form a compound subject.

Two (or more) simple subjects connected by a coordinate conjunction form a **compound subject.** Coordinating conjunctions join equal or like ideas within a sentence; examples include *and, or, but, nor, for, yet,* and *so.* The following sentences have the compound subject in bold print and the complete subject in italics. The coordinating conjunction is underlined.

*The **doctor** <u>and</u> her **staff*** work to keep health care costs down.
*The **Firestix** <u>or</u> the **Wildcats*** will win the baseball tournament in Columbia, Missouri.

The Predicate

NOTE SB.8

The predicate tells something about the complete subject.

The **predicate** is the part of a sentence that tells something about the complete subject. The predicate consists of a verb with or without phrases or words that modify the verb, serve as its object, or complement the verb. The predicate may be complete, simple, or compound.

THE COMPLETE PREDICATE

NOTE SB.9

The complete predicate includes the verb and all words directly related to it.

The **complete predicate** includes the verb and all the words directly related to it, including modifiers and objects. The following examples show the complete predicate italicized.

Cats *eat slowly.*
Basketball and football ticket prices *are increasing.*
The package *was sent by overnight express.*
Nancy *quickly completed her first assignment in her new job at the greenhouse.*

THE SIMPLE PREDICATE

NOTE SB.10

The simple predicate is the main verb in the complete predicate.

The **simple predicate** is the main verb in the complete predicate. The verb expresses action or a state of being. The simple predicate is in bold print in these examples of italicized complete predicates:

The team ***left*** *quickly.* (*Left* expresses action.)
The package ***was sent*** *by overnight express.* (*Was sent* states the action.)
The office and distribution center ***moved*** *last week to another part of the city.* (*Moved* expresses action.)

THE COMPOUND PREDICATE

NOTE SB.11

Two or more simple predicates connected by a coordinating conjunction form a compound predicate.

A **compound predicate** is formed when two (or more) simple predicates are connected by a coordinating conjunction. The compound predicate is in bold print in these examples of italicized complete predicates. The coordinating conjunction is underlined.

Cathy ***sails*** *weekly* <u>and</u> ***races*** *monthly.*
The college roommates ***ate*** *dinner* <u>and</u> ***went*** *to a movie.*
Manuel ***rode*** *the bus* <u>or</u> ***walked*** *to school each day.*
Hurricane Katrina ***destroyed*** <u>or</u> ***left*** *uninhabitable* 95 percent of the houses.

Subject and Predicate Identification

Practice recognizing subjects and predicates to improve your understanding of sentence structure. Analyzing sentence structure is easier if you start by locating the simple predicate (the verb); then ask *who* or *what* to identify the subject. The following examples illustrate this approach:

NOTE SB.12
Locate the simple predicate and then find the subject.

> The YMCA opened at 5 a.m. (The action word *opened* is the verb. What opened? The *YMCA* is the simple subject.)
>
> Tan manages the computer store. (The action word *manages* is the verb. Who manages? *Tan* is the simple subject.)
>
> Nikolas Pantuliano is 16 years old. (The verb *is* describes a state of being. Who is? *Nikolas Pantuliano* is the subject.)
>
> Patrick bought a new loft apartment and moved into it last month. (The compound action verb is *bought* and *moved*. Who bought and moved? *Patrick* is the simple subject.)
>
> Amalia and Eduardo worked together on a class project. (The action word *worked* is the verb. Who worked? The compound subject is *Amalia* <u>and</u> *Eduardo*.)
>
> Ching-yu works at the theatre in the evening and attends school during the day. (The action words *works* <u>and</u> *attends* are the compound predicate. Who works and attends? *Ching-yu* is the simple subject.)

The most common sentence arrangement is for the subject to be followed by the verb (e.g., **Chuck** *rebuilt* his *Volkswagen*). A sentence in which the subject follows the verb is called an **inverted sentence.** Inverted sentences may ask a question or begin with *here* or *there*. The following examples, with the subject in bold print and the verb in italics, illustrate this inverted arrangement:

NOTE SB.13
In most sentences, the subject precedes the verb.

NOTE SB.14
In inverted sentences, the verb precedes the subject.

> There *are* 20 **employees** in the front office.
> Here *is* the **umbrella**.
> Why *was* **he** absent?

To locate the subject and verb, restate the sentence in the standard order—subject, then verb, as in the following examples:

Inverted order:	There *are* 20 **employees** in the front office.
Standard order:	Twenty **employees** *are* in the front office.
Inverted order:	Here *is* the **umbrella**.
Standard order:	The **umbrella** *is* here.
Inverted order:	Why *was* **he** absent?
Standard order:	**He** *was* absent why?

In some of the previous examples, words or groups of words were ignored when the predicate and subject were being located. These parts of sentences will be considered in the sections that follow next.

Objects and Subject Complements

Objects and subject complements are important parts of sentences. They help to complete the thought expressed by the subject and the simple predicate. Understanding the functions of objects and subject complements will assist you in avoiding grammatical errors.

NOTE SB.15
Objects and complements help complete the sentence thought.

OBJECTS

An **object** is a noun or pronoun acted upon by another part of speech such as a verb or a preposition. Objects may be direct or indirect.

NOTE SB.16
Direct objects receive the
action of the verb.

A **direct object** receives the action of the verb and helps complete the thought of the sentence. The direct object answers the *what* or *whom* question raised by the subject and verb. Examples of direct objects are shown in italics in the following sentences:

Cathy teaches the *piano*. (Cathy teaches what?)

Suzy is ill. (Only action verbs can take direct objects; *is*, a linking verb, links the subject with a word that describes Suzy, the subject. A modifier coming after a linking verb [also called a state-of-being verb] is known as a *subject complement* and is explained in the next section of this Seminar.) See Seminar A, page 528 for linking or state-of-being verbs.

He ran *track* one semester. (He ran what?)

The recommendation assisted *Kern Kwong*. (The recommendation assisted whom?)

Restoration hardware adds *authenticity* to an older home. (The hardware adds what?)

NOTE SB.17
Indirect objects are nouns
or pronouns acted upon by
a subject, a verb, and a
direct object.

An **indirect object** receives the action that the verb makes on the direct object. The indirect object usually answers the question, "To whom or what is the action being directed?" Indirect objects are located between the verb and the direct object. You cannot have an indirect object if you do not have a direct object. Neither the direct object nor the indirect object ever appears as a prepositional phrase. You can locate the indirect object by inverting the sentence and mentally inserting the word *to*. In the following two sentences, the indirect object is in bold print and the direct object is in italics:

Alexis gave **Jonathan** the *photograph*. (The photograph was given *to* Jonathan.)

The realtor sold the new faculty **member** a *condominium*. (A condominium was sold *to* the member. The words *new faculty* are modifiers for the noun object **member**.)

SUBJECT COMPLEMENTS

NOTE SB.18
Subject complements
rename or modify the
subject.

NOTE SB.19
Linking verbs express a
state of being.

The **subject complement** is (a) a noun or pronoun that renames the subject or (b) an adjective that modifies (describes) the subject. In both cases, the subject complement follows a linking verb in the sentence. A **linking verb** (such as *is*, *was*, *has been*, *am*, *are*, and *seem*) does not show action. In each of the following examples, the subject and the subject complement are in bold, and the linking verb is in italics:

Peter and **Lauren** *are* good **friends**. (*Friends* is a noun that renames *Peter* and *Lauren*. The complete subject complement is *good friends*; *good* is an adjective modifying *friends*.)

The **dog** *was* **lazy**. (*Lazy* is an adjective that describes *dog*.)

Mary *has been* **ill**. (*Ill* is an adjective that describes *Mary*.)

The Hawaiian **holiday** on Maui and the Big Island *seemed* far too **short**. (The noun *short* is an adjective that describes *holiday*. *Far too short* is the complete subject complement and includes the adjective describing the subject and its related words—the adverbs *far too*.)

Phrases, Clauses, and Fragments

Being able to identify groupings of words—referred to as *phrases* or *clauses*—is important for understanding sentence structure. Also, you should be able to recognize sentence fragments and make conscious decisions about their use.

PHRASES

A **phrase** is a group of related words functioning as a part of speech. Phrases do not contain both a subject and a verb; phrases may contain one or the other or neither. Here are examples of phrases:

NOTE SB.20
A phrase is a group of words functioning as a part of speech.

Verb phrases: Verb(s) with related, connecting words: *will be mailing; may not fly; is considered; have been waiting; rested briefly and waited quietly*

Noun phrases: Noun(s) with related, connected words: *my home address; the fall semester; the lovely summer wedding; mother's flower garden; three men and five women*

Prepositional phrases: Preposition with related, connected words: *to college; before the concert; under the table; for a good reason; between the first and second years*

Adjective phrases: Adjective(s) with related, connected words: *pretty and smart; 15 years of age; three dozen; soothing or calming*

Participial phrases: Present or past tense verb form(s) including related, connected words and serving as an adjective or adverb: *having been promoted; seeing clearly; keying rapidly; waiting anxiously*

Infinitive phrases: Infinitive(s) (*to* plus a verb form) with related, connected words: *to play; to promote; to interact; to collaborate; to speak eloquently*

Gerund phrases: Gerund (a verb plus *-ing* ending) including related, connected words and serving as a noun: *your willingness to help; your accepting our offer; reading the daily newspaper; adding to the issue*

Using phrases as parts of speech—as adjectives, adverbs, and nouns—can make your writing more interesting. Phrases add variety and color. They can add strong words to your sentences and bring power to your writing. Finally, they can strengthen your writing by providing specific details and showing relationships. Note how the italicized phrases in the following examples add detail, variety, color, interest, power, and liveliness:

NOTE SB.21
Phrases can strengthen and add life to writing.

Mary Rose sings. (no phrases)
Mary Rose sings songs *in the shower.* (prepositional phrase)
Mary Rose sings *better-than-average soprano.* (adverbial phrase)
Mary Rose, *a better-than-average soprano*, sings *contemporary songs.* (adjective phrase, noun phrase)
Mary Rose sings *to gain musical experience.* (infinitive phrase)
A natural soprano, Mary Rose sings *contemporary songs.* (adjective phrase, noun phrase)
Serenading softly, Mary Rose sings *contemporary songs.* (participial phrase, noun phrase)

Understanding the purpose of the phrase is important. For example, prepositional phrases can serve both as adverbs and as adjectives. An adverbial phrase should be placed near the verb, adjective, or other adverb modified. If a phrase is serving as an adjective, it should be placed close to the noun it modifies so that the relationship is clear:

Incorrect: The members present were *of the National Business Education Association.*

Correct: The members *of the National Business Education Association* were present.

The prepositional phrase *of the National Business Education Association* serves as an adjective and modifies the noun *members.* This relationship is clearly understood if the modifying phrase is close to the noun.

CLAUSES

A **clause** is a group of related words including both a subject and a predicate. There are two kinds of clauses: independent and dependent. An **independent clause,** sometimes referred to as the *main clause,* expresses a complete thought. It can stand alone as a separate sentence. In the following examples of independent clauses, the simple predicates are shown in italic print, and the simple subjects are in bold:

Daniel *listens* daily to music on his mp3 player.
The business administration **program** *averages* 150 graduates yearly.

A **dependent clause,** also called a *subordinate clause,* does not express a complete thought; therefore, it cannot stand alone as a sentence. The dependent clause contains both a subject and a predicate but, because of its construction, depends upon another clause to complete the thought.

Most dependent clauses are introduced by a subordinate conjunction (such as *because, as, if, since, while,* or *when*) or by a relative pronoun (such as *who, which,* or *that*). Look at the subordinating conjunction or relative pronoun (shown in bold), the simple subject (in bold italics), and the simple predicate (in regular italics) in these examples of dependent clauses:

if the ***order*** *arrived* on Monday
that the ***product*** *meets* expectations

The basic difference between dependent and independent clauses is the use of a subordinate conjunction or relative pronoun at the beginning of the clause. Adding a subordinate conjunction to the beginning of an independent clause would make it a dependent clause. On the other hand, if you were to omit the subordinate conjunction or relative pronoun at the beginning of the previous illustrations of dependent clauses, those clauses would become independent clauses:

The order arrived on Monday.
The product meets expectations.

Subordinate conjunctions and relative pronouns should be selected carefully; interchanging them reduces the precision of your message. Two commonly interchanged relative pronouns are *that* and *which*. Use *that* for clauses essential to the meaning of the sentence and *which* for clauses adding information that would not change the sentence meaning if omitted. The nonessential clause that is adding information should be set off with commas as shown here:

Correct: The course that I took last summer was difficult. (essential to identify the course)

Correct: Cost Accounting, which I took last summer, was difficult. (adds nonessential detail)

Other subordinate conjunctions that are often confused are *because* and *since*. *Since* is the more specific term when the reference is to *time passing; because* is the best term when the reference means *the reason*.

Correct   Since James left town, my work load has increased. (refers to a *time* sequence)

Correct   Because you are my closest friend, I will miss you if you leave. (refers to a *reason*)

Use the relative pronoun *who* or *whom* when referring to a person or persons. If the pronoun is the subject of a verb, use the word *who*; if the pronoun is used as an object, use *whom*. The following sentences show the relative pronoun in bold, the noun to which it refers in italics, and nonessential clauses set off by commas.

Correct: *Mary Sue,* **who** received her degree from Stanford, teaches at UCLA. (who—subject of the verb *received*)

Correct: *Anyone* **who** needs an education can get one. (who—subject of the verb *needs*)

Correct: *Each* of the team players **who** left school last year graduates this year. (who—subject of the verb *left*)

Correct: Jacque is the *visitor* **whom** I met at the airport. (I met whom—object of the verb)

Incorrect: Swimming brings calm to busy *people* **whom** need a stress reliever. (should be *who*—subject of verb *need*)

SENTENCE FRAGMENTS

A **sentence fragment** is a group of words that may or may not have meaning. *Sentence fragment* is another name for an *incomplete sentence*. Note the following examples:

If the vacation is taken early (lacks meaning)
Ernesto, having been promoted (lacks meaning)
Best wishes for success (has meaning in context)

Although some sentence fragments that represent a complete thought may be used in informal business communication, the acceptability of their usage for formal writing is questionable. In letters, for example, writers may choose meaningful sentence fragments—such as *If only I had known!* or *And now to move on.*—to give life and personality to their messages. *Congratulations!* and *Yes!* are used often, also. Other writers do not use sentence fragments. For the most part, you will want to use only complete sentences: independent clauses that have a subject and verb and express a complete thought.

Sentence Patterns

A helpful approach to understanding sentence construction is to examine common basic sentence patterns. Although the English language is extremely flexible, the following patterns are the most frequently used:

1. Subject → Verb
   Elena → reads.

NOTE SB.25
Sentence fragments are incomplete sentences and may or may not have meaning.

NOTE SB.26
Some writers selectively use sentence fragments; others never use them.

NOTE SB.27
A common sentence pattern is subject → verb → object or complement.

2. Subject → Verb → Direct Object
    Elena → reads → a novel.

3. Subject → Verb → Indirect Object → Direct Object
    Elena → reads → Cruz → a novel.

4. Subject → Linking Verb → Subject Complement
    Gregory → is → lost.

5. Here (or There) → Linking Verb → Subject
    Here → is → your backpack.

Subject and Verb Agreement

NOTE SB.28
The subject and verb must agree in number.

One of the basic rules of sentence construction is that the subject and the verb must *agree in number*. If the subject is singular—refers to just one person or one thing—then the verb must be singular. If the subject is plural, the verb must also be plural. Your ability to identify the subject is essential to determining whether it is singular or plural. In the following examples, the subject is bold and the verb is in italics:

Singular:	The **pilot** *flies* the helicopter.
Plural:	**Pilots** *fly* helicopters to be able to land without an airstrip.
Singular:	The peak travel **season** to the Caribbean *is* January through April.
Plural:	Peak travel **seasons** *vary* by location.
Singular:	**Mary** *has made* reservations to fly to Bermuda in October.
Plural:	**Mary** and **Susan** *have made* reservations for a vacation in Bermuda.

Recall that adding an *s* to most subjects makes them plural and adding an *s* to most verbs makes them singular. If you are not sure whether the subject is singular or plural (for example, a word like *athletics*), look in a dictionary. Then use the verb that agrees with the number of the subject.

Words between the subject and the verb (intervening words) must be ignored when determining the correct number of the subject. In the following examples the subject and the verb are in bold, and the word or words to be ignored are in italics:

Singular:	The **man** *with the rackets* **is** an outstanding tennis player.
Plural:	The **men** *with the rackets* **are** tennis players.
Singular:	The **computer**, *as well as the printers*, **was** new.
Plural:	The **runners**, *other than Coach Bill*, **were** on time for the track meet.
Singular:	**Athletics gives** students an opportunity for teamwork and leadership.

NOTE SB.29
Compound subjects may take singular or plural verbs.

Recall that a compound subject is two (or more) subjects connected by a coordinating conjunction. Some compound subjects take singular verbs, and some take plural verbs. There are four possibilities:

1. When compound subjects are connected by *and*, they are plural and require a plural verb.
2. When compound subjects are connected by *or* or *nor* and both are singular, they take singular verbs.

3. When compound subjects are connected by *or* or *nor* and both are plural, they take plural verbs.

4. When compound subjects are connected by *or* or *nor* and one of the subjects is plural and one singular, the verb should agree with the number of the subject that is closest to it.

The compound subjects are in bold print, and their correct verbs are in italics in these examples:

Plural:	**Lawanna** and **Laquita** *are* freshmen at the university.
Plural:	The **pilot,** the **copilot,** and the **navigator** *fly* all the international flights.
Singular:	Neither **Nancy** nor **Art** *is* going.
Plural:	Jim's **books** and his **newspaper** *were left* at the restaurant.
Singular:	Neither **Kristen** nor **Amy** *attends* class regularly.
Plural:	Either **Marcus** or his **brothers** *arrange* the chairs before every meeting.
Singular:	**Tents** or a **cabin** *is* available for camping.
Plural:	A **cabin** or **tents** *are* available for camping.

Notice in the last example that the plural verb sounds better than the singular verb used in the previous sentence. In sentences with both singular and plural subjects, this is almost always true. Therefore, you might consider putting the plural subject closer to the verb.

Some words used as subjects are singular even though they may give the appearance of being plural. Examples of these words are *everybody, everyone, anybody, anyone, somebody, someone, nobody,* and *neither.* With these singular subjects, use singular verbs:

NOTE SB.30
Some subjects appear to be plural but are singular.

Singular:	**Anyone** *is* (not *are*) invited.
Singular:	**Everybody** *is* (not *are*) welcome.
Singular:	**Each** of the participants *attends* (not *attend*) a conference.
Singular:	**Neither** of the boys *was* (not *were*) late for the meeting.

Also, some words that end in *s* are singular. Use singular verbs with those words:

Singular:	**Aeronautics** *is* a field of interest to persons with a sense of adventure.
Singular:	The **news** about Sal's troubles *makes* me sad.
Singular:	**Economics** *is* an important field of study.

Other words appear to be singular but take a plural verb. *Data* and *criteria* are examples. The singular form of data is datum; the singular form of criteria is criterion. The singular forms of these two words are seldom used, but their plural counterparts are often mistaken for the singular form. Some nouns such as *proceeds* and *goods* are always singular.

NOTE SB.31
Some subjects appear to be singular but are plural.

Plural:	The **data** collected from research *show* that exercise is important.
Plural:	The job **criteria** *include* work experience and positive interaction with people.
Plural:	Her **earnings** *exceed* his income.

The name of one song, book, company, magazine, or article is singular even though the name is plural:

NOTE SB.32
Book, magazine, or song titles ending in *s* are singular.

Singular:	*"Spanish Eyes" has been* a favorite song of mine.
Singular:	**Starving Students, Inc.,** *is* located in Ft. Lauderdale.
Singular:	*Learning and Leading with Technology is* published monthly.

Subjects in plural form that are considered as a single unit or as a whole take singular verbs. Amounts, distances, and some compound subjects are examples of this:

Singular:	**Ten feet** *is* the distance to the end of the wall.
Singular:	**Five to seven pounds** *is* the average weight for a notebook computer.
Singular:	**Turkey and dressing** *is* a Thanksgiving favorite.

The words *few, both, many,* and *several* are considered plural and take plural verbs. For example:

Plural:	**Few** *expect* to become a millionaire during their lifetime.
Plural:	**Both** *were hired* before graduation.
Plural:	**Many** *have replaced* their land-line phone with a cell phone.
Plural:	**Several** *sing* in the college choir.

Collective nouns such as *board, faculty,* and *audience* may be singular or plural. If the group is acting as one, the verb should be singular. If the group members are acting as individuals, the verb should be plural:

Singular:	The **committee** *plans* to develop an academic code of honor this year.
Plural:	The **committee** *represent* different parts of the city.
Singular:	The **couple** *attends* all the high school plays.
Plural:	The **couple** *are* separated.

Pronoun and Antecedent Agreement

NOTE SB.33
Pronouns and their antecedents should agree.

NOTE SB.34
Pronouns are noun substitutes.

NOTE SB.35
Pronouns replace antecedents.

NOTE SB.36
Pronouns and their antecedents should agree in number.

To be grammatically correct in your communication, you will want to know and use another form of agreement—the *agreement of pronouns and their antecedents.* Recall that pronouns are noun substitutes. An **antecedent** is a word, phrase, or clause that is replaced by the pronoun. Most antecedents are nouns. The pronouns used as subjects, objects, or complements are *he, she, I, we, you, it, her, him, them,* and *they.* As a possessive, a pronoun is used as a modifier. Examples of possessive pronouns are *my, mine, our(s), your(s), his, her(s), its,* and *their(s).* Possessive pronouns do not use an apostrophe to show possession. *Its* used as a possessive pronoun should not be written as *it's,* which is the contraction for *it is.*

Pronouns and their antecedents must agree in three ways: (a) in number, (b) in gender, and (c) in a clear relationship. In the following examples of agreement in number, the antecedent is in italics and the pronoun is in bold print:

| Singular: | If a *worker* continues to arrive late, **he** or **she** will be counseled. |
| Plural: | *Robin* and *Dennis* reported on Monday, and **they** said the report is complete. |

Singular:	The *company* began **its** production on January 1.
Plural:	Company *employees* began **their** work the previous November.
Singular:	*Everybody* sat at **his** or **her** desk.
Plural:	The *representatives* from that state vote as **their** constituents dictate.
Singular:	*Software, Inc.,* is opening **its** fifth store.
Plural:	All Software, Inc., *employees* believe **their** company will continue to grow.
Singular:	Either *Michelle* or *Consuelo* will sell **her** bicycle.
Plural:	*Both Michelle and Consuelo* will sell **their** bicycles.
Singular:	The *number* is high; **it** exceeds 100.
Plural:	A *number* of birds eat **their** breakfast at the bird feeder in my yard.

The next set of examples of pronouns and their antecedents shows agreement in gender. The antecedent is in italics and the pronoun is in bold print:

Masculine:	*Rudolph* ran **his** best race at the Boston Marathon.
Feminine:	*Megan* cut **her** hair in a pageboy style today.
Mixed:	Each *man* and *woman* must send **his** or **her** vote before Wednesday's meeting.
Neuter:	The *meeting* begins when the president calls **it** to order.

NOTE SB.37
Pronouns and their antecedents should agree in gender.

Finally, there must be a clear relationship between a pronoun and its antecedent. Examples of unclear relationships and clear relationships follow:

Unclear:	Will attended the Las Vegas convention with his colleague, and he said the convention sales were low. (Antecedent not clear; who said the sales were low?)
Clear:	Will attended the Las Vegas convention with his colleague, and Will said the convention sales were low.
Unclear:	While Janice was home for the holidays, she called her friend Jennifer; she wanted to go to a movie. (Who wanted to see the movie? Janice or her friend Jennifer?)
Clear:	While Janice was home for the holidays, she wanted to go to a movie and called her friend Jennifer.

NOTE SB.38
Pronouns and their antecedents should clearly relate.

Parallelism

One other important form of agreement for constructing correct sentences is parallelism. **Parallelism** means using similar structure for words or word groups used in a similar fashion. This rule applies to items in a series; comparisons; contrasts; plural subjects or verbs; or other words, phrases, or clauses used in a sentence to express similar ideas. Express parallel ideas in a parallel form. Sentences without parallelism lack balance and consistency.

Parallelism is achieved by using the same grammatical form for the two or more parts of sentences that serve the same function. Using the same grammatical form means using noun with noun, adjective with adjective, verb with verb, adverb with adverb, phrase with phrase, or clause with clause. Parts of sentences serve the same

NOTE SB.39
Sentence constructions used for the same function should be parallel.

NOTE SB.40
Use the same grammatical structure for parts serving the same function.

function if they serve as a part of a series, a contrast, a comparison, a choice, or an expression of equality.

Several examples of parallelism are shown in the following illustrations. The parts of these sentences that are not parallel are shown in bold.

Series

NOTE SB.41
Parts of series should be
parallel.

Not parallel: Designing a garden, **dues collection,** and **organization of a garden club** are essential to maintain current beautification activities. (*Designing a garden* is a gerund phrase, *dues collection* is a noun phrase, and *organization of a garden club* is a noun phrase.)

Parallel: *Designing a garden, collecting dues,* and *organizing a garden club* are essential to current beautification activities. (All parts of the series are gerund phrases.)

Not parallel: Members of the class worked quickly, **with enthusiasm,** and **with a display of skill.** (*Quickly* is an adverb; *with enthusiasm* and *with a display of skill* are adverbial phrases.)

Parallel: Members of the class worked quickly, enthusiastically, and skillfully. (All parts of the series are *-ly* adverbs.)

Not parallel: The duties of the president are the following:

1. To preside at meetings (infinitive phrase)
2. Be sure *Robert's Rules of Order* is followed to conduct business (independent clause)
3. Know the constitution and bylaws (verb and its objects)

Parallel: The duties of the president are the following:

1. To preside at meetings (infinitive phrase)
2. To conduct business with *Robert's Rules of Order* (infinitive phrase)
3. To know the constitution and bylaws (infinitive phrase)

Contrast

NOTE SB.42
Parts of contrasts should
be parallel.

Not parallel: Lydia speaks Spanish eloquently, but **her writing of English is poor.** (Both are independent clauses but the clause structure is not parallel. The pattern of the first clause is *subject–verb–object–adverb*; the pattern of the second clause is *subject–prepositional phrase–verb–adjective.*)

Parallel: Lydia speaks Spanish eloquently but writes English poorly. (Both contrasting parts are verb-object-adverb combinations.)

Comparison

NOTE SB.43
Parts of comparisons
should be parallel.

Not parallel: Juan is not only proficient in algebra *but also in calculus.*

Parallel: Juan is proficient *not only in algebra but also in calculus.* (*not only. . .but also* are followed by parallel elements.)

Choice

Not parallel: You may choose to complete your lesson, practice piano, or **your room is to be cleaned.** (The choices are in a series that includes an infinitive phrase, a verb-object combination, and an independent clause.)

Parallel: You may choose to complete your lesson, to practice the piano, or to clean your room. (each item in the series is an infinitive phrase.)

NOTE SB.44
Parts of a choice should be parallel.

Expression of Equality

Not parallel: Carmen Martinez tutored a fourth-grade student and **fifth grade.** (The lack of the words *a fifth-grade student* implies that Carmen tutored the entire fifth grade.)

Parallel: Carmen Martinez tutored *a fourth-grade student* and *a fifth-grade student.* (The use of appropriate articles and modifiers in both places clarifies that two people were tutored.)

NOTE SB.45
Expressions of equality should be parallel.

The parallel constructions in these illustrations are precise, clear, and strong. Achieving parallelism in your sentences improves their readability. Because of their balance and consistency, parallel constructions communicate effectively as well as correctly.

Common Sentence Errors

Dangling modifiers and double negatives are common sentence errors you want to avoid. Good writers also avoid split infinitives.

NOTE SB.46
Avoid common sentence errors.

Dangling Modifiers

A **dangling modifier** in a sentence means that the relationship is not clear between a phrase and the word or words that it modifies. The modifying phrase is *dangling* if it is too far removed from the word it modifies. For clarity in your messages, avoid dangling modifiers. In each of the following examples, the modifier is in italics and the word to be modified is in bold print:

NOTE SB.47
Avoid dangling modifiers; place modifiers correctly.

Incorrect: *Idling loudly,* John shut off the **motor** of his car. (Who or what is idling?)

Correct: John shut off his car **motor** that was *idling loudly.* (Placing the dangling modifier closer to **motor** than *John* clarifies its relationship to the word modified.)

Incorrect: *While participating as a cheerleader for Northwood High,* my teacher gave **me** a new cheer. (Who was participating as a cheerleader?)

Correct: *While participating as a cheerleader for Northwood High,* **I** was given a new cheer by my teacher. (Modifier *While participating as a cheerleader for Northwood High* now clearly modifies the subject, **I,** in the rephrased sentence. The sentence could also be corrected by changing the introductory phrase to an introductory clause: While I was participating as a cheerleader for Northwood High, my teacher gave me a new cheer.)

Double Negatives

NOTE SB.48
Avoid double negatives—
negative adverbs and
negative verbs used
together.

A **double negative** is formed when a negative adverb (such as *no, not, hardly, barely,* or *scarcely*) is used in the same sentence with a negative verb (*cannot, could not, won't, didn't,* or other verbs plus *not*). Such constructions are illogical because their use actually forms a positive. Double negatives are grammatically unacceptable. In the following examples the negative adverbs are in bold print and the negative verbs are in italics:

Incorrect: I *couldn't* **hardly** understand what she said. (The negative verb *couldn't* and the negative adverb *hardly* are used in the same sentence.)

Correct: I *could* **hardly** understand what she said. (The negative verb has been removed from the sentence.)

Incorrect: Finishing this course *won't* do **no** good for your grade point average. (The negative verb *won't* and the negative adverb *no* are used in the same sentence.)

Correct: Finishing this course *will* do **no** good for your grade point average. (The negative verb *won't* has been changed to the positive verb *will.*)

Split Infinitives

NOTE SB.49
Avoid split infinitives; do
not place other words
between *to* and a verb.

An infinitive is formed by placing the word *to* before a present tense verb (examples: *to accept, to agree,* and *to feel*). A **split infinitive** is formed when an adverb or other words are placed between the *to* and the verb (to *bravely* accept, to *barely* agree, to *warmly* feel). Split infinitives are not correct grammar. Avoid them when possible. In the following examples, the infinitives are in bold print and the adverbs or other words that split the infinitives are in italics:

Incorrect: The Human Resource Department selected Pamela **to** *officially* **represent** her department at the company's annual conference. (The infinitive **to represent** has been split by the adverb *officially*.)

Correct: The Human Resource Department officially selected Pamela **to represent** her department at the company's annual conference. (The adverb *officially* was moved closer to the word modified: *selected.*)

Incorrect: Tina received an assignment **to** *as quickly as possible* **design** a presentation for ABC. (Several words, *as quickly as possible,* split the infinitive **to design.**)

Correct: Tina received an assignment **to design** a presentation for ABC *as quickly as possible.* (The words *as quickly as possible* have been moved to the end of the sentence so they do not split the infinitive.)

Some split infinitives seem to sound better than technically correct versions do. Usually, you can reword the sentence to avoid the problem, as seen in the following examples:

Technically correct: He decided **to change** *gradually* the procedures. (The wording *to change gradually* is awkward.)

Revision: He decided **to change** the procedures *gradually.* (This revision also avoids the problem of a split infinitive.)

Functions of Sentences

Sentences can serve one of four basic functions. These four functions are described here:

1. *Statements*. Sentences that state ideas or facts are **declarative sentences** and are followed by a period. For example:
   Cold weather arrived earlier than predicted.
   I believe that the school year should be 11 months.
2. *Questions*. Questions are called **interrogative sentences** and are followed by a question mark. For example:
   Will you attend the party?
   Did Connie miss her dental appointment?
3. *Requests or Commands*. Requests or commands, also known as **imperative sentences,** are followed by a period. Usually *you* is understood as the subject in a command or request. For example:
   [You] Please bring the file to our next meeting.
   [You] Refer to page 12 for examples of countries conserving their energy resources.
4. *Expressions of Strong Emotion*. Exclamations or **exclamatory sentences** express strong emotion and are followed by an exclamation point. For example:
   I congratulate you for graduating with high honors!
   Ah, what a glorious day it is!

NOTE SB.50
Sentences can serve as statements, questions, commands, or exclamations.

Types of Sentence Structures

To construct correct sentences, you should know the four basic sentence structures. The technical names of these sentence structures are *simple sentence, compound sentence, complex sentence,* and *compound-complex sentence.* Sentence structures are classified by the number and kinds of clauses they have. You read about the two kinds of clauses—independent (main) and dependent (subordinate)—earlier in this seminar.

Varying sentence structure helps to make your messages interesting. You can also use sentence structure to emphasize an idea by placing it in an independent clause or de-emphasize it by placing it in a dependent clause. The effective communicator understands and uses all four sentence structures.

NOTE SB.51
There are four sentence structures.

The Simple Sentence

The **simple sentence** consists of a single independent clause and no dependent clauses. You will recall that an independent clause has both a subject and a predicate and expresses a complete thought. The independent clause does not begin with a subordinate conjunction or a relative pronoun. Simple sentences can have compound subjects or compound predicates and can include phrases. Here are some examples of typical simple sentences with the subject in bold type and the verb in italics:

NOTE SB.52
Simple sentences contain one independent clause.

> **Cooper** *played* Frisbee toss. (simple sentence)
>
> A **view** of the Big Ben tower suddenly *appeared* through the trees in St. James Park behind Buckingham Palace. (simple sentence with prepositional phrases)
>
> **Milton** and **John** *attend* the same university. (simple sentence with compound subject)
>
> Because of the reporting date extension, **we** *can edit* and *proofread* our report again. (simple sentence with introductory phrase and compound predicate)
>
> **Mr. Manrique**, executive director of Ukropina Delivery, *plans* to retire next year. (simple sentence with descriptive phrases)

NOTE SB.53
Simple sentences are businesslike, but their overuse sounds choppy.

You can communicate an idea clearly using a simple sentence. This sentence structure gives the greatest emphasis to the idea because there are no distracting dependent clauses. The simple sentence is effective in composing business messages. It is a clear, concise, and efficient way of communicating—the simple sentence is businesslike. Overuse of simple sentences in a message, however, can result in choppy, singsong monotony—particularly if the sentences are all short. Note the choppiness in the following paragraph:

> I started the computer. I accessed the e-mail account. I launched the Google search engine. I received a listing of websites for airlines. I located the URL for LOT Airlines' website.

To make your writing more interesting and to de-emphasize and emphasize ideas, you will want to use a mix of sentence structures. Understanding different sentence structures will help you vary them in your messages.

The Compound Sentence

NOTE SB.54
Compound sentences contain two or more independent clauses.

The **compound sentence** contains two or more independent clauses (each with a subject and a verb) and no dependent clauses. In this sentence structure, two or more ideas share equal emphasis. Each independent clause could stand alone as a complete sentence because it expresses a complete thought. However, by pairing the ideas in one sentence, both ideas receive less emphasis than they would in separate simple sentences.

In the following examples, the subjects are in bold and the verbs are in italics. Note in these examples that the independent clauses in each compound sentence are joined with a comma and a coordinating conjunction or a semicolon:

> **Ronalee** *will take* the train to the conference, and **she** *will speak* on cellular biology at the 9 a.m. session.
>
> **Mr. March** *applied* for the position, but **he** *did* not *accept* the offer.
>
> **Janie** *is* a senior, **Jade** *is* a junior, and **Beau** *is* a freshman.
>
> **Kevin** *worked* for Blockbuster Video for three years; **Craig** *worked* for Boy Scouts of America for two years.

The use of the compound sentence structure enables you to give equal importance to two or more ideas. By putting them together in one sentence, you indicate a close relationship of the ideas.

The Complex Sentence

The **complex sentence** has one independent clause and one or more dependent clauses. Remember that a dependent clause depends on the independent clause to make a complete thought—-hence, the term *dependent clause.*

In the *complex sentence* structure, one or more ideas are subordinate to the main idea. The least important or negative ideas can be de-emphasized by placing them in dependent clauses; the main idea can be emphasized by placing it in the independent clause. Another advantage of the complex sentence is that a dependent clause can be used to explain, clarify, and strengthen the main idea. The dependent clauses commonly used in complex sentences are the following:

- Noun clauses—used as subjects and objects
- Adjective clauses—used to modify nouns and pronouns
- Adverbial clauses—used to modify verbs, adjectives, or other adverbs

As you know, a dependent clause contains both a subject and a verb and is introduced with a subordinating conjunction (such as *because, although, while, as soon as, if, whether,* or *when*) or a relative pronoun (such as *who, which,* or *that*). In the following examples the dependent clauses are in italics:

If taxes were lower than they now are, I could save money.
Although 99 percent of American retail stores stay open all year, most of them make more than half their profit during the November-December holiday season.
I will send you the check *that I received from your sister.*
You will want to know *that many call the independent clause the main clause.*
All *who are being promoted* will receive raises.
When new graduates seek employment, they should use their networks of friends, acquaintances, and relatives.

Complex sentences convey more than one idea. By its design, this structure causes some ideas to be de-emphasized and others to be emphasized.

Figure SB.1 and Figure SB.2 illustrate the importance of correct grammar and sentence structure in your communication; review these two examples of messages. Figure SB.1 is an example of a **poor** e-mail. Its writer will lose credibility because of the grammatical errors and poor sentence structure. Figure SB.2, a **good** version of the same e-mail, will gain credibility because of its correctness and varied sentence structure.

The Compound-Complex Sentence

The **compound-complex sentence** contains two or more independent clauses and one or more dependent clauses. This sentence structure offers a business communicator the advantages of both the compound and complex sentences. Ideas can be related, emphasized, and de-emphasized in this complicated structure.

The compound-complex sentence structure, however, can become long and cumbersome. Business readers want to be able to understand a sentence on the first

NOTE SB.55
Complex sentences contain one independent clause and one or more dependent clauses.

NOTE SB.56
Independent clauses emphasize ideas; dependent clauses de-emphasize them.

NOTE SB.57
Compound-complex sentences contain two or more independent clauses and one or more dependent clauses.

NOTE SB.58
Compound-complex sentences can be long and cumbersome.

needs work

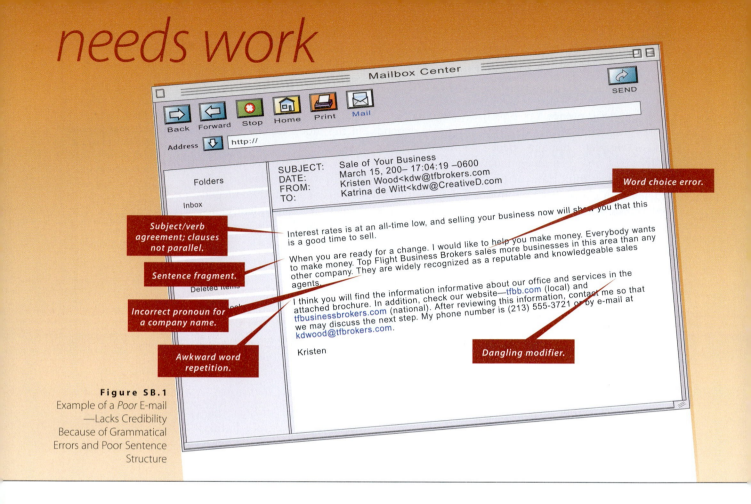

Figure SB.1
Example of a *Poor* E-mail
—Lacks Credibility
Because of Grammatical
Errors and Poor Sentence
Structure

reading. For this reason, this sentence structure is used infrequently in business messages. In the following examples of compound-complex sentences, the dependent clauses are in italics and the independent clauses are in bold print.

> **The bright star** *that we saw last night* **was the planet Venus,** and **the constellation** *that we saw Monday night* **was Orion.**
>
> *When you take your next flight on a commercial airliner,* **remember the first flight only 100 years ago; one man made the first flight on a little 12-horsepower biplane.**
>
> **The looting of the downtown stores,** *which took place after the flood,* **was a disaster for small businesses; 75 percent of small businesses affected by the looting went into bankruptcy within six months.**

APPLICATION EXERCISES

1. Key these sentences in a computer word processing program. For each independent clause, use bold font for the complete subject (the subject with its modifiers); use italic font for the complete predicate. Print a copy.

   a. The reputation for high fashion in Paris is the chief attraction that brings the world's best designers to work there.

   b. High school juniors take the SAT for college admission so that they will have an opportunity in their senior year to retake the test to raise their score.

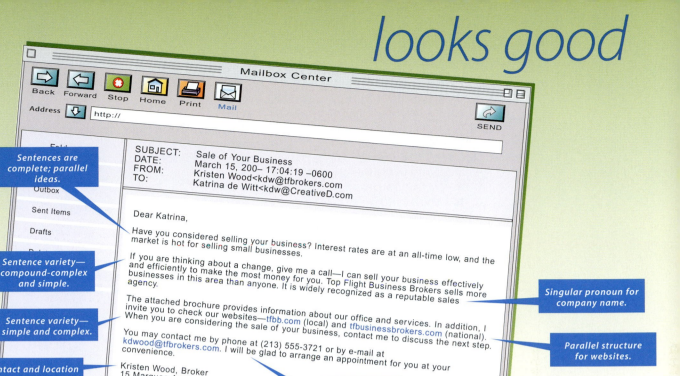

Figure SB.2
Example of a *Good* E-mail —Gains Credibility Because of Grammatical Correctness and Varied Sentence Structure

   c. The economy ranked as the top priority in a recent national poll.

   d. English skills are important in all occupations.

   e. The Schaus swallowtail butterfly, which is being raised and reintroduced in Florida, has been on the list of endangered species.

   f. Hobbyists who were not software professionals created many early software packages.

   g. Stars circled by planets are quite rare.

   h. Newly uncovered Guatemalan hieroglyphs help explain Mayan history.

   i. X-ray equipment is going digital; X-ray film is becoming obsolete.

   j. Why can't you install the additional memory in the new computer that I bought?

2. Open the electronic file of your sentences from Application Exercise 1. With word processing software, underline the simple subject and bold the simple predicate for each independent and dependent clause.

3. For the following sentences, identify the direct objects and indirect objects (if any). For each sentence, write the object(s) followed by the word Direct or Indirect.

   a. The department store clerk sold Patrick a new suit.

   b. Gordon gave Allen a haircut.

   c. Michael wrote an article about science.

   d. Angel Contreras gave Benito a book titled *Soy la Avon Lady and Other Stories*.

   e. Christopher Askew received an award for his singing.

4. Write or key the following sentences. Underline the linking verbs and use a circle or bold print to identify the subject in the following sentences.

   a. How do you feel?

   b. You look fabulous!

    c. Where are my gloves?

    d. One fourth of the library books on reserve are lost.

    e. Julie has been out of the country for two weeks.

5. Review the sentences in Application Exercise 4, and write the complete subject complement for each sentence.

6. For each of the following sentences, write the italicized word phrase as shown for each sentence and label it by the type of phrase.

    a. *Managing the restaurant* is Jeffrey's responsibility.

    b. Jane likes *to conduct meetings.*

    c. Billy laid the tile *in the bathroom.*

    d. *Haunted by his previous experience,* Rob did not return to the cabin.

    c. Betty found Megan *walking in the park.*

7. For each of the following sentences, write all dependent clauses the sentence contains and indicate the sentence structure (i.e., simple, complex, compound, or compound-complex).

    a. When Jim asked what decision he should make, his father referred him to a professional code of ethics.

    b. Overseas shipments of freight are to be insured for full value if their value exceeds $1,000.

    c. Pay for men and women should be equal if the work performed is of comparable worth.

    d. When the pizza is ready, let me know; I will ask our guests to come to the table.

    e. The College of Business Instructional Materials Center (IMC) is a full-service facility; when you need word processing, e-mail, fax service, or copying service, send your request to the IMC.

    f. Martin Luther King Jr. promoted the fundamental goal of the civil rights movement as a color-blind society where people were judged "not . . . by the color of their skin but by the content of their character."

    g. Graphic aids help make information understandable when the ideas are complex.

    h. Although not all the sales agents agreed, the home office changed the structure of the sales commissions; this change took effect in January.

    i. The National Weather Service predicted that warm weather would come to the Rocky Mountain area early this year because of global warming.

    j. During the last three years, research has revealed much new information about healthful living; but few people apply this knowledge because they have developed unhealthy habits.

8. In an electronic file, list the letter for each sentence in Application Exercise 7. Key the independent (main) clause(s) beside each letter. Bold the subject(s) and underline the verb(s) in these independent clauses.

9. Write or print the following sentences using the correct verb form for each:

    a. Forensics (is, are) required for the study of debate.

    b. Either Nancy or Peggy (is, are) going.

    c. *Communication Notes* (contain, contains) articles helpful to business writers.

    d. The committee (agree, agrees) with the new procedure.

    e. The board, rather than the officers, (vote, votes) on increasing fees.

    f. Everybody (is, are) expected to be present at the meeting.

    g. Data (indicate, indicates) that our original plans were correct.

    h. Each of the members (want, wants) to see facts on the issue before deciding how to vote.

    i. JC Industries (is, are) opening its new plant next week.

    j. What criteria (has, have) been established for selecting a new president?

10. Write or print the following sentences using the correct pronoun(s) for each sentence.

    a. The price you quoted is high; please explain (its, their) cost components.

    b. Either Christina or Lucy left (their, her) coat at Julio's house.

    c. Global executives must learn to handle cultural differences in (his or her, their) own way.

    d. (Him and I, He and me, He and I) introduced (his or her, their) dorm roommates.

    e. Every man or woman seeking employment should try to match opportunities with (his or her, their) qualifications.

11. Rewrite each of the following sentences to correct the lack of parallelism. Use correct punctuation for your rewritten sentences.
    a. The song challenged and was intriguing for me.
    b. The company paid its employees a high salary and was offering them good health benefits.
    c. Shahz was strong, optimistic, and a woman of courage.
    d. International companies look for executives who can quickly adapt to local customs and whose language skills show competency.
    e. Tom and Daniel play baseball and basketball but are not playing soccer.

12. Examine the following sentences for the common sentence errors of dangling modifiers, double negatives, parallelism, and split infinitives. Write a correct version of each sentence.
    a. He wouldn't never deny that he had a good time.
    b. Sailing on the ocean, a beautiful sunset filled the sky.
    c. The attendance clerk wrote the note to specifically excuse the boy from class.
    d. Walking on the beach, the seashells fascinated me.
    e. She tripped on the cord and resuming her walk was with difficulty.

13. Write a short paragraph that includes an example of each of the four functions of sentences—statement, question, command or request, and exclamation.

14. Write a short paragraph that includes at least one example of each of the four basic sentence structures—simple sentence, compound sentence, complex sentence, and compound-complex sentence.

MESSAGE ANALYSIS

Examine the following message. Rewrite the message to make it understandable. Vary the sentence structure. Correct punctuation, sentence fragments, split infinitives, dangling modifiers, double negatives, parallelism, errors in subject–verb agreement, and errors in pronoun and antecedent agreement.

If you watch a guard perform their duty at the Tomb of the Unknown Soldier. The seriousness with which they take their job is evident. However, you may not realize the level of commitment to perform this duty. Members of the guard must commit two years to the assignment, and live in a barracks under the Tomb. They cannot drink alcohol on or off duty, swearing in public is not allowed, and cannot disgrace the uniform in any way. In 2003 a hurricane was approaching Washington DC the U.S. Senate took two days off in anticipation of the storm. From the hurricane because of the potential danger the members of the guard for the Tomb was given permission to temporarily suspend the assignment. They respectfully declined. Marched in the rain; soaked to the skin, during the tropical storm. They said that guarding the Tomb was not just an assignment it was the highest honor that could be afforded to service personnel. The Tomb has been patrolled continuously, 24/7, since 1930.

seminar c

When you speak, the tone of your voice, the gestures you make, and the pauses you insert help your listeners understand what you are saying. When you write, punctuation helps your readers understand your message. Punctuation tells your readers where one thought ends and the next begins; it helps emphasize ideas and clarify meaning. Writing without punctuation is comparable to building a house without a blueprint.

This seminar reviews the punctuation that occurs most often in business writing. The material is not designed to eliminate the need for reference manuals. When you have a question about punctuation, check a reliable source.

NOTE SC.1
Punctuation marks add emphasis and clarity to a message.

NOTE SC.2
Check reference sources when you are uncertain about punctuation.

Terminal Punctuation

The three punctuation symbols that are used to signal the end of a complete thought are the period, the question mark, and the exclamation mark.

The Period

The **period** is the most frequently used ending mark of punctuation. It signals the end of a declarative or an imperative sentence. A declarative sentence makes a statement; an imperative sentence gives a command.

> The policy will take effect March 1. (declarative)
> The office will close at noon on Tuesday. (declarative)
> Lock the door when you leave. (imperative)
> Make three copies of the contract. (imperative)

A **polite request,** sometimes called a *courteous request,* requires action rather than an oral or written response. The writer would rather have the reader devote time to doing what has been requested than to writing or calling to say yes or no. A polite request ends with a period:

> Won't you take a few moments now to complete and return the survey.
> Will you please speak more slowly.

The period is also used when the writer asks an **indirect question**—a statement about a question:

> I wonder when the new server will be installed.
> Mr. Harper asked when I would be taking vacation.

NOTE SC.3
Periods are used to end
• Declarative and imperative sentences
• Polite requests that require action
• Indirect questions

The Question Mark

A **question mark** should be used with an interrogative sentence. An interrogative sentence asks for or requires a definite response. The response may be a single word, or it may be one or more sentences.

NOTE SC.4
Question marks are used to end direct questions.

Is Barbara in her office? (one-word response)

What arrangements have you made for your trip to Seoul? (a response of one or more sentences)

When a series of questions has a common subject and predicate, each question is followed by a question mark. Unless the questions in a series are proper nouns or complete thoughts, capitalize only the first letter of the sentence.

Have we determined when? where? why?

Do you like jazz? rock? rap?

Did you select maple? oak? cherry?

The Exclamation Mark

NOTE SC.5

Exclamation marks show
strong emotion.

An **exclamation mark** is used with an exclamatory sentence—one that shows strong emotion. Because of the dramatic effect it creates, the exclamation mark is used sparingly in business correspondence.

Yes! The color matches perfectly.

Hurry! Make your reservation today.

Excellent!

Sharp's will not be undersold!

Choosing Terminal Punctuation

When deciding which terminal punctuation mark to use, ask these questions:

- Am I expressing a strong emotion? (If yes, use !)
- Am I asking the reader to give me a response? (If so, use ?)

If you answer no to both questions, use the period.

Primary Internal Punctuation

Terminal punctuation marks help guide your reader through your message. Internal punctuation marks help him or her through each sentence. The comma and the semicolon are the most frequently used internal punctuation marks.

The Comma

NOTE SC.6

Commas separate items in
sentences.

The comma plays an important role in business writing. A **comma** separates items in a sentence and helps the reader correctly interpret each thought. By learning how commas are used and by mastering the rules for their placement, you will become a more effective business writer. Using commas incorrectly—omitting them where needed or adding them where they are not needed—can hamper communication. Consider these examples:

After you have eaten the leftover meat the vegetables and the dairy products should be placed in the refrigerator. (commas have been omitted)

In this sentence, the absence of commas makes the reader wonder what is to be eaten and what is to be put into the refrigerator. Because the message is confusing, additional communication is necessary. The message becomes clear when a comma is inserted after the word *eaten* and between each item in the compound subject:

> After you have eaten, the leftover meat, the vegetables, and the dairy products should be placed in the refrigerator.

NOTE SC.7
Too few or too many commas can hamper message clarity.

In the following sentence, clarity is lost because four commas are used where none is needed:

> This afternoon, we will meet with the chair, of the board, while her staff tours the new addition, to the factory. (commas are used where they are not needed)

The sentence should read as follows:

> This afternoon we will meet with the chair of the board while her staff tours the new addition to the factory.

Although the original versions of these sentences are extreme examples of comma omission and misuse, they illustrate the need for caution when using commas. The best way to ensure correct use of commas is to justify their placement.

NOTE SC.8
Be sure to justify each comma you use.

CALENDAR DATES

A complete **calendar date** consists of a month, a day, and a year. Whenever a complete calendar date occurs within the body of a sentence, the year is set apart from the rest of the sentence by commas. When a complete calendar date occurs at the end of an independent clause or a sentence, the final comma is replaced by a semicolon or terminal punctuation. Commas are omitted when the date consists of only the month and year or the month and day. If the military or international date form is used, no commas are needed.

NOTE SC.9
Use commas with complete calendar dates.

> On *June 17, 1932,* Carlson College held its first commencement ceremony. (Calendar date is complete.)
> Bob joined the firm in *February 1999.* (Date consists only of month and year.)
> The meeting has been rescheduled to *September 14.* (Date consists only of month and day.)
> I will have been with the company for 30 years on *17 January 2010.* (The military or international date form does not need commas.)

When a weekday is used with a calendar date, the date is set off by commas. The calendar date may be complete or incomplete.

> Our office will be closed on *Friday, July 3,* to enable our staff to have an extended holiday. (weekday with incomplete calendar date)
> The memorial was dedicated on *Tuesday, March 19, 2003.* (weekday with complete calendar date)

CONTRASTING EXPRESSIONS

Expressions that contrast with, limit, or offer a contingency to the main idea are set off with commas.

NOTE SC.10
Use a comma before an expression that contrasts with the main idea.

Jim, *not Joe,* is the nominee. (contrast)
The longer we stay, the later it will be when we get home. (contingent statement)
Sally will work this weekend, *but only if she gets an extra day off next week.* (limit)

GEOGRAPHIC LOCATIONS AND ADDRESSES

NOTE SC.11
Use commas with complete geographic locations.

A complete **geographic location** consists of a city and a state, province, or nation. When a geographic location is mentioned within a sentence, the name of the state, province, or nation is set apart from the rest of the sentence by commas. When an incomplete geographic location is named in a sentence, no commas are necessary.

Our favorite resort in *Palm Springs, California,* has a 27-hole golf course. (Palm Springs, California, is a complete geographic location.)
The new mall in *Silverdale* will open this fall. (The geographic location is incomplete.)
Have you ever visited *Acapulco, Mexico?* (The geographic location is complete; the question mark replaces the ending comma because the name of the country is the last item in the interrogative sentence.)

A mailing address is a type of geographic location. When a mailing address is presented in sentence form, use commas to separate its parts. No comma is placed before the ZIP code.

The showroom for Martin Electronics is at 612 West Buckley Avenue, Amherst, NH 03031.

INDEPENDENT ADJECTIVES

NOTE SC.12
A comma replaces the word *and* between independent adjectives

When two or more adjectives in a series independently modify the same noun, they are called **independent adjectives.** Commas are used to separate independent adjectives:

Avery is a *patient, caring, sincere* foster parent; Dyanne is a *well-known, well-respected* office automation consultant.

The adjectives in the first series independently describe Avery as a foster parent; those in the second series independently describe Dyanne as a consultant. The writer could have stated it this way:

Avery is a patient and caring and sincere foster parent; Dyanne is a well-known and well-respected office automation consultant.

Combining the adjectives, however, is more efficient for the writer and more pleasing to the reader. A good test of the need for commas and where they should be placed is to insert the word *and* between the adjectives. If the word *and* can be inserted without altering the meaning of the sentence, a comma should be used.

Sentence without punctuation: Reo gave a brief emotional acceptance speech.
Test: Reo gave a brief (and) emotional acceptance speech.
Correctly punctuated: Reo gave a brief, emotional acceptance speech.

The following example needs no commas. If we insert the word *and* between the adjectives, the sentence becomes awkward.

Sentence without punctuation: Roberto drives a shiny blue sports car. (The words *shiny, blue,* and *sports* describe the car, but they do so collectively, not independently.)

Test: Roberto drives a shiny (and) blue (and) sports car.

Correctly punctuated: Roberto drives a shiny blue sports car.

INDEPENDENT CLAUSES

When the independent clauses in a compound sentence are joined with a coordinating conjunction (*and, but, or, nor*), use a comma before the conjunction. If the sentence is 12 words or less, the comma may be omitted. The comma before the coordinating conjunction is also omitted when the sentence contains an introductory dependent clause in addition to the two independent clauses.

> The mountains and streams created a peaceful atmosphere, *but* Leona and Signe longed for the hustle and bustle of the city. (The coordinating conjunction joins the independent clauses.)
>
> Sally agreed to record the minutes of next week's meeting and post them to the website. (No comma is needed because the coordinating conjunction *and* does not connect two independent clauses.)
>
> The flavor is strong and the texture is smooth. (The comma before *and* may be omitted because the sentence is less than 12 words.)
>
> After the meeting ended, Joe collected the leftover handouts and Barb disassembled the equipment. (Comma omitted because sentence also contains introductory dependent clause.)

NOTE SC.13
When two independent clauses are joined by a coordinating conjunction, place a comma before the conjunction.

INTRODUCTORY CLAUSES

When a dependent clause *introduces* an independent clause in a complex sentence, a comma is used to separate the clauses. Introductory clauses commonly begin with one of the following words:

after	before	until
although	if	when
as	since	whenever
because	unless	while

When the dependent clause does not introduce the independent clause, a comma is not used.

> *If you book your flight online,* you will receive 500 bonus miles. (The dependent clause introduces the independent clause.)
>
> *When Bob phones,* tell him his travel authorization has been signed. (The dependent clause introduces the independent clause.)
>
> Be sure to replace the toner cartridge *before you leave*. (No comma is needed; the dependent clause does not introduce the independent clause.)

NOTE SC.14
Use a comma after a dependent clause that introduces an independent clause.

NONESSENTIAL ELEMENTS

Words, phrases, or clauses that are not necessary to the meaning or structure of a sentence are considered **nonessential elements.** Appositives, names used in direct address, introductory words, introductory phrases, nonrestrictive clauses, parenthetical expressions, and transitional expressions are all nonessential elements.

NOTE SC.15
Nonessential elements require one or more commas.

Each nonessential element requires one or more commas. A nonessential element that begins a sentence is followed by a comma. A nonessential element that ends an independent clause is followed by a comma or a semicolon; one that ends a sentence is followed by the appropriate terminal punctuation. A nonessential element that does not end an independent clause or a sentence is preceded and followed by a comma. To determine whether an item is nonessential, omit it from the sentence. If the meaning and structure of the sentence are complete, the item is nonessential.

NOTE SC.16
Use commas with nonessential appositives.

APPOSITIVES An **appositive** is a word or a phrase that immediately follows a noun and renames, describes, or provides additional information about it. When this additional information is not necessary to the meaning of the sentence, it is separated from the rest of the sentence by commas:

My oldest sister, *Sarah*, serves on the City Council. (The name Sarah is not essential to the meaning of the sentence; only one of the writer's sisters may be the oldest.)

My sister Sarah serves on the City Council. (The name is needed to indicate which of the writer's sisters serves on the council.)

My accountant, Chet Arthur, filed the application for me. (The name is nonessential information.)

NOTE SC.17
Commas separate a direct address from the rest of the sentence

DIRECT ADDRESS In order to make a sentence sound more personal and conversational, senders may insert the receiver's name. When a name is used in this manner, it is referred to as a **direct address:**

Mr. Wilson, you'll receive many hours of enjoyment from your new treadmill.

Thank you, *Manjeet*, for your efforts on our behalf.

Your speech was very inspiring, *Myrna*.

NOTE SC.18
An introductory word is followed by a comma.

INTRODUCTORY WORDS An **introductory word** is the first word in a sentence; it leads the reader to the independent clause and is separated from the clause by a comma. *Obviously*, *generally*, and *consequently* are examples of introductory words; others are used in the following examples:

Unfortunately, the exchange rate is not in our favor. (The introductory word is not essential to the meaning or structure of the sentence.)

Currently, I am coaching a youth softball team. (The introductory word is not essential to the meaning or structure of the sentence.)

NOTE SC.19
Commas are optional after introductory phrases.

INTRODUCTORY PHRASES An **introductory phrase** is a group of words that begins a sentence and introduces an independent clause. For simplicity and clarity, we recommend placing a comma after all introductory phrases unless they serve as the subject of the sentence:

While walking to work, Tim saw a two-car collision.

Without warning, Juan turned and walked away.

After entering your five-digit authorization code and hearing the tone, enter the area code and number.

Placing the fax machine near the photocopier has created a bottleneck. (No comma is needed; the phrase is the subject of the sentence.)

NONRESTRICTIVE CLAUSES Earlier in this section, you learned that an appositive provides additional, but nonessential, information about a noun; a **nonrestrictive clause** has the same function. One feature distinguishes an appositive from a nonrestrictive clause: An appositive is a word or a phrase—not a clause.

Nonrestrictive clauses frequently begin with *who* or *which*. They are separated from the rest of a sentence by commas. Some writers prefer to use the word *which* to begin a nonrestrictive clause and the word *that* to begin a restrictive (essential) clause.

NOTE SC.20
Nonrestrictive clauses provide additional information; use a comma before and after them.

> The play, *which was written by Rita Golden,* will be performed without intermission. (The clause is not essential to the meaning of the sentence.)
> The boxes *that are on the loading dock* must be moved immediately. (The clause is essential to the sentence.)
> The people *who want to speak with you* are seated in the lobby. (The clause is essential to the sentence.)
> Sally, *who visited Mexico City last spring,* plans to vacation in Toronto this fall. (The clause does not restrict the meaning of the sentence.)
> Please inform Senator Barjo that, *although we have supported him in the past,* we will oppose him on the sales tax issue. (The clause is not essential to the meaning of the sentence. Note that this nonrestrictive clause does not begin with *who* or *which*.)

PARENTHETICAL EXPRESSIONS When one or more words interrupt the flow of a sentence, a **parenthetical expression** is created. *In addition, for example, however, therefore, of course,* and *too* are common parenthetical expressions. These and other parenthetical expressions are separated from the rest of the sentence by commas.

NOTE SC.21
Parenthetical expressions interrupt the flow of a sentence; they should be preceded and followed by a comma.

> If you return on Monday, *however,* you will have time to visit the museum. (The word *however* interrupts the flow of the sentence.)
> The white blossom, *although less common,* is as beautiful as the red. (The words *although less common* interrupt the flow of the sentence.)
> The film is, *to quote the reviewer,* "extraordinary." (The words *to quote the reviewer* interrupt the flow of the sentence.)

TRANSITIONAL EXPRESSIONS A word or a phrase that links sentences or independent clauses is a **transitional expression.** When a transitional expression links two independent clauses, it is preceded by a semicolon and followed by a comma. When a transitional expression links two sentences, it is followed by a comma.

NOTE SC.22
Transitional expressions link independent clauses.

> The anticipated merger did not occur; *consequently,* the price of the stock fell by nearly 30 points. (The transitional expression links two independent clauses.)
> Your newest catalog had not yet arrived when we placed our order. *As a result,* we were unable to use the new price in calculating the total cost of our order. (The transitional expression links two sentences.)

Words such as *however* and *therefore* and phrases such as *of course* and *as a result* may be either parenthetical or transitional. The key is how they are used in the sentence.

The invoice, *therefore,* has been approved for payment. (The word *therefore* interrupts the flow of the sentence—it is parenthetical.)

The remaining items in the order were delivered yesterday; *therefore,* the invoice has been approved for payment. (The word *therefore* is used as a transitional word linking two independent clauses.)

SERIES

NOTE **SC.23**
Commas separate items in a series.

Three or more words, phrases, or clauses that form a subject, a verb, or an object create a **series.** Items in a series should be separated by commas. The final item usually is set apart from the others by the word *and* or the word *or.* For clarity, a comma should be used before the conjunction as well as between the other series items.

Jon, Kyle, and *Andy* are taking golf lessons. (The three names are part of a compound subject.)

Jason plays *bridge, chess,* and *backgammon.* (The items are the direct object of the verb *plays.*)

Up/down, near/far, and *thick/thin* are pairs of antonyms. (Each pair of words in the series is part of a compound subject.)

When the items in a series illustrate only a few of all possible options, a writer may use *etc.* to end the series. When this occurs, omit the word *and* but place a comma before etc.

The cruise ship has swimming pools, dining rooms, a spa, etc. (The conjunction *and* is omitted; a comma is placed before *etc.*)

The Semicolon

The **semicolon** is used to separate. It may also be used to join.

INDEPENDENT CLAUSES WITHOUT COORDINATING CONJUNCTIONS

NOTE **SC.24**
Semicolons join independent clauses when no conjunction is used.

A semicolon is used to connect two independent clauses not joined by a coordinating conjunction. The semicolon makes the reader aware of the close relationship between the independent clauses. Although each clause could be written as a separate sentence, joining them with a semicolon creates a smoother writing style.

Please sign and return the enclosed card; it requires no postage. (The clauses are closely related; no conjunction is used.)

The book was an action-packed thriller; I hope the film is, too. (The clauses are closely related; no conjunction is used.)

A comma mistakenly used to join independent clauses where no conjunction is present creates a *comma splice.* Writers should be careful to avoid this error.

Paul has asked for a paternity leave, he and his wife have adopted a baby. (incorrectly punctuated; comma splice)

Paul has asked for a paternity leave; he and his wife have adopted a baby. (correctly punctuated; semicolon joins independent clauses)

When closely related independent clauses are joined by a semicolon, the writer may omit duplicate words in the second clause and replace the material with a comma.

Last year we sponsored five concerts; this year, six. (Comma replaces duplicate words.)

INDEPENDENT CLAUSES WITH COORDINATING CONJUNCTIONS

When independent clauses are joined by a coordinating conjunction and either or both of the clauses contain commas, clarity is achieved by using a semicolon (rather than a comma) before the conjunction that joins the two independent clauses. In the example that follows, the second sentence uses a semicolon and is clearer and easier to read.

NOTE SC.25
Semicolons should be used to join independent clauses that contain commas.

> Mr. Samkoff, Mr. Cromwell, and Mrs. Fritz will move to the new building on May 3, but Mr. Martin, Mrs. Hazel, and Mr. Kinnard will not relocate until May 8.
>
> Mr. Samkoff, Mr. Cromwell, and Mrs. Fritz will move to the new building on May 3; but Mr. Martin, Mrs. Hazel, and Mr. Kinnard will not relocate until May 8.

SERIES ITEMS CONTAINING COMMAS

Using commas to separate items in a series could create confusion when one or more items within the series contain a comma. By using semicolons to separate the items within this type of series, the message is easier to interpret. In the example that follows, the second sentence—the one that uses semicolons to separate the series items—is much clearer.

NOTE SC.26
Use semicolons to separate long, complex series items that contain commas.

> The group will visit Vienna, Austria, Paris, France, Munich, Germany, and Naples, Italy, during its two-week tour. (unclear)
>
> The group will visit Vienna, Austria; Paris, France; Munich, Germany; and Naples, Italy, during its two-week tour. (clear)

The comma and the semicolon are punctuation marks that influence the clarity and readability of a message. Use them effectively to help your reader better understand your message.

Secondary Internal Punctuation

Several other punctuation marks are used within sentences to bring clarity, emphasis, and variety to writing. Those punctuation marks are discussed in this section.

The Apostrophe

As you write letters, memos, and reports, you will use the apostrophe in three ways: to form possessives, to form contractions, and to form plurals.

NOTE SC.27
Apostrophes are used to form possessives, contractions, and plurals.

POSSESSIVES

A **possessive** shows ownership. Both nouns and pronouns may be expressed as possessives. Figure SC.1 shows the possessive form of several nouns and pronouns. Recall that only nouns use an apostrophe in their possessive form. The apostrophe is placed either before the *s* ('s) or after the *s* (s') depending on the noun. The context of the sentence often will provide a clue to placement of the apostrophe. Seminar A contains detailed information about forming possessives.

Word	Possessive	Word	Possessive
she (pronoun)	her office	week (noun)	two weeks' vacation
we (pronoun)	our factory	employee (noun)	employee's desk
they (pronoun)	their engineer	employees (noun)	employees' lounge
he (pronoun)	his computer	Dale (noun)	Dale's idea
month (noun)	a month's salary	Dennis (noun)	Dennis' promotion

CONTRACTIONS

NOTE SC.28
Contractions are seldom
used in business
correspondence.

A **contraction** is a combination of two words in a shortened form. An apostrophe signals the omission of one or more letters in the contraction—*you're* for *you are, wouldn't* for *would not,* and *let's* for *let us.* Contractions are seldom used in business writing because they lack the formality desired in a permanent record. The opposite is true of *o'clock;* this contraction for *of the clock* is used when writers want formality.

When spoken, several contractions sound the same as possessive pronouns. These potentially confusing words are listed in Figure SC.2. If you are unsure about whether to use an apostrophe, remember this: A contraction *always* has an apostrophe.

PLURALS

For clarity, use an apostrophe to form the plural of a lowercase letter. Also use the apostrophe to form the plural of the uppercase letters A, I, M, and U. Without an apostrophe, these uppercase letters could be misread as words (As, Is, Us) or as an abbreviation (Ms).

Place x's before all items that apply.
How many A's did you earn last term?

The Colon

NOTE SC.29
Colons alert the reader
that something of
importance will follow.

The colon is often used as a clue to the reader that a *list,* an *explanation,* or an *example* will follow. The words that introduce the list should contain a subject and a predicate. The items following the colon may be words, phrases, or complete sentences. They may be displayed as part of the paragraph text or as a vertical list. The writer makes the placement decision based on the space available and the amount of emphasis to be placed on the items. A list will receive more attention than items

Word	Meaning
its	possessive form of pronoun *it*
it's	contraction of *it is*
their	possessive form of pronoun *they* (before noun)
they're	contraction of *they are*
theirs	possessive form of pronoun *they* (not before noun)
there's	contraction of *there is*
whose	possessive form of pronoun *who*
who's	contraction of *who is*
your	possessive form of pronoun *you*
you're	contraction of *you are*

presented in paragraph form. When displayed in paragraph form, items following a colon begin with a capital letter only when they are complete sentences; items in a vertical list always begin with a capital letter. When a sentence separates the lead-in from the list, no colon is used.

Bretta's reason for missing the meeting was simple: She was one of three passengers in the elevator when it stopped between the sixth and seventh floors. (explanation in paragraph form)

Several factors influenced our decision: personnel, space, and equipment. (listing in paragraph form; common nouns)

Three factors influenced our decision: (1) Additional personnel would be needed. (2) Space for expansion does not exist. (3) Our equipment is old and fragile. (explanatory list in paragraph form with numbered sentences)

NOTE SC.30
List in paragraph form.

The decision was influenced by the following factors. We must address all of them before we reconsider the proposal. (No colon is used because of the intervening sentence; no periods are used because the items are not complete sentences.)

NOTE SC.31
List in vertical form.

1. The need for additional personnel
2. The lack of space for expansion
3. The condition of our equipment

Our decision was influenced by personnel, space, and equipment factors. (No colon is used because the portion of the sentence before the series is not an independent clause.)

The colon has several other applications that occasionally occur in business writing. Those uses and an example of each are presented in Figure SC.3.

The Dash

A **dash** is used to separate. When using word processing or desktop publishing software, writers create solid lines known as an *en dash* and an *em dash*. An *en dash* is a solid line used to separate the low and high elements of a numeric or an alphabetic range by taking the place of *to* or *through*. An *em dash* is a longer solid line used when a writer wants to show a sudden change in thought or to place emphasis on what follows.

NOTE SC.32
Dashes separate.

In some software, such as MS Word, the en dash and em dash are available as symbols; the em dash may also be included as an autoformat feature created when two hyphens are keyed with no space before, between, or after them and the surrounding text. If the en dash is not available, use a hyphen with no space between it and the items it separates. Similarly, two hyphens (no space before, between, or

Use	Example
ratio	2:1 (2 to 1)
references	11:18–21 (volume:page numbers)
reference initials	DKH:jw (author:keyboarder)
salutations	Dear Mr. Waldorf: (mixed punctuation)
times	12:15 p.m. (hour:minutes)
titles, subtitles	*Time Management: Making the Most of Your Day*

FIGURE SC.3
Other Uses of the Colon

after) can be substituted for an em dash. Because of its strength and impact, the em dash should be used less frequently than other marks of punctuation.

Bilin—a B+ student—plays catcher for the softball team. (em dash; sudden change of thought)

Only one sales representative exceeded this month's goal—Dan Enwright. (em dash; emphasis)

Items 1–5 focus on demographics; items 6–10, on opinions (en dash; numeric range)

When main floor seating is nearly full, open balconies A–C. (en dash; alphabetic range)

The Diagonal

NOTE SC.33
The diagonal has
several uses.

The **diagonal** (also called the *slant* or *slash*) frequently indicates a choice or an alternative. The diagonal is also used in creating fractions and may be used with some abbreviations. No space is used before or after the diagonal.

Do you want bagels and/or muffins at the meeting? (Either or both may be served.)

The new manager will select his/her administrative assistant. (The gender of the new employee is unknown.)

2/3 (fraction)

11 1/2 (mixed number; space before fraction)

NOTE SC.34
In correspondence, avoid
using the diagonal with
a date.

When completing business forms, writers often use the diagonal as part of a date. The standard format is month/day/year; two character positions are allocated to each part. The emerging popularity of the international date style (day/month/year) and the confusion that could result make this format inappropriate for use in correspondence:

07/09/08 (July 9, 2008? September 7, 2008?)

The Ellipsis

NOTE SC.35
Ellipsis points indicate that
words have been omitted.

An **ellipsis** is an intentional omission of words. An ellipsis is signaled by **ellipsis points,** a series of three periods separated from each other and from what precedes or follows them by one space. Ellipsis points are used for emphasis in advertising. In other forms of business writing, ellipsis points are used to indicate that words have been omitted from a direct quotation. When the ellipsis occurs at the end of a sentence, add the terminal punctuation:

The fluctuations in currency exchange rates are interesting . . . and worth watching.

The owner's manual says the picture should be ". . . clear and crisp."

Ethel choked back tears as she began her acceptance speech by saying, "I am truly honored . . . ." (end of sentence)

The Hyphen

The **hyphen** is used to bring words together to show that two items are related. Because the purpose is to join, there is no space before or after a hyphen. Hyphens are commonly used in three ways: (a) to form compound words, (b) to join prefixes and suffixes to root words, and (c) to indicate where a word has been divided. The first two uses are more common and are explained in this section.

COMPOUND WORDS

The most frequent use of the hyphen is to form compound words. A **compound word** is two or more words used as one. Compound words may be nouns, verbs, or adjectives. Writing experts do not always agree on whether compound words should be hyphenated, written as two words, or written as one word; style preferences are continually changing. The best source of information about compound nouns and verbs is a current dictionary. The information presented in this section will help you determine when and how to hyphenate compound adjectives.

NOTE SC.36
Hyphens form compound words.

Compound adjectives may be permanent or temporary. Permanent compound adjectives include a hyphen as part of their dictionary entry; temporary compound adjectives do not. Permanent compound adjectives use a hyphen all the time; temporary compound adjectives contain a hyphen only when they come before a noun. Compound adjectives formed using an *-ly* adverb are never hyphenated:

NOTE SC.37
Compound adjectives may be permanent or temporary.

Ron Howard is a *well-known* film director. (permanent compound before a noun)
Patricia Cornwell is *well-known* as an author. (permanent compound not before a noun)
This is a *highly technical* procedure. (temporary compound; *-ly* adverb)
Our goal is to produce *high-quality* products. (temporary compound before noun)
Our goal is to produce products of *high quality*. (temporary compound not before noun)

Dictionaries may vary. Always consult the current edition of a well-known dictionary.

Sometimes two or more hyphenated compound words with the same base word appear in a series. In this case, the hyphen is used, but the base word may be omitted in all except the last item of the series. This procedure is called suspending a hyphen:

Leah will describe our *short-* and *long-term* forecasting techniques. (The word *term* is omitted in the first compound word.)
The announcement can be repeated at *5-, 15-,* or *30-minute* intervals. (The word *minute* is omitted in the first two compound words.)

PREFIXES

A **prefix** is one or more syllables added to the beginning of a word. Prefixes are followed by hyphens in a variety of situations. Figure SC.4 lists those situations and gives an example of each.

Prefix	Hyphenated	Example
ex	yes	ex-mayor; ex-officio
self	yes	self-addressed; self-employed
pre	generally not	prescreen; preemployment
re	to distinguish from word with different meaning	re-call; recall
non	generally not	nonflammable; nonresponsive
co	consult dictionary	co-owner; coworker
vice	consult dictionary	vice president; vice-chancellor

FIGURE SC.4
Hyphenating Prefixes

Whenever a prefix is added to a proper noun, the prefix is separated from the word by a hyphen:

mid-October   trans-Alaska

Parentheses

NOTE SC.38
Items that are not essential may be placed in parentheses.

Parentheses, like commas, may be used to separate nonessential information from the rest of a thought. If parentheses and commas were compared according to their strength, however, parentheses would be rated as weaker marks of punctuation. The information they contain may be so unimportant that the writer should consider eliminating it entirely. Names, dates, times, amounts, reference citations, abbreviations, area codes, phone numbers, addresses, and editorial comments are just a few of the items that may be enclosed within parentheses. If a writer chooses to use parentheses, certain requirements must be met:

1. Both left and right parentheses must be used.
   The stock will be listed on the New York Stock Exchange *(NYSE)*.

2. Commas, semicolons, periods, or other punctuation marks should be used as needed within the parentheses.
   The entree *(salmon)* will be served with a baked potato, broccoli with cheese sauce *(or, if you prefer, lemon butter)*, and a colorful fruit garnish.

3. The presence of parentheses should not affect the use of punctuation elsewhere in the statement or question.
   After she retired *(lucky woman!)*, Elsa moved to Idaho.

The Period

NOTE SC.39
Periods are used with
• Abbreviations
• Decimals
• Lists

Earlier in this chapter, you reviewed the use of the period as a mark of terminal punctuation. Although that use of the period is certainly the most common, it is by no means the only use. This section focuses on other uses.

ABBREVIATIONS

Abbreviations are shortened forms of words, names, or phrases; their primary purpose is to save time and space. As a rule, business writers restrict their use of abbreviations to those they believe their receivers will recognize.

The capitalization, punctuation, and spacing of abbreviations vary widely. Seminar D covers some of these issues. The most comprehensive source of information about abbreviations is a reference manual.

DECIMALS

A **decimal** is one method by which writers may express fractional components of a whole number. In business writing, use decimals when expressing money or measurements. Do not use a space before or after the decimal:

The official rainfall for June 24 was *.24* inches.
Kyle has averaged *10.3* points per game this season.
The second portage is the longest, *2.8* miles.
All units that vary from specification by more than *.0025* " must be rejected.

LISTS

When items in a vertical list are identified by numbers or letters, a period is used with them. Lists may be formatted in three ways; all three apply to either numeric or alphabetic listings:

NOTE SC.40
List formats vary.

- In one format, the number is indented and the text wraps to the left margin. This is true whether the text runs over one line or many.
- In another format, both the number and any runover lines of the text begin at the left margin. This, also, is true whether the text runs over one line or many.
- Still another option is to key the number at the left margin and hang indent the text. This is true whether the text runs over one line or many.

A minimum of two spaces should follow the period. When using word processing software, simply tab to the next position on the preset tab grid, or use the feature that creates bullets and numbers for a list.

The Quotation Mark

A **quotation mark** serves three different purposes in written messages: (a) to indicate that the writer is using the exact words of another individual, (b) to emphasize words that are unique or have a special meaning in a particular message, or (c) to identify literary or artistic works. In all cases, quotation marks are used in pairs—one is placed at the beginning of the quote or item of information, the other is placed at the end.

NOTE SC.41
Quotation marks show exact wording, give special emphasis, or identify literary or artistic works.

EXACT WORDS

Quotations may be indirect or direct. An **indirect quotation** paraphrases the words of a writer or speaker. A **direct quotation** uses exact words. Quotation marks are used only with a direct quotation. Use a comma to separate introductory words from quoted material displayed in sentence format:

> Mrs. Larson said, *"Third-quarter sales exceeded expectations."*
> *"Third-quarter sales,"* said Mrs. Larson, *"have exceeded expectations."*
> Mrs. Larson said that third-quarter sales exceeded expectations. (not a direct quote)

Using quotation marks to highlight someone's exact words works well if the quote is brief. When the quote is long, however, another display technique is more emphatic. If a direct quotation occupies fewer than four lines of type, place the text in quotation marks but do not indent the material:

NOTE SC.42
The length of a quote influences its display.

> In his inaugural address, Governor Snellgrover told the citizens of the state, "Education, jobs, and the environment are high-priority items." (short direct quotation)

If the quoted material occupies four or more lines of type, display it as a separate, single-spaced paragraph; indent the material from both the left and right margins. This indented format, together with information about the source of the material, makes quotation marks unnecessary:

> In his inaugural address, Governor Snellgrover told the citizens of the state,
>   During my campaign I promised to work to maintain the quality of life

that has made this state such a fine place in which to live. Education, jobs, and the environment are high-priority items. We must not lose what we have worked so hard to achieve; we must strive to make further gains.

EMPHASIS

Whenever you wish to emphasize a word or phrase, even if it is not part of a direct quote, consider displaying it in quotation marks. Humorous items, definitions, slang words or phrases, and technical terms used in nontechnical ways are good candidates for this type of emphasis. If words are emphasized with quotation marks too frequently, however, the benefits of this display are lost.

Although she wears a size 5 shoe, Robin is known to her friends as *"Big Foot."*
Etc. is the abbreviation for the Latin phrase meaning *"and so forth."*

LITERARY AND ARTISTIC WORKS

Use quotation marks to set off the title of any section of a published work:

Beth just learned that her article, "Consolidating College Loans," has been accepted for publication in *The Young Professional.* (article in a magazine)
"Houseplants" is the second chapter of Beth Bretaglia's book, *The Green Thumb Gardener.*
"Memory," a well-known song from the Broadway musical *Cats,* is one of the selections contained in *The Andrew Lloyd Webber Collection.* (song, musical, album)

WITH OTHER PUNCTUATION MARKS

Because quotation marks may be used to begin, end, or set off material within a statement or question, some guidelines must be set regarding the use of other punctuation when quotation marks are present. Figure SC.5 will be a helpful reference.

Three additional rules concerning the use of punctuation and quotation marks should be remembered in writing business letters, memos, and reports:

1. Punctuation may be included in a quotation. If the quote is taken from a printed source, the punctuation should be included where the original author inserted it—even if it is incorrect.
2. Ending punctuation may be placed before or after the quotation marks but never in both places. When a conflict exists, use the stronger mark of punctuation. Exclamation marks are stronger than both question marks and periods.

FIGURE SC.5
Quotation Marks with Other
Punctuation Marks

Punctuation Mark	Placement
period	inside quotation marks
comma	inside quotation marks
colon	outside quotation marks
semicolon	outside quotation marks
question mark	inside when quotation is a question; outside when the entire item is a question
exclamation point	inside when quotation is an exclamation; outside when the entire item is an exclamation

3. Direct quotes that occur in the middle or near the end of other statements or questions are introduced by either a colon or a comma.

The following items illustrate how the placement guidelines and rules may be applied:

Did the performance appraisal contain this statement: "Sandra has become the department's expert in database management"? (The entire item is a question.)

Seth was so moved by the opera that he was the first to rise and shout, "Bravo!" (Only the quote is an exclamation.)

This badly damaged package was marked "Fragile"! (The entire sentence is an exclamation.)

Other Uses for Punctuation

NOTE SC.44
Punctuation may be used as a delimiter or divider.

Punctuation marks may be used in a number of other ways, among them as delimiters or dividers within mathematical formulas, telephone and fax numbers, e-mail addresses, and Internet URLs:

(707) 555-1234   707/555-2468   1.800.555.9876
$x = 3/(2y \times 4)+5$ jp@tophat.org   http://www.vqun.com

Application Exercises

1. Carefully read each of the following items. Insert the terminal mark of punctuation that would be best in each situation. Choose periods, question marks, or exclamation marks.
   a. Theo asked whether he could leave 30 minutes early on Friday
   b. You're the greatest
   c. Which company provides your cell phone service
   d. The fire alarm is sounding
   e. When will the new carpet be installed
   f. Will someone please replace the bulb in the projector in Room 20
   g. Elevator 2 will be out of service for three days
   h. Please call after 3:30 tomorrow afternoon
   i. Our medical plan does not cover cosmetic surgery
   j. Be sure to get a receipt

2. Locate the dates and geographic locations in the following sentences. Determine whether commas are needed, insert them where necessary, and give the reason for their use.
   a. Barbara lives and works in Calgary Alberta but often travels to Winnipeg Manitoba to consult with personnel at the corporate headquarters.
   b. Hotel reservations have been made for Sunday May 26 through Saturday June 1.
   c. Are you available to meet on the first of May?
   d. The bankruptcy petition was filed Thursday May 15 2007.
   e. The minutes of the December 3 meeting were approved as distributed.
   f. Richard will retire in June 2010 and move to the home he and Phoebe are building in Lakeland Florida.
   g. The application must be signed and returned by April 16 to Rob Welch, HR Manager, Wilderness Adventures 6782 Mountain View Road Gillette WY 82731,
   h. The letter from The Royal Bank is dated 12 July 2008.
   i. Naples Florida formalized its Sister City agreement with Piemonte Italy in September 2007.
   j. The tournament begins next Thursday.

3. Read each of the following sentences, and insert commas where necessary between independent adjectives. Some items may be correct.
   a. The Lunar New Year is the longest most important Chinese festival.
   b. Mr. Able described the new president as a charismatic challenging leader.
   c. Wooden furniture treated with dark mahogany stain helps create a warm welcoming atmosphere.
   d. Josh led an interesting informative seminar.
   e. Chuck's vintage motorcycle drew the attention and admiration of parade watchers.
   f. Sami paused then made several insightful thought-provoking remarks.
   g. The consultant provided us with a very clear picture of what needs to be done.
   h. The soft soothing music playing in the waiting room calmed the patients.
   i. The warm glowing embers of the fire lingered long after the campers were asleep.
   j. The laundry was unable to remove the stain from Sarah's dark blue wool suit.

4. Insert commas where needed in the following sentences, which may or may not contain independent or introductory clauses.
   a. When you are in New Orleans this summer be sure to visit the French Quarter.
   b. Employment data are weak but other economic indicators look strong.
   c. The zoo director has requested both a photocopier and a fax machine but I think we should buy one unit that performs both functions.
   d. If you want more tickets call Matt at 555-2259.
   e. The efficiency apartment is more affordable but I prefer the view and space in the studio unit.
   f. As we discussed yesterday your account will be credited for $57.
   g. When the parking permits have been printed send an e-mail announcing when and where they may be purchased.
   h. Please verify the time and date of the next training session.
   i. Although Marge won the car her husband says he will be the one to drive it.
   j. Archie read the book last week and plans to see the movie on Saturday.

5. Locate the nonessential elements in each of the following sentences, and insert punctuation where needed. Indicate whether the nonessential element is an appositive, a direct address, an introductory word, an introductory phrase, a nonrestrictive clause, a parenthetical expression, or a transitional expression.
   a. The situation in my opinion has become critical.
   b. The new hotel which is located at Baron Avenue and East First Street has 950 guest rooms.
   c. Mr. Winston I look forward to meeting with you and your staff on the 19th.
   d. According to our records your last payment was received February 11.
   e. The portraits which were painted by Alex Renquist will be hung in the lobby.
   f. You will of course be fully vested in the retirement program.
   g. Yes two pedestrians witnessed the accident.
   h. The keynote speaker is Jackson Rutlege owner of Mocha Madness.
   i. Fortunately the negatives were not destroyed in the fire.
   j. We must find a way to curtail expenses otherwise our profitability will fall.

6. Insert commas where necessary to separate series items in the following sentences.
   a. Corporations must begin to address social issues such as diversity work-family balance equal rights and the environment.
   b. People attending the concert may park in lot A D or F.
   c. Your business card should include your phone number your fax number and your e-mail address.
   d. The airline has hubs in Philadelphia Cleveland Houston and Denver.
   e. The lease specifies that we must shampoo the carpets wash the windows and clean the oven before we vacate the apartment.
   f. Be sure to order more mugs hats and key chains.
   g. Seth Meg and Molly collaborated on the project.
   h. Rooms 316 317 and 318 will be remodeled next month.

     i.   Should I print the notice on yellow green or buff paper?

     j.   The weather is especially nice during May June and July.

7. Insert commas and semicolons where necessary in each of the following sentences. Explain the reason for each punctuation mark.

     a.   The policies have not changed but the procedures have been updated.

     b.   The plaques have been delivered but they have not yet been engraved.

     c.   The package was damaged during shipment therefore you are entitled to a full refund.

     d.   Mo said that he would be working late every night this week he indicated however that he will not be working this Saturday.

     e.   While employed by Smythe Brothers I worked in Ft. Collins Colorado Salem and Portland Oregon and San Bernardino California.

     f.   Once the logo has been redesigned we'll reprint our stationery internal forms however will not be reprinted until our current inventory is depleted.

     g.   We will break for ten but only ten minutes.

     h.   Thanks to you Sandy the project was a success we appreciate your efforts.

     i.   Sharon was angry when she learned of the defect she relaxed when she learned it would be repaired without cost.

     j.   Rochelle will write the news release Lilly will fax it to the media outlets.

8. Insert terminal punctuation marks, commas, and semicolons where appropriate; some items may be correct.

     a.   All representatives who exceed the quarterly sales goal will be eligible for the drawing.

     b.   The warranty expired on March 31 nevertheless we will approve your claim.

     c.   The recreational sports program offers a nice blend of individual and team sports classes include kayaking golf tennis and volleyball.

     d.   The first part of the test went fairly well I think but I will need to review my English spelling and mathematics before returning for the next section of the examination.

     e.   After reading your December issue I immediately subscribed the articles were outstanding.

     f.   Robert Brown president of Brown Brothers Albert Pyroz personnel director at Dataform Sylvia Jacobsen owner of a consulting firm and Amanda Newel records manager at BZP Corporation were all members of the panel discussing mid-life career changes.

     g.   The men's locker room has three showers the women's five.

     h.   I wonder what the next popular technology tool will be

     i.   Congratulations Madeline

     j.   The Bailey study which was conducted in California in 2007 challenges the results of earlier research.

     k.   You must get the data to Olivia by noon on Friday or a decision on the waiver will be delayed until next week.

     l.   Ben Zyck our representative in your area will phone you next week.

     m.   The contract calls for a bonus of 10 percent if construction is completed by June 23 2009.

     n.   We will of course send a copy of the proposal to Sean.

     o.   Cylene has a sincere positive attitude.

9. Decide whether the secondary internal punctuation marks have been used correctly in the following sentences. Make all changes that are necessary.

     a.   Did Director Jackson ask "Why we want to replace the printer"?

     b.   The visitors from abroad had difficulty understanding what Marvin meant by a "rock bottom price".

     c.   Three options are available. 1 Enter into a contract with a service bureau. 2. Hire temporary workers. (3). Ask our employees to work overtime.

     d.   The engineer thinks he can reform the mold rather than replace it.

     e.   Our business plan must contain short medium and long range financial projections.

     f.   To have a representative visit your office, call 651 (555/2333].

     g.   From 7 . . . 9 p.m. Thursday, each student who brings his:her ID card to the theater will receive $1 1_2 off the posted ticket price and a coupon for a free box of popcorn.

     h.   The title slide should be Language The Good The Bad and The Trendy.

i. Chapter 2, Sinks and Faucets, can be found on pages 126/134 of "Home Improvement Hints".

j. "Accept the challenge Ricardo said and you will reap the rewards."

Message Analysis

Make the changes needed to ensure that the following draft of a position description is punctuated correctly and formatted attractively.

As an industry leader, and a service provider to more than one million customers, Baker Bottling has excellent start-up opportunities for Delivery Rep/Sales in the Jamestown TN area.

Baker seeks an enthusiastic performance driven selfmotivated individual to join its marketing team. The qualified candidate must have 3 or more year's experience in sales, excellent communication skills, and a genuine commitment to providing superior customer service. In addition he-she must be able to meet applicable Department of Transportation, d.o.t., licensing requirements. A demonstrated commitment to the community and the profession are desirable.

Among the responsibilities this individual will assume are these . . . [1] acquire new customers, (2) make deliveries to customers, set up promotional displays, (d.) execute the companies' business plan; and ensure compliance with safety policies.

If you are interested in this exciting challenging opportunity send a letter resume and the names:addresses of 3 references to Lisa Blixt at Baker Bottling 2386 Sherman Road Jamestown TN 38556

seminar d

The word *style* is used in several ways in business writing. A person's ability to organize and express ideas is called style. The format of a letter, memo, or report may be referred to as style. Reference manuals are sometimes called style manuals. In this seminar, **style** is used to mean the basic rules for number display, capitalization, and abbreviation that apply to business writing.

Writers should be as concerned about correct usage as they are about their basic writing skills. Correct usage—usually called mechanics—and good writing skills work together to

- Minimize the number of distractions in a message
- Bring consistency to communication
- Reflect well on the writer
- Have a positive effect on the reader

Reference manuals differ in the way they approach style items. Materials in this seminar are based on *HOW 11: A Handbook for Office Professionals*, by James Clark and Lyn Clark.

NOTE SD.1
Style refers to rules for correct usage.

Numbers

Numbers play a major role in our lives. They represent, describe, and locate people and objects. Because numbers are used so widely, attention must be given to expressing them correctly in business writing.

Business writers use general style when expressing numbers. **General style** is a blend of two styles known as *formal* and *technical*. In general style, numbers are represented in words when formality is needed and in figures when clarity is desired.

NOTE SD.2
General style is used for expressing numbers in business writing.

General Guidelines

Several guidelines relate to the way numbers are expressed. Some of these guidelines are used frequently in business writing, others are used rarely. This section describes those guidelines that have frequent application in business correspondence and reports.

WRITING WHOLE NUMBERS

Whole numbers greater than ten are written in figures. This guideline applies only to whole numbers—those that have no decimal or fractional parts:

The bill shows that Art made *three* long distance calls last month.
Because of the storm, Carol's flight was delayed *two* hours.
The manufacturer predicts that the van will get *19* mph in city driving conditions.

NOTE SD.3
Write whole numbers greater than ten in figures.

WRITING ROUND NUMBERS

NOTE **SD.4**
Using figures draws
attention to large numbers.

Round numbers may be expressed in figures, in words, or as a combination of the two. To reduce the emphasis placed on a round number, use words. When emphasis is desired, use figures. Figures are often used in advertising for emphasis. Because numbers greater than a million may be difficult to read when expressed in figures, a writer may combine words and figures to achieve greater clarity:

> The science museum has hosted nearly *400,000* visitors since it opened.
> The band spent more than *three hundred* days on the road last year.
> The population of the country exceeds *15 million*.

BEGINNING A SENTENCE WITH A NUMBER

NOTE **SD.5**
Use words for numbers
that begin sentences.

Numbers that begin a sentence are expressed in words. If the number is large, rewrite the sentence:

> *Five* managers have requested early retirement.
> *Six thousand* runners have registered for the marathon.
> *Thirteen thousand two hundred seventy-seven* people attended the convention. (Awkward. See the following sentence.)
> The convention attendance was *13,277*. (improved version)

WRITING NUMBERS CONSISTENTLY

NOTE **SD.6**
Make numbers easy
to read.

Be consistent in expressing numbers, and strive for easy reading. When *related* numbers greater than and less than ten appear in the same sentence, use figures for all numbers. When *unrelated* numbers greater than and less than ten appear in the same sentence, follow the general guideline for writing whole numbers. Items in a series are always considered related.

> Children *6* and under are admitted free; adults *65* and older receive a *$2* discount. (related numbers)
> Today's shipment included *20* pairs of sneakers, *15* pairs of sandals, and *5* purses. (series numbers considered related)
> The tour group consisted of *15 people,* each of whom had at least *two suitcases.* (unrelated numbers)

When one of two adjacent numbers is part of a compound modifier, the first number is written in words. If the first number cannot be written in one or two words, display it as a figure also:

> The performance schedule includes *two 15-minute* intermissions. (adjacent numbers; compound modifier)
> The developer plans to build *175 3-bedroom* condominiums north of Ridgeway. (large number as part of adjacent number; compound modifier)

If two numbers are adjacent to one another, as in a series, punctuation and spacing enhance readability. When two unrelated numbers are adjacent to one another in a sentence, place a comma between them to make them easy to read:

> By *2006, 15* of the franchises had been remodeled. (easy to read)

PUNCTUATING NUMBERS

NOTE **SD.7**
Use commas in numbers
with four or more digits.

In numbers with four or more digits, a comma usually is used. The comma is omitted in identification, model, serial, house, page, and telephone/ fax numbers. It is also omitted in ZIP codes, years, decimal fractions, and metric measurements:

1,113	1,250,671	ID No. 9336
8723 Springfield Road	Serial No. 8512-C	page 1543
Cleveland, OH 44122-1856	2010	(715) 555-3821
3000 meters	Model 6518	.16824

Specific Guidelines

The general guidelines just presented will help you through many writing situations involving numbers. There are some specific guidelines, too, that should be mastered. As you read the material, you will encounter the term *ordinal*. **Ordinal** numbers show position in a series. *First, second, third, tenth,* and *seventy-fifth* are examples of ordinal numbers spelled out; *1st, 2nd, 3rd, 10th,* and *75th* are examples of ordinal numbers in figures.

NOTE SD.8
Ordinals show position in a series.

ADDRESSES

House or building numbers except *one* are written in figures when used within the text of a message. As part of the mailing address in a letter or on an envelope, *all* house and building numbers are displayed in figures; *one* is not an exception. Street names that are numbers are spelled out if ten or below and written as figures in all other cases:

NOTE SD.9
Use figures for house and building numbers in mailing addresses.

One Ordean Road (in text)
1 Ordean Road (in a mailing address)
906 West Third Avenue
1212 65th Avenue West
10 North 32nd Avenue

NOTE SD.10
Use words for street names ten and under; otherwise, use figures.

DATES

Cardinal numbers (1, 2, 3) are used for the day and the year. If the day is used without a month or if the day precedes the month, ordinal numbers (1st, 2nd, 3rd; first, second, third) may be used:

June 1954   May 28   January 1, 2007
the 1st and 15th (ordinal without a month)
the 2nd of October (ordinal number)
the seventh of March (ordinal number)

Some writers use the international (military) date form, but it has not received widespread acceptance in American business correspondence. The international date form should be used in correspondence sent to receivers outside the United States. Select the form used in the country to which you are writing. Here are two common international date forms:

NOTE SD.11
Use figures for the day and the year.

13 October 2009   2009.10.13 (year/month/day)

FRACTIONS

When a fraction appears alone, it is written in words. Use a hyphen between the numerator (top number) and denominator (bottom number) of a fraction written in words when the fraction is used as a compound adjective. When a fraction is part of a mixed number, express it in figures:

NOTE SD.12
Use words when a fraction stands alone; use figures when a fraction is part of a mixed number.

one fourth of the proceeds   a one-third share (adjective)
one twenty-seventh   3 2/3

Notice the space in the mixed number between the fraction and the whole number. Unless a typewriter or keyboard has a special key for fractions, this space is necessary for readability. Without the space the figure could be misread as 32/3 (thirty-two thirds).

MONEY

NOTE SD.13
Indefinite money amounts are written in words.

Money amounts are expressed in figures. If the money amount is a whole number, the decimal and zeros are omitted—even when whole and mixed dollar amounts occur in the same series. A comma is used in most money amounts of four digits or more. An indefinite amount of money should be written in words:

$7,093.32	$719	$11,500	several million dollars

The missing checks were for payments of $127.63, $250, and $325.50.

For amounts of money less than a dollar, use figures and spell the word *cent(s)*:

1 cent   39 cents

On orders, invoices, and other business forms, the symbol ¢ may be used. If definite amounts of money greater and less than one dollar occur in the same sentence, use the $ symbol and a decimal where necessary:

The three lowest bids were $1.19, $1.03, and $.96 per unit.

ORDINALS

NOTE SD.14
Use only one- or two-word ordinals; in other cases, rewrite.

If an ordinal can be expressed in one or two words, spell it in full. If the ordinal exceeds one or two words, rewrite the sentence to avoid the need for an ordinal. This restriction applies only to ordinals that appear within the body of a sentence. Refer to the sections on addresses and dates under the Specific Guidelines heading in this seminar for the proper use of ordinals in those items.

The cast was exhausted after giving its fifth performance in three days.

The president gave a gold watch to Fred Benson, who was celebrating his *thirtieth* anniversary with the company.

Dilton's *one-hundred-seventeenth* Customer Appreciation Sale will begin Monday, August 12. (Long ordinal; hard to read when written in words)

Dilton's has held a Customer Appreciation Sale for 117 years; this year's sale will begin Monday, August 12. (Improved version; sentence rewritten to avoid the need for an ordinal)

PERCENTAGES

NOTE SD.15
Use the word *percent* within text.

In nontechnical business communication, write *percent* as a word and express the number as a figure. Use the symbol % on forms or in statistical or technical tables. Include a zero before a decimal that does not begin with a zero:

In correspondence:

25 percent	$13^1/_4$ percent	76.2 percent	.05 percent	0.8 percent

In statistical or technical tables:

25%	$13^1/_4$%	76.2%	.05%	0.8%

At the beginning of a sentence, spell the number or reword the sentence:

Six percent of our budget is targeted for equipment purchases.

We have targeted 6 *percent* of our budget for equipment purchases.

TIME

To designate time with a.m. (midnight to noon) or p.m. (noon to midnight) use a figure; the colon and zeros are not needed for on-the-hour times. The word *o'clock* is used only with on-the-hour times; the number may be displayed as a figure for emphasis or written as a word for formality.

> On the first day of the sale, we will open at *9 a.m.* and close at *9 p.m.*
> We agreed to meet in the lobby at *7 o'clock* tomorrow morning. (emphasis)
> The reception will begin at *eight o'clock* this evening. (formality)

In all cases, be sure the time of day is clear:

> The train will arrive at *5:30.* (in the morning or in the afternoon?)
> The train will arrive at *5:30 this afternoon.* (clear)

To avoid confusion, writers usually use *midnight* rather than 12 a.m. and *noon* rather than 12 p.m. Omit *a.m.* when using *noon* and omit *p.m.* when using *midnight*. Include 12 when noon or midnight is used in conjunction with another time; the figure is optional when the terms are used alone:

> The doors will be opened at *6 a.m.* and locked at *12 midnight.*
> Lunch will be served at *noon.*

WEIGHTS AND MEASURES

Express the amount something weighs or measures in figures. Abbreviate the name of the weight or measure only on business forms or in statistical material.

> Use *1-inch* margins on the report.
> The heater will go on when the temperature falls below *68 degrees.*
> 65# (on a business form)   7" (on a business form)

NOTE SD.16
Designate time in figures or words based on content.

Capitalization

Early in your education, you were taught to capitalize proper nouns and the first letter of a word that begins a sentence. Few, if any, writers have difficulty with these practices. This section, therefore, will present other accepted rules for capitalization.

Academic Courses and Degrees

When referring to a specific course, capitalize the first letter of the main word(s). Do not capitalize general subjects other than languages. Degree names are capitalized only when used with a person's name and, in that circumstance, most always appear as an abbreviation:

> The spring schedule lists three sections of *Ethics and Technology*.
> Are you taking an *ethics course* this term?
> Dr. Harwood teaches *Finance* 200, 315, and 450.
> Dr. Harwood teaches *finance* courses.
> Before traveling to Europe, Paul took a *conversational German* course.
> Blake Colby, MD, recently earned a *master's degree* in health care management.

NOTE SD.17
Capitalize specific academic courses and languages.

Compass Directions

Names of specific geographical regions are capitalized. Do not capitalize general directions:

> The *East Coast* is bracing for hurricane season. (region)
> The Marks brothers have acquired the DeliMeat distributorship for the *Midwest*. (region)
> The parking lot on the *east* side of the building is being repaired. (a direction)
> Drive three miles *south* on Highway G, then turn west on Route 12. (directions)

Government

Principal words in the names of domestic and foreign government agencies, units, and organizations are capitalized:

> Environmental Protection Agency
> Royal Canadian Mounted Police
> United States Navy

Short forms of the names of national and international government bodies and their major divisions are generally capitalized. Writers should use short forms only when they are certain their readers will understand them:

> the Court (United States Supreme Court)
> the House (United States House of Representatives)
> the Corps (United States Corps of Engineers)

The short forms of the names of state and local government bodies are not capitalized unless used in formal communication. Terms such as *federal*, *government*, and *nation* are general terms, so they are not capitalized:

> Rex bought a 20-acre tract of land adjacent to the *county* line. (general reference)
> A *city* ordinance prohibits burning trash outdoors.
> The *federal* government requires commercial aircraft cargo to meet safety standards.

When in doubt about the capitalization of government and judicial body names, consult a reference book such as *HOW 11*.

Institutions and Organizations

The full names of institutions (churches, libraries, hospitals, and schools) and organizations (associations, companies, and clubs) and their divisions or departments are capitalized. Capitalize *the* only when it is part of the official title. Follow the style established by the organization or institution as shown on its letterhead stationery or in other written communication. The shortened, common noun version of institution and organization names is generally not capitalized except in formal documents:

> Ralph earned his degree at *The Ohio State University*.
> *The McCarren Library* has a good selection of audio books.
> Have you accepted the invitation to join *Pi Sigma Epsilon*?

Planning Committee	but	*the committee*
Intensive Care Unit	but	*the unit*
Investor Services Division	but	*the division*

Time

The most common reference to time in business writing is a date, but time can also be a reference to seasons, holidays, or events. The names of days, months, specific special events, holidays, religious days, and historical events are always capitalized. The names of decades and centuries are generally not capitalized; season names, however, are capitalized when combined with a year:

NOTE SD.21
Capitalize most references to time.

Tuesday, August 3	Flag Day
Kwanzaa	Sidewalk Sale
twenty-first century	the mid-nineties
Winter Carnival	Summer 2008

Titles

Titles (professional, business, military, service, religious, political, family, or nobility) are capitalized when used in a signature line, a mailing address, or a list. In correspondence text, however, they are treated differently. Titles are capitalized when they come before a personal name unless the name is there as an appositive. Titles are not capitalized when they come after a personal name or when they replace a personal name:

NOTE SD.22
Capitalization of personal titles depends on how they are used.

The *maintenance manager,* P. J. Perkins, described the changes in the safety code. (name clarifies)

Acting Dean Jean Sanders will present the certificates. (job title before personal name)

Josefina Ortiz, who was elected *mayor* last year, reported on economic development activities. (title following name)

After vacationing in Florida, *Ambassador* Portor returned to France. (title before a personal name)

The *president's* motorcade was delayed by traffic. (title used in place of personal name)

Abbreviations

Abbreviations save space and time, but their use in business writing should be limited to those that the reader will recognize and understand. If an abbreviation is to be used several times within a letter or report, the complete form—followed by the abbreviation in parentheses—should be used at the first instance. The reader will then understand the abbreviation when it occurs again:

NOTE SD.23
Use only those abbreviations your reader will understand.

The *Student Conduct Committee (SCC)* has filed its report. After the vice president has reviewed the SCC report, she will submit it to the Board of Governors.

Generally, an abbreviation follows the full-text format with respect to whether it is displayed in uppercase or lowercase letters—abbreviations for proper nouns use uppercase letters; abbreviations for common nouns use lowercase letters. Guidelines about whether to use or omit periods within the abbreviation are less clear. To be sure, consult a reference manual.

Acronyms and Initialisms

NOTE SD.24

Acronyms are pronounced as words; initialisms are not.

Acronyms and initialisms are special forms of abbreviations. **Acronyms** are words formed by using the first letter of each major word of a compound item. When abbreviations are formed from the first letter of major words in a compound item but the outcome is not pronounced as a word, the abbreviation is called an **initialism.** Business firms, government agencies, and professional groups are often known by their initialisms. Examples of both follow:

Association for Computing Machinery	becomes	ACM
Beginners All-purpose Symbolic Instruction Code	becomes	BASIC
U.S. Postal Service	becomes	USPS
Consolidated Omnibus Budget Reconciliation Act	becomes	COBRA
Cost-of-living adjustment	becomes	COLA
Initial public offering	becomes	IPO
Personal Digital Assistant	becomes	PDA

Business and Association Names

NOTE SD.25

Spell generic business names when used alone in a sentence.

Abbreviated words are often part of the name of a business firm. *Assn.* for Association, *Co.* for Company, *Corp.* for Corporation, *Ltd.* for Limited, and *Inc.* for Incorporated are examples. Abbreviate these items only when they are abbreviated in the business name; spell them in full when used independently within a sentence:

Adventure Travel *Corp.* offers whitewater rafting trips.
The *corporation* is based in North Carleston, South Carolina.

Courtesy and Personal Titles

NOTE SD.26

Courtesy titles should be abbreviated when they occur before a name.

Courtesy title abbreviations such as *Mr., Mrs., Ms.,* and *Dr.* are used before a personal name:

Mr. Juan Estrada   *Ms.* Rose Pardue
Mrs. Celia Wood   *Dr.* Edward Robier

NOTE SD.27

The individual's preference should be respected when using titles.

Unless a woman's specific title is known, use *Ms.* A woman should tell her correspondents the title she prefers. When the person's preference is known, that title should be used. If a writer's first name may be used by members of either gender (Pat, Terry, Lee), the writer should include a personal title in the signature line. This procedure should also be followed if a writer uses only initials (A. K. Jones; B. W. O'Brien). This technique, as well as other options, is illustrated in Chapter 6.

The personal titles *Junior* and *Senior* are abbreviated when they follow a name. Because they are considered part of the name, no commas are used:

Kenneth Langford *Jr.*   Hector Todd *Sr.*

Measurements

Measurements may be abbreviated when they occur frequently in tables or business forms. When used, they are displayed in lowercase letters, with periods if they represent one word and without periods if they represent more than one word. In most business writing, measurements are spelled in full rather than abbreviated. Metric units of measurement are always written without periods. Common measurements and their abbreviations are shown in Figure SD.1.

NOTE SD.28
Spell measurements in general correspondence.

Months/Days

Months of the year and days of the week should be abbreviated only on forms or in visual aids where space is limited. Two options are shown for days of the week, one with and one without periods. The style with periods is used most often:

NOTE SD.29
Use abbreviations sparingly for months and days.

Jan.	Apr.	July	Oct.
Feb.	May	Aug.	Nov.
Mar.	June	Sept./Sep.	Dec.

Sun.	Mon.	Tues. (Tue.)	Wed.	Thurs.	Fri.	Sat.
Su	M	Tu	W	Th	F	Sa

Personal Names

Abbreviations for personal names may take the form of an initial or a shortened form of the name:

NOTE SD.30
Names may be abbreviated by using initials or a shortened form of the name.

C. Luisa Diaz	O. C. Chatsworth
Wm. Baxter	Jamie P. Adams-Roy

An abbreviation is different from a nickname. An abbreviation is always shorter than the given name; it always ends with a period. Nicknames may be modifications of a given name (Katy for Katherine) or may be totally unrelated to the given name (George Herman "Babe" Ruth). Personal names should not be abbreviated unless space is limited, as in tabulations or enumerations. In business writing, restrict the use of nicknames to those that are modifications of given names (e.g., Don for Donald). Before abbreviating a person's name, be sure that the individual will not object to the use of the abbreviated form.

NOTE SD.31
Nicknames differ from abbreviations.

FIGURE SD.1
Measurement Abbreviations

Measure	Abbreviation	Measure	Abbreviation
centimeter	cm	miles per hour	mph
foot	ft.	pound	lb.
gallon	gal.	pages per minute	ppm
kilogram	kg	words per minute	wpm

Professional Titles, Designations, and Degrees

NOTE SD.32
Abbreviate designations
and academic degrees.

Many people choose to use their professional titles, designations, or degrees when conducting business. Whenever possible, write professional titles in full. Abbreviate designations and academic degrees:

Professor Bernard Lomax   Major Hal Zypt
Ronald P. Gilmore, CIO   J. J. Alvarez, CNA
L. N. Lee, DVM   Emily Hunter, CMA

NOTE SD.33
Use either a title or an
academic degree
abbreviation, not both.

When referring to a person who has the academic or medical credentials to be addressed as doctor, use either the title or the degree abbreviation, not both. If the title is used, place the abbreviation *Dr.* before the name. If the abbreviation for the degree is used, place it after the name; use a comma to separate the name from the abbreviation:

Dr. Jane Alexander   Jane Alexander, PhD

States/Territories/Provinces

NOTE SD.34
Abbreviate names
of states, territories,
and provinces when
they are part of a
complete address.

The official two-letter postal abbreviations for state, territory, and province names should be used when part of a complete address. In all other cases, the name of the state, territory, or province should be spelled in full. A complete list of the two-letter postal abbreviations used in the United States and Canada is on the inside back cover. Be sure to learn the postal address requirements of other countries to which you write.

Symbols

NOTE SD.35
Use only those symbols
that your receiver will
interpret correctly.

Symbols are a form of abbreviation. Figure SD.2 includes several standard symbols. A brief definition and an example of each are also provided. Symbols should be used sparingly in business writing. Include only those symbols that your readers will interpret correctly.

FIGURE SD.2
Frequently Used Symbols

Symbol	Definition	Example
&	ampersand (meaning *and*)	Dr. & Mrs. Wolff
*	asterisk (refers reader to a note)	Price*
		*subject to change without notice
@	at, each, per	17 @ $2.25 each
©	copyright	© Hale Publishing
®	registered trademark	Compaq®
°	degree	89°
/	diagonal, slash	and/or, s/he, http://, 5/11/02
¢	cents	79¢
$	dollars	$589.99
'	feet (apostrophe)	2'
"	inch (quotation mark)	10.2"
:	ratio (colon)	3:1
#	number (before figure)	#10
#	pounds (after figure)	100#
%	percent	75%
x	by or times (lowercase *x*)	2 x 4, 5 x 7
K	thousand	640K, $20K
<, >	less than, greater than	<20, >75

Time Zones

The world is divided into time zones. In Canada and the United States, each zone has its own abbreviation. In addition, one character in that abbreviation is changed to indicate whether those residing in the region are observing standard or daylight saving time:

NOTE SD.36
Time zones for both standard and daylight savings time are abbreviated.

EST	Eastern Standard Time	EDT	Eastern Daylight Time
CST	Central Standard Time	CDT	Central Daylight Time
MST	Mountain Standard Time	MDT	Mountain Daylight Time
PST	Pacific Standard Time	PDT	Pacific Daylight Time

Telephone directories often include a map of North America and show the areas covered by each zone. When writers ask receivers to phone them, they often include the time zone in the message. Typically, the time zone is displayed in parentheses following the hours during which telephone calls are received—for example, 9 a.m. to 4 p.m. (EST).

Other Abbreviations

So many abbreviations are used in business that it is impractical to include all of them in this seminar. Some of the most commonly used terms are listed in Figure SD.3.

NOTE SD.37
Consult references before abbreviating unfamiliar terms.

FIGURE SD.3
Other Commonly Used Abbreviations

Term	Abbreviation	Term	Abbreviation
account	acct.	manager	mgr.
additional	addnl., add'l	merchandise	mdse.
also known as	a.k.a.	money order	MO
amount	amt.	month, months	mo., mos.
as soon as possible	ASAP	national	natl.
attached	att.	net weight	nt. wt.
average	avg.	not applicable	NA
balance	bal.	not available	NA
care of	c/o	optional	opt.
charge	chg.	organization	org.
collect on delivery	COD	original	orig.
continued	cont.	out of stock	OS or o.s.
courtesy copy	cc	over-the-counter	OTC
credit	cr.	package	pkg.
depreciation	depr.	page, pages	p., pp.
destination	dstn.	paid	pd.
discount	disc., dis.	parcel post	PP
division	div.	part, point	pt.
extension	ext., Ext.	port of entry	POE or p.o.e.
fiscal year	FY	prepaid	ppd.
for example	e.g.	purchase order	P.O., PO
forward	fwd.	quantity	qty.
freight	frt.	quarter, quarterly	qtr.
gross weight	gr. wt.	received	recd.
headquarters	HQ, hdqtrs.	requisition	req.
hour	hr.	respond, if you please	R.S.V.P., RSVP
institute	inst.	self-addressed, stamped envelope	SASE
international	intl., intnl.	standard	std.
inventory	invt.	statement	stmt.
invoice	inv.	wholesale	whsle.

Notice that some of the abbreviations use capital letters; others use lowercase letters. Some of the abbreviations use periods, others do not. Because abbreviations are often associated with particular fields (e.g., education, law, medicine, transportation), you may encounter abbreviations with which you are unfamiliar. When this situation arises, consult a dictionary or reference manual.

Application Exercises

1. Choose the appropriate expression(s) for each number in the following items:
   a. Nearly (500/five hundred/5 hundred) students have preregistered for the (8-/eight-) week summer session.
   b. We replace (four/4) trucks in our (twenty-/20-) truck fleet every (thirty-six/36) months.
   c. Mail my reimbursement check to (523/Five Twenty-three/Five Hundred Twenty- three) (Second/2nd/2) Street South.
   d. The serial number on the Model (1222/1,222/twelve 22/twelve twenty-two) laser printer is (736,921-G/736921-G).
   e. PQG declared a (38-cent/thirty-eight cent/$.38) dividend.
   f. After spending nearly (three/3) hours on the road, we had traveled merely (one hundred fifty/150) miles.
   g. Please change my address from (763 - Fifth Avenue/763 - 5th Avenue/763 5th Avenue/763 Fifth Avenue) to (376 - Fifth Avenue/376 - 5th Avenue/376 5th Avenue/376 Fifth Avenue).
   h. The stock rose (1 1/4 / 11/4 / 1 and one-fourth) points in (two/2) days.
   i. By subscribing now, you'll get (15/fifteen) issues for the price of (10/ten), a savings of (50%/50 percent/fifty percent).
   j. (25/Twenty-five) years ago we were a fledgling startup; today we are a multinational corporation with a (two billion dollar/$ two billion/$2 billion/$2,000,000,000) annual payroll.
2. Correct the number errors in the following sentences.
   a. Introduced in May 2006, the Model 6,267-P has generated more than $2 million in sales.
   b. Install 21 4-light fixtures in each bathroom.
   c. Deliver the package to Mark Muntz at 113 South 4th Street.
   d. Insert the table on page six of the report.
   e. 17 minutes later, the power was restored.
   f. More than 2/3 of the tickets were sold during the first day they were available to the public.
   g. Sam was successful in negotiating a $.03 cent discount.
   h. Order three lateral files, three vertical files, and 10 dozen folders.
   i. On Wednesday, April 12th, Char Pullar will be in Cleveland for a book signing.
   j. The new inventory system software paid for itself 2 times over within the 1st 10 months we used it.
3. Each of the following sentences requires corrections in capitalization. Some words shown in lowercase should be in uppercase; some shown in uppercase letters should be lowercased. Correct the errors.
   a. The Internal Revenue service has pledged to improve customer service.
   b. The centers for Disease Control (cdc) reported an outbreak of german measles in the Western Suburbs of Dallas.
   c. Krystal c. McIntosh, a Broker with Lamplighter realty in Flagstaff, was recently elected President of the Arizona board of realtors (abr).
   d. according to a recent Report from the American Council on Science and Health, fluoridation of drinking water is a very effective weapon against tooth decay.
   e. The Summer Language program at Century college has been expanded to include arabic and mandarin Chinese.
   f. The vice president will represent the President at the Nato meeting.
   g. My new laptop pc uses a Wireless internet connection.

    h.   Each Summer, the residents of smithville gather at City park for a founder's day Picnic.

    i.   After the election, mayor Bennett removed the door on her Office to show the citizens of parker that she had an "open door" policy.

    j.   Stella, whose Bachelor's Degree is in Engineering, has applied for admission to the mba program at Central College.

4. Several company, organization, agency, and program names are listed here. By what abbreviation is each name most commonly known?

    a.   America Online

    b.   National Collegiate Athletic Association

    c.   National Broadcasting Corporation

    d.   Organization of Petroleum Exporting Countries

    e.   United Auto Workers

5. Each of the following items contains at least one abbreviation. Decide whether each has been used correctly. If the abbreviation is incorrect, change it.

    a.   Our 30-month cd has an A.P.Y. of 5.25 pct.

    b.   Our coach said we had >50% chance of winning the game & he was right!

    c.   Hartford, Conn.; Pittsburgh, P.A., and Orono, ME are possible sites for our new branch office.

    d.   Bagley # Sons, the co. for which Emi works, offers its employees a 10 percent disc. on the glassware it makes.

    e.   The reg. Monthly mtg. has been changed from Tu Sep. 6 to Thurs. Sept. 8.

MESSAGE ANALYSIS

Edit the following message to reflect correct use of numbers, capitalization, abbreviations, and symbols.

DATE:	*03 – September – 2008*
TO:	*Mister Ralph Harding*
	MANAGING PARTNER
FROM:	*Georgia m. Teague, C.M.A.*
SUBJ.:	*request for leave of absence [l.o.a.]*

Last week, I learned that my Mother has been diagnosed with pancreatic cancer. Her doc. indicates that she has approx. 3 mos. to live. My family & I have discussed several care options and agreed that I should move to St. Louis and live with her in our family home during her last months. My vacation days for this yr. have been used; there4, I respectfully request an unpaid LoA beginning September 15th.

Bill Harper and (Ms.) Charlene Webber are familiar with the work I've been doing on the Parden account, and they have agreed to see it through to its conclusion. I have assured them that I will respond to questions by phone and:or e/mail.

I would appreciate your notifying me of your decision within the wk.

seminar e

The words listed in this seminar are among those that can pose problems for writers. Words included in this list are misused or often confused with other words. The words are listed alphabetically by the first word in each set.

ADAPT	(verb) to adjust or modify
ADEPT	(adjective) skilled
ADOPT	(verb) to take or follow as one's own
ADVICE	(noun) suggestion, opinion, or recommendation
ADVISE	(verb) to counsel or recommend
AFFECT	(verb) to influence
EFFECT	(verb) to bring about or cause to happen; to create (noun) result, outcome, or consequence
AID	(verb) to help or assist
AIDE	(noun) a person who assists another
AISLE	(noun) a passageway for inside traffic
ISLE	(noun) a piece of land surrounded by water; island
ALL READY	(adjective) a state of complete readiness; prepared
ALREADY	(adverb) prior to a stated or implied past time
ALL RIGHT	(adjective) approval meaning satisfactory, safe, well, or acceptable
ALRIGHT	informal spelling of *all right*; not appropriate for business writing
ALL TOGETHER	(adverb/adverb combination) wholly as a group; a summation
ALTOGETHER	(adverb) wholly; completely
AMONG	(preposition) ordinarily refers to three or more people or things
BETWEEN	(preposition) ordinarily refers to two persons or things; refers to more than two persons or things when they function one-on-one in a group
AMOUNT	(noun) used with singular nouns and "mass" nouns—things that can be measured but not counted
NUMBER	(noun) used with plural nouns and items that can be counted
ANY ONE	(adjective and pronoun) any one person or thing in a group; always followed by *of*
ANYONE	(pronoun) any person at all

ANY TIME	(adjective and noun) an amount of time
ANYTIME	(adverb) whenever; at *any time whatsoever*
AS	(conjunction) introduces a clause
LIKE	(preposition) means "similar to"
ASSURE	(verb) to promise; to make a positive declaration
ENSURE	(verb) to make certain
INSURE	(verb) to protect against financial loss
BAD	(adjective) modifies noun or pronoun or used after linking (nonaction) verbs such as *is, was, feel, look,* or *smell*
BADLY	(adverb) used with action verbs
BIANNUAL	(adjective) occurring twice a year
BIENNIAL	(adjective) occurring once every two years
BIBLIOGRAPHY	(noun) a list of resources reviewed by an author for a paper or production
REFERENCE LIST	(adjective and noun) a list of resources cited in a paper
BIMONTHLY	(adjective) occurring every two months
SEMIMONTHLY	(adjective) occurring twice a month
CAN	(verb) have the ability to do something
MAY	(verb) expresses permission to do something
	(verb) indicates possibility or expectation
CAN NOT	not acceptable in business writing
CANNOT	(verb and adverb) unable to do otherwise
CANVAS	(noun) a firm, closely woven cloth
CANVASS	(verb) to survey or solicit in an area
CAPITAL	(noun) asset; uppercase letter; city that is the location of a government seat
CAPITOL	(noun) a state or national government building
CARAT	(noun) a unit of weight for gems
CARET	(noun) a proofreading symbol to show insertions
KARAT	(noun or adjective) a unit of weight for gold
CITE	(verb) to quote or mention
SIGHT	(noun) a view or spectacle; vision
SITE	(noun) a place, an area, or a location
COMPARE	(verb) to examine similarities and differences
CONTRAST	(verb) to examine differences
COMPLEMENT	(verb) to complete or to enhance
COMPLIMENT	(verb) to praise
COMPOSED	(verb) to have been formed by putting together; constituted
COMPRISED	(verb) to be made up of; to be included within or a part of

CONSUL	(noun) a government official residing in a foreign country to represent the commercial interests of citizens from the appointing country
COUNCIL	(noun) an advisory group
COUNSEL	(verb) to give advice
	(noun) advice
CONTINUAL	(adjective) a regular or frequent occurrence
CONTINUOUS	(adjective) occurs without interruption; ongoing
CREDIBLE	(adjective) believable
CREDITABLE	(adjective) good enough for praise; reliable
DISBURSE	(verb) to pay
DISPERSE	(verb) to break up or spread
EAGER	(adjective) to show enthusiasm or similar positive feeling
ANXIOUS	(adjective) to show great concern; to be worried or apprehensive
ELICIT	(verb) to draw out or bring forth
ILLICIT	(adjective) unlawful
EMINENT	(adjective) prominent
IMMINENT	(adjective) impending
ENVELOP	(verb) to wrap, surround, or conceal
ENVELOPE	(noun) a container for a written message
FARTHER	(adjective) a greater distance; a measurable amount of space
FURTHER	(verb) to move forward
	(adverb) to a greater degree or extent
	(adjective) additional
FEWER	(adjective) used with plural nouns and things that can be counted
LESS	(adjective) used with mass items that can be measured but not counted and with singular nouns
FISCAL	(adjective) relating to financial matters or periods of time
PHYSICAL	(adjective) concerned with the body and its needs
FLAIR	(noun) a natural talent or aptitude
FLARE	(verb) to blaze up or spread out
	(noun) a signal light
FORMALLY	(adverb) in a formal manner
FORMERLY	(adverb) in the past
GOOD	(adjective) of favorable quality; wholesome
WELL	(adverb) properly; skillfully
	(adjective) fit, in regard to state of health

IF	(conjunction) in the event that; even though; on the contrary; a wish contrary to fact
WHETHER	(conjunction) alternative conditions or possibilities; used with *or*, or with *or whether*
INTERSTATE	(adjective) between states
INTRASTATE	(adjective) within a state
IRREGARDLESS	an incorrect usage for *regardless*
REGARDLESS	(adverb) despite everything
REGARDLESS OF	(preposition) in spite of
LAY	(verb) to put or to place; past tense of the verb *lie*
LIE	(verb) to recline; to remain at rest in a horizontal position; to remain inactive
LED	(verb) past tense or past participle of the verb *lead*
LEAD	(verb) to guide in advance; to direct on a course (noun pronounced with a long *e*) a position at the front
LEAD	(noun or adjective pronounced like the past tense of the verb *lead)* a metallic element
LOOSE	(adjective) not fastened; not tight
LOSE	(verb) to misplace
MORAL	(adjective) pertaining to right and wrong; ethical
MORALE	(noun) a mental or emotional attitude of an individual or group toward a function or task; a sense of satisfaction or dissatisfaction.
PASSED	(verb) past tense or past participle of *pass*, meaning *to go by*
PAST	(noun or adjective) time gone by or ended
PERPETRATE	(verb) to bring about; to commit an act, such as an injustice
PERPETUATE	(verb) to continue something indefinitely
PERSONAL	(adjective) private; individual
PERSONNEL	(noun) a group of workers or employees
PRECEDE	(verb) to go or come before
PROCEED	(verb) to go forward with; to continue some action
PRINCIPAL	(noun) head of a school; a capital sum (adjective) something or someone *chief* or *primary*
PRINCIPLE	(noun) a rule or basic truth
ROLE	(noun) proper function of a person or thing; assigned responsibility
ROLL	(noun) a list of names; something wound around a core (verb) to move by turning or rotating

SET	(verb) to place; to position; to arrange
SIT	(verb) to take a seat; to remain in place
SHOULD	(helping verb) used only with first-person references; appropriate in formal writing; denotes future time; owed; was obliged to; past tense of *shall*
WOULD	(helping verb) preferred in business writing; used with first-, second-, or third-person references; expresses desire or intent; past tense of *will*
SOME TIME	(adjective/noun combination) a specific time
SOMETIME	(adverb) an indefinite time; occasionally
STATIONARY	(adjective) not movable; in a fixed position
STATIONERY	(noun) writing material
STATUE	(noun) a molded or carved image of something or someone
STATUTE	(noun) a law enacted by a legislature
THAN	(conjunction) used to show comparison
THEN	(adverb) at that time
THAT	(pronoun) refers to animals or things; introduces an essential (restrictive) dependent clause
WHICH	(pronoun) refers to animals or things; introduces a nonrestrictive or nonessential clause
WHO	(pronoun) refers only to persons; may introduce a restrictive or nonrestrictive clause
THOROUGH	(adjective) to the fullest level of detail
THROUGH	(preposition) to show movement into and out of; to specify methods; to show completion
THRU	should not be used in business writing; an informal abbreviation of *through*
TO	(preposition) movement or direction; intention or result
TOO	(adverb) also; to an excessive degree
TWO	(noun) a number
TOWARD	(preposition) in the direction of
TOWARDS	should not be used in business writing; secondary form of *toward*

Application Exercises

1. Select the appropriate word(s) in each of the following sentences.
    a. The speaker (complemented/complimented) the audience for the (role/roll) their questions played in keeping the follow-up discussion related to the (principal/principle) theme of his presentation.
    b. Vic has taken Gerry's (advice/advise) and offered to mediate the disagreement (among/between) Alex and Jamal.

   c. The teacher's (aid/aide) helped the students pick up the paper (lying/laying) on the floor.

   d. Susan performs her job as (good/well) as Judy did when she worked in this position.

   e. Maynard (continually/continuously) tries to (elicit/illicit) a positive response to his sales letters.

   f. (Some time/Sometime) next month, I will seek the (consul/council/counsel) of a (personal/personnel) trainer to try to (affect/effect) a change in my exercise pattern.

   g. Sarah (can/may) phone Adam and suggest that he invite (fewer/less) people to this year's seminar (than/then) were invited last year.

   h. The legislature passed a (biannual/biennial) budget of (capital/capitol) expenditures for the next two years.

   i. Edmond's (cite/sight/site) management team has (led/lead) the nation in productivity for the (passed/past) three years.

   j. Edith, (that/which/who) has never visited the city (that/which) is her state (capital/capitol), is the newly elected state representative from her district.

   k. Staff (moral/morale) has been (good/well).

   l. Let me know when you are (thorough/through/thru) with Part A; we can (than/then) (precede/proceed) with Part B.

   m. We (can not/cannot) travel (further/farther) down this road because we may (loose/lose) (too/to) much time (too/to) get to the city before dark.

   n. The plant closing was (imminent/eminent), and factory (personal/personnel) thought they were treated (bad/badly) when asked to relocate.

   o. Be sure to (cite/sight/site) the source of the data you use in preparing the (bimonthly/semimonthly) report for January and February.

2. Find and correct the word-use errors in the following sentences. If a sentence has no errors, write *correct*.

   a. The bride's two-karet diamond sparkled as she walked down the isle for the wedding.

   b. A bibliography should have only the resources sited in the manuscript.

   c. Can I have permission to address the student counsel next week?

   d. I would like to canvas the staff to get their opinions on adapting a 20-minute break period during the afternoon.

   e. Michelle is of Indian dissent, as was evidenced by her fiscal characteristics.

   f. Corinne asked to move her desk further away from the construction noise.

   g. Was it Jennifer that persuaded the principle to release the enrollment data which she calculated from the teachers' class roles?

   h. The audience believed Barry's story because it was creditable.

   i. We are anxious to see how good the furnishings in the outer office compliment the decor of the conference room.

   j. I asked our account clerk to order high-quality stationary and envelops.

   k. Irregardless of having a full schedule next Tuesday, I will find sometime to meet with you.

   l. The dog lifted its head as I past by but continued to lie on the floor.

   m. After you have analyzed the data which you received from Steve, summarize your results and send a copy to Bill which formerly worked on this project.

   n. Stephen and Juan moved towards the statute to set on the bench beside it.

   o. A large amount of people were anxious to attend the concert and preceded to the assembly hall before the doors opened.

Appendices

appendix a

Chapter 3 emphasizes the importance of giving proper credit for words or ideas that you use from other sources. This appendix gives guidelines for formatting citations within formal papers, reports, and manuscripts, as well as for preparing a list of sources at the end of a document. Using a style manual as a guide gives consistency to a written document. Two widely used style manuals are the *Publication Manual of the American Psychological Association (APA)* and the *MLA Handbook for Writers of Research Papers (MLA)*. In this appendix, you will find examples of different types of source documents formatted by both APA and MLA style guidelines.

Documentation Format—APA

The APA style is used in psychology and the behavioral and social sciences, including business and education. APA examples in this appendix conform to the fifth edition of the APA style manual published by the American Psychological Association. In this section, guidelines cover both in-text citations and the References or Reference List at the end of a document. The APA web page may be found at http://www.apa.org. Order information for a copy of this handbook can be found at http://www.apastyle.org/pubmanual.html.

Reference Citations in Text

The first time you use information from a specific resource, include a reference citation. Repeat the citation for that same source again if you have used information from another source since the previous citation. Also, if the material cited from one source extends to another page, repeat the citation.

For a text citation, APA style uses the author's surname and the year of publication in parentheses or the author's surname, the year of publication, and the page number from the original source. The citation enables readers to find complete resource information in the list of references at the end of the document. An item quoted directly from source material requires the author's surname, the publication date, and the page number where the quote was found. The following examples illustrate in-text citations by one author or multiple authors:

"Kentucky author Silas House draws inspiration from family and Appalachian roots" (Nipper, 2006, p. 47).

Nipper (2006, p. 47) says that "Kentucky author Silas House draws inspiration from family and Appalachian roots."

In a recent interview, Silas House, a Kentucky author, attributed his inspiration for writing to his family and his Appalachian roots (Nipper, 2006).

Japanese society expects a high level of individual conformity with detailed norms (Schneider & Silverman, 2000).

According to Schwan and Mitchler (2005), outdoor rooms that bring summer living outside have become popular in the South and Southwest.
To market successfully using a large customer database requires being able to identify prospects who are most like your best customers (Marshall, Nolan, Smythe, & Stein, 2006).

The last example shows a work by four authors. According to APA, a citation of a work with two authors should use both surnames each time the work is cited. For three to five authors, all authors are cited the first time but only the first author followed by et al. and the year are included in subsequent citations. The example with four authors would be shown in subsequent text citations as follows:

You should target customers whose needs match your services (Marshall et al., 2006).

Marshall et al. (2006) recommend that you target customers whose needs match your services.

The following examples show groups as authors and works with no authors. Group names are spelled out unless an abbreviation is easily recognizable. If the name is long, give the full name the first time; if the abbreviation is understandable, use it for subsequent citations. For works with no author, cite the first few words of the reference list entry (usually the title) and the year. For an in-text citation, put the title of an article or a chapter in quotation marks, and italicize the title of a journal, book, brochure, or report.

Group as the author:

The Ursula County School System (2006) attendance policy states . . . .

First citation as follows; subsequent citations use only USDA with the date:
Small farms in the United States are disappearing at a rapid pace (United States Department of Agriculture [USDA], 2005).

No author; abbreviated title with date:
Changes in the arts venue brought in new leadership ("Arts World Changes," 2004).

Cite personal interviews, telephone conversations, e-mail, letters, or memos in the text only. Such personal communications are not recoverable by others and, therefore, are not included in the reference list. The following examples show two ways that personal communication information can be cited in the document text:

M. G. Lane (personal communication, March 17, 2005) reported that . . . .

These statistics were verified (M. G. Lane, personal communication, March 17, 2005).

Reference List or Bibliography

A **reference list** is a list of works cited in the text of a particular paper, report, or manuscript; a **bibliography** is either a list of works for further reading or a list of works that provide background on the topic in addition to the sources cited in the text. If you are using APA style, the same formatting applies to lists that can be titled References, Reference List, or Bibliography.

All references cited in the text must be included on a reference list, and all resources in the reference list must be cited at least once in the text. All in-text citations must appear in the bibliography, but all resources in the bibliography might not be cited in the text.

The reference list at the end of a document begins on a new page with the title References or Reference List centered at the top margin. This list shows all information necessary to identify and retrieve each source.

The following guidelines will assist you with the development of an APA style reference list.

1. Complete information on all the works that have been cited in the document, and only sources cited in the document, are listed.
2. All dates and spellings are accurate for each source. Reference data must be correct and complete to enable readers to retrieve and use the source.
3. The reference list begins on a separate page with the list of sources beginning two lines after the title References or Reference List.
4. Each entry uses a **hanging indent** format. In hanging indent format, the first line of the entry begins at the left margin and all subsequent lines of the entry are indented one-half inch. Reference lists in manuscripts prepared for publication are double-spaced; however, reference lists in other types of papers and reports may be either double-spaced or single-spaced with double spacing between items.
5 Entries are in alphabetical order by the surname of the first author or by title if the entry has no author.
6. In the title, capitalize only the first word and proper nouns. This capitalization applies to book titles as well as chapter or article titles in other publications. However, each word in a magazine or journal name begins with either a capital letter or a lowercase letter, depending on the publication's normal style.
7. The names of books, magazines, and journals should be in italics.
8. For books, reports, brochures, and other nonperiodical publications, give the location and publisher's name. Use the city and state for location of the publisher. Baltimore, Boston, Chicago, Los Angeles, New York, Philadelphia, San Francisco, and other widely recognized cities do not require the state name.
9. Electronic resources include many kinds of publications. As a rule, Internet resources in the reference list give the author's name (if known), the date of the document (or n.d. if there is no date), a title, the date you retrieved the resource, and its Uniform Resource Locator (URL).

Internet Citations

Internet documents may be articles from newspapers, newsletters, or journals; research papers or reports; online books or brochures; or web pages. Electronic library resources may come from electronic databases. Include information in the reference list that will direct readers to the source document. Be sure that all URLs in the list work.

Specific information for citing electronic references using APA style formatting can be found at http://www.apastyle.org/elecref.html. Reference examples are given for Internet articles based on a print source, articles from electronic journals, Internet newsletters, electronic documents with no author and no publication date, documents from university websites, and journal articles from a library electronic database.

In-text citations of resources obtained from the Internet follow the same pattern as for other sources. The citation includes the author's name or a portion of the title followed by a document date or n.d. if there is no document date. The URL does not appear in the in-text citation.

Figure APA.1 shows examples of a variety of entries in a reference list using APA style. Study the examples in this appendix for wording and order of entries, capitalization, italics, and punctuation.

FIGURE APA.1
APA Reference List

	References
Internet article based on print source (no author).	Arts world changes for the better [Electronic version]. (2004). *Journal of Fine Arts, 5,* 12–14.
Newspaper article (one author).	Earnest, L. (2004, January 21). Investments: Diversification. *Kansas City Star*, p. B4.
Magazine article (one author).	Kridel, T. (2002, November). Trading spaces: The power of flash memory. *Laptop Mobile Solutions for Business & Life*, 78–86.
Encyclopedia article (one author).	Lorenz, J. R. (2002). Commodity exchange. In *World book encyclopedia* (Vol. 20, pp. 495–497). Chicago: World Book, Inc.
Unpublished paper presented at a meeting.	Merlin, T. I., Case, W., Wilson, T. Y., & Menlo, A. (2006, May). *Effective business practices of UPS.* Paper presented at the global symposium of the Automotive Warehouse Distributors Association, Dearborn, MI.
Internet-only journal article (no page numbers).	Miller, A. (2003). Mission impossible: Increasing female enrollment in computer science. *Online Computer World, 6.* Retrieved November 25, 2004, from http://www.elecjournals/ocw.volume6/ejj0030.html.
Journal article (two authors).	Moses, M. S., & Chang, M. J. (2006, January/February). Toward a deeper understanding of the diversity rationale. *Educational Researcher, 35*(1), 4–11.
Newsletter article from electronic database.	On-the-job interview: Survey shows value of temporary work as prelude to full-time job. (2002, October 15). *PR Newswire.* Retrieved November 10, 2002, from the InfoTrac College Edition database.
CD-ROM encyclopedia.	Psonga, M. S. (Ed.). (2006). *The psychological encyclopedia of literacy.* [CD-ROM]. Chicago: Literacy Associates.
Book, 2nd edition (two authors).	Schneider, L., & Silverman, A. (2000). *Global sociology* (2nd ed.). Boston: McGraw-Hill Higher Education.
Chapter in edited book (four authors).	Sundaram, A. K., Bradley, M., Schipani, C. A., & Walsh, J. P. (2000). Comparative corporate governance and global corporate strategy. In R. E. Grosse (Ed.), *Thunderbird on global business strategy* (pp. 110–150). New York: John Wiley & Sons, Inc.
Governmental agency Internet datafile.	United States Census Bureau. (n.d.). *Population profile of the United States: 2000* [Internet release]. Retrieved July 30, 2006, from http://www.census.gov/population/www/pop-profile/profile2000.html.
School district publication (agency author).	Ursula County Board of Education. (2004). Student attendance policy. *School board policies.* Falls City, IA: Ursula County School System.
Corporate report from its website.	World Bank. (2005). *The World Bank annual report 2005: Year in review.* Washington, DC: International Bank for Reconstruction and Development and International Development Association. Retrieved July 20, 2006, from http://www.worldbank.org/.
Daily newspaper article, electronic version.	Yardley, W. (2006, July 30). Police describe Seattle shooting as a hate crime. *The New York Times.* Retrieved July 30, 2006, from http://www.nytimes.com.

Documentation Format—MLA

The MLA style was developed by the Modern Language Association of America. The MLA style is used by writers in government, business, industry, the professions, and the media. MLA style is currently used by more than 125 scholarly and literary journals, newsletters, and magazines with circulation over one thousand. In addition, the MLA guidelines are used by hundreds of smaller periodicals and by many university and commercial presses. In 2003 the *MLA Handbook for Writers of Research Papers,* 6th edition, was written by Joseph Gibaldi. This book had its fourth printing in 2006. Examples in this section are based on this edition of the handbook. The *MLA Handbook* may be ordered from the MLA web page, located at http://www.mla.org. Documentation guidelines for the Modern Language Association are not published on the Web.

Reference Citations in Text

Periodically, you will use primary and secondary sources in writing. Individuals must be given proper credit whenever their works are used by others. The MLA referencing style, used in the humanities, is another method for citing sources. When you use the MLA style, you may use parenthetical citations in the text and an alphabetical list of cited works that appears at the end of the document.

The parenthetical citations in the text use the author-page method, without a comma between. For example, (Biggs 128) refers to a specific page and (Biggs 128–34) refers to an entire article. Use the last name of the author or authors (or editor, translator, or narrator). For three authors, cite all three last names (Greenfield, Parks, and Anderson 145–56). If the work has more than three authors, use only the first author's last name followed by et al. with no intervening punctuation (Biggs et al. 128). If no author is listed, use the title or a shortened version of the title: ("Study Finds"). A corporate author's name is cited in full or as a shortened version. Shortened titles should begin with the first word of the entry in the list of works at the end of the paper. This identifies the source for readers and enables them to locate it in the **Works Cited** list. If the author or title is mentioned as part of a sentence in the text, use only the page number within parentheses as the citation.

Works Cited List

The Works Cited list at the end of the document provides the information necessary to identify each source and to retrieve the material. The following guidelines will assist you with the development of a Works Cited list following MLA style.

1. The list contains information on all the works that have been cited in the document.
2. The MLA manual uses the title Works Cited for the list; however, other titles sometimes used for the list include Bibliography or Literature Cited.
3. The Works Cited list is placed at the end of the document.
4. The Works Cited list should begin on a separate page, and each page should be numbered, continuing the page numbers of the text.
5. The title Works Cited should be centered one inch from the top of the page with a double space between the title and the first reference entry. Double spacing is used within and between entries.

6. A hanging indent is used for each entry, with the first line beginning at the left margin and each subsequent line indented one-half inch from the left margin.
7. Entries are listed in alphabetical order, disregarding the articles *A*, *An*, and *The*.
8. Underline the titles of books, magazines, and journals.

Internet Citations

The *MLA Handbook for Writers of Research Papers* has complete guidelines that cover citing World Wide Web sources. Entries for types of web sources include scholarly projects, professional sites, personal sites, books, poems, articles in a reference database, articles in a journal, articles in a magazine, works from a subscription service, and postings to a discussion list. Refer to Figure APA.2 for examples of how to cite information from a website on the Internet, an online magazine article, and an online newspaper article, as well as a variety of print sources. Study the examples for wording and order of entries, capitalization, underlining, quotation marks, and punctuation.

FIGURE APA.2
MLA Works Cited List

Works Cited

Annotation	Entry
Internet article based on print source (no author).	"Arts World Changes for the Better." Journal of Fine Arts 5 (2004): 12–14. 5 Aug. 2006 <*http://www.musu.edu/jfa.html*>.
Newspaper article (one author).	Earnest, Larry. "Investments: Diversification." Kansas City Star 21 Jan. 2004: B4.
Magazine article (one author).	Kridel, Tim. "Trading Spaces: The Power of Flash Memory." Laptop Mobile Solutions for Business and Life. 1 Nov. 2002: 78–86.
Encyclopedia article (one author).	Lorenz, Jerry R. "Commodity Exchange." The World Book Encyclopedia. 10th ed. 2002.
Unpublished paper presented at a meeting.	Merlin, Talcott I., William Case, Thomas Y. Wilson, and Arnold Menlo. "Effective Business Practices of UPS." Global Symposium. Automotive Warehouse Distributors Association. Dearborn. 2006.
Internet-only journal article.	Miller, Andrea. "Mission Impossible: Increasing Female Enrollment in Computer Science." Online Computer World 6 (2003): 25 Nov. 2004 <*http://www.elecjournals/ocw.volume6/ejj0030.html*>.
Journal article (two authors).	Moses, Michele S., and Mitchell J. Chang. "Toward a Deeper Understanding of the Diversity Rationale." Educational Researcher 35 (2006): 6–11.
Newsletter article from electronic database.	"On-the-Job Interview: Survey Shows Value of Temporary Work as Prelude to Full-Time Job." PR Newswire 15 Oct. 2002. InfoTrac College Edition 10 Nov. 2002 <*http://www.infotrac-college.com*>.
CD-ROM encyclopedia article.	Psychological Encyclopedia of Literacy. Ed. Martin S. Psonga. CD-ROM. Chicago: Literacy Associates, 2006.
Book, 2nd ed. (two authors).	Schneider, Linda, and Arnold Silverman. Global Sociology 2nd ed. Boston: McGraw-Hill Higher Education, 2000.
Chapter in edited book (four authors).	Sundaram, Anant K., Michael Bradley, Cindy A. Schipani, and James P. Walsh. "Comparative Corporate Governance and Global Corporate Strategy." Thunderbird on Global Business Strategy. Ed. Robert E. Grosse. New York: John Wiley & Sons, Inc., 2000. 110–50.
Governmental agency Internet datafile.	United States. Census Bureau. Population Profile of the United States: 2000. 1 Jan. 2003 <*http://www.census.gov/population/www/pop-profile/profile2000.html*>.
School district publication (agency author)	Ursula County Board of Education. "Student Attendance Policy." School Board Policies. Falls City, IA: Ursula County School System, 2004.
Corporate report from its website.	World Bank. The World Bank Annual Report 2005: Year in Review. Washington, DC: International Bank for Reconstruction and Development and International Development Association, 2005. 20 July 2006 <*http://www.worldbank.org/*>.
Daily newspaper article, electronic version.	Yardley, William. "Police Describe Seattle Shooting as a Hate Crime." The New York Times 30 July 2006. 30 July 2006 <*http://www.nytimes.com*>.

appendix b

The title page.

EMPLOYEE INTEREST
IN A
COMPANY-SPONSORED FITNESS PROGRAM

States the subject of the report.

Prepared for

Tells to whom it is being submitted.

Jillian Erp

Human Resources Director

Prepared by

Tells who is submitting it.

Hank Thorp

Human Resources Specialist

Identifies the organization.

Nomar Printing Company

Gives the date of submission.

June 15, 2008

The title fly (not discussed in text).

EMPLOYEE INTEREST
IN A
COMPANY-SPONSORED FITNESS PROGRAM

May be blank or, as in this example, include the report title.

Nomar Printing Company

220 North Highway 367
Boise, ID 83705
(208) 555-0227 FAX (208) 555-1008

> *Authorization message (not discussed in the text).*

March 12, 2008

TO: Hank Thorp
             Human Resources Specialist

FROM: Jillian Erp   *JE*
             Human Resources Director

> *Gives authority to conduct the study.*

SUBJECT: **Research Authorization**

The Human Resources Committee has read, discussed, and approved your proposal to survey Nomar employees about their interest in a company-sponsored fitness program. As you point out in your proposal, our plans to renovate and expand our facilities offer a unique opportunity to investigate ways in which we can improve the quality of work life for our employees, especially in light of declining productivity levels over the past few years.

The Committee has set a July 15 deadline for the report and approved a $1,500 budget for your use in designing, field testing, printing, distributing, and analyzing the surveys. The Committee asks, however, that you submit the survey questionnaire for approval prior to distribution.

Please contact me if I or the Committee can be of assistance.

rt

> *Gives relevant information, such as deadline and funding.*

Nomar Printing Company

220 North Highway 367
Boise, ID 83705
(208) 555-0227 FAX (208) 555-1008

June 15, 2008

Transmittal message.

TO: Jillian Erp
          Human Resources Director

FROM: Hank Thorp   *HT*
          Human Resources Specialist

Sets the context and transmits the report.

SUBJECT: **Employee Interest Survey—Company-Sponsored Fitness Program**

As we agreed in March, I have surveyed a representative sample of Nomar employees to determine their interest in a company-sponsored fitness program, including the possibility of a company-sponsored fitness center. Here is the report of that study.

Response to the survey was outstanding; over 80 percent replied. The results suggest that there is strong interest in a company-sponsored fitness program. The concept of an on-site fitness center was also viewed positively.

Provides highlights of the study.

Based on the findings of the survey, I recommend that we develop proposals for a fitness program that includes an on-site fitness center.

Summarizes the recommendations.

I would appreciate your sharing this report with the HR Committee. If you would like me to discuss the results with the Committee members, please let me know.

dkh

iv

> The table of contents lists names and page numbers of all major sections.

TABLE OF CONTENTS

The list of illustrations contains the titles and page numbers of all visuals used in the report.

LIST OF ILLUSTRATIONS

TABLES

FIGURES

EXECUTIVE SUMMARY

Nomar plans to renovate and expand its current facilities. This growth provides the company with an opportunity to investigate ways in which employees' work life quality can be improved. A fitness program, possibly one including an on-site fitness center, is one of the options available to the company.

Research has shown that health and productivity are related and that work is one of the three top sources of stress for adults in the United States. Physical exercise has been identified as an effective method for controlling stress. Access to an on-site fitness center can be useful in reducing stress and raising productivity if the center offers a variety of activities in which employees may voluntarily participate.

In order to determine employee interest in a company-sponsored fitness program and an on-site fitness center, 500 employees were surveyed using a stratified random sample data-gathering technique. Over 80 percent of those surveyed responded.

Data collected through the survey show that Nomar employees are interested in improving their fitness and that they currently participate in a variety of activities. Those surveyed show strong support for a company-sponsored fitness program; a majority also favor construction of an on-site fitness center. The findings suggest that a center would be used regularly.

Based on the results of this survey, Nomar should pursue development of a company-sponsored fitness program that includes an on-site fitness center.

I. INTRODUCTION

The introduction assists the reader in understanding the rest of the report.

The background describes the problem in general.

Background

The daily routines, quotas, and deadlines under which most workers at Nomar Printing operate go hand in hand with stress buildup. Depending on the individual, work-related stress can be perceived as intolerable and threatening or as normal and stimulating. If individual workers have planned leisure activities that allow for the release of such daily stressors, then supposedly all is well within the working community. One area of concern, though, is the amount of time workers devote to gaining and maintaining a good fitness level. Without regular exercise, the workforce can become increasingly unmotivated or physically ill.

The statement of the problem specifies what was studied.

Statement of the Problem

Productivity at Nomar has declined steadily over the past three years despite increased wages.

Purpose of the Study

A representative of Allied Insurance, Nomar's health care provider, has suggested that offering employees a fitness program might improve productivity. The purpose of the study was to determine whether Nomar's employees are interested in a company-sponsored fitness program.

The purpose tells why the study was conducted.

Scope

The related literature reviews what has been published about this or a similar topic.

This study is limited to full-time, regular employees of Nomar who have been with the company at least one year.

The scope outlines the boundaries of the study.

II. RELATED LITERATURE

"Stress is unavoidable" (Krazen, 2003, p. 48). This was one of the conclusions in a study conducted by the Winthrow Group in 1999. The report of this study pointed out that stress can be produced by any demands placed on a person or any changes in his or her life. Money, interpersonal relationships, and job satisfaction are identified in the report as the top three sources of stress for adults in the United States.

Although stress cannot be avoided, it can be minimized. Dr. Joshua Carey of the Quincy Institute for Better Health states in a recent *Journal of Stress Science* article:

> Physical exercise seems to be effective in controlling stress. A planned exercise program will minimize physical and emotional reactions to pressure; it will help keep blood pressure, heart rate, and cholesterol at acceptable levels (Carey, 2007, pp. 78–79).

The concept that stress can be reduced through exercise is not new. In the mid-1990s, published articles suggested that exercise was linked with better health. Ethan-Rolle monitored the

1

energy levels of 150 adults between the ages of 35 and 45. During the two years of her research, she found that "physical activities such as walking, jogging, biking, and aerobics diminished stress and fatigue" (Ethan-Rolle, 2002, p. 103).

The strong relationship between exercise and stress reduction has important implications for business and industry. In 2001, the Sanders Corporation converted a portion of an unused warehouse into a physical fitness center for its employees. During the next five years, the company traced worker health, productivity levels, and facility use. The report prepared at the end of the research period indicated that Sanders' workers were in better health, productivity had increased, and the popularity of the facility had risen steadily (*West Coast Business,* 2004, p. 6c).

Not all the news is good, however. Some firms that have begun corporate wellness programs report that "workers are 'suspicious' of companies that try to become involved in aspects of their private lives" (Haugen, 2002, p. 38). To minimize the effects of suspicion, Haugen recommends that wellness programs be voluntary and that they include options to meet the varying interests and needs of employees (Haugen, 2002, p. 41). A similar study involving office workers in New York City (Trent, 2002, p. 118) yielded comparable results.

The procedures section describes the steps taken in conducting the study.

III. PROCEDURES

After the literature was reviewed, a questionnaire was designed, field tested, and revised. The questionnaire, which contained ten items, was designed to gather information about employees' current exercise patterns and their interest in a company-sponsored fitness program. A copy of the questionnaire, which was approved by the HR Committee on April 24, is in the Appendix.

In order to get responses from a cross-section of Nomar employees, a stratified random sample data gathering technique was used. With the help of personnel from the Human Resource Management Department and the Information Systems Department, questionnaires were distributed with the May 12 paychecks of 500 full-time Nomar employees who had been with the company for at least one year. Employees were asked to complete the survey and return it to the Human Resource Management Department within five working days. A second distribution was made on May 26 to those employees who did not respond to the initial mailing.

In formal reports that are simple and brief, analysis can be combined with findings.

IV. FINDINGS AND ANALYSIS

Responses were received from 408 of the 500 employees surveyed. This high response rate (81.6 percent) is one indication of the employees' interest in their health. The majority of the respondents (228; 55.9 percent) were men. Respondents ranged in age from 19 to 68; the median age of the respondents was 41. Respondents were fairly evenly distributed across all employment length categories with the average length of employment being 11 years.

Nearly two thirds (266; 65.2 percent) of the respondents felt they would like to be more fit. When asked why they were interested in improving their fitness level, 211 (51.7 percent) indicated they wanted to improve their health, 101 (24.8 percent) wanted to improve their physical appearance, and the remaining 96 (23.5 percent) wanted to have more energy. The national

3

trend toward health and fitness is reflected in the distribution of these responses. Data do not reflect whether this high interest in fitness is related to busy, stress-producing lifestyles.

Just over a third (143; 35 percent) of the employees who returned surveys currently participate in regular programs designed to maintain or improve their health. As shown in Table 1, employees participate in unstructured activities such as swimming, walking, and weight training as well as structured activities such as aerobics and exercise classes.

Findings are presented objectively.

TABLE 1   EXERCISE PROGRAMS IN WHICH NOMAR EMPLOYEES PARTICIPATE (N=408)

Illustrations are numbered by type and use descriptive titles.

Activity	Respondents Participating*
Walking	308
Weight Training	141
Aerobics	121
Swimming	95
Jogging	77
Exercise Classes	62
Racquetball	38
Cycling	16
Other	7
No Response	4

*Respondents could check multiple activities.

When data were examined to determine the effect of age, gender, and length of employment, no significant differences were found but observable differences were noted. Regardless of how long they have worked at Nomar, employees of both sexes and all ages participate in the activities listed in Table 1. Men and women between the ages of 19 and 30 run, cycle, and do aerobics while those 50 and older prefer to walk and swim. Readers should note, however, that the survey did not solicit information about how frequently employees participated in the various activities.

Employees were asked to indicate their level of interest in a company-sponsored fitness program. Considering the strong interest in fitness that was expressed in earlier responses, it is not surprising that 287 (70.3 percent) of those returning surveys indicated that their interest in a company-sponsored fitness program was "Very High" or "High." (See Table 2.)

The analysis shows important relationships.

TABLE 2   EMPLOYEE INTEREST IN A COMPANY-SPONSORED FITNESS PROGRAM (N=408)

Interest Level	Number	Percent
Very High	113	27.7
High	174	42.6
Moderate	66	16.2
Low	31	7.6
Very Low	24	5.9

When asked about the type of activities they would like to see included if the company developed a fitness program, respondents expressed a preference for an on-site walking/jogging path and an on-site fitness center. These responses loosely parallel the workers' current activity patterns. Refer to Table 3 for further information.

TABLE 3   PREFERRED FITNESS PROGRAM ACTIVITIES (N=408)

Activity	Number Selecting*	Percent
Classes	173	42.4
On-site Fitness Center	284	69.6
On-site Walking/Jogging Path	301	73.8
Paid Health Club Membership	37	9.1

*Respondents could check more than one item.

Additional analysis showed that 22 of those employees indicating they would like to have paid health club memberships also favored an on-site fitness center. The data do not reveal whether those who favored paid health club memberships are currently members of fitness centers or whether they would forgo those memberships if the company were to establish an on-site center.

Those respondents who indicated they would like to have an on-site fitness center included in a company-sponsored fitness program were asked how often they anticipated using such a facility. As shown in Figure 1, a majority of these workers said they would use the facility on a regular basis.

Figure 1. Projected Fitness Center Use

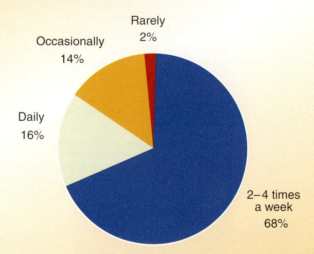

5

Those who indicated they would use an on-site fitness center were also asked to indicate the time of day at which they anticipated using the center. Findings suggest that use would be distributed fairly evenly across the before work, lunch break, and after-work time frames. Location and the availability of lockers and showers would likely influence use patterns. Refer to Figure 2.

Figure 2. Anticipated Times of Use

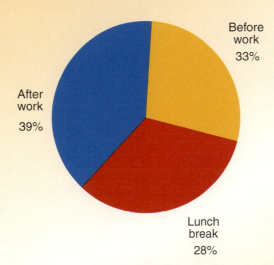

V. CONCLUSIONS AND RECOMMENDATIONS

Conclusions are drawn from the analysis of the findings.

Conclusions

1. Nomar employees are interested in becoming fit and/or maintaining their personal fitness.
2. Nomar employees, regardless of age or gender, engage in both structured and unstructured fitness activities.
3. Nomar employees are interested in having a company-sponsored fitness program.
4. A company-sponsored fitness program should include an on-site fitness center and an on-site walking/jogging path.

Recommendations

Recommendations are based on the study's conclusions.

1. Nomar should develop a company-sponsored fitness program.
2. Nomar should investigate the feasibility of establishing an on-site fitness center and on-site walking/jogging path.
3. Employees should be consulted regarding the facilities/activities they would like to see included in an on-site fitness center.

An appendix contains supportive supplementary material that is related to t he study.

APPENDIX

SURVEY QUESTIONNAIRE

7

NOMAR PRINTING COMPANY
Employee Interest Survey

Please complete the following survey, fold it to highlight the address, and return it by May 19. The number on the form will be used only to do a second mailing (if necessary). Once a sufficient number of responses has been received, data linking surveys and respondents will be destroyed.

No. _____

DEMOGRAPHIC DATA

Please check the most appropriate response or supply the requested information.

1. How long have you worked at Nomar?

    ❑ 1–5 years
    ❑ 6–10 years
    ❑ 11–15 years
    ❑ 16 years or more

2. What is your gender?   ❑ Male   ❑ Female

3. What is your age? _____

FITNESS INTERESTS

Please check the most appropriate response or supply the requested information. For some items, you may check more than one response.

4. Would you like to be more fit?   ❑ Yes   ❑ No

5. If your answer to Question 4 was Yes, why are you interested in being more fit?

    ❑ Better health
    ❑ Improved appearance
    ❑ More energy

6. In which of the following activities do you currently participate? Check all that apply.

    ❑ Aerobics
    ❑ Cycling
    ❑ Exercise classes
    ❑ Jogging
    ❑ Racquetball
    ❑ Swimming
    ❑ Walking
    ❑ Weight training
    ❑ Other

7. Please indicate the extent of your interest in a company-sponsored fitness program.

    ❑ Very high
    ❑ High
    ❑ Moderate
    ❑ Low
    ❑ Very low

8. If the company were to develop and sponsor a *fitness* program, which of the following items would you like to see included? Check all that apply.

    ❑ Classes (e.g., Health and Nutrition, Aerobics, Yoga)
    ❑ On-site fitness center (e.g., exercise equipment, free weights, etc.)
    ❑ Paid membership in private health club
    ❑ Walking/jogging path on the premises

9. If you checked *on-site fitness center* in item 8, how often would you anticipate using the facility?

    ❑ Rarely
    ❑ Occasionally
    ❑ 2–4 times a week
    ❑ Daily

10. At what time of day would you be most likely to use the facility?

    ❑ Before work
    ❑ During lunch break
    ❑ After work

Thank you for your input. Please fold and return by *May 19* to:

Hank Thorp
Human Resources Management Department
146 Building C

The reference list includes citations for all materials used as sources for the study.

REFERENCE LIST

REFERENCE LIST

Carey, Joshua. "Exercise Promotes Better Health." *Journal of Stress Science* 26:7 (February 2001): 78–79.

Ethan-Rolle, Madeleine E. "Run for Your Life." *Today's Healthy Living* 19 (June 7, 1986): 103.

Haugen, R. P. "Are Stress Reduction Programs Stressful?" *Today's Healthy Living* 22 (January 31, 1989): 38–41.

Krazen, C. B. *The Winthrow Group Report on Stress*, Report 108. Altoona, PA: Winthrow, 1999.

"Sanders on Top of Fitness Scene." West Coast Business, 17 December 2002: 6c.

Trent, Willis M. "Insurer Has Fitness Policy." *NYC Today* 35 (March 31, 2002): 118.

index

Two-Letter Postal Abbreviations

U.S. State, District, and Territory Names

Name	Two-Letter Abbreviation	Name	Two-Letter Abbreviation
Alabama	AL	Montana	MT
Alaska	AK	Nebraska	NE
Arizona	AZ	Nevada	NV
Arkansas	AR	New Hampshire	NH
California	CA	New Jersey	NJ
Colorado	CO	New Mexico	NM
Connecticut	CT	New York	NY
Delaware	DE	North Carolina	NC
District of Columbia	DC	North Dakota	ND
Florida	FL	Ohio	OH
Georgia	GA	Oklahoma	OK
Guam	GU	Oregon	OR
Hawaii	HI	Pennsylvania	PA
Idaho	ID	Puerto Rico	PR
Illinois	IL	Rhode Island	RI
Indiana	IN	South Carolina	SC
Iowa	IA	South Dakota	SD
Kansas	KS	Tennessee	TN
Kentucky	KY	Texas	TX
Louisiana	LA	Utah	UT
Maine	ME	Vermont	VT
Maryland	MD	Virgin Islands	VI
Massachusetts	MA	Virginia	VA
Michigan	MI	Washington	WA
Minnesota	MN	West Virginia	WV
Mississippi	MS	Wisconsin	WI
Missouri	MO	Wyoming	WY

Canadian Provinces and Territories

Name	Two-Letter Abbreviation	Name	Two-Letter Abbreviation
Alberta	AB	Nova Scotia	NS
British Columbia	BC	Ontario	ON
Manitoba	MB	Prince Edward Island	PE
New Brunswick	NB	Quebec	PQ
Newfoundland	NF	Saskatchewan	SK
Northwest Territories	NT	Yukon Territory	YT